International Studies of the

Committee on International Relations

University of Notre Dame

Chile and the United States, 1880–1962

Chile and the

United States, 1880–1962

The Emergence of Chile's Social Crisis and
the Challenge to United States Diplomacy

By FREDRICK B. PIKE

UNIVERSITY OF NOTRE DAME PRESS 1963

To my mother

PREFACE

Chile, with its widely respected tradition of mature conduct of foreign policy, has long occupied a position of importance in American Hemisphere diplomacy somewhat out of proportion to its small size (286,396 square miles) and population (less than 7.5 million in 1960). It seemed worthwhile, therefore, to study Chilean attitudes toward and relations with the United States and to investigate what impact these have had on other Latin-American countries. To develop this story, it proved necessary to devote more space to the internal history of Chile—its social, political, and economic development and its value judgments and intellectual currents—than to matters of a strictly diplomatic nature. Only in this way did it seem possible to show that Chilean diplomacy has been a natural, organic outgrowth of national attitudes and experiences.

I am grateful to the Henry L. and Grace Doherty Charitable Foundation for the research grant covering the 1959-1960 academic year that enabled me to undertake research in Chile. The University of Notre Dame also conferred a grant which facilitated research.

The United States Embassy in Santiago extended every possible aid in arranging interviews and in obtaining permission to use archival material. It was always helpful to discuss my project with the amazingly well-informed Public Affairs Officer, Hewson A. Ryan.

Research involving the use of published sources, books, pamphlets, journals, periodicals and newspapers, was conducted largely in the Library of Congress in Santiago, where the staff presided over by Director Jorge Ugarte Vial seemed constantly intent upon making my tasks easier and more pleasant to fulfill. A frequent visitor to the library, Oscar Smits-Rivera, rendered invaluable assistance upon numerous occasions. The Archives of the Ministry of Foreign Relations, housed in the National Library of which Guillermo Feliú Cruz is the Director-General, were used extensively. Samuel Villalobos, Custodian (Conservador) of the National Archives, and his assistants were helpful and considerate. Archival material is cited in the footnotes of this book with the abbreviation AMRE (*Archivo del Ministerio de Relaciones Exteriores*). The various *Memorias* of the Ministry of Foreign Relations are referred to as MMRE (*Memoria del Ministerio de Relaciones Exteriores*), together with the appropriate date.

The Committee on International Relations at the University of Notre Dame sponsored the publication of this book. Committee chairman Stephen D. Kertesz has offered unceasing assistance and counsel. I am indebted to him as well as to committee member M. A. Fitzsimons for having read this manuscript and offered valuable suggestions.

It was my extreme good fortune to enlist the services of Donald W. Bray of Los Angeles State College and his wife, Marjorie, as editorial readers for this manuscript. Their incredibly painstaking work, combined with their vast knowledge of Chilean history, brought about improvements on every page as well as helpful organizational changes. Dana G. Munro, recently retired from his teaching duties at Princeton University, generously devoted his time to reading the manuscript and many of his wise suggestions have been incorporated into the final version.

Of course, I alone assume responsibility for the views and opinions expressed in this book, none of which should be construed as necessarily bearing the approval of any of the individuals or organizations mentioned above.

The unflagging interest of my mother, June Braun Pike, in the progress of the work was always appreciated. The assistance of my wife, Pachita Tennant Pike, was indispensable. Her knowledge and understanding of Latin-American customs facilitated my work in Chile, and her wide circle of friends not only in Santiago but wherever we traveled in Latin America added to the pleasure of the year abroad. Her cheerful encouragement and patience, especially on days when research or writing went badly, were always invaluable assets in carrying the project to completion. I benefited also from the encouragement which my father, John Pike, extended and from the uncomplaining understanding of my children, Paulita, June Sarita, and "Federico," that writing schedules reduced the time I could spend with them in diversion.

Finally, because I do not wish this book to offend my Chilean friends, I acknowledge that when it alludes to the helpful influence that the United States could begin to exercise upon Chile, it often contrasts the best features of life in the United States with the worst in Chile. To help restore balance to the picture, I profess my gratitude to the people of Chile. By their ability to enjoy life through inward resources, by their graciousness, spontaneity, and respect for culture, they taught me the tragedy of the situation in which they and their fellow Latin Americans seem fated for the present to be influenced by, rather than to exert influence upon, the United States.

Fredrick B. Pike

South Bend, Indiana
June, 1962

CONTENTS

xiii

INTRODUCTION

Chile is a unique country in the American Hemisphere. Stereotyped United States impressions concerning Latin America have little applicability to Chile. With only a few exceptions, Chile has maintained political stability since 1830. Its citizens, in fact, incline to judge us in the United States as politically wild and unruly. They are well aware that three of our presidents have been assassinated while in office, and they are proud that Chilean political history has never been blemished by such an act of lawlessness and civil disrespect. Perhaps also they puzzle over the ceaseless precautions we must exercise to protect the lives of our presidents. Jorge Alessandri Rodríguez, elected as Chile's chief executive in 1958, makes a habit of walking alone and unguarded between his residence and the presidential palace.

Far from demonstrating the exuberance and ebullience which we generally ascribe to all Latins, Chileans are remarkably restrained in displaying emotions. They are addicted to sports, especially to "futbol" or soccer. Yet, they are more orderly and undemonstrative when watching a soccer match, and less apt to engage in rowdy demonstrations if a favored team loses or is the victim of questionable officiating, than typical football audiences in the United States. Perhaps these engaging national traits have helped win for Chile the unqualified respect of many United States observers. Furthermore, those who have actually traveled in Chile are inevitably beguiled by the beauty of the country. It is hard to worry about such nasty things as gnawing poverty, mounting anti-United Statesism, and the increasing likelihood of a Marxist or communist takeover when marveling at the land that Theodore Roosevelt understandably described as the most beautiful in the world.

In the course of living one year in Chile, I fell nearly completely

under the country's spell. One evening in Santiago I tried to list
some of the national characteristics that I most admired. The
result of this endeavor comprised a small portion of an article that
I wrote in the spring of 1960 with Donald W. Bray, a Fulbright
scholar who, ably abetted by his wife Marjorie, was then in the
process of making himself one of the most knowledgeable of men
concerning contemporary Chilean affairs. I quote now the pertinent
part of the article:

> In Chile there is a highly developed sense of decency and fair
> play. . . . The respect for freedom of expression and exchange
> of ideas seems at times more fundamental than in the United
> States. This is particularly noticeable in the broad diversity of
> opinions presented in the universities and in the press. Chileans,
> moreover, have a maturity, a self-containment, and an inner
> discipline which, combined with the rare willingness to think of
> adverse situations in terms of equally bleak alternatives, render
> them ill-disposed to rush to the barricades to defend momentary
> whims. To almost every political predicament except dictator-
> ship they respond with patience and forbearance. In spite of
> their refreshing individualism, Chileans possess a deeply in-
> grained acceptance of authority and devotion to stability, a love
> of institutionalism and constitutional regularity. Their lively
> sense of humor enables them to respond to occasionally absurd
> political situations with laughter and with satire, rather than
> with rebelliousness of spirit. Chileans have developed a police
> force—the famed *carabineros*—that for integrity, efficiency and
> courteous firmness is unmatched in Latin America. And it is
> revealing that the populace continues to feel a sense of national
> guilt over the 1938 cold-blooded assassination of sixty-two youths
> who spearheaded an attempted nazi revolution. Bloodier and
> less excusable acts have been readily forgotten elsewhere in the
> American Hemisphere, including the United States.*

I was won also by the sort of nationalism that one encounters
in Chile. The people exude a love of country that is childlike in
the finest sense of the word: genuine and unquestioning, but free
from the wild exaggerations and psychopathic quirks that have
vitiated much of modern nationalism. And as an investigator of

* Fredrick B. Pike and Donald W. Bray, "A Vista of Catastrophe: the Future
of United States-Chilean Relations," *The Review of Politics*, XXII, no. 3 (July,
1960), 394-395.

historical events and ideas, I could not help being amazed, delighted, and at the same time appalled by the literary energy of Chileans. Although the population of the country is small, barely exceeding 7,000,000 in 1960, the number of serious books that Chileans have written on various aspects of national development is astounding.

But all the while I could not help suspecting that in spite of their admirable qualities, the people of Chile were blithely courting a national catastrophe that will make such natural calamities as the May 1960 earthquake fade into insignificance. The catastrophe that appears to be approaching would have more than domestic implications. It could, in fact, represent a momentous step toward the sort of utter collapse of friendly relations between the United States and Latin America of which *Fidelismo* has been a harbinger.

Why has the situation in Chile become so critical? Basically, I think the reason is that Chile has clung to a set of values associated with a rapidly disappearing way of life. The cardinal feature of this way of life is a sociopolitical structure based on paternalism, and on the perpetual existence of a participating, privileged minority that is served by a nonparticipating, nonprivileged majority. This system has much to recommend it. Historically, in many areas of the world, it brought forth great cultures. In Chile it produced a style of life in many ways laudable, and surely in certain aspects superior to that in the United States.

It may be futile, however, to ask which is superior: the old sociopolitical structure or the new, with its emphasis on mass participation in political decision-making processes and in the material wealth that a nation is capable of producing. At least in Chile the point is that, for good or for ill, the once silent masses are in the process of rendering an overwhelming decision in favor of the new. Somehow they have caught the scent of the twentieth century. By the hundreds of thousands they are clamoring to join this new civilization even though many, in order to put themselves in a position to do so, have had to abandon the relative security of rural existence and move with their families into the indescribable slums that are mushrooming around those symbols of modern hope, the industrial, urban centers. The pressures now being exerted by the lower masses cannot indefinitely be resisted by Chile's ruling class.

This class, consisting of those who are politically articulate and participate in the market economy, includes still a small segment of aristocrats of the traditional type, even though Chileans overwhelmingly deny the existence of a genuine aristocracy in their country. Be that as it may, there are Chileans who own vast rural estates, who live from their accumulated holdings without working to produce additional capital, and who trace their lineage back to the colonial period. There is also an upper class, more similar to certain middle groups than to a traditional aristocracy. In fact, upper-class members can be distinguished from the more successful middle groups only by their longer background of wealth and influence, by their ownership of rural property extending back for several generations, and by their membership in several exclusive clubs, primary among which is the *Club de la Unión*. This last criterion, to confuse the issue still further, is losing its applicability in contemporary Chile.

In Chile's ruling class, middle groups are much more important both in numbers and influence than aristocratic and upper social elements. The middle groups range from millionaire industrialists, whose wealth is of recent origin and whose children may come to be regarded as upper class, to street-car conductors. The middle groups, in short, are made up of those people who do not depend primarily on manual labor for their livelihood but who are active in earning income, either through choice or necessity. Those in the middle groups live primarily in the cities and are literate. Many are university graduates and practice the professions, while others have not advanced beyond primary education. Some are wealthier than upper-class members, and some are poorer than those at the top of the lower mass.

The ruling class, the amalgam of upper and middle groups, has consistently resisted any move aimed at incorporating the lower masses, those who depend exclusively upon manual labor for survival and who are at best barely literate, into society. Frequently, middle groups have committed themselves more passionately than the upper class to preserving the gulf between those who guide and benefit from the course of national development, and those who are supposed to accept and suffer from it with resignation. Unless the resistance of the ruling class to social change abates, its members, who have frequently demonstrated wisdom, talent, and responsibility, may be swept away and replaced by men who initially at least possess less ability and whose exercise of power will not necessarily bring greater integrity or balance to national administration.

Decades ago, and quite unwittingly and indirectly, the United States began to foment the social revolution that in the mid-twentieth century challenges the old order in Chile and in many other Latin-American nations. Every United States missionary who preached the dignity of labor and praised the natural virtues of thrift, frugality, and sobriety, every affluent tourist who indulged his penchant for conspicuous consumption and displayed his amazing manufactured-in-the-United States gadgets, every United States business firm that established itself in Latin America and paid higher than prevailing wages to its employees at the same time that it introduced concepts of mass production, every wife of a United States businessman or diplomat who paid her domestic servants at above the local level, every medical improvement and material comfort introduced by the United States that made it possible to improve an adverse environment, and every United States movie, were agents of change. These agents have helped arouse the desire of the lower mass to participate in the political and, above all, in the economic life of the nation.

In a way, the mania for change that is now so apparent in Chile and elsewhere in Latin America, and which stems at least partially from United States influence, has helped open the door to the disciples of communism. If the example of the United States had not argued persuasively in favor of the revolutionary notion of the participation of the proletariat in society, then the doctrine of the dictatorship of the proletariat would not now be making such rapid headway. Still, the concept of the participation and rising expectations of the proletariat is a good one—or else, basically, there may be little that is good in the United States way of life. We would therefore be foolish to be ashamed of having helped introduce this concept into Latin America. But we now face a decision that many find frightening. Should we nourish the seeds of change that we unwittingly planted so that they will produce a mature body politic in which previously unassimilated multitudes can participate with dignity and liberty? Or should we continue to bolster, as in the past we have nearly always wittingly done, the old and the semifeudalistic political practices of Chile, hoping that the impetus to dangerous change that we unintentionally introduced will gradually dissipate its energy? If the decision is made in favor of this second alternative, as our actions have convinced many Chileans that it has been, then the participation of the proletariat will not in the conceivable future come about in Chile. Instead, there might be a communist-style dictatorship of the proletariat.

Chileans themselves face a momentous decision. Unless they wish their country to remain a museum-piece reminder of ancient cultural patterns, they must make a commitment to the sort of civilization that is currently evolving. Otherwise, as their museum piece gradually decomposes, they will not be in a position to gain access to what is best and most worthwhile in the new civilization.

Chile has dangerously delayed making a favorable commitment to those forces that have lately been rocking the newly-emerging areas of the world. In the United States we have been unaware of the extent of Chile's delay. Deceived by the undeniably attractive and appealing features of the nation and its political traditions, we have tended, at least until late 1961, to assume that all must be well. Latin-American authorities in this country have even fostered the myth that in the 1920's, under Arturo Alessandri, and again in the late 1930's, under the Popular Front government, Chile committed itself firmly to the new, and made giant strides toward assimilating its lower classes and providing them with the opportunity to participate in society. This naïvely false interpretation has helped to bring about the present crisis in Chile's domestic situation and in its long-range relations with the United States. If Chile in the 1920's or the 1930's had made the basic decision to bring its society into line with the demands of the twentieth century, then the present situation would not be so explosive. We find difficulty in understanding Chile today precisely because the country must now begin to do what experts in the United States mistakenly reported it already did forty or thirty years ago. Tragically, United States scholarship allowed itself to be fooled by outward appearances. The 1920 elections that elevated Arturo Alessandri to the presidency suggested to our observers that Chile had become a truly democratic republic. Actually, what we have praised as democracy in Chile since 1920 has amounted to little more than a system in which a small, privileged class has been gentlemanly in determining, through very limited electoral processes, which of its members would rule the country.

I strongly suspect that our Latin Americanists made similar mistakes in assuming that Argentina in 1916 and Colombia in 1930 initiated genuine attempts to proceed away from the paternalistic and toward the pluralistic society. Future research will have to decide on these matters. However, I am now convinced that Chileans fooled us thoroughly. They fooled us because, especially after 1920, they began to talk about social reform. Our mistake lay in assuming that social reform meant the same thing to Chileans that it meant to us. Social reform to us has meant a move toward pluralism: the active and as-nearly-as-possible equal participation in society of diverse social and functional interest groups. In Chile, social reform has meant, and for many continued even in 1962 to mean, a reawakening of the sense of *noblesse oblige* among the ruling classes so that through charity they could satisfy the needs of the lower classes and persuade them to remain uncomplainingly in their nonparticipating status.

In attempting to produce a detailed account of Chile in its relations with the United States, the year 1880 has been selected as the logical point at which to begin, although a brief glimpse of Chilean internal development and attitudes toward the United States between the attainment of independence and 1880 is included. Prior to the latter date, Chile and the United States had been involved in a series of relatively unimportant diplomatic incidents and arguments over pecuniary claims, and had engaged in insignificant commercial relations. In general, however, the two countries had consistently ignored each other. After 1880, the United States came to be regarded, along with Argentina, as Chile's principal adversary in international affairs. Furthermore, increasing economic contact did not serve to reduce Chile's anxiety over its relations with the United States.

In analyzing Chilean relations with the United States since 1880 it soon became apparent that 1933 was a point of demarcation between two distinct eras. The approach used in studying events between 1880 and 1933, therefore, had to be modified when it came to dealing with developments between 1933 and 1962. With regard to Chilean-United States relations prior to 1933, this book follows the traditional approach of diplomatic history. Various incidents, conferences, and treaties are discussed, and there is an occasional attempt to play the game of determining what Chilean diplomat made a fool out of what United States representative, or vice versa, at such-and-such a meeting. History of this sort has great relevance to Chilean relations with the United States between 1880 and 1933. In that period incidents and conferences largely determined the nature of diplomatic dealings between the two countries and influenced the attitudes with which one regarded the other. Diplomatic incidents and conferences produced the old-style crises in Chilean-United States relations. By the end of 1933, however, the major, long-smouldering sources of diplomatic disputation had been largely eliminated, and an era of uniquely warm relations seemed at hand.

In carrying the story to 1933, this book also devotes considerable attention to Chile's internal development. Only if the arrogant self-confidence and pride that characterized national attitudes in the 1880's are appreciated, and then contrasted with the stagnation and doubt of the first two decades of the twentieth century, is it possible to understand Chile's changing appraisals of the United States. Moreover, only in the light of Chile's endeavor to bring about national regeneration in the late 1920's do the policies toward the United States pursued by the Carlos Ibáñez administration (1927-1931) become meaningful. For these reasons, in relating the story of Chilean diplomacy with the United States prior to 1933, more attention is sometimes devoted to Chile's domestic history than to events of a strictly diplomatic character.

In dealing with the 1933-1962 period, still greater emphasis has been placed upon internal Chilean development, and points of interest in traditional diplomatic history are almost eliminated. The expectations of warmly amicable relations between Chile and the United States, apparently justified by the settlement of old issues of diplomatic discord in 1933, have not been fulfilled. The reason is that after 1933, or at least some time between then and 1945, the usual conferences, treaties, pacts, bargaining and alliance-seeking that once constituted the principal aspect of diplomatic intercourse ceased to exert overriding influence in determining Chilean attitudes toward the United States, or in shaping the pattern of relations between the two countries. Within the realm of traditional diplomacy, harmony has indeed continued to prevail. But increasingly since the 1930's, Chile's relations with and basic intellectual and emotional attitudes toward the United States have been molded by its mounting social problem, and by the reactions of Chilean thinkers to this problem. Chile's social problem has created a new type of crisis in its relations with the United States. The sort of solution that is eventually found to this social problem, and the role that the United States plays either in aiding or hindering the finding of a solution, will determine how the two countries will regard each other in the future.

This book attempts to trace the emergence of social ferment in Chile. It endeavors also to suggest the disastrous consequences of the tardy recognition by the United States of social ferment as the source of the new-style crises in hemisphere relations, and to describe the tenacious dedication with which Chile's directing classes, in spite of lip service to reform, cling to the status quo. The final four chapters of the book, therefore, which carry the story of Chilean-United States relations from the early 1930's to 1962, deal almost exclusively with the social problem in Chile and with the attitudes of political and intellectual groups, from extreme right to extreme left, toward various social questions. They deal also with what United States attitudes toward Chile's social problems are assumed to be by native Chileans.

In conducting research, I have relied almost exclusively upon Chilean sources. My main objective has not been to arrive in all instances at objective historical truth regarding Chilean-United States relations. Instead, I have endeavored to discover what Chileans think is true about their dealings with the United States. If one were interested in chalking up debating points, it would be worthwhile to prove, on the basis of documents available in Washington, that many Chilean interpretations of United States diplomatic actions are incorrect. What has concerned me has been the attempt to understand why anti-United Statesism is on the rise in Chile and why, from a Chilean point of view, this development is justifiable. Consequently, my book is more a history of Chilean attitudes and prejudices, especially as they apply to the United States, than it is strictly speaking a diplomatic history. Perhaps the only merit of such a book is that it may help some few people in the United States to understand the unfavorable impressions of their country entertained by many Chileans. Not until these impressions and their causes are comprehended can the United States proceed more effectively toward halting the process by which Chile may be transforming itself into an actively hostile force.

Chile and the United States, 1880–1962

1: A GLIMPSE OF CHILEAN DEVELOPMENT FROM INDEPENDENCE TO 1880

INTRODUCTION

POLITICAL STABILITY AND ECONOMIC PROGRESS

After winning its independence from Spain in 1818, Chile suffered through twelve revolution-filled years of political turbulence. Then in 1830 in a remarkable display of political maturity, Chileans terminated their partisan bickering and began to apply their efforts to the constructive end of developing their nation's potential.

That Chileans were able to achieve political stability by 1830—something that eluded certain sister republics for a century and more—has always constituted one of the more important sources of national pride. The tangible results of political stability were also noteworthy. Taking advantage of the order in the nation's political life and of the effectiveness of institutions and new legal codes, Chilean capitalists and landowners in the nineteenth century created one of the most flourishing economies in the American Hemisphere.

By 1872 Chile was a significant purchaser of French luxury goods,[1] and nine years later over 15,000 industrial and professional establishments were earning sufficient profits to oblige them to pay taxes to the national government.[2] In 1880 the country produced sizable quantities of coal and silver, and was the first or second largest producer of copper in the world.[3] It had by this time begun to emerge from the economic recession of the early 1870's, and its seventy-two urban centers classified in the census as cities received a total income from taxation of 4.6 million pesos.[4] The income of the national treasury in 1880 reached 65.5 million pesos.[5] The capital, Santiago de Chile, was a city of over 150,000

1

inhabitants, and the total national population exceeded two million.[6]

More important, Chile's energetic capitalist-adventurers, responding to the opportunity presented by the political anarchy in Bolivia and Peru, had begun to exploit the vast mineral treasures of these two republics. This fact was the underlying cause of the War of the Pacific which erupted in 1879. During the course of the military struggle, Chile succeeded in despoiling her two antagonists of nitrate-rich territories. The war and its outcome were probably as inevitable as the 1846-1848 conflict between the United States and Mexico. In both instances, a well-governed, energetic, and economically expanding nation had been irresistibly tempted by neighboring territories that were underdeveloped, malgoverned, and sparsely occupied.

CHILEAN CRITICISM OF THE PATTERNS
OF NATIONAL DEVELOPMENT

In spite of obvious national accomplishments, there is a surprising note of pessimism and criticism in the writings of many Chileans who have tried to explain fundamentally what transpired in the nation between independence and 1880. Of all contemporary analysts, perhaps the most brilliant was Miguel Cruchaga Montt, economist of the laissez-faire school and a professor of economics at the University of Chile. A prolific writer, Cruchaga published his major work in 1878, *Estudio sobre la organización económica y la hacienda pública de Chile*.[7] Examining his country's past, Cruchaga concluded that colonial practices had bequeathed a legacy that impeded economic progress, and suggested that Chile's only era of genuine development had been from 1830 to 1860, when economic restrictions had been relaxed. The following sixteen years, however, had been marked by stagnation. Partisan politics, an excessive increase in the number of public employees, a tendency toward monopoly, a decrease in initiative, an obsession for luxury and ostentation, and a lack of concern with technology were suggested as the reasons for stagnation. Cruchaga felt Chile's only hope for renewed development and progress lay in giving the lower classes some share in society. Education might encourage the masses not only to lead better moral lives, but equip them to produce, and therefore to earn, sufficiently to enjoy adequate material comfort. Education might also instill in the middle classes respect for the virtues of work, efficiency and frugality. Once these goals were achieved, Cruchaga hoped the Chilean aristocracy would abandon its inordinate devotion to economic activity, and, by turning itself to pursuits of mind and soul, produce a Chilean culture.

More modern writers have also been suspicious of Chile's progress to the eve of the War of the Pacific. Domingo Amunátegui Solar, brilliant twentieth-century writer and long-time rector of the University of Chile, noted that the tendency up to 1880 had been away from absolute government and toward greater influence of public opinion. Still, Amunátegui felt that the era had also witnessed the sowing of the seeds of demoralization and inertia that later overtook Chile.[8] Archconservative Alberto Edwards Vives, one of the most eloquent and brilliant spokesmen for his intellectual school until his death in 1932, argued that Chilean dissolution began in 1850. From that time on the aristocracy, forgetful of the anarchy from which its preceding generation had escaped in 1830, began to oppose governmental institutionalism and to indulge in the worst excesses of individualism.[9] A later conservative *pensador*, Jaime Eyzaguirre, has lamented that around the mid-nineteenth century, the mutually beneficial relationship between *patrón* and worker disappeared and the *patrón*, corrupted by French-like love of luxury, abandoned his estate to live in Santiago or in Paris.[10]

Other writers of the present era have found grounds for serious concern over Chilean development preceding the War of the Pacific. Francisco Antonio Encina, dean of Chilean historians, and Carlos Keller, versatile writer on nearly all topics, have been among those suggesting that economic progress in this era was based more upon the habits of the conquistador than those of the practical-minded businessman and entrepreneur. Wealth resulted from dramatic discoveries and rapid, profligate exploitation that was pursued without heed of future needs. The richest ore at various sites was exploited by Chilean discoverers who, as the yields became less spectacular, abandoned their mines rather than invest in the technological development needed to assure continuing, long-term profit. In the dramatic economic development of nineteenth-century Chile, therefore, little was accomplished toward providing the basis for a sound and enduring economic structure.[11] Finally, Marxian writers see in the period under discussion the beginning of the acute class struggle in Chile, with the traditional aristocracy and the men of new wealth uniting to suppress the laboring classes.[12]

With such a variety of interpretations concerning fundamental patterns in pre-1880 Chile, it seems essential to examine some of the more important developments between independence and the outbreak of the War of the Pacific. On the basis of such a survey, it may be possible to gain a clear impression of what sort of a country Chile was when for the first time in 1880 it began to receive serious attention from the United States.

ECONOMIC DEVELOPMENT

MINERAL WEALTH AND SOCIAL TRANSITION

The Portales era commenced on a resounding note of economic good luck.[13] The Chañarcillo silver mine began operation in 1832 [14] —a mine that yielded 450,000,000 of the 891,000,000 pesos worth of silver produced in nineteenth-century Chile.[15] The mining boom had commenced, and the age of fabulous silver strikes continued until 1870, the date of the discovery of the northern Caracoles vein. By the time of the Caracoles find, Chilean nitrate production had begun, and the country was already saddled with a dependence on extractive industries that rendered unlikely a balanced economic growth. In 1864, approximately 70 per cent of Chile's exports consisted of mine products, while by 1881 the figure had risen to 78.5 per cent.[16]

Behind these statistics lie many stories of personal vision, daring, energy, and often ruthlessness, that rival the success tales of men like Vanderbilt, Carnegie, and Rockefeller. In 1845, Juan Mackay, a man of redoubtable spirit, began Chilean coal exploitation. Seven years later Matías Cousiño appeared upon the scene, married the widow of Miguel Gallo, who had himself been a mining million-aire, and shortly began the work that would make him the principal figure in the Chilean coal industry. All of Cousiño's patience, con-fidence, influence, and wealth were necessary to bring about suc-cessful production in the Lota and Coronel fields south of Concep-ción. But the capitalist-adventurer overcame the long odds against him, and by the later years of his life was investing some of his coal millions in northern nitrate operations. He had become per-haps Santiago's most colorful millionaire, living in one of the more lavish of the many mansions constructed in the capital city during the mining bonanza.[17]

By the 1870's, increasing numbers of Chileans were gaining fortunes in northern nitrate operations.[18] One of them was José Santos Ossa, a daring explorer of the desert and the discoverer of the Antofagasta nitrate deposits.[19] Santos Ossa was also active in establishing the *Compañía de Antofagasta* which became the main nitrate operation in South America. It was almost exclusively a Chilean venture, with the principal founders being, in addition to Santos Ossa, Agustín Edwards Ross, Alfredo Ossa, and Juan Francisco Puelma.

As early as the 1850's, a new aristocracy, its wealth based on commerce, industry, banking, and above all on mining, was coming to occupy positions of social and political importance formerly re-served to landowners who could trace their lineage back to early colonial times. Agustín Edwards Ossandón, Gregorio Ossa, Tomás Gallo, and naturally Matías Cousiño, were the first outstanding representatives of this new class.[20] In 1857, the traditional land-lord aristocracy suffered a rude blow with the abolition of *mayoraz-gos* (roughly equivalent to combined primogeniture and entail), which facilitated redistribution of landed estates. A depression from 1858 to 1860, moreover, caused a disastrous decline in agrarian land values, impoverished many members of the old order, and permitted the new rich to acquire land and, thereby, social prestige and acceptance.

By mid-nineteenth century Chile was revealing a remarkable tolerance for allowing entry of new blood into the ranks of the social elite. Even more striking, by the latter part of the century the aristocracy was studded with the names of foreigners whose grandfathers had arrived in the country only around the time of the independence movement. From the United Kingdom had come settlers with the names of Ross, Edwards, Lyon, Walker, MacClure, Garland, Mac-Iver, Jackson, Brown, Price, Phillips, Waddington, Blest, Simpson, Eastman, Budge, Page and others; from France came the Cousiño, Subercaseaux and Rogers families, while from Slavic and German areas had come the Piwonkas and the Königs. A survey of Chilean biographical encyclopedias, of membership lists for such aristocratic organizations as the *Club de la Unión,* or of the roll of the stock-market founders,[21] and a scanning of prominent names in diplomacy, politics and the fine arts will reveal the prominence that these names have enjoyed from the mid-to-late nineteenth century to the present time. A conspicuous factor in this development was the "well-known preference" of Chilean ruling classes for marrying their children to financially successful immigrants and their descendants.[22]

The rapid transformation in Chilean society was noted by the leading Valparaíso daily, *El Mercurio,* in May of 1882. Of the fifty-nine personal fortunes in Chile of over one million pesos (of forty-eight pence), twenty-four were of colonial origin, and the remainder belonged to coal, nitrate, copper, and silver interests, or to merchants, all of whom had begun their march toward fortune only in the nineteenth century.[23]

OTHER ASPECTS OF ECONOMIC DEVELOPMENT

In the 1850's, the first of the true banks appeared in Chile. The year 1855 saw the establishment of the Bank of Valparaíso, which accepted deposits and engaged in discount activities. The famous agricultural mortgage credit agency (*caja de crédito hipotecario*) was founded in the same year,[24] for the purpose of providing long-term loans. The man who devised the basic patterns of this agency —long a landmark in Latin-American agricultural finance—was a young economist, Wenceslao Vial y Guzmán, who later played a leading role in founding the National Bank of Chile.[25] On the eve of the War of the Pacific, banking deposits had risen to close to sixty million pesos.[26] A law of 1860, extremely favorable in its provisions to bankers, had facilitated the dramatic rise of the Chilean banking system.

Between 1845 and 1860, the volume of Chilean commerce tripled.[27] A great boon to commerce was the completion in 1863 of the Valparaíso to Santiago railroad[28]—a feat for which the Yankee speculator and railroad builder Henry Meiggs was principally responsible. By 1874 the total of Chile's foreign trade, exports and imports, had soared to 157 million pesos. Great Britain took close to two thirds of the annual exports, and supplied the country with approximately one third of its imports. Following Great Britain in importance of commercial relations were France, Germany, and Peru. The United States, an insignificant factor in the commercial picture, was in eighth place.[29]

The mid-nineteenth century witnessed also the inception of scientific livestock raising, under the direction of such men as Ricardo E. Price, Tomás Eastman, Tomás Gallo, Agustín Edwards, José Tomás Urmeneta, Guillermo Brown, Manuel Bunster and Tomás Bland.[30] General agricultural production matched the gains of animal husbandry. During the 1844-1880 period, the value of agricultural exports was nearly one half that of the extractive industries.[31] Wine production was also becoming increasingly important, with the vineyards of Manuel Antonio Tocornal, José Tomás Urmeneta, and Magdalena Vicuña Subercaseaux gaining wide renown. By 1865, moreover, there were twenty-six breweries in Chile.[32]

Utilization of new land and encouragement of immigration, especially the attempt to lure Germans to the southern area around Lake Llanquihue, added also to the nation's economic development. Instrumental in making a reality of President Manuel Montt's (1851-1861) dream of German settlements was Vicente Pérez Rosales, an adventurer and writer of ingratiating style who had been at one time or another a farmer in Boldamávida, a producer of *aguardiente* in Colchagua, a merchant, a painter of theatrical posters and decorations, an herb doctor, a contrabandist on the Argentine pampas, a miner in Copiapó, and a gold-seeker in California.[33] Pérez Rosales accepted the post of colonization agent in the early days of the Montt administration and thereafter worked

indefatigably to attract German immigrants, as well as to prepare
a suitable settlement for them at Valdivia. He procured land for
the first group of colonists to arrive in the South, among whom
was Carlos Anwandter, destined to found a distinguished family in
Chile. In 1852 while seeking new settlement sites, Pérez Rosales
helped found Puerto Montt and Puerto Varas, and his paintings of
this area are considered almost as valuable as his charmingly
written *Recuerdos del pasado,* in which he described the early
German colonization efforts.[34]

Still, Chile did not attract large-scale immigration. In the
periods immediately preceding and following 1880, complaints
were often voiced that more people left Chile in search of better
opportunity than came to the land. Moreover, shortly after the
War of the Pacific, the total number of German citizens living in
Chile was not much more than four thousand. While most of
these were permanent settlers, over one third of the approximately
four thousand British citizens in the country were transients, listed
as sailors. There were also 2,835 Frenchmen, 3,226 Italians, and
only 710 United States citizens, of whom 231 were transient
sailors.[35]

ECONOMIC RECESSIONS

Notwithstanding the unmistakable signs of economic progress,
there were setbacks and indications of imbalances. A modern
writer, in fact, asserts that from 1844 to 1891 Chilean imports
were greater in value than exports, a situation that was both cause
and effect of inadequate and distorted economic development.[36]
A three-year economic crisis began in 1858, triggered by the closing
of the California and Australian markets to Chilean wheat. In
1873, Chile suffered a more severe and prolonged recession. Agricultural prices declined rapidly, and Chileans showed signs of
losing confidence not only in farming, but in mining as well.[37]
The situation worsened in 1874, in part because Henry Meiggs,
building railroads at the time in Peru, contracted for the services
of 30,000 Chilean laborers, mainly from the southern provinces.
The subsequent crop failure in that area was caused largely by
lack of workers.[38] Ascending to the presidency in 1876, Aníbal

Pinto faced a genuine crisis. There was an unfavorable balance of trade, gold was being exported and metallic money was becoming scarce. Pinto responded to the situation by asking and obtaining in 1878 authorization for government issue of paper money. Chile had taken the first step toward monetary inflation. But the move had not been inspired by the traditional landed aristocracy, the group most commonly blamed for the country's early experiments in calculated inflation. Rather, the measure was enacted by one of the administrations most hostile to the landowning-conservative groups that had held office in Chile. Subsequent laws of the Pinto regime established imposts on inheritances and donations, as well as upon rents. Finally, in 1879, a tax was levied on nitrate exports. These measures, in addition to the economic stimulus provided by the outbreak of war, enabled Pinto to finish his five-year term on a note of renewed prosperity.[39]

ECONOMIC THEORY AND LACK OF UNITED STATES INFLUENCE IN THE CHILEAN ECONOMY

Given the frontier characteristics of Chilean economic advances in the three generations following independence—the existence of unexploited land, the frequency of mine discoveries, and the small population—it was natural that laissez faire became the principal economic theory of the times. The denigrating of Spanish traditions after the wars of independence also influenced Chileans to shun the planned-economy features of colonial administration. And economic as well as intellectual intercourse with France and England served to foster the cult of economic individualism. Juan Gustavo Courcelle-Seneuil, a product of the liberal economic school of nineteenth-century France, became the main theoretician of Chilean capitalist practices.[40] From 1855 to 1863 he was technical adviser to the Ministry of the Treasury. Many have questioned the wisdom of his attempts to apply to a weak and relatively underdeveloped economy the practices which had been suitable to France and England. But no one denies the influence that he and his disciples, Zorobabel Rodríguez and Miguel Cruchaga Montt, exercised in directing the basic patterns of Chilean capitalism. By the 1860's, laissez faire had become so firmly entrenched a dogma that iconoclastic intellectual José Victorino Lastarria, prolific historian Diego Barros Arana, and future Chilean president Domingo Santa María—all of them known for their political liberalism—were scandalized by state encouragement of the construction and operation of the Valparaíso to Santiago, and the Santiago to Concepción railroads.[41]

So far as either commercial exchange or economic theory were concerned, the United States scarcely existed for Chile prior to 1880. The flurry of trade with California at the time of the gold rush[42] had lasted less than a decade, and United States immigration to Chile had been as negligible as its commercial intercourse there. For their theory, Chileans looked to French thinkers and Herbert Spencer rather than to United States economists.[43] Finally, the business practices developed in "the Great Republic of the North" were not emulated in Chile. The one major contemporary study of Chilean corporations, for example, prepared by Miguel Cruchaga Montt, showed almost no awareness of United States corporate finance.[44]

POLITICAL DEVELOPMENTS AND INTELLECTUAL FERMENT

The Age of Portales, 1830-1841,
and its Disputed Significance

In the years following independence, two opposing political groups arose in Chile. The Pelucones, or bigwigs, stood for firm-handed, highly centralized rule by traditional landowning aristocrats in league with men of more recently acquired wealth, with the Catholic clergy, and with the leaders of the armed forces. They were the forerunners of the Conservative Party. The Pipiolos, or greenhorns, advocated the rapid introduction of democratic practices, rule by intellectuals rather than by men of wealth and social position, federalism that would result in nearly autonomous provinces, and curtailment of Church power. They were the forerunners of the Liberal Party. The showdown between the two groups came in 1830 near the Lircay River, where a pelucón army under General Joaquín Prieto defeated the pipiolo forces, and thereby ushered in what can only be referred to as the age of

Portales. Although the *Pelucón* president from 1831 to 1841 was General Prieto, the main policy maker was Diego Portales.

A successful businessman whose sympathies had always been with the *Pelucones*, Portales was a nation-maker along the lines of Alexander Hamilton.[45] Born in Santiago in 1793, Portales had attained wealth and position by his talent and strength of character. He was fervently dedicated to fostering nationwide economic development. And he realized that this goal could not be achieved without political stability. Moreover, he was convinced that to challenge those groups which had since early colonial times exercised power in Chile could lead only to chaos. The traditions of the past, Portales felt, would have to be respected if Chile hoped fully to develop its national potential. The great contribution of Portales to Chile lay precisely in his success in reintroducing and strengthening traditional patterns so as to make possible genuine organic development within the framework of custom.

There is scarcely any disagreement among Chileans that Portales was the guiding spirit in molding their nation into a united whole, even though his life was cut short in 1837 by a mutinous group of Chilean army recruits. There is also a general consensus that the policies of Portales exemplified one aspect of national character that under most circumstances is laudable, moderation. Portales never went to the extremes of certain other Latin-American nation-builders. He may have insisted upon firm rule and exploited shamelessly the political advantages of Church-State union; but he never committed the bloody excesses of the Argentine Juan Manuel de Rosas, or wallowed in the religious fanaticism of the Ecuadorean Gabriel García Moreno. Beyond these points, there is little agreement in Chile on Portales. Rather, the man seems to be all things to all persons.

The 1920's and the early 1930's saw the name of Portales invoked by those who wished to use the methods of dictatorship in order to transform Chile into a modern, materially productive nation. Portales thus became something of a model for the first Carlos Ibáñez administration (1927-1931), and received high praise from the Chilean Nazi movement as well. Then, beginning in the mid-1930's, the Portales tradition came to be regarded as a symbol of hope by people grown weary and suspicious of reform notions, and anxious to return to stability, order, and authority, even though these political objectives might suffocate vitality and produce stagnation. In today's Chile it is still the fear of change and experiment, and the glorification of inertia and the status quo that underlie the pro-Portales sentiments entertained by so many of conservative persuasion.[46] It is ironic that the ruler who created the institutional basis for much of nineteenth-century Chilean development, who pursued a dynamic foreign policy, who fostered and abetted economic growth, and used the instrumentality of the national government to foster education, should become the hero of a group that seeks to make a virtue of lethargy.

The modern foes of Portales have been as varied as his defenders. For example, writers who regard democracy as a panacea in all times and places have objected to the authoritarian features of the Portales government, while anticlericals have abhorred the close ties between Church and State that Portales insisted upon.[47] For Marxists, Portales is no puzzle. He is simply a villain, perhaps the archvillain, of Chilean history; the man who reimposed all that was vile and oppressive in colonial times, thereby snuffing out the notions of equality and democracy that had appeared during the early national period, and inflicting upon the country the unrestrained rule of a vicious oligarchy.[48]

Attitudes toward Portales, and the decade or so in which his influence reigned supreme, determine the interpretation of intellectual trends and political activities in the 1840-1880 period. To the champions of Portales, the self-styled liberals who after 1840 worked toward the extension of suffrage rights curtailment of Church influence, and the introduction of party politics are heedless levelers, foolishly intent upon importing from Europe notions that were unworkable in Chile. They were also seekers after personal gain, desirous of replacing the institutional stability introduced by Portales with party maneuvering aimed only at obtaining political spoils. To the detractors of Portales, on the other hand, the intellectual and political leaders of dissent who gradually began to challenge the established order are not only defenders of the rights of man, but the only persons intelligently concerned with balanced economic development. A brief survey of the history of intellectual trends and changing political philosophy in the restive years from 1840 to 1880 will reveal the nature of developments that continue to the present time to nourish animated disputation among Chilean historians.

MAJOR TRENDS IN CHILEAN POLITICAL PHILOSOPHY, 1840-1880

Many of the principles espoused by the *Pipiolos*, who had been crushed at the Battle of Lircay in 1830, gradually re-emerged on the Chilean intellectual scene of the 1840's. In 1843 José Victorino Lastarria, the disparager of colonial traditions, the tireless campaigner for electoral liberty and limited presidential powers, and eventually the champion of Auguste Comte and Herbert Spencer, was elected to the Chamber of Deputies as the representative of Elqui and Parral. At the same time Santiago Arcos Arlegui and Francisco Bilbao were studying in France, and were being influenced by the romantic nationalism of Jules Michelet, as well as by the liberal ideas of political democracy and social equality. Both witnessed the fall of the king of France in 1848, thereby gaining added confidence that liberal republicanism was the inevitable tide of the future. At the end of the 1840's, Arcos and Bilbao had returned to Chile and were active in founding the Society of Equality (*Sociedad de Igualdad*).[49]

The restlessness of the times was reflected also in the 1850 publication by Lastarria and future national president Federico Errázuriz of *Bases de la reforma*. This gave voice to the most liberal aspirations of the era, demanding the denial of extraordinary presidential powers in times of alleged emergency, the granting of voting rights to all men eighteen years of age or over, regardless of literacy, autonomous municipalities, freedom of conscience, a one-house legislature elected by direct popular suffrage, and a one-term limitation on presidential tenure. Two years later another remarkable liberal document appeared, the *Carta a Francisco Bilbao*, written by Santiago Arcos and referred to as the first attempt in Chilean writing to suggest the class-struggle concept as a key to understanding national history.[50]

The list of advocates of liberal, democratic practices and of a more open society grew steadily during the generation beginning in 1840. Eusebio Lillo, probably the best-known Chilean poet of the nineteenth century and author of the verses of the national anthem, gave voice to some of his liberal ideas in the poem, A mi amigo Francisco Bilbao.[51] Poet Lillo joined with such historians as Diego Barros Arana, Benjamín Vicuña Mackenna, and Miguel Luis Amunátegui, and with such literary figures, journalists and politicians as Isidoro Errázuriz, Ambrosio Montt, Gregorio Víctor Amunátegui, Justo and Domingo Arteaga Alemparte, Ignacio Zenteño, and Vicente Reyes, to preach the need for reform and change. The rising liberal trend was also augmented by the writings of the French historian Claudio Gay, who for many years made his home in Chile.[52] In his eight-volume *Historia civil de Chile*, published between 1844 and 1871, the Frenchman gave expression to his encyclopedist tendencies, as well as to his prejudices against the "obscurantism" of Spanish traditions. Moreover, various Reform Clubs were founded, advocating greater human liberty through more democratic institutions, and urging stricter probity in public life. In 1861 the *avant-garde* daily, *La Voz de Chile*, began publication. Through this organ a talented group of journalists and politicians including the Gallo brothers, Pedro León and Angel Custodio, Isidoro Errázuriz, Abraham König, and, above all, Manuel Antonio Matta and Enrique Mac-Iver, the most important figures in the early history of Chile's Radical Party founded in 1863, issued blistering attacks against the status quo.

In addition to urging political and social reform, the self-proclaimed apostles of a new era instituted a spirited anticlerical campaign. Masonic influences undoubtedly contributed to this activity. In the early 1860's a Grand Lodge was founded in Valparaíso, and later in the decade the Justice and Liberty Lodge was established in Santiago. Moreover, the rise of the cult of positivism, which found in the writer Juan Enrique Lagarrigue a zealous defender and popularizer, helped undermine faith in the Roman Catholic Church.

More important than Masonry and positivism in causing the anticlerical orientation of nineteenth-century Chilean liberals were various indigenously rooted factors. To begin with, many of the

liberals genuinely believed that political democracy was the cure-
all for each of society's ills. Proceeding from this premise, they
felt it necessary to destroy the influence of the Church. Otherwise, they feared, there could be no true electoral freedom. The
scandalous manner in which churchmen, especially after 1860,
redoubled their efforts to infuse religion into politics, insisting that
all political issues were matters of conscience and therefore in the
final analysis to be determined by men of the cloth, confirmed
liberal suspicions and animosities. How could democracy function,
they wondered, if theologians rather than the will of the people
decided all matters, both temporal and sacred? One of the intellectuals most firmly convinced that political democracy could not
function until institutions were laicized and the political conscience liberated from artificial religious restraints was the landowning deputy and later senator, Claudio Vicuña Guerrero. Another prominent figure for whom anticlericalism was an indispensable ingredient of liberalism was the civil engineer, educator, and
politician, Eduardo de la Barra. His barbed pen and unmerciful
satirical wit inflicted some of the most devastating of all the blows
struck against the Church in Chile during the second half of the
nineteenth century.[53] Contributing also to a mounting stream of
anticlerical writings was La Linterna del Diablo, the first satirical
newspaper in Chile. Another paper of this style, El Padre Cobos,
ridiculed many aspects of the Church's temporal position in the
1870's.[54]

Alberto Edwards Vives is undoubtedly correct in asserting that
the religious question, above all others, gave rise to party politics
in Chile. This staunchly conservative analyst also provides what is
probably the most rational and objective explanation of the origins
of the Church controversy in Chile. He calls attention to the long
tradition of anticlerical sentiment in the country, noting that voca-
tions were as scarce in 1800 as in 1900, and affirming that in mid-
century, the churches in Copiapó, Valparaíso, and Concepción
were nearly empty every Sunday. Anticlericalism, Edwards opines,
was a spontaneous, popular movement, not one artificially contrived by the political action of liberal elements.[55]

This was the background, then, when one of the most uncompro-

mising and iron-willed men in modern Chilean history, Rafael
Valentín Valdivieso y Zañartu, became archbishop of Santiago in
1845. Valdivieso was convinced there could be no compromise
with the new, secular spirit of the times, and that right-thinking
men must band together to wage an unrelenting struggle against
the forces of evil. The many prominent social and political leaders
who grouped themselves with the Archbishop became the forerunners of the Conservative Party. From their very appearance on
the political scene, they joined in combat with the forerunners of
the Liberal, National, and Radical parties.

THE POLITICAL ARENA, 1840-1880

The liberal ideology, suppressed for nearly twenty years by
Presidents Joaquín Prieto (1831-1841) and Manuel Bulnes (1841-
1851),[56] reappeared as a powerful political influence during the
presidency of Manuel Montt (1851-1861), a true watershed between the old and the new in nineteenth-century Chile.[57] Indeed,
a harbinger of things to come was provided by an uprising in the
closing years of the Bulnes administration. Fomented by the
Society of Equality, as well as by the archconservative followers of
Manuel Camilio Vial, a one-time Minister of Interior for President
Bulnes, an armed insurrection erupted in 1849. It was crushed
without serious difficulty by the administration, and the Society of
Equality was dissolved, with many of its members being sent into
exile. Two years later, a military uprising which drew some liberal
support was put down by the Montt regime. Having been twice
crushingly defeated and harshly dealt with, liberal elements retired from the scene for a time to nurse their grievances. In their
discontent, they were soon joined by a most unlikely ally.

The conservative aristocracy dominant since 1830 was torn by
dissension in 1856 because of a jurisdictional dispute between
ecclesiastical and civil tribunals known as the "affair of the Sacris-
tan." The outcome was that the Chilean Supreme Court exiled
Archbishop Valdivieso, and was backed in its sentence by President Montt and his energetic cabinet leader, Antonio Varas.
Some members of the ruling classes assumed a pro-Church stand,
and came together to found the staunchly Catholic, proclerical,

Conservative Party—membership in which, according to author and statesman Abdón Cifuentes, brought one closer to God.[58] Many other Chilean aristocrats approved the stand of the Supreme Court and the president. This second group formed the National or Montt-Varista Party which, though anticlerical, stood for authoritarian government and was as aristocratic in its makeup as the rival Conservative Party.

Conservatives now had a common grievance with the forces that had been crushed by military action in 1849 and 1851 and that banded together in the mid-1850's to form the Liberal Party. Both Conservatives and Liberals opposed the National Party. Dislike of a common foe served to mask the fundamental differences between Conservatives and Liberals, and the two groups united to form the so-called Fusion. At this point, in 1859, Pedro León Gallo,[59] a former friend of President Montt and a successful mining magnate in Copiapó, led a revolt against the administration. Although the insurgents enjoyed the support of the Fusionists, Montt inflicted a speedy defeat upon them. The frustrated Conservatives and Liberals now harbored additional resentment against the National Party. The age of party dispute had begun in earnest.

Political events were as important as economic factors in providing for admission of new men into the ranks of the aristocracy. Political expediency caused the most conservative of Chile's blue-bloods, the followers of Manuel Camilio Vial, to unite with the upstart Society of Equality in the 1849 insurrection. And unalloyed political considerations created the Fusion, driving together the aristocratic Conservatives and the Liberals, many of whom could only claim a social status considerably beneath the top level. In the search for political allies, class distinctions often melted. The continuing divisions among the Chilean ruling classes served throughout the nineteenth century to break down upper-class social barriers, as the traditional elite faced the necessity of winning recruits from a social class that they might otherwise have preferred to ignore.

In 1861 the logical man to succeed Montt in the presidency was his loyal and able Minister of Interior, Antonio Varas.[60] But election, or rather imposition, of Varas might have stung the

Fusionists into renewed rebellion. Varas wisely stepped aside, and José Joaquín Pérez, a widely traveled diplomat and politician of conciliatory temperament, was named the National Party's standard-bearer. As the official candidate of the outgoing administration he was, of course, duly installed in the presidential office. Before long, though, Pérez began to cooperate with the Fusion, whose growing membership made it for a brief period the largest political group in the country. By the end of his term, Pérez had become almost exclusively dependent upon the Fusion for political support. But the moderate president's wise endeavor to provide sound and stable government, even at the price of slighting former political friends, was thwarted by growing dissension with the ranks of the Fusionists. Some Liberals who had felt uncomfortable with their Conservative coalitionists joined the newly organized Radical Party,[61] which in 1864 elected as its first deputies Manuel Antonio Matta, Tomás Gallo, Juan Nepomuceno Espejo, Ricardo Claro y Cruz, and Manuel Recabarren. The underlying purpose of the new party was to work uncompromisingly and intransigently for political democracy, greater social equality, parliamentary rather than presidential rule, decentralization, and, perhaps above all, for suppression of the Church's temporal influence. While the party energetically sought support from the new middle sectors, its main leadership came from a moneyed aristocracy, and its early guiding spirit was Manuel Antonio Matta. An austere patriarch, Matta in 1873 became the fourth president of Chile's most exclusive aristocratic social organization, the *Club de la Unión*.[62]

A coalition was soon effected between the Radical and National parties. Although the first ostensibly favored an extreme form of democracy and the second stood for political authoritarianism of the Portales type, both were united in their anticlerical sentiments. Faced now with a rival political alliance, and with its own ranks somewhat thinned by defections, the Fusion suffered a further blow with the death of Manuel Antonio Tocornal in 1867. The conservative Tocornal, perhaps more than any single man, had embodied the spirit of the Fusion, and his political sagacity had helped keep the two poles united. And, at about the same time, a Conservative attempt to impeach the Supreme Court on no firmer grounds than the high tribunal's anticlerical leanings, further disillusioned many of the Liberals in the Fusion who had not been willing to go to the extreme of joining the Radical Party. Notwithstanding internal tensions, the Fusionists succeeded in gaining election of their candidate, Federico Errázuriz, in 1871. Only grudgingly supported by the Fusion Liberals because of his allegedly proclerical leanings, Errázuriz had been opposed by José Tomás Urmeneta,[63] the nominee of the National and Radical parties. A rich industrialist and mineowner, Urmeneta had considerable support in Coquimbo, Talca, Ñuble, and Atacama. The Fusion, controlling the electoral process as the incumbent party, awarded Urmeneta a mere 52 electoral votes, while claiming 226 for its candidate.[64]

During the Errázuriz administration (1871-1876)[65] the sorely-tried Fusion finally split wide asunder. Basically the cause of this development was the issue of lay versus religious control of education. Conservative Minister of Education, Abdón Cifuentes, managed to steer through Congress a bill partially freeing private schools from supervision of the National Institute of Education, directed at the time (1873) by Diego Barros Arana.[66] The result of the Cifuentes bill was a lowering of educational standards in private, or church-controlled, schools. Barros Arana, moreover, whose aim as he described it was to strip history and learning in general of the miracles and other supernatural appurtenances with which a gullible and fanatical age had burdened them, promptly became engaged in a bitter polemic with proclerical education leaders. The outcome was the removal of Barros Arana from the post of director of the National Institute. This Conservative-directed maneuver thoroughly incensed most of the Fusion Liberals. Withdrawing at last from the unlikely coalition, they helped bring about by the end of 1873 the fall of Cifuentes from his cabinet post. The Conservatives were now without ministerial representation in the government, and from this point on Errázuriz sought to govern through a Liberal Alliance, made up of defectors from the Fusion, and members of the National and Radical parties. An indication of the new political orientation was afforded in 1875 when José Alfonso, a Radical Party luminary later to represent his country at the 1889 Washington Conference, was named Minister of Foreign Relations.

Under Errázuriz, many political reforms were enacted, the main results of which were to limit presidential power, to move Chile increasingly toward parliamentary rule, and to facilitate party control of politics. Presidential nominating conventions now became *de rigueur*, and in November 1875, the Liberal Alliance summoned such an assembly. Aníbal Pinto, a former Minister of War and Navy and a disciple of Andrés Bello—the Venezuelan-born intellectual who helped to lay the foundations of Chile's educational and legal structures—defeated the more moderate Miguel Luis Amunátegui who, with the sole exception of Barros Arana, had been the most influential educator in steering Chilean instruction toward a secular, scientific orientation.[67]

In December the so-called Convention of the People met. Representing a new political grouping called the Liberal Democratic Party, this Convention decided upon Benjamín Vicuña Mackenna as its presidential candidate.[68] Romantic historian, diplomat, statesman and journalist, Vicuña Mackenna was also a former reform-minded intendant of Santiago who had transformed the Cerro Santa Lucía from a slum and vice center into one of the continent's most lovely parks. For a time a member of the Fusion, Vicuña Mackenna campaigned in 1876 for a return to pristine liberal reform ideals, which he claimed had been submerged beneath a sea of demagoguery and purely theological disputation. His campaign, notwithstanding support from the Conservative Party, was doomed to failure. At this time in Chile it was still impossible to defeat the official candidate.

THE SOCIAL IMPORT OF CHILEAN POLITICAL AND INTELLECTUAL DEVELOPMENT TO 1880

It is obviously absurd to read modern developments into the 1880's, and to suggest that as of 1880 Chile had already begun to suffer from the effects of a social problem. As late as 1885, 30 per cent of the active population was listed as independent workers, including artisans and those who owned and worked their own farms. The vast majority in this category apparently enjoyed some element of security and the ability to provide for themselves economically. Another 24 per cent, the agrarian laborers, were at least the beneficiaries of a feudalistic system that provided for the most pressing material needs of life. The same was true of the 10 per cent classified as domestic servants. The problem of a city proletariat crowded together in slum areas and working for greedy entrepreneurs was one with which Chileans would come to contend only in the future. Mining, the most likely enterprise at the time in which large numbers of workers might be exploited by management, employed only 3.6 per cent of the labor force.[69]

Still, all of the intellectual ferment, the concern with new ideas and the introduction of political reform, had not created a tradition that would equip Chile to cope with a social problem once urbanization, mounting industrialization, and more intensive mineral exploitation had come to create a less personal economic structure and to make possible and apparently expedient exploitation of labor by capital. The traditional aristocracy that had triumphed in 1830, that was scarcely challenged in its exercise of power until mid-century, and that continued thereafter to express its aspirations through the Fusion, the National, and the Conservative parties, espoused consistently a social philosophy best described as paternalism. The fundamental belief was that the natural, divinely ordained social order called for the existence of an immobile lower class permanently entrusted with the meaner occupations. There was no reason to expect the laboring masses to rise in the social order, for this would merely upset the hierarchical structure established by providence. But lower-class status and poverty did not imply a stigma of any kind or suggest moral shortcomings. Those in the lower classes had the same end of eternal salvation as those in the aristocracy, and therefore possessed human dignity. They should, accordingly, be made reasonably comfortable by a paternalistic arrangement in which the *patrón*, conscious of the humanitarian obligations of the nobility, assumed some responsibility for the material and spiritual welfare of his wards.

The social goal of the nineteenth-century champions of liberalism in Chile, who found their political homes in the Liberal and Radical parties, was to give to the lower classes a chance to rise in

social status by extending to them education and suffrage opportunities. Within the framework of this outlook, it was no longer
necessary for the upper classes to take special precautions to provide comfort and security for the masses. Rather, the masses were
expected to solve their problems on their own initiative by taking
advantage of the avenues for advance which, theoretically, liberal
administrations would provide them. The success of many Chileans
by mid-century in following the Horatio Alger success formula
often served to convince spokesmen of the new order that adequate openings for advancement already existed, and that any
attempt to establish additional ones would constitute an economically inadvisable and morally unjustified pampering of dul-
lards. Positivism, secularism, and classical liberalism in Chile were
seldom so directly ruthless and openly dedicated to eradication
of the "unfit" as they were in the Mexico of Porfirio Díaz or even
in the post-Civil War United States when Spencer enjoyed his
great vogue. Still, there may have inhered in them tendencies
toward harsher physical exploitation, once an industrial-urban
order had appeared, than existed in Chile's conservative traditions.

Chile has suffered unfortunate consequences from the conflict
of two ideologies. On the one hand exists the liberal belief that
poverty is a disgrace, but that the humble man can and should
rise and thereby gain honorable status and the power of self-pro-
tection. On the other hand, endures the conservative belief that
poverty is no disgrace, and that lower groups must never aspire to
political articulateness or to a status of comfort that they can
themselves safeguard and augment. To gain even the tolerance or
forbearance of the liberals, the masses must attain precisely what
the conservatives are determined to prevent them from attaining:
self-improvement, self-assertiveness, and a rise in social status.
Through the years, beginning even during the later nineteenth
century, cross-pollenization between the two ideologies has occurred. Liberals, at least those who became successful, were enticed
by the practical convenience of a providentially-ordained stratified
society. They came to question the perfectibility of the lower class,
and thus grew increasingly indifferent toward supplying its members with opportunity to advance. Conservatives, influenced by

secular, material standards, began to question the feasibility of supplying paternalistic protection to groups that appeared to lack economic virtues and the capitalist mentality. Middle and upper groups tended therefore to join in a disparaging attitude toward the lower mass.

SOME NINETEENTH-CENTURY ATTITUDES TOWARD THE UNITED STATES

One Tradition: The anti-Yankee, Isolationist Spirit of Portales

Diplomatic contact between Chile and the United States commenced in a spirit of warm cordiality. In December of 1811 the first United States consul, Joel R. Poinsett, arrived in Santiago. This flamboyant diplomat from South Carolina gave enthusiastic encouragement to the Chilean independence movement and actually participated personally in some of the engagements that the patriots fought against Spanish royalist forces.[70] On several occasions during the wars of independence, moreover, Chileans were able to purchase arms and even ships in the United States. However, when Theodorick Bland arrived in Chile in 1817 as a United States commissioner to investigate affairs in the southern Americas he became involved in disputes between rival political factions and formed an unfavorable opinion of the patriots.[71]

Relations between the two countries were restored to an amicable basis when the United States extended diplomatic recognition to the independent republic of Chile on January 27, 1823. Hemen Allen from Vermont arrived in Santiago in April of the following year and was extended a warm, almost tumultuous greeting as the first envoy and minister plenipotentiary of the United States. In Washington, however, relations had already become tense. Chile's first envoy to the United States, Joaquín Campina, grew increasingly resentful toward the State Department when he was unable to obtain what he considered satisfactory terms for a treaty of friendship, commerce, and navigation. Not until 1834, in fact, was such a treaty signed and ratified.

In the meantime, the two countries had begun to argue over

pecuniary claims. During the wars of independence certain United States citizens, most of them masters or crew members of ships that were engaged in commerce in the southern Pacific waters,[72] had accused Chilean agents of confiscating considerable sums of cash as well as valuable goods from them. Protracted diplomatic debate ensued over this matter, with both sides frequently resorting to forceful and intemperate language. Against this background, United States diplomatic representatives "seemed unable to protect their country's interest and at the same time remain on friendly terms with the Chilean government." [73] Not until 1863 was the dispute finally settled, essentially in favor of the United States, by the arbitration of the king of Belgium.

Before the arbitration settlement, fresh incidents had led to further deterioration in Chilean-United States relations. In the 1840's United States Envoy Seth Barton became involved in a bitter dispute with the archbishop of Santiago, Valdivieso y Zañartu. The prelate disapproved of Barton's marriage to a socially prominent Chilean lady, and tried unsuccessfully to block the union. Barton, after scathingly denouncing the archbishop, left Chile in a rage, but not before the government of that country had demanded his recall.[74] The United States Legation in Santiago remained closed for almost a year after the departure of Barton. Nor did relations improve with the arrival of a new envoy. United States spokesmen at this time resented Chile's overt sympathy for Mexico during its war with the northern Colossus (1846-1848), while Chileans were indignant over the harsh treatment that many of their fellow citizens received in the California gold rush.[75] By 1855 relations had become so strained that the United States envoy in Santiago reported: ". . . the United States and her citizens are the object of constant and virulent attack and the chosen target of scurrilous abuse on the part of the press of the country. . . . It has even been proposed to expel them from the country and close the ports of Chile against their commerce." [76]

More important than unpleasant diplomatic incidents was the basic attitude of distrust and even hostility toward the United States displayed by Chile's great statesman Diego Portales. The import of President James Monroe's December 1823 address had not yet become clear to most observers, either in the United States or abroad, when Portales began to express disapproval of those concepts that came soon to be referred to as the Monroe Doctrine. "Be careful," wrote Portales, "of escaping one domination at the price of falling under another. We must distrust those men who take advantage of the work of our champions of freedom, without having helped us in any way." [77] The Portales attitude helped found a Chilean tradition of diplomacy which was in some ways as powerful in that country as the Washington Farewell Address and early Jeffersonian isolationism in the United States.

In regard to inter-American affairs, the four pillars of the Portales policy were: (1) resentment of the Monroe Doctrine, and the desire to set it at naught; (2) conviction that so far as commerce was concerned, Latin America should think principally in terms of trade with Europe and the world rather than simply with American Hemisphere republics; (3) desire for a strong Chile that could singlehandedly defend and implement foreign policy; and (4), as a consequence of the third point, a disinclination to co-operate in multilateral hemisphere ventures, even with the His-panic-American republics of southern South America.[78]

These four fundamental principles of foreign policy, directly opposed to expanding United States influence in the hemisphere and to any inter-American system, continued to attract statesmen throughout the nineteenth century and even as late as the 1930's. Nevertheless, as a formula for international relations, the Portales program had the field to itself for a relatively short time, being soon faced with the challenge of two policies basically opposed to it.

A SECOND TRADITION: HISPANIC-AMERICAN UNION TO THWART
UNITED STATES PRE-EMINENCE IN THE HEMISPHERE

The most widely held of these two policies was based upon an animosity toward the United States exceeding that of the Portales tradition. It went beyond the Portales position also in evolving a rather complete rationale, both cultural and economic in content, explaining in what respects the United States represented a danger-ous influence that must be resisted. But in total departure from the Portales program, advocates of this second approach to inter-American relations affirmed that the only hope for Hispanic America lay in union.

The strongest nineteenth-century exposition of this viewpoint is found in the *Colección de ensayos i documentos relativos a la unión i confederación de los pueblos hispano-americanos,* two volumes published in 1862 and 1867, under the auspices of the Santiago Society of American Union (*Sociedad de la Unión Americana de Santiago*).[79] This organization included some of the most notable of Chilean intellectuals, from Radicals Manuel Antonio Matta and Manuel Recabarren to Conservatives Manuel José Irarrázaval and Francisco de Borja Larraín.[80] The immediate cause for the formation of the Santiago Society had been the Spanish naval operations against Chile and Peru, in the course of which Valparaíso had been bombarded in 1866.[81] The Society urged Hispanic-American union as a means of preventing the recurrence of so humiliating an experience. Many of its members also expressed their disillusionment with and hostility toward the United States, and asserted that from the sort of union they recommended would come the strength that was needed to check the growing influence and ambitions of the northern giant.

In one of the contributions to the *Colección de ensayos,* Pedro Félix Vicuña made it clear that the United States had no place in any union involving the Hispanic-American republics.[82] Manuel Carrasco Albano went beyond this and affirmed that unless the *South* American republics united, the Latin race—as a significant factor in America—would disappear, overwhelmed by the greedy Anglo-Saxon monster of the North.[83] The strongest words of all in the collected essays were uttered by firebrand Francisco Bilbao.[84] Warning that idealism and human nobility were threatened by the expansionist ambitions of two empires, Bilbao averred that Russia, through the initial instrumentality of Pan-Slavism, hoped to spread the gospel of personal servitude and inequality throughout the world, while the United States sought to infest the globe with its materialistic individualism. "Russia retires at the moment to prepare a future ambush. But the United States extends more each day the predatory hunt which it has already undertaken. We

see fragments of America falling into the Saxon jaws of the vora-
cious serpent. Yesterday, Texas. Soon, northern Mexico will acknowledge a new sovereign." [85] Ultimately, prophesied Bilbao, all
Hispanic-American nations would become mere protectorates of
the United States—unless they united.

Bilbao attempted also to describe the process by which the
United States had transformed itself from the hope of humanity,
with the finest political institutions in the world, into a major
threat to culture and human dignity. Infatuated by early success,
the citizens of the United States had come to regard themselves
the equals of the occupants of Olympus. As rampant individualism
triumphed over social consciousness, the Yankee replaced the
American. Philosophy gave way to chauvinism, charity to industry, morality to pursuit of wealth, and justice to self-interest. The
"new" United States, Bilbao concluded, was incompatible with
and presented grave dangers to Hispanic America, which had not
yet lost faith in the spiritual destiny of man, which valued society
above the individual, which preferred beauty to riches, justice to
power, art to commerce, poetry to industry, generosity to covetous-
ness, and which placed obligations above self-interest. [86]

These opinions of the advocates of Hispanic-American union
could logically be expected from conservative defenders of colonial
customs. What makes them remarkable is that they are the views
of liberal, positivist thinkers, of radical reformers and vituperative
disparagers of Spanish traditions. In Chile, the liberal-positivist
movement did not produce the pro-United States sentiments[87]
that were evident among some of Latin America's nineteenth-century reform leaders. In addition to Bilbao, staunchly liberal and
rabidly anticlerical Isidoro Errázuriz spoke for many of the men in
his movement when he described the United States as atheistic,
materialistic, coarse, and crude.[88] And it is significant that the
group headed by Manuel Antonio Matta, which published that
organ of extreme dissent from the old order, *La Voz de Chile*, and
which furnished the nucleus of the Radical Party in the 1860's,
expressed strong suspicions of the United States. This group, moreover, consistently urged a union of Hispanic-American republics
as a means of thwarting the menace from the North.[89]

Anti-United States doctrines and the message of Hispanic-American union were preached by still another influential intellectual of liberal leanings, Benjamín Vicuña Mackenna.[90] Vicuña's ire against the United States had been aroused in the mid-1860's[91] during the course of an unsuccessful ten-month mission to that country for the purpose of purchasing warships for defense against the Spanish. A frustrated and embittered Vicuña decided that Anglo-American and Ibero-American peoples had nothing in common and that the Monroe Doctrine threatened rather than protected Latin America. Secretary of State William Seward, in Vicuña's opinion, characterized the entire United States civilization: he was brusque, lacking in broad culture, a bit vulgar, and animated only by a lust to advance his own interests.[92] Another unsuccessful seeker of United States assistance during the Spanish crisis was a statesman destined to wield considerable influence in future domestic developments and international relations, Luis Aldunate.[93] By 1865 he had come to the same conclusions concerning the United States as Vicuña, feeling that the Hispanic-American nations must develop their own strength through unity and shun intimate relations with the northern power. More important still, the Spanish bombardment of Valparaíso, which was passively witnessed by two United States cruisers, called forth the wrath of young Marcial Martínez, and awakened his indignation against what he felt to be the duplicity of the trustees of the Monroe Doctrine. Within fifteen years, Liberal Party stalwart Martínez, as his country's envoy in Washington, would have additional grounds for his distrust of the United States. Ultimately, he became the elder statesman of the anti-United States and pro-South American union position.[94]

A THIRD TRADITION: THE AMERICAN INTERNATIONAL
LAW APPROACH TO HEMISPHERE RELATIONS

Finally, there had arisen in Chile by 1880 a third important approach to inter-American relations. As with the two already described, it continued to influence Chilean attitudes well into the twentieth century. And within the precepts of this third program for hemisphere dealings, Chilean contributions to the inter-

American movement have been greater perhaps than those of any other nation.

The advocates of the third approach took as their point of departure an idealistic belief in the existence of basic ties, both practical and mystic, between all occupants of the American Hemisphere. Consequently, they urged the desirability of the close fraternity of all American states—a recommendation originally advanced in Chile by the patriots Father Camilio Henríquez[95] and Francisco Salas. But at the same time they entertained considerable misgivings about the United States. Accordingly, they urged the formulation of a code of American international law that would embody all of the New World hopes for protecting human dignity and achieving the equality of nations. Could such a code be framed and could sincere United States acceptance be obtained, then the Latin nations of the hemisphere could participate without fear, on a basis of equality, with the more powerful Anglo-Saxon America.

Andrés Bello planted the seeds in Chile of the American international law approach. He argued cogently for the principles of the equality of nations and nonintervention. Significantly, he also stated that Great Britain was one of the nations most opposed to these principles.[96] Going on from this conclusion, the great disciple of Bello, José Victorino Lastarria, in one of his major works which he began writing in 1865,[97] charged that Europe was no longer acting in accordance with the laws of progress. Democracy, said Lastarria, was necessary for progress, and Europe was suppressing democracy. Only in America might men still succeed in responding to the higher callings of their nature. Therefore, Americans should formulate a different body of international law from that which prevailed in Europe. In order to make American international law a reality, Lastarria advised Latin Americans to overcome their anti-United States prejudices, which, he held, were artificially nourished by the Pope and by most priests.

In criticizing Argentina on the grounds that it was acting contrary to the true American purpose by insisting on unilateral action and opposing all attempts at confederation, Lastarria was also, at least by implication, censuring the Portales approach to inter-

American relations. And by his insistence that an American system based on American international law must include the United States, he placed himself in direct opposition to the policy favored by many of his fellow liberals, including his close friend Francisco Bilbao.[98]

Lastarria has been one of the most influential of Chilean Americanists. It is because many of his countrymen continued to work along the lines of the inter-American ideas he defended that dealings between Chile and the United States have not abounded in still more frequent crises and disputes. The tragedy of relations between the two countries has been that United States actions after 1880 afforded such concrete grounds for fear and distrust that American international law came—increasingly for Chilean statesmen—to be regarded as a means of protecting Latin America against, rather than preparing the way for cooperation with, the United States.

2: CHILE'S DOMESTIC DEVELOPMENT, 1880-1892

INTRODUCTION

For the young Chilean nation, the years from 1880 to 1892 can be compared to adolescence. They spanned a period of development in which surging strength and confidence mingled with previously unexperienced doubts and a frantic search for purpose. The rousing War of the Pacific victory, achieved against seemingly overwhelming odds, led to a feeling of near omnipotence, and fostered sentiments of smug satisfaction over the apparent perfection of national institutions. But continuing internal dissension led ultimately to a civil war and the first overthrow of a constitutionally elected regime since 1830. And just as internal order was temporarily crumbling, an enforced diplomatic surrender to the United States dictated a sweeping re-evaluation of foreign policy. Emerging finally from this period of hectic activity and crisis, Chile entered upon years of relative calm that endured to 1920. But the era of success and hope, of failure and frustration, left its mark. Above all, it rendered the national leaders after 1892 indecisive as to whether Chile should brave the risks and uncertainties attendant upon pursuit of further growth, development, and maturity, or cling to the static comforts of youth.

VICTORY, INTERNAL DEVELOPMENT, AND AN ERA OF EXUBERANT CONFIDENCE

CHILEANS RESPOND TO SIGNS OF NATIONAL GREATNESS

The Treaty of Ancón, signed on October 20, 1883, was a milestone in Chilean history, and the culminating point in a series of military victories that was nothing short of fantastic.[1] At the outset of the War of the Pacific in 1879, the Chilean army of 2,400 had been pitted against 13,200 Peruvian and 3,232 Bolivian troops.[2] (The Bolivian forces included over one thousand officers.) And yet, within four years, Chile had humiliated her combined adversaries, had vastly expanded her national boundaries, had established her sovereignty over nearly 25,000 new subjects,[3] and, most important, had acquired control over rich nitrate deposits, destined to constitute the principal source of national income for the next three to four decades. While all of this was transpiring, ordinary governmental services had not been interrupted. Between 1880 and 1883, for example, the number of public schools increased by eighty-three, and the ratio of schools to students changed from 1:217 to 1:170.[4]

Traditional procedures of civilian government had proved their merits by maintaining domestic development and tranquility while simultaneously providing competent direction to the military effort. By the end of the war, then, the political institutions that had been evolving since 1830 were more firmly established than ever before. Because of this, newly appearing military heroes had little opportunity of capitalizing on war-won glory to gain political dominance. Instead, the army was content to find its full measure of satisfaction in its professional accomplishments, while leaving politics to the civilians. The sense of military professionalism was enhanced by the arrival in 1886 of a German training mission led by Emil Körner. The tremendous economic boom touched off by the successful war also helped to stifle any overflow of military activity into the political sphere. Expanding economic opportunities existed on so vast a scale that ambitious middle-class elements did not have to turn to military careers as a means of gaining security and perhaps an entry into politics.[5] The military remained, therefore, strictly military, and Chile escaped one of the worst impediments to political maturity that has beset the majority of other Latin-American republics.

It was also fortunate that one of the great stimulants to Chilean traditions of militarism came to an end in 1883. This year witnessed the final campaigns against the Araucanians, completing at last a military venture that Spaniards had commenced before the mid-sixteenth century. As a military problem, the Indians now ceased to exist. The lands which had once been battlefields became the theater for the peaceful though often unscrupulous operations of land speculators. Much of these territories were converted into agrarian colonies that welcomed large numbers of immigrants. Whatever the disposition of the Indian lands, the point was that what had once been a military concern became a purely economic matter, and the glorification of military virtue that had influenced the Chilean population for over three centuries of Indian campaigns ceased largely to operate.[6]

The economic development that accompanied and followed the War of the Pacific was so remarkable that Marxist writers feel justified in alleging that Chile's great military adventure was instigated by self-seeking capitalists in order to bring their country out of the business stagnation that had begun in 1878.[7] However absurd this allegation, the truth is that the war did provide Chile with the economic means for coming of age. Manuel Guillermo Carmona, Chief of the Commercial Statistics Office, sensed this fact when in 1881 he observed that economic advances had been no less spectacular than those of the Chilean army in Peru.[8] Three years later the Central Office of Statistics noted that the total value of general commerce—exports and imports—had soared to over 129 million pesos, compared to roughly 83 million in 1875.[9] With only 5.4 per cent of the Latin-American population in 1887, Chile conducted 13 per cent of the entire area's commerce and enjoyed the highest per-capita income of any republic south of the Rio Grande. More surprising still, the per-capita value of exports was higher than that of the United States.[10] Bank deposits also reflected the economic upsurge. Approximately 60 million pesos on the eve of the war, they had risen to double this amount by 1890.[11] A bright economic future seemed assured, and the claims of the Society for Industrial Development (*Sociedad de Fomento Fabril*) that Chile could soon be largely self-sufficient even in the production of finished products seemed perfectly reasonable to many of the nation's capitalists.[12]

The federal government shared with private capitalists in the spiralling national prosperity. Treasury income rose from 65 to 75 million pesos of eighteen pence between 1880 and 1890.[13] For this last year, nearly 15 million pesos of the national budget were allotted to public works.[14] And in the decade following the outbreak of the War of the Pacific, the value of nitrate exports jumped from 25 to 80 million pesos.[15] Increasingly, the government came to depend on nitrate export taxes for its revenue. In 1880, export taxes produced only 4.7 per cent of government revenue, while in 1890 they accounted for over 46 per cent of the national treasury's income.[16]

As Chile savored its new prosperity, a demographic shift was underway. Although, with the 1883 subjugation of the Araucanian Indians, much southern agricultural land was being settled and exploited for the first time,[17] the most striking aspect of population shifts was the move to cities. While over-all, national population between 1885 and 1895 increased only from 2.53 to 2.7 millions,[18] the inhabitants of Santiago grew in number from 189,000 to over a quarter of a million. The same decade witnessed a population increase in Concepción from 24,000 to 40,000, in Iquique from 15,000 to 30,000, in Antofagasta from 7,600 to 13,500, and in Valparaíso from 104,000 to over 122,000.[19] Wealth increasingly acquired an urban basis, as absentee landlords channeled funds into productive city ventures, as well as into conspicuous consumption—not only in Chile, but in Europe. Thus, when Augusto Matte, Chile's envoy in Paris, presided over a gathering of the Chilean community in the French capital to celebrate the fall of President José Manuel Balmaceda, he had to obtain the largest salon of the luxurious Grand Hotel. A smaller room would not have accommodated the numerous Chileans in Paris, among whom there appeared the aristocratic names of Blest, Vega, Errázuriz, Baeza, Gandarillas, Subercaseaux, Irarrázaval, Lyon, Larraín, Vial, Peña, Orrego, Amunátegui and Zañartu.[20]

With a background of military victory, an outer show of political stability and representative civilian government, and head-turning economic progress, Chileans came to regard themselves as something of a master race in Latin America. An editorial in El Ferrocarril averred in 1880 that Chile's military victories were winning for it the attention and admiration of the world, and would soon attract armies of immigrants and guarantee the realiza-

tion of a glorious destiny.[21] Military success also called forth
heightened pride in political institutions, as various newspapers suggested that the heroic feats would have been impossible without
the stability of legal and constitutional administration which Chile,
alone among Latin-American nations, had known how to achieve.[22]
Minister of Interior (and soon-to-be-president) Domingo Santa
María noted with justifiable pride in mid-1880 that it had not been
necessary to alter constitutional order to achieve military triumph:
"The integrity of the legal regime, preserved amidst such excep-
tional circumstances, is a source of glory for the republic, and an
eloquent testimony to the patriotism of the Chilean people." [23]
A little later, a patriotic writer noted with approval that Argentina
was beginning to advance toward stability by emulating Chile's
political institutions. "By developing along these lines," he declared, "Argentina has now attained the right to aspire to friendship
with Chile on the basis of equality." [24]

Other observers tended to attribute success to the superior
virtues of the Chilean nature. A newspaper editorial stated: "Our
triumphs are owing to the fact that . . . we are a people accus-
tomed to overcoming grave difficulties by our habits of great industry and labor." [25] In a different paper, an article concluded: "It is
reserved to Chile, land of peaceful habits, incessant labor, humanitarian sentiments and tranquil disposition . . . to give to our sister republics an example of what patriotism and dedication to work
can accomplish." [26] Then, there was the editorial that affirmed:
"Chile, through the effort and labor expended since the attainment of independence, has achieved a reputation of virtue and
industry not equalled by another country of this continent." [27] The
all-pervasive spirit of self-satisfaction ushered in during the early
1880's was probably best expressed in the Valparaíso daily, El Mercurio: "Chile's greatness is now immense and all other nations
acknowledge it. . . . How could its glory be greater? Is there any
other American nation that has accomplished so much?" [28]

Combined with pride in past attainments was an unbounded
confidence in the future, and a conviction that Chile was well on
the way to becoming one of the world's great powers. This attitude
was in the 1880's as much a part of the national outlook as was

ever Manifest Destiny in the United States.[29] Unfortunately, added to the natural exuberance and optimism of a young republic whose accomplishments provided a legitimate source of pride and emotional nationalism was a view of race that would, as the years passed, establish itself as one of the more significant features of upper- and middle-class attitudes. In more than one of the contemporary editorials may be found at least the implication that Bolivia and Peru were mere Indian pygmies trying to stand in the way of white Chile's destiny.[30] Suggestions were further advanced that racially heterogeneous nations in the American Hemisphere could never aspire to the heights which Chile was destined to attain.[31] Journalists also ascribed the allegedly scandalous conduct of Peruvian leader Nicolás Piérola to his Indian blood,[32] and described a Peruvian general as a typical Indian: false, dissimulating, ostentatious, and fatuous.[33]

SOME SIGNS OF ECONOMIC IMBALANCE

The spirit of the 1880's was hardly conducive to reform, and the warnings of a few concerned observers went largely unheeded. A blistering editorial denouncing the slum conditions in which urban lower classes lived, and demanding that something be done about cleaning streets so that city dwellers would not have to breathe polluted air,[34] produced no response. Equally ignored was a plea that adulteration of food and liquor be halted.[35]

Still, for those willing to probe beneath the surface, there were disturbing indications that not all was well, not even economically. The Society for Industrial Development warned that nitrate prosperity was ephemeral, and that only industrialization could guarantee the nation's future economic strength.[36] In 1884, Manuel Aristides Zañartu, later to serve as Minister of Treasury under President Balmaceda, published the first volume of *Luis Ríos*, in which he preached the need for economic nationalism, urged especially that tariffs be enacted to encourage new industries, and cautioned the nation against merely living off its nitrate wealth. From still other sources came essentially the same message, advising economic diversification, particularly industrialization, and pleading that Chile encourage technical education rather than cling to the educational goals of the Renaissance.[37] In a country that still suffered from an illiteracy rate of 65 per cent,[38] and in which an increasing urban proletariat would inevitably become disillusioned and restive unless provided with expanding economic opportunities, there were ample grounds for this advice, regardless of how little impact it created.

A few writers also grew wary of increasing British influence in the nitrate industry, and admonished their countrymen not to let their economic future fall into the hands of foreign monopolies. Even by the early 1880's, British financiers were actively initiating the process which by the middle of the next decade would place them in control of some 43 per cent of Chile's nitrate capital.[39]

Chilean official policy had originally facilitated the rise of British nitrate pre-eminence. A law of January 11, 1881, decreed that individuals or firms holding three fourths of the bonds issued by Peru in compensation for nitrate holdings nationalized in 1874 and 1875 would receive the particular claim or mining operation on which the bonds were issued, provided they paid to the Chilean government the cash value of the other one fourth.[40] By September, the law was amended to provide for delivery of mining concessions by Chile to those who produced one half of the Peruvian bonds, and paid the value of the other half in cash. Mines for which sufficient bonds were not presented were to be auctioned off to the highest bidder, with no advantage being given to Chilean nationals. The effect of this legislation was to deliver to foreign, and especially to British investors, a large portion of nitrate property.

In dramatic fashion, the British adventurer-capitalist John T. North proceeded to gain possession of most of the nitrate holdings of Tarapacá. Borrowing 600,000 pesos from the Chilean Bank of Valparaíso with which to begin operations, North in the very early stages of the War of the Pacific started to acquire Peruvian government nitrate indemnification bonds, often for as little as 11 per cent of the face value.[41] Other Englishmen followed the North formula, although never with quite such spectacular success, and by 1882 nearly 35 per cent of the nitrate deposits which Chile was in the process of wresting from Peru and Bolivia had been assigned to British interests.[42]

Chile's most eminent economist and long-time champion of laissez faire, Miguel Cruchaga Montt, grew alarmed about the situation. In the pages of the *Revista Económica*, which he had founded in 1886, he began to argue for national control over nitrates. His crusade was short-lived, for he died the year after founding his distinguished economics journal. But the cause was soon taken up by Francisco Valdés Vergara, one of Chile's best economic writers in the late nineteenth and early twentieth centuries. In 1889 Valdés published *La crisis salitrera y las medidas que se proponen para remediarlo*. The book denounced foreign monopolistic control over nitrates, and called for government action to end it.

The attention of other economic worriers was fixed upon the currency problem. Some of them found ominous the fact that even in a decade unrivaled in national history for its prosperity, the foreign debt increased from 93 to nearly 125 million pesos.[43] Furthermore, in the course of the War of the Pacific, the government had directly issued 28 million pesos in paper money, and this mildly inflationist step helped produce a decline in the peso's international exchange rate. The money problem became more severe after 1885, when the world prices for such Chilean exports as copper,[44] wheat, guano, and nitrates[45] declined appreciably. The Santa María administration (1881-1886) began to plan for retiring paper money, and for converting to metallic currency. The matter was still under discussion, however, when the Balmaceda regime was installed in 1886.[46]

INTERNAL DISSENSION AND CIVIL WAR

Pre-Balmaceda Bickering

President Aníbal Pinto (1876-1881), apparently lacking some of the political skill and force of leadership of his predecessors, found it increasingly difficult to keep the various factions of the Liberal Alliance united in some semblance of a cohesive whole. Frequent ministerial crises and cabinet changes became for a time a definite menace to stability. One of Pinto's ministers, José Manuel Balmaceda, actually felt that had it not been for the War of the Pacific Pinto might have fallen, the victim of a civil war.[47]

At the outset of Domingo Santa María's presidency, the old religious issue seemed, on the surface, to be as divisive a political force as ever. The president, dedicated to theological liberalism, was regarded by his detractors as little better than an atheist.[48] A bitter struggle in connection with naming a new archbishop for Santiago (the inflexible Valdivieso y Zañartu had died in 1878), and the endeavor to nationalize cemeteries and provide for civil marriage scandalized Catholic elements.[49]

Yet, in spite of these incidents, it was becoming clear during the Santa María tenure that the religious issue was losing the prominence once associated with it in national politics. Perhaps Chileans were becoming more secular-minded, perhaps they were simply becoming bored by issues that had so long been used as a rallying cry for political action. Whatever the reason, Chileans began to show that what interested them primarily in politics was not religion, but politics itself. Santa María incurred his strongest opposition by his alleged attempts to revive "monarchical," or Portales methods, and to frustrate the proper workings of incipient democratic institutions. In the 1882 elections for deputies, presidential intervention was so overt and flagrant that many of Santa María's former supporters turned against him. Among these was Radical Party member José Francisco Vergara, who had been the president's first Minister of Interior. Balmaceda then succeeded Vergara in this most important of cabinet posts.[50]

In large part, Santa María's difficulties stemmed from the manner in which various laws, especially the suffrage-broadening legislation of 1874, had liberalized political procedure. Owing to this political evolution, it had become more difficult for the president to dominate the nation's administrative and legislative institutions to the extent that had once been not only possible but legal. Increasingly also, a group of able, strong-willed parliamentarians, influenced both by principles of political theory and personal ambition, showed that they would no longer tolerate presidential dominance. Aiding their cause was the fact that freedom of the press had been an established fact since 1861. During the Santa María term, a number of fearless and talented journalists, includ-

ing Manuel Blanco Cuartín, Isidoro Errázuriz, Máximo Lira, Zorobabel Rodríguez, Fanor Velasco, and Augusto Orrego Luco dedicated themselves to exposing instances of unauthorized electoral
intervention.[51]

The 1886 elections occurred against a troubled background. Dis-
contented Conservatives, consistently denied cabinet posts during
the past decade, were inclined to boycott the polls, claiming that
graft and corruption rather than ballots determined election results. The Nationals and Radicals attempted to renew their old
coalition, but could not agree upon a candidate. Thereupon the
Radicals lost interest in the campaign, while the Nationals extended tepid support to the Liberal Alliance standard-bearer, José
Manuel Balmaceda. Aided by the pressures always brought to bear
in favor of the candidate officially favored by the incumbent administration, Balmaceda was duly elected to the presidential office.

BALMACEDA AND THE CIVIL WAR

Background Considerations. Inaugurated as president at the age
of forty-six, the tall, slender, and handsome Balmaceda was descended from the colonial aristocracy. As a young politician he had
associated in the *Club de la Reforma* with such advocates of
change as Lastarria and Matta, and the Gallo and Arteaga Alemparte brothers. He had been influenced by the political ideas of
such French thinkers as Rousseau and Montesquieu. For his economic concepts, however, Balmaceda turned away from the classi-
cally liberal French school as popularized in Chile by Juan Gustavo Courcelle-Seneuil, and took to heart the state interventionist
theories of Georg Friedrich List. The new president desired greatness for his nation with a fervor matched by few of the renowned
nationalistic patriots of the 1880's. But he was remarkable for his
times in assuming that a splendid future for Chile was not inevitable. In order to realize the full national potential, he was convinced that Chileans must critically analyze their situation, reject
many traditional procedures, carefully plan for the future, and be
prepared to make greater sacrifices for the nation's welfare.

While unquestionably a man of unusual vision and patriotic

zeal, Balmaceda seemed excessively theatrical to many of Chile's aristocrats—men who have always been suspicious of spectacular, colorful, out-of-the-ordinary, and even unusually talented personalities. Balmaceda was also an extreme egotist, who, as his ideas encountered opposition, came to look upon himself more and more as the only man who truly understood what was best for his country. If he could not sell his ideas by persuasion, then he would enforce them. Power became more and more an obsession with the president, and to maintain it he appeared willing to utilize almost any expedient. It is possible that many of the most noteworthy measures he supported in the last period of his rule were not the products of a rational projection of principle so much as they were desperate attempts to gain support from some new quarter as the leaders of the traditional political and pressure groups tended more and more to desert him.[52]

Politically Motivated Opposition to Balmaceda. Increasingly restive during the past several administrations, the Conservatives under the Balmaceda regime determined to make an all-out effort to end what for them had become an intolerable situation. They rallied behind a plan advanced by Manuel José Irarrázaval for establishing a political structure based on autonomous municipalities. Irarrázaval, a great idealist and something of a utopianist, apparently sincerely believed that autonomous communities constituted the best means by which every member of society might most fully develop his full, God-given, human potential.[53] Many other Conservatives probably regarded the plan simply as a convenient method of curbing the power of a central government that had become unfriendly, and of utilizing whatever influence the Church still maintained on the local level to establish a political system aimed essentially at protecting the interests of the Conservatives. Regardless of their sources of motivation, Conservatives were enraged by Balmaceda's evident desire to augment, rather than to diminish, presidential authority. And remembering Balmaceda as a one-time champion of anticlerical legislation,[54] Conservatives distrusted the conciliatory attitude toward the Church that he adopted upon becoming president.

Through its Central Committee (*Junta Central*), the Radical

Party in 1889 announced its opposition to the strong-president ambitions of Balmaceda: ". . . our system of government is, and
ought constitutionally to be, parliamentary, or the government of
the cabinet." [55] As with the Conservatives in their support of the
autonomous community, so also with the Radicals in their espou-
sal of parliamentarism, motivation was highly varied. Some Radicals thought only of political expediency. In recent years, their
party had made notable headway in local and provincial politics.
If presidential intervention should end, the party could certainly
elect a considerable bloc of national legislators. But so long as an
absolutist president out of sympathy with their cause maintained
power, the political future for the Radicals seemed bleak. Other
Radicals, and Manuel Antonio Matta was certainly one of them,[56]
were devoted to parliamentary government because of principles
and ideals, convinced that it was the most perfect of all political
forms.

The Liberal Alliance was itself split by personality issues, with
several factions supporting the political aspirations of different
men. Nearly all of the factions were outraged by what they considered presidential interference when Balmaceda began to groom
his close collaborator and cabinet member Enrique Salvador Sanfuentes to succeed to the chief executive office.[57] Nor were they
mollified when Sanfuentes withdrew his candidacy upon accepting
a new cabinet post, that of Minister of Interior, in 1890.[58] The
time had come, felt most politicians, to end once and for all presidential violation of the free electoral process.

A new political organization that appeared upon the scene in
1887, the Democrat Party (*Partido Demócrata*) distrusted all previously existing parties, and doubted that Balmaceda actually had
the national good at heart. Led by the lawyer Malaquías Concha,
who was concerned over the decline in purchasing power of urban
labor income during the 1880's, the Democrats demanded solution
to what they described as deplorable social problems. They criticized the Conservatives as representing landlord interests, the Nationals as being only concerned with bankers and the higher bureaucrats, the Liberals as defenders exclusively of landowners and
mine operators, and the Radicals as the champions solely of south-

ern *latifundistas*, northern mine owners, and the professional sectors. Their charge that Balmaceda did not really worry over the worsening plight of the laborers gained substance when during the massive 1890 strike in Iquique the president sent national troops to disperse the aroused workers. The resultant violence led to some three thousand casualties.[59]

To mounting political opposition, Balmaceda responded by ruling in an ever more arbitrary and authoritarian manner. He was condemned by every major newspaper—excepting the government-published *La Nación*—ranging from the Conservative *El Estandarte Católico*[60] to the anticlerical *El Ferrocarril*,[61] when in early 1890 he began to purge government agencies of his critics. "Is this political persecution madness, or is it crime?" asked *La Época*.[62] "The president [is] trampling on constitutional provisions . . . ," charged *La Patria* in Valparaíso.[63] And in the same city, *El Heraldo* concluded that the president no longer deserved the benefit of the doubt which the paper had previously extended him.[64] Opposition intensified during the remainder of the year.[65] *El Ferrocarril* charged that the presidential message of June 1 did not contain adequate guarantees for free elections.[66] When a few days later the president announced he would retain his cabinet despite lack of parliamentary confidence in it, *El Independiente*, *La Tribuna*, *La Libertad Electoral*, and *La Época* all joined with *El Ferrocarril* in charging tyranny.[67] Even before this, the Santiago press had delighted in running quotations made by Balmaceda when he had served from 1881 to 1882 as Minister of Foreign Relations to the effect that ministers must obey the wishes of congress.[68]

Writing to his Foreign Office in late 1890, Baron von Gutschmid, the Imperial Germany envoy in Chile, observed that Balmaceda's opponents included the most honored members of all political parties, and even the hero of the War of the Pacific, General Manuel Baquedano.[69] The Baron noted also the cool reception Balmaceda had received in Valparaíso, Talcahuano, and Concepción during a recently concluded tour of the South, and reported signs of active hostility upon the president's return to Santiago. The Chilean populace, stated von Gutschmid, was making apparent how ". . . little disposed it was to support the authoritarian internal policies that obtain at present." [70]

On January 1, 1891, Balmaceda delivered a "Manifesto to the Nation," declaring that as the national congress would not cooperate with him and refused to approve his budget, he would proceed to enact the provisions of his proposed budget, even in the absence of constitutionally required legislative approval. The president noted that elections for national deputies were only sixty days away, at which time the electorate would have the chance to endorse or repudiate his policies. But the opposition, perhaps not anticipating honest elections, would not wait. On January 7, against government orders, the fleet in Valparaíso weighed anchor and headed north, under the command of Jorge Montt. Accompanying the rebelling naval forces were Waldo Silva, vice-president of the Senate, and Ramón Barros Luco, president of the Chamber of Deputies. The now openly insurgent "congressionalists" declared their opposition to the president and called for the restoration of constitutional government. Balmaceda responded by promptly raising army salaries 50 per cent to assure loyalty. The civil war had begun. [71]

Economically Motivated Opposition to Balmaceda. In his January 1 "Manifesto," Balmaceda had justified his position on the grounds that chronic ministerial crises resulting from legislative interference in the province of the executive made stable political administration an absolute impossibility. [72] In this appraisal, the harassed president apparently overlooked the real crux of the matter. To a large extent his quarrel with the opposition rested upon economic rather than political considerations. Once he was removed, his successors agreed among themselves on basic economic and social policies. This being the case, despite all manner of cabinet turnovers, they did at least succeed in providing their country with political stability.

In essence, the Balmaceda approach to Chilean material development rested on a belief in the necessity of an expanding economy under government stimulus and supervision. The president apparently was undismayed by temporary deficit spending and forced currency expansion, [73] feeling confident that the inflationist tendencies of these measures could be more than absorbed by the economic expansion resulting from a deliberate pump-priming process. These fiscal beliefs also led Balmaceda toward a policy of government control over banking activities. In addition, he insisted adamantly that nitrate income be used to finance special national development projects, and that the costs of ordinary government administration and services be paid for by a series of additional internal taxes.

The major obstacle to implementation of these policies was that the moneyed classes accepted laissez faire as the inevitable law of economic progress—a law that could not be artificially stimulated or hurried by government manipulation. They were scandalized by the president's notions.[74] Had not economic individualism and national budgets that were generally balanced resulted already in remarkable prosperity? What need was there to experiment with new expedients? Why not use nitrate export taxes to finance ordinary government administration and services, avoid all measures of planned expansion, and allow the upper classes to go tax-free? In the final analysis, what country riding the crest of an apparent boom, with a small population, with no bitter social cleavage yet apparent, with vast, newly-opened frontier lands, with the prospect of further discovery and exploitation of natural resources, would seriously consider embarking, as Balmaceda urged, upon a policy of centralized social and economic planning?[75] The times seemed to suggest quite the opposite approach. Anarchy, wildly liberal ideas, and economic disruption had, at the inception of the Portales period, demanded that social and political leaders curb their individualism and cooperate in a tightly centralistic and often arbitrary administrative structure. Now, the wealth of the 1880's, combined with political stability so firm that it had withstood even the challenge of war, seemed to permit at last a loosening of the reins of government, and a certain license for individuals and regions to conduct affairs as they saw fit, and if they chose, simply to luxuriate in indolence.

If Balmaceda had succeeded in imposing his economic policies, there is little question that Chile would in the twentieth century have been in vastly better condition. The nation might even have escaped many of the horrors of the social problem that today threaten stability and progress. But Chile could have implemented the Balmaceda program only by crushing genuinely precious qualities in the national tradition: regard for political freedom and liberty of expression, fundamental revulsion for dictatorship, and distrust of self-proclaimed saviours.[76] Balmaceda fell because the 10 per cent or less of the population that constituted an effective body politic would not accept dictatorial imposition of basically distasteful policies. The vast majority of Chileans who were politically inarticulate served merely as uninterested spectators of the political drama.[77]

The central question of modern Chilean history is not why anything so inevitable as the fall of Balmaceda occurred. Rather, it is why those who overthrew him, many of them high-minded and self-sacrificing, were able to do no more than to lead their country into a period of apathetic drifting.[78] Because of the palpable failure of those who overthrew and followed him in power, Balmaceda's vague and often chameleon[79] program, which evolved in *ad hoc* manner toward extremes of central planning, was assumed by a later generation of Chileans to have borne the stamp of genius.

3: CHILEAN RELATIONS
WITH THE UNITED STATES, 1880-1892

THE WAR OF THE PACIFIC: ALARM AND SUCCESS

Early Rumors and Apprehension

That international diplomacy might deprive Chile of anticipated fruits of victory loomed as a possibility early in the course of the War of the Pacific. It was reported by December, 1880, that three plans for joint European action had already been proposed. Each time, according to Chilean diplomatic sources, the negative attitude of Germany's Bismarck had blocked these plans. But the talented writer-diplomat, Alberto Blest Gana, Chile's envoy both to France and the United Kingdom, was kept in a state of constant apprehension as he sought to ferret out and thwart intervention plans.[1] The two countries in which Blest Gana represented Chile were the main European sources of hostility to the Chilean position, as French and British capitalists held extensive Peruvian guano claims, and were thus concerned about the outcome of the war.[2]

High United States officials also evidenced concern over European intervention plans.[3] Fearing a possible violation of the Monroe Doctrine, William M. Evarts, Secretary of State during the Rutherford B. Hayes administration (1877-1881), decided the United States should take steps to end the war, and instructed his country's representatives in Lima, Peru, La Paz, Bolivia, and Santiago de Chile to offer good offices. Thomas A. Osborn, United States envoy in Santiago, received these instructions on July 18, 1880, and by August 9 the Aníbal Pinto administration had agreed to a peace conference under the auspices of the Washington government.[4] Proceedings became more complex with the August 27 arrival of Isaac P. Christiancy in Valparaíso. Christiancy, the United

47

States envoy in Lima, was suspected of pro-Peruvian sentiments. In particular, it was felt that he would work to block the expedition that Chile was preparing for the conquest of Lima. Rumors also began to circulate that the Yankee representative in La Paz, Charles Adams, had stated that if the forthcoming peace conference, which it was by now agreed would be held at Arica, failed to end hostilities, the United States would feel compelled to intervene directly to forestall European measures. This remarkable harbinger of the Roosevelt Corollary to the Monroe Doctrine alarmed the Chileans. When shortly the Arica conference[5] did end in failure, there was an attempt in Chile to blame Adams. The argument was that Bolivia and Peru, emboldened by Adams' alleged statements concerning United States intervention, had presented impossible demands.[6] Actually, the Chileans themselves had probably never taken the conference seriously. Instead, they regarded it as no more than a ceremony that would provide them with an opportunity to demonstrate their "greatness of spirit," and their dedication to the principles of international law and peaceful settlement of disputes.[7] El Ferrocarril had caustically observed that the mediation efforts had come too late: "There can only be mediation before the outcome of a war has been clearly decided." [8]

ENTER JAMES G. BLAINE

James G. Blaine is reported once to have said that if he had been Secretary of State at the time of the Arica conference, he would have found the means to enforce peace.[9] Certain it is that upon assuming direction of his country's foreign relations with the inauguration of the James Garfield administration in March 1881, Blaine began to play a forceful role in working for the end of hostilities. In implementing their new type of diplomacy, Blaine and his advisers failed utterly to take into account the martial spirit that had swept Chile. Infatuated by an early series of victories, that nation would not be content until it had made a good portion of Peru and Bolivia its own. To have blocked transfer of territory, as Blaine desired, would have required nothing less than the armed intervention of the United States. This far Blaine was not willing to go, hoping to achieve his ends through persuasion and machination. Given the mood of the Chilean people, these means were bound to prove inadequate. If Blaine had realized this from the outset, the first tragicomic crisis in United States-Chilean relations might have been avoided. Instead, the futile efforts of the United States soon came to be regarded in Chile as gross effrontery, contributing tellingly to the useless prolongation of war by giving hopelessly beaten adversaries the impression that their cause might be rescued at the last minute by "the great republic of the north." [10]

Even before the Garfield administration assumed power, an economically-motivated United States interest in the War of the Pacific had become apparent. A French corporation, known as Crédit Industriel, had for a number of years held certain guano and nitrate claims in Peru. It now sought to obtain a monopoly for exploiting these resources, hopeful that Peru, reeling under Chile's military offensive, might be willing to make almost any business concession in return for some guarantees against being despoiled of land. In pursuing its objectives, Crédit Industriel extended its operations to the United States, disposing there of some securities, with New York lawyer Robert A. Randall becoming a principal shareholder. The success of Crédit Industriel rested entirely upon enlisting United States support in preventing transfer of Peruvian lands to Chile. Should Chile acquire the coveted nitrate and guano territories, Crédit Industriel was doomed.

The corporation gained the services of Cuban-born Francisco de P. Suárez, a long-time resident of Peru who during the course of his years in that country had become closely associated with United States railroad builder and business promoter Henry Meiggs. Suárez was sent to Washington specifically to win the support of Secretary of State Evarts for Crédit Industriel's venture. It seems that Evarts expressed at least passing interest in the plans outlined to him. At any rate, Suárez was back in Lima by mid-March, 1881— by this time the Garfield administration had taken office—armed with an Evarts-written letter of introduction to United States Envoy to Peru Isaac P. Christiancy.[11] However, no cooperation was forthcoming from Christiancy who regarded the whole venture as impractical. Christiancy was convinced that only United States armed intervention could forestall Chilean annexation of Peruvian nitrate and guano lands, and he correctly guessed that his country was unwilling to go to that extreme.

Suárez was not discouraged, and entered into negotiations with Francisco García Calderón, a Peruvian intellectual who had designs on the presidency. García Calderón apparently offered assurances that if he came to be accepted as president of Peru, and if the United States promised to protect his country against territorial losses, he would do the bidding of Crédit Industriel.[12]

Hastily returning to Washington, Suárez combined his efforts with those of attorney Randall to persuade new Secretary of State Blaine to recognize García Calderón. Whether or not this lobbying was actually responsible for the precipitous extension of United States recognition to García Calderón is uncertain, but for reasons best known to himself Blaine did decide to confer his blessings upon this Peruvian leader—even though Envoy Christiancy had advised against recognition, terming García Calderón's election a farce.[13]

Suárez now returned to Peru, accompanied by a newly-named United States envoy, Stephen A. Hurlbut.[14] On August 2, 1881, Hurlbut presented his credentials to García Calderón, and at once precipitated a crisis in Chilean-United States relations by asserting that his country was disposed to intervene in ending the War of the Pacific.[15] Chileans were still more alarmed in September when Hurlbut dispatched a highhanded memorandum to Rear Admiral Patricio Lynch, commander of Chile's occupation forces in Peru, stating that the United States would not permit a territorial cession as the basis for a peace settlement.[16]

News of the memorandum created a sensation in Chile. Every major newspaper asserted, probably more hopefully than confidently, that Hurlbut had acted on his own and was not carrying out official United States policy.[17] In response to a frantic inquiry from the Chilean Ministry of Foreign Relations, General Judson Kilpatrick, serving then as United States envoy in Santiago and suffering through the final stages of a fatal malady, took pen in his shaking hand and composed a document "which all Chileans will ever read with respect and admiration." [18] In it, Kilpatrick, who had long referred to Chile as his second country and who had married one of its native daughters, assured Chile of United States friendship and disinclination to intervene, concluding that Hurlbut had not acted in accordance with official instructions. Understandably, Chileans were still uneasy, and from Paris Blest Gana extended the reasonable suggestion that efforts be made to ascertain if the United States had issued one set of instructions to Hurlbut and another to Kilpatrick. The Chilean Minister of Foreign Relations wasted no time in instructing Marcial Martínez, serving his country since January as envoy in Washington, to find out just what United States policy was.[19]

Martínez encountered great difficulty in providing the answer. Robert R. Hitt, Assistant Secretary of State and considered to be very close to Blaine, refused to commit himself, although he did complain with ample justification that his country's position was complicated by the fact that at times Hurlbut seemed more to represent Peruvian than United States attitudes, and that Kilpatrick was Chilean at heart.[20] In a later interview that he had with the Secretary of State himself, Martínez was assured that the Hurlbut memorandum to Lynch had not embodied the official attitudes of the United States.[21] But then, as Martínez was later to discover, he was not always given the full truth by James G. Blaine.

CHILEAN ALARM OVER BLAINE'S PURPOSES INTENSIFIES

The Chilean Foreign Ministry remained uneasy. Its officials, in fact, seemed to agree with prominent journalist Justo Arteaga Alemparte who flatly stated that the United States was acting covertly in the affairs of Chile and Peru. Arteaga Alemparte added: "Obviously, as is usually the case, the United States is impelled by economic considerations." [22]

What most alarmed the Foreign Ministry was the rumor that the Bolivian envoy in Washington had won Blaine's agreement to a plan calling for the formation of a powerful United States company that would exploit guano and nitrate resources both in Bolivia and Peru. The United States would safeguard the territorial integrity of these two countries against Chilean designs, while the newly-formed company would guarantee indemnity payments to the victorious nation.[23] Marcial Martínez was gravely concerned. For him, the worst imaginable calamity for Chile would have been United States economic control over Tarapacá. And he was convinced that precisely this was the "probable menace that now confronts us."[24]

Chileans were further alarmed by Blaine's desire to make their government pay at full face value all nitrate indemnity bonds issued—mainly to Chilean, British and German interests—by the Peruvian government in 1874 and 1875. This measure would have put an end to the system whereby Chile was facilitating transfer of nitrate holdings to those who held Peruvian securities, and would have cleared the way for acquisition of concessions by capitalists who had not previously been active in the area—notably, United States capitalists. Moreover, if Chile felt it would be forced to confer a staggeringly large monetary settlement on the holders of Peruvian securities, then it might have been disposed to accept a large cash indemnity, guaranteed by a United States-backed company, in lieu of land claims.[25]

A more serious danger of United States intervention arose from the claims of a new venture known as the Peruvian Company. Presided over by New York promoter Jacob R. Shipherd, this company—which in the final stages of negotiations combined with the old Crédit Industriel in order jointly to press claims—had fallen heir to various guano and nitrate claims against Peru originally held by two Frenchmen, Alexandre Cochet and Jean Theophile Landreau. The latter's brother, Jean Charles, was at this time a naturalized citizen of the United States. With accrued interest, the Landreau claims amounted to $300,000,000, and those of Cochet to $900,000,000. That both claims had been dismissed several years previously by the Peruvian government bothered the new Peruvian Company not in the least.[26]

Marcial Martínez voiced alarm over the pressure that this company, which he thought included among its directors former President U. S. Grant, was exerting on United States policy. On October 26, 1881, he wrote to his Ministry in Santiago: "It is

within the realm of the probable that Blaine, in league with Hurlbut and the Peruvian Company, has sought to act in a manner
contrary to the interests of Chile." [27] Some ten days later, Martínez
wrote: "The Peruvian Company claims may lead the United
States to deny Chile's land acquisition rights. Every time I raise
the matter with Hitt and Blaine, they are evasive." [28] Martínez
also noted that when Rear Admiral Lynch, tiring of what he considered the duplicity of García Calderón, had the Peruvian president arrested and taken to Santiago, ". . . the news had the effect
of a bomb explosion among the group of Shipherd, Grant, and
Blaine, and those connected with the Peruvian Company." [29]

The outspoken attitude of the Peruvian Company itself added
to the discomfiture of Martínez. A company brochure had stated:

> The success of the Peruvian Company is now assured. . . . The
> most powerful corporation that the world has known, born of a
> history more romantic than any dream of the *Arabian Nights*,
> is about to plant the flag of the United States in Central and
> South America, and to restore more than the lost glory of the
> Incas. . . . The Peruvian Company has a complete under-
> standing with the government at Washington, and no adjust-
> ment of the difficulties between Chile and Peru will be per-
> mitted that does not first of all provide for all American inter-
> ests.[30]

On November 25, 1881, moreover, Jacob Shipherd personally
wrote an incredibly arrogant letter to Martínez, saying that the
rights of the Peruvian Company were absolute, that Chile must
learn to accept the disappointment it naturally felt upon seeing
the fruits of war slipping away, and asserting that the United
States government would extend full aid and support to the Company's claims.[31]

Operating in the rumor-charged Washington ambient, Martínez
showed signs of confusion. On November 18, he made up his
mind that Hurlbut was an agent not of the Peruvian Company,
as he had originally suspected, but of Crédit Industriel.[32] Just before this he had stated that although there were ample grounds
for suspicion, he had still obtained no positive proof that Blaine
was involved in anti-Chile plots.[33] But confusion soon turned to

indignation. In December, immediately after Blaine had been replaced as Secretary of State, the instructions he had sent to Hurlbut in August were released by the State Department and published in papers both in Chile and the United States. Martínez thereby learned that all the while Blaine had been assuring him that he had not the slightest interest in the Peruvian Company—which he referred to as the totally discredited scheme of madmen—he had actually been instructing Hurlbut to press for recognition of the Landreau claims.[34] The final Chilean verdict on the whole affair was expressed by Joaquín Godoy who in April 1883 succeeded Martínez as envoy in Washington. Said Godoy: "There is clear proof that Blaine exercised undue pressure in favor of the Peruvian Company and Crédit Industriel." In view of this, Godoy dismissed as hypocritical the expression of United States friendship uttered by President Chester A. Arthur upon receiving him as Chilean envoy.[35]

CHILEANS PUZZLE OVER MOTIVATION FOR BLAINE'S INTERVENTIONIST POLICIES

Exactly what lay behind Blaine's interventionist policies has never been satisfactorily determined.[36] Although many Chileans continue to be convinced that Blaine had a personal stake in the Peruvian Company, more responsible writers—such as Francisco Antonio Encina and Gonzalo Bulnes, the son of former President Manuel Bulnes (1841-1851), who between 1911 and 1919 published in three volumes the best Chilean account of the War of the Pacific—concede that there is no direct evidence of this.[37] The best guess as to what Blaine had in mind may well have been made by Marcial Martínez, who conjectured that the Secretary of State was anxious above all to provide United States capitalists with an opportunity to challenge mounting British pre-eminence in the Pacific coast countries of South America. One-time Minister of Foreign Relations José Manuel Balmaceda concurred in this appraisal.[38] A further indication that Blaine might have regarded his mission as being to curtail British economic influence was provided by the attitude of Envoy Hurlbut, who was known to be violently anti-British, and who even regarded England as being in back of Chile's entire military effort against Peru and Bolivia.[39] Then, too, "highly placed and reliable" sources had quoted Blaine as saying he had decided to back the Landreau claims on the grounds that the British and Europeans had so many claims he felt the United States might as well acquire some of its own.[40] Finally, there appeared in the *New York Herald* of July 3, 1882, a statement attributed to former Navy Secretary George M. Robeson to the effect that if the U.S.S. "Monadnock" had been finished the previous summer, she could have been sent to Callao to prevent a "sister republic from being dismembered for the purpose of filling the pockets of English dealers and contractors." Envoy Godoy promptly reported this statement to his government.[41]

On the other hand, there were signs that policy was shaped by belief that the United States, given its rising world power, should now step in as the final arbiter of South American affairs.[42] In a letter to General Kilpatrick, Stephen Hurlbut had stated clearly that United States strength and power were now so unlimited that the nation could easily enforce any hemisphere policy.[43] Marcial Martínez, moreover, observed that a strong desire was evident in Washington to make the United States supreme policymaker for the hemisphere.[44] Finally, there was the letter allegedly written by Isaac Christiancy to Blaine, stating that a colony of 50,000 United States citizens in Peru could dominate that country, making it virtually a part of North America. From this base of operations, the United States could then dominate the rest of South America and, in the process, open up vast commercial markets.[45]

VICTORY OVER BLAINE

Just as it appeared that nothing in the natural order of events could spare Chile from some form of adverse United States intervention, the beleaguered republic received oblique assistance from the most unlikely source. Hurlbut in Peru so overplayed his hand, and proved so bungling and inept a representative, that he disgraced not only the cause of García Calderón, whose position in Peru he was trying to solidify, but at the same time the whole cause of the United States. In addition to entering into an agreement with the would-be president of Peru by which the United States was given a coaling station in Chimbote, Hurlbut received a personal concession to the railroad that Peru had been in the process of building from Chimbote to an interior coal mine. The latter agreement gave to the United States envoy the right to award the railroad project and the coal mine to any United States firm of his choice for a period of twenty-five years.[46]

This incredible arrangement placed United States intentions in such a compromising light that even Blaine was shocked. In his South American manipulations Blaine obviously had in mind more imposing goals than an unnecessary coaling station and a lucrative deal for Hurlbut. Worried about the adverse United States press reaction to Peruvian dealings, and probably concerned about damage that might be done his ever-present presidential aspirations, Blaine sent a cruel, sarcastic, and cutting letter to Hurlbut, disavowing the coaling station and railroad agreement.[47] Increasingly preoccupied over the irreparable damage his envoy's lack of discretion might be dealing his hopes, Blaine was even heard once to thunder when informed of a particularly overt anti-Chile utterance of Hurlbut, "He must have been drunk at the time." [48]

Martínez now expressed relief, confident that the crisis was over, and that Blaine, to offset the Hurlbut-inflicted damage, would assume a more statesmanlike attitude.[49] Moreover, Martínez was cheered by reports in Washington that Chester A. Arthur, who succeeded the assassinated Garfield to the presidency in September 1881, would replace Secretary of State Blaine with Frederick T. Frelinghuysen. Martínez referred to Frelinghuysen as a man who, although possessing little talent, was "at least honest and conscientious." [50]

But Blaine still had one final trick in mind which, if successful, would have resulted in last-minute success for his South American policy. On December 2, 1881, William H. Trescott and the Secretary of State's son, Walker Blaine, departed for the troubled area to the south with instructions to press for the Landreau claims, to prevent territorial cession in any peace settlement, and to attempt to recruit Argentine and Brazilian backing of United States policy should Chile prove recalcitrant.[51] Learning of the departure of Trescott and Blaine, Martínez sent a telegram of warning to his government, and then set out to try to discover the Secretary of State's purpose. Blaine succeeded totally in calming the Chilean envoy's suspicions, assuring him that the purpose of the new mission was in no way contrary to the interests of Chile. In writing to his Ministry of Foreign Relations on December 6, Martínez was full of confidence and gave no intimation that trouble might lie ahead.[52] When soon afterwards he learned the actual content of the Blaine instructions, Martínez exploded in fury. He regarded Blaine's actions as perfidious to the highest degree,[53] and from this point on became one of the most outspoken and constant critics of the United States that Chile has ever produced.

By the time Trescott and young Blaine arrived in Valparaíso, on January 4, the mastermind of their mission was no longer Secretary of State, and his instructions to the two diplomats had been repudiated by Frelinghuysen.[54] Faced with this turn of events, Trescott and Blaine had no recourse but to sign with Chilean Foreign Relations Minister Balmaceda the February 11 protocol of Viña del Mar, in which the Chilean principle that peace depended on territorial transfer was accepted. Although Trescott shortly tried to persuade Balmaceda to modify this provision, the able Foreign Relations Minister stood his ground. Chile had gained a clear decision in its bout with the United States.[55]

Chile's position became still more secure when the Arthur administration abandoned Blaine-initiated plans for a meeting of the American republics. In the later stages of his dealings with Chile and Peru, Blaine had come to favor the convening of such a conference, perhaps hoping to obtain the help of other Latin-American republics in bringing pressure to bear upon Chile and to provide his questionable and increasingly criticized South American policy with the aura of statesmanship.[56] Chile had been highly suspicious of the conference from the outset,[57] and it was with a feeling of relief and triumph that Joaquín Godoy informed his government from Washington that President Arthur in his December 4, 1882, address had canceled the conference plans.[58]

FRELINGHUYSEN AND A FINAL MOMENT OF ALARM

But Chile was not out of the diplomatic woods yet. Once again the spectre of European interference brought threats of preventive United States intervention—another harbinger of the Roosevelt Corollary. Chileans were pleased, it is true, by the tactful conduct of new United States Envoy Cornelius A. Logan[59] who arrived in September 1882—he had previously represented his country in Chile during the Grant regime. They promptly accepted the envoy's offer of United States good offices to facilitate a peace treaty with Peru. But they soon found cause for concern in the attitude of Secretary of State Frelinghuysen. In February 1883, Frelinghuysen told Godoy that if Chile did not speedily conclude its peace negotiations with Peru, there was a likelihood of European intervention. To avoid this, Frelinghuysen urged that Chile settle the conflict on the basis of annexing Tarapacá and submitting its claims on Tacna and Arica to the arbitration of the United States, Brazil, and Mexico.[60] Thus, for the first time emerged the United States attitude that disposition of Tacna and Arica should be settled by arbitration, a factor destined to complicate United States-Chilean relations until 1929. In March, the Secretary of State went so far as to threaten direct United States intervention unless a prompt peace settlement was signed. This time, in addition to citing the European threat, he justified his stand on the grounds that a continuing state of war between Chile and Peru might prove politically embarrassing to the Arthur administration.[61]

Chile found in Peruvian General Miguel Iglesias a man easier to deal with than Frelinghuysen. Convinced of the hopelessness of the Peruvian cause, Iglesias was willing to let Chile annex Tarapacá once and for all, and exercise a ten-year sovereignty over Tacna and Arica, at the end of which period final disposition would be decided by a plebiscite. The Treaty of Ancón, based on these provisions, was signed in October 1883, and the Chilean-Peruvian military conflict at last came officially to an end.

The troublesome United States, however, provided Chile with one last scare. In his December 5 message, President Arthur provided a strange foretaste of later Wilsonian policies by suggesting the United States might not recognize Iglesias until it could be proved that he was supported by the will of the people.[62] Fortunately for Chile, nothing came of this threat which, if acted upon, might have resulted in the fall of Iglesias and the nullification of the Treaty of Ancón. Still, Chileans were puzzled as to United States policy. Why had there been such a rush to recognize the highly questionable claims of García Calderón to the presidency, and such misgivings about extending diplomatic approval to Iglesias?

FINAL CONSEQUENCES OF WAR OF THE PACIFIC
DIPLOMACY ON UNITED STATES-CHILEAN RELATIONS

Out of the War of the Pacific came enduring Chilean distrust of the United States. It seemed beyond the realm of credibility that enlightened principles of statesmanship alone had induced the owner of vast territories that had once belonged to Mexico to espouse the high-sounding concepts of no territorial acquisition based on war. In the eyes of Chilean diplomats, Blaine's policy had meant that weak Peru should not be despoiled by strong Chile because a stronger nation still, the United States, sought to establish dominance over Peru and perhaps over all South America.[63] Chile understandably felt that it had been the victim in the first attempt of the United States to extend to South America the influence that it had previously exercised only in Mexico and the Caribbean.

In addition, the War of the Pacific more or less directly resulted in modifications and changes in Chile's relationship with Argentina, Spain and Germany: (1) Argentina emerged more than ever as a villain; (2) Spain was forgiven its sins of the past; and (3) Germany came to be regarded as a great benefactor and sincere friend. These developments were destined to exert a future impact of great importance on United States-Chilean relations.

During the War of the Pacific, Argentina had evidenced a desire to curb the rising power of Chile, even, if need be, by encouraging United States intervention in the affairs of South America. The usual Argentine role of steadfast opposition to all manifestations of United States tutelage in South America was, in this instance, abandoned. The Buenos Aires *La Prensa* in late 1881 actually went so far as to urge strong-armed United States methods to end the war, stating that Chile, dedicated to force and terrorism, could not be trusted to provide on its own an acceptable conclusion to hostilities.[64] And Godoy reported in annoyance from Washington the words of the new Argentine envoy, Luis L. Domínguez, when presenting his credentials in Washington. Said Domínguez: "My country will always be prompt to cooperate with the United States in order that peace and justice will remain the permanent bases of the well-being of all the nations of America." This statement, concluded Godoy, was another indication of Argentina's unfriendly attitude toward Chile, and of its willingness to join with the United States in humbling Chile.[65]

Argentina, it was also felt, had taken advantage of Chile's preoccupation in the War of the Pacific and its concern with threats of United States intervention to enforce an unjust boundary settlement (the Treaty of July 23, 1881) in which Chile was "despoiled" of Patagonia. The role of the United States envoy to Argentina in helping to formulate this treaty was held to be highly censurable,[66] adding to the impression that the two nations were in league against Chile.

The rapprochement with Spain, initiated by that country's friendly neutrality[67] and culminating in a Treaty of Peace and Amity (June 12, 1883),[68] paved the way for the rise in Chile of the cult of Hispanism, which glorified traditional cultural and spiritual values and disparaged modern notions of materialistic utilitarianism. This in turn helped mold unfriendly intellectual attitudes toward the United States.

Of most immediate and direct importance was the position of almost boundless esteem that Germany came to occupy as a result of the War of the Pacific.[69] Speaking of Balmaceda's success in blocking Blaine's designs, a Chilean author has concluded: "But in addition to our own brilliant diplomacy, it is to Germany that we owe thanks for protection against the Colossus of the North." [70] Balmaceda himself was warm and open in acknowledging his debt of gratitude to Germany.[71] And when Bismarck died in 1898, the president of Chile ordered his country's envoy in Germany, Ramón Subercaseaux, to adorn the coffin with an expensive tribute. What was the reason for this gesture? Simply that Bismarck was felt to have protected Chile during the War of the Pacific both against United States and European intervention.[72] Chileans, moreover, flattered themselves that Bismarck had shown such friendship to them because he admired their institutions, and considered them the "Prussians of Latin America." [73]

Little wonder then, that Guillermo Matta, popularizer of Masonry in Chile and brother of renowned Radical leader Manuel Antonio Matta, felt himself among friends upon his March 20, 1882, arrival in Berlin as Chile's envoy to the Imperial government. Shortly thereafter he related in glowing terms his reception by the Emperor and his conviction that Chile could assure its future greatness by expanding trade with Germany and encouraging German immigration. On the other hand, "Irish Catholic immigrants must be avoided, as they are not good workers, are a turbulent lot, and are prone to strikes." [74]

By March 1883, Matta was able to describe German success in blocking proposed United States, Italian, English, and French intervention,[75] and the following month he reported: "Germany has been, as you are well aware, the country which among all other foreign nations interested indirectly in the War of the Pacific has most steadfastly maintained a friendly neutrality." [76] By August he was praising the German attitude toward that cooperative Peruvian leader Miguel Iglesias—an attitude that contrasted sharply with that of the United States. The German Sub-Secretary of State had assured Matta that if Chile chose to consider Iglesias the de facto ruler, in the belief that the war might thereby be most speedily terminated, then Germany would not delay in extending recognition.[77] And it was at almost the same time that the German envoy in Santiago, Baron Schenck zu Schweinsberg, was instructed to assure Chile's Minister of Foreign Relations of the high respect and warm admiration which the Imperial government felt for the Chilean people and for their institutions.[78]

The flattering and strategically invaluable attentions conferred by Germany during the War of the Pacific, the arrival during the

Santa María administration of the first German teaching missions and the military advisory group headed by Emil Körner, combined with the tradition of German colonization in the south, exercised enduring effects on Chilean attitudes. By 1890, Germany was probably the most widely admired of all foreign countries in Chile.

ANOTHER MENACE AND SUCCESS SAGA: THE 1889-1890 WASHINGTON CONFERENCE OF AMERICAN STATES

BACKGROUND PREPARATIONS

To their alarm, Chileans realized by 1884 that there was still life in the plans for a conference of American nations under Washington sponsorship. The United States Congress appointed a commission in that year to sound out Latin-American republics on the idea. A favorable report was returned by the commission, and on July 13, Secretary of State Thomas F. Bayard began issuing invitations. By March of the following year, John J. Walker, sent by the United States to gain assurances of attendance from various Latin-American states, had won a cautious consent from Demetrio Lastarria, Chile's Minister of Foreign Relations.[79] Although from two sources in Chile there came praise and encouragement for the American conference idea,[80] the general tendency was to condemn the notion.

The preliminary approaches of Arthur's Republican administration (September 1881-March 1885), continued halfheartedly by the Democratic regime of Grover Cleveland (March 1885-March 1889), came to nothing. Not until late 1889 did United States desire to sponsor an inter-American conference bear fruit. In the meantime, Chile had another opportunity to demonstrate its distrust of such assemblies. A Montevideo meeting, held from August 1888 to January of the following year, had attracted delegates from Argentina, Brazil, Chile, Bolivia, Paraguay, Peru, and of course the host nation, Uruguay. Out of this conference on private international law had come treaties on civil and penal law, patents, and copyrights. Chile and Brazil had been the only two countries not to sign these treaties—which ultimately failed to gain ratification by any signatory country.[81] El Ferrocarril, moreover, had heaped scorn upon the whole Montevideo meeting, saying Chile was in no mood to discuss anything so futile and impractical as international law.[82] And *El Estandarte Católico* observed that international meetings were a waste of time, as the only way for a nation to gain world-wide recognition and security was through its own internal development.[83]

The Republicans returned to power with the Benjamin Harrison administration in 1889. Appointed once again to the Secretary of State post, James G. Blaine resumed his interest in convoking an inter-American conference. Chileans at once manifested their suspicions. One paper warned that no good could come from anything sponsored by the United States, a country animated only by greed. "Who can forget," the paper inquired, "that country's brutal plundering of Mexico, and the nefarious schemes of intervention against our interests entertained by Blaine?"[84] Another daily surmised that in back of the United States proposal was an attempt to wean Latin America away from Europe, the only area with which true spiritual and significant economic ties existed,[85] while a prominent statesman feared Blaine was hoping to resume the meddling he had been forced to abandon late in 1881.[86] From Washington, Chilean Envoy Emilio C. Varas wrote that although a conference under Democratic auspices might have been safe, a clear danger existed now that Blaine and the Republicans were back in power.[87] The principal fear was that the United States would back a compulsory arbitration plan that could jeopardize Chilean claims on Tacna and Arica.[88]

When the matter of sending a delegation to the conference was raised in the Chilean Senate, some parliamentarians expressed the thought that the envoy already in Washington could handle the matter by himself. The argument that Argentina was sending three delegates, and that the United States had named a commission of ten, persuaded the senators to send an additional delegate to aid Varas in the conference deliberations.[89] The man chosen by the executive for this mission was José Alfonso, a socially prominent justice of the Santiago Court of Appeals noted for his competence in economic and commercial law.[90]

The sparring that the Chilean Ministry of Foreign Relations

went through before consenting to participate in the conference, and the instructions given the delegates, indicated a substantial element of uneasiness. Due to Chilean insistence, Blaine had been brought to declare that the conference would attempt to provide only for the solution of difficulties that might arise in the future, and would refrain from considering problems originating prior to the sessions.[91] Even with the matter of retroactive arbitration excluded from the agenda,[92] and with Chilean acceptance of the conference invitation having been conditioned upon the understanding that its delegates would only discuss commercial and economic matters,[93] the Ministry of Foreign Relations took no chances. Varas and Alfonso were instructed absolutely to refrain from so much as voicing opinions on questions involving arbitration.[94] Their attitude was to be that although Chile regarded with favor the principle of arbitration as an ultimate goal, the time had not yet come to introduce such a concept into America. Arbitration would pose a threat to national sovereignty in America until a far greater community of interest and purpose had been fashioned.[95] Alfonso, moreover, reflected official Chilean policy when he insisted that the Washington meeting, scheduled to convene on October 2, 1889, was not a congress but only a conference, and therefore not authorized to do more than express opinions on topics discussed.[96]

The Challenge to Chile at the Conference

If Blaine had hoped to pressure Chile for a Tacna-Arica settlement—there is no positive evidence that he did—he soon found himself placed squarely on the defensive and his effectiveness limited by a resolution conceived apparently by Argentina and backed by Brazil.[97] Introduced in violation of agenda agreements arrived at prior to the conference, this resolution urged a treaty providing for general and obligatory arbitration, and declared unacceptable in America the past or future acquisition of territory through threat or use of military aggression. The primary purpose of this move, it seems, was to embarrass both the United States and Chile, placing the first on the defensive in regard to the Treaty of Guadalupe Hidalgo that ended the Mexican War, and the second in regard to the Treaty of Ancón.[98]

Alarmed at the bitter discussions provoked by the Argentine-Brazilian proposal, Blaine arranged for a February 19, 1890, private meeting with the delegates of Mexico, Argentina, Brazil, and Chile. Blaine and the Mexican delegate took advantage of this opportunity to argue that arbitration should not apply to questions affecting territorial integrity, and that American states should be given preference as arbitrators in settling American disputes. Although Brazil semed ready to compromise, Argentina stoutly resisted any modification of its original proposal, and Chile, following its official policy, refused to discuss any arbitration plan. The meeting, therefore, ended in failure.[99]

To Chile's relief, the conference as a whole rejected the extreme features of the original Argentine-Brazilian proposal. All that ultimately came of the matter was a watered-down Arbitration Treaty signed in Washington in May of 1890, excepting from compulsory arbitration disputes which had been already settled by treaty agreement. Argentina refused to sign the compromise treaty, now that the troublemaking clause directed against the United States and Chile had been removed. And not a single one of the seven countries that did sign the instrument ever ratified it.[100]

EMERGENCE OF FIRM CHILEAN ATTITUDES
TOWARD PAN-AMERICANISM

Shortly after these events, Alfonso asserted that the crowning event in a long life dedicated to public service and the study of international law had been his success in defending his country's interests at the 1889 Washington Conference.[101] In spite of the triumph of their country's representative, Chilean statesmen and journalists had come to entertain grave suspicions concerning the Pan-American movement. When the conference had considered the Argentine-Brazilian proposal, the Chilean press had screamed betrayal and intervention.[102] Once the sessions adjourned, the newspapers were agreed that Chile had been insulted and that no useful purpose could be served by future international American conferences.

The reason was clear. American conferences had come to be associated with pro-Peruvian intervention in settling the Tacna-

Arica controversy. Chileans were ready therefore to embrace completely the Portales approach to inter-American relations: isolationism and dependence upon development of internal strength sufficient to defend whatever diplomatic policy might be judged best to serve national interests. So strong was the desire to go it alone in foreign affairs that *El Ferrocarril* actually urged the virtual abolition of the diplomatic service.[108]

Within two years, however, a series of humiliating events had shattered Chile's confidence in its ability to protect national dignity unilaterally, and had caused the United States once again to loom, along with Argentina, as the chief threat to national well-being.

ANNOYANCE, ALARM AND HUMILIATION: CHILE NEGOTIATES WITH THE UNITED STATES IN 1891 AND 1892

RELATIONS DURING THE CIVIL WAR

By the time the congressionalists overthrew Balmaceda in August 1891, their leaders had come to resent the apparent preference of the United States for the cause of the "dictator." In the first place, State Department attitudes, so far as the now successful revolutionists were concerned, had always left much to be desired. Shortly after his arrival in Washington in June 1891, Pedro Montt, the confidential representative of the congressional forces, reported that the State Department was "disfavorably inclined toward our position." [104] And Manuel Antonio Matta, an early Minister of Foreign Relations once the revolutionists re-established regular constitutional government, averred that United States acts of favoritism to the dictator had been "a matter of notorious and public knowledge." [105] Little wonder, then, that Prudencio Lazcano, who had represented the Balmaceda administration in Washington, could write as late as July 18—only a few weeks before the government was toppled—that the United States attitude toward us has been ". . . noble and friendly. We can rest tranquil in the assurance that we have the full support of the United States and its statesmen." [106]

Still, many Chileans were willing to give Washington officialdom the benefit of the doubt, feeling that the unfortunate State Department attitude had resulted from the false, misleading, and partisan reports of Patrick Egan, United States envoy in Santiago. On these grounds, Pedro Montt in Washington was inclined to forgive the United States government,[107] as were various Santiago newspapers.[108] Even the *Boston Herald* attributed the inaccurate accounts on the Chilean civil war given out by the State Department to the partisanship of Egan, adding that it was disgraceful for any man who had worked so hard for the cause of Irish independence to have endeavored to saddle the Chileans with tyranny.[109]

Chileans who blamed United States attitudes on Egan's shortcomings rather than on State Department plots frequently charged the envoy with excessive lust for personal gain. He and his son, it was said, hoped to benefit from private transactions with Balmaceda. Indignation was voiced especially when Egan's son served as the lawyer for a company that received a railroad-building contract in Santiago, and also when he was placed on the payroll of the State Railroads of Chile.[110] Egan was even blamed, apparently without justification, for having engineered the contract which Balmaceda signed with the notorious North and South American Construction Company for building an impressive series of railroads in Chile. The company, evidently conceived and operated in a spirit of fraud and corruption by some United States capitalists having their headquarters in Louisville, Kentucky, never laid so much as a mile of track. Still, in 1896, owing to the blustering attitude of the United States State Department, the Chilean government felt compelled to pay 150,000 pesos as settlement for the company's weak claims against it.[111]

Egan's personal interest in a Balmaceda victory led him, in the judgment of congressional leaders, to unpardonably biased meddling during the civil war. Above all, the congressionalists were infuriated by a letter Egan wrote in connection with endeavors to end hostilities through the good offices of the United States. This letter to Rear Admiral M. B. MacCann, the officer who was in charge of the Pacific operations of the United States fleet and in contact with the insurgent leaders in Iquique, stated that in Egan's opinion Balmaceda could not be defeated, *"if the army re-*

mained loyal [italics added]." In relaying the Egan message to Isidoro Errázuriz, who was conducting foreign affairs for the revolutionist government in Iquique, MacCann failed to include Egan's qualifying phrase. Errázuriz was furious, wondering what good could come from United States good offices if its envoy had already made up his mind as to the outcome of the struggle. The congressional forces never forgave Egan—even when they learned the original, complete text of his letter.[112]

It may well have been prior animus toward Egan that led leaders of the congressional cause to place the worst possible interpretation on the innocent though foolish actions of United States Admiral George Brown. Urged on by curiosity, Brown sailed the U.S.S. "San Francisco" to Quintero Bay to observe the August 20 landing operations of a congressional army.[113] Soon the rumor was circulating that Brown had engaged in espionage activities, giving information to the Balmaceda forces about the number and deployment of congressional troops.[114] Ismael Valdés Vergara, an important insurgent leader and for many years thereafter a leading figure in Chilean politics, formulated these charges in a forceful letter that was published in several Chilean papers.[115] Conservative Party stalwart Ricardo Cox Méndez soon echoed these accusations,[116] and, more important, it is certain that M. A. Matta believed Brown's conduct to have constituted espionage.[117]

Matta was therefore ill-disposed to receive the September 17 note directed to him by Egan. Actually, this was only the second Egan note to Matta. The first had offered congratulations upon Matta's appointment to the post of Minister of Foreign Relations, employing much cooler language than Egan had customarily used when wishing new Balmaceda appointees well. In the September 17 correspondence, Egan complained about the scandalous charges that had been voiced against Brown, saying that they constituted a "studied insult to the navy and flag of the United States." [118]

A number of incidents in addition to Brown's indiscretion aroused the ire of congressional leaders. Most notable among these was the much-discussed "Itata" affair,[119] in which the United States prevented delivery of arms to congressional forces. By the end of the civil war, then, the leaders of the successful insurgent cause were convinced that they had been discriminated against, if not by the United States, then at least by its representative in Santiago.

Egan was fully aware of this fact. On September 8, just four days after he had been authorized to assume diplomatic relations with the junta temporarily governing in the name of the congressional forces, he had published in *La Libertad Electoral* a letter in which he referred to the animosity against him and the widespread Chilean conviction that his actions during the civil war had been decidedly partisan. This being the case, Chilean diplomats were probably justified in observing that the only proper action for Washington upon the end of the civil war would have been to recall Egan.[120] A puzzling question is why Chile did not take advantage of an early October offer, extended to Pedro Montt in Washington by a State Department official, to recall Egan without delay.[121]

For some Chileans, Washington's failure to disavow Egan's actions by recalling him was tantamount to proof that the envoy's partisanship had resulted all along not from personal chicanery alone, but from the opportunistically motivated official policy of the United States. Among men of this persuasion, the most widely held theory was that Blaine had taken Balmaceda's posture as an economic nationalist, in connection with which the Chilean president had assumed a firm policy with Mr. North and other English nitrate magnates, as an indication of incipient anti-British sentiments. Blaine suspected that these sentiments might be nourished by shrewd United States diplomacy. In fact, according to the theory, the Secretary of State optimistically expected that by backing Balmaceda he might gain for United States business the concessions that his War of the Pacific meddling had failed to obtain, and at the same time curb once and for all British financial preeminence in Chile.[122] With this in mind, the plot-theorists concluded, Blaine had chosen as envoy to Chile the most confirmed Anglophobe he could find.

Late in March 1889, Emilio C. Varas had written to his Ministry from Washington about the nomination of Egan to head the United States Legation in Santiago. Varas described Egan as one of the best-known Irish "home-rulers," who, having suffered persecution from the English courts in his native Ireland, had come to the United States in 1882 and had received his citizenship papers six years later. In concluding his memorandum, Varas had referred to the reactions of various United States newspapers to the Egan nomination. The tendency had been to question the wisdom of sending a rabid British-hater to represent the United States in a country where United Kingdom interests were so important. Some segments of the press concluded that the appointment was an affront to England, and that Egan was going to Chile only to start a commercial war against British interests. Finally, the *Omaha Herald*—Egan had lived in Nebraska— hoped that "Egan would remember when he is in Santiago that he is not the leader of an anti-British crusade, but the representative of this republic instead." [123]

Egan's reports to Washington suggest that he sometimes attempted to combine the two functions.[124] But the reports do not indicate whether Egan was supplying the sort of information he had been instructed to look for by Blaine, or whether he was simply, on his own, trying to influence the judgment of the Secretary of State. Certainly though, he did, and always with displeasure, stress the pro-British orientation of the congressional forces.[125] And, according to Pedro Montt, who represented the congressionalists in Washington, Egan kept supplying the State Department with information that the Chilean civil war was fomented by British elements, and that a Balmaceda defeat would prove detrimental to United States interests.[126]

In London, there was little doubt that Egan's attitudes reflected official Washington policy. Foreign Office official Philip Currie in November told Agustín Ross, Chile's banker-diplomat who represented the congressional groups, that the United States had worked through its envoy to bring about a Balmaceda victory, hoping as a result to exact a favorable commercial treaty and terminate the dominance of British capital.[127]

MOUNTING TENSION IN THE IMMEDIATE POST-CIVIL WAR PERIOD

The civil war had barely come to an end when the triumphant revolutionary leaders were angered by what they considered another sign of Egan's animus against them. The new problem arose from the large number of Balmacedistas who found asylum in the United States Legation upon the collapse of their cause. The German envoy in Chile reported on September 9: "The various American Legations have offered asylum to a number of the principal Balmacedistas, and now find themselves congested with them. This is particularly true of the North American Legation." [128]

This situation involved Egan and Matta in an ill-tempered correspondence. Within a short time Egan had written fourteen sharp letters protesting what he considered the harassing actions of Chilean officials in their surveillance of the United States Legation.[129] Egan was annoyed by demonstrations against the Legation which he claimed were organized by secret police, and charged that many persons were arrested and detained in prison for no other reason than that they had been seen entering and leaving the building. He demanded, moreover, that safe-conducts be issued to all who had been granted asylum on United States premises.

Matta defended the Chilean position in eleven spirited notes to Egan. He charged revolutionary plots and subversive schemes were being spawned by the Chileans in the United States Legation. He stated further that safe-conducts could not be issued as the Chamber of Deputies was preparing criminal charges against several of those in asylum, and he criticized Egan for having delayed a month in submitting the names of Chileans housed in the Legation.[130] In this whole matter, it was Matta's conviction that the United States was pursuing a policy of threats and intimidation and trying to assume functions of the Chilean government.[131]

In Washington, Blaine strongly backed the stand of his envoy, at one time justifying the demand for safe-conducts by the absolutely false assertion that Chile had issued eighty of these writs to refugees in the German Legation.[132] Blaine further offended Chilean sensitivities by repeating allegations, obviously received from Egan, that the newly installed government was planning to execute all those who had been granted asylum by the United States and to confiscate their property. To this unfounded charge, which to the Chileans indicated that Blaine regarded them as one of the turbulent, unstable, tropical republics that had not yet established proud legal traditions, Montt replied with dignity. He explained to Blaine that in Chile the death penalty existed only for assassins and that confiscation of goods was prohibited by the constitution.[133]

Matters built quickly to a climax. In a note of September 25 to Matta, Egan complained about not having yet received a reply to his protests of September 23 and stated that activities of Chilean officials stationed in the vicinity of the Legation were "so extraordinary and incredible that I do not know of any similar instances having occurred in any other part of the world toward the Legation of a friendly power."[134] The next day Egan refused to accept written explanations offered by Matta. Moreover, in a sharp note to the Foreign Relations Minister, he observed: "Considerations due to the country which I represent cannot be entrusted to the discretion of detectives of an inferior grade; nor can they depend upon the outcome of suspicions and fears that I must consider unformed [sic] and chimerical."[135] A few days later in composing another letter to Matta, Egan again indulged his penchant for insulting Chilean police: "According to the principles approved by you, the diplomatic immunities should be at the mercy of idle rumors or of the whisperings of detectives composed of persons drawn from the lowest social grade."[136] And then on October 16 —the date is important—Egan in another note to Matta let loose a still stronger blast against Chile's position on the asylum issue: "Only ignorance of international practices could have led Chile to assume such attitudes."[137]

On October 16, the notorious "Baltimore" incident occurred in Valparaíso. By this time, relations between the United States and Chile—or at least between Egan and Chile—had deteriorated to an alarming degree.[138] And, by way of background, it must also be noted that since the 1860's M. A. Matta had been a leader among those Radical and Liberal party politicians who viewed the United

States with extreme distrust and dislike and hoped for Hispanic-American unity as a means of gaining adequate strength to combat the influence of the Colossus of the North.[139] Another prominent Chilean diplomat in the new government, who had handled the conduct of foreign affairs for the congressional forces when the civil war was in progress and who would become Minister of Foreign Relations just after settlement of the "Baltimore" affair was Isidoro Errázuriz. From his days as a student at Georgetown University during the 1850's, Errázuriz had developed a violent dislike for the United States, regarding the country as spiritually and culturally bankrupt, tainted by notions of racial superiority, and intent upon enslaving the Hispanic-American peoples.[140]

Undoubtedly, Matta, Errázuriz and other highly placed Chileans felt disposed to use the "Baltimore" affair at least in part as a means of declaring to the United States the complete and total sovereignty of their nation. They hoped thereby to announce their refusal to countenance further South American meddling on the part of the Colossus.

THE 'BALTIMORE' AFFAIR: THE FIRST STAGES OF THE DISPUTE

Captain Winfield S. Schley of the U.S.S. "Baltimore" granted shore leave on October 16 to slightly more than one hundred of the ship's company. This, in itself, given the state of diplomatic tension then prevailing, may have been imprudent. Some Chileans remembered with resentment that in the final stages of the civil war the "Baltimore" had been used to transport a large number of Balmacedistas to safety in Peru.[141] At any rate, a group of the diversion-seeking sailors soon found themselves in a disreputable district of Valparaíso, where drink and women were most plentiful. About six in the evening, a fight erupted between them and a large number of Chileans. According to the next day's edition of the Valparaíso El Mercurio, the altercation began when two United States sailors engaged in an argument with a Chilean mariner, threw rocks at him, knocked him down, and then sought to flee. Hearing the commotion, numerous Chileans poured forth from the bars in the area and gave chase. Eventually forty policemen arrived and herded some thirty of the "Baltimore" crew and approximately ten Chilean sailors to a jail about ten blocks away. One United States sailor, *El Mercurio* reported, had been killed and five seriously wounded, while only one Chilean had been slightly injured. The paper charged that some of the United States sailors had been armed, and that earlier that day in a public bar a group of them had shown their disdain for Chileans and had loudly remarked that there would be a good fight in the evening.

Within four days Captain Schley had received instructions from Secretary of the Navy Benjamin Tracy to conduct an investigation of the incident. Schley hastily complied with these orders, and by October 22 the cabled findings of his investigation were already in Washington. Accepting the "careful investigation" conducted by Schley as having turned up the full and unquestionable truth on the matter, William F. Wharton, interim Secretary of State during an illness of Blaine, instructed Egan to inform Chile that: the "Baltimore" sailors had been entirely correct and orderly in their conduct; that they had been unarmed and had given no provocation; that the attack was apparently premeditated and made by armed men greatly superior in number; that the police, instead of protecting the United States sailors, had arrested them and then joined with the mob in administering beatings; and that as a result of these actions two United States sailors had been killed—one outright, while another died shortly after of injuries—and seventeen wounded. Wharton concluded that the United States could only view the incident as inspired by hostility to the sailors as representatives of the United States government, and expressed amazement that Chile had not as yet expressed regret.[142] On the basis of Wharton's instructions, Egan on October 26 prepared his first note on the "Baltimore" incident. In it, he largely repeated the message from Wharton, noting that under the circumstances his government felt that Chile should offer full reparation.[143]

This marked the beginning of another acrimonious correspondence between Egan and Matta. Already by October 27, when Matta replied to Egan's note, the main patterns of the debate had been established. Chile's Minister of Foreign Relations maintained that only the findings of the official inquest already in progress under the supervision of E. Foster Recabarren, first judge of the criminal court in Valparaíso, could be accepted by the Chilean government. The notion that the "Baltimore" sailors had been attacked as the uniformed representatives of the United States government was rejected out-of-hand. Further, the government of Chile would not know if an apology was due the United States until after the Valparaíso inquest had been concluded.

The investigation presided over by Judge Foster Recabarren was as distinguished for its length as the Schley proceedings had been for their brevity. Not until the end of December had it been completed. There were frequent United States requests that the matter be expedited,[144] and that the initial findings be made public even before the investigation had been completed. To these promptings, Matta invariably replied that given the separation of powers in Chile, which the recent civil war had in part been fought to safeguard, the executive could not intervene in judicial procedures. He also pointed out that constitutional law forbade publication of criminal proceedings until the entire investigation had been completed,[145] and attributed the Valparaíso tribunal's slow progress to the uncooperative attitudes of Egan, the United States consul in the port city, and "Baltimore" personnel.[146] Above all, Matta never tired of stressing that "Chile would defend the sovereign rights that inhere in every independent country." [147]

The Patrick Shields case, occurring in November, served to exacerbate relations between Egan and Matta. According to the Egan version, Shields, a sailor on the United States merchant ship "Keweenaw," had without provocation been jailed and repeatedly beaten. Matta replied in strong, almost abusive terms that a Chilean inquiry revealed a thoroughly intoxicated Shields had been taken to jail as an act of mercy, and that if physical examination showed him to be bruised and in bad condition, it was owing to chronic drunkenness and resulting falls. Finally, Matta informed his antagonist, the great Irish freedom-fighter, that the United States had no concern in the matter because Shields had been found to be a citizen of Ireland, "and therefore a subject of Her Majesty, the Queen of England." [148]

ENTER PRESIDENT HARRISON

In his December 8 address to Congress, President Benjamin Harrison referred at some length to the "Baltimore" affair, accepting as established fact not only the findings of the Schley investigation but also some questionable information supplied by Egan. An infuriated Matta shortly wired Pedro Montt, now Chile's envoy in Washington, instructions in which he stated that Harrison's speech had contained errors or deliberate inaccuracies. Matta referred in particular to the president's allegations that Chileans granted asylum in the United States Legation had been in physical danger, that Egan had been subjected to calculated provocations, that the police had joined in beating the "Baltimore" sailors, and that the original attack against them had been premeditated and an act of animosity directed toward the government that the sailors represented. Matta also charged that Harrison had been induced into error of judgment "in regard to our people and our government." [149]

Showing wise restraint, Montt never delivered to Blaine the text of the Matta instructions. The State Department, however, was apprised of the content from another source. On December 11, Matta had undergone interpellation by the Chilean Senate on his conduct of relations with the United States. In the course of this proceeding he had read his latest instructions to Montt. [150] The next day *El Ferrocarril* published the full text, which was immediately wired by Egan to Washington. Upon being assured by Matta that the newspaper version was essentially an accurate reproduction of his instructions to Montt, Egan brought an end to correspondence with the Ministry of Foreign Relations. He was, moreover, conspicuously absent from the December 25 inauguration of President Jorge Montt. [151]

Although Chile and the United States were not speaking to each other in Santiago, discussion of the "Baltimore" case continued without interruption in Washington. Pedro Montt had reported after an October 30 interview with Blaine, who had just resumed his illness-interrupted duties: "We have nothing to worry about from Blaine." [152] Nor in subsequent proceedings did Montt find reason to modify his optimistic appraisal. Not until late December did Blaine calmly inquire about the Matta circular. Montt replied that it represented instructions of the Chilean government to its agent and had never been formally presented to the State Department. Therefore, United States complaints concerning it were inadmissible.[153] Blaine then asked about the possibility of arbitration, if after the Valparaíso investigation was completed the United States and Chile still found themselves in disagreement, adding that Chile must be the country to request arbitration.[154] In reply to Montt's wire seeking instructions, Matta replied that Chile would accept arbitration.[155] When Montt relayed this information to Blaine on New Year's Day, he reported that the Secretary of State seemed pleased.[156]

This was the point to which negotiations had advanced when Matta was replaced in the Ministry of Foreign Relations by Luis Pereira. Warned from Europe about bellicose United States intentions—although not so cautioned by its agent in Washington—Chile regarded Matta's removal as a conciliatory gesture toward the Colossus. By January 19, as discussions between Montt and Blaine continued, it had been agreed that arbitration would be suggested by some third power and that the offensive portions of the Matta instructions would be withdrawn in writing—Blaine had first asked only for oral assurances on this matter.[157] At the same time, Pereira wired Montt to attempt to secure the recall of Egan. A thoroughly affable Blaine agreed to this on January 20, provided Chile did not give as the reason for its request the partisan attitude of Egan during the civil war.[158] By this date, then, Montt was convinced that all was proceeding toward an amicable settlement and that Chile had nothing to fear from the United States. Meanwhile, advice of a different nature continued to be received from Europe.

WARNINGS FROM EUROPE

The British Foreign Office did not at first regard the "Baltimore" incident as posing a serious threat of actual war. As late as mid-December, one of its officials assured Chilean Envoy Agustín Ross that the whole affair was no more than "the usual tendency of the United States to use strong and undiplomatic language even over trivial affairs." [159] At about the same time Ross heard indirectly from the New York banker August Belmont, who had been contacted through the Rothschilds in England, that matters were proceeding satisfactorily and that the dispute would probably be settled by arbitration. [160]

The New Year, however, was only a few days old when Ross began to receive danger signals. On January 4, a high Foreign Office official revealed that, according to confidential information just received from Washington, unless Chile apologized promptly the United States would declare war and seize nitrate territories as indemnity. [161] The news received in London continued to alarm Ross, and on January 18 he sent a telegram directly to President Jorge Montt. The ungrammatical use of English and the lapse in one instance into Spanish may have been owing to Ross's anxiety. "British Ministry believes today American question todavia it is very serious on account of American general opinion is in great excitement." [162] Previously Ross had informed his government that if United States forces were actually sent against Chile, not one European nation would come to his country's aid. [163]

Chilean diplomacy was also on guard in Germany during the period of crisis. Renowned conservative diplomat and historian Gonzalo Bulnes arrived in Berlin in mid-December to ascertain the attitude of the imperial government. Although he received assurances from the emperor himself of admiration for Chile, he also learned that Germany would extend no more than diplomatic assistance should the crisis with the United States worsen. [164] Then, on December 26, Baron Marshall von Bieberstein, the Minister of Foreign Affairs, informed Bulnes that the German Legation in Washington believed war between the United States and Chile to be imminent. [165] Through an exchange of telegrams, Bulnes learned that Chile's envoy in Paris, Augusto Matte, had received the same information from French sources. Matte and Bulnes were in accord that Chile must quickly perform an act of conciliation, and so advised their chancellery. [166]

HARRISON HAS THE LAST WORD

With receipt of these warnings from Europe,[167] the Chilean government was probably less surprised than its representative in Washington at the January 21 ultimatum prepared by James G. Blaine. In this document, which reached the Chilean Ministry of Foreign Relations on January 23 through intermediary Patrick Egan,[168] the United States Secretary of State declared that his president had examined the findings of the Valparaíso investigation—this material had been delivered in late December, and in every respect had sustained the version of the "Baltimore" affair originally advanced by Chilean diplomats. The new material, the Blaine ultimatum continued, had in no way persuaded the United States to alter its original contentions that: the attack against the "Baltimore" sailors had been motivated by a spirit of hostility toward the United States; that Valparaíso police officials had failed flagrantly in their duties; and that Chile was obligated to render adequate satisfaction and reparation. The ultimatum also demanded disavowal of the objectionable words in the Matta instructions to Montt, "which under ordinary circumstances would have justified United States severance of relations." Finally, Chile was advised that failure to offer prompt satisfaction would result in the automatic rupture of diplomatic relations, and that the matter of Egan's recall had for the moment been dropped.[169]

On January 25 President Harrison delivered a fourteen-page message to Congress, attaching thereto some of the pertinent documentation in the case. Ignoring the already achieved successes of diplomacy, a belligerent Harrison avowed that his government would protect its citizens in foreign lands against brutality and injury inflicted out of a spirit of animosity toward the United States. The president also complained that Chile had not yet replied to the January 21 ultimatum—which had been received by Foreign Minister Pereira on January 23, only two days before the presidential message!

A charitable interpretation of the message would have to be based on the assumption that the president was sincere and candid in a later declaration that he had not, at the time of the message, been informed of a January 23 letter sent by Pedro Montt to Blaine, in which the Chilean envoy reiterated his country's regret for the October 16 incident and disavowed the objectionable passages of the Matta circular.[170] Still, Harrison did omit important information by failing to mention the friendly January conferences between Blaine and Montt which had prepared the way for an amicable settlement.

The Harrison performance certainly fulfilled no legitimate diplomatic purpose. Even before it, Chilean President Jorge Montt had arranged to meet on January 25—the very date of the Harrison address—with his cabinet and the president of the Senate to consider the United States ultimatum. The Chilean response to the ultimatum that was formulated at this meeting denied that the "Baltimore" affair represented a calculated offense against the government of the United States. On the other hand, it disavowed the Matta circular, conceded that the Valparaíso investigation might not have been as rapid as "the president of the United States could have desired," and expressed willingness to allow the United States Supreme Court, or any other arbitration body preferred by Harrison, to settle the affair.[171]

With this reply in his possession, Harrison informed Congress on January 28 that there had been a gratifying change in Chilean attitudes, as a result of which he now looked forward to a peaceful solution of all difficulties. The implication that the strong message of January 25 had been responsible for the so-called change in the adversary's attitude was, of course, absurd. Chile's reply to the ultimatum was in the same spirit that underlay assurances given by Montt as early as January 4 in his consultations with Blaine.

The peaceful solution to the "Baltimore" difficulties foreseen by Harrison was indeed forthcoming, with the Chilean government providing for the payment of $75,000 to the families of the dead. But Patrick Egan took advantage of one last opportunity to maintain strained relations between the two countries before finally departing from Santiago. A brief resurgence of the Balmacedista movement led the Chilean government in 1893 to order the arrest of suspected plotters. Two of these were promptly given asylum in the United States Legation, from which one of them, the prominent Anselmo Blanlot Holley, made good his escape. Egan, professing to be puzzled by the occurrence, became once again the object of a merciless press attack. And, as was his wont, he replied in kind. The general Chilean attitude was probably best expressed by Eduardo Phillips, Chief of the Diplomatic Section of the Ministry of Foreign Relations, who described Egan in a letter to one of the newspapers as a person "utterly lacking in all elements of culture and courtesy, and ever-ready to descend to the level of invective and calumny." [172] Shortly before the September *Fiestas Patrias* in 1893, Chileans were gratified to learn of Egan's recall.

THE EFFECT OF THE 'BALTIMORE' AFFAIR ON CHILEAN ATTITUDES TOWARD FOREIGN AFFAIRS

The memory of the "Baltimore" affair was not soon effaced. To this day, the majority of Chileans can whip themselves into an anti-Yankee frenzy by recalling the martyred *Teniente* Carlos Peña. The legend of Carlos Peña—and despite the wide credence it enjoys,[173] it is pure legend—has it that final settlement of the "Baltimore" affair necessitated the sending of a Chilean warship either to Valparaíso or San Francisco, California, depending on the version, to strike its colors in atonement. Lieutenant Peña volunteered to perform the onerous task of actually lowering his country's flag. As the standard touched the deck, he turned to the band and directed it to play the Chilean national anthem. Then, clutching the flag to his breast, he shot himself through the heart.

Even without the addition of sentimental legends, the actual humiliation of the "Baltimore" settlement was great enough, and Chileans soon began speculating as to why the United States had turned an "insignificant event" [174] into an international incident. The extremely conservative and proclerical organ, *El Porvenir*, took advantage of the affair to launch an attack against the hated anticlerical, Radical Party leader, M. A. Matta, blaming his diplomatic ineptness for the regrettable event.[175] Other Chilean sources were more balanced and responsible in their endeavors to analyze the dispute. Oddly enough, Blaine in general was considered to have displayed a friendly attitude toward Chile and to have been

forced against his own inclinations to implement the wishes of a
bellicose and blustering president.[176] The willingness to exonerate
Blaine is remarkable in view of the fact that Chile's man in Washington, Pedro Montt, never seemed to realize the seriousness of
the situation, with the Chilean Foreign Ministry receiving its most
accurate accounts from London and Berlin. This fact might
logically have aroused suspicions that Blaine had once more pulled
the wool over a Chilean envoy's eyes—as he had done so successfully ten years before with Marcial Martínez.

No matter whether President Harrison or Secretary of State
Blaine had formulated "Baltimore" affair policy, the question remains as to why the United States had proceeded in so blustering
a manner. There were those who were willing to attribute this
merely to United States immaturity, and they found comfort in
a London *Times* comment reproduced in *El Ferrocarril*: "The
trouble is the Americans still suffer from a colonial mentality,
which makes them hypersensitive to imagined affronts to their
national dignity." [177] The Spanish envoy in London interpreted the
"Baltimore" affair as a manifestation of United States belief in its
racial superiority over Latins.[178] More penetrating analysts sensed
that by its strong-handed actions with Chile, the United States
was announcing to Latin America that the Colossus was now supreme director of all hemisphere affairs. Indeed, Washington's
conduct in the "Baltimore" affair does appear to have been a
harbinger of the 1895 Venezuelan boundary controversy note in
which Secretary of State Richard Olney informed British Foreign
Minister Lord Salisbury that the will of the United States was now
law in the American Hemisphere.

The usual suspicions of United States economic motives were
also in evidence. Many Chilean as well as English and German
diplomats attributed the threatening posture of the United States
to a desire to obtain a favorable commercial treaty and separate
Chile economically from Europe.[179] Also, a few Chileans perceived
the importance of Alfred Thayer Mahan's strong-navy gospel and
all of its implications of a new type of United States Manifest
Destiny. For them, United States actions in the dispute were explained by the wish of Navy Secretary Tracy and a clique of

admirals and global strategists to invent a war threat so as to obtain larger naval appropriations.[180]

Probably the most widely shared conclusion was that Harrison spoke of war, when in reality successful diplomacy had already guaranteed the maintenance of peaceful relations, because of political considerations. By arousing national enthusiasm and establishing his party as the fearless defender of the rights of persecuted United States citizens, he hoped to bolster his political fortunes for the 1892 elections.[181] It was also felt that Harrison had become convinced of the mass appeal of a belligerent attitude by the success of the *New York Herald* and the *New York World* in expanding circulation through whipping up a martial spirit.[182] The spectacle of a weak president, egged on by yellow journalism, setting at naught the success of diplomacy has, of course, a striking similarity to the events that actually did involve the United States in war with Spain a few years later.

Although regarding the Democratic success in the elections of 1892 as having removed any immediate menace,[183] many influential Chilean statesmen felt that Latin America must take steps at once to guard against future United States aggression. In a remarkable about-face from the Portales traditions of strict isolationism and disparagement of cooperation among American republics, which had enjoyed great vogue immediately after the War of the Pacific, these leaders turned to the Lastarria-fathered belief in the need for American international law and cooperation. M. A. Matta just before his death in 1892 wrote: ". . . such acts [of the United States in handling the "Baltimore" affair] can only come to an end when . . . aroused public opinion gives life to an international law for the Hemisphere that places the powerful and the weak on the same level. Even the fellow citizens of Harrison and Blaine must come some day to respect the urge which stirs in the continent of Columbus." [184]

But for most Chileans in this period, the international law approach seemed too impractical and flimsy a means of protecting the interests of Latin America. Increasingly, therefore, the notion of a Latin-American union, which, as originally advocated by men such as Bilbao and Vicuña Mackenna, could be directed against the influence of the United States, began to win new adherents. As the leading newspaper in Santiago put it: "In dealing with its foes, when they are great world powers, the Latin-American countries must unite." [185]

Perhaps it was fortunate for the future stake of the United States in southern South America that Chile was at this time unable to progress toward achieving unity with its neighbor republics. Any unity of action in the southern region, any strength adequate to resist the United States, demanded as its prime prerequisite cooperation between the two main Hispanic powers of the South, Argentina and Chile. Time and again in the twentieth century, the United States escaped a "freeze-out" in southern South America because of the inability of Argentina and Chile to cooperate in any common policy. In fact, Argentine-Chilean animosity was a significant factor in allowing Washington largely to dominate the Pan-American movement from 1889 to 1933.

Chile's previously existing distrust of the trans-Andean rival had been magnified by Argentina's conduct during the War of the Pacific and at the Pan-American conference in Washington. Boundary disputes still nourished hostile sentiments in 1892, and around the turn of the century led many Chileans to desire war with Argentina. Against this background, the "Baltimore" affair served to strike an additional blow against Argentine-Chilean rapport. As early as December 1892, the rumor began to circulate among Chile's high government circles that Argentina had offered the United States an offensive-defensive treaty in case the northern power decided to declare war on Chile. Not only this, but Argentina, so the story went, had offered to allow United States troops to cross its territory to invade Chile and had promised to supply the navy of the Colossus with coal. Never reliably confirmed, and indeed quite effectively denied, these rumors nonetheless were, and still are, widely believed in Chile.[186]

In 1892, Chile was at a loss for a policy to pursue toward the United States. All of the old approaches—isolationism, groping toward American international law, and Hispanic-American union —seemed either inadequate or impossible of attainment. Chile therefore chose to leave the Colossus, so far as was possible, alone and to cultivate ties with Europe. That this last procedure might even provide a defensive mechanism against the United States was suggested by Gonzalo Bulnes, Chilean envoy to Germany at the time. Commenting from Berlin on the settlement of the "Baltimore" affair, he wrote: "Now that Chile has escaped United States intervention by the policy of conciliation, it must build toward future strength by cementing its bonds with Europe. The future of South America lies with Europe." [187]

4: THE MORE THE COUNTRY CHANGES THE MORE ITS GOVERNMENT REMAINS THE SAME: CHILE, 1892-1920

YEARS OF POLITICAL FUTILITY

GENERAL POLITICAL PATTERNS

Chilean political history during the so-called parliamentary period is complex. Between 1892 and 1920 there were close to 120 total or partial cabinet changes, involving in each instance the naming of a new Minister of Interior—the head of the cabinet in the Chilean political structure. Between 1831 and 1885, the Ministry of Interior had changed hands only thirty-one times.[1]

Although the party structure remained relatively unchanged, there were enough splinter movements and shifts in the composition of coalitions and alliances to add further confusion to the picture. The Conservatives, regaining much of the strength and influence they had lost after the 1870's, continued to represent primarily the proclerical, large landholders of the central valley.[2] The Liberal Party became, if possible, more amorphous than in the past. Although including many landowners in its membership, its general orientation was more urban than rural. Its liberalism was of the classical school, with the principles of rugged individualism and laissez faire prevailing.[3] Beyond this it is dangerous to generalize, because of the many different varieties of Liberals which caused the party to divide into several distinct groups. There were Doctrinaires who refused ever to combine with the Conservatives in waging political battles; there were Coalitionists who cooperated with the Conservatives; and there were Liberal Democrats who, for the most part, had supported the ill-fated Balmaceda. Led by Enrique Salvador Sanfuentes, the Liberal Democrats staged a remarkable comeback from their civil war defeat, and in 1894

86

elected the largest bloc of deputies in the national congress. In their lack of principles and consistent issues, the Liberal Democrats stand as a symbol of Chilean politics during the era. They were ready to combine with any and all alliances and coalitions, or to leave them just as casually, provided political expediency so dictated.[4]

Throughout the parliamentary period the Radical Party steadily expanded its political influence.[5] Claiming to be a middle-class party, its strength actually depended as much upon the *latifundistas* of Concepción, the rich mining interests of Copiapó, and the successful businessmen of Santiago, as upon the teachers, bureaucrats, lower-echelon professional people, and artisans.[6] Although it professed advocacy of socialism in 1906, it meant by this little more than government attention to urban sanitation and hygiene projects. And all the while, the National Party—founded to defend aristocratic, anticlerical government—continued to attract numerous voters, even though its ideology came to consist of nothing more than political jockeying and maneuvering. There was also the Democrat Party which originated in 1887 for the purpose of making the lower middle class more politically articulate.[7] While it showed somewhat greater probity than other political groups, generally refraining from buying congressional seats, it tended increasingly to reflect the economic and social attitudes of the traditional parties.[8]

The complexity of politics in the parliamentary period is exceeded only by its unimportance. One political historian refers to the era as "the futile years," and to the various presidents who held office as "the faces that pass."[9] Still, all of the tactical bickering that led to the rapid formation and crumbling of various Liberal Alliances (always excluding the Conservatives) and Coalitions (including the Conservatives) is significant: it constitutes an unmistakable symptom of the national malaise that afflicted Chile following the civil war of 1891.

During the "futile years" there was little chance for the best-intentioned politicians to develop consistent programs of national development, for the political ambient was such that yesterday's implacable foe became today's ally as the result of a new cabinet crisis.[10] Furthermore, each party or party-splinter enjoyed what amounted to veto rights because of its ability to topple a cabinet by temporarily altering its political alliances.[11] Presidents did at least succeed one another in accordance with constitutional provisions. And the numerous cabinets that briefly served their country respected the public liberties of the middle and upper classes, maintained freedom of the press, improved communications, did not totally neglect education, and seldom resorted to graft and peculation to the extent often prevalent in less stable sister republics. Moreover, passions were kept in check as the most consistently discussed issue of the period was debated. This involved whether education should be state-controlled and considerably expanded, as the Radicals desired,[12] or dominated by the Church and not drastically augmented, as the Conservatives urged.[13]

Gentlemanly moderation, however, was sometimes no more than a veneer. Beneath it, politics could be vicious and sordid. The autonomous municipality law, long championed by idealistic Conservative Senator Manuel José Irarrázaval and enacted in 1892, was supposed to establish higher standards of government by freeing towns from dependence on the corrupt Santiago bureaucracy. Unfortunately, in its final effects, the law only served to indicate that local corruption could match or exceed that which was practiced on the national level. Early in the parliamentary period also, "bribery came to be a national institution." [14] By 1900, El Ferrocarril could observe:

> . . . venality has become the over-riding feature of our electoral system. . . . national and municipal offices are obtained by the candidates who can spend the most money . . . this practice is followed by all political parties. . . . A seat in the Senate now costs some tens of thousands of pesos, the deputy posts are almost as expensive, and even the municipal offices come at nearly as dear a price.[15]

SOME OF THE "FACES THAT PASS": POLITICAL FIGURES
IN THE PARLIAMENTARY PERIOD

Upon becoming president in 1892, Jorge Montt, who had led the naval uprising against Balmaceda that precipitated the civil war, announced his full faith in parliamentary administration. As a result, and without amendment to the flexible 1833 constitution, a political system based on congressional interpellation and censure of ministers was introduced. Congress also resorted to denying or delaying approval of budget requests to keep presidents in line, and, when it desired, obstructed implementation of presidential decrees.

The 1896 presidential elections were notable in that their results were not determined by the will of the outgoing chief executive. Montt, in fact, was a passive spectator. At the outset of the campaign, the first of many parliamentary-period Liberal Alliances was formed. Consisting of the Doctrinaire Liberals, the Democratic Liberals, the Radicals and the Democrats, the Alliance advanced the candidacy of the widely respected but cold and aloof Vicente Reyes.[16] According to some accounts Reyes lost the election because he refused to enter into a free-spending contest to bribe the electorate. He is said to have spent only five thousand pesos on the campaign, while Federico Errázuriz Echáurren, supported by the Coalition of Conservatives, Nationals and Coalitionist Liberals, spent over a million pesos.[17]

Federico Errázuriz, son of the previous President Errázuriz (1871-1876), continues to be regarded in vastly varying lights by different Chilean writers. Archconservative Jaime Eyzaguirre[18] pictures him as a model of probity who with dedicated singleness of purpose defended Chilean territorial integrity in boundary disputes with Argentina and managed through supreme statesmanship to avert war with that country. Those whose political affiliations do not lie with the Conservative Party regard Errázuriz as a weak and vacillating president who kept many good men out of office by his steadfast refusal to appoint any Radical Party member to a ministerial post, who surrounded himself with dissolute advisers not primarily concerned with national interests, and who backed down shamelessly before blustering Argentina and surrendered vast national territories.[19]

Errázuriz, whose rule produced twelve cabinet changes compared to the eight of Jorge Montt's, was in office when the electric trolley was introduced to Santiago in 1900. Two years later, the first electric street lights were installed in the capital. But Errázuriz was not on hand for the impressive ceremonies heralding this event. In 1901 he had become the first parliamentary-period president to die while in office.

The ensuing presidential elections pitted Liberal Alliance candidate Germán Riesco Errázuriz against the Coalition-supported Pedro Montt, son of former President Manuel Montt (1851-1861) and envoy in Washington during the "Baltimore" affair. Religion was an issue in the campaign, with José María Caro, theology professor of the Conciliar Seminary and ultimately the archbishop of Santiago, advising the faithful they could not licitly support the candidacy of Riesco.[20] In spite of this clerical admonition, Riesco triumphed.

The new president, a nephew of the first President Errázuriz and a cousin and brother-in-law of the second, proved to be a safe enough choice, as even the Conservatives came eventually to concede. He has been described as a staunch foe of any daring or imaginative plan, and as lacking all semblance of outstanding talent.[21] Still, Riesco presided with at least a modicum of skill over a period of economic expansion that exhibited more dynamism than most of the other years of the parliamentary era. Riesco also entered into the famous May Pacts of 1902 with Argentina which brought an end to a renewed war threat and stipulated that future boundary disputes would be settled by arbitration. Two years later, the Riesco administration signed a definitive peace treaty with Bolivia confirming Chilean ownership of the Antofagasta region.

Interesting political events were also transpiring. The 1906 Radical Party convention saw Valentín Letelier triumphant over Enrique Mac-Iver in a great debate. As a result, the convention decided by majority vote to proclaim the Radical Party's belief in socialism. And a number of outstanding senators now brought at least a high tone to the nation's sterile political debates. During the period José Tocornal, president of the Conservative Party, Fernando Lazcano, head of the Liberals, Enrique Mac-Iver, still titular head of the Radicals, Pedro Montt, president of the Nationals, and Vicente Reyes, leader of the Doctrinaire Liberals, all served with distinction in the Senate. Also at this time, Senator Juan Luis Sanfuentes, the brother of Enrique Salvador and described as a man who had no goals or ideals other than to advance his political career,[22] became head of the Liberal Democrats.

The elections of 1906 which came at the close of Riesco's term provided a good insight into the significance of contemporary Chilean politics. Pedro Montt, who had been defeated five years earlier when running as the candidate of the Coalition, now won the presidential office as the Liberal Alliance standard-bearer, defeating Coalitionist Liberal Fernando Lazcano.[23] The new chief executive managed to rule with only eleven different cabinets, an improvement over the seventeen of the Riesco administration. But a national disaster and an economic collapse, both occurring early in his term of office, called for more resolute action than Montt, suffering from bad health, seemed capable of providing.

In August 1906 an earthquake struck the port of Valparaíso. and for a time it was feared the very site of the city might have to be abandoned, so devastating had the damage been. One year later there was a stock-market collapse, and the national economy plummeted alarmingly. Finally in 1910, a brighter aspect of the economic picture was provided by completion of the trans-Andean railroad. President Montt traveled over the new facilities to Buenos Aires to attend the first centennial celebration of Argentine independence. A short time later he journeyed to Bremen seeking medical assistance. Treatment for his heart condition was unavailing, and he died in the German city in August 1910.

The new elections brought victory to Liberal Alliance candidate Ramón Barros Luco. The seventy-five-year-old "liberal" victor failed utterly to perceive the new forces that were emerging in Chile. Although the Democrats had supported him in the campaign, he never called any of their members to the cabinet, regarding their increasingly mild and innocuous party as too revolutionary. When the appointment of Radicals seemed unavoidable, he sought out only the most moderate members of the party. The descriptions of Barros Luco as "the personification of mediocrity," and "the old man who took a long siesta in the presidency," [24] seem apt. It was going to partisan extremes, however, to assert, as did one writer, that the presidential palace "had been disgraced by a man who practiced fraud and corruption on the scale of Byzantine rulers." [25] The very best insight into the Barros Luco administration is provided by the president's own political credo: "There are two kinds of political problems—those that have no solution and those that solve themselves." [26]

Barros Luco probably wondered which of the two categories described the problems that were so evident during his rule. For example, political disputes forced the president to change cabinets fifteen times. And the distrusted Democrats were able in 1912 to elect their first senator. In the same year, an army-navy political conspiracy collapsed only when Gonzalo Bulnes, whom the discontents had hoped to elevate to the presidency, disavowed the scheme at the eleventh hour.[27] The president probably experienced relief as his term came to an end, although he was upset during his last year in office by the effrontery of Pedro León Loyola. This young man, a former president of the Federation of Chilean University Students (FECH) delivered a funeral oration for those who were still governing Chile but were, for all practical purposes, dead.[28]

The defenders of Barros Luco reveal as much about his rule as do his detractors. The thoroughly conservative *El Diario Ilustrado* contended at the close of 1915 that Barros Luco had been a good chief executive precisely because he had been a do-nothing leader. Had he been an energetic president, working zealously to solve all national problems, concluded the paper, "he would only have brought catastrophe to our country." [29]

The 1915 presidential nominating convention of the Liberal Alliance produced more than the usual amount of fireworks, and seemed actually to indicate that some men were attempting to introduce real issues into politics. Striving to gain the convention's favor were such Liberals as the broadly cultured, humanitarian, and sincere reform-advocate, Eliodoro Yáñez;[30] the incorruptible, but now out-of-date, Vicente Reyes; and the fiery, energetic, sometimes demagogic, Arturo Alessandri. The Democrats' Malaquías Concha,[31] by now a somewhat tired crusader, the same party's first senator, Angel Guarello, and the old leader of conservative Radicalism, Enrique Mac-Iver, also played prominent parts in the proceedings that led ultimately to the selection of the comparatively colorless Javier Figueroa as the Alliance standard-bearer. The Coalition decided it was time to try to give to Juan Luis Sanfuentes the national presidency that he had pantingly coveted for many years, and so chose him its candidate. The electoral vote favored Sanfuentes by one ballot: 174-173.[32]

Domingo Amunátegui Solar, a shrewd political analyst intimately connected with events of this period,[33] feels that the years from 1915 to 1920 may have been the most crucial of the entire parliamentary period, and that had the presidency been occupied at this time by a capable man willing to accommodate to new conditions, and possessing vision and understanding of social developments, then all of the turbulence and radicalism of the 1924 to 1933 period might have been avoided.[34] Be that as it may, Sanfuentes responded to danger-signals by resorting to added repression, to the use of militia, and to the suspension of constitutional guarantees in the north.

Still, some aspects of the Sanfuentes administration are viewed with approval by many Chileans. Overwhelmingly he is admired for preserving Chilean neutrality in the first World War. Some contend also that Sanfuentes deserves commendation for bestowing ministerial posts (Public Works as well as Justice and Instruction) upon Democrats. And there is widespread agreement that appointment during his term of the eighty-year-old but still energetic Crescente Errázuriz[35] to the archbishopric of Santiago was a stroke of genius. The guiding spirit behind this appointment was Eliodoro Yáñez, who realized that the issue of Church-State separation must soon come to a head and wished therefore to secure the nomination of a moderate and enlightened primate.[36]

The 1920 presidential campaign pitted Arturo Alessandri of the Liberal Alliance against the Coalition's Luis Barros Borgoño, the proper, correct, and rather drab professor-politician.[37] Few people realized, perhaps least of all Alessandri himself, that the narrow victory achieved by the Alliance heralded the end of Chile's long political slumber.

SELF CRITICISM: THE FAVORITE NATIONAL PASTIME

WHAT'S WRONG WITH CHILE?

To people who as recently as the 1880's had regarded themselves as the natural leaders of Latin America and assured of a
brilliant future, the political stagnation between 1892 and 1920
was bound to prove disconcerting. By the beginning of the twentieth century one of the favorite literary pastimes for Chileans had
come to be answering the question: "What's wrong with
Chile?" [38]

National Party Deputy Julio Zegers, deciding something had
gone wrong, wrote the pamphlet ¿de quien es la culpa? [39] But the
most important early expression of alarm came from Radical Enrique Mac-Iver. In 1900 Mac-Iver's pamphlet, Discurso sobre la
crisis moral de la república, raised most of the points that Chilean
writers have been developing and debating to the present time. To
Mac-Iver, Chile no longer seemed a happy country. It had lost its
vigor and confidence; its main difficulties were no longer economic
but moral. "We are richer than in the past," he said, "but are we
progressing? Do we have higher ideals, or better national standards
of living?" Mac-Iver answered these questions with a resounding
no, and went on to lament the disappearance of a spirit of enterprise and energy. "Where today is the initiative that built our first
railroads, ports, docks, irrigation projects and all classes of industries?" Even the glorious War of the Pacific, the Radical leader
declared, now seemed futile. And Mac-Iver concluded: "At an
earlier time, when our energetic and progressive spirit was at its
height, we surged far ahead of other young republics, including
Canada, Australia, Brazil, Argentina and Mexico. How do we com-
pare with those countries today? Silence is the kindest answer."

From the mid-nineteenth century, and especially immediately
after the War of the Pacific, Chileans had regarded themselves
as the hardest working, most industrious people in America. Then
suddenly it seemed that everything had changed. As early as 1887,
Isidoro Errázuriz warned that unless his countrymen worked
harder they could never hope to develop their country.[40] Twelve

years later Emilio Rodríguez Mendoza, then at the start of a brilliant career in journalism, diplomacy and politics, stated that Anglo-Saxons are producers, "while we in Chile have lost all initiative." [41] Thereafter, Chileans leveled the accusation of laziness against the national populace with greater frequency. A typical example was an *El Diario Ilustrado* editorial of 1914: "We are paying for the consequences today of having to support a generation that has not learned to work." [42] Writing a few years after the parliamentary period ended, Alberto Cabero, the popular publicist and respected Radical Party politician, charged that the great Chilean mania had come to be consuming more without producing more. Chileans, concluded Cabero, had become a race of parasites.[43] At the same time the Catholic priest Guillermo Viviani Contreras stated: "Laziness is *the* Chilean evil, that affects all our classes." [44]

Chileans were not only concerned that laziness, at least in the opinion of many, had quite suddenly become a national characteristic.[45] They were also alarmed by an alleged moral breakdown in the country. Enrique Mac-Iver, for example, decided that public morality was in decline, and that this fact was responsible for all of the national problems.[46] Writing also in 1900, Deputy Maximiliano Ibáñez stated: "I note with sorrow a decadence in all the country. . . . At each moment we see within the administration the perpetration of acts of true immorality. . . . We are suffering from the symptoms of moral, political, and social decadence." [47] At approximately the same time Conservative leader José Miguel Echenique declared: "The moral evil [of Chile] has been generating itself, little by little, thanks to the silence of the parties and the cowardice and weakness of character of the majority of persons." [48] *El Mercurio* was also pessimistic about the moral estate of Chileans, noting in 1904 that even if the parties were able to enact enlightened programs, the country lacked men of integrity and dedication to implement them.[49] Several years later, the same paper complained that the public had become so inured to stories of official malfeasance that it was no longer possible to arouse the indignation of the people against even the most glaring acts of immorality.[50] *El Diario Ilustrado* was even more extreme in its denunciation of national life, charging that Chile was morally ruined.[51]

The administrative incompetence, inertia and public immorality that many Chileans claimed to detect in the national life led to discouragement over what had been one of the greatest sources of patriotic pride a generation earlier: political institutions. In 1912 a group of prominent Chileans,[52] ashamed of what they felt their political institutions had degenerated into, formed the League of Civic Action (*Liga de Acción Cívica*). Its purpose was to try to regenerate Chilean political life by insisting upon public honesty, and its underlying conviction was: "Progress that is not based on moral rectitude and civic virtue is ephemeral, and even more, an indication that decadence is at hand." [53]

If many Chileans were agreed that at some time around the turn of the century their nation had lost its old initiative and energy and had begun to suffer from the effects of a moral disintegration, they had still to explain what had caused these unwelcome developments. The Conservatives blamed the secularism of the age, and the fact that anticlerical, Masonic Radicals were gaining control of public education. Radicals and many Liberals in turn blamed the obscurantist, bigoted, medieval mentality of the clergy and its followers. But doctrinaire and theological explanations were no longer convincing to the majority of Chileans, and other answers were sought. In 1908 aristocratic Luis Orrego Luco published *Casa Grande*, one of the most controversial, widely read and discussed novels ever produced in Chile. The work delivered a strong indictment against the Chilean ruling classes, who were charged with giving themselves over to an orgy of conspicuous consumption and abandoning all sense of national responsibility and respect for spiritual and cultural values. Orrego Luco felt that behind the aristocracy's betrayal of its once-proud traditions lay the too rapid admission of the new rich.[54] It was his opinion that vulgar, crassly materialistic, irresponsible, uncultured, unpatriotic, quick-fortune makers had bought their way into the aristocracy and had contaminated the ruling classes and thereby the nation as a whole.

Two years later appeared a monumental work in Chilean literature, *Sinceridad: Chile íntimo en 1910*.[55] Made up of penetrating essays, and something of a forerunner of sociological studies, *Sinceridad* was written by Alejandro Venegas, a humble school teacher. Venegas lacked the connections of Orrego Luco, and his book was less widely read at the time than *Casa Grande*. But its influence through the years has been tremendous. Writing under the pseudonym of Dr. Julio Valdés Cange so that he would not lose his job, Venegas commented bitingly upon the moral decline in Chile, and eloquently called attention to the mounting social problem, placing the blame for it squarely upon the aristocracy. Like Orrego Luco, he felt Chile's ruling classes had degenerated from a patriotic group sincerely seeking national development, into a band of idle, time-wasting, conscienceless self-seekers. Venegas also expressed alarm over the foreign background of the new rich. For him, the takeover of social and economic leadership by first-generation Chileans was both a cause and effect of the breakdown of the old aristocracy.[56]

Socially prominent Orrego Luco and lowly-born Venegas agreed basically, then, that Chile was suffering from a moral decline which had begun when a responsible, energetic, progressive aristocracy transformed itself into a greedy, visionless plutocracy. That brilliant defender of the old order, Alberto Edwards Vives, concurred,[57] and prolific journalist Trancredo Pinochet Le-Brun repeated the same message ad infinitum in his books and in *La Opinión*, the newspaper he published from 1915 to 1920.[58] Radical Party publicist Alberto Cabero had another explanation. He believed that the nitrate wealth acquired as a result of the War of the Pacific had led to the decline of national character. Overwhelmed by the material prosperity that the rich northern desert showered upon the country, Chileans had lost their desire for self-improvement and progress, and become complacent, indolent wastrels, desiring only to be supported by the money that others— notably British nitrate entrepreneurs—earned.[59]

Other intellectuals traced the causes of national infirmity back much further than the War of the Pacific or the rise after 1850 of the new rich. For example, there was Nicolás Palacios, whose writings in the early twentieth century reflected extremes both of optimism and pessimism. He believed that the Chilean "race," comprised of the superior northern, "teutonic" Spaniards and an outstanding breed of Indians, was the finest to be found in the entire American Hemisphere.[60] Nevertheless, Palacios feared that the master race of the Americas was not responding to the challenges of a new age, and thus was failing dismally to live up to its potential. Francisco Antonio Encina carried this point of view further. In the most influential of all his books, *Nuestra inferioridad económica*, published in its first edition in 1912, Encina suggested that racial characteristics rendered Chileans inferior when it came to competing economically in the sort of world that had evolved since the Industrial Revolution. The Basque settlers, beginning to arrive in the seventeenth century, had made Chile great, for their moderation, practicality, and willingness to compromise had helped the nation to achieve political stability based upon soundly functioning institutions and respect for law. But the Basques had failed to bequeath to modern Chileans character traits that were conducive to progress in the twentieth century. Vision, daring, imagination, and the inclination occasionally to gamble, and to break the fetters of narrowly-conceived practicality, were necessary ingredients in the new formulas for economic success. And these were the very qualities that Basques seemed to lack. They were not capable of "thinking big" in matters of economics. Comfortable subsistence was their main concern.

Encina's interpretation of national character also took cognizance of the fact that Chileans were descended ethnically from Castilians and Andalusians as well as from Basques. Southern Spaniards, the original conquerors in the sixteenth century, had firmly established their customs, traditions and value judgments in Chile. As a result of environment and race, then, Chileans continued to share the characteristics of Castilians and Andalusians. Therefore, speculated Encina, they were inclined to spurn the habits of frugality and patient, plodding capital formation. They desired instead to strike it rich by some spectacular deed, and were not averse to dissipating their fortunes as quickly as they had acquired them.[61] The use of capital to generate more capital was a process entirely alien to Chileans—both as Castilian-Andalusians and as Basques. Although he felt that Chileans were, so far as the economic demands of the twentieth century were concerned, an inferior race, Encina did not despair. He believed that education had perpetuated and exaggerated the economic vices inherent in the national character. Therefore, if its orientation was drastically altered, education might eventually equip Chileans to compensate for their inferiority and to come to grips with the challenges of a new age.[62]

CHILE'S DECLINE IN INTERNATIONAL STANDING

Inferiority! This was a startling word for the recently proud and haughty Chileans to begin to bandy about. Worse still, inferiority seemed to manifest itself, as Enrique Mac-Iver first intimated, not only in domestic development, but in the relationship of Chile to other world powers. Undoubtedly, the "Baltimore" affair contributed to a sense of international impotence. Of more fundamental significance were the consequences of the War of the Pacific. In the period immediately following the war, Chileans had dreamed of extending their enlightened influence throughout Latin America and had been obsessed with notions of Manifest Destiny. By the time of the Washington Conference in 1889, their sense of mission in providing continental leadership had been replaced by a concern for protecting War of the Pacific gains against the schemes of jealous neighbors. The ambition to direct American affairs had given way to a merely defensive mechanism.

The perceptive author of Sinceridad was among the early writers to grasp this fact.[63] "For some thirty years," observed Venegas, "we dreamed of establishing our hegemony over South America. Now this dream has vanished. Much as it offends our pride, it is true. Every visitor who goes to Argentina and Brazil is impressed by our inferiority to these two countries." [64] Writing a few years later, Trancredo Pinochet lamented that Chile's role in relation to the rest of the world was no longer one of leading or even contributing, but solely of imitating.[65]

Particularly frustrating and puzzling for Chileans was the manner in which the nation's archrival, Argentina, seemed after 1900 to forge ahead as Chile stood still. In 1860, Chile had boasted a population larger than Argentina's; by 1914, the Chilean population was about 3.5 million while that of Argentina had reached eight million.[66] *El Ferrocarril* observed that in 1897 Chile's General Agency of Colonization could lure only 855 immigrants to the country, while in the same year Argentina attracted 105,143.[67] However, a vast majority of Chileans in 1900 undoubtedly shared the conviction of Liberal statesman Eliodoro Yáñez and Conservative diplomat Gonzalo Bulnes that Chile was superior both in virtue and in might to Argentina. Like Yáñez and Bulnes they were ready for war with the trans-Andean nation to teach it who was master in southern South America. By the 1920's, on the other hand, many were willing to agree with Gabriela Mistral that Chile, when it came to material progress and power, must recognize its inferiority to Argentina.[68]

THE CAUSES OF NATIONAL DECLINE

ECONOMIC FACTORS

In spite of continuing nitrate production and a resurgence in copper production beginning in 1912, there was much evidence that all was not well with the Chilean economy during the parliamentary period.[69] Between 1879 and 1918 the public debt rose from 156,000,000 to 692,000,000 pesos. One reason for this was the government's unwillingness to tax the wealthy classes to even the minimal extent that was coming to be customary in some of the other Latin-American republics.[70] Imposts upon inheritances and donations which had been suspended in 1881 were not restored until 1915, and then with a top rate of only 5 per cent. Lack of solid economic foundation was suggested also by the fact that in 1907 Chileans expended some 6,800,000 pesos on importing champagne, jewels, silks and perfumes, while devoting only 3,789,000 to industrial and agricultural machinery imports.[71] Moreover, between 1908 and 1920, milk production registered almost no increase, while the number of cows decreased and that of sheep rose only some 7 per cent. Worse still, between 1913 and 1920 the average per-acre wheat yield fell nearly 40 per cent.[72]

One of the most notorious aspects of Chilean economic practices during the parliamentary period was the indiscriminate use of paper money, which led inevitably to steady inflation. A plot theory has even been developed that attempts to explain virtually all Chilean difficulties by printing-press money. Writers as divergent in time, political ideas, and even nationality as Alejandro Venegas,[73] Henry Lane Wilson,[74] Frank W. Fetter,[75] Ricardo Donoso,[76] and Eduardo Frei,[77] as well as numerous Marxian publicists,[78] have looked upon Chile's long love affair with paper money as the result of a deliberate conspiracy on the part of landowners, abetted by bankers, to subjugate and exploit middle and lower classes.

This interpretation is inadequate in many respects. In 1892, for example, when the landowners and bankers were at the very peak of their power after the overthrow of Balmaceda, both groups opposed paper money and favored adoption of a strict gold standard.[79] Instead of opening the gates for paper-money emission, Congress at that time stabilized the peso at twenty-four pence.[80] The explanation sometimes offered by advocates of the plot theory is that it was not until 1898, because of a rapid increase of mortgage indebtedness after 1892, that the large landowners insisted upon an expansion of paper money[81] as a means of facilitating repayment. However, much of the new indebtedness had been incurred by humble frontier settlers in the area south of Concepción, and their desire for currency expansion could not be construed as a scheme of land-burdened aristocrats.[82] Much more important, by 1898 the landowning aristocracy of Chile had, as a single group, probably already lost the power to foist a paper-money scheme upon the country.[83] Wealth and power by this time had shifted dramatically toward the cities, and although the landowners still had a veto power they would have encountered grave difficulty in imposing their interests upon opposing urban sectors.

In 1898, however, the landowners were joined by a variety of essentially urban groups that for a number of reasons, some selfish and some patriotic, wished vastly expanded sums of paper money. El Sur, the Concepción-published newspaper that reflected the views of conservative southern landowners, was correct when it noted in 1898 that the real champions of paper money were the urban-oriented Liberal Democrats, the former followers of Balmaceda.[84] And Francisco Antonio Encina has seldom made a more penetrating interpretation of Chilean history than when he lays blame for the infatuation with paper money upon industrialization-seeking urban sectors. Singling out Manuel Aristides Zañartu, his son Enrique Zañartu Prieto, Malaquías Concha, and Alfredo Irarrázaval Zañartu for special censure, Encina shows that the champions of rapid industrialization regarded paper money, easy credit, and protective tariffs as the sure-fire means of achieving their objectives.[85]

Other factors caused men like Enrique Mac-Iver, who had previously been implacably opposed to soft money, to favor by 1898 a large paper emission. The two preceding years had been marked by economic difficulties. Foreign commerce had declined some 15 per cent, the nitrate market was glutted, and other commodity prices were falling alarmingly.[86] But budget expenditures, especially on armaments, had to be maintained at high levels because of the threatened war with Argentina. The war scare led also to the flight of foreign capital and to a run on banks. Treasury Minister Rafael Sotomayor saw no way out other than the printing of 50,000,000 pesos of paper money.[87] Undoubtedly, the majority of those who in 1898 concurred in this judgment regarded the measure as a temporary, emergency expedient.[88]

Unforeseen circumstances combined to keep Chile saddled for over twenty years with printing-press money. To begin with, those who had seen in paper money the means of industrialization seemed to be vindicated by developments between 1898 and 1906. The amount of new capital pouring into industrial corporations during this period far surpassed anything previously witnessed in Chile.[89] Then, in 1907, the bubble burst. Too large a number of the new corporations had been vastly overcapitalized, making inevitable a stock-market collapse. Most Chileans, however, refused to concede that there might be a direct causal relationship between paper money and the crash. They reasoned that the 1906 Valparaíso earthquake and the world-wide recession the following year were more responsible than domestic fiscal policies for Chile's economic plight. And no one was willing to urge tightening money in the midst of a depression, compounded as it was by the necessity of rebuilding the country's main port. So, an additional 40,-000,000 paper pesos were printed and circulated.[90]

It is evident that these events can scarcely be attributed to the designs of rapacious landowners. By 1914, moreover, the congressional representatives of this very group had come to favor converting to a metallic standard.[91] The economic dislocation produced by the first World War, however, made conversion unfeasible. Total treasury income fell from well over 96,000,000 pesos of eighteen pence in 1913 to 33,465,589 in 1915.[92]

Thus, Chile's money problem was not the result of an aristocratic plot. Moreover, a corollary of the plot theory, the belief that paper money was the principal cause of the worsening social problem during the parliamentary period, is untenable. Hard money would not have cured Chile's social problem—not unless the attitudes of the aristocracy had been fundamentally changed. Basically, what caused the nation's social ills was the inability or unwillingness of the upper classes and their middle-class allies to comprehend the inevitable consequences of the simultaneously worsening plight and rising expectations of the lower classes. It matters not whether the currency is hard or soft when national leaders insist upon being indifferent to the needs of half or more of their countrymen. Under such conditions, if money is dear or cheap it will be used exclusively for the advantage of a few.

THE RISE OF THE SOCIAL PROBLEM DURING
THE PARLIAMENTARY PERIOD

Scarcely a reputable Chilean writer failed to indicate his awareness of the social problem that was becoming increasingly acute during the parliamentary period. Proportionately, Chilean-published books decrying the miserable conditions in which a growing number of the population was compelled to live form a far more consequential part of national literary output than does the muckraker literature of the United States.[93] Newspapers of all political affiliations, prose authors and even poets[94] raised their voices in protest. Only one thing is more impressive than the volume of writing produced by Chilean exposers of social horrors: the utter failure of this literature to stimulate amelioration of the conditions described.

Already in 1896 *La Libertad Electoral*, which generally reflected Liberal and Radical Party beliefs, warned the nation that its social problem could usher in European-style radicalism. The difficulties did not lie, the paper contended, in the greediness or viciousness of Chile's urban lower classes, the *rotos*. Quite to the contrary, the *rotos* were singularly unconcerned with money and eminently virtuous. When they had been paid for their services in the civil war and placed aboard ships to be returned to the north, many had thrown their wages into the ocean, proclaiming that they had come to fight for freedom, not for money. The danger now, warned *La Libertad Electoral*, was that the *roto* was being made an alien in his own land. Because of this, his proverbial patience was wearing thin. At least 150,000 homeless *rotos* wandered each year through the country as social outcasts seeking some pittance for their labor. The paper concluded: "Some attention must be paid the masses if capital is to remain secure." [95] One of the most thorough exposés of deteriorating social conditions was the already-mentioned *Sinceridad* of Alejandro Venegas. Although the book was widely dismissed as the work of a crank, one literary critic, the French priest Emilio Vaïsse who wrote for *El Mercurio* under the pseudonym Omer Emeth, proved a notable exception. When a generation had passed, said Vaïsse, *Sinceridad* would be recognized as the only accurate social history of the times.[96]

An early statistical insight into the social problem was provided by the careful and reliable historian Luis Galdames. After extensive and diligent research, Galdames concluded that the average rural worker (*inquilino*) in Chile received some twenty centavos per day, or the equivalent of four cents, and that the average *inquilino* family never gained a combined yearly income exceeding the equivalent of twenty dollars. In the summer the rural laborers subsisted on fruit, and in the winter on preserved apples and small quantities of wheat. Male industrial workers, estimated Galdames, received approximately 3.80 pesos per day (less than eighty cents) while women and children were paid 1.80 pesos. Daily wages for the northern nitrate workers were somewhat better, rising as high as five to six pesos ($1.00 to $1.20) in the interior of Tarapacá and Antofagasta.[97] The northern worker, of course, usually died at a younger age than his southern counterpart, his life expectancy shortened by extremes of temperature and by lung diseases. His high wages, moreover, were effectively taken from him by the company stores and wine merchants. And like workers throughout Chile, he had to pay usurious interest rates when forced to borrow. Shortly after the end of the parliamentary period Conservative Senator Alejandro Huneeus inquired in the upper chamber[98] how it was that a man of means might borrow from the *Caja de Crédito Hipotecario* at 8 per cent, 7 per cent, or even 6 per cent,[99] while the working classes could only obtain credit from loan agencies which charged 48 per cent interest.

It was the plight of the northern worker that first made Chile's upper classes aware of the social problem. In 1904 a group of distinguished statesmen and landowners, most of them members of the Conservative Party, described in calm and moderate terms the horrors of working conditions in the north.[100] In the same year *El Ferrocarril*, usually the staunch defender of laissez faire, voiced its concern, urging that the government expand its services so as to administer to the needs of the northern workers. It noted that foreign operations in the nitrate pampa provided decent conditions for workers, and asserted that the national government's failure to induce domestic firms to do as well by their laborers was a betrayal of the Chilean race.[101] About a decade later an *El Mercurio* reporter, after accompanying several ministers of state on one of the numerous and fruitless government inspection tours of the north, wrote: "The government of Chile has not been willing to protect its own citizens even on its own soil. But this is not surprising, as it is the natives of Santiago who control our politics, and they are interested only in self gain." [102] Even the mouthpiece of the extreme right, *El Porvenir*, concluded that the northern workers had real cause for discontent. "Perhaps they are, as the government claims, paid enough, but they have inadequate houses, and no schools, hospitals, or churches." [103]

The social problem, as Galdames had discovered, was not confined to the north. Illegitimacy figures for the nation as a whole were on the rise. In 1850 illegitimate births accounted for 21 per cent of total births; by 1900 they were 31 per cent of the total, and by 1920, 38 per cent.[104] A Valparaíso newspaper[105] noted in 1895 that the Equitable Company of New York had stopped issuing life-insurance policies in Chile because of its hygienic backwardness, poor health conditions, and the resultant low life expectancy of the population. In the same year another paper claimed that infant mortality in Chile's major cities was three times as high as in similar-sized communities in the United States, England, Belgium, and Germany. It also asserted that in 1894 deaths had exceeded births by 11.58 per thousand in Valparaíso, and speculated that if steps were not taken to improve the situation the city's entire population could be wiped out within ninety years. As a solution for the problem, the newspaper advocated passage of laws which would force irresponsible lower-class mothers to practice methods of elementary hygiene, and imprisonment for those mothers who failed to comply with the laws.[106]

Increasing alcoholism was another manifestation of the social problem. Military hero General Estanislao del Canto, one of the first Chileans to concern himself with the matter,[107] noted that not until the 1890's had drunkenness become a serious national problem. "Now [in 1901] there is not a weekend when one third of the men in Chile are not drunk . . . [even though] upper- and middle-class men are temperate." [108] In a 1914 speech Deputy Manuel Foster Recabarren described his horror at visiting a lower-class neighborhood on a Sunday. All of the bars were open, he reported, and there was scarcely a sober man to be found. The deputy suggested that laws be enforced, noting that legally any bar where a person became intoxicated could be fined and upon the third offense closed. "But who," asked Foster Recabarren, "has ever heard of a bar being closed in Chile?" [109] He did not add that one impediment to an antidrunkenness campaign was the political power of the grape-growers. In the early 1920's, fourteen of the twenty-four largest wine producers were senators.[110]

A leading Santiago newspaper observed in 1916: "Among Latin-American nations, Chile is now gaining distinction as a country of alcoholics." [111] One year later, the newly-founded *La Nación* in a series of excellent articles on the deterioration of national health attributed the grave situation to alcoholism.[112] Shortly later, a group of leading public figures, including Eliodoro Yáñez, Enrique Zañartu Prieto, Dr. Lucas Sierra and Monsignor Rafael Edwards founded the Chilean League of Social Hygiene (LCHHS), specifically to combat alcoholism.[113] But *El Mercurio* was pessimistic about such efforts: "All of the antialcoholism efforts will mean nothing so long as the country refuses to provide workers with adequate houses and some means of safe and healthy diversion." [114]

The increasing severity of the social problem toward the end of the parliamentary period seemed to indicate that the attempt of reformers to appeal to the conscience of the ruling classes had failed. There was still the hope of appealing to the aristocracy's sense of the practical.[115] This, at least, was in the mind of Dr. F. Landa, long conspicuous in the ranks of those trying to safeguard national health, when he upbraided men of wealth for their indifference to the social problem. "They would not expect hungry and sickly horses or oxen to perform satisfactory labor for them, and yet they see nothing impractical about destroying the health of their human laborers." [116]

In 1920 appeared Pedro Prado's *Alsino*, one of the masterpieces of Chilean fiction. The novel is based upon the Icarus legend. Alsino, raised in sordid surroundings by alcoholic parents, yearns to fly and thus escape his spiritually suffocating ambient. To some degree, Alsino represents the sensitive Chilean reaching maturity during the parliamentary period and wishing somehow to flee the squalor of it all. A reflection of the nation's mounting social problem, *Alsino* could not have been produced a generation earlier.

THE MASSES AWAKEN AND THE RULING CLASSES RESPOND

Labor Unrest

The intensifying acuteness of the social problem was reflected in strikes and labor violence during the parliamentary period. The first actual strike in Chile occurred in 1887.[117] While the decade of

the 1890's produced little in the way of organized strikes or boy-
cotts, it was a period of considerable lower-class violence. Larceny,
arson, and generally rising crime rates were reported in Santiago
and its environs in 1892. A roving band of terrorists in that year
killed the owner of a rural estate (*fundo*) and gave thorough
frights to several others. A newspaper asserted that within four
months, 24,000 persons had been jailed in Chile.[118] Three years
later the press was much alarmed by reports of violence and disturbances in the northern nitrate area. The general consensus was
that the nitrate workers lacked real grounds for discontent and
were being aroused by unscrupulous agitators.[119] Then, in 1898,
La Libertad Electoral announced: ". . . socialism has emerged
among us." It referred to the July 20 demonstrations in Santiago
when Magno Espinosa and others had been jailed for preaching
socialism and inciting laborers to violence. "We must take active
measures," cautioned the paper, "to counteract this menace. . . .
To preach socialist doctrines is a crime." [120] Despite this pronouncement, at the end of the troubled 1890's Víctor Soto Román published a book extolling socialism's virtues. "Once the workers take
over the means of production, it will be necessary to work only
four hours a day to enjoy material comfort. . . . Ownership of
private property constitutes a crime." [121]

Chile's first strike of major significance began in December
1901. Centering in Iquique, it lasted sixty days, even though its
leaders had been promptly jailed.[122] Two years later the workers of
the South American Steamship Company (*Compañía Sud-Americana de Vapores*) went on strike in Valparaíso. President Riesco
had temporarily relinquished office, and Ramón Barros Luco was
serving as provisional chief executive. He refused to grant an interview to Democrat Party leader Malaquías Concha who wished to
explain the workers' demands. Violence soon erupted. The workers
burned the steamship company's office building. Troops were
called out and broke the strike by killing some thirty workers and
wounding an additional two hundred.[123] The same company's
workers again went out on strike in 1905, and this time the labor
dispute spread to the branch office in Santiago.[124] Also in 1905 the
lower classes of the capital city arose in a wild demonstration, in-

cited by an unfrocked priest calling himself Pope Julius. Preaching class hatred and violence, Julius persuaded some of his followers to attack the Good Friday procession on the principal thorough-fare, and a rock-throwing fracas ensued.[125]

It was in the north, though, that the nation continued to experi-ence its most severe labor violence. A harbinger of things to come was provided in 1906 when the Antofagasta workers, led by Luis Emilio Recabarren, went on strike to protest the rising cost of living. Several Spanish-born owners of loan agencies were murdered. The workers lost heart in their struggle when the warship "Blanco Encalada" opened fire on some demonstrators, killing or wound-ing close to one hundred.[126] In the following year, thousands abandoned the miserable life of the nitrate pampa and converged upon Iquique. Some professed willingness to return to work if the companies would simply cover the oven pits where the pulverized nitrate ore was processed at temperatures of over 250° Fahrenheit. Scores of workers had fallen into these pits and died in agony. The majority of men and their families, however, wished to return to the south, charging they had been lured to the nitrate camps under false pretenses. Rafael Sotomayor, Minister of Interior at the time, decided the northern laborers must be taught a lesson once and for all. If the workers continued to be recalcitrant, British and Chilean capitalists might grow wary and hesitate to increase their investments. Military forces were sent to the area, and on December 21 killed or wounded some two thousand men, women, and children gathered in a plaza when they failed to disperse within a stipulated five minutes.[127]

But the lower classes failed to learn their lesson. In 1908 there were twenty-nine important strikes.[128] A pamphlet by Peter Kropot-kin, the Russian aristocrat turned revolutionist, appeared in a Chilean edition in 1911 and attracted considerable attention by its assertion: "Our desire for justice will give us strength to burn, to kill, to submerge all the men and all the forces that today perpetrate infamies against us." [129] Tension grew during 1914 and 1915 due to the initial economic disruption caused by the World War. Between the beginning of August and the middle of Septem-ber 1914, 48,000 persons—unemployed laborers and their families

—left the Tarapacá and Antofagasta regions. Thousands of them, bitter and resentful, came to Santiago where numerous industries had already shut down or laid off workers.[130]

A temporary economic resurgence gave way in 1919 to a still more severe depression.[131] Both in 1918 and in 1919 the main Chilean labor organization (*Gran Federación Obrera de Chile*), aided by university students, staged "hunger meetings" in Santiago, with demonstrators demanding lower food prices and greater employment opportunities.[132] A protest rally in August 1919 attracted a crowd of 100,000.[133] There were disturbances again in the north and in the south. The government responded by declaring a state of siege—which entails suspension of constitutional guarantees—in the north, by dispatching troops to the south, and by imprisoning hundreds in Santiago. One of those jailed in the capital city, a student named Julio Revasio, committed suicide because of the suffering and indignities inflicted upon him. And by all of this, "the government only demonstrated the futility of trying to stem a social tide with terror." [134]

THE RISE OF LABOR ORGANIZATION

By 1906, Chilean workers had founded over two hundred mutual aid associations,[135] while certain segments of labor, notably the coal workers of Lota, the maritime workers of Valparaíso, and the carpenters of Santiago, had formed more aggressive union organizations.[136] But the first truly significant step forward in labor organization was taken in 1909 with the founding of the Labor Federation of Chile (*Gran Federación Obrera de Chile*), referred to generally as the FOCH. Originally led by the Conservative Pablo Martín Pinuer and calling for nothing more radical than mutual aid, consumer-credit cooperatives, sickness insurance, arbitration of labor disputes, and the eight-hour day, the FOCH soon took a decided turn toward the left. By 1917 it was an avowedly revolutionary organization, seeking to gain leadership over all urban labor. At its third convention in 1919 it demanded the end of the capitalist system, and two years later declared its allegiance to the Communist International.[137]

As the FOCH turned increasingly radical, its principal leader came to be Luis Emilio Recabarren. The Valparaíso-born Recabarren embraced ever more extreme positions as he struggled for social reform in Chile. Originally a member of the Democrats, he soon decided that this moderate party had consistently ignored lower-class needs in its political manipulations. Moving to the turbulent north and becoming a socialist, Recabarren ran for and was elected to the national lower chamber, but was refused his rightful seat by the hostile deputies. After traveling in Europe and Argentina, Recabarren returned to Chile to participate actively in spreading socialist doctrines and in organizing labor. In 1912 he founded the Socialist Labor Party (*Partido Socialista Obrera*), having by now determined to rely upon labor organization for the winning of immediate objectives and upon political action for the ultimate transformation of the entire socioeconomic structure. In the 1920's, the Socialist Labor Party transformed itself into the Communist Party of Chile.[138]

By the end of the parliamentary period socialists and communists had made the most notable gains in infiltrating and gaining control over the Chilean labor movement. But anarchists were also active. They appeared upon the scene in 1911 when they bombed a Carmelite convent in Santiago[139] and touched off a major scare in the capital city. Deputy Zenón Torrealba, commenting upon the scores of alleged anarchists jailed in 1912, noted: "I know at least half of the persons listed in *El Mercurio* as having been jailed. . . . They are not anarchists, but merely people interested in achieving conditions that will permit them to lead lives of basic human dignity. Here in Chile, whoever demands the right to express his opinion is branded an anarchist." [140] In 1919, a branch of the I.W.W. was founded in Chile and one of its members was Oscar Schnake, who would play a prominent role in the socialist movements of the 1930's. While the I.W.W. won several important intellectuals to its cause, and strongly influenced the Federation of University Students (FECH), it never achieved real strength in the labor movement.[141]

The Ruling Classes Respond
to the Awakening of the Masses

The response of the directing classes to the mass unrest that was
beginning to become apparent in 1892 was to enlarge the army and
police force. President Jorge Montt and Deputy Julio Zegers were
among the more insistent advocates of this approach.[142] *El Ferrocarril* also urged that armed forces in the northern nitrate region
be augmented so as to convince the capitalists that the government had their interests at heart.[143] Around the turn of the century,
El Porvenir stated that no political party representing the lower
classes should be allowed to exist.[144] This conservative newspaper
blamed labor unrest in Santiago on public education and freedom
of the press.[145] Several influential persons agreed with this analysis.
Senator Rafael Errázuriz Urmeneta asserted: ". . . the campaign
for compulsory primary education represents the wave of socialism
that is threatening to overcome us. There must always be ignorance
in the world, just as there must always be poverty, and to attempt
to remove either by legislative process is to try to upset the natural
balance of life." [146] The primate of Chile, Archbishop Mariano
Casanova, in 1904 also attacked the baneful effects of widespread
instruction.[147] The justification for public education, observed the
archbishop, was to make possible universal suffrage,[148] which in
turn could lead only to increased social dissension and the under-
mining of Church influence.[149]

Happily, other social attitudes were also in evidence. During
the early part of the twentieth century, concerned administrations
began to send missions of national legislators and ministry heads
to investigate affairs in the north. True, little was done to implement the recommendations of these missions. In the face of their
reports, presidents often "crossed their arms and did nothing." [150]
But at least the matter was being studied, and this indicated an
awareness that merely enlarging the army might not be an adequate solution.

In 1901 Liberal stalwart Tomás A. Ramírez published a work
in which he came close to betraying his party principles. He

asserted that the state had a duty to encourage social solidarity among the various classes.[151] By 1910 even the moderate *El Heraldo* of Valparaíso, representing primarily commercial and banking interests, had begun to expound upon the need for society to protect all of its classes. The classical economic theories had lost their validity, the paper stated, and the government must undertake public works projects, provide workers' homes, hospitals and schools, and enact legislation protecting the rights of workers.[152] The University of Chile furnished another indication of changing attitudes. In 1915 it introduced a course on social economy and labor legislation under the direction of Moisés Poblete Troncoso, a reform-minded intellectual destined to establish one of the most distinguished records of public service in his generation. Three years later Daniel Martner, another young man who would later achieve wide renown as an economist and social thinker, inaugurated a seminar on the economic sciences.[153]

One of the most notable examples of upper-class social awakening was provided by Enrique Molina. Probably his country's outstanding young philosopher in the early 1900's, Molina was one of the few Chileans interested in the theories of Lester Frank Ward, William James, and John Dewey. Moreover, he admired much of what he encountered in the newly-emerging school of pragmatism because he sensed that it was largely based upon a humanitarian-inspired reaction to the conscienceless operation of the so-called laws of liberal economics. Molina thought that pragmatism might have much to offer Chileans interested in social reform.[154]

Actually, most Chileans of the parliamentary period who professed interest in social reform had something quite different in mind than what Molina and the United States pragmatists envisioned. Given their religious, intellectual, and social traditions, most Chileans inevitably approached the quest for reform from a vastly different set of premises than those being developed in the United States. Aside from some of the extreme radicals who had appeared upon the scene by 1920—such as the Marxian socialists, the anarchists, and the communists—Chile's reformers operated from an essentially conservative orientation. As "respectable reformers," they shared with the staunchest defenders of the status quo certain fundamental concepts that rested upon the following five intellectual and emotional pillars:

1) Devotion to a hierarchical, stratified society, and a consequent opposition to the open society, to equality of opportunity, and to social mobility.

2) Devotion to paternalism and, as a consequence, abhorrence of any genuinely pluralistic system which would permit divergent social and functional-interest groups to participate by virtue of their own power and bargaining influence in what the nation had to offer.

3) Belief in economic development only to the degree necessary to allow those at the apex of society to exist above subsistence levels. Accordingly, a society aspiring to a wider distribution of material comforts was disparaged as materialistic and secular on the theory that it would pamper elements incapable of contributing to cultural and spiritual wealth.[155]

4) Belief that, given the "immutable" operation of the iron laws once posited by David Ricardo, a class of brute laborers must always exist. Furthermore, the existence of this class was considered a positive good, as it permitted gentlemen to devote themselves fully to the higher human callings.

5) Conviction that the lower classes realized what was best for them and did not want essentially to alter their status. Therefore, when revolutionary ferment appeared, it was viewed as the work of a few subversive troublemakers acting in a manner alien to national traditions.

What separated the defenders of the status quo from the respectable reformers was this. The defenders saw nothing wrong with the social system as it was currently functioning. Relying on the endless patience and passivity of the lower classes, they felt that even alterations and modifications in detail were unnecessary. The reformers,[156] although desiring to maintain all that fundamentally inhered in the five pillars cited above, were not opposed to certain slight changes. Whether motivated by truly humanitarian impulses, as many were, or by enlightened self-interest, they realized modifications must be made so as to keep the over-all system essentially intact. To the five, therefore, they added a sixth point: recognition of the need to ease the plight of the lower classes to such a degree that they would be willing to remain an inert element in the hierarchical, stratified structure. As the social problem was ameliorated, the lower classes were not to be given the means to defend their own position or to voice demands. Instead, the conscience of the upper classes was to be relied upon to provide the dispossessed with just enough in the way of improvement so that they would not think of challenging their betters.

The fundamental approach of Chile's directing classes—both standpatters and respectable reformers—to the social problem helps explain the manner in which the various political parties worked, from 1892 to 1920, toward what they regarded as improvement of social conditions.

THE SOCIAL PROBLEM IN CHILEAN POLITICS

The National and Liberal Democratic Parties. The contribution of the National Party to meeting the social crisis has been justly described by a Chilean writer as, with one exception, nothing. The single exception was the project to improve workers' homes advanced by the wealthy businessman and owner of *El Mercurio*, Agustín Edwards.[157] For the Liberal Democratic Party, the story was largely the same. Although the self-styled followers of the Balmaceda traditions did include several persons sincerely concerned with the country's main problem,[158] as a group they accomplished little if anything. In fact, it is said that whenever there was talk of curbing inflation, of using nitrate funds for special economic development and meeting ordinary national needs by directly taxing the wealthy, or of enacting even the mildest social-reform law, "Juan Luis Sanfuentes and his Liberal Democrats could always be counted upon to upset the ministry and join with à new alliance, seeking to further their own selfish interests as they neglected the country." [159]

The Conservative Party. Although the Conservative Party compiled the best record of any political group in introducing social-reform legislation during the parliamentary period, its fundamental concern was more with charity than justice. Perhaps, also, it sought to trade excessively on its close ties with the Church, relying on religion to provide solace for the suffering. Thus Carlos Walker

Martínez, onetime president of the party, stated in 1895 that the social problem must be solved primarily by spiritual means. To trust in material expedients, Walker feared, "would encourage secularism and deprive the spirit of control over the passions, opening the door to the excesses of the carnal appetites." [160]

Although the Conservatives may have underestimated the need for minimal material welfare as a necessary condition for real spiritual development among the masses, they did produce many leaders who had the interests of the lower classes sincerely at heart. Among these *patrones* whose dedication to the concept of *noblesse oblige* could not be questioned were Francisco de Borja Echeverría, an early advocate of land redistribution as a means of stemming communism's appeal to the lower classes,[161] and Juan Enrique Concha Subercaseaux. Like Borja Echeverría before him, Concha became a professor at the Catholic University of Chile.[162] As a teacher, a deputy, a senator, and a president of his party, he stressed that only by providing better conditions for workers could class conflict be prevented. Concha also dedicated much of his fortune and energy to a lower-class community (*población*) called Leo XIII, where most of the residents became actual owners of their homes.[163] Animated by the spirit of leaders such as these,[164] the Conservative Party played a leading role in winning legislative approval of workers' homes projects and popular credit banks.[165]

The Liberal Party. For a time the Liberal Party was too concerned with theological questions to devote much attention to the social problem. A Liberal newspaper in 1896 summarized the ideas of its presidential candidate, Vicente Reyes, in the following manner: ". . . he has favored liberty of conscience, civil marriage, separation of Church and state, secularization of cemeteries, lay education, the end of special juridical privileges for the clergy, and freedom of the press and assembly." The paper concluded that the ideas of Reyes ". . . could not be more completely liberal." [166]

By the early twentieth century, however, the Liberal Party was beginning to realize that liberal ideas required a broader basis than anticlericalism, and many of its members joined the ranks of the respectable reformers. Men like Marcial Martínez,[167] Jorge

Errázuriz Tagle,[168] Tomás Ramírez Frías,[169] Eliodoro Yáñez, Armando Jaramilla, Oscar Dávila, and Arturo Alessandri were firmly convinced that society's top echelon could only maintain its predominance by devising palliatives for the social problem. Although the legislative record of the Liberals in regard to social reform was not imposing,[170] they did at least publish many books and pamphlets on the matter,[171] helping thereby to awaken the public conscience.

The Radical and Democrat Parties. During the parliamentary period the Radical Party was, as it has generally been, divided. One section was led by Enrique Mac-Iver who doubted that workers could ever acquire sufficient culture to understand the problems of government, let alone to participate in it.[172] It was among the members of this wing of the Radicals that aristocratic statesman and onetime (1918-1925) Chilean Ambassador in Washington Beltrán Mathieu felt at ease. Mathieu, who withdrew from politics partially because he regarded association with the masses as beneath his dignity, once referred glowingly to Chile's parliamentary period as representing the rule of gentlemen.[173] Another wing of the party was led by Valentín Letelier, and included in its ranks Pedro Aguirre Cerda, Alfredo Frigoletti, Luis Salas Rimo, and Eugenio Frías Collao, an early director of the only state agency concerned with labor and social work to be established before 1924, the Office of Labor Statistics (*Oficina Estadística del Trabajo*). Although Letelier professed to believe in socialism, he also believed in social evolution,[174] and was convinced that the laws of social progress could not be rushed.

Given its internal dichotomy, it is hardly surprising that the Radical Party made little contribution to reform legislation. But there were standout exceptions in a generally dismal record. Ramón Briones Luco, as the deputy from Tarapacá, proposed a compulsory workers' insurance law[175] and more than any other man was responsible for the government railroad workers' retirement law. Moreover, Pedro Bannen and other Radicals assumed the initiative in gaining congressional approval of the compulsory primary education proposal in 1920.[176]

Even the most extreme of the respectable parties, the Democrat

Party, never established any real contact with the proletariat.[177]
While hoping that in some dim and distant future classes could
be eliminated through a gradual redistribution of wealth, it was
basically a party that wanted "everything for everyone within the
framework of the status quo." [178] Still, the Democrats, led throughout most of the parliamentary period by their founder Malaquías
Concha,[179] were active in the fight against electoral bribery and
cooperated in the enactment of labor arbitration, workers' compensation, and housing laws.[180]

THE UNDERLYING CAUSES OF CHILE'S INITIAL INATTENTIVENESS TO THE SOCIAL PROBLEM

GENERAL APPRAISAL

The failure of Chilean politicians to respond adequately to the
social problem during the parliamentary period cannot always be
taken as an indication of the indifference or mediocrity of these
men. Rather than guiding national development in Chile, politicians were largely manipulated by the force of events that had
transpired since the 1880's. Different at least in degree and intensity from those in other Latin-American republics, the main
features of Chile's late-nineteenth and early-twentieth-century development inevitably slowed the formulation and impaired the
effective implementation of social-reform measures.

THE RURAL-TO-URBAN TRANSITION

Between 1892 and 1920 the Chilean population increased by
only one-half million, rising from 3.3 to 3.8 million.[181] Yet the
demographic shift underway was startling. The urban population,
only 27 per cent of the total in 1875, had risen to over 43 per cent
in 1907.[182] From 1885 to 1895, the population of Santiago went
up over 30 per cent, and by 1907 had increased an additional 22
per cent. During the same two time-spans population in Antofagasta rose 58 per cent and 73 per cent, in Iquique 76 per cent
and 16 per cent, in Concepción 50 per cent and 27 per cent, and in
Valparaíso 15 per cent and 24 per cent.[183]

In short, the period from 1885 to 1907 witnessed the most

dramatic population shift in Chile's history. The serfs or *inquilinos* who had previously labored on the vast estates of southern Chile and the central valley flocked in unprecedented numbers to northern and central towns. In their migration, the rural masses passed directly from a feudal situation—in which they had been cared for paternalistically, had never learned to protect themselves in a competitive society, and had almost never acquired education—into the modern conditions of semi-industrial urban life. In the rural setting they had at least possessed sufficient skill to be useful to their *patrones*. In the cities they had no skill to offer. They comprised a vast pool of untrained, largely unproductive, brute labor. The rising industrial and commercial capitalists would have been more than human if they had done other than exploit the new urban masses. And even as the element of *noblesse oblige* disappeared from the employer-employee relationship when the rural masses crowded into the city, so also the bonds between the *patrón* and the *inquilinos* who remained on the agricultural estates were weakened as the landowners began to maintain their principal residences in Concepción, Santiago, or Paris.[184]

Under these conditions, human labor fell increasingly into disrepute. Adding to this lamentable development was the incorporation of eight thousand Bolivian and nearly seventeen thousand Peruvian laborers into the Chilean nation as a result of territorial changes arising from the War of the Pacific.[185] The presence of these foreign, "inferior," Indian or mestizo workers in the nitrate camps hardened Chilean consciences to labor exploitation in the north and indirectly in the nation as a whole. Moreover, the majority of the southern rural workers who in droves arrived in the cities of Chile were invariably partially Indian in ethnic origin. This was a considerable disadvantage to them, for after the final conquest of the Araucanians in 1883, white upper classes largely ceased to regard the national Indians as noble, worthy adversaries whose long-continued battle against the Europeans had helped forge Chilean character.[186] Indians came instead to be dismissed as lazy, cruel, fatalistic, and hopelessly inclined to drunkenness; as lacking in foresight and imagination; as uneducable and incapable of imitating the better qualities of their conquerors.[187] Even

Chilean mestizos were judged to be a bad lot, having acquired by their Indian blood all the character weaknesses of the inferior race. As Chile's main authority on these matters summed it up: "The union of superior and inferior races always produces a product less good than the superior parent."[188] Because of its racial composition, then, Chile's new urban laboring class came to be regarded by many as the proper object of harsh abuse. This initiated a kind of vicious circle in which such treatment goaded the urban proletariat into occasional acts of resistance and violence. The more the masses resorted to these means, the more they proved their depravity to the upper classes.

Given, moreover, the overwhelming acceptance of the principles of laissez faire,[189] it was natural that Chile's new capitalist class did not fret over labor conditions. Perhaps it was also natural that political democracy—once so hopefully and approvingly regarded in Chile—began around the turn of the century to be increasingly disparaged. Allowing the literate members of society to vote had seemed reasonable enough to the liberal aristocracy when Chile had been preponderantly rural and illiterate. But as the lower classes migrated to the cities they found greater opportunities, in spite of Conservative Party efforts to curtail public education, to attend at least a year or two of school, to learn to read and write, and thereby to acquire suffrage rights. In 1907, 54 per cent of the city dwellers were literate, compared to only 29 per cent of the rural population.[190] In the face of this development the upper classes decided that the only way to render the unreasoning canaille politically harmless was to pay them to vote according to the desires of their betters. This development, contributed to by politicians of nearly all varieties, was a clear indication of unwillingness to face the rigors of fostering a genuinely democratic system.

The economy of Chile as well as its population was shifting to the cities. In 1889, mining products worth over 55 million pesos were exported. The value of agrarian exports that year was less than 7.5 million.[191] In the twentieth century the importance of agriculture to the national economy declined further, as Chile began to import wheat and meat from Argentina.[192] By 1912, while

Chile exported animal products worth 20.7 million pesos of eighteen pence, vegetable products worth 19.8, and wheat worth 7.1, the value of mineral exports had soared to 336 million.[193]

Chile's biggest money-earner was nitrates, and contrary to the prevailing impression that exploitation of this natural resource was controlled by the British and other foreign groups, domestic capital accounted for well over half of total nitrate investments.[194] In addition, Chilean capital to the extent of over 30 million pesos of eighteen pence was invested in the 70-million-peso copper industry, and comprised the total of the approximately 153 million invested in the coal industry.[195] Chileans also took advantage of the protectionist policies adopted by their government in the early 1900's. By 1920, more than one half of the approximately 800 million pesos invested in nonextractive industry was native capital. Moreover, nonextractive industry by this time employed 30 per cent of the entire active labor force, and was creeping up on agriculture which employed 40 per cent.[196]

Socially, the important feature of Chile's move to the cities was the manner in which earlier, more quickly and more completely than in other Latin-American republics, a landed aristocracy either became, or merged with, an urban upper or middle class. A strictly landowning aristocracy dwindled in importance as absentee owners, continuing the process initiated in the middle of the nineteenth century, invested in urban pursuits and married into the new-money classes of the mushrooming cities. In addition, the urban rich found continuing opportunities to gain the distinction of rural landownership, especially when many older families of social prominence lost their fortunes in the 1907 stockmarket crash and were forced to sell their lands.[197] By the turn of the century, then, urban and rural interests were crossed and crisscrossed to such a degree as to make the distinction often meaningless.[198]

Resulting from these conditions was a closer union between new, urban-middle and old, rural-upper classes than was achieved elsewhere in Latin America. A hybrid aristocracy, together with urban middle-class supporters, came into being, and neither aristocrats nor middle sectors were under pressure to minister to the needs of the lower classes. The urban *noveaux riches*, both upper-

and middle-class, found it totally unnecessary to enlist the aid of the city proletariat in a struggle with the old order, for they had already joined or were in the process of joining the old order. Nor were the landowners willing, as occasionally they have been in Peru and other countries, to support social reforms of strictly urban application. In Chile, urban and rural interests were becoming too intertwined to permit landowners to pursue this policy. Similarly, because of interlocking features, urban interests were unwilling to press for rural reforms. Thus, upper and middle classes, old and new or potential aristocrats, and rural and urban sectors united in regarding the lower classes, wherever found, as fair prey.[199]

Contributing to this social pattern was the role of the immigrant in Chile. Although the limited immigration to the country did not have notable effects upon the population as a whole, it greatly affected the composition of the middle class.[200] In 1930, while foreigners accounted for only 2.46 per cent of the population, they comprised about 17 per cent of the urban middle class.[201] Insecure in status because of foreign birth, it was only natural that these middle-class elements would try to assure acceptance by emulating the standards and value judgments of the established aristocracy.

The circumstances under which urbanization occurred in Chile induced the upper and middle classes to join in their economic pursuits and intellectual attitudes. Both social sectors were at the same time driven to renounce the obligations, although not the abstract theory, of paternalism, to abandon the Chilean masses, and even to turn wantonly upon them. Professing the worthlessness of a high percentage of their country's inhabitants, Chile's favored classes began to lose confidence in the virtue of their nation. As this occurred, patriotism dwindled and indigenous culture remained in a rudimentary stage. The educated sectors, turning their backs upon the richness of their own folk traditions, became mere imitators and uncritical flatterers of foreign tastes and styles. Chile was in an age of stagnation.

5: INCREASING CONTACT
AND CHRONIC TENSION:
CHILE AND THE UNITED STATES, 1892-1920

THE TROUBLED NINETIES

FROM THE 'BALTIMORE' AFFAIR
TO THE PUNA DE ATACAMA DISPUTE

Patrick Egan's departure from Santiago in 1893 found Chile still resentful over the actions of the ebullient Irishman and his superiors in Washington. Totally lacking significant economic ties with the United States, Chile would have preferred to isolate itself from the antagonist with whom it had been sparring since 1880. But the perennial boundary disputes with Argentina made this impossible in the 1890's.

The region of the northwestern boundary between Chile and Argentina, extending between 23° and 26°52', was known as Puna de Atacama. Originally Bolivian territory, it had been conquered by Chile during the War of the Pacific and incorporated in 1888 into the province of Antofagasta. The following year, and again in 1893, Bolivia ceded Puna de Atacama to Argentina. Claiming that Bolivia was signing away land that belonged to Chile, the government in Santiago began to dispute the matter with Argentina, and the issue of Puna de Atacama was thus added to the chronic dispute over the boundary farther to the south.

By 1898 it had been decided to submit the southern boundary question to the arbitration of the British crown, and to reach accord on the Puna de Atacama disagreement, if possible, by direct diplomacy. Argentina and Chile both agreed to name five-man commissions which would meet jointly in Buenos Aires to settle this northern territorial dispute. If agreement was not reached, one man from each commission would be designated to argue his country's case before William J. Buchanan, United States envoy to Argentina, who would then make final settlement of the dispute.[1] With this arrangement having been accepted by both contending countries, the Chilean press commenced a propaganda campaign to convince the public of the unassailable validity of the national territorial claims.[2] Prevailing journalistic attitudes were epitomized by Valparaíso's El Mercurio which concluded that only because Chile was so secure in its claims was it willing to risk the possibility that disposition of Puna de Atacama would be made ultimately by Buchanan, a man described as a warm friend of Argentina with intimate ties in Buenos Aires society.[3]

The Buenos Aires sessions got under way on March 1, 1899, and before long the two five-man commissions were hopelessly deadlocked.[4] Chile then named Enrique Mac-Iver its single agent, and he entered into negotiations with an Argentine counterpart, José E. Uriburu, and with Buchanan. On March 25, Buchanan announced his decision, which gave a portion of the disputed territory to each of the litigants. The Valparaíso El Heraldo commented that Buchanan had rendered a Solomon-like judgment.[5]

Other Chilean papers were outraged. "The decision clearly favors Argentina," and "Buchanan revealed colossal ignorance," complained La Unión.[6] El Ferrocarril declared that even though the line established by Buchanan was arbitrary and utterly without justification, Chile must manifest its greatness of spirit and respect for international procedures by accepting the decision with resignation.[7] Despite the general opposition of the press, the Chilean Senate quickly ratified the boundary settlement. Several deputies, however, raised objections. The most outspoken were the Radicals Abraham König and Daniel Feliú, who openly questioned the integrity of Buchanan.[8] Their strong remarks may have reflected the attitude of Chilean negotiator Mac-Iver, leader at the time of the Radical Party.[9]

The outcome of the negotiations produced sustained debate in Chile, which reached a peak in 1902. Although Conservatives Gonzalo Bulnes and Joaquín Walker Martínez—with his "natural vehemence of spirit"—[10] strongly attacked the decision and referred to the prejudice of Buchanan,[11] it was primarily the Liberals, attempting to use the issue to discredit the Conservative administration of President Federico Errázuriz Echáurren, who expressed displeasure. A central figure in the dispute was the staunch anti-clerical, Diego Barros Arana, who had devoted much time to compiling an historical justification of Chile's claims and had suggested what he considered a proper boundary line in the Puna area.[12] Liberals blamed Conservatives for not having insisted upon this Barros Arana line, while Conservatives maintained the Buchanan decision gave Chile more land than Barros Arana had claimed.[13] The United States envoy in Argentina was caught in the cross fire of Chilean politics, and the country he represented became the object of renewed resentment in Chile.[14]

Significant for the future of hemisphere relations was the manner in which the entire boundary dispute with Argentina bound Chile and Germany still more closely together. Throughout the year 1898, the German Foreign Ministry reiterated its pro-Chilean sentiments to Ramón Subercaseaux, representing the Errázuriz government in Berlin. Subercaseaux was even told that Germany might render Chile direct help in the event of war with Argentina, "were it not for the established attitude of the United States." [15] Thus, it is revealed that the German government had already decided to respect the strong position assumed by the United States in supervising affairs of the hemisphere. The loss of potential German assistance provided Chile with another cause for resenting the tutelage that the United States was establishing over the New World.

Vastly more important than Puna de Atacama in inter-American relations was the manner in which another of the spoils of the War of the Pacific influenced Chile in its relations with Peru, Argentina, and the United States, and colored its whole attitude toward the Pan-American movement. The final disposition of Tacna and Arica, according to the Treaty of Ancón (October 20, 1883), was to be decided by a plebiscite to be held ten years after the celebration of the treaty. It proved impossible to hold the plebiscite in 1893. Indeed, no serious effort to submit the matter to a ballot by Tacna-Arica residents was made until 1924. In the meantime, the unsettled boundary question caused frequent crises between Chile and Peru, with Chile steadfastly insisting that it would resolve these crises as it alone saw fit. This attitude involved Chile in repeated discord with Argentina, which in the interest of promoting a South American balance of power consistently backed Peruvian claims. The Tacna-Arica issue also caused Chile to regard the United States with hostile suspicions, fearful always that the great power of the North might champion the Peruvian cause. Finally, the obsession with preserving absolute sovereignty and complete freedom to act only as the national interest might dictate in regard to Tacna and Arica—probably in the hope of ultimately annexing both territories—led Chile resolutely to oppose all inter-American peace plans involving pressure on nations to resolve differences through compulsory arbitration.[16] Thus, Chile took an extremely jaundiced view of the early Pan-American conferences.

CHILE AND THE PAN-AMERICAN MOVEMENT

THE MEXICO CITY CONFERENCE, 1901-1902

Chile's invitation to the Second Conference of American Republics, to be held in Mexico City, was received by Carlos Morla Vicuña, Chilean envoy to the United States, in February of 1900.[17] About the middle of the following month Henry Lane Wilson, representing the United States in Santiago, wrote Chilean Foreign Minister Rafael Errázuriz, asking for a prompt reply to the invitation. But Wilson, whose unrestrained criticisms of Chile's inflationist policies had already rendered him less than popular in Santiago circles,[18] had a long wait in store before he was able to obtain the desired reply.[19]

Chilean diplomats were extremely wary of the second meeting of American states, recalling the unpleasant incidents of the 1889 Washington Conference when, contrary to the previously agreed-upon agenda, various states had backed a proposal for compulsory arbitration of pending and future disputes.[20] Then on May 23, 1900, the Executive Commission of the International Union of American Republics, meeting in Washington, decided that the forthcoming Mexico City Conference should attempt to formulate an arbitration plan that would apply to all pending and future disagreements. For Chile, this was an ominous development. Writing in *El Ferrocarril*, Luis Orrego Luco summarized the prevailing attitude in his country: "Those who advocate arbitration, and possibly even obligatory arbitration, of pending disputes in Latin America do so only out of the desire to see Chile despoiled of its War of the Pacific gains. They care nothing for the actual principle of arbitration." [21] Such leading statesmen as Gonzalo Bulnes and Paulino Alfonso agreed with this appraisal, and accordingly advised that Chile boycott the Mexico City Conference.[22]

Up to a point, the Chilean Ministry of Foreign Relations was in accord with this advice. It decided not to send delegates to Mexico City unless assurances were forthcoming that the conference would not endorse the principle of compulsory arbitration.[23] Carlos Morla Vicuña in Washington was therefore instructed to work toward persuading the Executive Commission to frame a more specific agenda that would explicitly exclude discussion of broad and sweeping arbitration agreements. The energetic Morla, whose experience with conducting diplomacy in the United States dated from 1870 when he had been named secretary of the Washington Legation, and who at one time had translated Longfellow's *Evangeline* into Spanish, began at once to fulfill his instructions. His task was facilitated in January 1901 when Argentina's membership on the Executive Commission expired and the more tractable Ecuador replaced the bitter rival.[24]

As Morla negotiated in Washington, the Chilean Ministry of Foreign Relations, in a move apparently intended to enhance its bargaining power should it decide to send delegates to the conference, created a separate legation in Mexico City. Emilio Bello Codesido, a grandson of the great educator and codifier of laws, Andrés Bello, and a son-in-law of the deposed president, José Manuel Balmaceda, was named his country's first envoy exclusively to Mexico. Instructed to proceed to his post by a highly circuitous route, Bello traveled first to Paris to persuade elder statesman and writer Alberto Blest Gana to help represent his country in the event it did not boycott the Mexico City Conference. After his Paris discussions, Bello went to Washington, where he learned that Morla had succeeded in persuading the Executive Commission to exclude compulsory arbitration from the Mexico City agenda.[25]

Arriving finally in the Mexican capital on August 4, 1901, Bello began immediately to report difficulty in counteracting Peruvian and Bolivian propaganda. He was uneasy also over the "passionate" endeavors of Argentina to enlist Mexican backing for a compulsory arbitration proposal, in spite of the action by the Executive Commission.[26] Shortly, however, Bello reported that Mexico's Foreign Minister Ignacio Mariscal had offered assurances that his country was against compulsory arbitration and favored the sort of peace-maintenance machinery provided by the 1899 Hague Convention: voluntary arbitration of international disputes, specifically excluding matters already settled by treaty agreements.[27]

Not until receiving these assurances in early September did Eliodoro Yáñez, serving then as Chile's Minister of Foreign Relations, decide that his country should participate in the Second Conference of American Republics.[28] Bello was joined in Mexico City by Blest Gana, Augusto Matte, and the Conservative Party's firebrand and activist, Joaquín Walker Martínez, a late substitute for Carlos Morla who had died suddenly in Washington.[29] Sessions of the conference began on October 22, with nineteen countries in attendance.[30]

The first explosion came on November 6. In the secret sessions of one of the conference's special committees, Mexico, probably because of a claims dispute with the United States, introduced a resolution favoring compulsory arbitration, even of matters pending at the time. The Chilean representatives were furious, accusing Mexico of violating a previous pledge.[31] The Chilean position was strongly supported by the United States, with William Buchanan,[32] the very man who as envoy to Argentina had made the unpopular Puna de Atacama decision, speaking effectively against the broad arbitration proposal.[33]

Nevertheless, by December, ten countries,[34] led primarily by Argentina, were urging compulsory arbitration—although with many exceptions, restrictions, and loopholes—in the plenary sessions of the conference. With Walker Martínez entering into bitter exchanges with Argentine delegates,[35] it seemed likely for a time that the conference would break down completely. Chile and

Argentina actually threatened more than once to withdraw from the proceedings. But, after Chilean representatives conferred privately several times with President Porfirio Díaz, Mexico agreed not to press for inclusion of the compulsory arbitration proposal in the final acts of the conference.[36] In the meantime, Chile and Ecuador, backed by the United States, had proposed that American states simply subscribe to the arbitration provisions of the 1899 Hague Convention, and on a voluntary basis submit disputes to the Permanent Court of Arbitration. Ultimately, this suggestion was incorporated into a treaty that gained the unanimous approval of the countries represented in Mexico. Along with this treaty, however, the conference forwarded the troublesome compulsory arbitration proposal to the Mexican Foreign Relations Minister, with the request that he submit both documents to the various American republics for possible ratification.[37]

On still another issue Chile found itself crossing swords with Argentina and in accord with the position of the United States. The delegates at the Mexico City Conference accorded a special vote of homage to Argentine statesman Carlos Calvo, in recognition of his contributions to international law.[38] Then, with Argentina leading the way, the representatives of several republics[39] attempted to win conference approval of the principle that came ultimately to be known as the Calvo Clause: foreigners involved in pecuniary disputes in any nation may resolve their disagreements only by having recourse to the nation's regular judicial procedures, and may not appeal for special diplomatic protection from their own governments. Both Chile and the United States took exception to the principle that foreigners and nationals in any Latin-American nation must at all times receive equal treatment in pecuniary disputes. In this stand Chile demonstrated an ambivalence that was typical of its approach to foreign affairs. Although firmly insisting upon its own unlimited sovereignty, Chile took the position that many Latin-American countries were not yet sufficiently advanced to claim rights of absolute sovereignty.

The same attitude was demonstrated by Chile in regard to the so-called Calvo Doctrine, which was also debated at the Mexico

City Conference. This doctrine originated in a treatise on international law by Carlos Calvo in which he maintained the nonresponsibility of states for losses of aliens resulting from civil war and insurrection, on the ground that to admit responsibility would establish an inequality between nationals and foreigners. Particularly proud of its own good record of internal stability and therefore confident that it would never be victimized by what it was advocating, Chile argued that in cases arising from civil wars when nations had not taken adequate steps to safeguard property rights, foreigners sustaining property losses might appeal for diplomatic aid from their home countries in pressing their claims.[40]

A slight exception, therefore, could be made to El Mercurio's appraisal of Chile's role at the Mexico City Conference: "Chile went to the conference with the idea of defending the absolute sovereignty of all nations, and its success in this was total." [41] Much more inconsistent, so far as Chileans were concerned, was the record of Argentina. In the matter of the Calvo Clause and Doctrine, that nation had supported absolute sovereignty to a more total degree than Chile. Yet, when it came to compulsory arbitration Argentina had endorsed principles clearly opposed to unlimited national sovereignty. The Chilean Ministry of Foreign Relations was convinced that in the arbitration issue Argentina had acted contrary to its usual stand on sovereignty only to embarrass Chile in its international position.[42] It must be remembered that at the time of the conference Chile and Argentina were on the verge of war because of continuing territorial disputes. Both Joaquín Walker Martínez, representing Chile at the conference, and Eliodoro Yáñez, serving at the time as Foreign Relations Minister, actually favored war with Argentina.[43] They, and statesmen of like opinion, were therefore outraged and incensed when Argentina managed—agenda agreements to the contrary notwithstanding—to use the inter-American conference to strike a blow at Chile.[44] Little wonder that Yáñez concluded the sessions had been fruitless, and that Chile should refrain from attending inter-American conferences "until the political development of American states is sufficient to assure worthwhile results." [45]

With the major exception of hypersuspicious Marcial Martínez, who felt that Washington's delegates at Mexico City had acted primarily to extend the hegemony of their country over the hemisphere,[46] Chilean diplomats tended to be favorably impressed by United States actions at the Second Pan-American Conference.[47] Still, dislike of the over-all Pan-American movement had reached a new peak of intensity at Mexico City.

THE RIO DE JANEIRO CONFERENCE, 1906

By the time of the Third Conference of American States, held at Rio de Janeiro in 1906, Chilean attitudes had undergone some modification.[48] The boundary dispute with Argentina had been settled,[49] and it was not expected that the trans-Andean rival would again attempt to humiliate Chile through the Pan-American movement. On the other hand, Chile experienced mounting misgivings about possible United States plans to work through the Rio meeting to impose a settlement of the Tacna-Arica issue. Chilean Envoy in Washington Joaquín Walker Martínez suggested that President Roosevelt had such a notion in mind.[50] Indeed, the envoy's suspicions went beyond this. Six months before the opening of the Rio meeting Walker Martínez wrote his Foreign Ministry: "Each day the United States advances farther in its imperialistic pretensions against Latin America. It has a master plan and knows where it is going. We cannot stand by with folded arms. We must devise our own master plan for resisting United States aggression." [51] Obviously, Chilean good will toward the United States, fostered by the Mexico City Conference, had proved extremely short-lived. So far as Chile's continuing cooperation in any international union of American republics was concerned, the 1906 Rio meeting was of critical importance. If Chile and the Washington-dominated Pan-Americanism were not to come to a parting of the ways, then somehow the United States would have to assuage Chilean misgivings. Fortunately for the United States, Secretary of State Elihu Root was more than capable of dealing with this challenge.

When the Executive Commission of the International Union of American Republics began once more the work of preparing an agenda for a new conference, Felipe Pardo, Peru's envoy in Wash-

ington, contended that discussion of arbitration of pending disputes should be included. Chileans feared that the same old con-
troversies of the 1900-1902 period were about to be revived, and
were inclined to wash their hands of the whole affair by boy-
cotting the Rio Conference.[52] But Elihu Root and the Brazilian
Legation in Washington came to the aid of Walker Martínez,
with the result that the Chilean position in the agenda debates
prevailed. The approved agenda limited its arbitration references to
an expression of hope that those countries attending the Hague
Conference scheduled for 1907—to which all the Latin-American
republics had been invited—[53] would celebrate a general arbitration convention that could be approved and implemented in the
American Hemisphere.[54] Satisfied by these terms, Chile decided to
participate in the meeting, which began on July 23.[55]

Once the sessions were under way Chile discovered, as it had
previously both in 1889 and in 1901, that its position was not
adequately protected by agenda agreements. Shortly after the Rio
Conference's subcommittee on international law began its deliberations, Argentina suggested that delegates at the forthcoming Hague
Conference be urged to formulate an arbitration convention that
would determine "which matters will be subjected to compulsory
arbitration." Walker Martínez, a member of the international
law subcommittee, quickly raised his objections. When the subcommittee appeared to be hopelessly deadlocked, United States
delegate William Buchanan offered what he termed a compromise
proposal. According to Walker Martínez the Buchanan plan entailed compulsory arbitration of all differences that might in the
future arise between American states, and was therefore more
obnoxious than the original Argentine suggestion. A perturbed
Walker Martínez approached Elihu Root, who had arrived in Rio
on July 27, and much to his relief gained the full backing of the
United States Secretary of State. This assistance proved decisive.
Argentina and Peru resignedly accepted another Chilean victory on
the arbitration issue.[56]

This action by Root led most Chilean diplomats, at least for
the time being, to trust the United States, and caused them to
look with less hostility upon the Pan-American movement. The

major address that Root gave at the Rio Conference won more friends. In it the Secretary of State avowed that the United States desired no more territory, and wished only to work for the increasing prosperity of the hemisphere within a framework of perfect respect for the equality of all nations, however small. Chilean journalists praised this speech in glowing terms.[57] A short time later the secretary of the Chilean Legation in Washington declared that Root had brought about a complete change in the official attitude of the United States toward Latin America,[58] and had ". . . mollified the suspicions that Chile had once entertained concerning the great northern republic." [59] The young Alejandro Alvarez, only beginning the career destined to make him one of the hemisphere's outstanding statesmen and international law experts, reached a similar conclusion. He stated that Root in 1906 had managed to reunite the American republics, thus making it possible for the peoples of the hemisphere henceforth to work together in the common struggle to achieve the material and moral progress of the New World.[60]

The South American tour that Root undertook after his appearance at the Rio Conference brought him to Santiago on September 4.[61] He arrived at a time of grief for the Chilean nation, as the August 16 earthquake had nearly leveled the port of Valparaíso, and had claimed many lives. Nevertheless, Chileans responded warmly to their distinguished visitor. Root impressed reporters by his vast knowledge of Latin America,[62] and by his frequently expressed view that New World nations, because of their similar history, political institutions, and dedication to democracy, comprised a distinct and homogeneous entity in international affairs and possessed a common destiny that must be fulfilled through intimate cooperation. Those who heard Root's address at the presidential palace (La Casa Moneda) in Santiago were also impressed by the frank references to the friction that had marred earlier relations between the United States and Chile. Root went on to predict that unpleasant incidents, the inevitable consequence of contact between two young and proud nations that did not understand each other, would disappear as mutual intercourse and knowledge increased.[63] The newspaper La Ley best summarized the impact

that Root's four-day visit produced among Chileans. After referring to the past attitudes of Chile toward the United States,
the daily observed: "The days when American republics lived
within their own boundaries, fearful of contact with one another,
are now past." [64]

THE BUENOS AIRES CONFERENCE, 1910

The spirit of trusting the United States and even Pan-Americanism carried over to the Fourth Conference of American Republics, scheduled to convene in Buenos Aires in 1910.[65] Still, Chile
exercised the customary precautions before committing itself to
attend the sessions. Upon receiving the formal invitation on September 16, 1909, Agustín Edwards, brilliant millionaire-statesman
and owner of El Mercurio, serving then as Chile's Minister of
Foreign Relations, refused to render his reply until the complete
agenda had been prepared.[66] The focus then shifted to Washington, where the Executive Commission of the International Union
of American Republics undertook again the task of formulating a
program. Events followed the traditional pattern. At the Commission's November 10 session, the Peruvian chargé d'affaires in
Washington argued that the topic of compulsory arbitration
should be included on the agenda. Needless to say Aníbal Cruz,
Chile's envoy to the United States, objected strenuously. Cruz
pointed out the Rio meeting had agreed that arbitration was a
matter that affected not just Latin America but all of the world's
republics, and could therefore properly be considered only by
truly international conferences, such as those of the Hague. As no
country backed Peru's position, Cruz easily carried his point.[67] In
reporting to his Foreign Ministry, Cruz exulted: "Victory has been
the result of my diligent precautionary work carried out over a
long period of time." [68]

Receiving assurances from Cruz, Agustín Edwards accepted the
Argentine invitation on January 27, and proceeded to appoint the
largest and most distinguished delegation that had yet represented
Chile at a Pan-American conference. Heading the Chilean delegates was Miguel Cruchaga Tocornal, son of the distinguished
economist-statesman Miguel Cruchaga Montt and one of the most

renowned internationalists Chile has ever produced. At the time Chile's envoy in Argentina, Cruchaga Tocornal held the chair of international law at the University of Chile and was a member of the Hague's Permanent Court of Arbitration.[69] In addition to appointing a delegation that in its entirety was made up of distinguished public figures, Chile hastened to give other indications of its conversion to Pan-Americanism. By the time the Buenos Aires Conference began on July 12, Chile had ratified a greater number of the treaties and conventions produced at earlier inter-American meetings than any other major Latin-American republic.[70] Moreover, a high degree of optimism over the outcome of the conference was expressed by the Chilean press.[71] This was in stark contrast to the skepticism which journalists had demonstrated on the eves of the Washington, Mexico City, and Rio de Janeiro meetings. And, shortly before his departure for the Buenos Aires sessions, Aníbal Cruz, undoubtedly the most pro-United States envoy that Chile had sent to Washington since the War of the Pacific, bade a genuinely friendly farewell to President William Howard Taft and Secretary of State Philander C. Knox. Cruz took advantage of this opportunity to praise the United States for its Latin-American policy.[72]

Chilean hopes for a smoothly proceeding conference were fulfilled. Although Amérigo Lugo, representing the Dominican Republic, tried in mid-August to introduce the troublesome matter of compulsory arbitration into the proceedings, he failed absolutely to produce a favorable response. This led *El Mercurio* in Santiago to conclude that at last the Pan-American meetings had reached a level of maturity.[73] And upon conclusion of the Buenos Aires Conference, *El Heraldo* conceded that there might, after all, be something to the Pan-American movement: "In spite of what detractors say of the movement, the New World is distinct and bound together by unique ties. . . . we went through the same sort of independence struggles. . . . we admire and work toward democracy. . . . and in America, men of different national origins are accepted and assimilated to a degree not possible in Europe." [74] With attitudes of this nature coming to prevail, Chile was pleased and honored upon being designated the host nation for the Fifth

Pan-American Conference which, although originally scheduled for late 1914 or early 1915, was postponed because of the World War and did not convene until 1923.[75]

While the proposed conference was not held in 1914, there did occur in that year a diplomatic event that Chile found flattering. The United States Legation in Santiago was elevated to the status of Embassy and Henry P. Fletcher, who as an envoy for several years past had won the admiration and regard of social and diplomatic circles, was designated the first United States ambassador to Chile.[76]

There is more to relations between countries than friendly diplomatic gestures. Even while the United States and Chile were succeeding in establishing apparent mutual faith and friendship on the diplomatic front, a group of intellectuals and journalists in the string-bean republic maintained a steady anti-Yankee obligato. By 1914 their hostile declarations were beginning to reach crescendo proportions, and to be increasingly echoed in official diplomatic quarters. Eduardo Suárez Mujica, who was serving as Chile's envoy in Washington and who was raised to the rank of ambassador in that year, often waxed vitriolic in expressing his anti-Yankee prejudices.

Primarily responsible for the undercurrents of antagonism toward the Colossus between 1895 and 1900, and for the emergence of anti-Yankee sentiments as a national attitude of basic importance between 1900 and 1914—and especially during the last four years of the period—was the specter of United States imperialism and intervention.[77]

THE SPECTER OF UNITED STATES IMPERIALISM

CHILE'S CONCERN WITH UNITED STATES IMPERIALISM
AND INTERVENTION, 1895-1910

The Venezuelan Boundary Controversy, 1895. The Santiago press was generally although not unanimously[78] alarmed by the role the United States assumed in the boundary controversy between Venezuela and British Guiana. It took a particularly dim view of a strong note sent to Great Britain by Secretary of State

Richard Olney claiming that the Monroe Doctrine had become a part of international law and that the will of the United States would be enforced throughout the hemisphere. *El Ferrocarril* saw irony in the fact that "although the principles of the Monroe Doctrine were conceived by British Prime Minister Canning, the United States has seen fit to use the doctrine almost exclusively against the interests of England."[79] The Santiago daily also interpreted the actions of the United States as constituting proof of a desire to establish hegemony over all Latin America, and registered its bitter complaint: "Latin-American republics in the past fifty years have become capable of protecting their own interests. There is no longer danger of European aggression. Today we have more to fear from United States 'protection' than from European aggression."[80]

In Washington, Chile's Envoy Domingo Gana was even more perturbed. He felt that if the United States was able to sustain its attitude toward Great Britain, "then, in fact, the United States will have succeeded in establishing a protectorate over all of Latin America."[81] In a later letter, Gana complained that other Latin-American countries were not taking seriously enough the threat to hemisphere independence posed by the United States. He went on to reveal: "Secretary of State Olney recently confided to one of my colleagues that the only country in America on whose sympathies he could not safely count in the present circumstances was Chile."[82]

The Spanish-American War, 1898. The Spanish-American War presented further proof to Envoy Gana that the United States could not be trusted in its Latin-American dealings. Gana was convinced that Spanish policy toward Cuba was just, and that greed alone induced the United States to intervene in a situation that did not concern it.[83] Santiago newspapers were more outspoken still in their criticism. According to *El Ferrocarril*, the events leading up to the war simply afforded additional proof of United States desire to control Latin America and to separate the area from Europe.[84] *El Porvenir* was in complete accord,[85] and *La Unión* of Valparaíso warned that Latin America must now be on guard against rampant United States imperialism.[86]

The Panama Incident, 1903. The next incident that caused widespread discussion of the northern Colossus was the Panamanian revolt against Colombia, out of which the United States acquired the coveted canal rights from a speedily recognized independent Panama. Chileans were strongly divided in their reaction to these events. Some expressed the opinion that Colombia was a tropical, turbulent republic, unable to develop effective government, and therefore not to be pitied in its loss of Panama.[87] And the mood of many practical-minded Chileans was caught in the words of a particularly callous editorial appearing in *El Ferrocarril*: "If the business in Panama speeds the building of the canal, so vital to Chilean interests, then all should rejoice over the affair." [88]

On the other hand, a majority of Chile's leading newspapers responded to the news of the Panamanian revolution with anti-Yankee tirades. *El Diario Popular* urged Chile to extend sympathy to sister republic Colombia, "whose only crime has been to try to defend what belongs to her." [89] All Latin America, concluded *El Imparcial*, was now at the mercy of the United States, which tomorrow "will absorb Central America, and after that will humble Chile, Argentina, and Brazil." [90] *El Diario Ilustrado* advised Latin America to take careful note of United States actions in Panama, "for it is conduct of this sort that all of us can expect whenever the United States decides to extend its interest to us." [91] At least two papers warned that the menace of the United States was now so grave that Latin America must unite to resist it.[92]

The alarmist papers shared the views of Joaquín Walker Martínez, then Chile's envoy in Washington. So far as Walker Martínez was concerned, the Panama incident proved that in its dealings with Latin America the United States would always ignore the concept of the equality of states, and justify its predatory deeds by claiming they were the means of spreading civilization. Should it ever suit the purposes of the United States to establish naval bases at the Straits of Magellan, or to take over the nitrate fields of Tarapacá, Chilean sovereignty would be totally disregarded. Walker Martínez also drew attention to what had befallen the three Latin-American republics that, according to him, had thus far had the closest contact with the United States. If Chile wanted to escape the fate of Mexico, Colombia, and Cuba, then it ought to avoid, so far as possible, all intercourse with the United States. Unless Latin America became sufficiently alarmed by the situation, Walker Martínez predicted, the United States would pick off the southern republics one by one, establishing "protectorates" over each. To prevent such an occurrence, he urged the Foreign Ministry to alert Chilean writers and intellectuals to the menace,[93] so that they might sound the alarm before it was too late.[94]

The Roosevelt Corollary, 1904. In contrast to the outburst against the United States at the time of the Panama incident, Chilean response to the Roosevelt Corollary to the Monroe Doctrine—which in essence stated that the United States would intervene in the affairs of unstable and fiscally irresponsible Latin-American republics in order to forestall European intervention—was fairly mild.[95] True, Walker Martínez in his dispatches from Washington ranted against the new pronouncement, claiming it was now clear to all that the United States wished to establish an iron-handed protectorate over the entire hemisphere: "Soon all Latin America will be reduced to the status of Cuba. . . . With the Roosevelt Corollary, the Latin-American republics have lost the independence that they achieved in their wars against Spain."[96] But Walker Martínez conceded that his attitudes were not widely shared in Chile, and complained that the press and Congress were indifferent to foreign affairs.[97]

Indifference to the Roosevelt Corollary did indeed prevail in Chile, even though elsewhere in Latin America it produced a sensation. Only one Santiago daily seriously attacked Roosevelt's expansion of the Monroe Doctrine.[98] The reason for the Chilean attitude, according to one well-informed national author was the realization that the Corollary was "directed against backward countries that require treatment of this sort. The Roosevelt Corollary obviously has nothing to do with a stable, developed, mature country such as Chile."[99]

The Alsop Company Claims, 1909. Writing late in 1909 to the United States chargé d'affaires in Santiago, Chilean Foreign Minister Agustín Edwards observed: "Our government has never imagined that a relatively small pecuniary claim could assume such proportions as to lead to suspension of diplomatic relations." [100] And yet, a small pecuniary claim had brought the United States to the brink of severing diplomatic relations with Chile. It was the first major, widely publicized crisis in relations between the two countries since the "Baltimore" affair.

In the treaty of 1884 which established a truce between Chile and Bolivia, as well as in the definitive peace treaty which was signed in October 1904, Chile had agreed, with various reservations and exceptions, to assume responsibility for foreign claims against Bolivia originating in the territory that Bolivia was compelled to cede to the War of the Pacific victor. A commercial firm known as the Alsop Company, in which some United States citizens were stockholders, had held claims against Bolivia. In the 1890's the United States began seriously to apply pressure on Chile to meet the Alsop Company claims.[101] A United States-Chilean claims tribunal sitting in Washington decided in 1901 that the Alsop Company was strictly a Chilean enterprise. On this basis Chile argued that the Alsop claims should properly be settled in the Chilean courts and were outside the province of diplomatic intervention. Nevertheless, the United States persisted in championing its citizens who were Alsop stockholders. Hoping to end the matter by direct negotiations with the United States claimants, Chile sent Paulino Alfonso to Washington, authorizing him to offer 67,000 pounds sterling (the equivalent of $335,000) in settlement. These negotiations did not produce a settlement, and when their failure became apparent in 1905 Chilean Envoy Walker Martínez peremptorily declared that the claims had never been worth more than 43,000 pounds.

Three years later Chile agreed to accept the good offices of the United States in resolving the dispute. Alejandro Alvarez, attached to the Chilean Legation in Washington, worked closely and amicably with State Department solicitor James Brown Scott, and by 1909 agreement had been reached on terms generally favorable to Chile. But the Taft administration was scarcely installed when Secretary of State Knox let it be known that he found the agreement unsatisfactory and would reopen the case on the grounds that Chile was guilty of a denial of justice.[102] Under considerable pressure, the government of Chile by mid-September agreed in principle to submit the matter to arbitration.[103] But trouble had only commenced.

Chile insisted that any arbitration protocol must include provision for it to press its argument that the United States had no right to intervene in the matter as the Alsop firm was a Chilean company. Knox regarded the Chilean attitude as little short of impertinent, and insisted that arbitration be limited to deciding how much money Chile must pay the claimants.[104] Still hoping for a speedy settlement, Aníbal Cruz, Chile's envoy in Washington, renewed the old offer of 67,000 pounds sterling. Acting on the orders of Knox, First Assistant Secretary of State Huntington Wilson rejected this offer,[105] informing Cruz that Chile must offer at least one million dollars, or sign at once an arbitration protocol on the terms demanded by the United States.[106] On November 18, 1909, the United States chargé d'affaires in Chile delivered to that country's Foreign Ministry an ultimatum embodying the Knox demands. Chile was informed that if it did not at once yield, the United States Legation in Santiago would be closed.[107]

At this point Joaquim Nabuco, Brazilian envoy in Washington, came to Chile's aid. In a long talk with Knox on the night of November 23, he attempted to justify the Chilean position and explained that United States severance of relations would jeopardize the forthcoming Buenos Aires Conference.[108] In addition Nabuco sent an urgent note requesting the assistance of Elihu Root in the delicate negotiations. Nabuco closed this note with the admonition: "In the language of The Lusiads,[109] 'Father, come quickly and hasten to help me, as if you do not run, you may not find him who needs succor.' "[110] That Root came running is indicated by his November 29 note to Nabuco: "I received your note—your cry from Macedonia—just as I was leaving my apartment, but just in time to enable me to see Mr. Knox before leaving Washington. . . . I was quite sure from my talk with him that the Chilean matter would be settled without serious difficulty."[111]

Root's optimism was justified. Aníbal Cruz shortly reported to his government that Knox was a changed man,[112] and on December 9 in Santiago an arbitration protocol was signed on terms permitting Chile to question the right of the United States to press the Alsop claims. Chile, however, made a considerable concession, agreeing to submit the matter to the arbitration of the King of England rather than of the president of Brazil, as Chile preferred.[113]

Not all the credit for the happy outcome belongs to Nabuco and Root. Aníbal Cruz, although criticized in Chilean papers for having let his country down, was quite correct in saying that had it not been for the warm, personal friendship between himself and Knox, an amicable settlement might have been impossible to arrange.[114] If Chile had been represented in Washington at the time by such a bellicose diplomat as Joaquín Walker Martínez, the affair undoubtedly would have led to the rupture of diplomatic relations.

Despite the ultimately peaceful solution of the dispute,[115] Chilean passions were slow to subside. It proved difficult, for example, for the rising Liberal Alliance politician, Arturo Alessandri, to soften his condemnation of the bullying attitude of the United States. In 1909 Alessandri had told his colleagues in the Chamber of Deputies:

> In the streets, in the plazas, in the marketplaces, there is overwhelming agreement that Chile, at the point of cannons, has been forced to abandon its national honor. . . . It matters not that the offender is a strong and powerful nation, for the honor of our country is worth more than life itself.[116]

The following year Manuel Foster Recabarren, who argued Chile's case in the arbitration proceedings in London, observed that his countrymen had been foolish to oppose the United States on the grounds that international law precluded diplomatic intervention in the case. "When dealing with weak Latin-American countries, the United States cares as much about international law as about a radish." [117] Undoubtedly Foreign Minister Agustín Edwards expressed a minority viewpoint when he stated that the Alsop case had not altered the basic currents of mutual sympathy between Chile and the United States.[118]

Apprehension over Tacna and Arica, 1909-1910. In the entire sphere of diplomatic relations at this time, nothing was more apt to inflame the passions of Chilean statesmen than talk of outside intervention to arrange a final disposition of the Tacna and Arica territory. And precisely at the time of the Alsop controversy, the United States aroused suspicions that it was about to align itself with Peru and force Chile to accept an unfavorable settlement. Indeed, as early as September 1909 Aníbal Cruz had been warned at least by implication that unless Chile yielded in the Alsop matter, the United States might champion the Peruvian cause.[119] And in an early November conference, Knox had hinted to Cruz that the United States might back the Peruvian bid to include compulsory arbitration on the agenda of the Buenos Aires Conference, if Chile remained intransigent in the Alsop dispute.[120] Even after the Alsop case was settled, Chile continued to detect danger signs. From Buenos Aires, Miguel Cruchaga warned of Peruvian-United States negotiations, with Peru allegedly offering a coaling station at Chimbote in return for United States aid in the recovery of Tacna and Arica.[121] Sensing that the tide of diplomatic opinion in Washington was beginning to run against Chile's Tacna-Arica position, Aníbal Cruz inaugurated a brisk propaganda campaign to justify his country's stand.[122] Finally, in an interview with Huntington Wilson in April 1910, he impressed upon this State Department official the seriousness with which Chile would view United States intervention in the still smouldering Peruvian dispute.[123]

Conclusions. At the opening of the century Chile, by and large, had deemed it safe to ignore such signs of United States imperialism and intervention as the seizure of the Panama canal route and the enunciation of the Roosevelt Corollary. Confidently, Chile assumed that stable and mature countries need not fear the United States. In 1910 Chile was still one of South America's most stable and orderly republics. In spite of this, the specter of United States intervention had begun to cause serious concern. This led to a reappraisal of the recently evolved attitudes of friendship and trust toward the United States. The reversion to suspiciousness and hostility was clearly evident by 1913, when Chile began to play an active, even leading, role in the condemnation of all manifestations of expanding United States influence in Latin America. In particular, Chile by 1913 had taken up its cudgels against the previously tolerated cornerstone of Yankee Latin-American policy, the Monroe Doctrine.

MOUNTING CRITICISM OF UNITED STATES IMPERIALISM AND THE MONROE DOCTRINE, 1912-1913

In addition to the handling of the Alsop case, a number of other actions taken by the Taft administration had mildly alarmed many Chileans.[124] Thus the resolution introduced by Senator Henry Cabot Lodge and approved by the United States Senate in 1912 had caused concern.[125] The resolution, which came to be known as the Lodge Corollary, was intended to prevent acquisition of land rights in the Magdalena Bay region of lower California by a Japanese syndicate. The Lodge Corollary extended the application of the Monroe Doctrine to non-European countries and to foreign companies as well as foreign nations. Not, however, until Woodrow Wilson began to shape his own Latin-American policy did alarm become profound and widespread. Chileans were first dismayed by the speech that President Wilson gave in Mobile on October 27, 1913, in which he attributed many of Latin America's problems to the machinations of European, especially British, interests and implied that the solution would be to replace European with United States capital.

Elder statesman Marcial Martínez—who had sparred none too successfully with James G. Blaine during the War of the Pacific —described Wilson's Mobile address as a clear indication of United States intentions to establish economic control over Latin America, and ultimately political domination. "Blaine began the policy of United States imperialism in Latin America," charged Martínez, "and now his fondest hopes are embodied in the Mobile address." [126] Fast-rising diplomat-journalist Félix Nieto del Río obviously had the Mobile speech in mind when he wrote: "We do not want the United States to act as mining companies do— that is, establish company stores and force their wards to buy exclusively from them." [127] By the end of 1913, more and more Chileans were coming to agree that "Pan-Americanism as applied by Wilson aims at United States domination in Latin America, just as Pan-Germanism aims at Prussian control over Germany and even a larger area of Europe." [128] Considerable numbers of them had also become convinced that the Monroe Doctrine was the primary instrument by which the United States hoped to implement its nefarious scheme of mastering the hemisphere.[129] Precisely at the time that this conviction was spreading most rapidly among Chilean diplomatic and intellectual circles, former President Theodore Roosevelt arrived in Santiago. His presence touched off the strongest show of anti-Monroeism that the staid Chilean republic had ever staged.

The dynamic Roosevelt reached Santiago on November 21, 1913. El Mercurio had sought to prepare for his arrival by advising its readers: "Let us forget whatever unpleasant incidents we associate with Theodore Roosevelt . . . he is a typical product of United States civilization: vigorous, impulsive, not heedful of the consequences of his actions, strongly susceptible to error, but at the same time possessed of the noblest of humanitarian sentiments." [130] Unfortunately for Roosevelt, many Chileans were not inclined to be so lenient as El Mercurio advised. When the former president of the United States came to the University of Chile to present an address,[131] Marcial Martínez, as the oldest member of the law faculty, was prepared with a speech of welcome. Here was a precious moment of reprisal for the octogenarian who ever since he had been victimized by the deceitfulness of Blaine had harbored bitter resentment against the United States. Martínez took full advantage of the opportunity and in his speech—read for him by Jorge Errázuriz Tagle—proclaimed, among other points, that the Monroe Doctrine had ceased to exist: "It is dead." [132] When the Martínez-written introduction was completed, the symphony orchestra began to play Beethoven's Fifth Symphony, whereupon the presiding officials leapt to their feet, mistaking the strains for those of the United States national anthem. Such at least is the account provided by a probably unreliable Peruvian writer, strongly unsympathetic to Chile and Chilean culture.[133]

Whether or not this anecdote is true, Roosevelt was plainly ruffled by the events preceding his address.[134] Martínez had issued a direct challenge. In previous talks on his South American tour, especially in those presented in Montevideo and Buenos Aires, Roosevelt had said that the Monroe Doctrine was very much alive, but that now certain Latin-American states had reached a sufficient degree of maturity, strength, stability, and responsibility to interpret and enforce the doctrine along with the United States. Martínez declared that Chile wanted nothing to do with the doctrine on any terms. In this he was seconded by various elements of the press which stated: "The United States should cease proclaiming doctrines and begin to observe a line of conduct based on the principle of the equality of nations;" [135] and again, "We are tired of hearing about international doctrines whether enforced unilaterally or together with Argentina, Brazil, and Chile. The United States will have nothing to say to us until it recognizes a system of American law based on absolute equality of nations." [136]

Roosevelt's discomfiture continued. On November 25 when he spoke at the elegant and exquisite Teatro Municipal, Santiago's opera house, he was introduced by another Yankeephobe, the historian-journalist-diplomat Gonzalo Bulnes. Somewhat haughtily, Bulnes averred that Chile was not interested in continental doctrines that curtail national sovereignty, "for we are concerned only with mutually advantageous and practical policies that can be actually implemented." [137]

In Washington, Chilean Envoy Eduardo Suárez Mujica backed to the hilt the pronouncements of Martínez and Bulnes. Suárez Mujica did point out that Martínez had not spoken as the representative of the government. But he then proceeded to give to the United States press what he implied was the official Chilean interpretation of the Monroe Doctrine. This analysis was, if anything, more extreme than that of Martínez.

Countries that have reached a high degree of maturity and organization . . . have no reason to·regard with suspicion any international doctrine. . . . They will judge and decide for themselves, as their high interests dictate, the applicability in each instance of such a doctrine. . . . The utterances known as the Monroe Doctrine are not a principle of international law. . . . They are merely a declaration of the United States which

. . . might have been gratifying to Latin American republics when originally propounded.[138]

Obviously Roosevelt's visit to Chile brought to the surface strong anti-United States sentiments.[139] Had he arrived in the country sometime before 1900, his message that Chile had now reached the stage in which it could cooperate with the United States in enforcing the Monroe Doctrine would have greatly appealed to national pride and might have won him a hero's welcome. By the end of 1913 relations between the United States and Chile had deteriorated to such a degree that Roosevelt's peace offering was coldly spurned. Several reasons for this deterioration have already been discussed. An additional contributing factor was the Wilson administration's early approach to the Mexican crisis.

THE IMPACT OF WILSON'S MEXICAN DIPLOMACY ON CHILE, 1913-1915

Shortly after his March 1913 inauguration, Woodrow Wilson began to apply pressure against the administration of Victoriano Huerta who by force and guile had recently wrested the Mexican presidency from its rightful occupant, Francisco I. Madero. Many Chileans were outraged by what they considered the meddling of the United States.[140] Their attitude, as the anti-Yankee diplomat and author Galvarino Gallardo Nieto later described it, was that Wilson, by passing judgment on the constitutionality of regimes and insisting upon democratic processes in Mexico, had proved himself a more dangerous interventionist than Theodore Roosevelt. To some informed observers in Chile it also seemed incongruous that the United States, which they charged with denying voting rights to its own Negroes, should demand that Mexican Indians, "even less well prepared than the Negroes in the republic to the north, be given suffrage rights." [141]

Deep concern was displayed by various Chilean newspapers. El Mercurio, after describing General Winfield Scott's capture of Mexico City in 1847, stated that after the second United States conquest, the flag of Mexico would probably never again be raised in the capital city.[142] It predicted also that Yankee intervention in Mexico, which was judged almost certain to occur, would produce the same sort of consternation in Latin America that the advance of Islam had caused in Europe.[143] Another daily described the United States as an international bully,[144] and printed a cartoon in which a map of North America was cleverly turned into a leering Uncle Sam. Canada formed the cap, Florida was the hooked nose, the Mississippi River was the mouth (complete with teeth), Mexico was the flowing beard, and Cuba the pipe. Uncle Sam was saying: "How good I will feel when I have such a long beard and such a good pipe." [145]

Foreign Minister Enrique Villegas was as perturbed over the possibilities of United States intervention in Mexico as the alarmist journalists.[146] Proceeding upon the basis of a precedent established in 1910 in the face of a Peruvian-Ecuadorean boundary dispute,[147] Villegas began in August of 1913 to explore the possibility of settling the United States-Mexican difficulties through the good offices of Argentina, Brazil, and Chile—the so-called ABC powers.[148] Shortly after the bloody landing of United States troops at Vera Cruz, Secretary of State William Jennings Bryan accepted the Chilean-initiated offer of mediation by the ABC powers. The resultant Niagara Falls Conference convened on May 20, 1914.[149] Suspicion of United States intentions led Chilean representative Suárez Mujica, in accordance with instructions from his Foreign Ministry, to suggest that the conference agree to leave internal affairs of Mexico strictly in the hands of the Mexican government and to limit discussion to the international aspects of the problem.[150]

With this suggestion having been agreed to by the delegates at Niagara, the conference proceeded smoothly enough. When, shortly after its conclusion, the United States withdrew its forces from Vera Cruz, Chilean diplomats and journalists jumped to the conclusion that the Niagara meeting had been a resounding triumph. Envoy Suárez Mujica reported from Washington: "The ABC mediation has produced a sensation in the United States press, which realizes that for better or for worse this heralds the dawn of a new era in hemisphere relations." [151] Other high-ranking diplomats agreed that by their actions at Niagara the ABC powers had won a great victory for the doctrine of nonintervention.[152]

The press was likewise convinced that the South American republics had actually prevented war between the United States and Mexico.[153] El Diario Ilustrado went so far as to announce: "The equilibrium of the American Hemisphere is now largely in the hands of the three most advanced South American nations." [154]

Chileans were soon rudely restored to a sense of reality about the power of the ABC republics to mediate the affairs of the hemisphere. By the end of 1915 it was generally agreed that Wilson was still pursuing an interventionist policy and that the renewed attempts of the ABC nations, augmented by Bolivia, Guatemala, and Uruguay, to resolve the continuing difficulties between the United States and Mexico had been a flat failure.[155] A few months later Santiago's leading daily was ready to agree with an editorial that had appeared in the Buenos Aires La Razón: "United States action in attacking Mexico [General Pershing's pursuit of Pancho Villa] without consulting the ABC powers proves there is nothing to the supposed new continental policy except United States hypocrisy." [156]

Still, Chilean diplomacy helped salvage something worthwhile from the policy of ABC cooperation that had been brought into existence by the Mexican crisis. In March of 1915 the Foreign Ministers of the three countries[157] conferred in Santiago. The following May in Buenos Aires they signed a treaty calling for mutual cooperation and maintenance of peace.[158] Chile and Brazil even ratified the treaty, but Argentina, with its traditional aversion to international alliances and commitments, refused to do so.[159]

In exhibiting at least a temporary interest in cooperative action, Argentina, Brazil, and Chile were taking what conceivably could have been the most significant step in influencing hemisphere relations since the independence movements. Heretofore, although Argentina and Chile had often displayed active hostility to the Latin-American policies of the United States, they had never been able to present a united front to the Colossus. But as of 1915 the two most powerful countries of Hispanic South America, bulwarked by Brazil, were warily attempting to pursue a common hemisphere policy. This fact did not bode well for the future success of Washington in dominating the Pan-American movement.[160] In fact, it was this first glimmer of ABC unity that soon enabled Chile to play a decisive part in rejecting the most important feature of Woodrow Wilson's emerging Latin-American policy.

THE REJECTION OF WILSON'S PAN-AMERICAN PACT, 1913-1916

Chile received its first official word of President Wilson's proposed Pan-American Pact on the evening of December 20, 1913, when Colonel Edward M. House—a principal formulator of the pact—had an interview with Envoy Eduardo Suárez Mujica. Explaining the desire of the United States to sound out the ABC powers before presenting the plan to Latin America as a whole, Colonel House proceeded to outline a four-point hemisphere pact. Points one and two seriously alarmed Suárez Mujica, who had made up his mind sometime previously that President Wilson was intent upon making United States interests prevail throughout Latin America without consideration for the desires and rights of other republics.[161] The first point called for mutual guarantees by the American republics to maintain the territorial integrity and political independence under the republican form of government of all hemisphere nations except Canada—which was not included in any of the points of the Wilson plan. The second called for definite settlement within a year, by arbitration or any other means that the interested governments preferred, of all pending questions of limits and territories. If the one-year time limit expired with disagreements still unresolved, arbitration was to become obligatory. The third point, stipulating that the governments of each of the American republics should control the manufacture and export of arms and munitions, seemed harmless enough to the Chilean envoy, but his suspicions were again aroused as he heard the fourth and last point explained. This provided for final solution of all future difficulties between American republics by investigation and conciliation, and should these expedients fail, by arbitration—except when disputes affected the honor, independence, or vital interests of the contracting parties.[162]

Although assuring House that the proposed pact was in many ways praiseworthy, Suárez Mujica observed that the first point, calling for guarantees of territorial integrity, could prove highly unfavorable to Chile, "given its peculiar situation pertaining to pending disputes." [163] Obviously, the Tacna-Arica issue was uppermost in the mind of the Chilean, and he suspected a United States plot to force a possibly disadvantageous settlement on his country. Suárez Mujica further explained that the second and fourth points, with their implications of compulsory arbitration for both pending and future questions in the event other means failed to achieve solutions, were diametrically opposed to Chile's traditional position in hemisphere relations.

Immediately after the interview Suárez Mujica dispatched a telegram to Minister of Foreign Relations Alejandro Lira, urging that Chile oppose the pact suggested by the United States, not only because of the Tacna-Arica issue, but because a young nation confident of increasing strength and international importance should not "tie its hands and condemn itself to any limitation of its sovereignty for reasons of an altruistic nature." [164] Upon receiving this message, Lira exchanged telegrams with his country's representatives in Argentina and Brazil, and to his discomfiture learned that both of these countries were favorably disposed toward the Wilson plan. In spite of this, he instructed Suárez Mujica by cable to maintain a cold attitude toward the proposed pact.[165]

Rather than base its objections to the pact solely on the Tacna-Arica issue, the Chilean Foreign Ministry advanced a number of additional arguments against the United States proposal, some of them apparently valid and sincere, others rather contrived and far-fetched. Foreign Minister Lira complained that the pact would place a stable country like Chile in the same category with nations that had two revolutions a year. Worse, it would involve Chile, Argentina, and Brazil, along with the United States, in defending the republican form of government against a great number of revolutions throughout the hemisphere each year. Not only would this impose an intolerable burden on the stable countries, but it would cast them in the role of intervening in the affairs of sister republics.[166] Ultimately, therefore, the pact would result in the dominance of some American states over others.[167] Certain Chilean diplomats also argued that insistence upon the republican form of government was an infringement upon national sovereignty, assuming the possibility that someday an American republic might wish to establish a different type of political administration. Internal systems of government, it was suggested, could not be made the subject of treaties, because each country was sovereign within its own territory to choose whatever means of government it desired.[168] Finally, Carlos Castro Ruiz, a subsecretary in the Chilean Ministry of Foreign Relations who played a leading role in shaping Chile's opposition to the Pan-American Pact,[169] condemned the Wilson plan because of its lack of reciprocity. He pointed out it could hardly be expected that Latin America would intervene to protect United States territorial integrity or to maintain its republican form of government. But, under the leadership and instigation of the United States, intervention of this nature would be frequently directed against Latin-American republics. "The treaty, if skillfully exploited, would tend to erect a United States tutelage over Latin America, and might lead to commercial and political absorption by the United States of smaller, weaker Latin-American countries." [170]

Throughout 1914 and 1915, Secretaries of State William Jennings Bryan and Robert Lansing continued sporadically to discuss the pact with the ambassadors—the legations had by then been elevated to embassies—of the ABC powers. Chilean Ambassador Suárez Mujica steadfastly maintained a negative attitude.[171] A dispatch from Ambassador Henry P. Fletcher in Santiago further impressed upon Washington the gravity with which Chile regarded the matter. Fletcher warned that if the United States should proceed along the lines of the Wilson plan without the support of Chile, then that republic would develop an implacable hostility against the Yankees, which would tend to make it turn exclusively to Europe in its commercial and political ties.[172]

President Wilson now decided to resort to different tactics, and chose his appearance on January 6, 1916,[173] before the Second Pan-American Scientific Congress being held in Washington as the opportunity to publicize his more overt approach. This decision by the United States president turned the Congress into something of a contest between Wilson and Suárez Mujica. The

Chilean ambassador, who was the presiding official for the Congress, had hinted at his suspicions of the Wilson plan when he presented the address of welcome at the opening session in mid-December, 1915. In this and in subsequent pronouncements at the Congress Suárez Mujica criticized the Monroe Doctrine and suggested that no matter how it might be multilateralized by the Wilson plan so as to allow Latin-American nations to participate in its enforcement, it was still contrary to the only principle upon which Pan-Americanism could function: absolute equality and complete sovereignty of nations.[174]

When President Wilson's moment came on January 6, he urged Latin-American adherence to a slightly modified Pan-American Pact. The first point was unaltered, calling still for mutual guarantees of territorial integrity and political independence under the republican form of government. In the case of the second point, however, the one-year time limit for settling territorial disputes before being obliged to submit them to arbitration had been removed. Instead, it was stipulated that signatories would be asked to agree to compose their territorial disagreements through conciliation or international arbitration. Despite this change, the second point still implied to suspicious readers that compulsory arbitration was in order when other methods failed to resolve boundary disputes.[175] Nor did the slightly revised wording of the fourth point allay Chilean doubts.

Following Wilson's speech, the State Department began to deal individually with the Latin-American republics—excepting Mexico, Colombia, Haiti, Nicaragua, and the Dominican Republic—attempting to line up support for the Pan-American Pact. Ramón Subercaseaux, serving as Minister of Foreign Relations for the newly-installed Juan Luis Sanfuentes administration, resented Washington's decision to cease working through the ABC powers and took immediate measures to counteract the new United States approach. The scene of battle shifted now to Rio de Janeiro and Buenos Aires, where Chilean diplomats[176] worked feverishly to gain backing for their country's position. In the interest of preserving ABC unity Brazilian Foreign Minister Lauro Müller tended generally, albeit sometimes reluctantly, to support Chile, and did all in his power to persuade Argentina to do likewise. This was no easy task, as Argentine Foreign Minister José Luis Muratore and, most especially, Ambassador in Washington Rómulo Naón felt the Chilean stand was unreasonable and based only upon the wildly exaggerated suspicions of Ambassador Suárez Mujica. At several points, Argentina threatened to sign the Wilson pact separately, even though this would mean the end of ABC unity. In these proceedings, Argentina exhibited its customary desire to go it alone in conducting foreign affairs, while Chile gave evidence of the new approach that would soon become a cornerstone of its United States policy: dealing with the Colossus through the combined strength of several South American countries.[177]

Chile's campaign against Wilson's Pan-American Pact, hesitantly supported by Brazil and, in spite of threats, not sabotaged by Argentina in the final stages of negotiations,[178] played a major role in leading the United States to abandon the whole notion.[179] On the evening of February 28, 1916, Suárez Mujica learned from Lansing that the United States no longer considered the pact essential. The Secretary of State even conceded that in the hands of a Republican administration, the pact might have been converted into an instrument of imperialism and intervention.[180] Early the next summer Suárez Mujica, satisfied that he had succeeded in protecting his country's interests, resigned his ambassadorial post, pleading ill health.[181]

Chile's triumph in this issue had been due to the germ of ABC unity. Had it not been for the interest especially of Chile and Brazil in nurturing this germ, Chile would have been isolated in its opposition to the pact, and the outcome of the struggle might have been entirely different. Here was a clear example, from which diplomats could later profit, of what a united ABC stand could accomplish in dealing with the United States.

The conviction that the major South American countries should present a united front in hemisphere relations contributed also to Chile's next crisis with the United States. This arose over the issue of Chilean neutrality in the First World War.

THE FIRST WORLD WAR AND PRO-GERMAN SENTIMENT IN CHILE

Chile's Wartime Neutrality

A substantial tradition of pro-German sentiment existed in Chile upon the outbreak of the First World War. German settlers had made a striking contribution to national progress by developing the south. Numerous German teaching missions had strongly influenced the educational structure,[182] and many German technicians and scientists had notably advanced Chile's physical development. In April 1914 Chileans had revealed their admiration for the German nation by giving an ecstatic welcome to Prince Henry, brother of the Kaiser, on his good-will tour. The warmth of the popular greeting extended the prince was in marked contrast to the coolness with which Theodore Roosevelt had been received.[183] And once the war was under way, Chilean writers seemed never to tire of making the point that Germany had saved Chile from the evil designs of the United States and various European nations during the War of the Pacific.[184]

When the United States finally entered the struggle and began to apply pressure for the severance of Chilean diplomatic relations with the Central Powers, Chile all the more steadfastly persisted in its policy of neutrality. One influential writer justified Chile's stand by a line of reasoning that should have been effective with a United States audience, since it bore striking similarity to the position once defended by Washington and Jefferson. Chile, it was pointed out, had no direct concern with the war. It was a young country, working diligently to develop its own internal resources so as to guarantee a bright future. Consequently, it could not afford to become enmeshed in wars brought about by other nations.[185]

Despite the dispassionate logic of this particular argument, there was a pointedly anti-Yankee aspect to Chilean neutrality. One-time Foreign Ministry official Galvarino Gallardo Nieto wrote:

Let Chile remember the indignities inflicted upon it during the Alsop case discussions; let it remember the plight of Mexico, Colombia, Cuba, the Hawaiian Islands, Santo Domingo, Haiti, Nicaragua and the dollar diplomacy practiced in Costa Rica and

Honduras. Then let it decide if it wishes to side with the United States in the war.[186]

Moreover, Conservatives such as Joaquín Walker Martínez, Abdón Cifuentes, and Gonzalo Bulnes,[187] and Liberals such as Arturo Alessandri,[188] Ernesto Barros Jarpa (who would serve as Minister of Foreign Relations beginning in 1920), Marcial Martínez,[189] and Eliodoro Yáñez,[190] as well as elderly Radical leader Enrique Mac-Iver,[191] all regarded Chilean neutrality as an essential step toward creating a bloc of truly independent South American nations capable of standing up to the United States in hemisphere relations.[192] In pursuing the policy of neutrality Chile learned once again of the effectiveness of a South American alliance.[193] Many of the nation's diplomats acknowledged that without the insistence of Argentina's notoriously inflexible President Hipólito Irigoyen upon preserving neutrality, an isolated Chile might have been humbled, "deprived of its sovereign rights, and forced to heed United States wishes." [194]

Thus, Chilean neutrality rested upon a combination of anti-United States and pro-German sentiments.[195] Indications of the pro-German orientation of Chilean wartime policy were plentiful. For example, there was the simple fact that Gonzalo Bulnes, who had fallen in love with Germany and its civilization when representing his country there in the 1890's, was one of President Sanfuentes' most influential advisers.[196] There was also the fact that conservative elements in general, and especially the clergy, made no endeavor to disguise their passionate preference for the German cause. This group maintained that Germany represented the traditional cultural values, under attack by the forces of materialism and secularism unleashed by the French Revolution and carried to new extremes by the Anglo-Saxon civilizations of England and the United States.[197] Moreover, the Chilean army, because of sentimental and pragmatic considerations, was strongly pro-German, "especially its intellectual circles." [198] In the realm of sentiment, it was easy to recall that General Emil Körner, arriving from Germany in the mid-1880's, had become the real father of the modern Chilean army. A steady stream of German military missions had helped Körner mold the Chilean army into a unit of advanced professional efficiency. Throughout the First World War General Körner, living in retirement in Germany, kept Chilean government and military officials supplied with his pro-German observations, all carefully written in Spanish.[199] On pragmatic grounds, Chile's military leaders sympathized with Germany out of admiration for the proficiency and might of its war machine, which they regarded as invincible. As late as June 1918, Lieutenant Colonel Jorge Ahumada, Chilean military attaché in Berlin, continued with absolute certainty to predict a German victory.[200] Finally, racial considerations contributed to the pro-German sentiments of many Chileans. Nicolás Palacios in his popular *Raza chilena*, published first in 1911 and then in a second edition in 1917, argued that the Chileans were a superior race because of their descent from northern Spaniards, who were actually Teutons. These conclusions, which Palacios was by no means alone in propounding,[201] undoubtedly induced a substantial number of Chileans to side with their supposed racial counterparts in Europe.[202]

In the light of these circumstances, it was not strange that "Germanophiles in Chile were as abundant as mushrooms." [203] It was understandable also that an overt flaunting of United States wishes brought satisfaction to Chile during the course of the war. But once the Central Powers had been crushed, Chile grew alarmed and then panicky over the possible deterioration of its bargaining position in hemisphere relations. As had been true so often in the past, Tacna and Arica furnished the primary cause for concern.

CHILEAN FEAR OF UNITED STATES RETALIATION

Peru and Bolivia, respecting the obvious desires of the United States, had "been quick to fly to the support of the country of Mr. Blaine" [204] by severing relations with the Central Powers. Toward the end of 1918, therefore, Chile was gravely worried that these War of the Pacific foes might, by virtue of their World War cooperation, win United States support for their territorial aspirations. Accordingly, a group of Chilean notables[205] assembled at Santiago's Turf Club (*Club Hípico*) on September 18 and drafted a message to President Wilson, congratulating him upon his announced peace formula and obliquely assuring him that Chilean neutrality had never assumed an anti-United States orientation.

An opportunity quickly presented itself for President Wilson to indicate that he was not placated by this message. The president directed some pointed words to Beltrán Mathieu when receiving him as Chile's new ambassador in November: "The triumphant conclusion of the war gives assurance that henceforth no nation can venture to seek only its own aggrandizement at the expense of others, or hope upon such an enterprise to prevail." [206] The following month Wilson rattled his saber more loudly. Taking cognizance of a new flare-up in the chronic territorial dispute between Chile and Peru, he directed a strong message to the Chilean government. In it, Wilson stated that Chile and Peru had obligations to international society to take immediate steps to re-establish friendly relations. [207] President Sanfuentes replied in forceful language on December 7: "Chile has been at peace with all countries for thirty-five years, and has been capable during that time of resolving with justice all disputes with its neighbors." Sanfuentes concluded with the assertion that the Treaty of Ancón—providing that disposition of Tacna and Arica would be determined by a plebiscite—was the governing instrument in the present discord, and that Chile would know how to preserve peace within the framework of the treaty terms. [208]

These bold words constituted a façade, masking basic Chilean inquietude about the success of Peruvian propaganda not only in Washington, but in Paris and London as well. Actually, there was fear that unless Chile made amends to the Allied Powers, the proposed League of Nations might be inclined to restore Tacna and Arica to Peru. [209] The clear danger confronting Chile led a number of its writers to turn out an imposing volume of books, articles, and pamphlets justifying their nation's stand concerning Tacna and Arica. [210] And in Washington, Ambassador Mathieu instituted a crash program of propaganda to prove his nation's admiration for the United States and deny that its neutrality had been tinged with anti-Yankee sentiments. [211] Félix Nieto del Río was rushed to the United States to assume command of the propaganda campaign. As a member of El Diario Ilustrado's staff in 1914, Nieto

del Río had written a series of bitterly anti-United States articles.[212] But circumstances had now changed, and the talented journalist went to absurd extremes to curry United States favor. In
an article appearing in the September 1, 1919, *New York Sun* he
even made the preposterous assertion that a strong wave of public
sentiment might soon lead Chile to emulate the United States and
enact a prohibition law.[213]

To augment the propaganda efforts of Nieto del Río, Chile sent
to the United States two of the ablest members of the *El Mercurio*
staff: Ernesto Montenegro and Carlos Silva Vildósola. This move
at least brought a greater measure of integrity to the campaign,
as Silva Vildósola had been one of the outstanding defenders of
the Allied cause throughout the war, and the pro-United States
articles which he was soon turning out had the ring of sincerity.[214]
Also in the endeavor to win good will, Amanda Labarca, already
one of Chile's most renowned woman intellectuals,[215] was sent to
the United States to arrange for an exchange of university professors. Finally, Eliodoro Yáñez headed a mission that traveled to
both the United States and Europe attempting to offset the effects
of Peruvian propaganda and to present the Chilean argument that
the Treaty of Ancón was absolutely binding in the Tacna-Arica
dispute.[216]

Chilean propaganda efforts apparently enjoyed some success.
At least, the feared foreign intervention was not forthcoming. But
it was irksome for Chile to discover that actions taken during the
First World War in an attempt to liberate the nation from United
States influence had, in the final analysis, only brought about a
greater dependence upon the favorable disposition of the Colossus.[217]

THE RISE OF ECONOMIC AND CULTURAL NATIONALISM AND
THE CONTINUING SEARCH FOR A UNITED STATES POLICY

CHILEAN CONCERN WITH INCREASING UNITED STATES
ECONOMIC PENETRATION, 1892-1920

Especially in the later years of the 1892-1920 period, distress
over the economic penetration of the northern master-capitalist

nation contributed to Chile's frequent manifestations of anti-United States sentiments. A brief glance at statistics reveals why this would be so, for the increasing importance of United States trade and investments to the Chilean economy, most particularly after 1910, is indeed striking.

In 1896, the total value of goods exchanged between Chile and the United States was slightly less than $3,000,000.[218] In both exports and imports, the United States occupied fourth place in Chilean commerce, behind England, Germany, and France, in that order. Two years later Frank G. Carpenter, a Yankee journalist who traveled through Chile, commented upon the insignificance of United States trade and capital in the Chilean economic structure. Outside of Grace Company operations—the company had established its Valparaíso office in 1881 and a Santiago branch in 1885 —Carpenter could find only one large-scale operation owned by Yankee interests. This was the silver mining and refining "kingdom" of New York capitalist George Chace. The owner of several of the richest silver mines in northern Chile, Chace also operated a profitable silver and copper refining plant in Iquique.[219]

The Chilean commercial picture had changed by 1910. At that time the United States absorbed about $22,650,000 worth of Chilean exports—80 per cent of this was represented by nitrates— virtually the same amount as Germany. The United Kingdom was still in first place by a considerable margin, buying over $40,000,-000 worth of Chilean products, but France had ceased to be an important purchaser.[220] In the same year Chile bought $12,271,000 worth of goods from the United States, $32,035,000 from the United Kingdom, $24,035,000 from Germany, and $6,434,000 from France.[221] By 1913, Chile's export-import figures with the United States, Germany and the United Kingdom had all increased slightly, but the relative position of the three countries was unaltered.[222] The First World War drastically transformed the Chilean commercial structure, eliminating Germany and propelling the United States far ahead of Great Britain. In 1920, Chilean exports to the United States were valued at $115,803,000, and imports reached $47,000,000—figures that represented 54 per cent of Chile's entire foreign trade. In contrast, the value of exports to the United Kingdom was $55,000,000, while imports were $39,-160,000.[223]

The increase of direct United States investments in Chile was also striking. Although in 1912 these investments totaled scarcely more than $15,000,000,[224] the next eight years witnessed a remarkable upsurge. The Guggenheim interests, already by 1912 the owners of the rich copper mine of El Teniente, located in Sewell in central Chile, shortly later acquired the fabulous Chuquicamata mine in the north. After investing over $1,000,000 in the mine, the Guggenheim-controlled Chile Exploration Company began actual production at Chuquicamata in mid-May 1915, employing some 3,500 workers.[225] Beginning also in 1915, Bethlehem Steel undertook the extraction of northern Chile's iron ore and within four years had exported 143,000 metric tons.[226] By 1916 Grace and Company had offices in nine Chilean cities, and the National City Bank of New York had established a branch in Santiago.[227] As the decade of the 1920's began, direct United States investment in mining, industry,[228] and commerce in Chile had soared to over $250,000,000,[229] while loans and portfolio investments amounted to an additional $100,000,000. At this time, approximately one third of all United States private funds directly or indirectly committed to Latin America were invested in Chile.[230]

To Chileans this fact did not represent an unmixed blessing. The presence of United States-financed operations in the country produced inevitable friction. By 1920 charges were being voiced in the Chilean Congress that United States copper firms imposed subhuman working conditions on their unfortunate laborers.[231] Other United States operations were accused of controlling the votes of their employees, thereby securing election of "puppets" to the national Congress.[232] More important, influential Chileans were becoming convinced that the United States was bent upon obtaining economic control over Chile as well as the rest of Latin America, and was using the Pan-American movement to accomplish this end.[233] El Mercurio summed up this attitude: "In the Chilean Congress and in other informed circles, the prevailing opinion is that Pan-Americanism represents merely a materialistic attempt on the part of the United States to gain economic mastery over Latin America." [234] Chilean suspicions of United States intentions, especially of Wilson's apparent desire to have United States capital replace that of Europe in Latin America, were pointedly expressed at the Buenos Aires Financial Conference held in 1916. At the opening session of the conference, to which the United States had sent a distinguished delegation headed by Secretary of the Treasury William Gibbs McAdoo, Chilean representative Armando Quesada Acharán proclaimed: "Closer economic ties between the United States and Latin America must not, in any way, interfere with the maintaining and increasing of economic relations with Europe." [235] And as the First World War came to an end, Chileans became obsessed with the economic menace posed by the United States, fearing that the Yankees might initiate a dumping policy which would wipe out the recent gains scored by domestic industry. [236] In this respect, Eliodoro Yáñez asserted that Chile was threatened by a calamity worse than international war. [237]

It is significant that economic nationalism was not introduced as a major issue into Chilean politics until sometime after 1910, precisely the period in which United States economic influence first became apparent. [238] An early, half-hearted attempt of President Balmaceda to rally Chileans against the peril posed by British economic pre-eminence had won only a handful of supporters. [239] But the new efforts, directed against the United States, won a considerable following. [240] Many of Chile's most respectable citizens were attracted to the Nationalist Union (Unión Nacionalista). Founded in 1913, this organization was led by such prominent men as Francisco Antonio Encina, the distinguished upper-class historian-essayist, and Guillermo Subercaseaux, perhaps the most renowned Chilean economist and banker in the first third of the twentieth century. The Nationalist Union, which briefly transformed itself into a political party in 1915, attempted to bring an "economic and sociological orientation" to Chilean politics. In particular, it urged nationalization of foreign-controlled industries and greater governmental economic planning. [241]

Other signs heralded the birth of economic nationalism in Chile.

Santiago in 1917 witnessed an imposing ceremony honoring Argentina's prolific author and fiery lecturer Manuel Ugarte, one of the most outspoken Yankeephobes ever to arise in Latin America. Upon this occasion both Marcial Martínez and Eliodoro Yáñez agreed that warnings of the Argentine writer against United States imperialism were now more timely than ever, in view of the new Yankee commercial invasion.[242] About this time, Chileans also shuddered at the implications of a story told by the eminent journalist Trancredo Pinochet Le-Brun. While in New York, Pinochet claimed to have met a Spaniard who wanted to go to Chile to raise chickens, but who insisted upon postponing his departure until he had become a United States citizen. When queried as to this decision, the Spaniard explained: "If I am a United States citizen and someone steals chickens from me in Chile, the fleet will be sent to my aid." [243]

Far and away the most significant point raised by the champions of economic nationalism was the assertion that foreign dominance of the national economy was an unmistakable sign of Chilean decadence and inferiority. The underlying contention here was that if Chile ever wished to become a modern republic, it must develop the technical skills and habits of industry for which it had heretofore relied upon foreigners. Francisco Antonio Encina made this point in his classic *Nuestra inferioridad económico*.[244] Trancredo Pinochet had the same thing in mind when he urged Chileans to study in the United States in order to acquire technological proficiency. To allow Yankees to come to Chile to introduce advanced scientific methods would only result in greater United States dominance of Chile's economy. However, once well-trained Chileans returned from the United States, they would be able to stir their laggard compatriots into exercising their latent talents. Thus, Chileans would begin to develop their country by their own efforts. With this process once initiated, it would be possible to oust the foreigners.[245] But if Chileans refused to follow this policy, he warned, "then we will remain a fossilized reminder of a bygone age, or else become the subjects of more economically advanced nations." [246]

FEAR OF UNITED STATES CULTURAL PENETRATION

The Spanish-American War had helped call into being in Chile the cult of Hispanism, although the way had been prepared for this development by the Chilean-Spanish rapprochement during the War of the Pacific. A fairly comprehensive system of value judgments, Hispanism places dignity, status, and manners above talent and tangible accomplishments, the supernatural graces believed to flow from the Catholic faith above deeds that produce good results on the mundane level, dogma above curiosity, authoritarianism above democracy, family above communal good, permanent, stratified order in the social structure above flux, and resignation to the physical ambient above endeavors to reform and improve it. Hispanism also honors the traditional more than the new, and the graceful and artistic more than the functional and the practical. Finally, as the name implies, Hispanism entails veneration of Spain and Spanish civilization as the foundation of virtue, morality, and culture, and as the vital source of all that is good in the New World.

A remarkable prediction made in 1845 by former President Joaquín Pinto about Chilean political development has applied with even greater validity to intellectual patterns and value judgments. Said Pinto: "But you who know the character of our country must realize that we will never utilize the methods of democracy as practiced in the United States of America, but rather the political principles of Spain." [247]

The historical writings of Crescente Errázuriz, ultimately to become the archbishop of Santiago, accomplished the preliminary work necessary to make devotion to Spain an historically justifiable position in Chile. His publications, which began to appear in the 1870's,[248] refuted the charges of consistent Spanish depravity in colonial Chile that had been spread by such liberal, anticlerical writers as Diego Barros Arana, Miguel Luis Amunátegui, and José Victorino Lastarria.[249] But it was only with the outbreak of the Spanish-American War that a sizable number of Chileans, often led and encouraged by the Spanish clergy,[250] made the rendering of homage to the greatness of Spain something of a national vogue.[251] It soon became a commonplace that Spain with its moral and spiritual splendor was being attacked by the crude worshippers of power and material affluence.[252] Although the motherland might go down to defeat, "Spanish valor was still worth more than all the gold of the United States." [253] The war, moreover, and the general suspicion that the Colossus would by one means or another impose a colonial status upon Cuba seemed an indication to some Chileans of United States contempt for the Latin race and therefore a warning of the sort of treatment that all Latin America could expect from Anglo-America.[254]

With the Spanish-American War, Chileans began for the first time to concern themselves seriously over the dangers of United States cultural penetration. Not only avowed Hispanists but a wide variety of intellectuals joined in the endeavor to protect traditional cultural and spiritual values—many of them urging united action with other Hispanic-American nations so as to oppose the common menace.[255] Consequently, the great Uruguayan writer, José Enrique Rodó, probably the most famous critic of the allegedly anticultural utilitarianism of the United States and champion of concerted Hispanic-American effort to resist it, was lionized by Chilean intellectuals, and his warning against Yankee cultural penetration was spread by eager disciples.[256]

During the course of the Spanish-American War, one of the points soon to be developed in *Ariel y Calibán*—the best known book of José Enrique Rodó, published in 1901—was anticipated by an editorial appearing in the conservative newspaper, *La Unión*. The writer described two United States warships (the "Oregon" and the "Iowa") which had recently visited Valparaíso, and compared the entire United States to its two instruments of war: "Grey in color, monsters of strength, but ugly and stolid in design when contrasted with Chile's graceful, light, and delicate vessels. . . . In essence the North American ships are nothing more than brute power . . . and in their appointments they are merely functional and always ugly." [257]

In the two decades following the war, Chilean writers produced an impressive amount of literature glorifying traditional values, which they exhorted their nation to preserve unsullied.[258] Tran-

credo Pinochet Le-Brun began to urge greater technological progress in Latin America so that these nations could acquire the might
to protect and develop further their superior culture. And in a
work published in 1918 he dismissed Pan-Americanism as the
"sweetheart dress that the Colossus donned in order to court Latin
America." The Colossus was not interested in a marriage of love,
but one of economic expediency. Latin Americans were therefore
called upon to unite in resisting the encroachments of the United
States way of life, described as the very antithesis of all the noble
sentiments that Latin civilizations epitomized.[259]

The assumed struggle between secularism and materialism on
one hand, and culture and morality on the other also guided many
of the judgments of Emilio Vaïsse, better known by his pseudonym of Omer Emeth. In 1910 the wrath of this literary critic
for *El Mercurio* was aroused by a new publication of Enrique
Molina, a young but already widely respected Chilean *pensador*.
In the book under discussion Molina had praised certain aspects of
United States pragmatism. Emeth was shocked, and asserted that
pragmatism inevitably destroyed all spiritual values.[260] Ten years
later Emeth objected to the characterization of the United States,
in a new Molina book, as a moral country. "No country," asserted
Emeth, "in which there were 124,000 divorces in one year could
be considered moral." [261] And in 1925, when attacking still another
of Molina's works, Emeth observed: "In any one of the Old
World Latin nations there is more intellectual, moral, and religious vitality than in the United States." [262]

To Moisés Vargas, a high official in the Ministry of Public Education, United States schools reflected the national character.
Students were encouraged to concern themselves only with the
practical. Theory and beauty were ignored and the soul of the
students was allowed to atrophy. Only in physical training programs were United States schools superior to those of Chile.[263] To
the conservative organ *La Unión*, New York City, with its infernal
machines that shattered the nerves and removed the human element in economic and even social relations, was a frightening
microcosm of United States civilization.[264] To Eduardo Suárez

Mujica, representing his country in Washington, the greedy, covetous trusts, alleged to be virtually unchecked in their power, stood as the major symbol of United States culture,[265] while to Conservative Party leader Carlos Walker Martínez, the typical United States politician—uncultured, undignified, immoral and unscrupulous, but diabolically skilled in masterminding sordid deals—was the embodiment of the main national characteristics.[266]

Thus, fear of cultural as well as of economic imperialism, combined with a multi-faceted distrust of Washington diplomacy to determine Chile's early twentieth-century attitudes toward the United States. The question was: what could Chile do to protect its traditional values and its vital interests against the advancing tide of United States dominance in the American Hemisphere?

CHILE SEARCHES FOR AN EFFECTIVE POLICY TOWARD THE UNITED STATES

The Diego Portales tradition of suspecting the United States seemed to have been vindicated once again in the years between 1893 and 1920. But his admonition that Chile must pursue a policy of isolation was more than ever outmoded, if for no other reason than the importance that United States capital had assumed to the Chilean economy by 1920. The José Victorino Lastarria concept of finding in American international law a means of curbing the imperialistic tendencies of the United States and making it respect the principle of the absolute equality of nations did not receive serious attention until after 1920. In the meantime, statesmen began to investigate the feasibility of pursuing the Francisco Bilbao-advocated policy of acquiring strength to resist United States influence through diplomatic cooperation with other Latin-American nations.

Unlike Argentina, which throughout the period under discussion generally exhibited a penchant for going it alone when dealing with the United States, Chile—adopting a realistic appraisal of its own impotence—tended to favor presenting some semblance of a united Latin-American front to Washington. The decline of confidence and the mounting sense of inferiority, resulting from the general stagnation of the parliamentary period's wasted years, rendered Chile little inclined to grapple alone with the United States.

But what countries should comprise a united Latin-American bloc? Obviously troublemakers like Peru and Bolivia had no place in such a grouping. Moreover, there were many "tropical, turbulent, Indian" republics with which proud and race-conscious Chile did not wish to deal on terms of equality.[267] Nevertheless, a few isolated Chilean voices did cry out for the creation of a solid Latin-American bloc. Invariably, they justified their pleas on grounds of the need to resist the United States. Their programs, therefore, bore a striking similarity to the union plans that Bilbao and others had formulated in the 1850's and 1860's. In short, Chile's interest in Latin-American unity up to—and for that matter, well beyond —1920, arose principally from antagonism toward the United States.[268]

While Chile during the parliamentary period contributed little of practical significance to the formation of a united Latin America —it could not begin to do so until the dispute with Peru was settled—it assumed leadership in fashioning a South American, ABC power bloc.[269] A united ABC front gave promise for a brief period of being an effective instrument for blocking United States influence in South America. But ABC unity was short-lived, ending with Brazil's entry into the First World War. The rapport between Chile and Argentina survived a bit longer, but was always extremely tenuous,[270] and came to a spectacular end with the 1923 Pan-American Conference in Santiago.

Between 1892 and 1920 Chile resorted to one other means of offsetting United States influence. This was the attempt to strengthen ties with Europe in the hope that the Old World powers might act as a counterbalance to the United States.[271] But this approach was singularly ineffective in solving the "United States problem." England came increasingly to respect the wishes of the Colossus in American Hemisphere relations, and Germany, the ally toward which Chile looked most hopefully in the endeavor to thwart United States designs,[272] was crushed in the First World War. In the 1920's, therefore, Chile would face the task of beginning anew the search for a utopian United States policy: one that would provide Chile with the means to block United States diplomatic moves in South America that might redound to the disadvantage of Chilean national interests or pride.

6: CHILE ALMOST BREAKS WITH THE PAST: DOMESTIC DEVELOPMENT, 1920-1933

ALESSANDRI FAILS TO MAKE THE BREAK

Alessandri's Background

Arturo Alessandri, along with José Manuel Balmaceda and Carlos Ibáñez, is one of the three truly important Chilean presidents to have ruled the country since 1880. The manner in which he governed during his two presidential terms, 1920-1925, and 1932-1938, has determined to a large extent the nature of Chilean development since the end of the parliamentary period.

Alessandri brought a broad and varied background to the presidency. Born in 1868 in Linares, he was educated in Santiago where he earned his law degree in 1893. As an attorney for various foreign and domestic corporations, he acquired a reputation as a "sort of liberal conservative, although displaying on occasion interest in measures of social reform." [1] In addition to practicing law, Alessandri gained election in 1897 to the national Chamber of Deputies, representing Curicó, immediately south of Santiago province. The following year he served for a short period as Minister of Treasury. Ideally suited to politics, Alessandri rose rapidly in the ranks of the Liberal Party. He was intelligent, extremely quick-witted, an excellent writer, and naturally combative in temperament. In addition, his superb talent for oratory soon won respect for him among his colleagues in the Chamber of Deputies.

In 1915 Alessandri campaigned for election as senator from the far northern province of Tarapacá. It was in this campaign that he became for the first time an outspoken champion of social justice. The delighted masses of the nitrate pampa began to refer to him as the "Lion of Tarapacá." In the course of the campaign he fought a duel with Minister of Interior Pedro N. Montenegro—neither was injured—whom he accused of partial responsibility for the miserable social conditions in the north. Alessandri won the senate seat, and in 1918 served briefly as Minister of Interior.

There was abundant evidence to indicate that Alessandri was not a revolutionary to the degree sometimes suggested by his fiery oratory. Basically, he seemed to wish to adopt only a few changes in order to preserve a society similar to the nineteenth-century model.[2] In accepting the presidential nomination of the Liberal Alliance in 1920, Alessandri declared that the social problem had to be solved, "not only for reasons of humanity, but for considerations of economic expediency and for *conserving* [italics added] the social order." [3] That Alessandri was sufficiently moderate in his social philosophy not to shock traditionalist groups is indicated by the political debates of the 1920 presidential campaign, which failed to produce any genuine dispute on the social issue. Although social reshuffling was occasionally called for by Alessandri and his adherents, it is revealing that the man who most consistently campaigned for the Liberal Alliance by attacking the oligarchy was Rafael Maluenda. Doubt concerning the sincerity of this aspect of the campaign is occasioned by the fact that Maluenda even in 1920 was an essentially conservative individual who had dedicated himself to bringing about a still closer alliance between the Chilean middle class, of which he was a member, and the traditional upper classes.[4] In 1923 Maluenda was singled out by a well-informed observer as a defender of conservative, Hispanist values,[5] and today it would be difficult to find a more steadfast advocate of the status quo than this director of *El Mercurio*.

The 1920 platform of the Liberal Alliance, moreover, contained many planks that appealed to conservative interests.[6] And, it was only owing to entirely fortuitous political incidents that the National Union (the alliance of conservative political groups) failed to nominate as its standard-bearer against Alessandri the well-nigh universally respected Ismael Tocornal. In social thinking, Tocornal was fully as advanced as Alessandri.[7]

THE SIGNIFICANCE OF THE ALESSANDRI INAUGURATION

Chile may have been closer to civil war in 1920 than at any time since 1891. Economic dislocation following the end of the First

World War had resulted in vast unemployment, in strikes, and in labor violence. In this troubled ambient, anarchists and communists were working to bring about genuine revolution and class warfare. The government in 1919 had found it necessary to declare a state of siege in the depressed mining region.[8] The middle of the following year in far southern Magallanes a number of striking workers were shot down as they attempted to flee their union building, which had been set on fire.[9] At about the same time in the area just south of Concepción an eighty-three day coal workers' strike, marked by violence and attempts at harsh repression, ran its course. Even the most conservative elements in Chile began to wonder how much longer the proverbial patience of the lower classes could be relied upon. There were unmistakable indications that unless the ruling sectors made at least a few conciliatory gestures to the masses a wave of violence might sweep the land that prided itself on stability and order.

The inauguration of Arturo Alessandri was a conciliatory gesture to the hungry masses. The number of ballots recorded as cast for him was so close to that of his opponent, Luis Barros Borgoño, that the electoral tribunal established to determine the outcome could have ruled either way. But there were factors other than number of votes to be taken into consideration. By his demagogic speeches Alessandri had during his presidential campaign established closer ties with the Chilean lower classes than any previous candidate. No other presidential aspirant had ever bothered to make glittering promises to the forgotten Chilean proletariat. The poverty-stricken multitudes, who have since become skeptical, were in 1920 willing to accept at its face value the emotional oratory of Alessandri. Not questioning his sincerity, they enthusiastically flocked to his cause.[10] However, only those relatively few who were not disfranchised owing to illiteracy could give him their votes. Scarcely more than 8 per cent of the population participated in elections at this stage of Chilean political development.[11] Thus, notwithstanding the fact that it is often described as a victory achieved by the lower classes, the election of Alessandri was the result of votes from middle- and upper-class elements.

Politically sophisticated members of the opposition, realizing

that the Liberal Alliance was by and large as dedicated to preserving the old social structure as the National Union, knew that no
real damage would come to the established order by allowing Alessandri to be installed as president. They understood also that
Barros Borgoño was a symbol of the past twenty-eight years of
aristocratic, parliamentary rule, in short of stagnation and social
injustice. They did not object then when, guided by expediency,
the electoral tribunal decided in favor of Alessandri. The alternative choice might have meant civil war. So, while the masses had
not elected Alessandri, their devotion to him was instrumental in
assuring his inauguration.

Despite the essential dedication to the status quo of most voting
Chileans, regardless of whether they supported or opposed Alessandri, the year 1920 marked the beginning of a new and vital era in
Chilean history. From this time on Chile's leaders began to take
cognizance of the social problem, and this fact vastly altered the
traditional political climate. Until 1920, the ruled masses had
generally remained unquestioningly submissive to the rulers. Now
a change was occurring. Politicians in each of the major parties
sensed this, and accordingly began to acquire or at least to feign an
interest in the aspirations of the lower classes. Chilean politics suddenly became fraught with dynamic controversy, as the country's
rulers—representing an amalgam of urban and rural, middle- and
upper-class interests—debated how Chile should adjust to the new
social forces. For the first time since the civil war of 1891 Chile
had a vital and timely political issue.

What had injected the social question into Chilean politics was,
above all other factors, the nation's continuing population shift to
the cities. As Alberto Edwards has observed, Chile's population in
1920 was only three times as large as in the days of Portales, but
the urban population was twenty times greater.[12] By 1930, nearly
42 per cent of the Chilean populace lived in cities of 5,000 or
over.[13] During the decade of the 1920's, Santiago's population increased 31.7 per cent, Concepción's went up 19.2 per cent, Viña
del Mar's 33.4 per cent, and Iquique's 21.6 per cent.[14] Santiago in
1930 had close to 700,000 inhabitants. Combined with Concepción, Valparaíso, and Iquique, it accounted for approximately one-

third of the entire national population.[15] And the growth of the Chilean cities was due overwhelmingly, as it had always been, to internal migration, for between 1920 and 1930 the annual average by which immigrants arriving in the country exceeded emigrants was only 3,650.[16]

THE RULE OF ALESSANDRI, 1920-1924

The principal national question in 1920 concerned what Alessandri would do in the face of rapid urbanization and the accompanying demands of an urban proletariat. In analyzing Alessandri's approach it is only fair to keep in mind the incredible difficulties confronting him during his first four years of rule. To begin with, his campaign platform had been one largely of dissent, and it was not easy for him to switch to a positive, constructive program.[17] A more imposing difficulty was the division of the political parties in their approach to the social problem. Whatever he might wish to do or refrain from doing in regard to the matter, Alessandri could not even count on the united support of any of the parties in the Liberal Alliance. On the left wing of the Radical Party, for example, there was Deputy Pablo Ramírez, who stated that the 1920 elections should be the point of departure for a genuine and sweeping social revolution in Chile.[18] Radical Deputy Carlos Pinto Durán agreed, asserting that his party must transform itself into an instrument of social reform and dynamic progress. But Pinto Durán realistically observed: "There are very few Radicals who share these opinions." [19] The truth of this observation is suggested by the attitudes of old-time Radical leader Enrique Mac-Iver, who was convinced that Alessandri was bringing ruin to Chile by arousing lower-class interest in politics. This, feared Mac-Iver, would give the masses sufficient temerity to challenge "the only classes that know how to govern Chile." [20] Nor could Alessandri count on united, consistent support from the Liberals, as their party had "one foot in the National Union and the other in the Liberal Alliance." [21] Finally, the Democrats seemed to be as divided as ever between those interested in real social reform, and those concerned simply with advancing their careers.[22]

Plagued by dissension within and among the Liberal Alliance

parties that had supported him, Alessandri had also to contend with his political enemies in the National Union. Even in 1919, Conservative senators had unsuccessfully championed a labor code as comprehensive as anything Alessandri put forward in his first four years of rule.[23] After the election of Alessandri, the Conservatives continued their efforts to establish closer ties with the lower classes by posing as their only real defender.[24] Conservatives probably would have worked still more assiduously for social justice if they had controlled the executive branch of government and had thereby been in a position to receive credit among the masses for reform legislation. Be this as it may, they still vied quite successfully with Alessandri for lower-class support, thereby compounding the "Lion of Tarapacá's" political difficulties.

Alessandri also faced imposing economic problems.[25] As late as the end of 1922 the unemployment rate in the north had not been substantially lowered. The development and manufacture of cheaper synthetic forms of nitrate had drastically curtailed the demand for the natural Chilean product. Exploitation of many nitrate fields had ceased altogether.[26] On a tour of the depressed northern area, Minister of Interior Ismael Tocornal was shocked by the conditions of poverty that he encountered.[27] And in Santiago, between January and November of 1921, over 40,000 unemployed sought assistance from the Office of Labor.[28] In attempting to deal with the emergency, Alessandri resorted to paper-money issues, with the result that in 1925 the value of the peso was only half of what it had been in 1920.[29] Largely because of renewed inflation, the cost of living moved rapidly ahead of real wage increases.[30]

Although the vast economic difficulties made dramatic progress unlikely, regardless of policies pursued by the government, the national situation was not ameliorated by the listless incompetence of Alessandri's administration, nor by the low caliber of advisers with whom he surrounded himself.[31] He was unable to lead Chile even a step away from the old routine of sterile political maneuvering. Within four years he had appointed sixteen different cabinets,[32] but had been utterly incapable of goading Congress into speeding up the leisurely pace with which it was studying the ad-

ministration's labor and social security programs. The left wing
of the Radical Party began to charge an administration sellout to
the vested interests,[33] and in mid-July 1923 brilliant journalist Joaquín Edwards Bello wrote: "The country is disgusted. . . . the
tyranny of injustice and fraud prevails in order that the interests
of a small privileged group may be better served." [34]

At this juncture Alessandri decided to try bargaining with his
recalcitrant Congress. He promised free and honest elections for
March 1924, if a few minimum-wage laws, which comprised a
thoroughly insignificant portion of the over-all administration-sup-
ported program, were approved. The laws, intended to ameliorate
some of the worst abuses in the labor-capital structure, were duly
passed by Congress. Immediately, Liberal Alliance politicians,
alarmed by the amount of money the National Union was raising
for the March elections, began urging Alessandri to renege on his
part of the agreement. The president acquiesced and armed bands
were placed at the polls to prevent National Union adherents from
voting. In spite of this scandalous electoral intervention, the
Liberal Alliance triumphed by only a narrow margin.[35]

The newly-elected Congress proved no more cooperative than its
predecessor. Perhaps in an endeavor to win its good will, Alessandri
encouraged the Congress to pass a bill giving its members a salary
of two thousand pesos (about $120.00) per month, both for sena-
tors and deputies. In many ways this was an enlightened measure,
making it possible for talented Chileans of low income to serve
their country in the national congress. But the timing of the salary
law was disastrous. Congress had still not approved the long-pend-
ing labor and social code, unemployment continued to exist on a
massive scale, and many bureaucrats and military personnel had
not been paid for months.[36]

On September 3, a number of army officers were present in the
legislative galleries and gave vocal expression to their dissatisfaction with the just enacted congressional salary law. The following
day there were similar demonstrations, and on September 5 an
army-inspired coup d'état brought an end to ordinary constitutional
procedure. Alessandri, reduced to a mere puppet of the military,

obtained asylum in the United States Embassy and submitted his resignation as president on September 8.

An astute observer of Chilean politics has attributed Alessandri's failure to bring order and reform to the country to the following factors: the opposition of the senate, the loss of the enthusiastic support of the masses as the administration failed to fulfill campaign promises, the mistakes arising from the inexperience of the new administration, and the "doubtful moral character of some of Alessandri's assistants." [37] Perhaps there was a more fundamental reason for Alessandri's failure. Actually, given the prevailing attitudes of the leaders both in the Liberal Alliance and in the National Union, there was little reason to expect energetic attention to the fundamental issue of national life: the social problem. Alessandri and the majority of those who backed him were in accord with the Conservatives in the belief that the old system was still fundamentally viable and that the basic patterns of social and political hierarchy and stratification could be preserved. Obviously, private charity had failed to keep the masses content. It was still hoped, however, that governmental paternalism might succeed in supplying a modicum of material welfare to the proletariat, thereby making them content to remain in their place without challenging their betters. It was precisely in this regard that Alessandri encountered an insuperable difficulty. The economy of the country was in no condition to support the social benefits program the administration suggested, *unless* the upper classes were taxed. Very few of the political leaders, and certainly not Alessandri, were willing to resort to this expedient. Basically, what the governing classes had in mind, whether they were Liberals, Conservatives, Radicals, or Democrats, was a system of paternalism that could be financed through the ordinary national revenues—consisting principally of export taxes—augmented perhaps by additional regressive taxes, thus leaving the upper-income group essentially free from direct imposts. There was simply not enough government income to finance such a system in the 1920-1924 period. The "revolution of 1920" was never envisioned by most of its instigators as anything more than a program of mild palliatives; but it was unable to furnish even the palliatives.

MILITARY INTERVENTION, 1924-1925

Three factors were uppermost in leading to military intervention in Chilean politics, commencing with the September 5 *coup*.[38] To begin with there was the element of simple opportunism, apparent primarily in the desire of the officers to gain better salaries and living conditions.[39] In addition there was a group in the army that, ashamed of Chile's drifting and inertia during the past generation, wished to head a national revitalization movement, based fundamentally upon the attempt to find a solution to the social problem.[40] Finally, there existed a reactionary element that was opposed to the increasing articulateness of the masses which had been accelerated to some degree by Alessandri. This group wished to restore the country to the days of parliamentary rule when the social problem had been ignored. The champions of reaction in the armed forces were the first to gain control of the government following the September military power-grab.

On September 5 Alessandri had submitted to the military by appointing General Luis Altamirano Minister of the Interior. Altamirano then selected as the remainder of the short-lived cabinet Colonel Juan P. Bennett, Admiral Francisco Neff, and three civilians: Emilio Bello Codesido of the Democratic Liberal Party, Gregorio Amunátegui of the Liberals, and Angel Guarello of the Democrats.[41] When Alessandri on September 8 submitted his resignation, Congress refused to accept it, voting the president instead a six-month leave of absence. This move annoyed the military members of the new cabinet who wanted to be rid of Alessandri once and for all. At the same time, these men realized the need to gain popular support before proceeding to move overtly against the "Lion of Tarapacá." Accordingly they pressured Congress to pass the long-discussed labor and social code. Congress duly approved laws granting full legal protection to labor organizations, providing for labor contracts with many restrictions on employers, and establishing unemployment and accident insurance. Only one senator and one deputy opposed the legislation which erected the foundation for the Chilean labor-protection structure that endures to the present day.[42]

Having mollified public opinion by forcing through the labor legislation, the military members of the cabinet proceeded to show their true colors. Applying some pressure, they obtained the resignation of the civilian members on September 10. This left Altamirano, Bennett, and Neff in power as a self-styled junta of government (*junta de gobierno*). The junta at once canceled the presidential leave-of-absence arrangement, accepting instead Alessandri's resignation. Next, the junta disbanded Congress, promising at the same time promptly to hold presidential elections. But the junta had no intention of allowing the public will to prevail. Now rid of Alessandri, it wished to see the powers of government placed in the hands of a safe and reliable individual who would regard the events that had transpired since 1920 as a bad dream to be quickly effaced from memory. Therefore, the junta gave tacit approval to the candidate nominated by the National Union, Ladislao Errázuriz. General Bennett demurred mildly, realizing the danger of turning the presidency over to a man who was so overtly a symbol of the past. But his voice was not heeded.[43]

Profoundly alarmed by political developments, Eliodoro Yáñez wrote to Joaquín Edwards Bello, the man he had chosen to help mold the newspaper *La Nación* into one of the country's finest:

> Like you, I believe that among the circles of Santiago there is a profound incomprehension of the universal movement toward democracy. . . . To advance today a presidential candidate who embodies the conservative, oligarchical tendencies, is to jeopardize the future tranquility of the country. . . . The transcendent phenomenon of modern times is the admission of the popular classes into political life. Throughout the world the defenders of classical liberalism have been learning this truth, and Chile will be no exception. The evolution that has been occurring has brought an end to castes, to special privileges, and to authoritarianism, and has raised attentiveness to the social problem, which is in large measure an economic problem, to the first level of state obligations.[44]

Yáñez was not alone in realizing what was best for the national interests. The majority of the armed forces' officers opposed the restoration to power of a discredited oligarchy. Since the early part of the century, and particularly after 1912, army officers—

generally in the lieutenant to lieutenant-colonel category—had begun to concern themselves over the background of abject poverty from which the majority of enlisted men came. The officers, mainly of middle-class origins, began at the same time to resent the mean estate in which low salaries and spiralling inflation forced them to live. And they worried that upon their death there would not be adequate protection for surviving family members. In short, the army officers acquired an interest in their country's social problem.[45] Waxing impatient over continuing national stagnation, they dreamed of playing a role in restoring Chile to the grandeur of the 1880's—and more, of transforming their country into a modern and dynamic continental leader.

Young officers, many of them inspired by such a vision, met on September 4 and formed the military junta (junta militar), hoping that through this organization they might be able to turn the coup planned for the following day into a genuine revolution of national revitalization. Originally numbering twenty-three, the military junta membership soon rose to thirty-five army officers, most of them majors.[46] Prominent among the junta's members were Carlos Ibáñez del Campo, Bartolomé Blanche, Marmaduke Grove, Oscar Fenner, Alejandro Lazo, Mario Bravo, and Arturo Ahumada.[47]

Realizing that its purposes were being betrayed by the three conservative military men who controlled the government after September 10, the military junta began to advance its own program, one that called for an increased degree of state economic planning aimed at achieving rapid national progress. Specifically, the military junta advocated calling a constituent assembly in which all social, political, and administrative groups would have representation, creating a ministry of labor, establishing price controls on goods of prime necessity, and raising the wages of laborers. The hope that the military junta placed in its program is revealed in a bulletin distributed to its members: "When we succeed in our self-imposed mission of regenerating the country and placing it upon a new and sound basis, then the page that we are writing in history will redound to the eternal glory of the armed forces.[48]

In a move of particular significance, the military junta tried to establish close connections with the urban proletariat and with labor organizations, so as to provide its program of national revitalization with a broad base of support. This was one of the few times that Chilean middle-class sectors, outside of a handful of communists, had seriously endeavored to form an alliance with the lower classes. Playing a leading role in the move to unite army and proletarian elements was one of the most worthy figures of Chilean political and military annals, the largely unacclaimed Bartolomé Blanche, soon to be appointed Subminister of War.[49]

Although the military junta purposely tried to avoid contact with traditional circles,[50] it soon found itself subjected to pressures from them. Ismael Tocornal tried in vain to persuade the military junta to resolve its growing disagreement with the junta of government,[51] while Eliodoro Yáñez encouraged it to maintain its role of opposition.[52] By working through the military junta, as well as by organizing the friends of the exiled Alessandri and the left-wing Radicals, Yáñez hoped to block the imposition of Ladislao Errázuriz as president of the republic. His plans sustained an apparently severe setback when the older army leaders, supported by the traditionally conservative navy, brought about the suppression of the military junta. But the victory of those who insisted upon pretending that Chile was the same in 1925 as in 1900 proved short-lived. On January 23, 1925, another bloodless military coup d'état took place, led by Carlos Ibáñez and Marmaduke Grove. The junta of government was ousted, the candidacy of Ladislao Errázuriz was suppressed, and Arturo Alessandri was invited to return to serve out the remainder of his presidential term.[53]

For a time it seemed that the navy and other conservative elements would resort to civil war to reverse the unwelcome turn of events. But Agustín Edwards in a brilliant mission of mediation dissuaded the naval officers from their intentions.[54] With a calm and settled atmosphere at last prevailing, a newly-appointed, three-man junta[55] awaited the return of the "Lion of Tarapacá."

THE LAST DAYS OF THE FIRST ALESSANDRI ADMINISTRATION AND THE RISE OF CARLOS IBÁÑEZ, 1925-1926

Alessandri reassumed his presidential powers on March 20, 1925. He had eight months still to serve of his original five-year term.

Enjoying the support of the army and of Ibáñez who became
Minister of War, he was able now to embark upon a program of
solid achievements. A permanent electoral registry was created to
inscribe voters and guarantee the honesty and freedom of elections,
a nominal impost was placed on incomes that exceeded ten thousand pesos per year,[56] and upon the recommendation of a United
States financial commission headed by Edwin Kemmerer a Central
Bank was established, with one of its functions being to peg the
peso at the equivalent of $0.1217.[57]

During this second installment of his term Alessandri presided
also over the birth of a new constitution. To frame the instrument
the Chief Executive summoned a consultative commission consisting of approximately 200 individuals representing all the political parties, as well as industry, commerce, and the liberal professions. The constitution drafted by the commission was notable
for the political and social changes introduced, and for the alteration of Church-State relations.[58]

Politically, the constitution ended the parliamentary system of
government which had prevailed since 1892, restoring to the chief
executive the broad and sweeping powers originally intended by
the framers of the 1833 instrument. According to the new charter,
the president, who was to be elected to a six-year term by direct
suffrage and could not stand for immediate re-election, enjoyed
power to dismiss at his own discretion the cabinet, members of
which could not be deputies or senators. The 1925 constitution
included also an important labor and social code that, theoretically at least, substituted state planning for the old concepts
of classical liberalism.[59] The state was declared to have the duty to
limit rights of property ownership in the interest of the common
good, to safeguard the rights of labor, and to provide for social
security and the maintenance of public health.[60] Finally, the new
instrument provided for the separation of Church and State. This
hotly contended measure, urged by Radicals and many Liberals
and opposed by Conservatives, produced the most spirited political
discussion since the turn-of-the-century debate as to whether there
should be war with Argentina.

In 1922 Father Alejandro Vicuña had published a book pre-
dicting the moral ruin of all Chile if separation occurred.[61] A

large and powerful group of Catholics agreed with this dire prediction. Thus, Conservative Party president Juan Enrique Concha
Subercaseaux stated in 1923: "We are opposed to separation of
Church and State because we oppose an atheistic state." [62] In his
April 1923 pastoral letter, Gilberto Fuenzalida Guzmán, bishop of
Concepción, accused Masons of having introduced the concept of
secularism into Chilean politics and added: "Today we face a new
menace. An anti-Christian party [the Radical Party] has unleashed
a doctrinaire campaign against the religious duties of the State and
against the rights of the Church." [63] In the same period, the executive commission of the Conservative Party condemned the Radical-
Liberal supported program as an all-out attempt to destroy the
Catholic faith.[64] On April 24, 1923, the widely admired and generally moderate archibishop of Santiago, Crescente Errázuriz,
issued a pastoral admonishing all Catholics that they must reject
in toto the attempt to separate Church and State. Such a move,
the prelate continued, would signify an affront to God, a public
and solemn declaration on the part of Chile that God does not
exist. Action of this sort, stated Errázuriz, would mean that "the
Christ of the Andes ought no longer to extend His blessings to
us." [65]

A year after the Errázuriz pastoral, a manifesto appeared in the
conservative organ, *El Diario Ilustrado*. Signed by over 300 prominent members of Chile's high society, the document declared that
the move to separate Church and State was a declaration of war
against Jesus Christ, and called on Chileans to be ready to find
sublime martyrdom in defense of God.[66] The August 2, 1925, issue
of *El Diario Ilustrado* contained a declaration signed by Luisa
Fernández de García Huidobro, president of the Patriotic Union
of Chilean Women Leaders, Enrique Cañas Flores, national secretary of the Young Catholics of Chile, Teresa Ossandón Guzmán,
president of the Association of Young Catholic Women, and
Natalia Rubio, president of the Women's Syndicates, condemning
the proposed constitution and the lay state. The declaration
stated: "All Catholics who love God, who confess God and defend Him publicly and privately have the moral obligation not to
accept the denial or rejection of God Himself, which is incorpo-

rated into what is intended to be the highest political instrument of the nation." Far-right groups also founded the organization known as TEA (Tenacity, Enthusiasm, Abnegation), which among other activities blew up the house of the Grand Master of the Masonic Lodge in Santiago, and carried out a physical attack against Minister of War Luis Brieba.[67]

President Alessandri issued a call for a plebiscite to be held in September 1925 to consider the newly drafted constitution. Conservatives overwhelmingly opposed the instrument, primarily because of the separation provision. Aware of their impotence to prevent its approval in a national balloting, some of them began to disparage the notion of consulting the will of the people. Thus Gonzalo Bulnes testily observed: "There are not three hundred persons in Chile competent to judge a constitution." [68]

On entirely different grounds, the Radical Party also opposed ratification of the new constitution. The party justified its stand by charging that the instrument contained the seeds of executive tyranny.[69] Expediency was probably the real factor in determining the Radical position. Radicals had by this time come to enjoy great success in congressional elections. But they were still unable to coordinate their strength on a nationwide basis to the extent necessary to elect a president, and therefore preferred the continuance of parliamentary government.

Conservatives and Radicals, however, were not able to combine in opposing the constitution. Voters at the plebiscite were to be asked to choose one of three alternatives: total approval of the constitution, total rejection, or approval of the instrument provided it was altered to permit the continuance of parliamentary government. Conservatives desired the second alternative and Radicals were committed to the third. Realizing they could not obtain majority support for their respective preferences, both Conservatives and Radicals abstained, by and large, from going to the polls. The constitution was approved therefore through a plebiscite in which less than half of the registered voters participated.[70]

With the constitution officially sanctioned by the votes of at least some of the people, the Chilean hierarchy decided to accept their defeat gracefully. They issued a joint pastoral expressing hope for the future safety of the Church, and conceding that at least the State had thus far refrained from such acts of persecution as had accompanied separation in so many other countries.[71]

Alessandri had his new constitution, and therefore appeared to have succeeded where Balmaceda had failed: the fundamental law of the land now clearly provided that in matters of administration the office of the executive was supreme over the legislature. But Alessandri was still plagued by difficulties. Minister of War Carlos Ibáñez announced his candidacy for the forthcoming presidential elections, and then refused to heed Alessandri's urgings that he resign his cabinet post before beginning his active campaign. Perceiving that even under the new constitution he could control neither his cabinet nor the military, Alessandri for the second time renounced the presidential office. His original term was still two months short of expiration.[72]

Ibáñez, although he had the support of the right wing of the Liberal Party and of many Conservatives,[73] offered to withdraw from the contest if the nation's political parties could form a united front and agree to support one candidate. It is commonly suggested that Ibáñez was simply making a hypocritical gesture, confident that the politicos would find it impossible to choose a single candidate.[74] Be this as it may, the major parties were able to unite in supporting the candidacy of Emilio Figueroa Larraín. A man of integrity, common sense, and ingratiating personality, Figueroa had been a firm supporter of Balmaceda, and had subsequently served his country with distinction in various high diplomatic posts.

When the political parties complied with the conditons he had imposed, Ibáñez withdrew from the campaign. However, last-minute opposition to Figueroa was provided by the Social Republican Union of Chilean Wage Earners (*Unión Social Republicana de Asalariados de Chile*). Professing to represent proletarian interests and enjoying support from many communists and Marxian socialists, the Wage Earners demanded total nationalization of the means of production. With José Santos Salas as their standard-bearer the Wage Earners, who had organized their political machinery in only a few days' time, won approximately 75,000 votes in the October elections. While Figueroa Larraín was handily elected, receiving over 184,000 ballots,[75] the left had given an impressive indication of its strength.[76]

The Figueroa inauguration, occurring on December 23, impressed various Chileans as something of a Bourbon restoration. *El Mercurio* revealed its apprehension, observing that the working classes of Chile were now articulate as never before, and that the key to the success of the new regime would be its ability to deal in an enlightened manner with the social problem. The Santiago daily was plainly doubtful that Figueroa could respond adequately to the central challenge of the times.[77] Moreover, Figueroa lacked two qualities demanded by the troubled situation: driving energy and the ability to assert strong leadership at moments of crisis.[78] It was soon apparent that he was able neither to suppress nor to utilize the new social forces in Chile. Nor was he competent to cope with powerful reactionary interests that still hoped to restore the pre-Alessandri status quo. Above all, he could not resolve the old issue that had led to the downfall of Balmaceda: the clash between executive and legislative power.

The Chamber of Deputies in 1926 elected as its president the staunch Conservative, Rafael Luis Gumucio. Unhappy with the new constitution, especially its provision for Church-State separation, Gumucio was apparently anxious to embarrass and even to topple the Figueroa administration, hoping that in the resultant confusion and power scramble the Conservatives could acquire control, scrap the 1925 constitution, and nullify the political and social innovations of the past several years. Under Gumucio's leadership, the deputies in 1926 refused to approve the proposed budget. Exercising a power granted by the new constitution, Figueroa decreed the budget to be in effect even though it lacked congressional approbation. Nevertheless, Figueroa was greatly distressed by the situation, feeling he could not effectively govern without the full support of Congress. Manuel Rivas Vicuña, appointed Minister of Interior at this time of crisis, by using tact and resorting to skillful maneuvering, finally won the approval of the deputies for the budget. This accomplishment provoked a split within the cabinet. Minister of War Ibáñez was convinced that the times required stronghanded action rather than tact and maneuvering. He maintained that the president should, by utilizing legally provided emergency powers, impose his will upon Congress and thereby infuse life into the new constitution that had not as yet actually begun to function. Ibáñez soon succeeded in having himself elevated to the Minister of Interior post. After announcing the cabinet change, President Figueroa, presumably not inclined to contend further with the ponderous national problems, resigned the executive office.

In the subsequent presidental elections of May 22, 1927, which were considerably less than a shining example of free, democratic processes, an unopposed Ibáñez received over 230,000 votes.[79] A man who three years earlier was a little known major in command of the national cavalry school was now the president of the republic.[80]

IBÁÑEZ THE MAN

Although never an original political theorist, Carlos Ibáñez del Campo was little less than a genius in the art of political maneuvering, of manipulating men, and of extracting and blending together the ideas of others. This consummate opportunist who loved power as an end in itself was also one of the most complex, enigmatic persons ever to dominate a Latin-American country.[81] His personality seemed almost to consist of contradictions. Personally honest, Ibáñez did not demand this virtue of the relatives and friends with whom he surrounded himself in office. While he was capable of cold-blooded scheming and manipulating—and did not shy away from the occasional use of force and violence to obtain and to regain power—he was incapable of plunging to the depths of depravity or terrorism in pursuing his objective. Like Getulio Vargas of Brazil, Carlos Ibáñez possessed the redeeming feature of moderation. But the Ibáñez character was essentially marred by a certain lack of integrity. In obtaining his ends, Ibáñez seemed consistently to prefer the use of guile and cunning to candor. He did what the expediency of the moment dictated, rather than what principles commanded. Perhaps he acted in this manner because he lacked a morally rooted set of purposes which he strove consistently to achieve. Had Ibáñez possessed deep moral convictions he might have been the greatest figure in Chilean politics. And yet, possessing them, might he not have been a bloodthirsty fanatic?

In 1927 the supreme accomplishment of Ibáñez was to achieve a balance between leading and being led by the dynamic forces that had begun to impél Chile toward a genuine national rehabilitation. There is no question that Carlos Ibáñez, like most of the members of the short-lived military junta, had felt he had a principal role to play in the mission of restoring disciplined constitutional regularity and of reordering the national existence so that Chile might emerge as a strong, prosperous, modern republic. It is equally certain that Ibáñez could not himself have sparked a movement of national regeneration. Still, he knew how to coordinate the seething forces of the era into an effective whole, and how to dash down extremists of all types so as to prevent disparate energies from canceling each other out. Because of these abilities, Ibáñez managed to preside over the four most active, fruitful years of national existence that Chile had enjoyed since the War of the Pacific. The institutional structure that has governed Chile down to the present day was fashioned by Ibáñez between 1927 and 1931.

A new, vibrant optimism pervaded Chile after 1925, resulting in large measure from the return of prosperity. Chileans began to exude confidence that their country was well on the way to reacquiring the daring spirit of progress, somehow lost during the parliamentary period. National power and affluence seemed an imminent likelihood. Ibáñez caught this mood of the times, and attacked the extreme rightist forces that opposed activism and change. On the other hand, he stopped far short of being a real revolutionist. He was enough of a traditionalist to lash out also against the extreme left that desired a genuine social upheaval. Ibáñez did more to ease the material suffering of the lower classes and to provide them with education than any man who had held presidential powers in the twentieth century. And yet he insisted upon doing this in a strictly paternalistic manner. He did not wish labor to obtain sufficient power to protect its own interests.

Throughout his life Ibáñez consistently advocated, and occasionally actually worked for, amelioration of the social problem. But the wily politician never pursued this goal with the singleness of purpose of a dedicated crusader. Often, in fact, he betrayed the interests of the masses. Yet as the Ibáñez funeral procession in 1960 made its way from the Santiago Cathedral to the cemetery, tens of thousands of the dirty and the ragged, the lame and the undernourished, struggled for a last look at the coffin, pulled out their handkerchiefs to wave a token farewell to the doughty general who had succumbed to cancer, and then successfully stormed the cemetery gates—which had been rudely closed—so that they might see the coffin placed finally in the ground. Anyone who witnessed these events cannot doubt that Ibáñez had managed somehow to establish a bond of sympathy with the Chilean masses. They knew he had often betrayed them, and they loved him still. Ibáñez had a way like that with people.

IBÁÑEZ DECIDES THE COUNTRY NEEDS HIM, 1926-1927

It is frequently assumed that by early 1925 Ibáñez was already wildly ambitious to become president of Chile. Yet it is possible that not until sometime after April of 1926 did he come to feel that circumstances demanded that he take charge of the country's destinies. In that month Ibáñez appeared in the Chamber of Deputies to defend the army against a series of charges that it was plotting to take control of the government. In denying these assertions and disavowing his own political ambitions, Ibáñez gave a remarkable exposition of his views on Chile's immediate situation and of his hopes for the nation's future. Since 1920, he recalled, he had been vitally concerned over Chilean decadence and over the proper role of the army in a program of national regeneration. The parliamentary period had represented the dictatorship of irresponsibility. This was ended finally by the September 5, 1924, coup d'état. Spurred on at this time by overwhelming public opinion and desiring to act in accordance with its proud tradition as the founder of the republic and defender of national dignity and honor, the army moved to end the period of stagnation. Without army action, declared Ibáñez, Chile would not have had its social and sanitation laws, its tax on incomes, its central bank, or its retirement fund for public employees. The politicians must now assume responsibility in carrying forward Chile's new and progressive program. But if politicians persisted in placing their own self-interest above the nation's good, then, stated Ibáñez: ". . . the army will know its duty." [82]

Upon hearing these courageous and perceptive words from the Minister of War, the deputies staged the sort of scene that might well have convinced a witness that little could be expected from Congress in providing the form of leadership that Chile so urgently needed. Shouting, gesticulating, and prancing about, the deputies seemed all to talk at once. For many minutes the president of the chamber, Rafael Luis Gumucio, was unable to restore order. When a semblance of calm finally returned, Ibáñez tried to continue his observations and to defend an education plan that the administration was backing. But the shouted insults of heckling deputies led by Jorge Alessandri, one of Arturo's sons, made it impossible for Ibáñez to develop his argument. When the military man finally left the chamber, it is likely that whatever confidence he might once have had in the abilities of Chile's traditional politicians to provide worthy leadership was shattered. Probably it is to the credit of Ibáñez that within a year he acted in accordance with his conviction that unusual and even extraconstitutional measures were necessary to pull Chile out of the morass in which the politicians seemed content to allow their country to remain.

Sources of Support for Ibáñez

Once in the presidency, the fifty-year-old Ibáñez proceeded to demonstrate his uncanny ability to win support from amazingly varied quarters, appearing indeed to be all things to all men. The chameleonic leader appealed to far-right groups as the man who would return his country to the iron discipline of the Portales era.[83] Conservative Party president Arturo Lyon Peña delighted at first in the Ibáñez administration, expecting from it a curtailment of suffrage rights, a repudiation of "the monstrous belief in equality," and a general restoration of power to the landowners, "who alone understand how to govern." [84] On the other hand, José Santos Salas, the extreme leftist champion of the proletariat whose presidential bid in 1925 had been supported by communists, regarded Ibáñez on the eve of his election as the indispensable man for the republic.[85] Santos expected Ibáñez to take drastic measures to elevate the lower classes and to reduce the power of the traditional aristocracy. Similar expectations led the Democrat Party[86] as well as Juan Antonio Ríos, Dr. Leonardo Guzmán, and other Radical Party members to support the Ibáñez administration.[87] Ibañista Radicals found the political philosophy of their early leader Valentín Letelier useful in justifying their position: "There are times when alleged concern with traditional personal liberty acts only to block real social progress. In such times, the true liberals are those who advocate authoritarianism." [88] Liberal Party member Ismael Edwards Matte admired Ibáñez for defending economic individualism,[89] while somewhat strangely another Liberal, Jorge Gustavo Silva, praised the president for his willingness to abandon classical liberalism and to introduce a suitable measure of socialism.[90] El Mercurio congratulated Ibáñez for restoring responsibility and respect for work.[91] Journalist Carlos Silva Vildósola was delighted by the administration's concern with education and fiscal stability, while fellow-journalist Augusto Iglesias thanked Ibáñez for having at last fulfilled in Chile the dream of Balmaceda[92]—whatever that meant. Finally, devout Catholic Jorge Délano saw in Ibáñez' rise to power the repudiation of materialistic capitalism.

THE CULT OF FASCISM AND THE ADVOCATES OF THE
CORPORATE STATE ADD TO THE SUPPORT OF IBÁÑEZ

Chile's fascistically-inclined intellectuals also approved of Ibáñez, regarding him as Chile's man of destiny. Beginning in the mid-1920's, it had become quite fashionable to sing the praises of fascism. As early as 1923, El Mercurio had concluded that the only people who said evil things about fascism were communists, while Las Ultimas Noticias almost simultaneously had proclaimed:

"What Chile needs is a Mussolini." [93] Three years later *El Mercurio* periodically accorded fulsome praise to fascism, and implied that Chile should follow the patterns being established in Spain by Primo de Rivera.[94]

Fascism seemed particularly to appeal to Chilean churchmen. In part, this was a reflection of the situation in Europe, where many of the clergy had welcomed the ideology of the corporate state. In a 1924 pastoral Bishop Gilberto Fuenzalida Guzmán of Concepción praised fascism for the manner in which it had restored morality to Italy, while at the same time solving all of that country's major problems.[95] Bishop Martín Rücker of Chillan was impressed with the accomplishments of Italy under Mussolini, and regarded fascism as the only means for stemming communism.[96] Perhaps fascism's most assiduous propagandist in Chile was Father Guillermo Viviani Contreras who, by 1919, was convinced that liberalism on one hand and socialism on the other were destroying cultural and spiritual values and that the world could only be saved by a return to the corporate structure of the middle ages.[97] In 1927 the priest was certain that Benito Mussolini and Miguel Primo de Rivera had begun to apply the world-saving formulas.[98] With the signing of the accord between Mussolini and the Vatican in early 1929, the encomiums which churchmen heaped upon the Italian dictator and his system of government reached a new peak. Archbishop Crescente Errázuriz stated that by signing the pact Mussolini had provided the Church with one of the great days in its history,[99] while the official organ of the Chilean hierarchy concluded that Italy was showing the world how to triumph over the evils of the liberal creed.[100] Not only had Mussolini routed the defenders of pseudo-democracy, the ecclesiastical journal added, but he had crushed the doctrines and the parties of international Masonry.[101]

Many Conservatives now gave enthusiastic support to the concepts of the corporate state, often motivated by their continuing dismay over the separation of Church and State accomplished by the 1925 constitution. Traditionally, the Conservative Party had been the Catholic party.[102] So long as Church-State union had prevailed, Catholic groups had found encouragement of government-administered social justice measures a valuable means of gaining credit for the Church and Conservative Party among the lower classes. With separation of Church and State, however, the Church and the Conservative Party could no longer directly benefit from state-enacted social legislation. Rather, the Liberal, Radical, and Masonic bureaucracy that had gained control of national institutions would become the beneficiary.[103] Conservatives were alarmed not only because the power position of the Church would decline, but because they feared that social programs devised by a non-Catholic oriented group would lack moral foundation and guidance.

The principal objective of Conservatives following approval of the 1925 constitution was to curtail or overthrow the anticlerical middle- and upper-class alliance that had by shrewd organization and political sagacity, abetted by the fact that suffrage was denied to the vast majority of the population, scored a striking victory. One means would have been to agitate for greater extension of voting rights, banking on the traditional utility of the faith in influencing the masses. Because of their social philosophy, Conservatives were resolutely opposed to direct democracy. The acceptable method, therefore, appeared to be to work for social betterment through channels outside of, and at a subsidiary level to, the central government's bureaucracy, that is, through Catholic Action groups and charity organizations operated privately or in conjunction with local government. The increased tempo of Catholic social work after 1925 was striking,[104] and at least in part this was owing to the desire of the Church and its allies to gain the good will of the masses and through their support to begin to move toward adoption of a new national charter providing for a corporate state.

Once a corporate-state structure was adopted the Church and its supporters could, by exercising their influence at the grass-roots level of all functional-interest groups, secure representatives of those groups in the national legislative body who were safely Catholic. Thus, the tainted bureaucracy would be dethroned. Beyond this, a small aristocracy of owners and employers, demanding nothing more than equal representation with the rank-and-file workers in each guild or syndicate that was empowered to choose delegates to the national corporate assembly, could dominate the political structure and forestall the rise of genuine class competition and the give-and-take of social pluralism. The paternalistic, stratified social structure would thus be safeguarded.

This is what the corporate state signified to many of its Chilean advocates. It is readily understandable, then, that in the period immediately following the separation of Church and State—between 1925 and 1930—conservative Catholic elements would begin to express strong favor for the corporate state and to find encouragement in indications that the government of Ibáñez might be drifting toward fascism. It would be entirely misleading to suggest that support for fascism and the corporate state during the Ibáñez regime came exclusively from conservative Catholics. But it is significant that the most carefully rationalized support for them, favoring them as philosophically good, came from Catholic rightists. Other elements favored fascism and its corporate political structure only because they regarded them pragmatically as the means most likely to bring rapid material development to Chile.

Indications of pro-fascist sentiments were abundant among military officers.[105] And high officials in the Ibáñez government made no effort to hide their admiration of fascism. Minister of Foreign Relations Conrado Ríos Gallardo referred to fascism as the only force of national rejuvenation in the world, and praised Italy as the first country in Europe effectively to contain communism. Minister Ríos added: "Chile has been the first country in South America to do so." [106] Armando Labra Carvajal, an important Radical Party member and Subminister of Interior for Ibáñez, published in 1928 El fascismo, a book arguing that governments based on classical liberalism were archaic mementos of the past. Fascism, asserted Labra, had made Italy prosperous and therefore should be practiced by all countries desiring rapid economic advance.[107] The pages of the official government newspaper featured pro-fascist articles by some of the country's leading journalists,[108] one of whom announced that throughout the world fascism would inevitably replace the discredited forms of parliamentary and liberal democratic government.[109]

Taking advantage of the cult of fascism in Chile, Ibáñez enjoyed hearing himself described as a Chilean Mussolini.[110] An official circular of the Chilean Ministry of Foreign Relations, distributed to all diplomatic agents abroad, drew a parallel between Ibáñez and Mussolini, while Guillermo Gacitúa, Chile's consul in Boston, described Ibáñez—with the approval of the ambassador in Washington, Miguel Cruchaga—as a New World Mussolini.[111] Furthermore, Ibáñez made frequent requests to the Chilean embassies in Italy and Spain to provide him with information about the systems and techniques of government being developed by Mussolini[112] and Primo de Rivera.[113] In response to these requests, he received from his diplomatic agents in 1928 such advice as:

> . . . the concept of liberty should not become a dogma in which we believe only because of faith rather than rational considerations. . . . The state must expand its operations, and concern itself with social problems. The political school of classical liberalism is daily losing more partisans. . . . Left to their own resources, the people of Chile cannot evolve satisfactorily; they require force to stimulate, guide, counsel and command them.[114]

These words undoubtedly convinced Ibáñez all the more of the validity of what journalist Joaquín Edwards Bello had written earlier in the same year: "The Chilean . . . is docile and anxious to find discipline. Without firm control, our people have never produced good results." [115]

Despite his apparent infatuation with fascism, Ibáñez rejected the extremes of the new Italian and Spanish systems. Against the counsel of his own ministers he left the Chilean private educational system relatively free, refusing to transform the schools into propaganda mills.[116] Nor did Ibáñez ever try to control public opinion to the extent attempted by more zealous fascist dictators.[117] Still, without question, Ibáñez found the cult of fascism in Chile useful to his purposes, and adorned his administration with many fascist trappings.

Ibáñez Represses His Enemies

There were, of course, many Chileans who despised fascism and all of its accoutrements. They joined with other citizens who for a wide variety of reasons opposed Ibáñez. The members of the opposition were not long in discovering that theirs was a dangerous position. Those who opposed too strenuously were apt to find themselves either in jail or banished from the land. Labor leaders in particular were dealt with harshly, usually on the pretext that international communism, in collusion with Chile's labor organizations, was plotting to gain control of the country. The Red menace, probably exaggerated by Ibáñez, also proved most effective as an excuse for disposing of a broad assortment of other political opponents.[118] Ibáñez, furthermore, curtailed freedom of the press, subjecting the papers to rigorous censorship.[119] In a shockingly arbitrary action he seized Eliodoro Yáñez' distinguished daily, *La Nación*, in 1927, and converted it into the mouthpiece of the government.[120]

THE ACCOMPLISHMENTS AND THE SHORTCOMINGS OF THE IBÁÑEZ ADMINISTRATION

Having established his right to do as he pleased, free from effective political opposition, Ibáñez proceeded to accomplish much in the way of lasting benefit for Chile.[121] The public services were reorganized and for the first time some degree of scientific efficiency was introduced into the Chilean bureaucracy.[122] An institute of industrial credit—it was transformed into the State Bank (*Banco del Estado*) in 1953—was created to encourage industrialization. The entire structure of agricultural credit was overhauled so as to make loans available for small-scale landowners and to encourage agricultural colonization.[123] In 1929 agricultural cooperatives were established and the Ministry of Southern Property—forerunner of the present Ministry of Lands and Colonization—came into being. George McBride, who a few years later wrote the classic study on the shortcomings of the Chilean landowning structure,[124] was highly encouraged by the Ibáñez approach to agriculture, seeing in it considerable promise for solution of the multi-faceted agrarian problem.[125]

Perhaps the greatest of all the Ibáñez-regime contributions was the education reform law of 1928,[126] largely the work of Education Minister José Santo Salas—who shortly thereafter quarreled with the dictator and went into exile. This reform measure constituted the most enlightened endeavor that Chileans have undertaken in the twentieth century to create an educational system capable of turning out men with practical knowledge and respect for work and technology.[127] The new education law was warmly praised by such distinguished intellectuals as Luis Galdames and Gabriela Mistral, but roundly denounced by conservative elements.[128]

Promising advances in economic development were also made during the years of the dictatorship. The rates of production of copper, iron, nitrates, and coal in the 1926-1930 period were far ahead of those of 1921-1925.[129] The tariff protection and easier credit provided by the Ibáñez administration stimulated the industrialization process and for the first time in the nation's history industrial capital came to exceed agricultural investment.[130] Ibáñez also undertook an impressive program of public works, some basically worthwhile, others simply ostentatious.

To finance these projects foreign loans totalling more than $95 million were floated.[131] There were scattered complaints about the increase in the foreign debt, but given the prevailing optimism over the possibilities for expansion of the Chilean economy it was generally easy for government economists to counter misgivings about the loans. Finance Minister Pablo Ramírez, who was the master-planner of the entire Ibáñez economic program, looked forward confidently to borrowing an additional billion dollars in the 1931-1933 period.[132] The depression, of course, made Ramírez look like something less than the financial wizard for which Ibáñez and others had taken him. By 1931, Chile found itself saddled with a foreign debt it could not service, and with no possibility of obtaining additional credit from abroad.

Even before the depression struck it was apparent that beneath the veneer of prosperity existed signs of economic malaise—in addition to excessive foreign borrowing. From 1925 to 1929 nitrates accounted for about 50 per cent of Chilean exports and copper for 30 per cent.[133] Lack of diversification in Chile's foreign-exchange earning potential therefore continued to be marked. Much more ominous, so far as many Chileans were concerned, was the manner in which foreign-investment capital, especially from the

United States, appeared to be taking over the economy. Foreign capital in Chile rose from $723,000,000 in 1925 to $1,017,000,000 in 1930.[134] Moreover by this latter year, foreign capital exceeded the total of national investments in manufacturing and industry[135] as well as in mining,[136] and was not far behind native capital in commerce.[137] In the eyes of critics, Ibáñez failed to place sufficient imposts upon the operations of foreign capital. More unpardonable still to Chile's economic nationalists was the manner in which Ibáñez and Pablo Ramírez allegedly sold out to Guggenheim interests in the formation of the COSACH (Compañía de Salitre de Chile) nitrate monopoly.[138]

Reliance on foreign loans, refusal to take effective steps to bring about sufficient domestic capitalization, indiscriminate encouragement to the entry of foreign capital, and acceptance of a social security system that did not consistently reach down to the most needy, all combined to foster a strange economic structure. The aristocracy was still largely untaxed, and the middle class was supported, through housing, social security, and retirement plans, by a government that was supported by foreign capital and regressive taxation revenue. Obviously, the accomplishments of Ibáñez fell somewhat short of the national regeneration he had promised the country.

The Fall of the Ibáñez Administration

Once the world-wide depression had begun and Chile's sources of foreign capital ran dry, there was insufficient money to finance social security and public works plans. Unemployment rose, and tales of governmental incompetence and corruption circulated increasingly. Under these circumstances the administration found it impossible to maintain its image as the indispensable force of national revitalization. By July 1931, in a desperate bid for new support, Ibáñez decided to appoint a cabinet of traditional rightist politicians. Upon learning of this, Ibáñez' private secretary and confidante René Montero, traveling at the time in the United States, dispatched an airmail letter complaining that the new cabinet appointments compromised the spirit of the administration. He advised the formation of an emergency military cabinet with perhaps two civilians, one being the Minister of Social Welfare, who should be a person from the ranks of the laboring classes. What Montero had in mind apparently was the imposition of a stronger military rule, accompanied by a more convincing display of administration interest in social reform.[139] Ibáñez, however, found the notion of extreme military dictatorship abhorrent. He had, moreover, been suffering from a protracted illness and seemed to have lost his energy and ability to make decisons. Pablo Ramírez, upon whose advice he had relied so heavily, was in Europe, and Ibáñez complained that the only influential person on whose support he could count was Bartolomé Blanche. Even though the troops were apparently still loyal to him, Ibáñez felt that he could not cope with a nationwide general strike that erupted in July. He resigned the presidency on the twenty-sixth of that month and went into exile in Argentina.[140]

The overthrow of Ibáñez resulted from the cooperation of groups that were divergent and even directly opposed in their orientation. Communists and other leftist elements wished to oust Ibáñez because of the repressive measures he had used against them. Beyond this their motivation was varied, but the establishment of some sort of a socialist dictatorship as well as the enactment of stringent curbs on foreign capital would have been to their general liking. Various elements in the Liberal Party opposed Ibáñez because of his interference with free-enterprise capitalism and, in their opinion, excessive attention to the lower classes. In general, these same Liberals wished to lure additional foreign capital by offering the most generous terms conceivable. Other political leaders, among them many of the Democrats and a few Radicals, most notably Gabriel González Videla, wanted to be rid of the dictator because they felt he had not done enough for the lower classes. The expectations of Conservatives had not been fulfilled by the Ibáñez regime, and many of them had concluded that the dictator would have to be overthrown before the union between Church and State could be re-established, and the influence of social levelers crushed. The incipient nazi movement wished the removal of Ibáñez on the grounds that he had betrayed the true principles of fascism. Finally, in all political parties there were opportunists who wanted to oust Ibáñez simply so that they might themselves reacquire power, as well as sincere defenders of democratic processes who hoped for the restoration of personal liberties and administrative integrity. The forces which temporarily eliminated Ibáñez from Chilean politics were, in short, as complex and as divided in regard to ultimate objectives as those which had elevated him to power.

Compounding the political confusion was the fact that the primary obstacle to Chilean stability in 1920 still confronted the country in 1931. This was the social problem which, mainly ignored until 1927, had subsequently received passing governmental attention but which became still more acute once the depression began.[141] With myriad opposing political forces operating against a background of striking social injustice, the return to constitutional order within a semi-democratic framework seemed a utopian aspiration. That Chileans were able to accomplish this goal within slightly more than two years is a remarkable testimony to the inherent national devotion to stability and to the status quo.

COMPETING SOCIAL AND POLITICAL IDEOLOGIES
IN CHILE: FROM 1920 TO THE EARLY 1930's

RIGHTIST AND CATHOLIC GROUPS

That the Conservative Party had learned nothing during the 1920's was indicated when, shortly after the overthrow of Ibáñez, it elected as its president Rafael Luis Gumucio, a man who in 1926 and 1927 had schemed for the restoration of parliamentary rule and who subsequently had been exiled by the dictator.[142] Apparently the majority of the Conservatives agreed with journalist Fidel Muñoz Rodríguez who from the pages of *El Diario Ilustrado* averred in 1931 that the restoration of parliamentarianism and Church-State union, combined with removal of government interference in the economy, would solve all the national ills.[143] Apparently also the Conservatives still agreed with their prominent members who a few years earlier had attributed the country's problems to social reforms that had permitted the masses to question authority.[144] Nor were they yet ready to quarrel with the newspaper article of 1923 lamenting the advances of medical science in Chile on the grounds that resultant reductions in infant mortality would allow the inferior classes to reproduce too rapidly and result in the degeneration of the race.[145]

The Conservatives ran true to form in 1932. They elected as the party president Héctor Rodríguez de la Sotta. An admirer described Rodríguez as: ". . . the one member of his party whose political and social ideas had been the least altered or contaminated by the changing times." [146] Proving that this praise was well deserved, Rodríguez declared in 1932: "We must fight to restrict suffrage. . . . the suffering and the mean circumstances which beset the poor and which the sociologists say is wrong, we Christians say is proper. . . . For in our concept as Christians, poverty is the estate most rich in the means through which man realizes his eternal destiny." [147] And Arturo Lyon Peña, a former president of the Conservatives, was almost as uncontaminated by the changing times as Rodríguez. In 1930 Lyon Peña had urged a reduction of real-estate taxes. To make up for the revenue losses that would result he suggested that the base for the income tax be reduced so that this impost would apply to even the lower classes.[148] Some three years later the same man was arguing that public education had ruined Chile by increasing literacy rates and thereby extending suffrage.[149] He and fellow Conservative Agustín Zegers Baeza argued that electoral laws must be changed so as to restrict suffrage drastically.[150] Conservatives were obviously concerned that nearly 10 per cent of the Chilean population had gained the right to vote.[151]

It did not require great perceptiveness for journalist and literary historian Raúl Silva Castro, writing in 1933, to observe that there were many people in Chile who did not believe in democracy.[152] A number of Liberals,[153] such as Raúl Marín Balmaceda,[154] agreed with the Conservatives that the country could only be saved by a rightist dictatorship which would safeguard a stratified, hierarchical social and political order. The newspaper El Imparcial generally reflected the views of the far right element of the Liberal Party when it contended in 1932 and 1933 that dictatorship was essential for Chile.[155]

By no means all articulate Catholics agreed with the "Christian" concepts of social philosophy expounded by Héctor Rodríguez de la Sotta and approved by many Conservatives and Liberals. Economist and banker Guillermo Subercaseaux, for example, affirmed that the social justice formulas of the papal encyclicals must be applied in Chile if that country hoped to avoid chaos.[156] The Social Catholic Union (*Unión Social Católica*), Chile's largest Catholic action group, was still strongly committed to improving the material lot of the masses and eliminating the class conflict, although it did not favor state action to achieve these goals.[157] During the 1930's the number of Catholics preaching the need to elevate the lower classes to a position of greater dignity and comfort rose steadily. Believing generally that paternalism was the only acceptable means for accomplishing this goal, some of the reform-minded Catholics advocated greater private charity, some favored a form of Christian state socialism,[158] and some favored the corporate state. But they agreed—as did, indeed, the Young Conservatives' Club (*Juventud Conservadora*)—that the most commonly expressed social concepts of the Conservative Party were dangerously outmoded.[159] In addition, there were many Chileans who, caring little about the Christian social gospel, were convinced that in order to preserve as much of the old paternalistic order as possible, considerable concessions would have to be made to the lower classes. Writers of this persuasion had produced a formidable body of literature by the early 1930's.[160]

COMMUNISM AND MATERIALISTIC SOCIALISM

Between 1920 and 1933 communism and both Marxian and anarchistic socialism made some headway in infiltrating the Chilean labor movement. In 1921 the Federation of Chilean Laborers (FOCH) with close to 100,000 members decided to adhere to the Communist International. Four years later similar action was taken by the 12,000-member railroad union.[161] The independent organized labor movement was interrupted during the Ibáñez administration, but in October 1931 the leaders of some of the unions that had been suppressed by the dictator met in Santiago and founded the General Confederation of Laborers (*Confederación*

General de Trabajadores), or CGT.[162] Boasting an initial membership of 10,000, the CGT called for abolition through revolution of the capitalistic system, for total elimination of private property, and for suppression of all government institutions. Its aim, in short, was anarchistic communism. The CGT militantly rejected international affiliations and for that reason launched an all-out struggle against the Moscow-dominated FOCH.[163]

The split between communists and extremist socialists who held out for national control was also apparent in political activity. When the Socialist Labor Party (*Partido Socialista Obrero*) convened in Rancagua in 1922, its founder, Luis Emilio Recabarren, desired the group to associate itself with the Third International of Moscow. Despite vigorous opposition by Manuel Hidalgo, who insisted on some degree of national control, Recabarren's position prevailed, and so the Chilean political scene came for the first time to include a Moscow-led party. But the Chilean communists received serious setbacks in the mid-1920's. Disillusioned over the apparent rise of military rule in Chile, Recabarren—who had been a recent visitor to Russia—committed suicide in December 1924. Furthermore, known and suspected communists were either imprisoned or driven from the country during the Ibáñez administration. With the fall of the dictator, however, the power of Chile's Communist Party began steadily to rise. Late in 1931 its existence was officially recognized, which meant that henceforth it could register and present candidates for local and national elections. In the same year Carlos Contreras Labarca became the party's secretary general, an office he energetically filled until 1947. The entry of Contreras, who had been a leader of the Chilean Federation of University Students (FECH) from 1920 to 1922, into the Communist Party signified an important change in the history of Chilean communism. Previously dominated by labor elements, communism in the 1930's became increasingly a movement of Chilean intellectuals.[164]

Noncommunist but extremist socialists—the great majority of whom subscribed to Marxian interpretations—also entered into their most active period after the fall of Ibáñez. By the end of 1931 there were four important socialist political organizations.[165]

Severely curtailed in their effectiveness because of lack of unity, Chilean socialists in 1933 decided to establish a common front and formed the Socialist Party (*Partido Socialista*) with one-time anarchist Oscar Schnake as secretary general. Rejecting international communism on the grounds that it sought world power rather than amelioration of social problems, the Socialist Party did subscribe to Marxian materialism and to the concept of the class struggle. According to the party, the state represented only the capitalist class. After this class had been stripped of power and after a brief period of proletarian dictatorship, the traditional state institutions would disappear, leaving only various workers' groups that would control the means of production. All of this, stated the party, could be accomplished by gradual and generally peaceful means. Finally, the Socialist Party stressed the need for the solidarity of Latin America's lower classes, and urged the creation of an anti-imperialist continental bloc of socialist republics.[166]

In these last two points, Chile's Socialist Party resembled the most famous of all Latin America's indigenous, Marxist-oriented movements, the APRA (*Alianza Popular Revolucionaria Americana*), founded in 1924 by Peruvian Víctor Raúl Haya de la Torre. The APRA, in fact, won several distinguished followers in Chile, among them Gabriela Mistral and Joaquín Edwards Bello.[167] Chileans, however, would not in large numbers acquire interest in a movement which, like the APRA, dedicated itself above all else to raising Latin America's abandoned and disparaged Indian elements to the level of full participation in national existence. With a pure-blooded Indian population of only some 150,000, and with an anti-Indian-and-mixed-blood prejudice as an important facet of the national character, Chileans in general regarded the APRA with hostility.

NAZISM

The National Socialist Party (*Partido Nacional Socialista*) came into official existence in April, 1932. It has been described as the one nazi group in all Latin America which thoroughly succeeded in absorbing the European philosophy of national socialism.[168] Chilean nazism, however, was not merely imitative. In a number of

ways it was a genuinely indigenous phenomenon, intimately connected with many of the more important traditions of national
life that had developed after independence and especially after the
1891 civil war.

In preaching the need for national regeneration and revitalization, the nazi movement echoed the words that intellectuals and
politicians of all schools had been uttering since the turn of the
century, and reflected in particular the spirit that had led to the
September 5, 1924, coup d'état, to the intervention of the military
in politics, and to the rise of Carlos Ibáñez. In their assertion that
Chile required strong-handed leadership along the lines of the
Portales tradition and in their contention that democracy was discredited as an effective form of government, the nazis merely repeated what an imposing number of disgruntled national figures
had been saying ever since the congressional victory over Balmaceda. In professing the existence of laws of material progress
which could be discovered and successfully applied by people
willing to throw off the fetters of dogmatism and superstition, the
nazis established rapport with the strong tradition of Chilean
positivism. On the other hand, by insisting that all human problems were essentially moral in nature and that Chile required a
moral reawakening even more urgently than it needed material
progress, nazism appealed to traditional Catholic elements. By the
early 1930's, a growing number of Catholic social reformers also
agreed with the nazi conclusion that liberal, individualistic capitalism was an evil system which destroyed human values and which
must give way to an economic structure emphasizing the common good and placing society above the individual. Moreover, even
a few Liberals[169] had come to agree with a cardinal tenet of the
nazi program: liberal capitalism, ineffective in resolving the major
problems of economically backward nations, must yield to a measure of state-planning.

Chile's economic nationalists, increasing rapidly in numbers and
in influence after the First World War and especially after the
great depression, nodded approval to the nazi assertions that the
dominance of foreign capital was an indication of national decadence. They agreed also that the influence of foreign capital

would inevitably disappear in the course of a nationwide moral
reform which was to include a thorough overhauling of the educational structure. Nazi dismay over abandonment of the Ibáñez
educational reforms after the fall of the dictator was shared by
many. In demanding renewed educational reform, the nazis did in
fact only reiterate what writers had been observing for years: that
the Chilean system of instruction produced citizens who might
have been fitted to the culture of previous centuries but who represented a drag on Chile's attempt to enter the modern, industrial
age. While the far right might have been suspicious of this aspect
of the nazis' program, it was reassured by the fact that the National
Socialists obviously intended to rule through a hierarchical, paternalistic social order. The lower classes, the nazis said, were to be
provided with material comfort and education so that they might
become efficient workers; but they were to be kept in their place
and taught not to challenge their superiors or to aspire to rise
above their station. Finally, a large proportion of the members of
all the traditional parties in Chile agreed with the nazis that the
social problem was the primary reason for their country's backwardness, and that until it was at least partially resolved national
progress could not be anticipated.[170]

Chilean nazism benefited also from the considerable demagogic
talent of its supreme leader, Jorge González von Marées. More than
just a demagogue, González was a brilliant writer and perceptive
analyst of the vital national problems.[171] Furthermore, many of the
country's more highly regarded and stable intellectuals—the most
prominent being Carlos Keller—joined the nazi movement. This,
combined with the fact that the National Socialists won many of
their recruits from upper-class youth, gave their party greater re-
spectability than had been enjoyed by most previous groups dedicated to drastic reform. Effective press support [172] contributed also
to the success of the Nazi Party, as did the zeal of many of its
adherents. And, as would be expected, Chilean nazism profited
from the same factors that had earlier nourished the cult of Italian
and Spanish fascism: extreme rightists regarded National Socialism
as an effective instrument for crushing atheistic communism,[173]
while practical-minded individuals uninterested in ideological or

theological issues admired the technical proficiency of German nazism with its ability to get things done.[174]

Picturing itself at first as a reasonably moderate movement and playing down the antisemitism of German nazism, Chile's National Socialist Party grew increasingly extreme as the 1930's progressed. More and more in its propaganda the party resorted to bitterness and invective rather than to rational justifications. Abandoning the original contention that the reforms it advocated might be introduced in an orderly, gradual manner, the party began to speak out frankly in favor of violence and revolution, with González von Marées proclaiming in the Chamber of Deputies: "The nazis will triumph by reason or by force, with the law or against the law, and if necessary by the spilling of blood." [175] The increasing stridency of nazi propaganda, and the mounting stream of anti-Jewish and anti-Masonic diatribes that began eventually to pour from the party's two principal organs, *Acción Chilena* and *El Trabajo*, helped account for the inability of the National Socialists to gain lasting, widespread support.[176] At the height of its power, the Nazi Party managed only to win 18,150 votes[177] and to elect three deputies to the national Congress: González von Marées representing Santiago, Fernando Guarello representing Valparaíso, and Gustavo Varas representing Temuco. But more important than the number of votes obtained was the nazi claim, probably not wildly exaggerated, that the party had a membership of 40,000, drawn largely from the youth of the better families, many of whom were below the legal voting age of twenty-one.[178]

Given the degree to which nazism in Chile reflected so many of the major national currents, and taking into account also the strength of the German colony and the traditional tendency for Chileans to admire and to emulate Germany, it appears at first glance somewhat strange that the National Socialist Party did not gain more general approval. Probably four factors account for the ultimate failure of nazism to attract large membership from the more mature upper-class groups: (1) dislike by the aristocracy of extremist, "upstart" Jorge González von Marées; (2) aversion of the ruling class, priding itself on its traditions of orderliness and stability, to the nazi's glorification of violence and revolutionary change; (3) alarm of the upper classes over nazi insistence upon forming a new elite, based not on birth, wealth, and traditional status, but on intellectual talents and ability to comprehend the "laws" of national progress; and (4) fear that a powerful new party might totally upset the customary political balance which, for the upper classes, had been generally satisfactory. All four of these factors would also have rendered nazism repugnant to the Chilean middle classes, consistent defenders at this time of the aristocracy and its values. Chilean nazism failed, moreover, to win large lower-class support because, unlike communism, it did not glorify the laboring sectors. Instead, it blamed much of Chilean backwardness on lower-class depravity and degeneration and held out to the masses the prospect of hard work and rigorous reform without any compensating promise of proletarian control of government. Finally, the National Socialist Party did not establish close ties with the army. Although it did in 1938 somewhat reluctantly support the candidacy of Carlos Ibáñez for the presidency, it preferred to keep the army at arm's length, while allowing a civilian, intellectual elite to control party policy. Nor did the nazi program of providing military training for its young recruits please Chile's professional military leaders.[179]

CHILE, STRUGGLING AGAINST ECONOMIC AND POLITICAL CHAOS, RETURNS TO STABILITY AND THE STATUS QUO, 1931-1933

The Economic Collapse in Chile

In addition to the ideological warfare raging as never before in its twentieth-century history, Chile faced the obstacle of a general economic breakdown in its quest for stability. Accompanying this collapse was chronic labor unrest. December 25, 1931, for example, has come to be known as the "Tragic Christmas." On that day, strikes which had originated in Copiapó and other northern centers were violently suppressed, with scores of casualties resulting.[180]

A study produced by the League of Nations[181] agreed with the conclusions of the president of W. R. Grace and Company: "Chile was hit harder by the effects of the depression than any other nation in the world." [182] Even the cold statistics of the depression in Chile produce a rather vivid picture of catastrophe. Sale of copper and nitrates, upon which Chile depended for more than 70 per cent of its national income, declined from over $27,000,000 in 1929 to about $3,500,000 in 1932.[183] Between October 1929 and October 1930, imports fell 88 per cent and by 1932, were less than one fifth of what they had been in 1929.[184] Adding to the dismal situation was a tragic crop failure in 1931. As unemployment rose —100,000 joined the ranks of the unemployed in 1931 alone—[185] the cost of such staples as oil, rice, sugar, beans, flour, milk, bread, potatoes, and beef went up between 82 per cent and 138 per cent in the course of two years. Moreover, between 1929 and 1932 real salaries declined 40 per cent.[186] The amount of money in circulation initially dropped from 500,000,000 pesos (worth about twelve cents each) in 1929 to 350,000,000 in 1931. Then the government resorted to inflationary expedients, and by June of 1932, 800,000,-000 pesos were in circulation. Within the next ten years the amount rose to over two billion.[187] The process that would ultimately result in a peso to dollar exchange rate of nearly 1,500:1 had begun.

POLITICAL CHAOS IS FOLLOWED BY ALESSANDRI'S REELECTION

Given this background of economic distress, the successors to Ibáñez did not face an easy task in governing Chile. When the dictator fled the country in late July 1931, he turned his executive powers over to Pedro Opazo Letelier, president of the Senate, who in turn delivered the provisional presidential powers to Minister of Interior Juan Esteban Montero. In accordance with constitutional regulations, Montero arranged for new presidential elections and, wishing to be a candidate himself, surrendered his executive authority to the distinguished Radical, Manuel Trucco. The Liberal, Conservative, Radical, and Democrat Parties promptly declared in favor of Montero's candidacy. Arturo Alessandri, recently returned from Europe and unable to understand why the major parties did not favor his own presidential aspirations, decided nevertheless to oppose Montero in the 1931 elections.[188] The result was a sweeping victory for Montero, who took office in high hopes that he could serve out his six-year term. His actual tenure was closer to six months.

At heart, Montero was more a spokesman for the traditional aristocracy that had controlled Chile during the parliamentary period than a leader for the reform-minded national figures who since 1920 had been trying to modernize the nation.[189] In his thinking on the social problem he seemed to crystallize the attitude that was coming to prevail among both the upper and middle classes: the laboring masses had failed to respond appreciatively to the paternalistic gestures extended them since 1920; therefore, a pox upon them. Montero failed utterly to understand the fundamental reasons for manifestations of popular discontent. Proletarian tumults were to him merely an indication of lack of respect for authority.[190] He and his financial advisers, moreover, appeared to be more convinced than even Herbert Hoover and Andrew Mellon had been that the traditional formulas of classical, laissez-faire capitalism would solve the problems of the depression—and that if they did not it was nevertheless better to live by them than to resort to dangerous experimentation.

His outmoded ideas, his lack of firmness, and his disinclination to fight to retain power doomed Montero. Against a background of street demonstrations, Colonel Marmaduke Grove, commander of the air forces, masterminded a coup d'état on June 4, 1932.[191] With the Santiago garrison refusing to support the administration, Grove and his followers occupied the presidential palace and Montero resigned. A junta was promptly named, made up of General Arturo Puga as a distinguished figurehead, Eugenio Matte Hurtado, a prominent founder and leader of various Chilean socialist groups, and Carlos Dávila, the opportunistic onetime ambassador to the United States and writer for La Nación. The driving force in the new government was provided by Matte Hurtado and the equally dedicated socialist, Colonel Grove. It was not surprising, therefore, when the junta proclaimed Chile a Socialist Republic. But the measures adopted by the triumphant socialists proved too extreme for Carlos Dávila, who plotted against the administration and was therefore removed from the governing junta. He managed quickly to turn the tables on his adversaries, and on June 16 replaced the socialist junta with one of his own choice. With Dávila at the helm—he was proclaimed provisional president on July 8 —and with Grove a prisoner on Easter Island, Chile began to experiment with moderate, "sane socialism." "Socialist" Dávila appointed "fascist" Carlos Ibáñez ambassador to Argentina. Political labels obviously meant very little, and Ibáñez may or may not have been sincere when he proclaimed his sympathy for the goals of Dávila's socialistic regime on the grounds that it was trying "to revive and expand the move toward social justice instituted in 1927." [192]

There is no need to follow in detail the complex political history of the period. Rafael Luis Gumucio in the book ¡No mas!, published in 1932, points out that within a 101-day period in 1932 six different governments controlled Chile. Finally, on September 13, General Bartolomé Blanche tried to bring the country back to its senses. Assuming provisional executive powers through a coup d'état, Blanche announced that presidential elections would be held the following October 30.

In the ensuing contest Enrique Zañartu Prieto, who had been in Chilean politics for a very long time without ever truly distinguishing or disgracing himself, ran for the Liberals. Rafael Luis Gumucio tried for the Conservative nomination,[193] but was bested by Héctor Rodríguez de la Sotta. Released from his Easter Island imprisonment, Colonel Grove ran for the Socialists, and Elías Lafertte, at the beginning of a long career of dedicated service to the cause of international communism, represented Chile's Communist Party. But this time Arturo Alessandri was not to be denied. Drawing support from the Radicals and Democrats, from many Liberals, and probably from a majority of the Conservatives, Alessandri obtained 184,754 of the 339,709 votes cast.[194] Rightist strength has seldom been more impressive. Between them, candidates Alessandri, Zañartu Prieto, and Rodríguez de la Sotta obtained 80 per cent of the total vote,[195] leaving leftists Grove and Lafertte together with only 20 per cent of the ballots cast.[196]

Absent from the 1932 elections were two traditional political groupings, the National Union and the Liberal Alliance. This fact heralded the advent of a new era in Chilean politics. Previously, one sector of the Liberal Party had generally supported, even if reluctantly, the National Union, and another had backed the Liberal Alliance. Increasingly after 1932, the Liberal Party tended to join ranks and as a unified whole to combine with the Conservatives in waging political battle. This development greatly facilitated the return of the country to the sort of control that a variety of divergent forces had since 1920 almost succeeded in ending. Among the politically articulate classes, Conservatives and Liberals were by the early 1930's probably the most conspicuous opponents to renewed reform efforts. Had they remained divided, and had the Liberals remained divided among themselves, Chile might not have turned back so resolutely toward the status quo.

THE RETURN TO STABILITY

Because of changed conditions in Chile, Alessandri during his second term (1932-1938) was able to rule more in accord with his basically conservative preferences than had been possible at the time of his first term. There were still elements that clamored for change and reform, perhaps more stridently than in the 1920's; but Alessandri was able to withstand their demands, largely by consistently relying for his political support on the new Conservative-Liberal alliance. Furthermore, while men of means and position had on the whole toyed with social reform in the 1920's, many of them abandoned these activities in the following decade. Given the economic collapse occasioned by the depression, it was quite clear to them that they would themselves have to make direct contributions and sacrifices if the plight of the masses was to be alleviated. Easy and painless social reform was no longer a possibility.

In the 1930's the military, once Alessandri's nemesis, also cooperated with the president in restoring to Chile its customary stability and apathetic acceptance of the social problem. A decade before, certain elements among the military had become infatuated with a sense of national destiny such as had not been evident in Chile since the early days following the War of the Pacific. In part, at least, it was the self-assumed mission of revitalizing the country and resolving the social problem that had led to military intervention in politics and to the establishment of ties between military personnel and the urban masses. The depression, combined with the frustrations resulting from the inadequate leadership of the Ibáñez regime, brought an end to dazzling dreams and the mission complex passed out of vogue among military circles. Abandoning its ephemeral interest in politics, the military returned to its professional pursuits, ready when the need arose to protect the civilian government against disgruntled masses. Conservative army elements, moreover, who had harassed Alessandri in the 1920's because of their desire to return to the traditions of the parliamentary period, saw no need to pressure the president during his second term. He was ruling in full accord with their desires.

To make certain that the army remained out of politics the privately organized Republican Militia (*Milicia Republicana*) came into existence at the beginning of the second Alessandri administration. Enjoying the backing of many of the most respected elements in Chilean society and politics, and perhaps secretly supported by Alessandri, the Republican Militia dedicated its efforts to preventing military interference in politics and even threatened civil war if the army officers again abandoned their barracks for the political arena.[197]

By the end of 1932 Chile's governing classes had led their country out of the period of political chaos. They had restored stability. But they were about to provide renewed proof that no country can achieve notable progress in the modern world—unless it resorts to totalitarianism—when it excludes a third or more of the population from true participation in the national existence.

7: CHILE'S EMERGING HEMISPHERE LEADERSHIP AND RELATIONS WITH THE UNITED STATES, 1920-1933

TACNA AND ARICA AND THE EMERGENCE OF A NEW HEMISPHERE POLICY, 1920-1926

A New Approach to the Tacna-Arica Controversy

In conducting foreign affairs, Arturo Alessandri was more imaginative and more inclined to break with the past than he ever was in dealing with domestic problems. Alessandri perceived clearly that the tide of internationalism was rising in the world. International organizations and plans for the maintenance of world peace were the talk of the hour in 1920. This very fact rendered Chile's traditional foreign policy untenable. Prior to 1920, largely because of its desire to settle the Tacna-Arica issue solely as it saw fit and entirely free from outside pressures, Chile had maintained an isolationist orientation, jealously guarding every vestige of national sovereignty. By the time of Alessandri's first inauguration, there were grounds to fear that the new League of Nations might bring irresistible pressure upon Chile to resolve once and for all a dispute that had been a source of hemisphere ill-will since 1884,[1] and that had produced genuine crises on nine occasions.[2]

Quite aside from the League of Nations issue, the advantages of a Tacna-Arica settlement—even if Chile were to lose a bit of territory—began to become apparent to a growing number of Chilean statesmen. Foremost among them were Arturo Alessandri himself and his first Minister of Foreign Relations, the twenty-six-year-old Ernesto Barros Jarpa.[3] Both men realized that by resolving the persisting controversy, Chile could free itself from the fear it had lived under ever since the War of the Pacific: foreign, especially United States, intervention to force an unfavorable territorial disposition. With this fear removed, Chile could abandon its defensive and distrustful attitude toward the United States-led Pan-American movement and assume a role of leadership in hemisphere relations. Above all, a Tacna-Arica settlement would facilitate the accomplishment of South American unity, so that the Latin republics might deal with the United States from a position of strength. Besides simply encouraging friendly relations with Peru, a Tacna-Arica solution would remove a chronic source of antagonism with Argentina[4] and possibly lead to the adoption of cooperation as a substitute for the traditional balance-of-power relationship between the two major republics of Spanish South America. Therefore, in the search for a new and effective United States policy—one that would check the increasing dominance of the Colossus in hemisphere affairs—the Alessandri administration turned first to the Tacna-Arica problem.[5]

At a banquet given for him by United States Ambassador in Santiago Joseph Shea on April 16, 1921, Alessandri gave the first public indication of the change in Chile's hemisphere policies. The president expressed his desire for a final solution to the Tacna-Arica problem, adding that he was certain the United States would lend its moral support to the endeavor.[6] A short time later Chilean Ambassador in Washington Beltrán Mathieu forwarded to the State Department the text of Alessandri's April 16 address and received assurances that Secretary of State Charles Evans Hughes was profoundly interested in the matter.[7] The following June in his message to Congress, Alessandri again referred to his hope for a Tacna-Arica settlement. By mid-December the Chilean Ministry of Foreign Relations, in an exchange of cable communications with officials in Lima, was suggesting the possibility of United States arbitration if direct consultation between Chile and Peru should again fail to resolve the territorial dispute.[8]

Informed of renewed contact between Chile and Peru, Washington instructed its representatives in Santiago and Lima to offer United States good offices in facilitating final disposition of Tacna and Arica.[9] Both disputants promptly accepted the offer and appointed delegates to argue their respective cases in Washington.[10]

The understanding was that if these delegates could not reach an agreement, they should consider submitting the dispute to the arbitration of the United States.

The Washington sessions were initiated in the Pan American Union Building on May 15, 1922, with Secretary of State Hughes delivering an address to which all of the accredited diplomatic representatives in Washington were invited.[11] Discussion soon began to center about whether a plebiscite provided for in the 1883 Treaty of Ancón, by which Chile and Peru had ended their War of the Pacific hostilities, might still be a workable means for settling the dispute even though the specified ten-year time limit had long since expired. The original plebiscite arrangement, constituting Article III of the Treaty of Ancón, had considered Tacna and Arica as a whole, stipulating that both areas would go to the country receiving the majority of votes in a balloting to be held by 1893. Within a month, negotiations between the Chilean and Peruvian delegations in Washington reached an impasse,[12] and both countries requested the direct assistance of Secretary Hughes.[13] The result of the ensuing discussions was the Washington Protocol of July 20, 1922. In this instrument, Chile and Peru agreed to submit the question of the plebiscite to the arbitration of the president of the United States. In the event the president decided the plebiscite should be held, he was empowered to spell out the conditions of balloting. If he decided the plebiscite was not feasible, he was to be allowed to offer the good offices of the United States in seeking a different solution.[14]

The terms of the arbitration protocol represented an apparent diplomatic triumph for Chile, as most of its statesmen were optimistic that a plebiscite would result in a victory for their country.[15] Peru, on the other hand, had hoped that the arbitration process would be based on terms sufficiently broad to permit the president of the United States to make an equitable disposition without the plebiscite. Notwithstanding the seemingly favorable terms of the protocol, many Chilean politicians resolutely opposed the instrument and sought to block its ratification in both chambers of the national Congress. Two factors were primarily responsible for opposition to the protocol. To begin with, traditionalist statesmen[16] were horrified by Chile's departure from its time-honored insistence upon unilateral settlement of the dispute. Utterly unimpressed by the new drift toward internationalism and arbitration, they regarded Washington's entry into the matter, even on terms favorable to Chile, as a violation of national sovereignty.[17] Secondly, opposition to the protocol impressed many congressmen as a politically advantageous stand. Precisely in July, the month in which the Washington Protocol had been signed, the promising attempts to unite the Liberal Alliance and National Union factions of the Liberal Party had come to an end, with the Liberals dividing more bitterly than ever.[18] Joining with many Conservatives, the National Union Liberals began violently to attack the protocol, hoping thereby to discredit the Alessandri administration. While they managed in Congress to censure Foreign Relations Minister Barros Jarpa and thereby to force his resignation, they were not able to prevent ratification of the protocol, even though in the Senate they nearly succeeded in attaching reservations that would have deprived the instrument of all effectiveness.[19]

On March 5, 1925, President Calvin Coolidge announced his decision that the Tacna-Arica matter should be settled by a plebiscite, to be held under United States supervision.[20] The announcement found Chilean politics still in a state of chaos, with Alessandri just about to resume his rule of the country following the January coup d'état which had overthrown the junta of government.[21] In the frenzied power struggle still under way, many Chilean politicians tended to regard plebiscite preparations not as the means of settling a long-standing and vexatious international question, but as a situation out of which to make political capital. The Chilean delegation to the plebiscite commission, which had opened its sessions in Arica on August 5 under the direction of General John J. Pershing,[22] had begun by October 20 to worry that Chile might not win the sort of carefully controlled and supervised plebiscite upon which Pershing and his aidés were insisting. Their apprehension arose in part from the suspicion that United States agents were consistently inclined to accept claims of long-term residence in the disputed area and consequent right to vote in the plebiscite when advanced by Peruvians, and to reject similar assurances when offered by Chileans. Accordingly, the Chilean delegates in a secret communiqué recommended that their government consider seeking some solution to the dispute other than that of the plebiscite.[23] Of course, for those who had had anything to do with planning or ratifying the July 20 protocol, it was not politically safe to admit that the instrument could be disadvantageous to Chile. Therefore, while political leaders in the recently restored Alessandri administration continued to express their absolute faith in a Chilean electoral victory, to urge a prompt holding of the plebiscite, and to blame Pershing and the United States for all delays, various elements in Tacna and Arica began to receive orders from Santiago to stage incidents that would disrupt Pershing's efforts to arrange for the plebiscite.[24]

By the beginning of November 1925, Pershing was justifiably lashing out against Chilean officials for their failure to cooperate in establishing suitable conditions for a just plebiscite.[25] Toward the end of the month the United States general stated that Chilean actions made an honest electoral process impossible and suggested that the territorial dispute be settled by awarding Tacna to Peru. Immediately, Pershing was bitterly assailed by the head of the Chilean delegation to the plebiscite commission, Agustín Edwards,[26] and was accused of having demonstrated a pro-Peruvian bias from the moment of his arrival in Arica.[27] The press joined in flailing Pershing, attributing the delays in holding the plebiscite to the general's collusion with Peruvian agents.[28] Rumors began now to circulate that Yankee agents were driving Chileans out of their homes in Tacna, replacing them with Peruvians,[29] and that the United States was planning to land troops to supervise the plebiscite.[30]

The disgruntled Pershing announced on January 27, 1926, that he was departing at once from Arica. He was shortly replaced by General William Lassiter, whom the Chilean politicians and journalists were soon attacking even more passionately than they had Pershing. Lassiter declared that the plebiscite was unpractical, and proposed that the problem be settled through the good offices of the United States. Shortly after, the Chilean government accepted the offer of good offices with the face-saving qualification that attempts to arrange for a plebiscite were not to be interrupted.[31] Many Chilean writers were less reasonable than their government. They attacked Lassiter unrelentingly for having suggested a procedure that could lead to alteration of the original Coolidge arbitration decision that the Tacna-Arica matter be settled by a plebiscite.[32] Lassiter's suggestion was taken as an insult to Chile, and the general was compared to the hated James G. Blaine. Once again, it was asserted, the United States was plotting to despoil Chile of territory.[33] Jingoist elements made the most of the situation. Many signed petitions to the effect that they preferred death to the loss of national territory.[34] Others accused the United States of wanting to dispense with the plebiscite and enforce its arbitrary decision on Chile as the first step toward establishing hegemony over all South America.[35] Arturo Alessandri charged that through the actions of Lassiter, the United States had revealed gross ignorance of what was properly entailed in international arbitration. Therefore, the United States could no longer pretend to enjoy a position of special pre-eminence in hemisphere relations. "During my five years in office," stated Alessandri, "I worked to give true life to Pan-Americanism. . . . But now I will devote all the energies that remain to me in preaching that. . . . We [the Latin-American republics] must arise, and together, in union, proclaim: Latin America for the Latin Americans." [36]

Alessandri, Barros Jarpa, and other statesmen had started bravely down new paths of international diplomacy in 1920. But the Chilean tradition of political stagnation and insistence upon placing personal political gain above national interests, as well as the continuing strength of honest isolationist convictions, totally stifled their well-conceived efforts. Final solution of the Tacna-Arica question awaited the advent of an administration that had the strength to rise above customary political maneuvering and to impose by sheer strength a new orientation in foreign affairs. As of 1926, Chile had still not found a satisfactory basis for dealing with the United States, or with the other republics of the hemisphere.

CHILE AND THE CONCEPT OF AMERICAN INTERNATIONAL LAW,
1920-1926

In officially receiving William Miller Collier as the new United States ambassador on September 29, 1921, President Alessandri had referred to the Monroe Doctrine. Because the European threat to America had long since disappeared, Alessandri averred, the Monroe Doctrine had ceased to be anything more than an expression of the moral solidarity of the hemisphere.[37] Actually, most Chilean statesmen were convinced, as was Alessandri himself, that the Monroe Doctrine and the moral solidarity of the New World republics were mutually exclusive concepts. In their view, moral solidarity in the hemisphere was dependent upon recognition of the equality of all American nations: this very recognition was directly opposed to the United States tutelage over Latin America that a broadly-interpreted Monroe Doctrine seemed designed to foster.

Alejandro Alvarez was one of the Chileans who had devoted the most thought to the problem of the irreconcilability of United States pretenses and ambitions, as embodied in the expanded Monroe Doctrine, with hemisphere solidarity. Alvarez, who in 1920 was at approximately the halfway point in his long career, had already become one of his country's most active and distinguished figures in diplomacy and international law,[38] and had formulated a fresh approach to Chile's role in hemisphere relations. In the Alvarez approach may be found the fusion of several traditional and seemingly contradictory attitudes that had first emerged in the nineteenth century. As suspicious of United States ambitions, as incensed about the imperialism of the Colossus as ever Portales and Bilbao had been,[39] Alvarez nonetheless subscribed wholeheartedly to the Lastarria thesis[40] that certain indissoluble ties, based upon a common and unique heritage, bound the New World republics together. However reluctantly, Alvarez did accept intellectually the impossibility of a New World divided between two opposing blocs, one represented by the United States, the other by the Latin-American countries. In addition, Alvarez was practical enough to realize that by 1920 economic considerations prevented Chile or any other Latin-American nation from living in the splendid isolation from the United States that many abstract thinkers still advocated.[41]

And yet the fact remained, so far as Alvarez was concerned, that the United States was not a trustworthy partner in hemisphere relations.[42] What was the way out of the dilemma in which numerous considerations counseled the maintenance of close relations with the United States, while at the same time that very nation appeared unwilling to respect the rights of Latin-American nations and to deal with them as equals? To Alvarez, the way out was American international law.[43]

At the 1901-1902 Pan-American Conference in Mexico City, where Alvarez had been one of his country's representatives, a commission of two jurisconsults had been appointed to begin work on preparing codes of private and public international law. In 1906, at the Rio de Janeiro Conference, this commission was expanded and charged with preparing specific reports on the codification of private and public international law that applied to America.[44] The Rio Commission of American Jurisconsults proved ultimately to be the main instrument in winning Latin-American approval for the Alvarez-championed concept of American international law. But for a number of years the Chilean statesman had little assistance in his mission. As early as 1905 at the Third Latin-American Scientific Congress held in Rio de Janeiro, Alvarez presented an address on the concept of American international law and won approval of the delegates for his assertion that the fundamental legal procedures governing relations among American Hemisphere republics differed from those applicable in the Old World.[45] Three years later at the 1908 First Pan-American Scientific Congress, which met in Santiago, Alvarez gained majority acceptance of this same thesis.[46]

In 1910 Alvarez published an important work[47] revealing that his suspicions of United States imperialism and his enthusiasm for American international law were both rising in intensity.[48] Within a very few years after that, Alvarez had finally resolved how to utilize American international law to contain the menace of the United States. The key to the problem, as Alvarez saw it, was for all of the southern republics firmly to support the few Latin-American and even United States statesmen who had begun to insist that the two fundamental and unique principles of American international law—not to be found in traditional international law—were absolute equality of New World republics and nonintervention by any of them in the affairs of another.[49] Alvarez hoped that ultimately the United States would come to honor these principles. In that event, the United States could become a trustworthy member of a regional, American Hemisphere organization.

Fully aware of the vast difficulties involved in taming the Colossus, Alvarez was not surprised when in 1910 and again in 1912[50] the United States resolutely opposed the notion of American international law—an interesting rehearsal of the major debate that was to be staged on the issue at the 1928 Havana Pan-American Conference.[51] As a means of pressuring the United States into accepting the concept of American international law, Alvarez hoped to utilize the instrumentality of South American unity.[52] He was convinced that the southern republics had to deal with the United States from a position of some strength, not only so as to win that country's recognition of the principles of equality of nations and absolute nonintervention, but also in order to persuade it to live by these principles once it had recognized them. Equally as committed as Alvarez to the necessity of South American unity in the quest for United States acceptance of the alleged principles of American international law were Miguel Cruchaga Tocornal [53] and Ricardo Montaner Bello,[54] two Chilean statesmen-intellectuals who enjoyed world-wide reputations as international law authorities.

By 1926 Alvarez had conceived another means of putting pressure on the United States. Perceiving that the cardinal tenet of the United States Latin-American policy was still prevention of European intervention in the American Hemisphere, Alvarez tried, as had Chileans since 1920,[55] to use the essentially European League of Nations as a counterpoise to United States influence. His two-pronged tactical procedure was to obtain overwhelming Latin-American acceptance of the concept that American international law was an essential, underlying principle of Pan-Americanism, and then to obtain closer rapport between the League of Nations and the Pan-American organization. If this endeavor to involve the League in helping to guarantee a system of American international law began to give indications of success, then, felt Alvarez, the United States would become alarmed by the specter of European intervention in the hemisphere and in order to forestall it would accept voluntarily what was most desired by the Latin-American republics: namely, the principles of equality of nations and nonintervention. Once the United States subscribed to these principles, the Latin-American nations would consider recourse to the League unnecessary, and thus the likelihood of European intervention, so dreaded by Washington, would have been removed.[56]

The impotence of the League of Nations, of course, robbed the ingenious Alvarez plan of practical effectiveness. All the same, the Chilean statesman had demonstrated remarkable prescience in perceiving that a threat from Europe might be the only way of inducing the United States to subscribe to the concept of American international law. Ultimately, it was just such a threat, posed not by the League of Natons but by Hitler, that produced the results for which Alvarez had struggled. But in the meantime Alvarez and other Chilean diplomats returned to the attempt to pressure the United States by means of the strength that could result from genuine South American unity. As had proved true so often before, however, Chile and Argentina, upon whose cooperation the emergence of a South American power-bloc depended, were unable to join together in pursuing a common policy. This inability was strikingly demonstrated at the 1923 Pan-American Conference held in Santiago, where the bonds of unity between Chile and Argentina, laboriously fashioned beginning in 1914 but gradually weakened after 1919, were rudely sundered.

At the opening sessions of the 1923 conference,[57] both President Arturo Alessandri and provisional conference President Luis Izquierdo[58] referred to the ties between all New World republics and stressed the need for the codification of American international law.[59] The Chilean position in this regard was made even more emphatic by a special study that Alejandro Alvarez had prepared for presentation to the conference.[60] But Argentina staunchly opposed the new approach to hemisphere relations championed by Chile. The notion of American international law impressed Argentina as being simply another manifestation of the unacceptable "America for the Americans" postulate.[61] The Argentine desire was still to avoid close commitments to a regional hemisphere system, to maintain particularly close ties with Europe, and essentially to go it alone in dealing with the United States. Accordingly, Argentina was not prepared to accept the Chilean conclusions that a Pan-American organization including the United States had become inevitable and that the only practical procedure was for Latin-American republics to remove the potential dangers of this organization by transferring its old and tottering structure to the new foundation of American international law. Led by Daniel Antokeletz, the Argentine delegation at the Santiago meeting scathingly denounced the concept of American international law and directed many sharp words of criticism against Chilean statesmanship.[62]

While the Argentine policy of favoring the continuation of virtual isolationism in dealing with American Hemisphere republics was undoubtedly best for Argentina, the Chilean-sponsored approach was best for Latin America. It would have placed each of the republics under the protective shell of American international law—a shell intended primarily to guard against the blows of United States intervention. For the first time, Chile had emerged as a hemisphere leader, not concerned exclusively about its own national considerations, but interested in the hemisphere as a whole. The clash with Argentina, however,[63] thwarted the Chilean endeavors and rendered temporarily fruitless the new tendencies in Alessandri's international program.

THE IBANEZ REGIME STRENGTHENS THE NEW TENDENCIES IN CHILE'S AMERICAN HEMISPHERE POLICY, 1927-1931

CHILE POPULARIZES AMERICAN INTERNATIONAL LAW CONCEPTS

In addition to his troubles with Argentina, Arturo Alessandri was consistently hamstrung in his foreign policy objectives by domestic opposition. Many Chilean statesmen disapproved the fresh approaches to hemisphere relations that had been conceived by Alvarez. Opposing the new tendencies were such prominent national figures as Eliodoro Yáñez and Chilean Ambassador to Brazil Alfredo Irarrázaval. These men wished Chile to refrain from any meaningful Pan-American commitments so as to preserve absolute sovereignty and to rely upon ties with Europe[64] and Ibero-American unity to offset the influence of the United States. In short, much as Argentine statesmen, they believed basically in an approach to hemisphere relations which maintained two Americas: Ibero-America and the United States. The notion that American international law could render the United States a safe partner in a hemisphere-wide association they regarded as dangerously unrealistic.[65]

Alessandri had never been able to crush the internal opposition to his new hemisphere policies, but the case was entirely different after Carlos Ibáñez seized power in 1927. The dictator and his advisers decided that a Pan-American movement in which the United States would play an important role must be accepted as one of the inevitable facts of life in American Hemisphere relations.[66] With this decision made, Chile was automatically committed to a new role of inter-American cooperation, whether the majority of the politicians liked it or not. Still, Ibáñez and his Foreign Ministry officials feared and distrusted the United States and were bitterly opposed to all of the expanded interpretations of the Monroe Doctrine, which they regarded as the spearhead of imperialism.[67] Consequently, they grasped at the Alvarez thesis that American international law might be the means of guaranteeing restraint on the part of the United States in its dealings with Latin America. In addition, they were convinced that Latin America must achieve the strength of union if it was to succeed in the desire to block United States imperialism.

The approach of the Ibáñez regime to hemisphere relations was clearly revealed at the 1927 Rio de Janeiro meeting of the recently reactivated Commission of American Jurisconsults. Much to the dismay of Alfredo Irarrázaval in Rio,[68] the Foreign Ministry appointed Alejandro Alvarez to represent Chile at the jurisconsults' sessions, and backed him fully in his championing of American international law, which he described as the only means that would enable "Latin America to contain the aggressive policies of the United States." [69] With Alvarez leading the way,[70] the Rio Commission of Jurisconsults approved a code of American international law that included the principles of absolute equality of nations, nonintervention, recognition of *de facto* administrations regardless of how they had acquired power,[71] and equal treatment for foreigners and native citizens in all pecuniary disputes arising in any nation that was a member of the Pan-American organization.[72]

As Chile's representative in Rio, Alvarez worked also to reestablish Chilean rapport with Argentina—the *sine qua non* for an effective Latin-American power-bloc capable of exerting effective pressure on the United States. The degree of success achieved by Alvarez in this endeavor was phenomenal. Argentina, which had scornfully rejected the notion of American international law at the 1923 Pan-American Conference, enthusiastically embraced it at Rio only four years later. Indeed, one of the Argentine delegates to the Rio sessions, Carlos Alcorta, agreed to write a book on American international private law, for which Alvarez would supply the introduction.[73] Reporting triumphantly to his Foreign Ministry, Alvarez observed: ". . . never at any international conference have there been such close and cordial relations between Argentine and Chilean delegates as those that prevailed at Rio." [74]

The on-again rapport between Chile and Argentina was almost off again at the Sixth Pan-American Conference that convened at Havana, Cuba, on January 16, 1928. The reason was that Argentina displayed a willingness, if not a desire, to end once and for all the entire Pan-American movement. This attitude was revealed after Charles Evans Hughes, head of the United States delegation, indicated that his country would never consider abandoning its rights of intervention, allegedly sanctioned under certain circumstances by international law as interpreted by leading authorities throughout the world.[75] Chile was prepared to be more patient than Argentina in the face of Hughes' bluntness. Significantly, Ibáñez had appointed as the head of the Chilean delegation Alejandro Lira, a man noted for his support of the Alvarez approach to hemisphere relations, and fully committed to the belief that, for better or for worse, the United States must be included in any hemisphere association.[76] Accordingly, Chile played the role of conciliator at Havana, attempting to moderate the attacks that other Latin-American delegates, particularly those of Argentina, were eager to deliver against the United States. Quite patently, the Chilean desire was to keep the Pan-American movement intact, in the hope that eventually pressure upon the United States to accept the principles of American international law might prove effective.[77]

Chile continued its role of suspicious but hopeful cooperation with the United States at the Washington Conference on Arbitration and Conciliation held from December 10, 1928, to January 5 of the following year.[78] This conference had been conceived at the 1928 Havana Pan-American meeting. Panamanian delegate Ricardo J. Alfaro had attempted to introduce a resolution demanding obligatory arbitration of all pending and future American disputes. Alejandro Lira strenuously objected to the proposal, and a compromise measure was approved, calling for a special conference to meet within a year to attempt to arrive at an agreement on arbitration and conciliation, "with as few limitations and reservations as possible, other than those necessary to guard the sovereignty of nations." [79] Considerable skepticism prevailed in Chile concerning the Washington Conference, the general consensus being that the United States would never agree to enter into broad and sweeping arbitration agreements which would limit its alleged rights to act unilaterally. Similar skepticism was observable elsewhere in Latin America, and Argentina—nursing resentment over the United States stand at the Havana Conference—refused even to send representatives to Washington.

Much to the surprise of the Chilean delegation, the United States exhibited a sincere interest in creating genuinely effective machinery for solving disputes between American states, even though this very machinery might deprive the Colossus of its traditional power to settle hemisphere discord simply by imposing its will. The unexpected attitude was interpreted by Chilean statesmen to mean that Washington was becoming aware that old-style, strong-armed action in the hemisphere might be economically dis-advantageous, causing Latin-American nations to become not only wary of granting concessions to United States business but even anxious to strengthen commercial ties with Europe.[80]

The apparently new United States approach to hemisphere rela-tions involved Chile in a difficult dilemma. On one hand, the will-ingness of the United States to curtail once jealously-defended rights to act unilaterally in the hemisphere seemed to suggest the possibility that the Colossus might be moving toward acceptance of the Chilean-championed concepts of American international law. On the other hand, the new United States attitude placed Chile once again in an embarrassing position with respect to the Tacna-Arica matter. When on January 5, 1929, the Washington Conference delegates approved a Treaty of Inter-American Con-ciliation, Chile felt compelled to sign with reservations specifically excluding from the conciliation process all questions pending at the time.[81] In order to be able to take advantage of the apparent shift in United States policy,[82] Chile would have to resolve the Tacna-Arica question. Only then would Chile be in a strong posi-tion to participate in the shaping of a system of American Hemi-sphere arbitration and conciliation based upon the principle of the equality of American nations.[83]

FINAL SETTLEMENT OF THE TACNA-ARICA DISPUTE

Many elements combined to produce a situation which led the Ministry of Foreign Relations to deem it imperative to put an end to the Tacna-Arica dispute. At the 1927 meeting of jurisconsults in Rio, sharp exchanges had taken place between the Chilean and Peruvian delegations. It was apparent, therefore, that no truly united South American stand in favor of American international law could be achieved until the boundary dispute was finally set-tled. At the same Rio meeting Alejandro Alvarez had observed that since the First World War the cause of compulsory arbitra-tion had made such headway that Chile was no longer secure in the anti-arbitration concessions it had won from the Pan-American conferences at Mexico City (1901-1902) and Rio de Janeiro (1906).[84] Chile, moreover, considered itself at a disadvantage throughout the sessions of the 1928 Pan-American Conference at Havana, for President Coolidge had remained inscrutable as to his objectives in exercising United States good offices in the Tacna-Arica dispute. Chilean diplomats suspected that Coolidge, by keeping them in a state of apprehension as to his intentions, had hoped to be able to pressure their country into favoring the United States position in any debate that might arise at Havana. While Chilean policy had by this time come independently to rest upon belief in basic accord with the United States, it was still galling to occupy so precarious a bargaining position.[85]

Arriving in Washington in the summer of 1927, Ambassador Carlos Dávila bore with him instructions to work zealously toward solution of the Tacna-Arica matter.[86] The chain of incidents that facilitated Dávila's implementation of these instructions was initiated many miles from Washington, on a ship proceeding northward up the Pacific coast of South America. Much to the surprise of the Chilean representatives travelling to Havana for the Sixth Pan-American Conference their ship was boarded at Callao by several members of the Peruvian delegation. Probably even more surprising, the Chileans struck up a friendly relationship with the Peruvians, one that continued not only for the remainder of the voyage, but throughout the Havana Conference.[87] Following the conclusion of the Havana sessions, Chilean and Peruvian statesmen began an unofficial exchange of ideas—regular diplomatic relations had been severed since 1910. By the end of June, United States Secretary of State Frank Kellogg, who for months had been trying to facilitate an amicable agreement between the two countries,[88] was informed that the time was propitious for him publicly to suggest the renewal of diplomatic relations between Chile and Peru. Kellogg made the proposal on July 9, and shortly Emilio Figueroa Larraín was sent as Chilean ambassador to Lima.[89]

Now that diplomatic relations were restored, Chile and Peru resorted to direct diplomacy in the endeavor to make final disposition of the Tacna-Arica territory. While the Chilean press for the first time in more than fifty years was pouring forth expressions of warm friendship and admiration for Peru,[90] negotiations between the two countries came to a swift and satisfactory conclusion. On

April 16, 1929, Emilio Figueroa won Peruvian President Augusto
B. Leguía's consent to the terms offered by Chile: Arica to remain
in Chilean hands, and Tacna to be returned to Peru together with
a Chilean cash settlement of $6,000,000. With these terms already
agreed upon secretly, a dramatic touch was given to the proceedings by allowing the Spanish fliers Francisco Iglesias and Ignacio
Martínez Jiménez, who had recently crossed the Atlantic in their
plane, the "Jesús de Gran Poder," to fly the official Chilean offer
from Santiago to Lima. Thus motherland Spain was given a sym-
bolic role in presiding over the reconciliation of her recalcitrant
offspring.[91]

In the meantime, the United States Department of State had
never ceased to exercise its powers of friendly persuasion in urging
the two countries to resolve their differences. Frank Kellogg, in
fact, believed that his efforts were instrumental in preventing the
breakdown of negotiations. He therefore remained in his post as
Secretary of State several weeks longer than he had intended so
as to be on hand in an official capacity when the negotiations were
at last crowned with success. Thus it was that Kellogg was able
to convey to President Hoover the information that Chile and
Peru had come to a secret agreement. Acting then in his capacity
as the presiding official of the negotiations which the United States
had been conducting for some three years, Hoover on May 15 "suggested" that Chile and Peru compose their differences on the terms
actually already agreed upon.[92] The Hoover recommendation was,
of course, promptly accepted by the reconciled disputants.[93]

At last, Chile was able to abandon the opposition to broad and
sweeping American Hemisphere arbitration and conciliation, held
resolutely since the Washington Conference of 1889. The reservations with which the January 5, 1929, Washington Treaty of Inter-
American Conciliation had been signed were promptly withdrawn.[94]
Now, with its own position in the hemisphere no longer vulnerable,
Chile stood ready to prod the United States to go all the way in
accepting the premises of American international law. No longer
was there the danger that the United States might retaliate by
threatening to intervene in the Tacna-Arica dispute.

Settlement of the controversy with Peru at once provided Chile with the means to apply pressure on the United States through the instrumentality of South American unity. Chile and Peru, for example, could now present a united front to the United States.[95] Also, new opportunities for intimate and consistent cooperation with Argentina were now opened. Ever since the War of the Pacific, Argentina had played the balance-of-power game in South America, frequently siding with Peru and Bolivia[96] in their claims against Chile. With the Tacna-Arica accord, the last of these claims appeared to have been settled. It is significant that when the old statesman-diplomat and chronic Yankee-baiter Gonzalo Bulnes was asked about his reaction to the Tacna-Arica agreement, he prefaced his favorable remarks with the observation that he was in favor of South American unity—especially, Chilean-Argentine unity.[97]

The administration regarded the Tacna-Arica settlement largely in the same light. The official government newspaper *La Nación* declared that the plebiscite, if held, might have given both Tacna and Arica to Chile. But, it editorialized, this would have been merely a legal decision and would not have paved the way for true friendship and solidarity among South American nations.[98] Carlos Ibáñez, speaking shortly after the announcement of the final settlement, intimated what the event meant to him. "The Tacna-Arica accord has been another step in the program of national resurgence that I have been leading." [99] It is not difficult to understand what Ibáñez had in mind when making this statement. Having at last struck off the shackles of isolationism, Chile now hoped to lead the American Hemisphere states toward the sort of relationship that had been foreseen by its statesmen—particularly, Alejandro Alvarez—more clearly than by most of those of the other New World republics. In providing the sort of apolitical ambient necessary for solution of the Tacna-Arica controversy, Carlos Ibáñez made his greatest contribution to Chilean resurgence and the reacquisition of international prestige.[100]

CHILEANS MANIFEST A SENSE OF IBERO-AMERICAN UNITY

Ibáñez and his advisers hoped that at last they had found a satisfactory policy toward the United States, one in which Yankee acceptance of and respect for the principles of American international law could be induced by the strength of a united Ibero-America. The concept of relying on the strength of unity to curtail the imperialistic tendencies of the United States had won many advocates during the 1920's, and by now was clearly a part of government policy. When Enrique Bermúdez arrived late in 1928 as the new Chilean ambassador in Buenos Aires, he said that the fundamental purpose of his mission was to bring about closer union between Chile and Argentina.[101] Previous Ambassador Gonzalo Bulnes had stated the same sentiment, rejoicing particularly over the re-election of Hipólito Irigoyen as Argentine president in 1928. Bulnes recalled that during the First World War Irigoyen had stood shoulder to shoulder with President Sanfuentes of Chile in resisting United States pressures for severance of relations with the Central Powers.[102] In addition, *El Mercurio* on February 9, 1928, reported an interview with Conrado Ríos Gallardo in which the Minister of Foreign Relations expressed his deep satisfaction over the increasing cooperation and unity between Chile and Argentina in hemisphere policy. And *La Nación* on the same date noted that Ibáñez was pursuing Chilean-Argentine unity more diligently than had any president in Chilean history.

Once Chile undertook to resolve its differences with Peru, it seemed for the first time to become interested not only in cooperation between the southernmost republics of the continent, but in a more extensive Ibero-American unity. Republics previously dismissed contemptuously as tropical, turbulent, Indian nations now began to concern its diplomats. This was demonstrated by Chilean reaction to United States actions in Nicaragua. The country that had taken the United States acquisition of Panama lightly, and that had regarded the Roosevelt Corollary as suitable for treatment of weak and inferior republics, became emotionally aroused over the Coolidge administration's intervention in Nicaragua that commenced in 1926.[103]

When Enrique Villegas, long-time Chilean delegate to the League of Nations, retired from that post in 1929, he addressed a group of delegates from the other Latin-American nations, urging that they avail themselves of their experiences of cooperation at Geneva in order to fashion some permanent measure of Ibero-American unity. More than ever, said Villegas, such unity was necessary, as the Washington-dominated Pan-American movement "has so far been sterile and produced only academic results." [104]

UNITED STATES ECONOMIC PENETRATION IN CHILE

Confident of the ultimate effectiveness of American international law backed by Ibero-American strength as a means of stemming imperialism, the Ibáñez administration encouraged United States investments in Chile and saw little occasion for alarm in the growing economic dependence upon the once-dreaded Colossus—even though by the end of the 1920's this dependence had become striking indeed. The Ibáñez attitude toward foreign investments rested also upon the hope that once the reformed Chilean educational structure began to produce men well trained in the modern technological procedures and imbued with respect for capitalist values, Chileans would automatically begin gradually to take over the economic management of their country. Meanwhile, foreign assistance seemed essential.[105]

United States investments in Chile, direct and indirect, had by 1920 already reached the imposing total of $200,000,000;[106] by 1928 they had soared to approximately $400,000,000.[107] During the 1920's, the dominance of United States direct-investment capital had become particularly striking in the Chilean copper industry. In 1920 United States capital made up 82 per cent of the total invested in copper exploitation; by 1924 it accounted for 91.83 per cent, and Chilean capital owned only 5.5 per cent of the industry.[108] By 1927, moreover, the Guggenheim interests had purchased the Lautaro nitrate operation from British investors, becoming thereby the principal power in nitrate production.[109] Here, so far as Chilean economic nationalists and Yankeephobes were concerned, was an ominous situation. Worse still was the fact that total foreign capital invested in Chile, of which United States holdings accounted for some 60 per cent, represented an average of 36 per cent of the aggregate capital investment in Chile during the 1925 to 1929 period. Between 1930 and 1933, foreign money had come to constitute an annual average of 52 per cent of the entire capital invested in Chile.[110]

Chile's commercial dependence on the United States also increased perceptibly during the 1920's. Toward the end of the decade Chile obtained over 30 per cent of all its imports from the United States. The second largest supplier of import goods, the United Kingdom, sent merchandise valued at only slightly more than one half of that obtained from the United States.[111] Moreover, by the late 1920's, between one fourth and one third of the entire value of Chilean exports went to the United States. In the single year of 1926, Chile shipped goods to the United States worth some $96,000,000. Included in this amount was close to 40 per cent of national mining exports.[112]

In the early 1920's, before the Ibáñez administration, Chileans had voiced alarm about the increasing dominance of foreign capital. Leftist Deputy Nolaso Cárdenas in 1920 accused the United States owners of the Chuquicamata and El Teniente copper mines of pressuring the administration into using the armed forces to crush strikes.[113] In 1923 Conservative stalwart Manuel Rivas Vicuña asserted that Chile, and in fact Latin America as a whole, enjoyed only political independence and must begin to strive for economic freedom.[114] Three years later Ricardo Latcham, who has distinguished himself among Chilean writers for expressing strongly-held ideas and prejudices with strong words, warned that soon the United States would exact from Chile the same sort of price it had earlier collected from the Dominican Republic, Colombia, and the Philippines.[115]

As the tide of foreign economic penetration rose during the Ibáñez regime, there were many Chileans who felt that the government was not adequately protecting national interests. From Buenos Aires Chilean Ambassador Gonzalo Bulnes warned in 1928 that the United States would soon wield a virtually monopolistic control over northern Chile's nitrate and copper resources. Once this came to pass, Bulnes gloomily concluded, Chile would be no more than a vassal of the United States.[116] Although partially muzzled by the Ibáñez press censorship, economic nationalists were still able to give some expression to their dissatisfaction from 1927 to 1931. After the dictator's fall, the charges against the allegedly predatory United States capitalists increased sharply in number and intensity.[117] The general frustration and bitterness engendered by the depression also served to encourage attacks against Wall Street, the favorite symbol of the capitalistic system that many Chileans supposed to be outmoded. The tirades against United States economic policies were frequently combined with warnings about that country's cultural imperialism, which was pictured as threatening to replace Chile's superior spiritual and cultural values with purely materialistic standards.[118]

MOUNTING OPPOSITION TO THE UNITED STATES GIVES WAY TO A NEW RAPPROCHEMENT: 1931-1933

AN ALL-OUT DRIVE TOWARD IBERO-AMERICAN UNITY

The desperate consequences of the depression in Chile, coupled with the callous indifference of the United States to the problems of the southern republics—as manifested by a tariff policy that dealt a crippling blow to trade relations[119]—evoked a new variation of the ever-present theme that all or at least some of the Latin-American republics should unite in the endeavor to end their dependence on the unreliable Colossus of the North. Even before Ibáñez fell, Foreign Relations Minister Antonio Planet had been working toward a customs union of the more southern nations of Latin America, one purpose of which would be to combat United States economic dominance in the southern hemisphere.[120] Once Ibáñez had gone into exile, the anti-United States storm broke in earnest. Temporarily abandoned was the desire to form a South American bloc as a means of forcing the United States to act with justice in a hemisphere organization. For many political and economic leaders, the main objective now came to be the formation of a South American power-bloc, based on economic and political cooperation between Chile, Argentina, Uruguay, Paraguay, Brazil, and Peru, as a means of enabling these republics permanently to sever most of their economic ties with the United States.[121] Going beyond the concept of South American cooperation as a defense against the United States, the Radical Party's Desiderio González Ossandón called upon all of the republics below the Río Grande to pool their efforts to attack "gringo" economic dominance.[122] Socialist and right-wing journalists[123] joined in giving vigorous support to this proposed line of action, as did aristocratic Luis Orrego Luco,[124] inflammatory pamphleteer J. Schneider Labbé,[125] Liberal Party elder statesman Eliodoro Yáñez, and banker-economist Guillermo Subercaseaux.[126]

In his letters written to the Ministry of Foreign Relations in 1932, Chilean Ambassador to the United States Miguel Cruchaga Tocornal revealed between the lines the frustration and resentment he felt as he conducted his country's affairs in Washington.[127] The activities related by Cruchaga indicated the galling degree to which Chile had become dependent upon the whims of the United States. He spent hours of his time investigating and worrying about every rumor as to what the United States intended to do in regard to tariff policy, in regard to copper purchases, and in regard to pressing for payment on Chilean bonds temporarily in default. Never had Chile felt so totally controlled by the unpredictable attitudes of a foreign power.

Upon leaving his Washington post late in 1932 to serve as Minister of Foreign Relations for the re-elected Arturo Alessandri, Cruchaga assumed a leading role in the effort to eliminate Chile's humiliating subservience to the United States. Cruchaga, in fact, became the prime mover in the endeavor to cement the firmest and most intimate ties between Chile and Argentina, as the preliminary step toward creation of an effective South American union of economic and political cooperation.[128] On February 1 and 2, 1933, he met with his Argentine counterpart, Carlos Saavedra Lamas, in the western Argentine town of Mendoza.[129] There the two ministers signed a fourteen-article agreement, reaffirming their dedication to continental—but significantly, not hemisphere—fraternity in meeting the vast problems facing the Latin-American republics.[130] Of the fourteen points agreed to at Mendoza two were aimed directly against the United States. First, Chile and Argentina pledged cooperation in ending the Chaco War between Bolivia and Paraguay, an action that was clearly meant to indicate

·their displeasure with United States-led efforts to establish peace.[181] Second, they expressed joint approval of the Saavedra Lamas Anti-War Pact, which contained as one of its important provisions the principle of absolute nonintervention. Saavedra Lamas intended the Anti-War Pact at least in part as a challenge to be hurled at the United States at the next Pan-American meeting, scheduled for late 1933 in Montevideo.[132]

Accord having been reached with Argentina on matters of hemisphere relations, Miguel Cruchaga next gave his full support to the efforts being led by Maximiliano Ibáñez, an elderly and widely respected Liberal Party statesman, to obtain a commercial treaty between the two nations. The result was an agreement signed in the spring of 1933, which put an end to tariff schedules that had long caused strained relations between the two republics.[133] Congressional debate on the ratification of the treaty revealed the significance that intimate ties between Chile and Argentina assumed for well-informed politicians. Democrat Deputy Armando Chanks stated that the treaty would bring the two southernmost republics of the continent together on a firmer basis than ever before, and constitute the first step toward a union of Ibero-American republics that would enable them to protect themselves against all menaces that might originate in the hemisphere.[134] In urging ratification of the treaty before the Chilean Senate, Miguel Cruchaga emphasized the need for Argentine-Chilean unity as a starting point for genuine cooperation among all the Ibero-American nations. He alluded in terms of glowing praise to a recently published book by Fernando Illanes Benítez[135] arguing for South American economic cooperation as a means of combating the influence of foreign capital.[136]

By mid-1933, then, it was becoming increasingly clear that the traditional international discord between Chile and Argentina, from which the United\States had frequently profited in maintaining its own leadership over the Pan-American movement, was being effectively eliminated. Moreover, this new development was consciously fostered by important Chilean statesmen precisely in order to end United States dominance in hemisphere relations.[137] Some policy makers and intellectuals would not have been satisfied with ending United States dominance. They looked forward to eliminating its participation in the affairs of Latin America.

A NEW UNITED STATES IMAGE IN CHILE, AND THE 1933 PAN-AMERICAN CONFERENCE

By the end of 1933, however, there were influences in Chile operating to oppose a freeze-out of the United States from the southern continent. The Alejandro Alvarez-inspired point of view still found many supporters who recognized the necessity of continuing to have close relations with the United States and who counted on American international law to curb that country's dominance. Undoubtedly, Miguel Cruchaga, long a champion of the American international law concept, hoped to see this policy prevail. He hoped also that a united Chilean-Argentine stand might induce the United States to assume a favorable attitude. But the Chilean Minister of Foreign Relations wished also to be prepared with measures that would enable Latin America increasingly to go it alone after 1933 should the United States continue to refuse to accept the principles of equality of nations and nonintervention. These two sources of motivation had accounted for Cruchaga's actions after he had returned to Chile from his ambassadorial post in Washington.

The hopes of American international law enthusiasts were bolstered with the inception of the Good Neighbor policy which created a new United States image for many Chilean leaders, inducing them to look more tolerantly toward the northern republic. With the election of Franklin D. Roosevelt and the inauguration of vigorous new policies, the United States began to impress influential Chileans as a country that was undergoing a profound change for the better. Faced with the internal suffering and misery resulting from the world depression, the onetime Colossus seemed to be abandoning its attitude of smug superiority and to be transforming itself into an understanding and sympathetic good neighbor, one that did not know all the answers. It was less inclined to accept the chronically depressed conditions of the southern republics as proof of Latin-American inferiority. Rather, it was willing to cooperate with these countries as equals in the attempt to modify the practices of capitalism so that it might be transformed into a system that would benefit all classes and restore dignity and purchasing power to those who had lost or never adequately possessed them. At last, progressive Chileans seemed to have something in common with the United States. Chile's chargé d'affaires in Washington, Benjamín Cohen,[138] caught the spirit. Given its newly emerging attitudes, the United States, predicted Cohen, would abandon its old ways of imperialism.[139]

While the new image that the United States was beginning to project favorably impressed many Chilean statesmen, there was still widespread agreement in late 1933 that the northern republic and the entire Pan-American movement would be on trial at the seventh meeting of the American states.[140] With avid interest, Chile awaited United States reaction to the principles of American international law that, according to the approved agenda, would be discussed at the forthcoming conference in Montevideo. The United States, it was clear, would be called upon in two instances to take a stand on the vital matter of nonintervention. At the suggestion of Chile, it had been agreed that the Saavedra Lamas Anti-War Pact, containing the nonintervention clause, would be discussed at the Montevideo sessions, with the objective of gaining approval from all the American states that had not yet signed the instrument.[141] In addition, the Seventh Pan-American Conference was committed to considering the American international law proposals formulated in 1927 by the Rio Commission of American Jurisconsults.[142]

To the vitally important conference that convened on December 3, 1933, Chile sent a distinguished delegation headed by Foreign Minister Cruchaga.[143] Perhaps more striking than the ability and prestige of the Chilean delegates was the absence from the group of Alejandro Alvarez. The man who had been largely responsible for the emergence of the Chilean policy for the hemisphere that advocated a Pan-American system including the United States and based upon American international law had, by 1933, become the object of President Alessandri's strong personal dislike.[144] Ironically, then, Alvarez was absent from the meeting that made the initial move toward implementing the ideas he had tirelessly championed for more than twenty years.

Nevertheless, the delegation that the Alessandri administration sent to Montevideo was prepared to respond favorably to any conciliatory gesture that the United States might make in respect to American international law. The crucial point of the conference came during the plenary sessions of December 22 when Secretary of State Cordell Hull, head of the United States delegation, agreeably surprised many Latin Americans by accepting the general principle of nonintervention, and then aroused their customary ire by stating that his country would insist upon certain reservations. Unlike many of their fellow delegates, the Chileans accepted Hull's explanation that while Latin America had no grounds to fear intervention during the Roosevelt administration, a short conference could not formulate definitions and establish interpretations pertaining to nonintervention. Hull offered assurances that the United States hoped these tasks could be accomplished speedily after the conclusion of the conference. In the meantime he maintained that the State Department must follow the principles of international law as generally recognized and accepted if differences of opinion should arise as to what constituted intervention.[145]

On the whole, the Chilean press was also satisfied by the United States stand. Journalists ranging from moderate left to extreme right accepted the Hull statement on nonintervention as satisfactory for the immediate situation. Moreover, they praised the United States for having embarked upon a dramatically new approach in its relations with Latin America, one that would undoubtedly lead in due time to full acceptance of the concept of American international law.[146]

Other aspects of the conference enhanced the image of the United States for many Chileans. The Hull proposals for reciprocal tariff reductions were warmly praised. The Chaco War truce, which the Chilean delegation at Montevideo played a much publicized role in helping to negotiate, contributed also to friendly relations by ending the long-smouldering dispute over which of two rival groups of American neutrals was properly qualified to attempt to restore peace between Paraguay and Bolivia.[147] By the time the delegates had finished their business at Montevideo, even the rightist Santiago daily *El Imparcial*, usually a bitter assailant of the United States, was willing to concede that the Seventh Pan-American Conference had been the most successful of them all and that the new attitudes displayed by the United States had been responsible for this fact.[148]

In Montevideo, then, at the end of 1933, the Pan-American movement had begun to proceed in the direction that farsighted Chilean statesmen had sporadically advocated since the days of José Victorino Lastarria and resolutely espoused since 1920. So far as American Hemisphere political questions were concerned, the United States took at Montevideo the first step toward accepting commitments and restrictions that would render it a safe neighbor in the eyes of Latin-American republics. However, there was realization in some circles that the vital issues confronting Pan-Americanism were beginning to change. Domingo Melfi, one of Chile's leading writers and political analysts who covered the conference proceedings for his government's newspaper, *La Nación*, expressed only guarded optimism about the future of Pan-Americanism.[149] While granting that the growing acceptance of the tenets of American international law was gratifying, Melfi declared that José M. Puig y Cassauranc, the Mexican Minister of Foreign Affairs who headed his country's delegation at Montevideo, had perceived the real issue that would at some future time threaten the effectiveness and the very existence of the Pan-American organization. Puig y Cassauranc had warned that the basic concern for the American Hemisphere was already shifting from political to socioeconomic considerations. The primary challenge now was to provide social justice and to assimilate into society the millions of the hemisphere's dispossessed. The inter-American movement, advised the Mexican, must regard as its *raison d'être* the stamping-out of social inhumanity. If it failed in this, success in other ventures would be merely superficial, and could not mask the fact of fundamental failure.[150]

The words of Puig y Cassauranc constitute in some ways the most consequential pronouncement made at the Montevideo Conference. By ignoring them during the course of the ensuing generation, the hemisphere's leaders had by 1960 brought the inter-American movement to the very threshold of failure.

8: THE CHILEAN RIGHT
AND THE UNITED STATES

RIGHTIST DOMINANCE OF CHILEAN POLITICS

THE BACKGROUND OF RIGHTIST POLITICS, 1933-1962

In spite of warnings from abroad, such as the one heard at Montevideo in 1933, and from its own writers and public officials, Chile has failed in the years following the re-election of Arturo Alessandri and the return of political stability to ameliorate its social problem. One reason for this is that traditionalist, rightist groups—which are actually made up more of middle than of upper social sectors—have not been sincerely willing to work for basic social reform. Since 1933, an unofficial alliance of the two main rightist parties, Conservative and Liberal, has either directed policy or wielded a generally effective veto power.

Originally divided primarily by the religious question, these two parties have been in accord on social issues ever since the Liberals discovered in the second half of the nineteenth century that they could gain access to privileged circles without having to resort to the genuinely democratic expedients they had at first championed. By the turn of the century, Conservatives had been joined by one branch of the Liberal Party in the political affiliation known as the National Union. Then, in the 1920's, relations between the two parties tended to worsen, as Conservatives were outraged over the support that many Liberals gave to the campaign to separate Church and State. However, once separation was finally effected under the 1925 constitution, Conservative dismay began quickly to abate as it became apparent that the new constitution would neither contribute directly to the advance of atheism nor result in persecution of the Church. A few die-hard elements still favor the corporate state and neofascistic programs᷑ as the means of rectify-

243

ing the moral damage that the country allegedly sustained from the 1925 constitution. But the majority of Conservatives have since the 1930's accepted the practical advisability of abandoning the religious question in order to cooperate with the Liberals in resisting the forces of social change.

A contributing factor to this development has been that Conservatives have come gradually to see that even though Liberals might lack religiously-grounded belief in the necessity for a stratified, hierarchical, paternalistic society, they have in actual practice become effective guardians of just such an order. At one point in the nineteenth century the traditional faith appeared to be the essential bulwark against social modification. In later periods, purely secular considerations began to create equally formidable barriers to change. As early as the 1920's, moreover, certain Catholics began to agitate for radical alteration of society. More recently, the Catholic-oriented Christian Democrat Party and even an important member of the Church hierarchy, Bishop Manuel Larraín of Talca, have dedicated their energies to the quest for fundamental social reform. Obviously, the Church was no longer the formidable deterrent to change it had been in an earlier period. Conservatives, therefore, ceased to regard union of Church and State as essential. Even without union, the 1925 constitution soon demonstrated that it could be an effective instrument for perpetuating the status quo. When the Conservatives realized this, they found it possible to accept the instrument and to cooperate with the Liberals in protecting the social order that both espoused.

Frequently joining with Conservatives and Liberals to buttress the status quo has been another political entity tracing its history back to the second half of the nineteenth century, the Radical Party. Generally since 1932, at least in municipal and congressional elections, it has been the party of greatest voting strength, normally receiving more ballots than either Conservatives or Liberals. Chilean Radicalism, however, suffers from a basic schizophrenia. Since early in this century it has had a leftist branch demanding sweeping social reform and even socialism and a rightist sector identifying itself in political philosophy with Conservatives and Liberals. In the 1930's, the leftists prevailed and the party cooperated with socialists and even with communists in pushing effectively for reform. In the 1940's the Radicals talked more about reform but did less about it than they had in the 1930's. During the 1950's the rightist bloc reacquired control, and since 1958 the party has united with Conservatives and Liberals to oppose the reform measures advocated by the newer political groups.

ALESSANDRI FAILS TO RISE
TO THE NATIONAL CHALLENGE, 1932-1938

In the early 1930's, a wide variety of groups gave lusty expression to the desire for far-reaching social change. Communists, socialists, Trotskyists, anarchists, and nazis vied for followings, and the Radical Party showed serious interest in social reform. A young group within the Conservative Party began to evince discontent with the traditionalist approach of party elders and in 1937 founded the National Falange, forerunner of today's Christian Democrat Party. The 1930's may well have been the period of sharpest intellectual and social ferment in Chile's twentieth-century history. The time seemed to demand a leader of vision and magnetism to seize upon all of the evidences of impatience with the stagnation of the past and to harness Chile's pent-up energy to a program of national progress dedicated to assimilating previously ignored population elements.

This was the challenge confronting Arturo Alessandri during his second administration. It was hardly to be expected that he would be able to meet the demands of the 1930's, for in his first term (1920-1925) he had revealed a dedication to conserving the essence of the old order and an inability to come to grips with new forces. After 1932 Alessandri sided increasingly with those who were set upon maintaining Chile's traditional economic and social patterns and sought primarily the support of the Conservative-Liberal alliance. These policies dealt a crippling blow to the reform movement that had since the early 1920's threatened the status quo.

THE POPULAR FRONT STRUGGLES TO REVIVE
CHILE'S REFORM MOVEMENT, 1939-1941

By the end of his administration in 1938, Alessandri had managed to return Chile to essentially the same groups that had governed before 1920. Congress was safely in the control of the Conservative and Liberal parties and except for a bloody pre-election incident, Alessandri would have been able to turn his office over to the officially-supported candidate, Gustavo Ross, an archconservative who had served as his Minister of Treasury. An attempted nazi *coup* on Septmeber 5 was easily suppressed, but the *carabineros* (national police) then shot down in cold blood sixty-two youthful members of the National Socialist Party who had already surrendered to them. Chileans, who are traditionally noted for their moderation, were outraged by this senseless act of cruelty which was committed in the very heart of Santiago. Blame for the deed was attributed to the administration, and rumors circulated that Alessandri had been personally responsible. Carlos Ibáñez, the candidate of the National Socialist Party in the 1938 elections, was withdrawn from the campaign as a result of the unsuccessful *coup* and virtually on the eve of the balloting the nazis threw their support to the coalition known as the Popular Front. Although previously implacable foes of this coalition of Radical, Socialist, and Communist parties, the nazis chose now to cooperate with the group in order to strike back at the hated Alessandri through his favored candidate, Ross. With the unexpected nazi support and with many voters casting their ballots against Ross as a protest over the nazi assassination incident, the Popular Front won an extremely close election.

With Congress still controlled by the Conservatives and Liberals and apparently with some electoral debt to pay the nazis, there seemed little likelihood that the Popular Front could work effectively toward solving the social problem. Progress in this direction seemed all the more improbable in view of the fact that the head of the Front and new president of Chile, Pedro Aguirre Cerda, was regarded by many as a representative of the right wing of the Radical Party. He had, in fact, as a member of the party's central committee voted against formation of the Popular Front.[2]

Ironically, a cruel assault by nature, in the form of a devastating earthquake, made it possible for the Front to move ahead with a successful program of reform and national revitalization. The January 24, 1939, earthquake which centered around south-central Chillán killed perhaps 50,000, injured 60,000, and left 70,000 homeless.[3] Faced with this catastrophe, some rightist elements in Congress revealed a willingness, however hesitant, to cooperate not only in rebuilding the afflicted areas, but in reordering to some degree the entire Chilean economic structure.[4]

During a three-year period, the Popular Front accomplished more in the way of economic and social reform than has been achieved in any equal time-span between 1930 and 1962. Progress, however, came to an end with the death in 1941 of Aguirre Cerda, who had proved a more progressive and dynamic leader than expected. Internal dissension among the elements comprising the Front had already resulted in its dissolution. Wartime prosperity and a binge of inflation and speculation, moreover, dulled the Chilean appetite for reform. The result was that the attainments of the Popular Front proved more ephemeral than John Reese Stevenson foresaw when in 1942 he published his optimistic and carefully researched book, *The Chilean Popular Front.*[5]

THE RADICAL PARTY IN CONTROL OF THE PRESIDENCY, 1942-1952

From 1942 to 1952, the presidential office was filled by two members of the Radical Party: Juan Antonio Ríos, a pro-fascist Ibañista in the late 1920's who died in office in 1946, and Gabriel González Videla, long regarded as a leader of Radicalism's left wing. Some positive progress was made, especially by the González Videla administration (1946-1952). Still, given the continuing power of the Conservative and Liberal groups, as well as the increasing effectiveness of the right-wing element within the Radical Party, it proved impossible to launch a direct assault against social injustice. Radical Deputy Sebastián Santandreu in 1948 congressional debates reflected the thought of some elements in his party when he expressed colossal boredom with reform endeavors. "What if," he asked his colleagues, "people are dying from hunger and exposure in Chile? The same thing is happening all over the world." [6]

Probably the most impressive accomplishment of the González Videla term was the transformation wrought in the president's hometown, La Serena. This beautifully situated coastal city at the northern edge of the central valley was turned into a model community. Slums were cleared, handsome new buildings were erected, and many fine schools, particularly well-equipped technical schools, were constructed. La Serena today is one of the most hopeful sites in all of Chile. Had the Radicals won the 1952 presidential elections, they intended to carry out a similar revamping of Iquique.

However, Chileans had grown discouraged and dismayed by the inflation which the Radical presidents had not curbed and which had resulted in declining purchasing power for salaried groups and wage earners. They were dissatisfied also with bureaucratic proliferation, inefficiency, and corruption. Overwhelmingly in 1952 they gave their support to a man whose symbol was the broom and whose promise was to sweep out all the refuse that had accumulated during the period of the Radicals' somewhat slipshod rule. Carlos Ibáñez was the man with the broom.

THE SECOND IBÁÑEZ ADMINISTRATION, 1952-1958, AND SUBSEQUENT POLITICAL EVENTS

Carlos Ibáñez, for the first time president of Chile by free and constitutional elections, faced a difficult task. In the first place, his principal formal political support had come from two entirely disparate parties: the fascistically-inclined Agrarian Labor Party and the Marxian-oriented Popular Socialist Party. Further, Chile was not the same country it had been when Ibáñez ruled it dictatorially but energetically, 1927-1931. At that time, the republic displayed interest in change and improvement and a willingness to experiment. Influenced by heady ideologies from abroad as well as by locally-sparked movements, Chileans dreamed of a real transformation. Taking advantage of these conditions, Ibáñez had provided dynamic leadership, even though some of the goals toward which he proceeded as well as the methods he employed were questionable. Between 1952 and 1958, Ibáñez presided over a country that had sunk into spiritless lethargy. It might have been aroused by a truly charismatic leader, but Ibáñez did not possess this quality to a sufficient degree. It might also have been called forth from complacency and dejection by a real whip-wielder. But Ibáñez seemed satisfied simply to serve out his term by resorting to political machination and manipulation, and he avoided an all-out struggle to acquire the extraordinary power that would have been needed to revitalize the country. Although toward the end of his regime Ibáñez seemed increasingly to side with the left, and even relegalized the Communist Party—outlawed in 1948—and moved to curtail campaign bribery just before the 1958 elections, he was never able to curb the power of the Radicals, Conservatives, and Liberals. Many of the 135 ministers of state with whom he desperately experimented in the attempt to find a working combination came from the latter two parties. Ibáñez himself played the vital role in squelching a moderate, long-overdue attempt to reassess and raise the tax rates on agrarian property. The lords of the land thereby won continued immunity from equitable taxation.[7]

In 1958, with the election of Liberal Jorge Alessandri Rodríguez, one of Arturo Alessandri's several prominent sons and the recipient of Conservative support in his presidential bid, the Conservative-Liberal alliance regained effective control of the country. In the 1960 municipal elections, the combined vote of the two parties was approximately 363,000, roughly one third of the total ballots cast and larger than the vote received by any single party.[8] This was a clear indication of the extent to which new middle sectors had flocked to support the traditional aristocratic parties. Moreover, the ruling alliance could count on support in almost every instance from the Radical Party, the largest single vote-winner in the 1960 elections, despite that group's avowals of political independence intended to quiet the rumblings of its minority of dissident leftists.

It has been customary to point to Chile's long continuing conservative rule as one factor helping to account for the generally cordial relations which the country maintained with the United States after 1933. If this be so, then the future position of the United States in Chile is compromised by the fact that the groups with which it has so harmoniously dealt have been conspicuously associated with perpetuating the social injustices which have victimized the lower classes and excluded them from true participation in the national life. A critical reassessment of United States endorsement of the Chilean ruling elite is therefore in order. This reassessment becomes all the more urgent when it is understood that in Chile the rightists, however careful they have been to play down the fact, are more basically antagonistic to the United States than noncommunist leftists.

ANTI-UNITED STATESISM OF THE CHILEAN RIGHT

SPIRITUAL AND CULTURAL ANTI-UNITED STATESISM

In the nineteenth century, many so-called radical thinkers in Chile held ideas that the mid-twentieth century would have branded stuffily conservative. By and large they seemed to feel that the lower classes should derive their satisfaction from the development of inward values rather than enjoyment of material comfort. They doubted that political articulateness was of use to the masses in helping them to develop their human potential. They tended, therefore, to join with conservative thinkers in concluding that the United States, because of its groping toward political and economic democracy, and because of its concern with material development including encouragement to citizens of all classes to compete in acquiring wealth, was initiating a dangerous leveling process in which the higher spiritual and cultural values would be replaced by materialistic, hedonistic standards. Even men like Isidoro Errázuriz[9] and Francisco Bilbao,[10] considered leftist extremists a century ago, agreed in this appraisal.

Gradually, in the twentieth century, the position of the left has shifted. Left-of-center, noncommunist reformers have come to recognize the need for an acceptable level of material well-being for all classes if the majority of society's members are to develop adequately their spiritual and cultural potential. Political and economic democracy they no longer find abhorrent. Nonetheless, many noncommunist leftist elements continue to be convinced that the United States is basically without culture. They assume, then, either that the United States system has really not produced sufficient political and economic democracy, or else that because of basic character deficiencies the citizenry of that country has not known how to use political articulateness and widely dispersed material comfort to produce a culture.

The right has been more consistent. It has continued to dislike the end-product of United States life, dismissing it as lacking culture, grace, beauty, as well as widespread appreciation of aesthetic and spiritual values. It has continued also to blame United States social, economic, and political usages for having inevitably produced the end-product of a cultureless and spiritually starved society. Therefore, the right has been steadfast in wishing to maintain the traditional Chilean social, economic, and political patterns in order to retain intact its allegedly superior culture and morality.

Typical of rightist attitudes are the anti-United States utterances of Jaime Eyzaguirre. Considered by many to be Chile's leading Catholic *pensador*, Eyzaguirre remains to this day as implacable a critic of the United States as he was in 1944 when he wrote:

> As Catholics, we cannot expect that a world ruled by laic and antireligious powers, as found in the United States, or by Protestants, as found in England, or by atheistic and materialistic leaders, as govern Nazi Germany and Communist Russia, will find peace and justice within a universal Christian order. Nor, as Hispano-Americans, can we honestly expect from these imperialistic powers the gift of world political order based on equality and justice. Our hope is that rivalry between these global powers will give us the relative independence in which we can realize cultural and political unity, the essential basis for our future greatness.[11]

Four years after Eyzaguirre published these views, Carlos Keller—an intellectual who considers his attitudes to be based upon the spirit of Catholicism—called upon the elite of Latin America to unite to preserve a *culture* that was threatened by the democratic and therefore cultureless *civilization* of the United States.[12]

Closely connected with, and in fact often indistinguishable from, currents of spiritually-culturally motivated anti-United Statesism is Hispanism. How the cult of Hispanism, introduced as a serious intellectual force in Chile at the time of the Spanish-American War, gathered strength from 1900 to 1920 has been described earlier.[13] To a far greater degree than most other Latin-American countries, Chile in the twentieth century has demonstrated consistent devotion to the beliefs that inhere in Hispanism. This fact was recognized when a Spanish mission was sent to Chile in 1928 to found the Hispano-Chilean Cultural Center. Luis Olariaga, head of the mission, was delighted by the warmth of the reception, and enthusiastically observed: "Chile, above all other New World republics, has come to recognize the transcendent importance of its inheritance from Spain, and to appreciate that its deep-lying admiration for Spain has helped it to resist the flood of incompatible Anglo-Saxon and North American materialism." [14] Five years before this, the Spaniard Emilio Castelar after an extended tour through Latin America had published the same conclusion in his *Los valores españoles en América*. It is understandable, then, that the literature produced in Chile which clearly embodies the value-judgments of Hispanism continues to be abundant, and to be written by some of the country's most notable intellectuals. [15]

POLITICAL CONCEPTS OF THE CHILEAN RIGHT
AND ANTI-UNITED STATESISM

Although exhibiting pride and often smug satisfaction in his country's democracy, the Chilean's concept of democracy is often directly opposed to United States viewpoints. For example, a leading member of the Conservative Party noted for his progressive spirit, Eduardo Cruz-Coke, observed approvingly in a 1946 publication that Chile was "the country whose democracy is the responsibility of the [social] hierarchy." [16]

Some years before this, in 1933, when considerably less than 10 per cent of the Chilean population enjoyed suffrage rights Arturo Lyon Peña—onetime president of the Conservative Party—complained that the privilege of voting had been extended to people incapable and unworthy of exercising it and that right-thinking men were no longer in control of the nation. [17] Also in the early 1930's the well-known and widely respected Miguel Luis Amunátegui Reyes had praised oligarchy, or rule by a select few, as not only the ideal but the only practical mode of government and had advised Chile to restore those happy days when this type of political system had prevailed. [18] Furthermore, during this period a right-wing newspaper published an article urging suppression of free public education on the grounds that it allowed many of the "unqualified" sons of artisans and *campesinos* (rural laborers) to attend secondary school, where they acquired "unjustified" desire

for political participation.[19] Finally, as recently as 1958, Christian
Democrat Congressman Rafael A. Gumucio reported that a prominent Catholic University professor of constitutional law had
allegedly noted that bribery was a necessary corrective to lower-class suffrage.[20]

Dislike of the United States because of its democracy—common
among Chilean rightists—is matched by their respect and admiration
for criticisms that the Yankees themselves may make of democracy.
Of the books by United States authors that have become well
known in Chile, Lothrop Stoddard's *The Revolt Against Civilization* produced one of the most profound impressions. Translated
into Spanish in 1923 by the Chilean medical doctor Lucas Sierra
(as *La amenaza del sub hombre*), the work also appeared in serial
form in the Santiago daily *Las Ultimas Noticias*. It was taken as
a warning against any move that threatened the traditional aristocracy, and as an admonition to the upper classes not to become
"misguided superiors" by sympathizing with basic reform drives.[21]
Undoubtedly, the misgivings about democracy that some new conservatives in the United States have been voicing since the mid-
1950's will evoke a favorable response when they become known
among Chilean rightists.

SOCIAL CONCEPTS OF THE CHILEAN RIGHT
AND ANTI-UNITED STATESISM

The social structure and aims of the United States are unappeal-
ing to many Chileans. Particularly offensive is the acceptance of
social mobility and of the degree of class competition that is inevitable in a pluralistic society. Chile's directing classes, even if
they concede the need for social reform, remain generally committed to the stratified, non-open, hierarchical society. Within this
structure they are willing to encourage "fraternity," but certainly
not equality, nor necessarily even liberty, at least so far as the
lower classes and minorities are concerned. "Fraternity" is to be
achieved through the paternalism and charity practiced by the
aristocracy. And "fraternity" is to be guaranteed by seeing that
the lower classes are not allowed to become powerful enough to
challenge their leaders and demand their rights. They must re-

main content, in short, to accept gratefully what is bestowed upon them from above, without ever claiming anything from their superiors.

This spirit was well summarized in a letter that Ambassador to the Holy See Ramón Subercaseaux directed in 1928 to the Chilean Ministry of Foreign Relations. Subercaseaux lamented that social action movements in Chile and elsewhere in the world had not produced hoped-for results because many of their leaders, including even a few priests, had forgotten that the true end was the achievement of social solidarity based on paternalism. As a consequence, the immoral class conflict had vitiated most reform movements. The valid goal of social reformers, asserted Subercaseaux, was not to change the circumstances of men, but to encourage greater love of them as they are, no matter how mean the conditions in which they live.[22]

This attitude is expressed by a multitude of Chilean politicians and intellectuals who are often self-proclaimed champions of social justice. Over one hundred of them have published twentieth-century works that although advocating some reform are as hostile to basic United States social, economic and political patterns as to Russian communism.[23] A striking feature of this body of literature is the accord which the authors, even those of the most recent years, have maintained with the 1928 views of Subercaseaux.

UNLIKELY FRIENDS AND UNLIKELY FOES
OF THE UNITED STATES IN CHILE

In view of the multi-faceted anti-United Statesism of the traditional, rightist forces that continue to govern Chile, the question arises as to why conservative rule has been conducive to generally amicable relations between the two countries during the 1933-1962 period. There are two obvious answers. To begin with, United States actions have generally had the effect of aiding rightist sectors in maintaining the established order. Secondly, the men controlling the Conservative, Liberal, and Radical parties have consistently stifled intellectual and idealistic aversion to the United States in order to accept the practical, material benefits accruing from dealing with it and from according its capital a position of vast importance in certain sectors of the Chilean economy. Influx of United States and foreign capital in general has largely freed the ruling sectors from the burden of personally contributing to the economic development of their nation. They regard, moreover, a close association with the United States as a convenient bulwark against the sort of radicalism that a number of leftist parties have come to advocate.

Perhaps hoping that their ties with the United States may be turned still further to their advantage, rightist authors sometimes picture that country as practicing still a sort of McKinley-era rugged individualism and laissez-faire capitalism, in which capitalists unfettered by "initiative-stifling" taxes (meaning anything over 10 per cent of income) are allowed virtually a free hand in the social and economic spheres. The moral that rightists read into this distorted description of the United States is that because the Yankee nation is prospering by it, Chile can become prosperous by imitating it.[24]

Unfortunately, the United States has not succeeded in correcting this inaccurate picture of its capitalism that rightist "friends" as well as Marxian foes are wont to paint. Thus, it has excluded from its list of admirers most sincere advocates of national reform. What should make the United States particularly wary of allowing this situation to continue is the uncertain nature of the friendship of the now governing groups. If reform-minded elements in Chile should come to power and undertake basic economic and social alterations, the rightist camp because of its underlying philosophical attitude not only will fail to object to, but will probably derive inner satisfaction from, any anti-United States actions to which the reform regime resorts.

On the other hand, the noncommunist left in contemporary Chile (to be discussed in the next chapter) has outgrown the attitudes of a generation ago when Arturo Alessandri was regarded as a leftist. Today, many of the reformers of the noncommunist left have come to embrace the ideology of social mobility, direct democracy, pluralism, and some degree of class competition. They oppose the United States because its alliance with Chile's right has placed it in apparent opposition to the very principles to which they aspire.

Being disliked among noncommunist leftists because of what, when judged in the Chilean ambient, it merely seems to be, the United States must concentrate upon projecting a more accurate image of its national life. To do this would entail a certain disengagement from supposed friends on the right and the establishment of closer ties with groups previously avoided because of leftist outlook. If the United States is to proceed consistently along these lines, it must first face up to the fact that the traditionalist groups in Chile for whom friendship has been reserved are, in spite of their charm, sophistication, broad culture, gracious way of life, and unquestioned anticommunist fervor, the guardians of a social system that growing thousands are finding intolerable. Yet, not until 1961 did the United States begin to waver in its uncritical support of these groups. It thereby contributed to a situation in which inhered the increasing likelihood that its influence, along with that of the groups it backed, would be swept away before the advancing tide of the very principles which it has long championed within its own boundaries.

9: THE CHILEAN LEFT
AND THE UNITED STATES

SOCIALISM AND THE DEFENSE OF THE HIGHER HUMAN VALUES

.In the early 1930's many idealistic Chileans, motivated by considerations of Christian social morality, turned to socialism. In part, they were led in this direction by the world depression, which they tended to regard as the inevitable outcome of the unbridled lust of private capitalists, particularly United States capitalists. If unfettered individualism had failed to produce an acceptable social order, then, it was reasoned, socialism must be the means by which economic and social justice could be achieved.

In a book published in 1930,[1] the noted Chilean journalist Jorge Gustavo Silva argued that only socialism could provide the masses with the longed-for better life. In the same year Silva was elected president of the First National Congress of Cooperatives, a post from which he was effectively able to propagate his ideas. Two years later the prestigious and generally conservative newspaper *El Mercurio* suggested editorially that socialism might not actually be the threat it had originally appeared. The editorial speculated that a combination of socialism and capitalism might be necessary to produce harmony in the social order.[2]

Convinced that only socialism could bring about morality in social relations, Ricardo Latcham—a staunch defender of traditional values, of Hispanism, and of the Catholic Church—[3] declared himself a socialist in the 1930's. Latcham, moreover, ignored a strongly-worded castigation of Father Raimundo Morales who asserted that it was not possible to be a socialist and remain a Catholic.[4] Other Catholics were similarly unpersuaded by the words of Father Morales. Some of them, including Jorge Sanhueza

Donoso and Carlos Cariola, joined the staff of *Wikén*. This out-spoken, socialist weekly which began publication in 1932 contained such features as articles by Joaquín Edwards Bello advocating nationalistic communism, free from ties with Russia,[5] and editorial attacks upon the bankers and Jews of the United States who allegedly had corrupted the government and society of that country.[6] The lively weekly also featured the cartoons of Jorge Délano, better known by his pseudonym of Coke, who is perhaps the most talented political cartoonist that Chile has produced in the twentieth century. At one time conservative in his inclinations and associated with *El Diario Ilustrado*, Délano came in the 1930's to feel that only socialism could remedy the ills which capitalism had brought to the Western world.[7]

In the same period influential writer Trancredo Pinochet Le-Brun, who had always defended the superior cultural and spiritual values allegedly possessed by Chile, embraced socialism as the only effective instrument for perpetuating these values.[8] Father Alejandro Vicuña, who in earlier pronouncements had shown opposition to much of what was modern in the world,[9] turned also to socialism as the means of preserving Christian standards. In the 1930's he was sometimes referred to as "the communist priest." [10] Even the eminently respectable professor of labor law at the University of Chile, Francisco Walker Linares, charged in his 1935 lectures that capitalism had ignored the material, social, and spiritual betterment of the laboring classes that had created its wealth. Walker Linares urged adoption of socialism.[11]

It was understandable that such attitudes on socialism, generally tinged with anti-United Statesism, would be widely held during the period of the world depression. For many Chileans, however, not even the renewed vitality of capitalism in the United States and elsewhere in the Western world provided reassurance about the system in general. Largely, this is because Chileans have not become aware of how capitalism, outside of Chile and of Latin America in general, has evolved and assimilated certain features once regarded as socialistic in the endeavor to protect human values and to bring social benefits and economic protection to all classes.

In 1943 diplomat-author Galvarino Gallardo Nieto maintained that the United States was in the throes of a moral malaise because of the excessive attention to material considerations that was an inevitable product of the capitalist system, and argued that only some measure of socialism could protect the higher human values.[12] Similar convictions continue to lead numerous Chileans to espouse socialism and reject capitalism. In 1951 the eminent professor and writer, Julio Heise González, averred that capitalism tends to dehumanize men and to bring about an absolute separation between morality and economic practices.[13] Juan Gómez Millas, rector of the University of Chile, stated at a 1960 round-table discussion in Santiago between Adlai E. Stevenson and various Chilean intellectuals that the United States was interested only in things, not in men.[14] Gómez has long believed that this type of value distortion is an inevitable feature of any capitalistic system and accordingly has advocated the usages of socialism.[15]

THE CHRISTIAN DEMOCRAT PARTY

The tendency to embrace socialism as a means of combating the excessive materialism and dehumanizing elements attributed to capitalism was a factor in the emergence of the Christian Democrat Party. This reform-oriented group originated in 1937 as the National Falange. The guiding impetus came from young liberal Catholics, including Eduardo Frei, Bernardo Leighton, and Manuel Garreton Walker, who had been influenced by the social views of such men as the progressive Jesuit, Father Jorge Fernández Pradel.[16] The new party received important encouragement when the long-time pillar of the Conservative Party, Rafael L. Gumucio, temporarily joined its ranks.[17]

In its early days the National Falange received little voter support. Its difficulties were compounded in the 1940's when reformist Conservative Eduardo Cruz-Coke led a move that resulted in the founding of the Conservative Social Christian Party (*Partido Conservador Social Cristiano*) with a platform very similar to that of the Falange. In the 1950 Santiago municipal elections, the Falange polled only 6,860 votes compared to the 25,602 of the Conservative Social Christians. The Falangists persevered, however, and in the late 1950's the Cruz-Coke-led party dissolved, with most of those who had supported it either finding their way back into the Conservative Party or else aligning with the Falange.

With the political field of Catholic-oriented reform left largely to itself, the Falange began rapidly to gather strength. Changing its designation in 1957 to the Christian Democrat Party (*Partido Demócrato-Cristiano*), it began to prepare for the following year's presidential elections. Christian Democrat Senator Eduardo Frei was selected as his party's standard-bearer. Senator Frei finished third in the 1958 balloting, receiving approximately one fourth of the total votes cast. In the March 1961 congressional elections, the Christian Democrats won some 212,000 ballots, surpassing for the first time the Conservative Party which obtained approximately 197,000 votes.[18] They had also by that time won for themselves a position of leadership in the Christian Democrat movement in Latin America as a whole.

Chile's Christian Democrats regard social pluralism and political democracy as essential goals. They also accept religious pluralism as an established fact of national existence. In working toward the just social order, they are willing to cooperate with the many Chileans who are Masons or religiously indifferent as well as with the Protestants who have come to constitute roughly 8 per cent of the population. These attitudes scandalize old-guard Catholic groups who have engaged the Christian Democrats in one of the bitterest pamphlet wars in modern Chilean history.[19] Christian Democrats also cause consternation among traditionalists because they appear to accept the need for a limited form of the class struggle as a means of achieving social justice. According to their political philosophy, when a Christian Democrat administration attains power, it must aid and encourage the masses to acquire genuine political articulateness. The masses will then be able to force the upper classes to make the fundamental social and economic concessions that conscience alone could never have induced them to grant. Once the affluent groups have been goaded into accepting a new order based upon distributive justice, the Christian Democrats expect the class struggle to be replaced by amicable cooperation between the different classes.

Advocating what they term the "Communitarian Society," Chile's Christian Democrats profess that capitalism as practiced in the United States is opposed to Christian morality. Christian Democrat journalist Jaime Castillo attacks old-style liberalism as thoroughly evil and un-Christian and unfortunately assumes that the United States is still run according to the concepts of Herbert Spencer.[20] Jacques Chonchol and Julio Silva, two important intellectuals of the Christian Democrat movement, agree with Marx that private capital is the root of nearly every evil, and hence advocate abolishing private ownership of all save consumer goods.[21] Moreover, in practically all of his writings, Eduardo Frei refers to the need for replacing the crude lust for profit that inevitably vitiates capitalism with the spirit of Christian brotherhood.[22] And Máximo Pacheco Gómez, author of an important work on Christian Democracy in Chile, avers that modern capitalism is based still upon the teachings of Adam Smith, David Ricardo, and Thomas Malthus, and is therefore unacceptable.[23]

THE SOCIALISM OF THE RADICAL AND DEMOCRAT PARTIES

Since the early twentieth century, it has been fashionable in Chile for religiously nonaffiliated parties that profess interest in social reform to advocate socialism. Thus, in its famous 1906 convention the Radical Party, despite the furious opposition of Enrique Mac-Iver, declared its adherence to socialism. As the years passed, it became clear that there was no reason for Mac-Iver to have been alarmed. The rightist bloc maintained much of its strength among the Radicals and the party seldom used its power to raise the standard of living of the Chilean masses or to reorder the national social structure.

In the early 1930's, with socialism apparently making notable headway in Chile, the Radicals felt it would be advisable to reaffirm their belief in the doctrine. They went even further and at their 1932 Viña del Mar convention accepted the concept of the class struggle. But they did not really mean it. As 1933 debates in the Chamber of Deputies revealed, what the Radicals had in mind was only sufficient amelioration of the social problem to remove any fundamental threat to the traditional Chilean class relationship and thereby to restore social harmony.[24]

Another revealing insight into the social philosophy of one wing of the Radical Party was provided in 1957 by successful business leader and politician, Hernán Brücher. Speaking in the national lower chamber, Radical Deputy Brücher implied that the lower classes should not attempt to advance by contending with their superiors. Rather, they should rely on the paternalistic tutelage of the middle class and acknowledge that all benefits which they might enjoy had come to them because of the largess of their social betters.[25]

The Democrat Party (*Partido Demócrata*) founded in 1887 always claimed to be dedicated to sweeping social reform, and occasionally acted in accordance with this avowal. The party toyed with many socialistic ideas and early in the twentieth century advocated establishment of a socialist government. In the 1930's, moreover, Democrat Senators Juan Pradenas Muñoz, Virgilio Morales, Fidel Estay, and Raúl Puga often backed the legislative proposals of such genuine socialist senators as Jorge Waccholtz, Guillermo Azócar, and Hugo Grove.[26] But the real character of the Democrat Party was accurately described as early as 1922 by Fidel Muñoz Rodríguez. The party, said Muñoz, issued too many insincere proclamations and accepted too many members who did not believe in socialism or in social reform. The result was that the lower classes were losing faith in the party.[27] Subsequent developments have tended to bear out the Muñoz charge and by 1962 the Democrat Party had virtually disappeared from the political scene.

MARXISM AND COMMUNISM

Marxian Socialism in Chile

The Socialist Party, founded in 1933, united the various noncommunist, Marxian socialist groups that had previously existed as separate and antagonistic entities. Renewed quarrels, however, over matters of doctrine and methods of procedure soon brought an end to unity, and led to the formation of splinter socialist parties. One of these, the Popular Socialist Party (*Partido Socialista*

Popular), had by 1950 surpassed the Socialist Party in political strength.[28] Then, in 1958, the Marxian socialists managed once again to resolve their differences and joined together to form the United Socialist Party, today known simply as the Chilean Socialist Party (*Partido Socialista de Chile*).[29]

This new amalgamation of Chilean Marxists receives energetic leadership from such men as Senators Salvador Allende, Raúl Ampuero, and Aniceto Rodríguez. Among ideological purists it is handicapped by the fact that many of its members, at the time when they belonged to the Popular Socialist Party, cooperated with the fascistically-inclined Agrarian Labor Party to elect Carlos Ibáñez president of Chile in 1952. By strong leadership and aggressive propaganda, the Socialist Party is attempting to counteract the impression that Chilean socialism is inevitably associated with sellouts to the right. The electorate, however, appears to be somewhat skeptical.

An important reason for skepticism is the fact that the Radical and Democrat parties, describing themselves as socialist, have—because of the power and influence which both once possessed and which the Radicals continue to enjoy—done more to create an image in Chile of what socialism stands for than have doctrinaire, Marxian socialists. Perhaps it is for this reason that Chilean socialism is now apparently in decline. Socialist parties used to enjoy overwhelming success when competing with communists for lower-class support. However, in the December 1959 elections for the executive committee of the Single Center of Chilean Workers (*Central Unica de Trabajadores de Chile*), the principal labor confederation, socialists lost several seats, leaving the communists in clear control of the organization that had traditionally been led by noncommunist Marxists. Even more significant, in the March 1961 national congressional elections, the communist slate was supported by 154,130 voters, while the Socialist Party gained a disappointing 147,883 ballots.[30] In the United States, England, and West Germany socialism has lost ground because of the successes of rejuvenated capitalism. In Chile, socialism is losing power because of the failure of unaltered patterns of classical capitalism to provide solutions to the major national problems, and because of the widely-held suspicion that socialism has all too often compromised with the defenders of laissez-faire, nineteenth-century liberal capitalism. Growing numbers of Chileans are thus placing credence in the boast of the communists that they alone are capable of bringing about reform.

THE COMMUNISTS AND THEIR ALLIANCE
WITH THE MARXIAN SOCIALISTS

Under Carlos Contreras Labarca, its secretary general from 1931 to 1947, the Communist Party steadily gained strength. In the March 1941 congressional elections, it received some 55,000 votes. Five years later its support was instrumental in gaining election of Gabriel González Videla to the Chilean presidency. After the 1947 municipal elections, in which communists scored notable gains, the party overplayed its hand, attempting by terroristic methods to take over the entire Chilean labor movement. González Videla responded by requesting and obtaining congressional approval in 1948 of a "Law for the Permanent Defense of Democracy" that declared the Communist Party illegal. The actual effect of the law was merely to make the communists change the name of their party. As members of the rapidly organized Proletarian Party, and later of other parties, they continued to be active in Chilean politics. Just before the 1958 presidential elections the Communist Party was relegalized.

In 1956 communists had combined with the various socialist groups that existed at the time to form the Popular Action Front (*Frente de Acción Popular*), or the FRAP. Basically, the FRAP has been an uneasy alliance, in part because of the awareness of most noncommunist Marxian socialists that international communism is more interested in acquiring world power than in solving the social problems of Chile.[31] Still, the cooperation dictated by expediency has produced notable results. The 1958 presidential elections saw FRAP candidate Salvador Allende come within approximately 35,000 votes of being elected president of Chile.[32] The margin of victory for Liberal-Conservative candidate Jorge Alessandri Rodríguez seems to have been provided by an unfrocked priest, Father Antonio Raúl Zamorano, called the "Cura of Catapilco," who advocated a leftist program and won 40,000 votes which otherwise would probably have been cast for Allende. In the March 1961 congressional elections, the FRAP registered a greater increase in voting strength than any other Chilean political organization.

Not only are communists now attracting more votes than their socialist partners in the FRAP alliance, but among Chilean intellectuals they enjoy a respected position. Several of them hold important university teaching posts, and their party receives additional *réclame* because Chile's great poet, Pablo Neruda, is a communist.

Chilean communists and Marxian socialists have produced an imposing volume of literature in the past generation. In fact, the works in which they plead their economic doctrines probably exceed in number those devoted to defending capitalism.[33] In 1955, moreover, Guillermo Feliú Cruz, a non-Marxian historian respected as one of Chile's outstanding intellectuals, observed that most notable Chilean scholars developed in the preceding thirty years had been strongly influenced by Marxian ideology and had concluded that classical capitalism and democracy had outlived their usefulness.[34] Feliú Cruz also noted that the nearly simultaneous appearance—in the early 1950's—of important works by three of Chile's leading scholars, Julio César Jobet, Hernán Ramírez Necochea, and Julio Heise González,[35] had established a new trend in Chilean historiography whereby the country's past was reinterpreted in accordance with the theories of materialistic determinism and the class conflict.

ANTICOMMUNISM, CHILEAN AND UNITED STATES STYLE

Unquestionably, a large majority of Chileans continue to hold anticommunist sentiments. But these sentiments have not always served to lead them into a united front with the United States in combating the Moscow menace. Aware of the intransigence of the defenders of the established order, many noncommunist Chilean reform advocates maintain that they must cooperate with communists in order to transform society. They believe that communist support and advice in the initial stage of the change process will help them achieve an efficient economic organization and a rigorous system of capital formation. When the right moment comes, they are confident they can cast off the agents of Moscow. With material rehabilitation accomplished, they hope then to provide the populace with opportunities to share in a broad cultural life that is rooted in permanent philosophical and theological values compatible with national traditions.[36] However naive they may be in these hopes, they are not willing to accept the United States approach that communists must at all times be shunned.

Moreover, many Chilean anticommunists mistrust either the effectiveness or the motivation of the United States in its endeavors to eradicate communism throughout the hemisphere and the world. Alejandro Silva de la Fuente, for over fifty years a prominent journalist of rightist persuasions, suggested in 1956 that only Catholic countries could be effectively anticommunist. He feared that the United States would, because of its secularism and religious pluralism, inevitably weaken in the struggle against communism and hence could not be looked to by Chileans for leadership.[37] Even before Silva de la Fuente published these observations, journalist Armando González Rodríguez had commented upon the tendency of conservative Chileans to regard Catholicism as the only effective bulwark against communism.[38]

On the other hand, leftist but noncommunist reform elements distrust the motivation rather than the ultimate effectiveness of United States anticommunism. They wonder if in Latin America the Yankee-led anticommunist crusade has not been employed simply to bolster the position of rightist friends, with the expectation that they would respond by protecting all the more zealously United States economic investments. They wonder, in short, if United States-style anticommunism is a form of imperialism aimed at safeguarding the status quo. *AntiKomunismo*, the famous work published in 1955 by ex-Guatemalan President Juan José Arévalo (1945-1950), is probably the most influential book by a Latin American linking United States anticommunism to imperialism aimed at bulwarking aristocratic ruling cliques. The book has been popular in Chile, where it has gone through two editions.

Furthermore, the mistaken notion that United States capitalism still functions as it did in the late nineteenth century, leading to the concentration of capital in the hands of a few and the heartless exploitation of the masses,[39] leads many Chileans to resist joining with the Yankees in a concerted drive against communism. Christian Democrat Jaime Castillo, for example, in El problema comunista[40] is from thirty to sixty years behind actual developments in his description of the social effects of United States capitalism. On the basis of this out-of-date image, he decides that the United States is thoroughly indifferent to social justice. From this premise follows the inescapable conclusion that Chilean reformers who realize that social justice is the only effective block to communism can find no common ground with the United States.

ECONOMIC NATIONALISM

FOREIGN CAPITAL AS A SYMBOL OF CHILEAN DECADENCE

With the consistent exception of the Conservatives and Liberals, Chilean political parties during the twentieth century have all manifested a considerable degree of economic nationalism. As United States capital has come to dominate foreign investment in Chile, economic nationalism has become almost indistinguishable from anti-Yankeeism.

The genuine contributions made by foreign capital are recognized by most of Chile's noncommunist economic nationalists. Still, they feel that the time must come when Chile assumes for itself greater control over all aspects of its economic structure. They regard, moreover, the dominance of foreign capital as a symbol of national decadence. Alejandro Venegas, in the remarkable book Sinceridad published in 1910, was one of the first Chileans to interpret the rising influence of foreign capital as a symptom of national decadence and stagnation. Two years later Francisco Antonio Encina expressed similar views in his Nuestra inferioridad económica, and Alberto Cabero in 1926 repeated the thesis in Chile y los chilenos. In the 1930's, the Chilean nazis were among the most outspoken economic nationalists to regard the commanding position of foreign capital as an indication of deficiencies in national character.[41] Since that time, similar views have continued to be expressed by numerous writers who, although differing in political affiliation, have been united in desiring new and even revolutionary approaches to national problems.[42] Any movement, therefore, that calls upon Chileans to begin to tap latent resources of character and to strive energetically to develop the national potential, will probably rest upon a program of economic nationalism that will have strong anti-United States overtones—unless and perhaps even if the United States has in the meantime succeeded in identifying itself with the forces of change and social reform.

Chile's economists, in overwhelming majority, have in recent years developed an increasingly hardy strain of economic nationalism. Although the policies they advocate have not yet been implemented by national administrations, their views are gaining ever wider acceptance among college students, intellectuals, labor leaders, and many political groups.[43]

One of the complaints most frequently voiced by the economic nationalists concerns the failure of foreign capital operations and foreign financial advisers to consider Chile's economic problems in terms of the country's social conditions.[44] In this respect, Chileans were particularly critical of the Klein-Saks mission, maintaining that it typified the inadequate approach of United States capitalist interests to the Chilean situation. This mission, undertaken by a private United States firm that was retained by President Carlos Ibáñez to advise on economic policy in the mid-1950's, was accused by numerous Chileans, not all of whom were sincere,[45] of failing to consider the relationship between economics and the explosive problems attendant upon the existence of a large percentage of the population that was denied the minimum requirements of human dignity. While the Klein-Saks anti-inflation recommendations, said the critics, might have resulted in balanced budgets and fiscal soundness and thus have aided business, they would not have produced a "trickle-down" to marginal economic groups. Instead, it was alleged, the recommendations ignored the urgent pressures of the social problem and would indeed have resulted in initial worsening of lower-class conditions.[46]

ECONOMIC NATIONALISM, REFORM ASPIRATIONS,
AND THE THIRD POSITION

Since the mid-nineteenth century, there has been a desire on the part of Chileans to achieve Latin-American unity as a means of offsetting United States cultural influence[47] and preventing direct intervention.[48] Beginning in the 1930's, Chile's interest in unity has been increasingly a manifestation of the desire to escape economic dependence upon the United States. In part, this has been because Chile's leftist reform elements have grown ever more fearful that the presence of United States capital, both public and private, constituted an obstacle to solution of the social problem. Their fear arose from the inevitable indirect influence in Chilean affairs that investments of great magnitude gave to the United States, and from that country's apparently calm acceptance of the social problem as a perpetual feature of Chile's national existence. To many Chileans it appeared that the only way to curtail the allegedly baneful influence of the United States on internal development was to strike at Yankee economic might in Chile. They understood that simply to drive out Yankee capital without providing for alternative financial resources to stimulate economic expansion would be ruinous. The economic integration of Latin America was often regarded as the alternative to dependence upon United States capital.

Juan Gómez Millas reflected these attitudes in 1942 when he urged Latin Americans to unite to put an end to United States influence that was frustrating their aspirations for progress.[49] After the Second World War the number of Chileans championing a Third Position for Latin America grew impressively. A Third Position meant to them a united Latin America that would gradually become strong enough to end its economic subservience to the United States and to establish independence from the wishes both of Washington and Moscow in formulating foreign and domestic policy.[50] Noncommunist reform advocates in Chile, discouraged by United States policies, looked with increasing favor upon the Third Position movement in the years between 1945 and 1961. They felt that officials in Washington and their representatives in the field, failing to recognize the seriousness of the social problem, had thought purely in terms of conserving the status quo and of traditional economic-aid programs that benefited only those already well established in the market economy. Because it was accused of these attitudes, the United States was held partially responsible for the poverty and misery in which the Chilean masses continued to live.

To hold United States influence to some degree responsible for social conditions was often no more than an attempt by Chileans to escape reckoning for their own shortsightedness by shifting the blame to outsiders. Furthermore, United States representatives were accredited to the existing governments in Chile, had to deal with them in reasonably friendly manner, and could not go about publicly denouncing their actions. Still, had it been the policy of Washington to insist that its representatives in Chile broaden their base of contacts, and had the State Department used the influence of polite propaganda and mild economic pressure to favor the cause of social reform, then the United States would have assumed a posture that could not have been overtly repudiated by the established governments and that would have been lauded by those seeking reform. Instead, the policies actually pursued by the United States prior to 1961 made inevitable anti-Yankee sentiments among the noncommunist left and contributed unnecessarily to the rising tide of economic nationalism.

10: SOCIAL CONDITIONS IN MID-TWENTIETH CENTURY CHILE: OLD PROBLEMS ACQUIRE NEW URGENCY

UNITED STATES MISAPPRAISALS OF CHILEAN SOCIAL CONDITIONS

THE SITUATION AS THE UNITED STATES HAS SEEN IT

The misappraisals made by United States observers, who have erred by way of excessive optimism because they have failed to probe beneath surface appearances, have sometimes encouraged their country to proceed as if no urgent social problem existed in Chile. In 1931, for example, upon his return to New York after an extended stay in Chile, Spruille Braden reported that the communist threat to that country had virtually disappeared. He added: "In Chile there is much less difference between the rich and the poor than in any country of the world that I know. . . . a tremendous leveling in life has occurred there. . . . The Chilean today confronts his hard situation with serenity." [1]

At the time Braden made this remarkable statement, statistics revealed that the annual average income for approximately 90 per cent of the entire Chilean labor force was one thousand pesos, roughly the equivalent of eighty dollars.[2] The million workers represented by this statistic had perhaps experienced a leveling process, but not of the sort to which Braden had alluded. Furthermore, the lower-income sectors and reform-minded elements showed that they were not, after all, serene: they established the short-lived Socialist Republic in 1932; they flocked to join socialist and communist organizations throughout the 1930's; and in the 1938 presidential elections they helped achieve victory for the candidate of the Radical-Socialist-Communist Party alliance.

By no means have all United States observers formulated naively optimistic appraisals concerning Chile.[3] In 1936 George McBride in a classic study of Chilean agrarian society[4] painted a bleak and accurate picture of the master-and-man structure and depicted the horrors of the marginal existence led by thousands who were virtually serfs. Some twenty-five years later, the *New York Times* published factual, hard-hitting editorials on Chile's appalling social conditions. But the disconcerting message for some reason has never been taken to heart, and the United States has continued largely to judge Chile by the writings and utterances of suave and distinguished upper-class writers and diplomats who constantly offer assurances of their country's progressivism. This approach is clearly demonstrated in the book *Chile through Embassy Windows*,[5] in which Claude G. Bowers, United States ambassador in Santiago from 1939 to 1954, heaped uncritical praise upon all the superficial aspects of Chilean life and judged the country by its lustrous veneer. *The Atlantic Monthly* in one of its 1959 "Reports" [6] found Chile a nation where major problems were being resolved. In the same year, upon returning from his Latin-American tour, President Eisenhower displayed confidence and noted that when visiting a Chilean housing project he could tell by looking into the eyes of the occupants that he was viewing a happy people. These happy-eyed people gave the majority of their votes in the 1958 presidential and in the 1961 congressional elections to the Marxist ticket.

THE SITUATION AS OTHERS HAVE SEEN IT

Other foreign observers and many Chileans have not been so easily deceived. In 1923 the French writer André Bellesort in *La jeune amérique*[7] noted that Chile, although appearing to be politically the best organized of the Latin-American republics, was undermined by the existence of a lower class so miserable, so bereft of hope, that it had neither sufficient energy nor class consciousness to aspire toward improvement. Nearly fifteen years later Radical Party Senator Gabriel González Videla, later to serve his country as president, implied in one of his most brilliant speeches in the upper chamber that the French writer's gloomy appraisal was still applicable. If the Chilean rightists, asserted González Videla, lost a proportion of their livestock equal to that of the annual human loss occasioned by infant mortality and abortion, they would take immediate steps to remedy the situation. But in the face of the manpower loss to the Chilean race, they assumed always a calm attitude and spoke of the inevitable balance of nature. With considerable eloquence González Videla pleaded that Chile begin to utilize the potential of all classes of the population; that it take special pains to safeguard the health of the young and to provide them with adequate schools, so that a Chilean's ability to rise in society would be limited only by his own capacity.[8] This impassioned denunciation of Chile's social structure was timely in 1937. It would have been equally timely at the beginning of the 1960's.

CHILE'S CULTURE OF POVERTY*

The Statistics of Poverty and Wealth

Statistics must be called upon to support so critical a generalization. According to figures compiled by the Chilean Development Corporation (*Corporación de Fomento de Producción*), the real income of all groups in Chile grew approximately 40 per cent between 1940 and 1953. Distribution of this income, however, worked to the disadvantage of lower-class manual laborers. These workers, comprising roughly 57 per cent of the active population, won an increase in effective remuneration of only 7 per cent. The real income of white-collar workers rose an estimated 46 per cent, and that of proprietors, of the self-employed and of workers in the various services soared 60 per cent.[9] Little wonder, then, that Roberto Jadue Saba in a 1960 study affirmed: ". . . from 1940 to 1954 there has been a regressive redistribution of total income, carried out at the expense of the lower-income groups."[10]

This conclusion, confirmed in a later study by Helio Varela,[11] becomes all the more meaningful in the light of a reliable estimate that in 1942—before the retrogressive redistribution process was well under way—77 per cent of the working force did not earn sufficient income to provide a single man with a decent and respectable

* The term "Culture of Poverty" is borrowed from the title of a paper presented in Urbana on October 12, 1961, by the University of Illinois' brilliant anthropologist, Oscar Lewis.

mode of life. Only 0.3 per cent enjoyed income adequate to provide the minimal standards of respectable living for a family of four.[12]

The deterioration of the social situation in Chile can be traced in part to the failure of upper-income groups to contribute to national well-being. The British economist Nicholas Kaldor, on the basis of statistics compiled by the Chilean Development Corporation and the United Nations' Economic Commission for Latin America, estimated in 1956 that Chile's wealthiest groups pay 14.7 per cent of their income in taxes, while spending 64.3 per cent on consumer goods.[13] The increasingly regressive nature of the Chilean tax structure, noted in 1957 by the International Monetary Fund,[14] is further demonstrated by the fact that government revenue derived from direct taxes declined from 4.3 per cent of total treasury income in 1946, to 4.0 per cent in 1952, while income derived from indirect taxes increased in the same period from 7.8 per cent to 9.2 per cent.[15] Moreover, between 1940 and 1950, the portion of government income obtained from internal taxes, exclusive of customs revenue, has varied between the low rates of 13.2 per cent and 16.2 per cent.[16] This has led several economists to believe that if the large amount spent by Chilean upper classes on conspicuous consumption could be captured by the government through progressive taxation and channeled into productive ventures, Chile could realize annual capital-formation figures comparable to those of highly developed countries and make notable gains toward solving social and economic problems through use of domestic resources.[17]

The situation depicted by the above statistics makes all the more incredible a recent pronouncement by Liberal Party stalwart and prominent businessman Domingo Arteaga. In a communiqué widely publicized in 1960, Arteaga objected to plans calling for a mild increase in upper-level income taxes to help meet the expenses of reconstructing southern Chile after the catastrophic May earthquakes. Arteaga, repeating charges previously made by Liberal Party President Gregorio Amunátegui, argued that Chilean upper classes were already overtaxed. He suggested that the current emergency be met at least in part by having workers contribute without remuneration an extra hour of work each day! [18]

Other statistics say in different ways what has already been revealed. Thus, economist Jorge Ahumada has published figures showing that the top 5 per cent of Chile's higher income group enjoys a mean annual income twenty-two times greater than the average income of laborers. Put in other terms, this means that 5 per cent of the population receives slightly more than a third of total national income, and that close to 60 per cent, made up of laborers and their families, gains one fifth.[19] The same situation has been noted by Radical Party economist Alberto Baltra. In 1957 Baltra expressed alarm over the fact that per-capita consumption of upper income groups was fourteen times greater than that of manual and white-collar workers.[20]

The grinding lower-class poverty to which these figures attest has led many to question the wisdom of President Jorge Alessandri's anti-inflation measures. In 1959 and 1960, Alessandri fought inflation essentially by calling upon workers to make the first and the greatest sacrifice—a policy that had also been urged by United States advisers in the 1955-1956 Klein-Saks mission. Workers were asked to accept wage readjustments of one third of the increase in cost of living. This outraged even the usually moderate Daniel Armanet, long-time director of the excellent monthly, *Economía y Finanzas*. Armanet asserted: "To maintain salaries almost unalterable when the level of prices has risen, is mathematically the same as to lower them when prices have remained stable. This, in a country of low living standards, is an intolerable measure." [21]

What do some of the statistics that have been cited mean, when translated into concrete examples of human existence in Chile? What are some of the inescapable conditions of life for Chile's city-dwelling lower classes?

THE URBAN POOR

Illiteracy and Illegitimacy. National illiteracy figures and educational survey data suggest that over one fourth of the urban lower classes are either illiterate, and therefore disfranchised, or else educated only to the extent of being able to spell out laboriously the simplest words. Even more suggestive of governmental inattention to social problems is the fact that illiteracy rates have tended to remain rather constant between 1930 and 1952, amounting in both years to approximately 25 per cent of the population.[22] The Chilean education structure has not, during the past generation, been given the funds or direction necessary to enable it to keep pace with the population increase. Much of the potential of the Chilean population, therefore, remains unrealized. This situation is all the more lamentable in view of the fact that in previous generations, Chile was one of the leaders among Latin-American nations in educational advances.

In addition to the handicap of illiteracy, many of Chile's urban lower classes suffer from the stigma of illegitimacy. The over-all rate of illegitimacy continues to hover around 30 per cent,[23] which implies that close to 50 per cent of the lower classes are illegitimate.

Housing Conditions. In 1941, a government housing agency estimated that 152,000 new units would have to be constructed within the next nine years to house adequately the anticipated population increment. Even if these units had been constructed, nothing would have been done for those living in overcrowded, unsanitary squalor as of 1941. But, in the nine-year period the number of units actually constructed was 50,903.[24] Statistics for 1941 and 1942 showed that of the 6,100 children brought to court on various criminal charges, 95 per cent came from sub-standard homes, or else had no homes at all.[25] Allocation of public funds for housing projects, nonetheless, aroused the ire of Senator Fernando Alessandri Rodríguez who argued in 1943 that private enterprise alone must be allowed to provide houses for the needy. Senator Alessandri maintained that the United States had relied exclusively upon private enterprise in its housing projects, and admonished Chileans to follow this enlightened procedure.[26]

A government census, the results of which were published in 1955, declared that 30 per cent of the population was housed in units not meeting minimal sanitary standards.[27] Experts, moreover, estimated that between 1953 and 1959 the number of urgently needed housing units rose from 400,000 to 500,000.[28] Another aspect of the problem was underscored by an economist who noted in 1957 that Chilean rentals take one of the highest percentages of income of any country in the world.[29] One consequence is the prevalence of *callampas* (literally, mushrooms), slum areas made up of shacks constructed by squatters which simply grow spontaneously without planning, authorization, or control.

Even more discouraging is the blatant disregard for human dignity which the government has sometimes shown in constructing slum-clearance projects. "Lo Valledor" in Santiago is an example. Its approximately 11,000 units are capable of providing shelter for between 50,000 and 80,000 persons. But its wooden huts of concentration-camp uniformity into which thousands can be crowded impress many viewers, be they housing experts or amateur observers, as an outrage to humanity. Unheated, lacking a sewage system and indoor water, separated by barbed wire, with an outdoor toilet boasting not the slightest semblance of privacy, they create an ambient which seems calculated to deprive their occupants of any hope for a decent existence. Nowhere else in Latin America has this writer seen such a dreary array of flimsily slapped-together wooden crates masquerading as a government housing project. The few Chilean upper- or middle-class members who have seen "Lo Valledor" typically shrug their shoulders when queried about the matter, and note that such houses are all the lower classes deserve, and are at least better than the *callampas* which they ostensibly replace. The last is a debatable contention. The *callampa* shacks at least demonstrate an originality and spontaneity in construction and design that might actually be more stimulating to the imagination and the psyche of their dwellers than the stolid sameness of the "Lo Valledor" huts.

Alcoholism and Undernourishment. Chilean doctors and students of social conditions have long been convinced that per-capita alcohol consumption is higher in Chile than in any other Latin-American country. The striking fact of this situation is that upper and middle classes are, it is commonly agreed, reasonably temperate. This means that the lower classes must do much more than their share in driving up consumption figures. This seems in particular to be a function of the lower-class men—for their women are not noted for drinking excesses. In various urban slum areas it is estimated that from 20 per cent to 30 per cent of the men are chronic drunkards, who can be expected to spend the majority of weekends on prolonged binges.[30]

The 1944 statistics pertaining to arrests made for drunkenness give some interesting insights into the problem: of those detained that year for public intoxication, only 3 per cent had a secondary education, and 16 per cent were illiterate; moreover, the instances in which manual workers were arrested for drunkenness came to approximately one fifth of the total number of unskilled laborers in Chile.[31]

The habitual drunkenness of a large portion of lower-class workers produces notable effects on Chilean productivity. Industrial accidents occur at the highest rate on Monday, and absenteeism is also highest on that day.[32] There is a commonplace joke in Chile that Monday is a sort of unofficial holiday, the so-called San Lunes, or Blessed Monday.

Lower-class chronic drunkenness arises in part from the fact that, given relative food and wine costs, wine is often the cheapest source of caloric energy. Therefore, many men can scarcely afford not to be drunkards.[33] Closely connected to drunkenness, then, is the problem of undernourishment. In 1945, careful investigations revealed that only 14 per cent of the primary school students did not show evidence of long-term undernourishment.[34] At about the same time Senator Guillermo Azócar described in the upper chamber how one could stand on any street corner of Santiago and observe the degeneration of the Chilean race in the parading files of the sick, lame, deformed, and underfed. The senator further observed that whenever he began to discuss this matter, he was soon induced to desist because of the bored and annoyed expressions of his colleagues.[35] In the years following Azócar's gloomy appraisal, the problem of undernourishment has become more acute. Recent studies indicate that the average height of Chileans is now actually declining because of malnutrition.[36]

Disease and Infant Mortality. Given the background already described, it is only natural that Chile has long had one of the highest tuberculosis rates, as well as one of the shortest spans of average life expectancy, of all the Latin-American republics.[37] In addition, it is likely that one out of every four children born to urban, lower-class parents will die before reaching the age of five. The infant mortality rate in Chile is still one of the highest in the southern hemisphere.[38]

GENERAL OBSERVATIONS ON CHILE'S URBAN LOWER CLASSES

Because of the conditions in which they live, urban lower classes are generally regarded by their social superiors as the dregs of humanity, incapable of contributing anything except the brute labor which makes it possible for the upper classes to pursue their "higher cultural calling." Once a year, however, the humble laborers do have a holiday dedicated to them, the day of the Chilean *roto* (literally, broken one). They are then privileged to hear on the radio or at mass gatherings flowery oratory which proclaims the virtues and superiority of the Chilean lower classes. If they could read, they might also marvel at some of the books which convey the same message.[39] In this way, privileged-class orators and writers offer assurances that the *rotos* have not been wronged, for, as the reasoning goes, they continue to be superior to lower classes elsewhere in the world.

There is little opportunity for the *roto* to advance into a social position in which he can command true respect. The fact that the middle class of Chile is growing proportionately rather more than the population as a whole[40] is often taken as an indication of social mobility, the assumption being that lower classes are moving up to middle-class position. There is much need for careful sociological surveys to examine this question, but there are grounds for suspicion that the appearance is deceptive. Not only have fallen aristocrats swelled the ranks of the middle class, but immigration has played a vitally important role in increasing its numbers.[41] Thus in 1940, Chile's 107,273 foreign-born found, to an overwhelming degree, their social place in the middle class.[42] It is therefore arguable that Chile's growing middle class does not evidence significant opportunity for native lower-class social advancement.

Leading a subhuman, marginal existence, denied any likelihood that they or their children will greatly improve their lot, the Chilean *rotos* survive on the basis of their incredible stamina, patience, resignation, inward resources, and a zest for life that even the most adverse circumstances cannot totally crush. The women in this class, especially, struggle heroically to provide their children with the most essential elements of food and clothing so that they need not join the hordes of juvenile beggars roaming city streets.

It is the *roto* children who particularly arrest the attention of visitors to the poorer districts of Chilean urban centers. In the attentive and alert expressions of so many of them, promise, ability, and intelligence seem clearly revealed. It is when contemplating this youth that many Chileans and foreigners alike are apt to wonder how much longer a social system that dooms to frustration their precocious talent can continue to survive. Under present conditions, the twinkling eyes and the laughing faces are apt to give way within a short time to sullen masks. Chile's Nobel Prize-winning poetess Gabriela Mistral commented in the early 1920's upon the early age at which the lower-class Chilean child lost the habit of falling into spontaneous laughter.[48] The present writer will never forget a 1960 trip to the coal-mining city of Lota. There, as the late-afternoon sun was beginning to set on an unforgettably beautiful scene of tree-covered hills sloping down to a pounding surf, a group of women was seen proceeding down the town's main street. There must have been over a hundred of them, glum-expressioned, sallow-complected, their faces lined and distorted by concern, anxiety and, undoubtedly in many cases, by sickness. In the course of the half an hour or more in which they were observed, scarcely a handful so much as smiled. Almost silently, as if in a state of depression and disassociation from their surroundings, they slowly trudged toward their homes. They were dressed in the dark blue uniforms of the Chilean public schools. Their ages must have ranged from twelve to eighteen.

Aspects of Rural Chile

The social conditions of agrarian life are no better than those encountered in urban regions. In rural Chile there still endures an outmoded, nonproductive, semifeudalistic land and social structure that denies to the serf (*inquilino*) any right to share in the riches of society beyond what his master may paternalistically dole out to him. It is a fact, moreover, that although Chile's gross agricultural output has increased slightly since the early 1940's, per-capita productivity has notably declined.[44] The failure of agricultural production to keep pace with rising needs in Chile has been one significant factor contributing to the post-Second World War inflation and has also forced the nation to import huge quantities of food. During the 1950's Chile, with some of the finest land resources in Latin America, capable according to most authorities not only of feeding its own population but of providing food for sister republics as well, devoted an annual average of approximately one sixth of its foreign currency expenditures to food imports.[45] How has this incredible situation come into being? One authority asserts: "The basic reason underlying the failure of Chilean agriculture to keep up with growing needs may have to be sought in its semi-feudal structure." [46]

Chilean agricultural land is still concentrated in the hands of a few. It is estimated that 9.7 per cent of agrarian property holders own 86 per cent of the arable land, while 74.6 per cent own 5.2 per cent. In the provinces of Santiago, Valparaíso, and Aconcagua the situation is even more unbalanced, with 7 per cent of the landowners possessing 92 per cent of the land.[47] Many of the large-estate owners are urban *nouveau riche* elements that have acquired land relatively recently. Others, though descendants of traditionally landowning families, have at some period in the twentieth century acquired urban and foreign economic interests which furnish the major portion of their income. For neither group of landowners does essential livelihood depend upon productive use of rural property. Furthermore, a sense of responsibility to the common good has never developed to the extent necessary to induce them to increase output. A study prepared by the Economic Commission for Latin America in 1953 revealed that vast areas of land in Santiago and Valparaíso provinces, although well suited to intensive farming, were not under cultivation. The study showed further that 35 per cent of the landholders who owned arable land that was neither under cultivation nor in pasture were simply not interested in augmenting production.[48]

The owners of the larger rural estates, the very men who have shown the least interest in raising production, obtain the greatest proportion of the agricultural credit that is available in Chile. The result is that the funds extended to agrarian applicants by the State Bank (*Banco del Estado*) are more often operational than improvement loans. With inflation during the 1950's frequently causing a rise in cost of living that exceeded 20 per cent annually, many landowners discovered they could come out ahead by borrowing money for operation expenses at 15 per cent to 18 per cent interest. The owners of medium-sized holdings who, as a group, have traditionally shown the greatest incentive to raise productivity,[49] have in actual practice been discriminated against in obtaining credit.

The large estate owners' lack of interest in productive management as a means of bringing food to the hungry is illustrated by the fact that in 1961 the number of extensive rural holdings offered for sale in Chile was considerably more than the market could absorb. Worried by the mounting pressure for legislation that would require effective utilization of land, the owners, who are not primarily dependent upon income from their agrarian operations, were trying to dispose of their farm property. They simply did not want to be bothered with introducing advanced methods of production.

The lack of concern which the landowners have shown for the basic needs of the lower classes is evident also in the type of relations which many have maintained with their serfs. The National Society of Agriculture (*Sociedad Nacional de Agricultura*), the most powerful association of landowners, has customarily exerted its full force and influence to deny to the rural worker the right to enter into agrarian syndicates or cooperatives. The power of the landowners is reflected also in the fact that the majority of rural laborers are not included in the benefits of the social security laws.[50] Moreover, there is little desire on the part of many landowners to elevate the educational and cultural level of these laborers, to turn them into well-fed, efficient workers with incentives for greater output. Given their basic social and economic attitudes, nothing could interest these landowners less. This situation once led Gabriela Mistral to observe: "Our rural barbarism is enormous." [51]

The consequence of the rural barbarism which still prevails is the maintenance of an inefficient labor pattern, with workers remaining docile and unskilled and without incentive for self-improvement. These workers have never experienced what it is to pit themselves against a challenge and, by aggressiveness and imagination, by modifying old means and adopting new, to master it. They have remained, therefore, a stolid, nonassertive, inertia-bound mass, totally unassimilated into a modern economic structure.[52] When they flock to the cities, as many have done in the mid-twentieth century,[53] they bring with them none of the confidence that arises from having mastered a task. Their only psychological baggage is lack of imagination, fatalistic resignation, suspicion of what is new, and the response of removing the hat when the boss addresses them. They are wholly unprepared to defend their rights in a new urban environment, and hence they simply swell the ranks of easily exploitable labor. Their continuing influx into the cities is probably one reason why urban labor forces have thus far been rather inarticulate, and why the task of the organizer is difficult in the extreme.[54]

The continuance of semifeudalism, then, has contributed to the chronic undernourishment of vast population segments, to the disrepute of manual labor in general and to the freezing of urban manual laborers in their lowly social position, and to the difficulty of erecting a modern economic structure in the cities. The plight of the urban underlings cannot be fundamentally bettered until the rural landowners are either goaded into contributing to the over-all needs of the nation, or until they are stripped of their present power and influence.

THE MIDDLE CLASS AS A CONTRIBUTING
FACTOR TO THE CULTURE OF POVERTY

MIDDLE CLASS-UPPER CLASS ALLIANCE

It is possible to blame the landowners rather directly for the deterioration of Chilean agriculture, and indirectly for the poverty
and stagnation of the urban centers. It is logical to assess Chile's
urban middle class—many members of which are also landowners
—with a major share of the direct responsibility for the plight of
the lower classes in the cities. Chile's urban middle sectors have
traditionally demonstrated colossal indifference to the social problem and have dedicated themselves to defending the value-judgments of the upper classes.[55]

The readily observable traits of the middle class have led to the
introduction into the Chilean vocabulary of the word *siútico*. A
siútico is a middle-class individual who emulates the aristocracy and
its usages and hopes to be taken for one of its members.[56] It is
generally agreed that Chile's middle class abounds in *siúticos*.

Because of their desire to assume upper-class attitudes, middle
group members have developed very little consciousness of themselves as members of a distinct class. It is extremely difficult to
detect opinions, customs, and value-judgments in Chile that are
demonstrably middle class. Almost the only clear middle-class
trait has been the tendency to shun the lower mass and to embrace
the aristocracy. This fact may stem in part from the fact that
historically, as has already been noted,[57] the Chilean aristocracy has
in general been more open to entry by middle-class elements than
in other Latin-American countries.

Also fostering an alliance between middle and upper social sectors was the fact that the anticlericalism which erupted in nineteenth-century Chile probably received more direction and impetus
from the aristocracy than was common in other of the southern
republics. Elsewhere in Latin America, anticlericalism appears to
have been more nearly a middle-class movement. In Chile, of
course, the middle class did contribute to the anticlerical movement
and to the acceptance of the philosophy of positivism. But these
activities did not pit the Chilean middle class against the aris-

tocracy. Rather, they allied the middle class with at least that portion of the aristocracy that was included in the Liberal and Radical parties.

A large number of Chilean writers have turned their attention to the middle class. In 1919, *El Mercurio* editorialized that the middle class had traditionally remained aloof from political and social agitation. The paper held that the middle class, concerned with protecting its dignity, had customarily supported the position of the established ruling sectors.[58] Later in the same year other *El Mercurio* editorials commented that because of the manner in which the upper class had opened its ranks to the middle, there were really only two classes in the country: the united upper and middle, and the lower.[59] It is also revealing that the first attempt to mold the middle class into a cohesive, articulate group, leading in 1919 to formation of the Middle Class Federation (*Federación de la Clase Media*), produced a platform which, although containing a mild warning to the oligarchy to refrain from some of its more notorious abuses, said absolutely nothing about aiding the lower classes.[60] A decade later, Santiago Macchiavello speculated that Chile's main ills had stemmed from exploitation of the lower by the middle class, and from the attempt by members of the latter to pose as aristocrats and therefore to shun all useful and productive work.[61] In the early 1930's, when Chile was suffering from the effects of the depression, *El Mercurio* noted approvingly that in these times of crisis, the Chilean middle class had once again demonstrated its customary responsibility by siding with upper classes in the attempt to cope with economic disruption.[62]

Journalist Jorge Gustavo Silva observed in 1930: ". . . in whatever profession they enter, middle class elements seek to obscure their humble origins and to convert themselves, even at the risk of appearing ridiculous, into aristocrats and oligarchs."[63] A much more scathing attack against the middle class was delivered by Gabriela Mistral. She charged it with having turned viciously upon the manual laborers and with having failed to contribute to balanced national development.[64] The great poetess noted also the revulsion felt by novelist Pedro Prado for the middle class because of the manner in whch it had harassed the humble people.[65] Distinguished author Domingo Melfi suggested in 1948 that the plot situation which had most intrigued Chilean novelists in the twentieth century was the rise of a middle-class hero into the aristocracy, either by the acquisition of wealth or by a judicious marriage. To Melfi, this indicated the lack of middle-class consciousness.[66] Other journalists and critics, as Raúl Silva Castro, Manuel Rojas, and Hernán Díaz Arrieta (pseud., Alone), have agreed that middle- and upper-class authors alike have tended to ignore in their fiction the theme of Chile's social problem and the plight of the masses.[67]

Raúl Alarcón Pino, author of the principal—but nonetheless superficial—university dissertation that has been written on the Chilean middle class, notes that the main vice of this sector is its adoration of the aristocracy's way of life.[68] Alarcón Pino asserts that the Chilean middle class has always wanted to be taken for the aristocracy and that it has remained steadfastly unconvinced that it has any common purpose with the lower classes.[69] Much the same message is conveyed by Francisco Pinto Salvatierra, who argues that the overriding cause of Chilean stagnation, which threatens to become actual retrogression, is the total indifference of the middle class to the mounting social and economic problems of the masses.[70]

As much as any single Chilean writer and intellectual, Julio Vega has studied the role of the middle class. Vega has concluded that in Chile there is no artisan tradition. The artisan's chief desire is that his son should enter one of the professions that is recognized as the province of the upper classes.[71] Members of the lower middle class, Vega observed, will spend most of their income on clothes and housing, trying to present an upper-class façade. The result is that not enough of the budget is allocated for food and consequently some middle-class members are actually more undernourished than the lower classes.[72]

An observer of the social scene in 1951, Julio Heise González, offered assurance that the middle class had begun finally to develop a class consciousness, to emancipate itself from prejudice, to withdraw from the traditional aristocracy, and to approach the proletariat. Two pages later in the same work he seemed to contradict himself when he stated that members of the middle class were perpetuating their poverty by their conspicuous consumption, apparently in the desire to create the impression that they belonged to a higher social level than actually they did.[73]

The number of authors who have commented upon the middle-class betrayal and exploitation of the manual laborers is legion.[74] Not only because of their impressive number, but because of their close agreement, their charges cannot be lightly dismissed. This writer's own observations and conversations in Chile have confirmed, moreover, that the country is still to a large degree characterized by a close association between upper and middle groups which works to the disadvantage of the lower mass.

Probably the attitudes of Chile's middle class have produced an important superficial advantage for the country. Because this group has in its political, social, and economic thinking so closely reflected the attitudes of the aristocracy, there has been almost no disruption as middle sectors have won increasing power in Chilean politics. This has contributed notably to Chilean stability. The role assumed by middle sectors may also have contributed to economic and social stagnation.

Obviously, not all middle-class members uphold aristocratic values. As of 1962 there were many signs that some middle groups might sincerely be seeking an alliance with the lower classes and not (as in the past) simply trying through hypocritical promises to play the game of political opportunism. Stung by inflation and with their hopes for expanding opportunity frustrated by Chile's lack of real growth, some middle-class supporters of the Christian Democrat Party, of the activist wing of the Radical Party, and of the FRAP alliance, seemed intent upon siding with the lower masses in a genuine attempt to alter the traditional sociopolitical structure. Some of the young members of the Conservative Party seemed also to fit into this category. This was a relatively new development in Chilean politics, one that could in the years ahead prove to be of great significance.

EDUCATION AND THE CLASSES

Since early in this century Chilean educators and intellectuals have been writing books pointing out the inadequacy and outmoded orientation of the national educational structure. One of the features most commonly criticized is the lack of attention to technical education, with the accompanying overemphasis of the philosophical approach. This not only has slowed the rate of economic progress, but has meant that the typical middle-class product of the national educational system—which is, incidentally, largely controlled by middle-class, Radical Party bureaucrats—has been taught to think like an aristocrat of the past century and to hold in disdain manual labor and those who perform it.

As early as 1910, Alejandro Venegas in *Sinceridad* charged Chilean education with turning out stuffy sycophants of the aristocracy, utterly devoid of interest in the common good and unable to contribute to the vitally needed economic progress of their country. Two years later, Francisco Antonio Encina suggested in his *Nuestra inferioridad económica* that the type of education received made it impossible for the average Chilean to respond adequately to modern economic challenges. In 1916, *El Mercurio* observed: "We have among us thousands of university graduates who are true monuments of uselessness, and at the same time a living indictment of our national educational system." [75] The early 1920's saw several Chilean congressmen complaining that education only prepared their countrymen to become doctors, lawyers, architects, and engineers versed exclusively in theory, and did nothing to prepare a person to develop the nation's natural wealth.[76] Many national congressmen also agreed that Chilean education helped preserve class prejudice and at the same time implanted disdain for labor and technical proficiency.

The later criticisms that have been heaped upon education are well summarized in the writings of Amanda Labarca, who for longer than she might care to recall has been one of Chile's outstanding *pensadores*, feminists, and educators. Possessing faith in the ultimate role of the middle class in moving Chile ahead, Labarca feels that a superannuated educational system has unduly delayed this class in fulfilling its destiny.[77] Coming to the heart of the problem, another writer-educator asserted in 1950 that education must begin to emancipate itself from the social prejudices which lead 99 per cent of those entering the *liceo*—somewhat the equivalent of the United States high school, but organized around an entirely different curriculum and dedicated to a different social purpose—to want to be professionals, so as to gain access to the world of the aristocracy. Educators, it was further alleged, have passively permitted the continuing neglect of those studies that would be genuinely useful in developing the country.[78]

Chilean education, unfortunately, withstood the short-lived challenge of dictator Ibáñez' (1927-1931) reform program. It seems still to pursue an eighteenth-century ideal, wishing to produce persons trained in languages, metaphysics, and the arts, rather than in handicrafts, nutrition, or social and economic planning. It emphasizes also memorization of the pronouncements of the sages of bygone eras, rather than imaginative adaptation to new circumstances. Gunnar Myrdal once noted that these characteristics, found in many underdeveloped countries, represent a dangerous cultural lag.[79] Certainly in Chile they have operated to cement an alliance between upper and middle classes, to produce callous ennui in the face of social problems, and to stymie physical progress. They have contributed also to the unwarranted expansion of the personnel in the various services by encouraging disdain for technological skill and productive labor. In 1930, 35.5 per cent of the active population was employed in rendering services. By 1949, the percentage stood at 41.4 per cent. During the same period the percentage of those occupied in the production of goods, that is, in agriculture, industry, construction, and mining, decreased from 64.5 per cent to 58.6 per cent.[80] These figures underline an appraisal made by Enrique Molina in 1942: "Chileans are highly civilized in regard to consuming, but primitive when it comes to producing." [81]

RACIAL CONSIDERATIONS AND THE CLASSES

The majority of Chile's lower classes display recognizable Indian features, often manifest in some degree of skin-darkness. On the other hand, the great majority of the middle and practically the entirety of the upper classes do not clearly exhibit physical characteristics attributable to Indian blood. This fact has exercised profound effects upon the nation's social structure and has contributed to the incredible slowness of the ruling classes in concerning themselves with the crushing burdens of the lower classes.

Racist interpretations are commonplace in Chile. Early in the twentieth century, Nicolás Palacios in a very popular book, *La raza chilena*,[82] suggested that Chilean superiority to other Latin-American populations stemmed largely from the predominance of Basque or Gothic blood. In later times one of the most convinced of Chile's many racists has been the distinguished historian Francisco Antonio Encina, who basically repeats the Palacios assertions about the superiority of Gothic blood.[83] Julio César Jobet appeared to be largely justified when he accused Encina in 1949 of believing in the racist theories of Joseph Arthur de Gobineau and Houston Stewart Chamberlain.[84] Similar charges could be leveled against such Chilean *pensadores* as Carlos Keller, the late Alberto Edwards Vives,[85] and a multitude of lesser writers. The prevalence of racist interpretations among Chilean intellectuals may well be one reason why nazism made such inroads among the youth of Chile's better-educated families.

If Chilean superiority is regarded as the consequence of Basque or Gothic blood, what place is left for the Indian and those who share his blood? It is not necessary to search far in Chilean literature for the answer. Politician and author Alberto Cabero argued that Chileans are superior to Peruvians because there are few Indians and mixed-bloods in Chile.[86] Statesman and foreign-policy expert Galvarino Gallardo Nieto noted that one of the obstacles to attainment of the Pan-American ideal is that white countries such as Chile cannot be expected to deal as equals with Indian, tropical, turbulent nations.[87] Writing in the 1930's when he was president of the State Bank, Guillermo Subercaseaux cautioned Chileans not to copy Mexican socialism: Chile, he opined, should not be influenced by the practices of inferior races, but should look more toward Europe and other Latin-American countries where the European heritage had not been corrupted by Indian legacies.[88] Diplomat-author Emilio Rodríguez Mendoza was outraged when a Guayaquil (Ecuador) daily published a picture in which he appeared with two other Chileans over the caption, "The Araucanian diplomats." [89] Rodríguez, who at another time was justifiably accused by Gabriela Mistral of harboring anti-Indian prejudices,[90] was quick to assert that he had no Araucanian blood.

The anti-Indian literature produced in Chile is vast.[91] A random sampling of some of the published opinions illustrates the broad aspects of the prejudice that is an important national characteristic. One writer asserted that high infant mortality among the lower classes results from the stupidity and proneness toward uncleanliness and drunkenness bequeathed by their Indian blood;[92] another stated that the mental inferiority of Araucanians is recognized by almost all Chileans;[93] while from still a different source came the pronouncement that the racial superiority of the white upper classes made unavoidable the exploitation of the inferior, mixed-blood, lower classes.[94] A prominent army general contended that Indians are lazy, dirty, irresponsible, and that southern Chile was doomed unless Indian influence was eradicated by European immigration.[95] A noted intellectual was even more pessimistic, observing that because Chilean lower classes in general were contaminated by Indian blood, national progress was unlikely unless a veritable flood of white immigration descended upon the entire country.[96] Echoing this pessimistic tone, another writer suggested that the Indian mentality, which could not advance beyond concepts of subsistence production, was responsible for Chile's problems.[97] On the other hand, there have been many writers who although defending the Indian have sadly noted the prevailing tendency to hold aborigines and those sharing their blood in contempt,[98] and to consider the Indians and mixed-bloods as an impediment to national progress.[99]

The anti-Indian prejudice may explain why the visitor to Chile is assured over and over again, "We have no Indians, and therefore no Indian problem, here." The typical Chilean attitude was expressed once by Deputy Ricasio Retamales who during congressional debates interjected: "What, are there still Indians in Chile? I think not." [100] For a Chilean who is proudly nationalistic and optimistic about the progress potential of his country, and who is at the same time dedicated to belief in the inferiority of Indians and mestizos, it is convenient to forget the overwhelming evidence of Indian blood among the lower classes and the fact that, as Benjamín Subercaseaux has observed, the Chilean lower class is distinguished primarily by its color.[101] It is possible that the cruel treatment of the mixed-blood lower classes has stemmed from the fact that the upper and middle sectors would really be happier if somehow the reminder of Indian inheritance in Chile could be stamped out.

Upper-class criteria have even permeated down to the lowest social strata. Skin tone is the first feature that many of the humblest folk look to in assessing the physical qualities of a new-born child. If light, the child is beautiful (*precioso*); if dark, it is ugly (*feo*). This is a tragic indication of the psychological trauma which, in addition to material adversity, afflicts the lower classes.

The factor of Indian blood has contributed in telling manner to middle-class rejection of the lower classes. Priding itself on its whiteness, the middle class by and large believes in the inferiority of Indians and mixed bloods. Clinging to the aristocracy, it has erected a psychological barrier between itself and at least one third of the population. To a subtler but to just as deep-rooted an extent as in Peru, Ecuador, Bolivia, and Guatemala, the Indian problem, or a variant of it, is involved in Chile's social and economic ills.

THE TWO CHILES

The profound consequences of the social problem have created in Chile two distinct modes of existence separated by well-nigh unbreachable barriers. There is a Chile of the rulers and the assimilated portion of the population, a Chile noted for its stability, orderliness, sophistication, culture, and enlightened legal and political institutions. There is another Chile made up of people who can best be described (in words made famous by Arnold Toynbee) as an internal proletariat: in society but not of society. Put in other terms, it is safe to say that while Chile is a nation ostensibly with a population of over 7,000,000, considerably less than 5,000,000 actually participate or will participate upon reaching maturity in the vital currents of national existence. The other more than 2,000,000 exist in a category that is somewhat similar to serfdom or slavery. Because of their situation they are themselves demoralized, and bereft of hope and vitality. Perhaps worse, the presence of an immobile, inert mass of still docile and fatalistic workers demoralizes, corrupts, and enervates those who take advantage of them and imparts a viciously derogatory connotation to the word labor.

The gulf between the two population elements has prevented Chile from producing the consistent, dynamic, and energetic drive that is necessary to impel an underdeveloped country into the modern era. A nation that purposely prevents intercourse, communication, mobility, and cross-pollination among the social classes automatically limits its potential for progress in the sort of world that exists in the twentieth century. What is more, in the long run, it invites a devastating social revolution.

11: THE UNITED STATES
AND THE TWO CHILES

INTRODUCTION

THE UNITED STATES AND THE CHILEAN RULING GROUPS:
ALLIANCE FOR STAGNATION

In Chile, especially since the 1920's, many of the most active intellectual and political groups have been dedicated, either actually or verbally, to correcting the evils of a social structure that is repressive and inflexibly unprogressive. They have, in short, been concerned with fusing the two Chiles into one. This task inevitably entails considerable social and economic change. Where are large segments of the Chilean people now inclined to seek their patterns of change? It would be comforting to reply that they turn to the United States. Actually, it is the communist world that holds out programs of transformation that increasingly allure. Why is this?

Traditionally, the United States has fairly bristled with hostility in the face of new ideas and notions of change in Chile. The seeming desire to champion the status quo stems in part from the singular success of the United States in fashioning domestic policies that have produced an affluent society with a broad basis of economic and political participation. Radical notions of reform and change, therefore, insofar as they relate to the United States itself, are suspect and in many instances rightly so. Unfortunately, conservative criteria arising from this domestic context are projected for the evaluation of conditions in Chile and probably other foreign lands: areas where all too often there is very little in the way of interclass relationships and economic practices that is worth conserving.

In its dealings with Chile, the United States appeared to align itself unquestioningly with the traditional groups of privilege, seeming to feel that if only they were allowed to preside over a free-enterprise system, the social deformities of the country would somehow be ameliorated. The Chile of the dispossessed has not, until very recently, directly concerned the United States. To a certain extent, this is because there has been a tendency to assume that private capitalism will function in Chile as it now operates in the United States. Actually, Chilean capitalists have not been forced to heed the lessons brought home to United States business leaders after 1929. Their basic policies are still founded upon belief in suppressing rather than in cooperating with lower classes, upon small-scale production and excessive per-unit profit, upon government protection—but never government regulation—and upon special privileges which make possible the perpetuation of superannuated means of production.

POLICY CONSIDERATIONS

CAPITALISM AND DEMOCRACY

The failure to abandon the naive assumption that capitalism functions more or less the same in Chile as in the United States has resulted in the increasing loss of power of Washington diplomats to communicate with vast sectors of the Chilean population. So far as Chile's lower classes and reform leaders are concerned, capitalism has been synonymous with social injustice.[1] When United States spokesmen continue to announce in Chile that all problems can be solved through free-enterprise capitalism, without making it clear that the form of capitalism in mind is not necessarily that practiced in Chile, they convince the reformers that the United States stands in opposition to basic social readjustments.

To heap praise upon Chileans for their democratic procedures is to err in a similar manner. Chilean democracy is obviously quite different from the United States concept of what the word means. If there were genuine democracy in Chile, then the lower classes probably would have the means of protecting their interests. In Chile, however, even since the enactment of women's suffrage, only about one seventh of the population goes to the polls. Chilean democracy and Chilean capitalism have gone hand in hand toward producing outrageous social injustice. United States spokesmen, therefore, would be well advised to qualify and distinguish when they laud democracy as the only system of government. They must occasionally drop the hint that by democracy they do not have in mind the sort of political hierarchical control that characterizes Chilean politics.

UNITED STATES INVESTMENTS AND AID

During their 1960 visits to Latin America, President Eisenhower, Adlai E. Stevenson, and Senator George Smathers, in defending their country's hemisphere policies, all stressed that United States citizens have direct investments of over nine billion dollars—the total has declined since the Cuban expropriations—in the southern Americas and that between 1945 and 1960 governmental agencies of their country had poured 4.2 billions in the form of loans and grants into the Latin-American republics. In Chile, reiteration of these facts did not have the impact hoped for by good-will emissaries, at least not among the reform-minded elements. The truth is that all of these loans, grants, and direct investments have done very little to solve the basic problems of Chilean society. United States capital has been funneled into the Chilean economy from the top. The "trickle-down" assumption, which as the Marshall Plan demonstrated was to a large extent valid in Western Europe, does not appear to apply in Chile where, as has been noted, the proportion of the national income received by wage-earning sectors has since 1940 been declining. Given the basic structure of Chilean society and the presence of chronic inflation, increased productivity and higher per-capita income figures have tended to benefit only the directing classes, and to increase even further the distance between them and the masses. Because much traditional aid to Chile has gone primarily to improve the position of a group at the apex of society, it has made those beneath more suspicious than ever of capitalism and increasingly susceptible to the blandishments of communism.

To a considerable degree, Point IV and I.C.A. (forerunner of A.I.D.) assistance, however well intentioned, have fitted into this pattern. The better methods of agriculture which, for example, they have taught, will always go primarily to help the 9.7 per cent that own 86 per cent of the arable surface—unless combined with a program that enforces socially responsible use of the land. Under present conditions, better farming methods have often been utilized to reduce the labor force, to cut down on land under cultivation, and to raise export crops that do not contribute to solution of the domestic problem of undernourishment. Moreover, training bureaucrats, as some aid missions have done, more efficiently to administer, let us say, an archaic, retrogressive tax system, does little to enhance national well-being. Increasing the efficiency of an outmoded structure is at best a face-lifting operation—and as futile as giving a face-lifting to someone who is dead. These considerations cause many Chilean reformers to shudder when they see United States technical experts arrive in their country. Given the past orientation of over-all relations with Chile, these technical experts have operated to preserve the status quo.

Instead of making aid dependent, as in the past largely it has been, upon the willingness of the recipient country to balance its budget and refrain from any practice that seems to deviate from free-enterprise capitalism, the United States must insist resolutely, as it has begun tenuously to do, upon attaching different sets of strings. An overhauling of domestic structures, aimed at social amelioration, must be the price of assistance. If it were clearly understood among all social sectors in Chile that United States economic help would henceforth be conditional upon the enactment of progressive taxation legislation, upon efficient use of land and/or redistribution of it, and upon the undertaking of vast housing and education projects, the Chilean rulers would be hard pressed to withstand the pressure. Even in the 1950's, with the United States operating as a factor to aid them in their standpattism, they found it increasingly difficult to resist the clamor of the left for change. If the United States began to some degree to side with the underprivileged, it would help guarantee a lessening of social injustice and would at the same time act to prevent the noncommunist left from gravitating increasingly toward the communist world.

Such a policy would, of course, lead the privileged classes to hurl charges of intervention.[2] The truth is that given their relative power and economic standings, almost anything that the United States does or refrains from doing inevitably produces serious repercussions in Chile and could therefore be regarded as intervention. Past actions have actually amounted to intervention to buttress the status quo.

Chile can be expected to react officially with initial distaste to United States reform pressures, not only because of the stubborn conservatism of the directing classes, but because traditionally Chilean statesmen have played a role of leadership in the Latin-American endeavors to end United States intervention. Their insistence upon nonintervention arose in the nineteenth century, and reached a peak of intensity during the 1920's. At that time one of the main concerns of Chilean statesmen was absolute sovereignty. Seemingly, a nation had not "arrived" until it was able to act exactly as it pleased and to avoid the restrictions of international commitments.

The nonintervention semantics, then, were conceived in an isolationist spirit, when political rather than economic and social considerations were uppermost. Moreover, they appeared at a time when there were auguries of economic prosperity and a dazzling future. In the late nineteenth century and again in the 1920's, Chile did not feel the need for massive outside aid. Except for conventional private loans and investments, Chile seemed capable economically of going it alone.

As of 1962, all of this had changed. Facing what is primarily a social and economic problem, Chile cannot go it alone. The ability to provide the masses with a rising standard of living has become the prime prerequisite for "arriving" as a nation, and this can be achieved only through cooperation and interdependence. One of the most important tasks facing the United States is to persuade Chilean and Western Hemisphere jurists in general to begin to work toward formulating a new concept of nonintervention that will not preclude measures aimed at encouraging the economic cooperation needed to improve social conditions. If this is not done, a partly outmoded legalistic formula will hinder fulfillment of whatever plans the United States devises to assist Chile and the other republics of Latin America.

THE SOCIAL CIRCLE OF UNITED STATES GOVERNMENT PERSONNEL

It would be useful for the State Department to begin now to be no more than formally correct to politicians and intellectuals notoriously dedicated to preserving the old aristocratic-proletariat structure and to display special interest in those public figures and writers committed to social reform. Until the United States repudiates practices which have been cementing relations with Chile at the top while losing it not only at the bottom but at all levels genuinely interested in the bottom,[3] vast and influential segments which represent the Chile of the future will continue to be abandoned to the agents of communism. All the more will this be true if United States government personnel continue largely to refrain from contact with students, laborers, and labor leaders.

An example of what has been wrong with the traditional United States approach to Chile, and also of how past shortcomings can be rectified, was provided by the experiences of Richard Rose in 1959. While studying in Chile this young United States architect became interested in designing a cheap but attractive house that could be utilized in slum clearance projects. To learn what the lower classes wanted in a home, he lived among them for a considerable time. By this unorthodox procedure, Rose incurred the displeasure of embassy personnel. Despite the obstacles placed in his way by United States officials, Rose carried his project through to completion and constructed a dome-shaped concrete dwelling that was the most handsome and probably the most practical unit in the "San Gregorio" housing project in Santiago. Rose in one year may have done more than embassy, Point IV, and I.C.A. staffs had done in a decade to show Chilean lower classes that some "gringos" can be interested in them as human beings.

United States representatives might also give encouragement to those members of the traditional ruling groups who seem willing to break with the past and to institute reforms aimed at national betterment. The story is told that in the late 1950's an aristocratic landowner near Talca changed his paternalistic-type estate into a

highly technological operation, an innovation looked upon in
horror by the tradition-bound landowners in the vicinity. In 1958,
the United States ambassador canceled plans to spend a weekend
with the progressive landowner, apparently to avoid the risk of
offending feudalistic traditionalists.[4] Actually, the only policy that
can save the position of the United States is to run the risk of
affronting the feudalists and to pat on the back the progressively
inclined—and to do it openly.

AN UNFLATTERING IMAGE OF THE UNITED STATES IN CHILE

The Chileans have not had a chance to find out what the American dream, as it is dreamed in the United States, is all about. For
many of them the personification of the United States would be a
man of youthful physical energy directed by a middle-aged, con-
formist mentality, who mistakes pompously-repeated inanities for
thought, and nostalgia for vision; who nullifies occasionally good
intentions and dissipates vigor and wealth by supporting all that
is dying.

The charge that the United States is a purely materialistic
country has been increasingly voiced by Chilean intellectuals since
1945. One reason for the revival of this old canard is that the
United States appears to be more interested in giving the propertied
classes that comprise one Chile the opportunity to expand their
material possessions than in helping the dispossessed of the second
Chile to gain the opportunity to rise to a status of human dignity.
This impression results from the fact that United States aid has
apparently gone, in general, to help the "haves." The impression
is fostered by the naive praise of free-enterprise capitalism and
democracy, and by the failure to recognize that the distorted
practices of these economic and political systems has in Chile
served to intensify social suffering. The United States thus appears
to desire to export to Chile merely the formalistic shell of its way
of life, without the social justice that has been developed by its
capitalistic and democratic practices.

Unless a different kind of impression can be created, many
Chileans will become more firmly convinced that United States
civilization rests upon as unadulterated a form of materialism as

communism, the only difference being that Yankee practices—as actually observed in Chile—seem to operate against the masses, while those of the communists—as described by skillful propagandists—favor them. The situation is alarming and paradoxical. More than ever a large portion of the Chilean population has decided to struggle with militant insistency toward what is fundamentally implied by the materially successful and socially mobile structure of the United States. At the same time, the United States is repelling those very people by its stuffy devotion to what was safe and proper in yesterday's world of diplomatic procedure.

A NEW UNITED STATES APPROACH
TO CHILE AND LATIN AMERICA?

THE ALLIANCE FOR PROGRESS

When President Kennedy announced the plans of his Alliance for Progress in March 1961 (the substance of these plans had been anticipated by representatives of the Eisenhower administration in August of 1960 at an economic conference in Bogotá, Colombia), he was, if words are to be taken at their face value, making the United States a witting instrument of change in Latin America. In embarking upon a drastically different policy toward Latin America—one that seemed calculated to correct the more obvious shortcomings of United States-Chilean relations alluded to in this and the preceding three chapters—the United States was pursuing a two-pronged approach. From the top it was attempting to pressure Latin-American governments into adopting internal reforms, by making future aid and loans dependent upon such social-reform measures in recipient countries as modification of land-use patterns and capital-formation methods. From the bottom, it was seeking to establish contact with lower-class elements and aid them to become participants in society so that they might protect their own interests and wrest long-overdue concessions from the ruling classes.

One new means for accomplishing this second goal has been the community development program to which a Peace Corps group had by September 1961 been assigned in Chile. The purpose of this group was to lead people in poor communities to assume an active role in solving for themselves the problems confronting them. The principal feature of community development is that schools, sanitation facilities, clinics, and better houses must not be furnished for the people. Rather, the people must have instilled in them the desire to build such facilities for themselves. In this way, there is brought about the development of "the most important resources a country has—its personal resources." [5]

Prior to announcement of the Alliance for Progress approach, the common assumption in the United States had been that Chile and other Latin-American countries had already entered upon a stage of modern industrialization and that increasing investments of private foreign capital within the existing economic and social framework would be conducive to over-all national development. [6] The Alliance for Progress seemed to be based upon the realization that economic problems in Latin America were the result of social as well as exclusively economic factors and could not be solved by economic means alone. Thus, the basic Alliance ideology was in accord with the observations made by economist William Glade in 1961:

> . . . , while the best available purely economic policies will necessarily take years to effect meaningful changes in income levels, other quite important elements of economic welfare are susceptible to quicker increases through 'social reform' type measures which themselves need not require heavy expenditures so much as organizational changes and which can be designed, moreover, in some cases, to provide incentives for productivity. . . . Social reform . . . , is no longer simply a desirable concomitant of growth in output. It is, or is rapidly becoming, a prerequisite of growth—as much an integral part of a development program as any instrument of monetary control or any tax measure. [7]

Since 1920, various sectors of Chilean urban and rural laborers have probably achieved some economic gains. But the slight benefits that were occasionally won have not been accompanied by expanding opportunities for the lower classes to participate effectively and with dignity in the society in which they live. As a result, Chile's pattern of socioeconomic development only accelerated the move toward sweeping social revolution. This is why it has become essential for the United States to try to encourage Chileans basically to modify that pattern.

POTENTIAL CONFLICT BETWEEN THE SPIRIT OF THE ALLIANCE FOR PROGRESS AND OF THE MONROE DOCTRINE

In addition to providing previously ignored social outcasts with opportunities for genuine participation in the national life, Chile faces difficult tasks of capital formation if genuine economic advances are to be made. Given the past failures of private capitalism to respond to the challenge of capital formation, Chilean reform-advocates of every political affiliation insist that it will be necessary, at least at the outset, to rely on certain socialistic and even Marxian methods. Should a reform administration come to power in Chile the United States would be faced with certain psychological difficulties, for the majority of its citizens subscribe to the notion that in the name of the revered Monroe Doctrine all "un-American" practices must be excluded from the entire hemisphere.

If the basic principle of the Monroe Doctrine—America for the Americans under the leadership of the United States—is not to be enforced simply by the military might of the Colossus, then there must be a genuine spirit of solidarity between the Yankee nation and the Latin-American republics. In the mid-twentieth century, however, Chile has been prominent among the republics of the southern Americas that no longer feel bound by mystical ties to the United States. Basically out of sympathy with many patterns, real and imagined, of United States life, Chileans have increasingly longed to establish some sort of a Third Position. Also, Chilean reform-seekers have become more and more convinced that formulas of progress for underdeveloped countries cannot be obtained from the United States.

By encouraging change throughout the hemisphere, as ostensibly it has begun to do with the formulation of the Alliance for Progress, the United States may be hastening the day when it will have to deal with a Chilean government that has resorted at least temporarily to expedients that appear to be "un-American," and therefore opposed to the principles of Monroeism. Still, in Chile there may be no other means by which new social elements can acquire purchasing power and education, gain bargaining power in the sociopolitico complex, and help ultimately thereby to usher in a system of effective democracy and social pluralism.

The United States: from the Despair to the Hope of Progressive Chileans?

By the end of the Second World War, the traditional Latin-American policies of the United States, based from the very outset upon a Monroe Doctrine that was gradually expanded, and later upon the concept of nonintervention and encouragement of free-enterprise capitalism, were no longer capable of contributing to long-term friendly relations with Chile. Belatedly, in August of 1960, the United States unveiled a new Latin-American policy. As applied to Chile, it will produce many unforeseen problems and probably will not immediately or even soon achieve the warm and enthusiastic friendship which the United States tends to regard as its due. For the United States to transform itself from the despair into the hope of Chile's reform-oriented elements will require many years and repeated acts of good faith. Still, the fresh approach could, if seriously pursued, halt the process by which Chile has gradually become a center of potentially overt hostility to the United States and facilitate the eventual emergence of close and cordial relations. By the Alliance for Progress approach, the United States has provided itself with the potential means to demonstrate that the social consequences of economic practices concern it, not just within its own confines but throughout the entire hemisphere. If it begins to take advantage of these means, the United States can face with some confidence the task of gaining the respect of those Chileans, and of all those Latin Americans, who wish themselves to acquire, or to help their less fortunate citizens to acquire, security, dignity, and opportunity.

NOTES

CHAPTER 1

[1] Marcial González, *El crédito y la riqueza en Chile* (Santiago de Chile, 1872). Henceforth, unless otherwise specifically indicated, all books cited are published in Santiago.

[2] *Anuario Estadístico de Chile, 1881-1883* (1884), pp. xii-xiii.

[3] Carlos Arangua R., "Analizando los problemas: la situación del cobre," *Panorama Económica*, no. 163 (March 29, 1957), 123.

[4] *El Ferrocarril* (Santiago daily, 1855-1911), February 21, 1883.

[5] *Anuario Estadístico*, 1920 (1921), I, 14-15. The value of the Chilean peso fluctuated considerably in the nineteenth and twentieth centuries. In 1880, with the peso still relatively sound, it was worth on the London market 30⅞ pence or roughly the equivalent of US $0.64. By 1905, it had sunk to approximately 17 pence, or about US $0.33, while by 1925 its value was 6 pence, or US $0.1217. For more complete conversion tables see Frank Fetter, *Monetary Inflation in Chile* (Princeton, N.J., 1931), pp. 13-14.

[6] In 1875 Chile's population was 2,075,971, and in 1885, 2,527,320. The Argentine population in 1869 was 1,737,076. See *La Nación* (Santiago daily, 1917—), February 9, 1928. Between 1843 and 1875, the Chilean population increased at an annual average of 3.35 per cent. From 1875-1907, the rate was only 1 per cent. See Julio César Jobet, *Ensayo crítico del desarrollo económico social de Chile* (1955), p. 156.

[7] A second edition of the work, in two volumes, was published in Madrid in 1929.

[8] Domingo Amunátegui Solar, *El progreso intelectual y político de Chile* (1936), pp. 9-11.

[9] Alberto Edwards Vives, *La fronda aristocrática*. This is one of the most widely read books ever published in Chile. In 1959 it was in its eleventh edition.

[10] Jaime Eyzaguirre, *Fisonomía histórica de Chile* (1948), pp. 99, 101, 106, 130-138, 150-151. This is one of the most brilliant syntheses of Chilean historical development, although written from an almost absurdly extreme Hispanist point of view.

[11] See Encina, *Nuestra inferioridad económica* (1912) and Keller, *La eterna crisis chilena* (1931).

[12] See Jobet, *Ensayo crítico*.

[13] General works dealing with economic development in Chile from 1830-1880, and not specifically cited elsewhere in these notes, include the following. Miguel Cruchaga Montt, *Tratado elemental de economía política*, con prólogo por Guillermo Subercaseaux (Madrid, 1928 edition), and *Salitre y guano* (Madrid, 1929 edition). Dirección General de Contabilidad de Chile, *Resumen de la hacienda pública de*

Chile desde 1833 hasta 1914 (A bilingual, English-Spanish publication, printed in London without date). Marcial González, *Estudios económicos* (1889), and *La situación económica de Chile* (1874). Daniel Martner, *Estudios de política comercial chilena e historia económica nacional*, 2 vols. (1923). This is one of the first attempts at a general economic history of republican Chile. Manuel Miquel, *Estudios económicos y administrativos sobre Chile desde 1856 hasta 1863* (1863). Evaristo Molina, *Bosquejo de la hacienda pública de Chile desde la independencia hasta la fecha* (1898). Jack B. Pfeiffer, "Notes on the Heavy Equipment Industry in Chile, 1800-1910," *Hispanic American Historical Review*, XXXII, no. 1 (February, 1952). Agustín Ross, *Chile, 1851-1910: sesenta años de cuestiones monetarias y financiaras y de problemas bancarios* (1911). This is an authoritative work by a leading banker-businessman. Marcelo Segall, *Desarrollo del capitalismo en Chile: cinco ensayos dialécticos* (1953). The work deals mainly with the nineteenth century, and is written from a decidedly Marxist point of view.

[14] See Roberto Hernández, *Juan Godoy, o el descubrimiento de Chañarcillo*, 2 vols. (Valparaíso, 1932).

[15] Oscar Alvarez Andrews, *Historia del desarrollo industrial de Chile* (1936), p. 90.

[16] *Ibid.*, p. 131.

[17] Jobet, *Ensayo crítico*, pp. 35, 58-59. See also Roberto Hernández, *El salitre: resumen histórico desde su descubrimiento y explotación* (Valparaíso, 1930).

[18] Some of the more successful nitrate operators were Pedro González de Candamo, Diego de Almeida, José Antonio Moreno, Juan López, José Santos Ossa and his sons Manuel and Alfredo, Pedro León Gallo y Goyenechea and his brothers Tomás and Angel Custodio, Francisco Puelma, José Antonio Barrenechea, and Daniel Oliva. The reader is referred also to Mario Muñoz Guzmán, *Grandes figuras de la historia minera de Chile: Don José Tomás de Urmeneta, vencedor de Tamaya* (1947. Pamphlet).

[19] See the series of articles by Salvador Soto Rojas, "Chile minero: homenaje histórico a los fundadores de su riqueza," beginning in the April 26, 1921, edition of the Santiago daily, *Las Ultimas Noticias* (1904—).

[20] See the excellent study by Julio Heise González, *La Constitución de 1925 y las nuevas tendencias político-sociales* (1951), pp. 126-130. Pagination is based on the work as first published in the *Anales de la Universidad de Chile*, no. 80 (4° trimestre, 1950).

[21] See Luis Escobar Cerda, *El mercado de valores* (1959). This excellent work by a Harvard trained economist who served in 1962 as Minister of Economy contains a good analysis of the rise of corporate finance after 1850, and reveals the prevalence of first- and second-generation Chileans among the founders of the stock market.

[22] Heise González, *op. cit.*, p. 154.

[23] *Ibid.*, p. 132. Other works dealing with nineteenth-century social transition and not cited elsewhere in the notes include the following. Domingo Amunátegui Solar, *Historia social de Chile* (1936). This work carries the story only to 1857, in which year Amunátegui considers the old-style Chilean aristocracy to have disappeared once and for all. Francisco Antonio Encina, "Evolución social, política y económica del pueblo chileno," *Boletín de la Academia Chilena de la Historia*, Año VI, no. 10 (1° semestre, 1938), and no. 11 (2° semestre, 1938). Guillermo Feliú Cruz, *Un esquema de la evolución social de Chile en el siglo XIX* (1941). This pamphlet-length study is among the best essays produced by Feliú Cruz, one of Chile's out-

standing contemporary historians. Alejandro Fuenzalida Grandón, *La evolución social de Chile* (1906), and "La novela social contemporánea: ¿podrá ser invocado en el porvenir como fuente de información acerca de las costumbres y de las ideas de nuestro época?" *Anales de la Universidad de Chile*, LXXXV (1889). Julio César Jobet, "Síntesis interpretativa del desarrollo histórico nacional durante la segunda mitad del siglo XIX," *Atenea*, Año XII, no. 250 (April, 1946), and no. 251 (May, 1946). Abraham König, *Reseña histórica del Club de la Unión* (1886). This work, by a leading member of the Radical Party in its early days, gives a good insight into various aspects of social development. Jaime Larraín García Moreno, *Evolución social de Chile* (1955). Extremely conservative in tone, the work suggests that social evolution after the administration of Manuel Montt has constituted retrogression. Malaquías Concha, "El movimiento obrero en Chile," *Revista Económica*, no. 11 (March, 1888). This is a good study by one of the earliest champions of social reform, and the principal founder of the *Partido Demócrata*. Hernán Ramírez Necochea, *Historia del movimiento obrero en Chile . . . siglo XIX* (1957). Although written with blatant Marxist prejudices, the study is carefully researched, and contains much valuable information. Carlos Vicuña Fuentes, *La tiranía en Chile*, 2 vols. (1938, 1939). The first volume deals largely with nineteenth-century evolution. Vicuña, a lifelong campaigner for social and political reform, is a highly impressionistic writer, and his works abound with provocative interpretive insights. Benjamín Vicuña Mackenna, *Historia crítica y social de la ciudad de Santiago, 1541-1868*, 2 vols. (1924, 1926 edition), and *Historia de Valparaíso*, 2 vols. (1936 edition).

Social transformations in nineteenth-century Chile are also reflected in the novels of Alberto Blest Gana, the most successful novelist of the period who, after achieving success, spent most of his life in Paris. See in particular his very popular *Martín Rivas*, which has gone through an incredibly large number of editions.

[24] See *La Nación*, July 3, 1933, and José Bernardo Lira, *La caja de crédito hipotecario* (1884).

[25] Javier Vial Solar, *El diluvio: estudio político* (1934), pp. 35-36.

[26] Heise González, *op. cit.*, p. 135.

[27] Jobet, *Ensayo crítico*, p. 42.

[28] The classic study on Chilean railroads is Santiago Marín Vicuña, *Los ferrocarriles de Chile* (1916 edition).

[29] Oficina Central de Estadística en Santiago, *Sesto Censo Jeneral de la población de Chile levantado el 26 de noviembre de 1885* (1890), II, 496.

[30] Heise González, *op. cit.*, p. 135.

[31] The value of mine products exported, 1844-1880, was 523,967,996 pesos of eighteen pence; that of agricultural produce was 238,967,996. See Jobet, *Ensayo crítico*, p. 55.

[32] Alvarez Andrews, *Historia del desarrollo*, p. 135.

[33] Encina, *Nuestra inferioridad económica*, p. 80. See also Guillermo Feliú Cruz, *Pérez Rosales: apuntes* (1934. Pamphlet), and *Vicente Pérez Rosales: ensayo crítico* (1946).

[34] Pérez Rosales, *Recuerdos del pasado: 1814-1860* (1949 edition). See also Emilio Rodríguez Mendoza, *Pérez Rosales* (1934), pp. 97-103. Pérez was also sent to Germany to recruit settlers. He enjoyed fabulo.s success, and to facilitate his task wrote the famous *Ensayo sobre Chile* (1859). Other early works on Chilean

colonization include the following: Ignacio Anguita, *Breve estudio sobre la colonización en Chile* (1897); Agustín Correa Bravo, *Los extranjeros ante la ley chilena* (1894); Louis Dorte, *El porvenir en Chile de los emigrados europeos*, translated by A. Labin (1884); and Benjamín Vicuña Mackenna, *A Sketch of Chile, Expressly prepared for the use of Emigrants from the United States and Europe to that Country* (New York, 1866). See also Alberto Hoerll, *Los alemanes en Chile* (1910).

[35] Oficina Central, *Sesto Censo*, p. 496.

[36] Jobet, *Ensayo crítico*, p. 45.

[37] Guillermo Edwards Matte, *El Club de la Unión en sus ochenta años: 1864-1944* (1944), p. 29.

[38] Alvarez Andrews, *Historia del desarrollo*, p. 124.

[39] Domingo Amunátegui Solar, *La democracia en Chile* (1946 edition), pp. 198-199. See also Alberto Blest Gana, "La situación financiera de Chile en 1878," *Revista Chilena*, Año V, Tomo XIII, no. 1 (April, 1922).

[40] See Diego Barros Arana, *Don Juan Gustavo Courcelle-Seneuil* (1949), and Leonardo Fuentealba Hernández, *Courcelle-Seneuil en Chile: erores del liberalismo económico* (1946).

[41] Francisco Antonio Encina, *Historia de Chile desde la prehistoria hasta 1891*, XVIII (1950), 359.

[42] In 1850, Chile had exported wheat to California valued at nearly 2.5 million pesos of 46 pence. See Heise González, *op. cit.*, p. 128.

[43] The influence of Spencer in Chile is repeatedly stressed by Alejandro Fuenzalida Grandón in his prize-winning, two-volume biography of José Victorino Lastarria, *Lastarria y su tiempo* (1817-1888): *su vida, obras e influencia en el desarrollo político e intelectual de Chile* (1911).

[44] Cruchaga Montt, *Sociedades anónimas en Chile y estudios financieros* (Madrid, 1929 edition). Moreover, nearly the entirety of Chile's 1880 external debt of 92,-986,667 pesos had been financed by German and English banks. United States banks had not yet entered the field of foreign financing. See *Anuario Estadístico, 1920* (1921), I, 36-37.

[45] For studies of the Portales period, 1830-1841, not cited elsewhere in the notes, see the following works. Domingo Amunátegui Solar, *Nacimiento de la república de Chile: 1808-1833* (1930). The death of Amunátegui cut short his *Teatro político, 1810-1910* (1946), when the work had only progressed as far as the 1812 period. R. L. Barahona, "Portales: su época y su obra," *Revista Chilena de Historia y Geografía*, XLVI (2° trimestre, 1923). Ernesto Barros Jarpa, *La "segunda independencia"* (1956). Barros Jarpa, Minister of Foreign Relations during the first Arturo Alessandri and the Juan Antonio Ríos administrations, praises Portales for inspiring Chile's war against the Andrés Santa Cruz-dominated federation of Peru and Bolivia. Aurelio Díaz Meza, *El advenimiento de Portales* (1932). Historian Díaz Meza is an admirer of colonial traditions. Agustín Edwards, *The Dawn, 1810-1841* (London, 1931). This is one of the many fine books by the long-time editor-owner of Chile's leading daily, *El Mercurio*. Alberto Edwards Vives, *Páginas históricas* (1945. Posthumous). The work deals mainly with the 1833 constitution and the work of Portales. F. A. Encina, "Las ideas y los conceptos políticos en Chile entre 1817 y 1830," *Boletín de la Academia Chilena de la Historia*, Año IX, no. 20 (1° semestre, 1942). Jaime Eyzaguirre, "Las ideas políticas en Chile hasta

1833: apuntes para su estudio," *ibid.*, Año I (1° semestre, 1933). Hugo Guerra
Baeza, *Portales y Rosas: contrapunto de hombres y políticas* (1958). Domingo
Melfi Demarco, *Portales* (1930. Pamphlet). Eugenio Orrego Vicuña, *Andrés Bello*
(1953 edition). Ramón Sotomayor Valdés, *Historia de Chile bajo el gobierno del
General d. Joaquín Prieto*, 4 vols. (1900-1903 edition), and *El Ministro Portales*
(1954 edition). These are two painstaking studies by the outstanding conservative
historian of the nineteenth century. Benjamín Vicuña Mackenna, *Don Diego
Portales* (1937 edition). This may well be the most penetrating of all the Portales
studies. Oscar Waiss, *Antecedentes económicos y sociales de la constitución de 1833*
(1934. *Memoria de Prueba*). The onetime leading Trotskyist of Chile does a Charles
Beard-like job on the 1833 constitution. José Zapiola, *Recuerdos de treinta años,
1810-1840* (1945 edition). In addition, two general works cover this period: Diego
Barros Arana, *Historia general de Chile*, 10 vols. (1930-1935 edition), and F. A.
Encina, *Historia de Chile desde la prehistoria hasta 1891*, 20 vols. (1942-1952).

[46] See Alberto Edwards, *La fronda aristocrática*, and Jaime Eyzaguirre, *Fisonomía
histórica*. The reader should also consult Eyzaguirre's *O'Higgins* (1954), in which
the independence leader receives considerable censure because of his "French notions." See also F. A. Encina, *Portales*, 2 vols. (1934).

[47] See Amunátegui Solar, *Progreso intelectual*, p. 41, and *Democracia*, pp. 3-81.

[48] See Jobet, *Ensayo crítico*.

[49] For works on Arcos, a millionaire socialist, and Bilbao, see the following. Carlos
Acuña, *Nacimiento de la nueva Bilbao* (1944). Pedro N. Cruz, *Bilbao y Lastarria*
(1944). Cruz, an extreme conservative, sees Bilbao and Lastarria as devils incarnate.
Pedro Pablo Figueroa, *Historia de Francisco Bilbao* (1898). Gabriel Sanhueza,
Santiago Arcos (1956). On the Sociedad de Iqualdad, see José Zapiola, *La Sociedad
de la Iqualdad y sus enemigos* (1902).

[50] Julio César Jobet, "Notas sobre la historiografía chilena," in Ricardo Donoso,
et al., *Historiografía chilena* (1949), pp. 347-349.

[51] See *El Ferrocarril*, July 16, 1910.

[52] See Diego Barros Arana, *Don Claudio Gay* (1876).

[53] See Eduardo de la Barra, *Francisco Bilbao ante la sacristía* (1872), and *Saluda-
bles advertencias a los verdaderos católicos y al clero político: cartas sobre las jesuitas*
(1871).

[54] Ricardo Donoso, "La satira política en Chile," in Donoso, *et al.*, *op. cit.*, pp.
131, 138.

[55] Edwards, *La fronda aristocrática*, pp. 93-95. Additional works not cited elsewhere in the notes pertaining to the religious question and the rise of radicalism
in intellectual and political trends are as follows. Guillermo Juan Carter Gallo, "El
liberalismo," *Anales de la Universidad de Chile*, LII (1878). Miguel Cruchaga
Montt, *De las relaciones entre la Iglesia y el estado en Chile* (Madrid, 1929 edition).
Very proclerical in nature, the work considers events up to 1878. Isidoro Errázuriz,
J. M. Balmaceda, and A. Orrego Luco, *La Iglesia y el estado: discursos pronunciados
en el Congreso* (1884). This is a collection of speeches by three of the leading
anticlerical members of Congress. Julio César Jobet, *Los precursores del pensamiento
social de Chile*, 2 vols. (1955, 1956). This is a collection of short biographical
sketches by a leading Marxist writer. José Victorino Lastarria, *Lecciones de política
positiva* (1874), and *La reforma política* (1868). Arturo Lois Fraga and Mario
Vergara Gallardo, *Librepensadores y laicos en Atacama* (1956). The work contains

good sketches of M. A. Matta and other figures of Chilean Radicalism. It is surprising how many Radicals and freethinkers have come from the North. Benjamín Subercaseaux in his *Chile, o una loca geografía* (1956, 11th edition) goes so far as to assert that all that is fresh and original in Chile is introduced from the North, and speculates that a reason for this is that the nature of northern land has prevented latifundia. Fabio Muñoz H., *Don Pedro León Gallo, 1830-1877* (1903). Tomás Ramírez Frías, *El liberalismo y la cuestión religiosa y social en Chile* (1910). A long-time champion of social reform and workers' rights, Ramírez feels that Chilean religious attitudes are an impediment to realization of his goals. Benjamín Vicuña Mackenna, *Los girondinos chilenos* (1902).

Some works not cited elsewhere in the notes which are of value in gaining an insight into intellectual and literary trends in the period include the following. Domingo Amunátegui Solar, "Bosquejo histórico de la literature chilena," *Revista Chilena de Historia y Geografía*, VI (2° semestre, 1913), XI (3° trimestre, 1914), XIII (1° trimestre, 1915), XIV, XV, XVI, XX (4° trimestre, 1916), through XXXV (2° trimestre, 1920). This is perhaps the best single source on nineteenth-century writers of fiction, prose, poetry, history, philosophy and political essays. Gabriel Amunátegui Jordán, "Justo y Domingo Arteaga Alemparte: ensayo biográfico y juicio crítico," *Anales de la Universidad de Chile*, CXLII (2° semestre, 1918), and CXLIII (1° semestre, 1919). Fidel Araneda Bravo, "Don Ramón Sotomayor Valdés," *Boletín de la Academia Chilena de la Historia*, Año V, no. 9 (2° semestre, 1937). This is a good study of the conservative historian. Mariano Casanova, "Filosofía de la historia bajo el punto de vista católica," *Anales de la Universidad de Chile*, XVIII, no. 3 (1860). Casanova, an extremely conservative archbishop of Santiago, attacks the liberal historiography of Barros Arana and others. Pedro N. Cruz, *Estudio sobre literatura chilena*, 3 vols. (1940 edition). The Cruz thesis seems to be that only the religiously devout produced worthwhile literature. Ricardo Donoso, *Tres historiadores del siglo pasado: Amunátegui, Vicuña Mackenna, Barros Arana* (Buenos Aires, 1941). One of the most distinguished of today's "liberal" historians, Donoso has high praise for three liberal historians of the past century. See also his *Veinte años de la historia de "El Mercurio"* (1929), which carries the story of one of Chile's leading newspapers up to 1864. Francisco Antonio Encina, *La literatura histórica chilena y el concepto actual de la historia* (1935). Encina makes no attempt to disguise his scorn for most nineteenth-century historians. His judgments of Barros Arana, whom he charges with distorting the colonial tradition and totally ignoring the spiritual aspect of man, are particularly harsh. *El Estandarte Católico* (1874-1891) was one of the Santiago dailies expounding the position of the extreme conservatives and proclerical elements. It frequently engaged in feuds with the strongly anticlerical Valparaíso daily, *La Patria* (1863-1896), founded by Isidoro Errázuriz. For a general history of Chilean journalism see the carefully researched, encyclopedic work of Raúl Silva Castro, now the director of the National Library, *Prensa y periodismo en Chile, 1812-1956* (1957).

[56] See Diego Barros Arana, *Un decenio de la historia de Chile, 1841-1851*, 2 vols. (1913).

[57] See the highly laudatory work of Alberto Edwards, *El gobierno de don Manuel Montt* (1933). Particularly useful works on general political development, 1840-1880, are: Domingo Amunátegui Solar, *La democracia en Chile* and *El progreso intelectual y político de Chile*; Ricardo Donoso, *Desarrollo político y social de*

Chile desde la Constitución de 1833 (1942) and *Hombres e ideas de antaño y hogaño* (1936); Alberto Edwards, *Bosquejo histórico de las partidos políticos chilenos* (1903) and *La fronda aristocrática*. There follows below a listing of some additional works on the political events of the period.

Paulino Alfonso, *Los partidos políticos de Chile* (1913). *Anales de la Universidad de Chile*. Appearing since 1843, sometimes as a quarterly, sometimes as a semi-annual, this has been one of the most valuable outlets for Chilean *pensadores*. *El Araucano*. Published every other day, 1830-1877, this paper contained extracts from the Congressional records, and had one of the best coverages of foreign relations. Justo Arteaga Alemparte, *Nuestros partidos y nuestros hombres* (1886). Manuel Blanco Cuartín, *Artículos escogidos de Manuel Blanco Cuartín, con una introducción de don Juan Larraín*, vol. XI of *Biblioteca de Escritores de Chile* (1913). A leading journalist, Blanco in 1866 joined the staff of *El Mercurio* of Valparaíso and for twenty years was one of the guiding spirits of the paper. He had previously been associated with Zorobabel Rodríguez on the staff of the conservative organ, *El Independiente*. Blanco described himself as a laic conservative, averring that between his type of conservatism and that rooted in theocracy there was a world of difference. Fernando Campos Harriet, *Manuel de historia constitucional de Chile* (1951). Carlos Concha Subercaseaux, *Los partidos políticos chilenos* (1905). Concha was for years a leading figure in the Conservative Party. Agustín Edwards MacClure, *Cuatro presidentes de Chile, 1841-1876*, 2 vols. (Valparaíso, 1932). This is an excellently researched, extremely well-written study by a leading member of the Liberal Party. *El Ferrocarril*. This Santiago daily, published from 1855 to 1911, was perhaps the outstanding nineteenth-century Chilean newspaper. It expounded the concepts of the classical liberal school, was moderately anticlerical, and enjoyed the services of some of the leading journalists and literary figures of the period. Luis Galdames, one of Chile's most distinguished historians, has two works pertaining in part to the period under discussion: *Evolución constitucional de Chile* (1925), and *Historia de Chile* (1944 edition). Julio Heise González, *Historia constitucional de Chile* (1950). This modest compendium is in no way in the same class with Heise's *La Constitución de 1925*. Manuel José Irarrázaval, *Colección de discursos parlamentarios*, 2 vols. (1892, 1893). Irarrázaval was one of the most important members of the Conservative Party. René León Echaiz, *Evolución histórica de los partidos políticos chilenos* (1939). Ambrosio Montt, *Discursos y escritos políticos* (1879). This is a valuable work by a leading figure in Chilean politics. Martín Palma, *Los tres presidentes que no serlo: Antonio Varas, Benjamín Vicuña Mackenna, Manuel Baquedano* (1881). Ramón Sotomayor Valdés, *Historia de Chile durante los cuarenta años trascurridos desde 1831 hasta 1871*, 2 vols. (1875, 1876). This is one of the major works by the distinguished conservative historian. See also his *Noticias autobiográficas y epistolario* (1954 edition).

Biographical reference works include: Pedro Pablo Figueroa, *Diccionario biográfico de Chile* (1897); Enrique Amador Fuenzalida, *Galería contemporánea de hombres notables de Chile, 1850-1901* (Valparaíso, 1901); José Joaquín Larraín Zañartu, *Chile: figuras contemporáneas* (1882); Augusto Orrego Luco, *Retratos: Amunátegui, Gambotta, Cánovas del Castillo, J. M. Charcot, José Victorino Lastarria, Simón B. Rodríguez* (1917); and Ramón Pérez Yáñez, *Forjadores de Chile*, 2 vols. (1943, 1944). One of the most valuable of all reference works for the entire 1810-1950 period is Luis Valencia Avaria (compiler), *Anales de la república: textos constitu-*

*cionales de Chile y registros de los ciudadanos que han integrado los poderes
ejecutivo y legislativo desde 1810*, 2 vols. (1951).

[58] See Armando Donoso, *Recuerdos de cincuenta años: José Victorino Lastarria,
Isidoro Errázuriz, José Toribio Medina, Enrique Mac-Iver, Abdón Cifuentes, Vicente
Reyes, Crescente Errázuriz, Gonzalo Bulnes, Estanislao del Canto, Jorge Boonen
Rivera, Eduardo de la Barra, Marcial Martínez* (1947), p. 143.

[59] See Pedro Pablo Figueroa, *Historia de la revolución constituyente, 1858-1859,
escrita sobre documentos completamente inéditos* (1889); Fabio Muñoz H., *Don
Pedro León Gallo, 1830-1877* (1903); and Guillermo Rojas Carrasco, *Don Pedro
León Gallo: su vida y su actuación* (1931). Along with M. A. Matta, Gallo was
one of the main founders of Chile's Radical Party.

[60] See Joaquín Díaz Garcés, "Don Antonio Varas," *Revista Chilena*, Año II,
Tomo V, no. 15 (August, 1918).

[61] Works on the early Radical Party include: Eduardo de la Barra, *El radicalismo
chileno* (1875); J. Arturo Jabalquinto, *Figuras del radicalismo* (1885); Yerko
Koscina Peralta, *El radicalismo como partido político: su genesis y su doctrina*
(1956. *Memoria de Prueba*); Armando Labra Carvajal, *La política radical* (1912);
Ramón Liborio Carvallo, *Ojeada histórica sobre el Partido Radical* (1910); and
Nicolás Federico Torres, *El radicalismo chileno: su origen, su historia, su programa,
sus tendencias, su porvenir y sus enemigos* (Coquimbo, 1896).

[62] See Edwards Matte, *El Club de la Unión*, pp. 29-30.

[63] See Abraham König, *El candidato de la Convención: d. José Tomás Urmeneta*
(1871).

[64] Amunátegui Solar, *La democracia en Chile*, pp. 9-12.

[65] Works on Errázuriz and his administration include: Alfonso Bulnes, *Errázuriz
Zañartu: su vida* (1950 edition); Isidoro Errázuriz, *Historia de la administración
Errázuriz* (1885); and Lucas Grendi Casanueva, *Reseña histórica de la administra-
ción de don Federico Errázuriz* (1901).

[66] See Carlos Orrego Barros, *Diego Barros Arana* (1952).

[67] See Diego Barros Arana, *Don Miguel Luis Amunátegui: candidato a la Presidencia de la República* (1875), and Carlos Morla Vicuña, *Don Miguel Luis
Amunátegui* (no date).

[68] See Benjamín Vicuña Mackenna, *El Partido Liberal Democrático: su origen,
sus propósitos, sus deberes* (1876).

[69] Oficina Central de Estadística, *Sesto Censo Jeneral, 1885*, II, 496.

[70] See William Miller Collier and Guillermo Feliú Cruz, *La primera misión de
los Estados Unidos de América en Chile* (1926). Collier was a popular United
States ambassador to Chile during the 1920's. See also W. R. Manning, *Diplomatic
Correspondence of the United States Concerning the Independence of the Latin
American Nations* (New York City, 1925), I, 6, 11. A satisfactory biography of
Poinsett is J. Fred Rippy, *Joel R. Poinsett, Versatile American* (Durham, North
Carolina, 1935). Poinsett later became the first United States envoy to Mexico, in
which post he incurred the undying hatred of Mexican conservatives. See, for exam-
ple, José Fuentes Mares, *Poinsett, historia de un gran intriga* (México, D.F., 1951).

[71] See Eugenio Pereira Salas, *La misión Bland en Chile* (1936).

[72] See Pereira Salas, *La actuación de los oficiales navales norte-americanos en
nuestras costas, 1813-1840* (1936), and *Buques norteamericanos en Chile a fines
de la era colonial: 1788-1810* (1935).

[73] Graham S. Stuart, *Latin America and the United States* (New York, 1943), p. 421.

[74] Henry Clay Evans, Jr., *Chile and its Relations with the United States* (Durham, North Carolina, 1927), pp. 71-72, 122-126.

[75] The best study of the Chileans in California is Roberto Hernández, *Los chilenos en California*, 2 vols. (Valparaíso, 1930). See also Camilio Branchi, "Chilenos en California: el caso Bambiaso," *Atenea*, Año XXXII, nos. 355-356 (January-February, 1955); Enrique Bunster, *Chilenos en California* (1954), a deceptively entitled work, as only one of the stories deals with this topic; Juan Nepomuceno Espejo, letter of September 23, 1849, to the Santiago daily, *El Progreso*, and reprinted in *Revista Chilena de Historia y Geografía*, CXIV (December, 1950); and Eugenio Pereira Salas, *Bibliografía chilena sobre el "Gold Rush" en California* (no date).

[76] W. R. Manning, *Diplomatic Correspondence of the United States, Inter-American Affairs, 1831-1860* (Washington, D.C., 1935), V, 210. Additional information on early relations between Chile and the United States is contained in the following works. Agustín Bianchi Barros, *Bosquejo histórico de las relaciones chileno-norteamericanas durante la independencia* (1946). Eduardo Lamas G., "Don Ambrosio Montt," *La Revista de Chile*, II, no. 7 (April 1, 1899). Montt was one of the early figures to object to exploitation of Chile's lower classes. He was also one of the few Chilean *pensadores* with a genuine admiration for the United States. Alejandto Magnet, *Orígenes y antecedentes del panamericanismo* (1945). Ricardo Montaner, *Historia diplomática de la independencia de Chile* (1941). *Norteamericanos notables en la historia de Chile* (1953). This is a collection of five reliably written pamphlets dealing with Joel R. Poinsett, William Wheelwright, Henry Meiggs, Charles Whitney Wooster, and the Délano family. Eugenio Pereira Salas, *La misión Worthington en Chile* (1936). William Roderick Sherman, *The Diplomatic and Commercial Relations of the United States and Chile, 1820-1914* (Boston, 1926).

[77] See Luis Carcovich, *Portales y la política internacional hispanoamericana* (1937), p. 5. This monograph is a careful and reliable study.

[78] This latter attitude is well expounded in an *El Ferrocarril* editorial, October 13, 1880.

[79] The *Colección de ensayos i documentos* is an exceedingly important work, and the necessary point of departure for understanding the strong anti-United States currents still associated with most manifestations of Chilean desire for Latin-American unity.

[80] Other prominent members of the *Sociedad de la Unión Americana de Santiago* were Manuel Blanco Encalada, Pedro Godoy, Vicente Reyes, Justo Arteaga Alemparte, Pedro Moncayo, and Guillermo Blest Gana.

[81] For material on Chile's war with Spain see *Foreign Relations of the United States*, 1866, Part 2, pp. 349-413.

[82] "Unica asilo de las repúblicas hispano-americanas," I, 176-255.

[83] "Memoria presentada ante la Facultad de Leyes de la Universidad de Chile, por Manuel Carrasco Albano, en el mes de Marzo de 1855, sobre la necesidad y objectos de un congreso sud-americano," *ibid.*, I, 257-274.

[84] "Idea de un congreso federal de las repúblicas (a paper read in Paris in 1856)," *ibid.*, I, 275-299.

[85] *Ibid.*, pp. 280-281.

[86] *Ibid.*, pp. 284-287. See also Francisco Bilbao, *La américa en peligro* (1923 edition). Additional indications of the desire for Hispanic American union combined with anti-United States sentiments are found in an article published by Manuel Amunátegui in the July 28, 1860, Lima daily, *El Comercio*, as well as in Manuel Montt, "Mensage al cuerpo legislativo de 1860," Cámara de Senadores, *Boletín de Sesiones Ordinarias, 1860*; in Zorobabel Rodríguez, "Unión americana: modo de hacerla efectiva sin necesidad de la intervención de los gobiernos," *Revista de Sud América*, Tomo III, no. 11; in Ignacio Zenteño, "Unión hispanoamericana," *El Ferrocarril*, March 8, 1860; and in "Unión de la América del sur," *ibid.*, March 3, 1860.

[87] *La religión de la humanidad* (1884), the principal work of Juan Enrique Lagarrigue, Chile's most important popularizer of positivism, has strong overtones of anti-United States sentiment.

[88] April 5, 1852, letter of Isidoro Errázuriz to his father, Ramón, in *Revista Chilena de Historia y Geografía*, LVIII (3° trimestre, 1928). The vogue of romanticism in nineteenth-century Chile, influencing both Conservatives and Liberals, served also to awaken distrust of the United States, whose practicality, lack of sentiment, and apparently ruthless efficiency were regarded with distaste. The dominance of romanticism in Chile is well described by Domingo Amunátegui Solar, "Bosquejo histórico de la literatura chilena," *Revista Chilena de Historia y Geografía*, Tomo XXVII. Finally, the Masonic movement in Chile embraced many anti-United States overtones. See Benjamín Oviedo, *La masonería en Chile: bosquejo histórico* (1929).

[89] Amunátegui Solar, *Progreso intelectual*, pp. 110-111.

[90] See Carlos Castro Ruiz, "La doctrina Monroe y el gobierno de Chile," *Revista Chilena*, Año I, no. 3 (June, 1917).

[91] Even before this, Vicuña Mackenna had expressed dislike for many aspects of life in the United States. See his *Páginas de mi diario durante tres años de viaje, 1853, 1854, 1855*, 2 vols. (1856).

[92] Vicuña Mackenna, *Diez meses de misión a los Estados Unidos de Norte como agente confidencial de Chile* (1867), I, 190-191. See also the same author's *Historia de la guerra de Chile con España, 1863-1866* (1883).

[93] Additional evidences of anti-United States feeling arising out of Chile's "War" with Spain are found in: Joaquín Edwards Bello, *El bombardeo de Valparaíso y su época* (1934); Carlos E. Grez Pérez, *Los intentos de unión hispanoamericana y la guerra de España en el Pacífico* (1928); and Manuel Antonio Matta, *Documentos para la historia diplomática de Chile en su última guerra con España* (1872).

[94] See interview with Marcial Martínez in *La Nación*, January 22, 1917.

[95] Camilio Henríquez was a liberal-minded priest who took a prominent part in the Wars of Independence, believed in separation of Church and State, admired the United States, and founded the first Chilean newspaper, *La Aurora*. See José A. Alfonso, *Camilio Henríquez y sus principios políticos* (1934), Miguel Luis Amunátegui, *Camilio Henríquez* (1889), and Raúl Silva Castro (editor), *Escritos políticos de Camilio Henríquez* (1960).

[96] José Victorino Lastarria, *La América*, vol. X of *Obras completas* (1909), 17-19, 210.

[97] *Ibid.*

[99] See *ibid.*, pp. 201, 203, 215, 238, 248, and Alejandro Fuenzalida Grandón, *Lastarria y su tiempo*, I, 354-374. On Lastarria one should also consult Luis Oyarzún, *El pensamiento de Lastarria* (Valparaíso, 1953).

CHAPTER 2

[1] Listed below are some of the main works written in Chile on the War of the Pacific. Pascual Ahumada Moreno, *Guerra del Pacífico*, 9 vols. (Valparaíso, 1886), and "Guerra del Pacífico: recopilación completa de todos los documentos oficiales, correspondencias y de mas publicaciones referente a dicha Guerra," *Anales de la Universidad de Chile*, LXV (1884). L. Alfredo Arenas Aguirre, *Encina contra Encina: reestablecimiento de la verdad sobre la Guerra del Pacífico* (1958). Diego Barros Arana, *Historia de la Guerra del Pacífico*, 2 vols. (1880-1881). Luis Barros Borgoño, "Don Aníbal Pinto," *Revista Chilena de Historia y Geografía*, no. 88 (May-August, 1936). Emilio Bello Codesido, *Anotaciones para la historia de las negociaciones diplomáticas con el Perú y Bolivia* (1919). Anselmo Blanlot Holley, *Historia de la paz entre Chile y el Perú, 1879-1884* (1919). Gonzalo Bulnes, *Guerra del Pacífico*, 3 vols. (1911-1919, second edition 1955). This is the standard work published in Chile on the war, and one of the best pieces of scholarly research ever done in that country. General Jorge Carmona Yáñez, *Baquedano* (no date). Adolfo Calderón Cousiño, *Breve historia diplomática de las relaciones chileno-peruanas* (1919). *Diario Oficial*, published in Santiago, 1882-1883, contains good information on the progress of the war. Francisco Antonio Encina, *Historia de Chile*. Volumes XVI, XVII, XVIII (1950-1952) deal with the War of the Pacific. Volumes XIX and XX carry the history of Chile to 1891. To say that in his treatment of the War of the Pacific Encina has relied heavily upon Bulnes is to understate the case. Still, the work has more value than Arenas Aguirre, cited above, would concede. Isidoro Errázuriz, *Hombres y cosas durante la Guerra* (1882). Jaime Eyzaguirre (editor), "Cartas de don Domingo Santa María a don Domingo Gana," *Boletín de la Academia Chilena de la Historia*, Año XX, no. 50 (1° semestre, 1954). The Chilean president, writing to his envoy in Mexico, deals among other points with the difficulties he is having with the Church during the War. Jorge Inostrosa C., *Adios al séptimo de la linea*, 5 vols. (1959 ed.). An all-time best-seller in Chile, this is an historical-novel treatment of the War of the Pacific. One interesting point brought out is the influence of the Masonic-Catholic conflict in Chile upon the conduct of the war.

[2] *El Mercurio*, January 27, 1881.

[3] Oficina Central de Estadística, *Sesto Censo Jeneral de la población de Chile levantado el 26 de noviembre de 1885* (1890), I, xiv.

[4] *El Ferrocarril*, January 29, 1883. The number of public schools in 1882 was 703. There were also at this time 529 private schools. Total enrollment for public and private schools in 1882 was 79,230, representing an increase of 14,330 over 1880 figures.

[5] Oficina Central de Estadística, *op. cit.*, II, 496.

[6] The final Indian campaigns are well described by Encina, *Historia de Chile*, XVIII, 257-278. The same author alludes briefly to the methods by which unscrupulous interests acquired much of the land wrested from the Indians, pp. 369 ff.

On this latter point see also Julio César Jobet, *Ensayo crítico del desarrollo econó-mico-social de Chile* (1955), p. 70, and Aníbal Pinto, *Chile, un caso de desarrollo frustrado* (1959), p. 66. Chamber of Deputies debates also shed light on this subject. See, for example, Cámara de Diputados, *Boletín de sesiones extraordinarias, 1895-1896*, Sesión of December 20, 1895, and speech of Democrat Deputy Saturio Bosch, *Boletín de sesiones ordinarias, 1933*, Sesión of July 19, 1933.

[7] See Jobet, *op. cit.*, p. 65.

[8] *El Ferrocarril*, November 19, 1881.

[9] Oficina Central de Estadística, *op. cit.*, II, 496. Special commerce, exports and imports, rose from 74 to nearly 119 million pesos during the same period. Hernán Ramírez Necochea, *Balmaceda y la contrarevolución de 1891* (1958), gives figures indicating that Chilean international commerce increased from approximately 65 million pesos in 1870 to 90,881,170 in 1885, and 135,567,341 in 1890. Jobet, *op. cit.*, p. 80, is in substantial but not complete accord with Ramírez.

[10] Aníbal Pinto, *op. cit.*, pp. 45-46. Another good source for economic statistics during the period is *Anuario Estadístico de la República de Chile, 1890, 1891, 1892*, vol. XXVIII. Some other works dealing with economic developments of the period are listed below. Guillermo E. Billinghurst, *Los capitales salitreros de Tara-pacá* (1889). Roberto Hernández, *El salitre: resumen histórico desde su descubri-miento y explotación* (1930). Máximo Jeria, "La industria forestal en el Perú y en Chile," *El Ferrocarril*, February 8, 1898. Marcial González, *Estudios económicos* (1889). *Revista Económica*. This journal was founded in 1886 by Miguel Cruchaga Montt and Félix Vicuña. Upon Cruchaga's death the following year, the journal was taken over by Zorobabel Rodríguez, one of the most articulate champions of uninhibited laissez faire. Ramón Santelices, *Los bancos chilenos* (1893). Enrique Zañartu Prieto, *Manuel Aristides Zañartu, o historia y causas del pauperismo en Chile*, con prólogo por Emilio Rodríguez Mendoza (1940). This is Zañartu Prieto's biography of his father who, as Minister of Hacienda under Balmaceda, helped organize plans for a *Banco del Estado*, thus anticipating the Edwin Kemmerer mission in Chile by more than a quarter of a century. Manuel Aristides Zañartu was also one of the first advocates in Chile of economic nationalism as is seen in his *Luis Ríos*, vol. I (1884). Zañartu never completed this work in which he puts his own economic ideas in the mouth of Luis Ríos, a fictitious lawyer and agricul-turalist. Ríos argues with Professor Núfiez who represents the typical laissez faire economist.

[11] Jobet, *Ensayo crítico*, p. 80.

[12] The *Sociedad de Fomento Fabril* was founded in 1883, with Agustín Edwards Ross serving as its first president. The guiding spirit of the organization, however, was Guillermo Puelma.

[13] *Anuario Estadístico*, 1920, I, 14-15. Figures given by Jobet, *op. cit.*, p. 80, are somewhat different, showing that government income of 15 million pesos before the war rose to 58 million in 1890. Ramírez, *Balmaceda*, p. 16, states that the 1879 figure was 15 million pesos of 33 pence, while that for 1880 was 53 million of 24 pence.

[14] Ramírez, *op. cit.*, p. 122.

[15] See Jobet, *op. cit.*, p. 80, and Encina, *Historia*, XVIII, 280-325.

[16] *Anuario Estadístico*, 1920, I, 14-15.

[17] Nearly 1600 persons were settled in southern agricultural colonies between the

beginning of 1888 and the end of 1889. See Santiago Macchiavello Varas, *Política económica nacional: antecedentes y directivas* (1929), p. 83.

[18] *La Nación* (Santiago daily), February 9, 1928.

[19] Dirección General de Estadística, *X Censo de la población efectuado el 27 de noviembre de 1930* (1935), I, 46-50.

[20] The lavish event occurred on January 7, 1892, and was reported a few weeks later in the Santiago press.

[21] *El Ferrocarril*, August 3, 1880.

[22] See, for example, *ibid.*, August 3, 1880, September 18, 1881. Editorial writers who never tired of singing their country's praises included R. Ramón Nieto, Alvaro Vial, Enrique Subercaseaux, J. Samuel Molina Gómez, and Juan Agustín Barriga.

[23] *Ibid.*, August 29, 1880.

[24] *Ibid.*, October 1, 1881.

[25] *Ibid.*, September 4, 1880.

[26] *El Mercurio*, December 17, 1880.

[27] *Ibid.*, October 11, 1880.

[28] *Ibid.*, January 22, 1881.

[29] See, for example, *El Ferrocarril*, July 16, October 18, November 9 and 17, 1880.

[30] *Ibid.*, July 6, 1880.

[31] *El Mercurio*, January 6, 1881.

[32] *Ibid.*, October 19, 1880.

[33] *Ibid.*, October 26, 1880.

[34] *El Ferrocarril*, August 3, 1883.

[35] *Ibid.*, November 27, 1883.

[36] Sociedad de Fomento Fabril, *Boletín No. 1*, 1889.

[37] *El Ferrocarril*, July 16, 1880.

[38] Oficina Central de Estadística, *Sesto Censo Jeneral . . . 1885*, II.

[39] Jobet, *Ensayo crítico*, p. 117. Ramírez, *Balmaceda*, p. 21, is even more extreme when writing on this subject, alleging that by 1890, 70 per cent of the nitrate industry was controlled by enterprises having their headquarters in London. Although caution must be exercised in accepting figures presented by Marxist writers on "foreign imperialism," Jobet and Ramírez, especially the latter, have done extensive research on this particular matter, and there is some likelihood that their figures may be reliable.

[40] José Miguel Yrarrázaval Larraín, *La administración de Balmaceda y el salitre de Tarapacá* (1953), pp. 3-4.

[41] *El Ferrocarril*, June 12, 1895, has a brief but valuable account of Mr. North, obtained largely from the April 23 Paris *Figaro*. See also Encina, *Historia de Chile*, XIX, 400 ff.

[42] Yrarrázaval, *op. cit.*, pp. 6 ff. Ramírez, *op. cit.*, pp. 24 ff.

[43] *Anuario Estadístico*, 1920, I, 36-37.

[44] Between 1883 and 1885, copper prices fell from 66.1 pounds sterling per ton to 48. Chilean production, moreover, declined from 600,790 tons during the 1871-1880 period to 362,281 tons for the years from 1881 to 1890. Many plants were idle, and considerable unemployment existed. See Ramírez, *op. cit.*, pp. 146 ff.

[45] Nitrate prices declined 25 per cent in 1883. See Oscar Alvarez Andrews, *Historia del desarrollo industrial de Chile* (1936), pp. 134-135.

⁴⁶ See Yrarrázaval Larraín, *El gobierno y los bancos durante la administración de Balmaceda* (1953), pp. 4-6.

⁴⁷ Alberto Edwards, *Bosquejo histórico de los partidos políticos chilenos* (1903), p. 96. Some other useful works dealing with political events of the times and not cited elsewhere in this chapter include: Pedro Pablo Figueroa, *Los principios del Liberalismo Democrático* (1893); Luis Galdames, *Evolución constitucional de Chile* (1925); Julio Heise González, *Historia constitucional de Chile* (1950); Enrique Mac-Iver, *Discursos políticos i parlamentarios de 1868-1898*, revisado por él mismo i compilados con su autorización por Alberto Prado Martínez, 2 vols. (1899); and Nolasco Préndez P., *Los candidatos liberales para 1885* (Valparaíso, 1885). Some of the more useful newspapers of the period are next listed. *Chillán Times*, published weekly, 1876-1906, was one of the best newspaper voices of the South. *La Época*, published as a Santiago daily, 1881-1892, was famous for its literary coverage. *El Estandarte Católico*, a Santiago daily published 1874-1891, was the organ of clericalism and the Conservative Party, *El Ferrocarril* (see note 58, chapter I) was the best daily in Chile until the late nineteenth century. *El Heraldo*, published in Valparaíso, 1888-1953, was generally a voice of advanced liberalism. *La Libertad Electoral*, a Santiago daily published 1886-1901, was conceived, as the name would imply, in the principle of urging electoral reform and opposing presidential intervention. *El Mercurio* began publication in Valparaíso in 1827 and from 1900 on appeared in different editions both in that city and Santiago. After 1880 its owner was Agustín Edwards Ross, the banking, mining, insurance and land tycoon. By the end of the century, it had probably become the outstanding national paper. *La Patria*, published in Valparaíso from 1863 to 1896 was the voice of radicalism and anticlericalism. *La Unión* of Valparaíso, founded in 1885, continues to this day to be one of the leading voices of the conservative, clerical position. For further information on these and other papers of the period see Raúl Silva Castro, *Prensa y periodismo en Chile, 1812-1956*. Another source of local information during this time was *Revista Chilena*, published in Santiago, 1875-1888.

⁴⁸ See, for example, the extremely unsympathetic biography written by archconservative Carlos Walker Martínez: *Historia de la Administración Santa María* (1890).

⁴⁹ Edwards, *Bosquejo*, pp. 99-101, and Ricardo Donoso, *Desarrollo político y social de Chile desde la Constitución de 1833* (1942), pp. 91 ff.

⁵⁰ See Edwards, *op. cit.*, pp. 102-106; Donoso, *op. cit.*, pp. 94 ff.; and Domingo Amunátegui Solar, *La democracia en Chile* (1946), pp. 215-220.

⁵¹ Amunátegui Solar, *El progreso intelectual y político de Chile* (1936), pp. 130-131.

⁵² There follows a very incomplete bibliography of some of the main works most readily available in Chile dealing with Balmaceda and the civil war of 1891 which are not cited elsewhere in the notes for this chapter. Luis Aldunate, *Desde nuestro observatorio: estudio de la actualidad* (1893). This is an illuminating account by one of the most distinguished of contemporary statesmen in Chile. José Manuel Balmaceda, *Discursos y escritos políticos de don José Manuel Balmaceda, 1864-1891*, compilados con la autorización de la familia por Alberto Prado Martínez (1900). Rafael Balmaceda, *La revolución y la condenación del Ministerio Vicuña* (Buenos Aires, 1893). Written in exile, the work is highly pro-Balmaceda. Julio Bañados Espinosa, *Balmaceda: su gobierno y la revolución de 1891*, 2 vols. (Paris,

1891). Bañados, an important official of the Balmaceda administration who remained loyal to the last, wrote this highly partisan and often inaccurate work while in exile. Orozimbo Barbosa, *Como si fuera hoy: recuerdos de la revolución de 1891* (1929). This pro-Balmaceda account by a general in the forces that remained loyal to the president was well received at the time of publication. During the 1920's the cult of Balmaceda was at its height. Enrique Blanchard-Chessi, "La revolución de 1891;" *Zig Zag*. This study began in the December 18, 1909, issue of the weekly *Zig Zag* and continued in various subsequent editions through the first part of 1915. It is a valuable study and one of the first objective works written in Chile on the events leading up to the civil war and the struggle itself. Ricardo Cox Méndez, *Recuerdos de 1891* (1944). The outspoken, long-time Conservative leader Cox Méndez makes no attempt to disguise his dislike for Balmaceda. Luis Enrique Délano, *Balmaceda: político romántico* (1937). This is a sympathetic account, and *romántico* is probably the best adjective there is for Balmaceda. Víctor Eastman, *Balmaceda, don José Manuel, Presidente de Chile, 1886-1891, y el conflicto con el Congreso Nacional* (Latacunga, Ecuador, 1935). This is one of the several reasonably objective studies produced by a long-time diplomat and amateur historian. Alfredo Edwards Barros, *Balmaceda: su vida y su actuación como Primer Mandatorio hasta el 1° de enero de 1891* (1936). Francisco Antonio Encina, *La presidencia de Balmaceda*, 2 vols. (1952). This writer considers the work one of the most perceptive studies by the prolific dean of Chilean historians. Isidoro Errázuriz, *Embustes y truhanerías de Mauricio Hervey, corresponsal especial del "Times"* (Valparaíso, 1892). Firebrand Errázuriz delivers an outspoken attack against the pro-Balmaceda London *Times* reporter. See also Maurice Hervey's, *Dark Days in Chile: an Account of the Revolution of 1891* (London, 1892). Guillermo Feliú Cruz, "Un documento sobre Balmaceda: ¿escribió Balmaceda una justificación de sus actos después de la revolución de 1891 para el *New York Herald?*" *Revista Chilena*, Año VI, Tomo XIV, no. LV (September, 1922). Feliú Cruz thinks the disputed letter, in which Balmaceda blames his fall on the betrayal of a few generals, is authentic. The more rabid Balmacedistas regard the letter as a forgery, for it reveals a decided pettiness of spirit. Valentín Letelier, *La tiranía y la revolución, o sea, las relaciones de la administración con la política estudiados a la luz de los últimos acontecimientos* (1891). The first part of the title reveals the attitudes of the important Radical Party leader and *pensador*. Augusto Matte and Agustín Ross, *Memoria presentada a la Excma. Junta de Gobierno* (Paris, 1892). This is the interesting report of the agents of the congressional forces in Europe. Eugenio Orrego Vicuña, *Un canciller de la revolución* (1926). This is an objective account of Manuel María Aldunate Solar, Balmaceda's last Minister of Foreign Relations. Félix Pinto Ovalle, *Vindicación de Balmaceda: documentos, autógrafos y grabadas inéditos de la revolución de 91* (1925). This is another of the books in the move to glorify Balmaceda during the 1920's. Emilio Rodríguez Mendoza, *Los últimos días de la administración Balmaceda* (1899. Tomo 67 de la Colección Guerra Civil de Chile: folletos diversos. Library of Congress, Santiago). Joaquín Rodríguez Bravo, *Balmaceda y el conflicto entre el congreso y el ejecutivo*, 2 vols. (1921, 1925)—another item in the Balmaceda glorification movement. Ricardo Salas Edwards, *Balmaceda y el parlamentarismo en Chile: un estudio de psicología política chilena*, 2 vols. (1914, 1925). A leading figure of Conservative politics, Salas Edwards produced in these two volumes a valuable and generally objective study. The author does not regret his original anti-Balmaceda position. Fanor Velasco, one-time sub-secretary of Foreign Relations and student of diplomacy has written several works on the civil war: "La revolución de 1891," *Revista Chilena*, Año VI, Tomo XV, no. LVI (October, 1925); *La revolución de 1891; diario desde el 5 de agosto de 1890 hasta el 20 de agosto de 1891* (1914); *La revolución de 1891: Memorias* (Posthumous. Second edition, 1925). José Miguel Yrarrázaval Larraín, *El Presidente Balmaceda*, 2 vols. (1940), and *Tres temas de historia: Portales "tirano" y "dictador;" la perdida de la Patagonia; causa y resultados de la revolución de 1891* (1951). Conservative stalwart Yrarrázaval is one of the most careful and reliable historians that Chile has produced in the twentieth century. His works on Balmaceda are extremely valuable, and offset the Marxist interpretations of the civil war that have come to enjoy such vogue in Chile. Julio Zegers, *Memorandum político de 1889, 1890 y 1891* (1892). Zegers, an important political personality and one of John T. North's Chilean lawyers, was violently anti-Balmaceda.

[53] On the sincere reform aspirations of Irarrázaval see Jaime Eyzaguirre, *Chile durante el gobierno de Errázuriz Echáurren, 1896-1901* (1957), p. 26. See also José María Cifuentes, "Don Manuel José Irarrázaval: 6 de noviembre de 1834-14 de febrero de 1896," *Boletín de la Academia Chilena de la Historia*, Año II, no. 4 (2° semestre, 1934); Manuel José Irarrázaval, *Colección de discursos parlamentarios*, 2 vols. (1892, 1893), and *La comuna autónoma: discursos precedidos de la biografía de este ilustre hombre público*, recopilado por Manuel Alberto Guzmán (Valparaíso, 1890); and Javier Vial Solar, "Don Manuel José Irarrázaval; reminiscencias," *Boletín de la Academia Chilena de la Historia*, Año II, no. 4 (2° semestre, 1934). This last is a valuable eighty-page survey of Irarrázaval's role in Chilean politics up to his death in 1896.

[54] See Bañados Espinosa, *Balmaceda*, I, 32-53.

[55] *El Ferrocarril*, February 2, 1889.

[56] In referring both to Matta and Irarrazaval, Jaime Eyzaguirre, *op. cit.*, p. 27, is undoubtedly right when he says: "These sincere men had few sincere followers." For more on the frustrated hopes of these two idealists see Juan de Dios Vial, "Matta y Irarrázaval," *El Imparcial*, August 9, 1935.

[57] *El Ferrocarril*, June 13, 1890.

[58] Conservative Senator Manuel José Irarrázaval charged that Balmaceda offered the Conservatives control of half the seats in both chambers of congress if they would agree to support the candidacy of Sanfuentes. The Conservatives refused the deal. See Edwards, *Bosquejo*, p. 115.

[59] Julio César Jobet, *Luis Emilio Recabarren: los orígenes del movimiento obrero y del socialismo chileno* (1955), pp. 55 ff.

[60] *El Estandarte Católico* had as early as October 10, 1889, distinguished itself for its anti-Balmaceda editorials. This Conservative, clerical instrument was suppressed during the course of the civil war, but its spirit was carried on by *El Porvenir*, founded in 1891.

[61] See *El Ferrocarril*, February 8, 1890.

[62] *La Epoca*, February 7, 1890.

[63] *La Patria*, February 7, 1890.

[64] *El Heraldo*, February 7, 1890.

[65] Some of those who expressed themselves most strongly against Balmaceda and the journals which they used to disseminate their attacks are listed below: Máximo

R. Lira, editor of *El Mercurio*; Adolfo Guerrero and Gonzalo Bulnes of *La Libertad Electoral*; Zorobabel Rodríguez of *La Unión*; Javier Vial Solar of *El Independiente*; Augusto Orrego Luco and Vicente Aguirre Vargas of *La Época*; Enrique Valdés Vergara of *El Heraldo*, which was ultimately suppressed by Balmaceda; Isidoro Errázuriz of *La Patria*; Fr. Rodolfo Vergara Antúnez of *El Estandarte Católico*; and M. A. Matta of *El Atacameño*. See Augusto Iglesias, *Alessandri: una etapa en la democracia en América* (1959), p. 184. For some of the strongest of the early anti-Balmaceda diatribes published in the prestigious *El Ferrocarril*, see editions of April 13, 24, 27 and June 11, 1889.

⁶⁶ *El Ferrocarril*, June 3, 1890.

⁶⁷ See editions of June 12 and 13.

⁶⁸ *El Ferrocarril*, June 29, 1889.

⁶⁹ In addition to the prominent persons mentioned by the German envoy, the young Arturo Alessandri, then in his fourth year of law studies, was rabidly anti-Balmaceda. This attitude, which in later life he reversed, was owing largely to the influence of such professors as Valentín Letelier, Miguel Luis Amunátegui and Abraham König, all fervent advocates of electoral freedom and parliamentary government. See Alessandri, *Revolución de 1891: mi actuación* (1950). See also *Memorias íntimas, políticas y diplomáticas de don Abraham König*, compiladas por Fanor Velasco (1927).

⁷⁰ Letter of Baron von Gutschmid to General Caprivi, German Secretary of State, December, 1890, in *Los acontecimientos en Chile: documentos publicados por la Cancillería Alemana* (1892), pp. 3-5. The astute observations of the German envoy represent one of the more valuable sources on the Chilean civil war, and make it clear that from the outset the Germans were backing the winner.

⁷¹ Donoso, *Desarrollo*, pp. 91-102.

⁷² *El Ferrocarril*, January 1, 1891.

⁷³ The inflationist tendencies of Balmaceda were always given by Radical leader Enrique Mac-Iver as a major reason for his opposition to the president. See Armando Donoso, *Recuerdos de cincuenta años* (1947), pp. 130-131. *El Ferrocarril* editorials of May 2 and July 18, 1889, May 8, 1890, and December 24, 1891, harshly criticized Balmaceda's inflationist tendencies. Strongly opposed to Balmaceda for the same reason was banker Agustín Ross. See Frank W. Fetter, *Monetary Inflation in Chile* (Princeton, N. J., 1931), p. 61. See also Agustín Ross, *Los bancos de Chile y la ley que los rige* (Valparaíso, 1886), *Chile, 1851-1910: sesenta años de cuestiones monetarias y financieras y de problemas bancarios* (1911), and *La cuestión económica* (Valparaíso, 1888). See also Guillermo Feliú Cruz, *Chile visto a través de Agustín Ross* (1950).

⁷⁴ The Marxian interpretation is that aroused Chilean businessmen, especially bankers, aided and abetted by foreign capitalists, most notably British nitrate interests, brought on the civil war. Hernán Ramírez Necochea in *La guerra civil de 1891: antecedentes económicos* (1951), argues this thesis strongly. Further research in London provided him, he felt, with additional documentation for his interpretation, and in 1958 he published the more thorough *Balmaceda y la contrarevolución de 1891*. The already cited studies of Francisco Antonio Encina and José Miguel Yrarrázaval Larraín argue persuasively, so far as this writer is concerned, against the Ramírez interpretation. See especially the two Yrarrázaval monographs, *La administración de Balmaceda y el salitre de Tarapacá* (1953), and *El gobierno y los bancos*

durante la administración de Balmaceda (1953). For additional information on this matter see Osgood Hardy, "Los intereses salitreros ingleses y la revolución de 1891," and J. Fred Rippy, "Iniciativas económicas del 'Rey del Salitre' y sus socios en Chile," *Revista Chilena de Historia y Geografía*, CXII, no. 13 (January-July, 1949).

[75] The incredible extremes to which the business community went in resisting even the slightest suggestion of government attention to economic matters is suggested by the editorials of *El Ferrocarril*, January 23, February 8, and June 12, 1889. Furthermore, the Santiago daily *El Chileno* (1883-1924), around the turn of the century the most widely read paper in Chile, although ostensibly dedicated to the social philosophy of Leo XIII's *Rerum Novarum*, actually reflected more of Herbert Spencer than the Pope in its editorials.

[76] A more negative approach to the fall of Balmaceda might have it that the man of vision was toppled because Chileans are ". . . a people of the last minute. We never act until the water is already up to our neck. We reason little . . . we live full of confidence, expecting the gifts of good fortune." See Máximo Jeria, "La industria forestal en el Perú y el Chile," *El Ferrocarril*, February 8, 1898.

[77] Even Julio Bañados Espinosa, the staunch Balmacedista who stayed on to the bitter end and served as the beleaguered president's last Minister of War and Marine, concedes the indifference of the masses in the war. See his *Balmaceda . . .*, II, 52-54. See also Ives Javet, *La opinión pública y la revolución de 1891* (1942. *Memoria de Prueba*).

[78] The tragedy of this situation was perceived as early as 1894 when Francisco Valdés Vergara published in Valparaíso his *La situación económica y financiera de Chile*. On p. 29 Valdés states: "It is sad to confess, but it is certain, that with the best intentions of serving the country, of stimulating its progress, of purifying its politics, the men who made the [1891] revolution and those of us who were its servants have brought more damage than benefit to Chile."

[79] For example, Balmaceda appealed at first to the striking workers of Iquique for support in 1890. When this move aroused unexpectedly bitter opposition among political circles in Santiago, he responded by sending troops. The resultant slaughter of workers was a fundamental reason for the fact that the northern *rotos* flocked to join the armies that overthrew the president. In 1887 the Balmaceda policy called for national ownership of at least seventy nitrate operations, and he borrowed over a million pounds from the House of Rothschild to finance this plan. By 1889 he decided private citizens of Chile should own this property, and that the government should withdraw from direct ownership. When Chilean capitalists failed to purchase the mines, probably preferring that foreigners assume the risks of operation in an age when nitrate prices might further plummet, Balmaceda began to advocate a policy of increasing government supervision over nitrate production. At first an opponent of soft money, he later came to advocate increased paper emission by private banks, and only in the last stages of his struggle began to advocate a national bank that would have stripped private bankers of their past privileges.

CHAPTER 3

[1] See Gonzalo Bulnes, *Guerra del Pacífico* (1955 edition of the three-volume set originally published 1911-1919), II, 235, and *Memoria del Ministerio de Relaciones*

Exteriores i de colonización presentada al Congreso Nacional de 1882, pp. vii-viii. Henceforth, the various foreign relations *Memorias* will be cited as MMRE, followed by the year. Alberto Blest Gana, *Memoria comprensiva de los trabajos mas importantes ejecutados por la Legación de la república en Francia i Gran Bretāna,* in *ibid.,* pp. 137-172. See also Ricardo Montaner Bello, "La labor diplomático de don Alberto Blest Gana," *Revista Chilena,* Año V, Tomo XIII, no. 42 (July, 1921).

² See Manuel Jordán López, *Historia diplomática de la Guerra del Pacífico* (1957. *Memoria de Prueba*), pp. 96 ff. This is the most valuable single-volume treatment of the subject. It follows largely the treatment of Bulnes and Encina but occasionally is based upon more extensive documentation. See also Francisco Antonio Encina, *Historia de Chile desde la prehistoria hasta* 1891 (20 vols., 1949-1952), XVIII, 266-271; V. G. Kiernan, "Foreign Interests in the War of the Pacific," *Hispanic American Historical Review,* XXXV, no. 1 (February, 1955), 14-36; and J. Fred Rippy, "British Investments in the Chilean Nitrate Industry," *Inter-American Economic Affairs,* VIII (Autumn, 1954), 3-11.

³ Encina, *op. cit.,* XVII, 389-411.

⁴ For some aspects of the Pinto administration's dealings with the United States see Aníbal Pinto, "Apuntes en los años de 1880 y 1881," *Revista Chilena,* Año VI, Tomo XIV, no. 52 (July, 1922).

⁵ See *Las Conferencias de Arica: documentos* (1885). For material on the United States position in regard to the War of the Pacific, see "The War in South America," Sen. Ex. Doc. 79, 47th Cong., 1st Sess., and E. M. Borchard, *Opinion on the Question of the Pacific* (Washington, D. C., 1920).

⁶ See Bulnes, *op. cit.,* II, 499-501; Jordán López, *Historia diplomática,* pp. 103 ff.; and MMRE, 1881, pp. 65-101.

⁷ *El Ferrocarril,* October 15 and November 20, 1880. *El Mercurio,* October 19, 1880.

⁸ *El Ferrocarril,* October 9, 1880.

⁹ Marcial Martínez, Envoy Extraordinary and Minister Plenipotentiary of Chile in the United States, to the Chilean Ministry of Foreign Relations, November 6, 1881, *Legación de Chile en los Estados Unidos de N. América,* 1881, II, Archivos, Ministerio de Relaciones Exteriores. These archives will henceforth be cited as AMRE.

¹⁰ For indications of Chilean convictions that United States meddling prolonged the war see: Bulnes, *op. cit.,* III, 65; and Jaime Eyzaguirre (editor), "Cartas de don Domingo Santa María a don Domingo Gana," *Boletín de Academia Chilena de la Historia,* Año XX, no. 50 (1° semestre, 1954). These letters written by the Chilean president to his envoy in Mexico reveal great preoccupation over United States manipulations. The renowned journalist Justo Arteaga Alemparte wrote several articles on this subject for *Los Tiempos.* See, for example, the September 5, 1881, edition. See also *El Ferrocarril* editorial, January 28, 1883. Finally, the remarks made by Blaine in 1889 that far from intervening in the War of the Pacific the United States confined its actions to preventing European intervention were regarded by Chileans as a ludicrous distortion of fact. See *La Libertad Electoral,* August 5, 1889.

¹¹ Bulnes, *Guerra del Pacífico,* III, 41.

¹² *Ibid.,* 41-46.

¹³ Joaquín Godoy to the Chilean Ministry of Foreign Relations, November 18,

1882 ("Misión del Señor Joaquín Godoy como ajente confidencial de Chile en los EE. UU."), *Legación de Chile en los EE. UU. de N. América, Misión del Señor J. Godoy desde junio 29, 1882, AMRE.* When it came to enjoying public support and wielding effective power, Nicolás Piérola could advance far better claims to the Peruvian presidency than García Calderón, and even the not always perfectly informed United States press seemed aware of this fact. Godoy to the Chilean Ministry of Foreign Relations, April 17, 1882, *ibid.*

[14] See also Jordán López, *Historia diplomática,* p. 108.

[15] See Luis Guillén Atienza, *El principio de no intervención y las doctrinas americanas* (1949. Memoria de Prueba), p. 15.

[16] Jordán López, *Historia diplomática,* p. 110.

[17] See, for example, *El Diario Oficial,* October 11, 1881; *El Ferrocarril,* October 9 and 10, 1881; *El Mercurio,* October 10; and *Los Tiempos,* October 9, an article signed by Justo Arteaga Alemparte.

[18] *El Mercurio,* December 5, 1881.

[19] Confidential letter of M. Valderrama, Chilean Minister of Foreign Relations, to Envoy Martínez in Washington, September 12, 1881, *Correspondencia: ajentes diplomáticos de Chile en el exterior, 1878-1881, AMRE.* Confidential letter of J. M. Balmaceda, Chilean Minister of Foreign Relations, to Martínez, September 27, 1881, *ibid.*

[20] Martínez to Chilean Ministry of Foreign Relations, October 8, 1881, *Legación de Chile en los EE. UU. de N. América, 1881, AMRE.* The letter was marked absolutely confidential.

[21] Martínez to Chilean Ministry of Foreign Relations, October 15, 1881, *ibid.*

[22] *Los Tiempos,* September 5, 1881.

[23] *El Mercurio,* September 3, 1881.

[24] Martínez to Chilean Ministry of Foreign Relations, November 6, 1881, *Legación de Chile en los EE. UU. de N. América, 1881, AMRE.*

[25] José Miguel Yrarrázaval Larraín, *La administración de Balmaceda y el salitre de Tarapacá* (1953), p. 6.

[26] Bulnes, *op. cit.,* III, 55-66; Jordán López, *op. cit.,* pp. 108 ff.

[27] Martínez to Chilean Ministry of Foreign Relations, October 26, 1881, *Legación de Chile en los EE. UU. de N. América, 1881, AMRE.*

[28] Martínez to Ministry, November 6, 1881, *ibid.*

[29] Martínez to Ministry, November 6 and 21, *ibid.*

[30] Martínez referred to the brochure and enclosed a United States newspaper clipping concerning it in his October 14 letter to the Ministry, *ibid.*

[31] Martínez included the Shipherd communiqué with his November 26 letter to his Ministry, *ibid.*

[32] Martínez to Ministry, November 18, *ibid.*

[33] Martínez to Ministry, November 16, *ibid.*

[34] Martínez to Ministry, December 19, *ibid.* See also MMRE, 1882, p. 2, and Marcial Martínez, *Memorandum delivered by the Minister of Chile to the Secretary of State, stating the actual condition of affairs on the Pacific Coast* (Washington, D.C., 1881).

[35] Godoy to Chilean Ministry of Foreign Relations, June 29, 1882, *Legación de Chile en los EE.UU. de N. América, Misión de Sr. J. Godoy desde junio 29, 1882, AMRE.*

[36] A friendly and extremely well-documented study of Blaine's motivation is Russell H. Bastert, "A New Approach to the Origins of Blaine's Pan-American Policy," *Hispanic American Historical Review*, XXXIX, no. 3 (August, 1959). In the light of sources available in Chile, the Bastert interpretation appears somewhat overly favorable to Blaine.

[37] Bulnes, *Guerra del Pacífico*, III, 55; Encina, *Historia de Chile*, XVIII, 18 ff.

[38] *MMRE*, 1882, pp. 126-127.

[39] See Bulnes, *op. cit.*, III, 70, and article by Kiernan cited in note 2 for this chapter. If Chile was being backed in its war efforts by England, various Chileans did not realize it. *El Mercurio*, October 5, 1880, charged that England and France were acting in a manner contrary to the interests of Chile and asked: "Can it be that the European diplomatic representatives to Peru have been affected by their ties and marriages to the seductive daughters of the Rimac?"

[40] Martínez to Chilean Ministry of Foreign Relations, December 18, 1881, *Legación de Chile en los EE.UU. de N. América*, 1881, II, AMRE.

[41] Godoy's informant was the July 3, 1882, *New York Herald*. The pertinent article was clipped and sent by Godoy to the Chilean Ministry of Foreign Relations. It is bound, by mistake, with the April 17, 1882, letter of Godoy to the Ministry, *Legación de Chile en EE.UU. de N. América*, 1882, AMRE. Sentiments similar to those of Navy Secretary Robeson were voiced by various United States Senators during debate on a naval appropriations bill. See *New York Times*, July 6, 1882.

[42] *La Epoca*, December 5, 1881, gave United States desire to act as the supreme arbiter of all hemisphere relations as the reason for intervention. Alejandro Magnet, *Orígenes y antecedentes del panamericanismo* (1945), p. 259, shares this appraisal to a large extent.

[43] *MMRE*, 1882, pp. 62-64.

[44] Martínez to Chilean Ministry of Foreign Relations, November 6, 1881, *Legación de Chile en los EE.UU. de N. América*, 1881, II, AMRE.

[45] See Antonio Varas H., "Reminiscencias históricas y diplomáticas," *Revista Chilena de Historia y Geografía*, LXXVII (September-December, 1935), 71. Varas, the eminent, contemporary Chilean statesman was also suspicious that the United States wished to convert Peru into a protectorate. See also "Correspondencia de don Antonio Varas: Guerra del Pacífico," *ibid.*, XXV (1° trimestre, 1918), XVI (2° trimestre, 1918), and XVII (3° trimestre, 1918); and Alberto Cruchaga Ossa, *Correspondencia de Antonio Varas: cuestiones americanas* (1929).

[46] See Bulnes, *Guerra del Pacífico*, III, 74, and Encina, *Historia de Chile*, XVIII, 16.

[47] Javier Vial Solar, *Páginas diplomáticas* (1900), pp. 50-55.

[48] Martínez to Chilean Ministry of Foreign Relations, November 18, 1881, *Legación de Chile en los EE. UU. de N. América*, 1881, II, AMRE.

[49] Martínez to Ministry, November 21, *ibid.*

[50] Martínez to Ministry, November 6, *ibid.*

[51] Bulnes, *op. cit.*, III, 81, and Encina, *op. cit.*, XVIII, 28 ff.

[52] Martínez to Ministry, December 6, *Legación* . . . , 1881, II, AMRE.

[53] See Armando Donoso, *Recuerdos de cincuenta años* (1947), pp. xi, 428-429, and the long *memoria* by Martínez, dated April 19, 1882, and included in *MMRE*, 1882, pp. 97-134. See also Marcial Martínez, *Opúsculos sobre asuntos interna-*

cionales, Vol. III of *Obras completas* (1919), and Francisco Javier Ovalle Castillo, *La personalidad de don Marcial Martínez* (1918). See also Chapter I, note 94.

[54] See R. H. Bastert, "Diplomatic Reversal: Frelinghuysen's opposition to Blaine's Pan-American Policy in 1882," *Mississippi Valley Historical Review*, XLII (March, 1956), 653-671.

[55] Jordán López, *Historia diplomática*, pp. 112 ff., and MMRE, 1882, pp. 1-45.

[56] Such, at least, was the opinion of Foreign Relations Minister J. M. Balmaceda. See MMRE, 1882, pp. xxvi-xxxi.

[57] See Nemisio Martínez Méndez, *El Congreso Internacional Americano en Washington* (1892). Martínez Méndez was a highly placed official in the Ministry of Foreign Relations. See also *La Epoca*, June 26, 1882, and *El Ferrocarril*, January 25, 1882.

[58] Joaquín Godoy, Envoy Extraordinary and Minister Plenipotentiary of Chile in the United States, to the Chilean Ministry of Foreign Relations, August 16, 1882, *Legación de Chile en los EE.UU. de N. América, Misión de Sr. J. Godoy desde junio 29, 1882*, AMRE. See also Godoy to Ministry, December 9, *ibid.*, and MMRE, 1882, pp. 61-67. Chilean success in the conflict with the United States apparently went to the heads of some writers. Julio Bañados Espinosa, *Balmaceda: su gobierno y la revolución de 1891* (Paris, 1894), I, 27-31, for example, states that Chilean resistance forced the United States to change its policies, and to re-place Blaine with Frelinghuysen. The Garfield assassination is not so much as mentioned.

[59] MMRE, 1883, pp. lxii-lxiii.

[60] Godoy to Ministry, February 28, 1883, *Legación de Chile en EE.UU. de N. América*, 1883, AMRE.

[61] Godoy to Ministry, March 19, 1883, *ibid.*

[62] Godoy to Ministry, December 10, *ibid.*

[63] Benjamín Vicuña Mackenna felt that Blaine, in his South American policies, symbolized the dollar mania and moral disintegration of the post-Civil War United States. See his pamphlet *Blaine* (1884). A somewhat similar opinion is advanced by the present-day writer Alejandro Magnet, *Orígenes*, pp. 265 ff. For additional material on United States-Chilean relations during the War of the Pacific, refer to Chapter II, note 1. See also Jacinto López, *Historia de la guerra del guano y el salitre o Guerra del Pacífico entre Chile, Bolivia y el Perú* (New York, 1930), and Herbert Millington, *American Diplomacy and the War of the Pacific* (New York, 1948). Moreover, the all-time Chilean best-seller, Jorge Inostrosa's semi-historical *Adios al séptimo de la linea*, 5 vols. (1959 edition), has recently given new voice to the anti-United States sentiments justifiably fostered in Chile during the War of the Pacific.

[64] The editorial is quoted in the October 3, 1881, *El Mercurio*.

[65] Godoy to Chilean Ministry of Foreign Relations, November 15, 1882, *Legación de Chile en los EE.UU. de No. América*, 1882, AMRE.

[66] See Jaime Eyzaguirre, *La soberanía de Chile en las tierras australes* (1958); F. A. Encina, *La cuestión de límites entre Chile y la Argentina desde la independencia hasta el tratado de 1881* (1959); Manuel Rodríguez Mendoza, *La política internacional de Chile en sud-américa: el problema de la paz o de la guerra* (1893), p. 71, and Sergio Villalobos R., "Darwin y Chile." *Atenea*, CXXXIII, no. 384 (April-June, 1959), 44-45.

[67] *MMRE*, 1881, p. 18.

[68] *MMRE*, 1883, pp. xv-xvi.

[69] See Miguel Cruchaga Tocornal, "Actitud de Alemania durante la Guerra del Pacífico," *Boletín de la Academia Chilena de la Historia*, Año XVI, no. 40 (1° semestre, 1949). This article, by the eminent statesman who served during part of the First World War as his country's envoy to Germany, abounds in warm praise for Bismarck and the general German attitude.

[70] Guillén, *El principio de no intervención*, p. 71.

[71] *MMRE*, 1882, pp. vii-viii.

[72] *La Libertad Electoral*, August 2, 1898. *La Unión*, December 2, 1898.

[73] Encina, *Historia de Chile*, XVIII, 266.

[74] Guillermo Matta, Envoy Extraordinary and Minister Plenipotentiary in Germany, to Chilean Ministry of Foreign Relations, July 14, 1882, *Legación de Chile en Alemania, 1882-1883*, AMRE. Also included in this set of correspondence is the valuable, fifty-seven page, handwritten *memoria* prepared by Matta and dated April 14, 1883.

[75] Matta to Ministry, March 14, 1883, *ibid.*

[76] Matta to Ministry, April 14, *ibid.*

[77] Matta to Ministry, August 31, *ibid.*

[78] Schenck to Chilean Foreign Minister Luis Aldunate, December 21, 1883, *Gobierno y ajentes diplomáticos de Alemania en Chile, 1881-1886*, AMRE. See also the report prepared in Berlin by Guillermo Matta covering the September 3, 1885, to September 18, 1886, period, in *MMRE*, 1886. Matta praises Germany unstintingly and notes that it had become the second most important country in Chile's foreign commerce.

[79] See Nemisio Martínez Méndez, *El arbitraje obligatorio ante los congresos panamericanos* (1910), pp. 12-13. See also *La Libertad Electoral*, July 4, 1889, and *MMRE*, 1889, pp. xv-xviii.

[80] *La Libertad Electoral*, July 4, 1889, and Ignacio Calderón, *El Congreso de Washington y su misión* (Iquique, 1889).

[81] See Magnet, *Orígenes*, p. 263, and *MMRE*, 1889, pp. lxxiii-lxxv, lxxxvii-ccxiv. Chile was represented in Montevideo by Guillermo Matta and Belisario Prats. The report of the Chilean delegation's secretary, Francisco E. Noguera, pictures Chile as being the least cooperative of the nations represented, due to its insistence upon protection of absolute sovereignty.

[82] *El Ferrocarril*, February 5, 1889.

[83] *El Estandarte Católico*, July 5, 1889. Similar notions were expressed by *El Ferrocarril*, July 3, which dismissed all international meetings as an appeal by great nations to the vanity of lesser ones so that the strong might more easily crush the sovereignty of the weak. Chile was advised, therefore, not to attend the conference, the only result of which would be to reduce her absolute freedom of diplomatic action. See also Gaspar Toro, *Notas sobre arbitraje internacional en las repúblicas latino-americanas* (1898). Appearing originally as a series of articles in the September and October, 1898, editions of *El Ferrocarril*, the work is strongly isolationist in tone, ridicules the Pan-American movement, expresses aversion to arbitration, and indicates suspicion that the United States hopes to force Chile to arbitrate the Tacna-Arica matter.

[84] *El Estandarte Católico*, July 5, 1889.

[85] See *El Ferrocarril*, November 7, 1889, and Gonzalo Bulnes, Envoy Extraordinary and Minister Plenipotentiary of Chile in Germany, to Chilean Ministry of Foreign Relations, February 5, 1892, *Legación de Chile en Alemania*, 1892, AMRE. Bulnes reports that among German statesmen the feeling is common that Pan-Americanism merely represents a United States attempt to wean Latin America away from European commerce. Germans regard Chile as the main obstacle to this United States desire, and the Minister of State expressed to Bulnes his admiration of Chile's role in thwarting Washington at the 1889-1890 Washington Conference. See also Magnet, *Orígenes*.

[86] Martínez Méndez, *Arbitraje obligatorio*, pp. 5-8.

[87] Emilio C. Varas, Envoy Extraordinary and Minister Plenipotentiary of Chile in the United States, "Informe de la legación de chile en los EE. UU. de N. América, October 15, 1889," pp. 10-14, in *Legación de Chile en los Estados Unidos de N. América*, 1889, AMRE. See also MMRE, 1889, p. 95.

[88] José Alfonso, *El arbitraje internacional en la Conferencia Americana de Washington* (1892), pp. 6 ff., and Eduardo Phillips, *El Congreso Internacional Americana de Washington* (1890), pp. 4, 24, 28.

[89] Cámara de Senadores, *Boletín de sesiones ordinarias*, 1889, Sesión 10°, June 28, 1889.

[90] See *El Ferrocarril*, August 17, 1889, and Emilio Varas to Chilean Ministry of Foreign Relations, October 8, 1889, *Legación de Chile en los Estados Unidos de N. América*, 1889, AMRE. See also the biography of Alfonso written by his two sons: José A. and Paulino Alfonso, *Don José Alfonso; ministro de estado, ministro de la Corte Suprema, diplomático, consejero de estado* (1910).

[91] Alfonso, *Arbitraje internacional*, p. 11.

[92] Martínez Méndez, *Arbitraje obligatorio*, pp. 12-13.

[93] Alfonso, *Arbitraje internacional*, p. 6. *El Estandarte Católico*, July 5, 1889. Phillips, *El Congreso Internacional*, p. 8.

[94] In instructing the Chilean delegation to refrain absolutely from discussions involving arbitration, Foreign Relations Minister Demetrio Lastarria declared that no arbitral tribunal could ever function successfully without invading the sovereign rights of American nations. See MMRE, 1890, pp. xxxii-xxxv.

[95] Alfonso, *Arbitraje internacional*, pp. 6, 24.

[96] José Alfonso to Chilean Ministry of Foreign Relations, December 8, 1889, *Legación de Chile en los Estados Unidos de N. América*, 1889, AMRE.

[97] For background on Chilean-Brazilian relations, see Juan José Fernández, *La república de Chile y el imperio de Brasil: historia de sus relaciones diplomáticas* (1959).

[98] Alfonso, *Arbitraje internacional*, pp. 8-9.

[99] *Ibid.*, pp. 11-20.

[100] See Fernando Matte Hurtado, *El arbitraje en América, especialmente en Chile* (1922. *Memoria de Prueba*), and R. Acevedo Parraguez, *Aspectos jurídicos del antiguo y del nuevo panamericanismo* (1947), p. 18. The countries that signed the treaty were Brazil, Ecuador, Guatemala, Haiti, Nicaragua, El Salvador, and the United States. Other works that deal in part with the conference include Alejandro Alvarez, *Las conferencias panamericanas* (1911); Henry Clay Evans, Jr., *Chile and its Relations with the United States* (Durham, N.C., 1927); Manuel Hernández Trejos, *Las conferencias internacionales americanas y su contenida económica* (1947.

Memoria de Prueba); Ismael Huidobro, *Las cuestiones aduaneras ante los congresos pan-americanos* (1911. *Memoria de Prueba*); Lupsi Orrego Luco, *Los problemas internacionales de Chile: el arbitraje obligatorio* (1901); James Brown Scott, *American International Conferences, 1889-1936* (Washington, D.C., 1938); William Roderick Sherman, *The Diplomatic and Commercial Relations of the United States and Chile, 1820-1914* (Boston, 1926); and Manuel J. Vega, "El arbitraje obligatorio: un incidente histórico," *El Mercurio*, February 25, 1919.

[101] Alfonso, *Arbitraje internacional*, p. 5.

[102] *El Ferrocarril*, May 1, 1890; *El Heraldo* (Valparaíso), May 9, 1890; *La Libertad Electoral*, May 10, 1890; *El Mercurio*, May 1, 1890; *La Patria*, May 1, 1890.

[103] *El Ferrocarril*, May 10, 1890. See also *El Comercio* (Valparaíso), May 12, 1890, and *El Estandarte Católico*, May 9, 1890.

[104] MMRE, 1893, I, 143.

[105] Manuel Antonio Matta, *Cuestiones recientes con la Legación y el Gobierno de los Estados Unidos de Norte América* (1892), p. 20. In this volume published just after his removal as Minister of Foreign Relations, Matta reproduced much of the correspondence he exchanged with Egan and with officials in Washington. There is also an accompanying text.

[106] Prudencio Lazcano, Envoy Extraordinary and Minister Plenipotentiary of Chile in the United States, to Chilean Ministry of Foreign Relations, July 18, 1891, *Legación de Chile en los EE. UU. de N. América*, 1891, AMRE.

[107] MMRE, 1893, I, 143.

[108] See the long and important editorial in *El Ferrocarril*, October 15, 1891. While not exactly friendly to Egan, *El Ferrocarril* felt some Chilean papers had unduly maligned him. *La Libertad Electoral*, September 8, 1891, expressed a favorable opinion of Egan. Julio Bañados Espinosa, *Balmaceda: su gobierno y la revolución de 1891*, II, 728, praises what he terms the impeccable impartiality of Egan. As Bañados was a rabid Balmacedista, his praise of Egan is perhaps significant.

[109] *Boston Herald*, September 1, 1891.

[110] Ross to Chilean Ministry of Foreign Relations, February 19, 1892, *Legación de Chile en Gran Bretaña*, 1891-1892, II, AMRE, and *El Ferrocarril*, October 13, 1891, and February 19, 1892.

[111] The State Department actually backed the company's full claims of 6,334,203 pesos against Chile. But company representatives proved somewhat easier to deal with than their country's government, and thus Chile was able to settle for 150,000 pesos. See MMRE, 1896, pp. 75-76. The charges that Egan was largely responsible for engineering the whole questionable arrangement are found in *El Heraldo*, January 14, 1892. For additional information on this matter see *El Ferrocarril*, October 22 and 23, 1891, and Domingo Gana, Envoy Extraordinary and Minister Plenipotentiary of Chile in the United States to the Chilean Ministry of Foreign Relations, July 9, 1895, *Legación de Chile en los EE. UU. de N. América*, AMRE. In this letter, Gana describes the threatening attitude of Secretary of State Richard Olney. See also his letters of September 8, 19, 29 and October 29, *ibid.*, as well as *Cámara de Senadores, Boletín de sesiones extraordinarias 1888-1889*, Sesión 4°. For the Chilean Supreme Court investigation of the matter see the report prepared by its Fiscal, Ambrosio Montt, *Visita del fiscal de la Corte Suprema, recaída sobre la presentación de d. Juan A. Palazuelos a fin de que se le reconozca como agentes de la "North and South American Construction Company"* (1891), and

also Montt's *Dictames del Fiscal de la Corte Suprema de Justicia de Chile*, Vol. I, *Materias diplomáticas* (1894). Also helpful is Pedro N. Gandarillas, *Contestación a la demanda presentada al Tribunal Arbitral por la "North and South American Construction Co." contra el Fisco* (1890).

[112] J. M. Barros Franco, *El caso del 'Baltimore'* (1950), pp. 32-26. See also *Memoria relativo a las negociones de paz a invitación del Gobierno de los EE. UU. de Norte, por conducto del Almirante MacCann* (1892), and *Memoria de la revolución de 1891* (1892), AMRE, p. 204.

[113] Barros Franco, *op. cit.*, p. 31.

[114] See *El Ferrocarril*, October 22, 1891.

[115] *Ibid.*, October 27, 1891, and *El Heraldo*, November 4, 1891.

[116] Cox Méndez, *Recuerdos de 1891*, p. 317.

[117] See *Zig Zag*, the Santiago-published weekly, June 25, 1948, p. 51.

[118] Patrick Egan, Envoy Extraordinary and Minister Plenipotentiary of the United States in Chile, to M. A. Matta, September 17, 1891, *Gobierno y Legación de EE. UU. de N. América en Chile, 1891*, AMRE.

[119] The Chilean interpretation of the troublesome incident was that the United States government had resorted to an unduly narrow and unjustified interpretation of neutrality laws to prevent delivery to the congressional forces at Iquique of arms purchased in the United States—and very possibly loaded onto the "Itata" outside of United States territorial waters. Chileans were confirmed in their viewpoint when in 1891 the United States Court for the southern district of California, located in San Diego and presided over by Judge E. M. Ross, decided that the law had not been violated in the arms transaction and dismissed all charges. Egan's assertion that only the "unreflective element" in Chile was aroused by United States actions in the "Itata" affair produced further resentment. See Barros Franco, *El caso del 'Baltimore,'* p. 39. See also Osgood Hardy, "The 'Itata' Incident," *Hispanic American Historical Review*, V (May, 1922), 195-226, and *Oral Arguments in the District Court of the United States for the Southern District of California, before Honorable E. M. Ross, District Judge, by Charles Page and Stephen M. White, Esquires, for Defendants and Claimants, and Oral Argument of William W. Goodrich, Esquire, for Compañía Sud-Americana de Vapores* (San Francisco, 1891). The general Chilean interpretation of the incident is also presented by the Argentine Martín García Merou, *Historia de la diplomacia americana: política internacional de los Estados Unidos* (Buenos Aires, 1904), II, 191.

[120] Matta, *Cuestiones*, p. 24. See also *El Ferrocarril*, September 17 and October 14, 1891. Agustín Ross felt also that so long as Egan remained in Santiago there could not be friendly United States-Chilean relations. See Ross, Envoy Extraordinary and Minister Plenipotentiary of Chile in the United Kingdom, to the Chilean Ministry of Foreign Relations, February 19, 1892, *Legación de Chile en Gran Bretaña, 1891-1892*, II, AMRE.

[121] The offer was extended by John W. Foster. MMRE, 1892, I, 147.

[122] See Barros Franco, *op. cit.*, p. 19; J. Fred Rippy, "Iniciativas económicos del 'Rey del Salitre' y sus socios en Chile," and Osgood Hardy, "Los intereses salitreras inglesas y la revolución de 1891," *Revista Chilena de Historia y Geografía*, no. 113 (January-June, 1949). See also Hernán Ramírez N., *Balmaceda y la contrarevolución de 1891* (1958).

[123] Emilio C. Varas to the Chilean Ministry of Foreign Relations, March 28,

1889, *Legación de Chile en los EE. UU. de N. América*, 1889, AMRE. The *Omaha Herald* editorial was in the April 2, 1889, edition. See also Maurice Hervey, *Dark Days in Chile: an Account of the Revolution of 1891* (London, 1892).

[124] This fact was naturally resented by the British in Chile, who allegedly attempted to stir up anti-Egan sentiments. See Barros Franco, *op. cit.*, p. 39.

[125] Egan to the United States Department of State, March 17, 1891, quoted in Ramírez, *Balmaceda*, p. 195.

[126] Pedro Montt to Chilean Ministry of Foreign Relations, July 18, 1891, MMRE, 1892, I, 144.

[127] Agustín Ross to Chilean Ministry of Foreign Relations, November 9, 1891, *Legación de Chile en Gran Bretaña*, 1891-1892, II, AMRE. Moreover, Prudencio Lazcano, representing the Balmaceda government in Washington, notified his government that Blaine and his close friend Charles R. Flint were vitally interested in obtaining trade reciprocity with Chile. Lazcano to Chilean Ministry of Foreign Relations, July 18, 1891, *Legación de Chile en los EE. UU. de N. América*, 1891, AMRE. See also Ramírez, *Balmaceda*, pp. 230-231.

There was a readiness on the part of many to conclude that England was behind the anti-Balmaceda movement. Given this attitude a letter of Agustín Ross to the triumphant leaders of the revolution is somewhat remarkable. "Although public opinion in England favors our cause more than in any other country, the government has not observed toward us even what I would consider an attitude of proper neutrality." See Ross to his Ministry of Foreign Relations, *Legación de Chile en Gran Bretaña*, 1891-1892, II, AMRE. And two weeks later, Ross complained that the British government lacked confidence in the junta recently established in Chile. Ross to Ministry, September 19, 1891, *ibid.*

[128] Baron Gutschmid to Caprivi, September 9, 1891, *Los Acontecimientos en Chile: documentos publicada por la Cancillería Alemana* (1892), p. 205.

[129] Matta, *Cuestiones*, pp. 1 ff. The notes exchanged between Matta and Egan on the matter of asylum during the September 23-November 30 period are in *Estados Unidos i Chile: notas cambiada entre la Legación de los Estados Unidos de Norte América i el Ministro de Relaciones Exteriores de Chile, a propósito de las cuestiones suscitas entre ambos países* (1891). See also Egan to Matta, September 23, 1891, *Gobierno y Legación de EE. UU. de N. América en Chile*, 1891, AMRE, and Barros Franco, *El caso del 'Baltimore,'* p. 47.

[130] Matta, *Cuestiones*, pp. 1-2.

[131] *Ibid.,* p. 4.

[132] Pedro Montt to Chilean Ministry of Foreign Relations, December 4 and 8, *Legación de Chile en los EE. UU. de N. América*, 1891, AMRE.

[133] Montt to Ministry, October 30, 1891, *ibid.*

[134] Egan to Matta, September 25, 1891, *Gobierno y Legación de los EE. UU. de N. América en Chile*, 1891, AMRE.

[135] Egan to Matta, September 26, *ibid.*

[136] Egan to Matta, October 10, *ibid.*

[137] Egan to Matta, October 16, *ibid.*

[138] *El Ferrocarril*, for example, had for a number of days been republishing anti-Egan material that had appeared in other Chilean papers, and even in those of the United States. The culminating point was a long *El Ferrocarril* editorial on October 15.

[139] See notes 79, 80, and 89, Chapter I.

[140] See note 88, Chapter I.

[141] Barros Franco, El caso del 'Baltimore,' p. 40.

[142] Ibid., pp. 41 ff.

[143] Egan to Matta, October 26, 1891, in Matta, Cuestiones, pp. 5-6.

[144] Ibid., p. 8.

[145] El Heraldo, November 4, 1891.

[146] Barros Franco, op. cit., pp. 44-45. El Ferrocarril, December 24, 1891. In Washington, moreover, Pedro Montt pointed out to Blaine that the "Itata" affair had occurred three months before the "Baltimore" incident, and that not even a first-instance decision had yet been reached in the United States. Montt to Chilean Ministry of Foreign Relations, December 28, 1891, Legación de Chile en los EE. UU. de N. América, 1891, AMRE.

[147] Matta to Egan, October 27, 1891, in Cuestiones, pp. 7-8. See also the excellent series of articles dealing with the "Baltimore" affair that appeared in La Opinión (Santiago daily of socialist orientation, 1932-1957), beginning June 28, 1932 under the title, "Recuerdos del tiempo viejo: el incidente del 'Baltimore.' "

[148] Egan to Matta, November 23, 1891, and Matta to Egan, November 25 and December 3, in Cuestiones, pp. 9-10.

[149] Undoubtedly, what prompted Matta to make this statement was President Harrison's charge that events attendant upon the fall of Balmaceda had brought about the dissolution of order and the unleashing of passions, ". . . as frequently occurs in Central and South American republics." Given the Chilean sense of superiority and pride in political institutionalism, Harrison could not have delivered a more galling insult. See Matta, Cuestiones, pp. 17-18.

[150] The higher chamber approved the actions of Matta, deciding that the United States had not been insulted. The senators evidently agreed with the Matta line of reasoning: "Since when has the belief that a president, even of the United States, can be badly informed and fall consequently into errors, become an offense?" Ibid., p. 20. For the interpellation proceedings see Cámara de Senadores, Boletín de sesiones ordinarias, 1891, Sesión of December 11, 1891.

[151] See MMRE, 1892, I, 155-156. The December 12 note of Egan to Matta as well as the latter's December 14 reply are in Cuestiones, pp. 135-138. The latter reads in part: "Except for a few words, the telegram [as reported in El Ferrocarril] is correct. Furthermore, no clarification is possible, as the telegram simply reviews the norms by which Montt in Washington should guide himself."

[152] Montt to Chilean Ministry of Foreign Relations, October 30, 1891, Legación de Chile en los EE. UU. de N. América, 1891, AMRE. In his interview with Blaine, Montt dismissed the "Baltimore" affair as one of those incidents frequently precipitated by seamen, and received no rejoinder. Instead, the Secretary of State assured him that the United States would take no steps until the Valparaíso investigation had been completed. In response to Blaine's question as to whether the investigation would be finished by the time Congress adjourned in early December, Montt replied that while he could not give absolute assurance, he regarded it as almost a certainty that it would be. Some two weeks later, Montt even had words of praise for the friendly attitude of Harrison when the President formally received him as Chile's Envoy Extraordinary and Minister Plenipotentiary.

At the same time, Montt reported a rapid calming of United States emotions over the "Baltimore" affair. See Montt to Ministry, November 9, *ibid.*

[153] Montt to Ministry, December 28, 1891, *ibid.* See also *MMRE*, 1892, I, 155-156.

[154] "Memoria del Ministro de Chile en EE. UU. de América," in *Legación de Chile en los EE. UU. de N. América*, 1892, AMRE.

[155] *MMRE*, 1892, II.

[156] Barros Franco, *El caso del 'Baltimore,'* p. 60.

[157] Montt to Pereira, January 19, 1892, *ibid.*, p. 61.

[158] *MMRE*, 1892, II, 160. See also telegram of Blaine to Egan, January 21, 1892, in Matta, *Cuestiones*, p. 132.

[159] Ross to Chilean Ministry of Foreign Relations, December 24, 1891, *Legación de Chile en Gran Bretaña*, 1891-1892, II, AMRE. In this letter, Ross reports on his interview with Philip Currie, sub-Secretary of State for the British Foreign Office.

[160] Ross to Ministry, December 22 and 24, 1891, January 8, 1892, *ibid.*

[161] Ross to Ministry, January 8, *ibid.*

[162] This telegram text is cited by Ross in his January 22 letter to the Chilean Ministry, *ibid.* And, in his February 4 letter, Ross aptly observes that his January 18 telegram had at least prepared the Chilean government for the emergency which President Harrison's January 25 speech precipitated.

[163] Ross to Ministry, November 9, 1891, *ibid.*

[164] Gonzalo Bulnes, Envoy Extraordinary and Minister Plenipotentiary of Chile in Germany, to Chilean Ministry of Foreign Relations, early January (no specific date, but letter was apparently written between January 4 and 8), 1892, *Legación de Chile en Alemania*, 1892, AMRE.

[165] *Ibid.*

[166] *Ibid.*

[167] Moreover, *El Ferrocarril* both on December 24, 1891, and the following January 14, expressed the opinion that the United States was preparing for war against Chile.

[168] *MMRE*, 1892, II, 93.

[169] For text of ultimatum, see *ibid.*, II, 161.

[170] Barros Franco, *El caso del 'Baltimore,'* p. 67.

[171] *Ibid.*, pp. 70-72, and *MMRE*, 1892, II, 98.

[172] See "Recuerdos del tiempo viejo," *La Opinión*, July 3 and 5, 1933. See also *MMRE*, 1894, pp. xxxii-xlvi.

[173] See *El Mercurio*, February 7, 1943, and *Diario Aleman por Chile*, October 27, 1941. The best account of the Peña legend is in Barros Franco, *op. cit.*, p. 11.

[174] *La Epoca*, January 25, 26 and 27, 1892, *El Ferrocarril*, January 26, and *La Libertad Electoral*, January 25 and 26, 1892, all quite properly referred to the "Baltimore" incident as insignificant.

[175] *El Porvenir*, January 26, 1892. The majority of papers disagreed with *El Porvenir*, and upon Matta's death on June 22, 1892, published paeans of praise in his behalf, and recalled his courage and vigor in standing up to the United States. See *El Ferrocarril*, June 24 and 25, *La Libertad* (Talca), June 24, *El Mercurio*, June 24, and *La Patria*, June 23.

[176] Barros Franco, in his often cited study, exonerates Blaine. And in Washington, Pedro Montt continued to enjoy the warmest personal relations with the former Secretary of State. See *El Ferrocarril*, February 2, 1892. See also Montt to Chilean Ministry of Foreign Relations, October 30, 1891, *Legación de Chile en los EE. UU. de N. América*, 1891, AMRE.

[177] The November 16, 1891, London *Times* article was reproduced in *El Ferrocarril*, January 14, 1892.

[178] Agustín Ross to Chilean Ministry of Foreign Relations, December 22, 1891, *Legación de Chile en Gran Bretaña*, 1891-1892, II, AMRE.

[179] Ross to Ministry, January 6 and 22, 1892, *ibid*. Gonzalo Bulnes to Ministry, early January (no specific date), 1892, and February 5, 1892, *Legación de Chile en Alemania*, 1892, AMRE.

[180] Emilio C. Varas, Chilean envoy in Washington in 1890 had observed that the primary obsession among many United States government circles was navy expansion. See "Memoria del Ministro de Chile en los EE. UU. de América al Ministro de Relaciones Esteriores, April 10, 1890," in *MMRE*, 1890, pp. 337-341. Agustín Ross, writing from London on January 22 and February 4, 1892, expressed the feeling that naval expansionists were responsible for the United States threat of war. See *Legación de Chile en Gran Bretaña*, 1891-1892, II, AMRE.

[181] Ross to Ministry, November 9 and December 22, 1891, and January 22, 1892, *ibid*. Gonzalo Bulnes to Ministry, early January and February 5, 1892, *Legación de Chile en Alemania*, 1892, AMRE. M. A. Matta also believed United States actions to have been politically motivated. See his *Cuestiones*, pp. 24 ff. See also *El Ferrocarril*, April 7, 1893.

[182] Ross to Ministry, November 9, 1891, *op. cit.*

[183] *El Ferrocarril*, April 7, 1893.

[184] Matta, *Cuestiones*, p. 25.

[185] *El Ferrocarril*, March 25, 1892.

[186] The alleged Argentine offer to the United States can be studied in the January 12, January 18, and February 2, 1898, letters of Domingo Gana, Chilean Envoy Extraordinary and Minister Plenipotentiary in Washington, to the Chilean Ministry of Foreign Relations, *Legación de Chile en los EE. UU. de N. América*, 1898, parte I, AMRE. These communications, among other points, refer to the December 1892 note of Aníbal Cruz, at the time Chile's representative in Washington, which was probably the first official reference to the matter of Argentine-United States collusion. See also MMRE, 1892, II.

Domingo Gana, after a careful investigation, decided that Argentina had neither sought an offensive-defensive alliance with the United States, nor offered transit rights across the country for troop movements. But Gana noted: "I do have grounds to think that Mr. [E. C.] Zeballos [Argentine Minister of Foreign Relations at the time of the "Baltimore" affair] made assurances to the United States Minister in Buenos Aires that in case of war between Chile and the United States, Argentina would extend tolerance and even certain facilities to the United States." Gana to Ministry, February 8, 1898, *ibid*. Barros Franco, *El caso del 'Baltimore,'* believes the worst about Argentina, making much of the fact that Brazilian Minister in Washington Salvador Mendonça told Chilean Chargé d'Affaires Aníbal Cruz in 1892 about the whole nefarious Argentine plot. Gana, however, in his 1898 reports found the Mendonça charges wildly exaggerated, a point Barros Franco does

not mention. *El Ferrocarril*, moreover, in providing a good coverage of the matter in its February 24, 1898, edition, dismissed the more extreme anti-Argentine charges as "not containing a grain of truth."
[187] Bulnes to Chilean Ministry of Foreign Relations, February 5, 1892, *Legación de Chile en Alemania*, 1892, AMRE. Two final works that may be consulted on the "Baltimore" affair are Mario Vergara, *El imperialismo yankee en Chile: resumen histórico del incidente del U.S.S. 'Baltimore'* (without date), and Eugenio Orrego Vicuña, *Un canciller de la revolución* (1926). The latter work, dealing with Manuel María Aldunate Solar, Balmaceda's last Minister of Foreign Relations, has good background material on Egan's relations with the Balmacedistas.

CHAPTER 4

[1] Alberto Edwards and Eduardo Frei, *Historia de los partidos políticos chilenos* (1949), p. 133. The section of the book dealing with the history of political parties since 1891 is written by Senator Frei. The book will subsequently be referred to as *Partidos*.
[2] On the Conservative Party during this period, see the book written by one of its most distinguished members: Rafael Luis Gumucio, *El Partido Conservador* (1911).
[3] A member of the conservative wing of the Liberal Party has written a useful history of this period: Benjamín Vicuña Subercaseaux, *Las ideas liberales en Chile* (1909).
[4] Edwards, Frei, *Partidos*, p. 134.
[5] Some of the useful works on the Radical Party during this period are the following. Angel C. Espejo, *El Partido Radical: sus obras y sus hombres* (1911). Armando Labra Carvajal, *La política radical* (1912). Ramón Liborio Carvallo, *Ojeada histórica sobre el Partido Radical* (1910). Good sketches of several figures in the Radical Party are included in Arturo Lois Fraga and Mario Vergara Gallardo, *Librepensadores y laicos en Atacama* (1956). Invaluable for gaining an insight into the Radical outlook is *La Libertad Electoral*, a Santiago daily published 1886-1901.
[6] Jaime Eyzaguirre, *Fisonomía histórica de Chile* (1948), p. 147.
[7] See Héctor de Petris Giessen, *Historia del Partido Democrático: posición dentro de la evolución política nacional* (1942), and Pedro Segundo Prado, *Diccionario biográfico de los Demócratas de Chile* (1923).
[8] Arturo Olavaría Bravo, *La cuestión social en Chile: los partidos políticos chilenos frente a la cuestión social* (1923), p. 100.
[9] Edwards, Frei, *Partidos*, p. 131. Useful sketches, biographies and autobiographies of prominent political figures during the period include the following: Virgilio Figueroa, *Diccionario histórico, biográfico y bibliográfico de Chile*, 2 vols. (1926, 1931). Enrique Amador Fuenzalida, *Galería contemporánea de hombres notables de Chile*, 1850-1901 (Valparaíso, 1901). Abdón Cifuentes, *Memorias*, 1836-1928, 2 vols. (1936). Nicomedes Guzmán (editor), *Autorretrato de Chile* (1957). The book contains views on Chile and the Chileans from Ercilla to the present time. Francisco Javier Ovalle Castillo, *Hacia la política chilena: retratos de la época contemporánea* (1922). This is one of the best collections of short biographies of men prominent during the parliamentary period. Ramón Pérez Yáñez,

Forjadores de Chile, 2 vols. (1943, 1944). Carlos Pinto Durán, *Diccionario personal de Chile* (1921). Emilio Rodríguez Mendoza, *Alfredo Irarrázaval Zañartu: adición a como si fuera ayer* (1955). A biography of a leading Chilean statesman and diplomat by one of Chile's most distinguished journalists, as well as an important politician and statesman. See also Rodríguez' charmingly written biographical sketches, *Como si fuera ahora.* . . . (1929), and *Como si fuera ayer* (1919). Armando Rojas Molina, *Semblanzas* (1944). The book consists of short biographies of prominent Chileans from the Carrera brothers to Gustavo Ross and Carlos Ibáñez. Raúl Silva Castro, *Cuarenta años de vida pública: don Gonzalo Urrejola* (1936). Ramón Subercaseaux, *Memoria de ochenta años: recuerdos personales, críticas, reminiscencias históricas, viajes, anecdotas*, 2 vols. (1936). These are valuable reminiscences by one of Chile's ultraconservatives. Ismael Tocornal, *33 años de vida pública* (1930). Tocornal was long a prominent figure in Chilean politics and society. Benjamín Vicuña Subercaseaux, *Gobernantes y literatos* (1907). Francisco Undurraga, *Recuerdos de ochenta años, 1855-1943* (1943). See also Fidel Araneda Bravo, *Hombres de relieve de la Iglesia Chilena*, 2 vols. (1947).

[10] See *El Mercurio*, January 12, 1904.

[11] Some valuable general works on the political history of the era and not specifically cited elsewhere in the notes for Chapter IV include the following. Jénaro Abasolo N., *La personalidad política y la América del porvenir* (1907). The author felt the country would emerge from its decadence if intellectuals played a more prominent part in politics. Arturo Alessandri, *Recuerdos de gobierno* (1952). The work deals with the early political career of Alessandri. He died before writing a proposed second volume. José A. Alfonso, *El parlamentarismo y la reforma política en Chile* (1909). Hernán Castro Nordenflicht, *El parlamentarismo y la administración pública* (Valparaíso, 1902). Carlos Concha Subercaseaux, *Los partidos políticos chilenos* (1905). The book is useful, but clearly reveals that it was written by a Conservative. Alberto Edwards, "Breve reseña histórica de la política chilena," *Pacífico Magazine* (June, 1916). Roberto Espinoza, *La evolución democrática* (1918). Luis Galdames, *Evolución constitucional de Chile* (1925). Galvarino Gallardo Nieto, *Los partidos políticos* (1898). This is one of the earliest works by a socially prominent statesman and diplomat noted for his outspokenness. Julio Heise González, "La democracia y el parlamentarismo," *Atenea*, Año XXVII, no. 309 (March, 1951). This is a valuable article by one of Chile's leading professors and intellectual figures. Antonio Huneeus Gana, *La Constitución de 1833: ensayo sobre nuestra historia constitucional de un siglo* (1933). Luis Izquierdo F., *Nuestro sistema política ante el Senado* (1916). Izquierdo was at the time Minister of Interior and extremely conservative in his politics. Adolfo Ovalle Vicuña, "La nueva era," *El Ferrocarril*, October 22, 1901. *Pacífico Magazine* was published monthly, 1913 to 1921. It was one of the better magazines of the period, containing excellent fine arts criticisms, as well as essays on national and international happenings. Alberto Edwards frequently wrote in it under the pseudonym of Miguel de Fuenzalida. Moisés Poblete Troncoso, *Nuestro seudo régimen parlamentario*, con un prólogo por el Diputado de Antofagasta, Antonio Pinto Durán (1919). Eduardo Poirier, *Chile en 1910* (1910). Poirier, a leading Central-American diplomat stationed in Chile, wrote one of the most valuable descriptions of the country at this time. *La Revista de Chile* was published as a semimonthly, 1898 to 1902. It contained materials taken from the Congressional Records, and

valuable abstracts of university theses and other studies. Raúl Ripamonti, *Del régimen parlamentario en Chile y en especial de la inestabilidad ministerial* (1922). "Treinta años de anarquía política," *Pacífico Magazine* (May, 1916). This is an extremely valuable study dealing with ministerial instability. *Zig Zag*, founded in 1905, soon became one of Chile's most valuable weeklies.

[12] For some of the opinions of the anticlerical advocates of expanded public education see Francisco de B. Guerrero, *Justificación de los Liberales de Chile ante la conciencia católica* (1895), Valentín Letelier, *La lucha por la cultura* (1895), and Roberto Munizaga Aguirre, *Algunos grandes temas de la filosofía educacional de don Valentín Letelier* (1952). It is interesting also to consult the Masonic magazine, *La Verdad*, published monthly, 1907-1923, and *Centenario del nacimiento de Augusto Comte celebrado por Iglesia Positivista de Chile* (1898).

[13] Ricardo Donoso, *Desarrollo político y social de Chile desde la Constitución de 1833* (1942), p. 103. The book will be referred to hereafter as *Desarrollo*.

[14] The quotation, originally from Domingo Amunátegui Solar, *La democracia en Chile* (1946), is found in Edwards and Frei, *Partidos*, p. 142.

[15] *El Ferrocarril*, March 6, 1900. See also Abraham König, "Necesidad de reformar el sistema de elección presidencial," *Revista Chilena de Historia y Geografía*, L (2° semestre, 1924). König was a leading member of the Radical Party, and the *Revista Chilena de Historia y Geografía*, one of the country's most distinguished publications, was founded in 1911 by the eminent intellectual, Enrique Matta Vial. See Guillermo Feliú Cruz, "Enrique Matta Vial: su vida, su obra y su acción en el desarrollo de la cultura intelectual chilena," *ibid.*, XLVIII (3° trimestre, 1922). For additional material on electoral dishonesty during the parliamentary period see José de la Maza, *Sistemas de sufragio y cuestión electoral* (1913), Augusto Orrego Luco, *Al margen de una jornada electoral* (1915), and *El Mercurio*, July 19, 1906. In the last reference appears the story of the laborer Antonio Flores who contributed the bribe he had received for voting to the Director of the Society of Schools for the Proletariat, realizing that only through lower-class education could vote-purchasing be eliminated.

[16] See Francisco Javier Ovalle Castillo, *Don Vicente Reyes, una de las grandes figuras del Partido Liberal* (1918). See also Armando Donoso, *Recuerdos de cinquenta años: José Victorino Lastarria, Isidoro Errázuriz, José Toribio Medina, Enrique Mac-Iver, Abdón Cifuentes, Vicente Reyes, Crescente Errázuriz, Gonzalo Bulnes, Estanislao del Canto, Jorge Boonen Rivera, Eduardo de la Barra, Marcial Martínez* (1947).

[17] The electoral college vote of 137 obtained by Errázuriz was short of the required majority, and hence the matter was decided by Congress. There, the 62-60 outcome was owing largely to the relatives of Errázuriz who held congressional office. See Domingo Amunátegui Solar, *La democracia en Chile*, p. 303.

[18] Eyzaguirre, *Chile durante el gobierno de Errázuriz Echáurren, 1896-1901* (1957). For another favorable appraisal of the administration see Jorge Huneeus Gana, *Balance de la administración Errázuriz y del gobierno conservador* (1900).

[19] Amunátegui, *Democracia*, pp. 304 ff. Donoso, *Desarrollo*, pp. 105-106. See also Ricardo Donoso, "Omisiones, erores y tergiversaciones de un libro de historia," *Atenea*, XXXIV, no. 377 (September-October, 1957), and no. 378 (November-December, 1957). In these articles, Donoso delivers a blistering attack against the Eyzaguirre book on Errázuriz Echáurren.

[20] José María Caro, "Respuesta a un católico sobre sus deberes cívicos en la presente campaña presidencial," El Porvenir, March 26, 27, 28, 1901. See also Germán Riesco, Presidencia de Riesco, 1901-1906 (1950), a favorable biography written by the president's son.

[21] Amunátegui, Democracia, p. 319.

[22] Ibid., p. 319.

[23] On the 1906 campaign see Luis Galdames, La democracia en peligro (1906) and El pueblo y los candidatos (1906), as well as Julio Zegers, Don Pedro Montt y don Fernando Lazcano (1906).

[24] Edwards, Frei, Partidos, pp. 178-182. See also Carlos Pinto Durán, ¡Como se hunde el pais! Desgobierno, clericalismo, oligarquía, corrupción, decadencia (1917).

[25] Luis Alberto Cariola, "La Liga de Acción Cívica, su fundación y rol que ha desempeñado," El Mercurio, January 1, 1913.

[26] Donoso, Desarrollo, p. 112.

[27] See General Jorge Boonen Rivera, Participación del ejército en el desarrollo y progreso del país (1917).

[28] El Diario Ilustrado, September 16, 1915.

[29] Ibid., December 22, 1915. See also Francisco Javier Ovalle Castillo, El presidente de la república de Chile, Ramón Barros Luco (1917).

[30] See Joaquín Edwards Bello, Don Eliodoro Yáñez, "La Nación"y otros ensayos (1934), and Fernando Santiván, Don Eliodoro Yáñez: el hombre y su obra (1925).

[31] See Oscar Alfonso Godoy, D. Malaquías Concha: su vida, sus obras, su glorificación (1923), Luis A. Trejo Oyarzún, Luis Malaquías Concha: hombre de la democracia (1936), and Enrique Turri Concha, Malaquías Concha, el político (1958. Memoria de Prueba).

[32] Congress in plenary session, however, gave Sanfuentes a somewhat more comfortable margin, choosing him 77 to 41. See Amunátegui, Democracia, p. 353.

[33] See Homenaje de la Universidad de Chile a su ex-rector don Domingo Amunátegui Solar en el 75° aniversario de su nacimiento, 2 vols. (1935), and Raúl Silva Castro, Don Domingo Amunátegui Solar, su vida y sus obras (1934).

[34] Amunátegui, Democracia, pp. 355 ff.

[35] See the posthumously published memoirs of Crescente Errázuriz, Algo de lo que he visto: memorias (1934).

[36] El Mercurio, May 6, 1960.

[37] See Enrique Vergara Robles, Biografía de don Luis Barros Borgoño (1949), and Raúl Silva Castro, Don Luis Barros Borgoño, 1858-1943 (1944).

[38] Some of the works dealing with the alleged decadence of Chile, and not specifically cited elsewhere in this chapter's notes include the following. Florentino Abarca, La decadencia de Chile (1904). Guillermo Feliú Cruz, "La anarquía: pesimismo, 1891-1924," one of the chapters in his Chile visto a través de Agustín Ross (1950). Abraham König, La Constitución de 1833 en 1913 (1913). Enrique Oyarzún, Discursos parlamentarios (Concepción, 1913). Oyarzún was an early advocate of economic nationalism who regarded foreign capital's takeover in Chile as a sign of national decadence. Nicolás Palacios, Decadencia del espíritu de nacionalidad (1908). Samuel Valdés Vicuña, La solución del gran problema del día (1895). Among other points, Valdés blames the decline in copper production upon Chilean lack of initiative and ingenuity. Carlos Vicuña Fuentes, La tiranía en Chile, 2 vols. (1938, 1939).

[39] Zegers published his work in 1904. See also Roberto Huneeus, "Don Julio Zegers," *Pacífico Magazine* (May, 1918), published in the year of Zegers' death. Gonzalo Bulnes was another leading Chilean of conservative convictions who felt something was wrong with Chile, asserting that intellectual giants like Barros Arana, Vicuña Mackenna, and the Amunátegui brothers were products of an epoch superior to that of the early twentieth century. See *El Ferrocarril*, December 4, 1904.

[40] Isidoro Errázuriz, *Tres razas* (1887), pp. 26-27.

[41] Rodríguez, *Ante la decadencia* (1899).

[42] *El Diario Ilustrado*, October 10, 1914.

[43] Alberto Cabero, *Chile y los chilenos* (1926), p. 338. This has been one of the more widely-read books published in Chile.

[44] Guillermo Viviani Contreras, *Sociología chilena: estudio de sociología general aplicada a nuestra país* (1926), pp. 153-154.

[45] Gabriela Mistral was convinced that the predominant trait of national character was laziness. See her *Recados contando a Chile* (1957), p. 21.

[46] Mac-Iver, *Discurso sobre la crisis moral de la república* (1900), p. 15.

[47] Quoted in Aníbal Pinto, *Chile: un caso de desarrollo frustrado* (1959), p. 66. See also Maximiliano Ibáñez, *El régimen parlamentario en Chile* (1908).

[48] Pinto, *op. cit.*, p. 66.

[49] *El Mercurio*, January 12, 1904.

[50] *Ibid.*, July 12, 1913.

[51] *El Diario Ilustrado*, September 16, 1915. See also Pedro Aguirre Cerda, "Carta abierta," a ringing denunciation of moral turpitude in Chile, *La Nación*, October 17, 1919, and the speech of Conservative Deputy Manuel Rivas Vicuña, Cámara de Diputados, *Boletín de sesiones ordinarias*, Sesión of January 24, 1919.

[52] Prominent Chileans in the League included Vicente Reyes, Miguel A. Varas, and Manuel Egidio Ballesteros.

[53] See *El Mercurio*, January 1, 1913, and Galvarino Gallardo Nieto, *La Liga de Acción Cívica y los partidos políticos* (1912).

[54] See Ernesto Montenegro, "La novela chilena en medio siglo," Universidad de Chile, *Desarrollo de Chile en la primera mitad del siglo xx* (1953), II, 324-327. There are two other excellent studies that should be consulted: Arnold Chapman, "Don Luis Orrego Luco y la vida en Chile," *Atenea*, Año XXV, no. 278 (August, 1948), and Domingo Melfi, "La novela *Casa Grande* y la transformación de la sociedad chilena," *Anales de la Universidad de Chile*, CVI, no. 69-72 (1948). In a far less skillful novel, *Gran Mundo*, Tomás Gatica Martínez in 1910 also delivered a scathing attack on Santiago's higher society.

[55] Chile's distinguished journalist and critic, Armando Donoso, has stated that along with Juan Montalva's *Mercurial eclesiástica*, José Victorino Lastarria's *Manuscrito del diablo* and Alcides Argüedas' *Un pueblo enfermo*, *Sinceridad* ranks as one of the most important works conceived in America. See also Enrique Molina, "La filosofía en Chile en la primera mitad del siglo xx," Universidad de Chile, *Desarrollo*, II, 466.

[56] In addition to *Sinceridad*, see Alejandro Venegas, *Cartas al Excelentísimo Señor Don Pedro Montt sobre la crisis moral de Chile en sus relaciones con el problema económico de la conversión metálica* (1909), and *La procesión de Corpus* (1908). See also Julio César Jobet, "Alejandro Venegas Valdés, precursor del socialismo,"

La Opinión (a socialist daily, 1932-1957, published in Santiago), September 20, 1946, and Enrique Molina, *Alejandro Venegas (Dr. Valdés Cange): estudios y recuerdos* (1939).

[57] Edwards, *La fronda aristocrática* (1959), pp. 174-176. See also Raúl Silva Castro, *Don Alberto Edwards* (1933).

[58] One of the most distinguished contributors to Pinochet's *La Opinión* was Amanda Labarca H. Two of the books which reveal Pinochet's thought during this period are *La conquista de Chile en el siglo xx* (1909) and *Oligarquía y democracia* (1917). More recently, Julio Heise González, *La Constitucion de 1925 y las nuevas tendencias político-sociales* (1951), pp. 138-139, has written about the moral deterioration of the Chilean aristocracy during the parliamentary period.

[59] Cabero, *Chile y los chilenos*, esp. pp. 334-345. The distinguished economist and journalist Francisco Valdés Vergara agreed with, indeed he anticipated, the Cabero thesis. In 1913 he argued that Chile's troubles stemmed from the self-indulgence of the upper classes enriched by nitrate earnings. The aristocracy, he charged, was acting like an heir who spends money without even bothering to learn the size of his inheritance. *El Mercurio*, May 27, 1913.

[60] Palacios, *Raza Chilena*. The influential work was published first in 1911 and again in 1918 in a two-volume edition.

[61] Carlos Keller also talks about the conquistador mentality of Chilean capitalists in the opening portions of *La eterna crisis chilena* (1931).

[62] In *La educación económica y el liceo* (1912), Encina delivers a strong and cogent indictment of Chilean education's failure to equip students for meeting the primary challenges of modern life. Other works published during the parliamentary period which make this point include the following. Pedro Aguirre Cerda, *Estudio sobre instrucción secundaria* (1904). This was the *Memoria de Prueba* of the distinguished Radical, and ultimately Popular Front president of Chile. José Alfonso, *La educación inglesa y la educación chilena* (1901). Francisco Araya Bennett, *Observaciones para una reforma de nuestra enseñanza* (1921). Luis Galdames, *Educación económica e intelectual* (1912). Guillermo González, *Memoria histórica sobre la instrucción pública* (1914). Alfredo Ovalle Vicuña, "Evanjelios chilenos," *El Ferrocarril*, July 30, 1898. This extremely fine article urges practical education and less training for the aristocratic professions. Chile's schools are accused of training nothing but pedants, orators, and lawyers. The need to curtail metaphysics and emphasize physics is stressed. Carlos Pinto Durán, *La educación pública de Chile es inadecuada y deficiente* (1911). Manuel Rivas Vicuña, *Instrucción del pueblo* (1903). Darío E. Salas, *La instrucción primería obligatoria* (1910), and *Nuestro educación y sus deficiencias* (1913). See also Emilio Rodríguez, *Ante la decadencia*.

[63] Even before Venegas, *El Ferrocarril* had editorialized on April 2, 1895: "It is indisputable that the flag of Chile no longer flies with the same proud grandeur of bygone years above our Legations in foreign lands. . . . its white star has lost the splendor of former years in the eyes of many neighbor republics."

[64] Venegas, *Sinceridad*, pp. 246-247.

[65] Pinochet, *La conquista*, esp. pp. 65-120.

[66] *La Nación*, February 9, 1928.

[67] *El Ferrocarril*, October 27, 1898.

[68] September 26, 1928, letter of Mistral to Emilio Rodríguez, accompanying the November correspondence of Ambassador in Madrid Rodríguez to the Chilean

Ministry of Foreign Relations, *Correspondencia recibida de las legaciones de Chile en España y Portugal*, 1928, AMRE.

[69] Below are listed a few of the more useful works on Chilean economic development during the parliamentary period. Carlos Aldunate Salas, *Leyes, decretos y documentos relativos a las salitres* (1907). Ernesto Barros Jarpa, Alberto Edwards, Luis Pérez, G. Gallardo Nieto, *Chile: geografía económica* (1923). Alejandro Bertrand. *La crisis salitrera* (Paris, 1910). Dirección General de Estadística, *Anuario estadístico de la república de Chile*. This valuable statistical work was published from 1910 to 1927. Alberto Edwards, Alfonso Lastarria and Armando Donoso, *Chile: 1915* (1915). The most complete description of Chile available at the time, the work includes statistical data and information on geography, politics, the army, railroads, public organization, national economy, etc. Luis Escobar Cerda, *El mercado de valores* (1959). Joaquín Errázuriz, *De la constitución de la propiedad salitrera y de la renta que ha producido al estado* (1913). Roberto Espinoza, *Cuestiones financieras de Chile* (1919). Frank W. Fetter, *Monetary Inflation in Chile* (Princeton, New Jersey, 1931). Fetter was a technical advisor for the Kemmerer mission that assisted Chile and other South American countries to organize central banking institutions in the 1920's. Javier Gandarillas and Orlando Ghiglioto S., *La industria de salitre en Chile, traducido del alemán y consideralmente aumentado* (1908). Roberto Hernández, *El salitre: resumen histórico desde su descubrimiento y explotación* (Valparaíso, 1930). Maximiliano Ibáñez, *La cuestión económica* (1894). Enrique Kaempffer, *La industria de salitre ye el yodo* (1914). Santiago Marín Vicuña, *Los ferrocarriles de Chile* (1916). Daniel Martner, *Estudios de política comercial chilena e historia económica nacional*, 2 vols. (1923). Martner, who studied in Germany, produced in these two volumes one of the finest económic studies published in Chile. He was a strong economic nationalist, and is much admired today in socialist circles. See also his *Historia de Chile: historia económica* (1929). Two volumes were announced for this study, but only the first appeared. Also valuable is Martner, "Nuestros problemas económicas," *Anales de la Universidad de Chile*, CXLII (1° & 2° semestre, 1918). Augusto Orrego Cortés, *et al.*, *Chile: descripción física, política, social, industrial y comercial de la república de Chile* (1903). Luis Orrego Luco, *Chile contemporáneo* (1904). Luis Orrego Luco, *et al.*, *Chile: organización política y social* (1903). José Joaquín Prieto M., *La industria salitre: su historia, legislación y desarrollo* (1945. Memoria de Prueba). Armando Quesada Acharán, president of the Radical Party in 1920 and rector of the University of Chile during the first Ibáñez administration, wrote several valuable economic studies, among them the following: "La economía social," *Anales de la Universidad de Chile*, CXVII (2° semestre, 1905); "La historia y el método de economía política," *ibid.*, CXXII (1° semestre, 1908); "Introducción al estudio de la economía política," *ibid.*, CXVII (2° semestre, 1905). República de Chile, *Estadística comercial* (published 1893-1910), and *Sinopsis estadística* (1890-1925). Zorobabel Rodríguez, one of Chile's most zealous defenders of laissez faire and rugged individualism, wrote two works during the early years of the parliamentary period: *Estudios económicos* (Valparaíso, 1893), and *Tratado de economía política* (Valparaíso, 1895). Guillermo Subercaseaux, *Cuestiónes fundamentales de economía política teórica* (1907), *Estudios políticos de actualidad* (1914), and *Historia de las doctrinas económicas en América y en especial en Chile* (1924). Subercaseaux was a deputy, a professor of economics at the University of Chile, a Minister of

the Treasury (1923), and director of Chile's state bank during the 1920's. Francisco Valdés Vergara, *Problemas económicos de Chile* (Valparaíso, 1913), and *La situación económica y financiera de Chile* (Valparaíso, 1894).

[70] Cabero, *Chile y los chilenos*, pp. 330-331. For the Chilean tax structure at this time see also Patricio Barros Lynch, *Un cuarto de siglo de legislación tributaria chilena* (1927) and Alberto Edwards, "Nuestro régimen tributario en los últimos cuarenta años," *Revista Chilena*, Año I, Tomo I, no. 4 (July, 1917). Published from 1917 to 1930, the *Revista Chilena* was, like the *Revista Chilena de Historia y Geografía*, founded by Enrique Matta Vial. See also the work of the distinguished Catholic champion of social justice, Julio Philippi, "La reforma del sistema tributario fiscal," *Revista Chilena*, Año II, V, no. 15 (August, 1918).

[71] Pinto, *Chile: un caso de desarrollo frustrado*, p. 75.

[72] "Resumen de agricultura," *Anuario Estadístico de 1920*, I, 131.

[73] See Venegas, *Sinceridad*, and *Cartas*, as mentioned in note 56.

[74] Wilson at the time was the United States envoy to Chile. See his report on paper money's ruinous effects upon the lower classes published in Washington and bound in *Legación de Chile en los EE. UU. de N. América*, 1898, II, AMRE.

[75] See reference to Fetter, note 69.

[76] Donoso, *Desarrollo*, pp. 106-107.

[77] Edwards, Frei, *Partidos*, pp. 167 ff.

[78] See Julio César Jobet, "Movimiento social obrero," Universidad de Chile, *Desarrollo de Chile en la primera mitad del siglo xx*, I. For additional works by Jobet, see note 28, Chapter X. For Marxist and communist literature in general, see note 30 of that chapter.

[79] The representative of the landed aristocrats, President Jorge Montt, stressed in his speech of June 1, 1892, the need for stabilizing the peso at twenty-four pence. See Cámara de Senadores, *Boletín de sesiones ordinarias*, Sesión of June 1, 1892. *El Porvenir*, the archconservative voice of the landowners in Santiago violently disapproved of paper money. See its editions of January 16 and 29 and June 15, 1892. A similarly conservative organ, *La Unión* of Valparaíso, was equally outspoken in condemning paper money. See its editions of June 15, 1892, and January 24, 1895. Bankers such as Agustín Ross and Agustín Edwards were also opposed, as Frank Fetter, *Monetary Inflation in Chile*, p. 68, brings out. See also Amunátegui, *Democracia*, p. 288. For additional indications of anti-paper-money sentiments see *El Ferrocarril*, December 1, 1891, May 25 and June 15, 1892, and January 12, 1895; *La Libertad Electoral*, June 15, 1892; and *El Mercurio* (Valparaíso), January 24, 1895.

[80] *El Ferrocarril*, one of the journalistic voices of the moneyed classes, consistently exhibited unconcern with the plight of workers, championing the law of the jungle and survival of the fittest, and actually arguing in the March 14, 1895, edition that the northern nitrate workers—easily among the worst victims of labor exploitation in the hemisphere—were overpaid. Yet, *El Ferrocarril* was always one of the loudest opponents of paper money. Obviously it was convinced that the law of survival of the fittest would function quite satisfactorily under a gold standard.

[81] Fetter, *op. cit.*, p. 76, notes that mortgaged indebtedness increased from something over 36 million pesos in 1892 to over 57 million in 1898.

[82] See *El Ferrocarril*, October 24, 1895.

[83] See final section of this chapter, "The Rural-to-Urban Transition."

[84] *El Sur*, July 23, 1898.

[85] Encina, "Estudio prelímina: la evolución histórica de Chile que se desarrolla en este libro," prologue to Guillermo Feliú Cruz, *Chile visto a través de Agustín Ross*.

[86] Between 1870 and 1900, prices of primary goods exported by Chile fell some 50 per cent. See Encina, *Nuestra inferioridad económica*.

[87] Amunátegui, *Democracia*, p. 316. Eyzaguirre, *Chile durante el gobierno de Errázuriz Echáurren*, pp. 83-86.

[88] For more material on the monetary issue see Roberto Espinosa, *Cuestiones financieras de Chile* (1909), and *La reforma bancaria y monetaria de Chile* (1913); Agustín Ross, *Chile, 1851-1910: sesenta años de cuestiones monetarias y financieras y de problemas bancarios* (1911); and Guillermo Subercaseaux, *El papel moneda en Chile y ensayo sobre la teoría del valor* (1898). It is also useful to consult Chilean Senate and Chamber of Deputies debates under the heading "Retiro del curso forzoso y reestablecimiento de la circulación metálica."

[89] Fetter, *op. cit.*, p. 121.

[90] As a result of paper issues, the peso declined from a value of twenty-four pence in 1892 (about 47.5¢) to 8.25 pence in 1915 (about 16.5¢). *Ibid.*, pp. 13-14.

[91] Alejandro Silva de la Fuente, *Punto final* (1956), p. 176.

[92] Daniel Martner, *Estudios de política comercial chilena e historia económica nacional*, II, 624. Moreover, from 1913 to 1914, total import-export figures fell from 725,828,252 pesos of eighteen pence to 573,177,310. See *El Mercurio*, March 28, 1915. Also in 1915 the nitrate industry was in a crippling slump, with more than one hundred operations closed. See *Memoria de Hacienda*, 1915, p. lxvii. See also Oscar Alvarez Andrews, *Historia del desarrollo industrial de Chile* (1936), p. 171.

[93] A) *Contemporary material on the social problem not specifically cited elsewhere in the chapter*. Claudio Arteaga (pseud. Clarín), *Leyes urgentes para el pueblo* (1920), and *Los problemas internos de Chile* (1919). Arteaga was one of the journalists most concerned with the social problem. F. de Bèze, *El suicidio en Chile* (1899). Julio P. Bravo Hayley, *La abolición de la esclavitud en Chile y su relación con nuestros problemas sociales* (1917). Camilio Carrasco Bascuñán, "El proletariado rural en Chile: apuntes sobre sus males y medios de corregirlos," in *Contribución del Centro Industrial y Agrícola al IV Congreso Científico y 1° Pan Americano* (1908). Gabriel Carrasco, *Del Atlántico al Pacífico, y un argentino en europa: cartas de viaje* (Rosario, Argentina, 1910). Arturo Contreras G., *El derecho de los pobres* (1904). Isidoro Errázuriz, *Historia de la administración Errázuriz* (1885). This was one of the first books written in Chile showing real comprehension of the just-appearing social problem. Luis Galdames, *La lucha contra el crimen* (1903). Osvaldo Labarca Fuentes, *Del privilegio de pobreza* (1909). Juan Enrique Lagarrigue, "Sobre la cuestión social," *Las Ultimas Noticias* (Santiago daily), January 20, 1919. Luis Lagarrigue, *La cuestión social* (1895), and *Incorporación de la proletariado a la sociedad moderna: nociones positivas sobre el trabajo, la producción, el salario, el capital y la propiedad* (1920). Juan Enrique and Luis Lagarrigue were brothers, and the principal proponents of positivism in Chile. Santiago Marín Vicuña, *Problemas nacionales* (1917). Gabriela Mistral and Guillermo González, *Deber cristiano* (1922). These essays contend that the Chilean masses have become a sad, disheartened, sick, ignorant, and lazy people due to the worsening social problem. A. Moraga Porras, *Higiene social: cartilla anti-tuberculosa* (1918). Tomás

Ramírez F., *Apuntes de medicina legal* (1907), and *Elementos de medicina legal aplicada* (1917). Carlos Vicuña Fuentes, *et al.*, *Don Pedro Godoy* (1946). As young men, Vicuña and Godoy were among the first in Chile to object to the increasingly miserable conditions suffered by the lower classes. Julio Vicuña Luco, *Condiciones de vida del proletariado* (1915. *Memoria de Prueba*). Guillermo Viviani Contreras, *La cuestión social en Chile* (1919). The Oficina Estadística del Trabajo, founded in 1908, published some of the most valuable and authoritative works of the parliamentary period depicting the social problem. Under the direction of such men as Simón B. Rodríguez, Eugenio Frías Collao and Moisés Poblete Troncoso, the Oficina waged an admirable struggle for reform. This government agency published such works as: *Los accidentes del trabajo en Chile y en el extranjero* (1913); *Boletín de la Oficina del Trabajo*, an annual appearing from 1911 to 1927; *Estadística de la asociación obrera* (1910); and *Las habitaciones obreras en Chile y en el extranjero* (1911). See also: Frías Collao, *El trabajo en la industria salitrera* (1908); Simón B. Rodríguez, *Estadística del trabajo* (1908), and *Malthus, Z. Rodríguez y el socialismo cristiano* (1906); Ricardo Donoso, "Una figura singular: d. Simón Rodríguez," *Atenea*, Año III, no. 3 (April, 1926); and Augusto Orrego Luco, *Retratos: Amunátegui, Gambotta, Cánovas del Castillo, J. M. Charcot, José Victorino Lastarria, Simón B. Rodríguez* (1917).

B) *Awareness of the Social Problem as Revealed in Contemporary Fiction.* A. Acevedo Hernández, *La raza fuerte* (1922). Eduardo Barrios, *Páginas de un pobre diablo* (1923, 3rd ed.). Marta Brunet, *La flor de Quillén* (1924), and *Don Florisondo* (1926). Baldomero Lillo, one of the greatest writers Chile has produced, excelled at depicting the horrors of life in the coal-mining areas. See his *Sub terra* (1904), and *Sub sol* (1907). Pedro Prado, *Un juez rural* (1924). Like other Prado novels, this pleads for social solidarity. Juliot Ramírez, *El rancho* (1920). For works dealing with the fiction of this period see Pedro N. Cruz, *Estudio sobre literatura chilena*, 3 vols. (1940); Guillermo Muñoz Medina, "La generación literaria de 1900 y Augusto Thompson," *Atenea*, Año XII, no. 116 (February, 1935); Luis Ignacio Silva, *La novela en Chile* (1910); Raúl Silva Castro, *Historia crítica de la novela chilena, 1843-1956* (Madrid, 1960), *Panorama de la novela chilena, 1843-1953* (México, D.F., 1955), and with Homero Castillo, *Historia bibliográfica de la novela chilena* (México, D.F., 1961); Emilio Vaïsse (pseud., Omer Emeth), *Estudios críticos de literatura chilena* (1940); Benjamín Vicuña Subercaseaux, *Memoria sobre la producción intelectual en Chile* (1909); and José Miguel Vicuña, "Antecedentes del movimiento intelectual de Chile desde la Guerra del Pacífico hasta 1920," *Atenea*, Año XXXV, nos. 380-381 (April, 1958).

C) *Later Works Referring to the Social Problem of the Parliamentary Period.* Claudina Acuña Montenegro, *El problema de la mendicidad en Chile* (1923). Arturo Alessandri, "Las cuestiones económicas, el régimen parlamentario, y la cuestión social en Chile desde 1891 hasta 1925," *Atenea*, Año XVII, no. 299 (May, 1950). Karl Brünner, *Santiago de Chile: su estado actual y su futura formación* (1932). Ricardo Donoso, *Las ideas políticas en Chile* (1946). Augusto Iglesias, *Alessandri, una etapa en la democracia en América* (1959), esp. "La rebelión proletaria," pp. 231-324. See the same author's *Revolución ideológico* (1929). Pedro I. Ljubetic V. and Marcia Ortiz, *Estudio sobre el origen y desarrollo del proletariado en Chile* (1954. *Memoria de Prueba*). Ricardo Marín Molina, *Condiciones económicos sociales del campesino chileno* (1947). René Montero, *Orígenes del problema social en Chile* (1926). Jorge Gustavo Silva, *Nuestra evolución político-social, 1900-1930* (1930).

[94] Poet Carlos Pezoa Véliz, born in Santiago in 1879, came to be known as the poet of the humble classes. Born of poor parents, he struggled against poverty throughout his life. Jorge González Bastías and Carlos R. Mondaca were two other poets concerned about the plight of the poor. See Hernán de Solar, "La poesía chilena en la primera mitad del siglo xx," Universidad de Chile, *Desarrollo de Chile en la primera mitad del siglo xx,* II, 306 ff. See also Hernán Ramírez N., "La poesía popular y la conciencia proletaria en Chile—última decada del siglo XIX," *El Siglo* (the communist daily published in Santiago), November 26, 1954.

[95] *La Libertad Electoral,* January 31, 1896.

[96] See Domingo Melfi, "La novela *Casa Grande.* . . . ," *Anales de la Universidad de Chile,* CVI, nos. 69-72 (1948).

[97] Luis Galdames, "Los movimientos obreros en Chile," in *Cuarto Congreso Científico, 1° Panamericano, celebrado en Santiago de Chile el 25 de diciembre de 1908 al 6 de enero de 1909* (1910), II. See also Ramón Angel Díaz R., *Del trabajo de las mujeres y los niños en la industria* (1910). Although the turn of the century was a period in United States history that has become notorious for low labor income, skilled industrial workers earned around $20.00 per week, and unskilled $10.00. The annual average wage of industrial workers in the 1880-1910 period never rose above $600, but was often close to this figure which was generally regarded as the minimum wage for maintaining a decent standard of living. Wages for agricultural laborers in the Middle West around the turn of the century were approximately a dollar a day without board, and seventy-five cents with board. See Samuel Eliot Morison and Henry Steele Commager, *The Growth of the American Republic* (New York, 1942), II, 161, and John A. Ryan, *A Living Wage, its Ethical and Economic Aspects* (New York, 1906).

[98] The Huneeus address was referred to by Conservative Deputy Fernando Varas, Cámara de Diputados, *Boletín de sesiones ordinarias,* Sesión of July 11, 1933.

[99] For material on the Caja de Crédito Hipotecario see Luis Barros Borgoño, *Caja de crédito hipotecario* (1931); José Bernardo Lira, *La caja de crédito hipotecario* (1894); Juan Venegas Quevedo, *La caja de crédito hipotecario* (1951. *Memoria de Prueba*), and the pamphlet *Antecedentes relativos a la caja hipotecario* (1918). See also Jorge Schneider Labbé, *Crédito popular* (1921. *Memoria de Prueba*), and E. Valdés Tagle, *La cuestión obrera y el crédito agrícola en Chile* (1911).

[100] Paulino Alfonso, R. Errázuriz Urmeneta, Luis A. Vergara, R. Bascuñán, Francisco de Borja Echeverría, Antonio Huneeus, Enrique A. Rodríguez, and D. Urzúa, *Problema obrera del norte* (1904). Other works dealing with the rigors of life for the northern worker include the following. Belisario García, *La verdad sobre los problemas económicos y sociales del norte* (1921). Marciano Martínez, *La vida en la pampa: historia de un esclavo* (Iquique, 1895). Trancredo Pinochet Le-Brun, *El 'Infierno' del Dante y la pampa salitrera* (1918). Manuel Rodríguez Pérez, *El trabajo y la vida obrera en Tarapacá* (1913). Floreal Recabarren, *Historia del proletariado en las provincianas de Tarapacá y Antofagasta* (1954. *Memoria de Prueba*). See also Alfaro Calderón, Carlos and Miguel Bustos González, *Reseña histórica de la provincia de Tarapacá* (Iquique, 1936).

[101] *El Ferrocarril,* April 22, 1904.

[102] *El Mercurio,* April 6, 1913.

[103] *El Porvenir*, December 21, 1913. See also Cámara de Diputados, *Comisión parlamentaria encargado de estudiar las necesidades de las provincias de Tarapacá y Antofagasta* (1913). *La Nación*, January 15, 1917, reported on the findings of another commission sent to investigate conditions in the north. The commission included Deputies Enrique Oyarzún, Julio Philippi, and Juan Enrique Subercaseaux.

[104] León Alterman P., *El movimiento demográfico en Chile* (1946. *Memoria de Prueba*), p. 64, and *La Nación*, September 18, 1918. See also Alberto Cabero, "Un opinión discordante acerca de las causas de la baja nupcialidad y de la alta natalidad ilegítima en Chile," *Revista Chilena*, Año IV, Tomo X, no. 32 (July, 1920). Cabero argued that the reason for Chile's high illegitimacy rate was not, as the Church claimed, the civil marriage law. The cause lay instead in the miserable lower-class living conditions. See also Manuel Iturrieta Sarmiento, *De los hijos ilegítimos no reconocidos solemnemente* (1898), and Moisés Poblete Troncoso, *Legislación sobre los hijos ilegítimos: cuestión social* (1912).

[105] *La Opinión*, February 14, 1895.

[106] *El Ferrocarril*, August 14, 1895. See also "Como se vive en los conventillos de Valparaíso," *Zig Zag*, May 18, 1918.

[107] See Guillermo M. Bañados, *Apuntes para un diccionario marítimo-militar chileno* (1924).

[108] *Discurso pronunciado por el Jeneral Estanislao del Canto en la reunión jeneral de las lojias y sociedades de temperencia* (1901).

[109] Cámara de Diputados, *Boletín de sesiones extraordinarias, 1913-1914*, Sesión 68°, January 15, 1914.

[110] Arturo Olavaría Bravo, *La cuestión social en Chile*, pp. 70-82. .

[111] *El Mercurio*, February 13, 1916.

[112] See, for example, *La Nación*, April 14, 1917.

[113] *Ibid.*, September 2, 1918.

[114] *El Mercurio*, January 3, 1922. For additional material on alcoholism see *Alcoholismo y la reglamentación de las bebidas alcohólicos* (1897); Antonio Cárdenas Soto, *El alcoholismo en Chile* (1909); and Zenén González R., *La embriaguez: sus consecuencias, penalidad de ella, medios de combatirlo* (1919). For material on lower-class housing problems, the following works may be consulted. Arturo Alessandri, *Habitaciones para obreros* (1893. *Memoria de Prueba*). Ernesto Aragón, *Las habitaciones para obreros* (1900). Consejo Superior de Habitaciones Obreras, *Memoria de su labor* (1919). Abel Gutiérrez, *Habitaciones para obreros* (1919). Osvaldo R. Marín, *Las habitaciones para obreros* (1903). Jorge Munita Infante, *El problema de la habitación barata* (1921). Julio Pérez Canto, *Las habitaciones para obreros: estudio presentado a la Sociedad de Fomento Fabril* (1898).

[115] Emilio Rodríguez Mendoza had this approach in mind as early as 1910 when he wrote: "As a nation we can never advance materially until we concern ourselves also with social progress, and begin to work toward the solution of our social problem." See Rodríguez, "Política nueva," *El Mercurio*, July 27, 1910.

[116] Dr. F. Landa Z., "Nuestro sistema educacional y la pasividad económica de la población de Chile," *ibid.*, January 1, 1922. Another indication of recognition of the social problem was the demand raised by many reformers for equality for women, whose political participation might make government more humanitarian. Some of the feminist literature of this period includes the following works: *Acción Femenina* was a monthly, beginning publication in 1922, dedicated to advancing women's

rights. Delfín C. Araya G., *Igualdad jurídica y social de ambos sexos* (1917). Claudio Arteaga, "La mujer esclavizada por las leyes," a series of articles appearing in *El Mercurio.* The concluding installment, January 5, 1922, summarized the main points made in, the series, and referred to the unsuccessful attempts of Luis Claro Solar and Ramón Briones Luco to persuade Congress in 1912 to pass women's rights legislation. Guillermo Burgos, *De la emancipación de la mujer* (1917). Carlos Calderón Cousiño, *El feminismo y el código civil* (1919). Carlos Carriel Herrera, *Apuntes sobre la situación jurídica de la mujer en Chile* (Chillán, 1911). Luis Constenal J., *Condición jurídica de la mujer en Chile* (1910). Margarita Gallo Chinchilla, *La mujer ante la legislación chilena* (1945. Memoria de Prueba). Manuel E. González, *Situación de la mujer en nuestra legislación social* (1918). Luis Gutiérrez A., *Administración y disposición de los bienes de la mujer casada* (1918). A great feminist, and one of the great female intellectuals Chile has produced is Amanda Labarca H. See her *Actividades femeninos en los Estados Unidos* (1914); *Femenismo contemporáneo* (1947); "Nuestra situación y la de otras mujeres," *El Mercurio,* a series of articles beginning February 27, 1922; and "Una embajada de mujeres," *ibid.,* February 26, 1923. Andrés Sepúlveda G., *La mujer y nuestro código civil* (1917). Jorge Solís de Ovando, *Los derechos de la mujer* (1922). Roberto Urzúa Puelma, *La mujer ante la sociedad y la ley* (1917). Julio Zegers, *Los derechos civiles de la mujer en la legislación chilena* (1918).

[117] Cabero, *Chile y los chilenos,* p. 391.

[118] *El Ferrocarril,* June 21, 1892.

[119] *Ibid.,* March 14, 1895.

[120] *La Libertad Electoral,* August 3 and 5, 1898.

[121] Víctor Soto Román, *La cuestión social* (1900), pp. 14 and 49. Other indications of socialism in the parliamentary period are found in the following works. Alfredo Arenas Aguirre, *Crónicas sobre revolución y evolución social en Europa y en Chile* (1925). The author is against private property. Eugenio Matte Hurtado, *Nuestra cuestión social* (1920). Matte Hurtado was one of Chile's leading socialists in the 1920's and 1930's. Francisco Pinto Salvatierra, *El obrero* (1896). Pinto played an important role in Chile's first Socialist Party. Evaristo Ríos, *El socialismo y algunas faces de su doctrina* (1919). Luis Sartori Alvarez, *La dialéctica y la interpretación del movimiento sindical chileno* (1936). Olegario Ugarte Vial, *Apuntes sobre el socialismo* (1917). For additional information on early socialism in Chile see the documentation for Chapter X, especially notes 1-13, and 30.

[122] Julio César Jobet, *Luis Emilio Recabarren: los orígenes del movimiento obrero y del socialismo chileno* (1955), p. 12.

[123] Amunátegui, *Democracia,* p. 325. Edwards, Frei, *Partidos,* p. 157.

[124] Donoso, *Desarrollo,* pp. 107-108.

[125] Germán Riesco, *Presidencia de Riesco,* pp. 127-128.

[126] Amunátegui, *Democracia,* p. 329.

[127] *Ibid.,* pp. 340 ff. Edwards, Frei, *Partidos,* p. 155. Augusto Iglesias, "Revolución ideológica," *El Mercurio,* January 5 and 6, 1908.

[128] Jobet, "Movimiento. . . . ," Universidad de Chile, *Desarrollo de Chile en la primera mitad del siglo xx,* I, 71. See also Carlos Roberto González, *Las huelgas* (1908).

[129] Peter Kropotkine, *A los jóvenes* (1911).

[130] Interview with Eugenio Frías Collao, *El Mercurio,* April 4, 1915.

[131] Nitrate sales which soared to 110,503,935 pesos in 1918 fell to 27,759,338 in 1919. See Fetter, *Monetary Inflation in Chile*, p. 147. Treasury income, 94,918,327 pesos of eighteen pence in 1918, slumped to 32,398,526 the following year. See Daniel Martner, *Estudio de política comercial chilena e historia económica nacional*, II, 624.

[132] Edwards, Frei, *Partidos*, pp. 156 ff. The student organization, FECH, was directed at the time by Santiago Labarca, who cooperated closely with the labor demonstrations.

[133] Jobet, "Movimiento . . . ," *Universidad de Chile*, *op. cit*. See also Alberto Mackenna S., ¿Cual es el origen del gran desorden de Santiago?" *El Mercurio*, January 22, 1919.

[134] Edwards, Frei, *Partidos*, pp. 157 ff.

[135] See Oscar Parrao S., *Historia de la mutualidad en Chile* (1923).

[136] Jobet, "Movimiento. . . . ," *Universidad de Chile*, *op. cit*. See also Oscar Alvarez Andrews, *Apuntes históricos del movimiento sindical* (1934); Aristodemo Escobar Zenteno, *Compendio de legislación social y desarrollo del movimiento obrero en Chile* (1940); Tulio Lagos Valenzuela, *Bosquejo histórico del movimiento obrero en Chile* (1941); Moisés Poblete Troncoso and Ben G. Burnett, *The Rise of the Latin American Labor Movement* (New York, 1960); and Guillermo Viviani Contreras, *El sindicalismo* (1919).

[137] The writings of Recabarren include the following works: *Los albores de la revolución social en Chile* (1912), *El socialismo* (1912), and *Ricos y pobres* (1910).

[138] See Jobet, *Luis Emilio Recabarren*, and Fernando Alegría, *Recabarren* (1938).

[139] See Zig Zag, January 6, 1912.

[140] Cámara de Diputados, *Boletín de sesiones extraordinarias*, Sesión 70°, January 3, 1912.

[141] See Amunátegui, *Democracia*, pp. 358 ff., and Jobet, "Movimiento . . . ," *Universidad de Chile*, *op. cit*., I, 75-77. See also Santiago Labarca, *Figuras de agitadores* (1923); Osvaldo López, *Diccionario biográfico obrero de Chile* (1912); and L. R. Ramírez, *Socialismo y maximalismo* (1919).

[142] See Montt's address of June 1, 1892, in Cámara de Senadores, *Boletín de sesiones ordinarias*, Sesión of June 1, 1892. Zeger's statements can be found in Cámara de Diputados, *Boletín de sesiones ordinarias*, Sesión 5°, June 21, 1892.

[143] *El Ferrocarril*, March 14, 1895.

[144] *El Porvenir*, July 27, 1898.

[145] *Ibid.*, August 3 and 4, 1898, and subsequent August editions.

[146] Cámara de Senadores, *Boletín de sesiones ordinarias*, Sesión 31°, July 30, 1902.

[147] The archbishops's remarks were reported in *El Ferrocarril*, December 6, 1904. This was a period of lively debate on the education front, because the Radical Party had begun to agitate for obligatory primary instruction. See *La instrucción primeria obligatoria ante el Senado: el proyecto de ley y el informe de la comisión: los discursos de Senadores Raimundo Silva Cruz, Pedro Bannen y Enrique Mac-Iver*.

[148] At this time there was little to indicate that Chilean education was making much headway in reducing illiteracy. In 1907, of the 715,000 children in Chile between ages six and fourteen, only 267,000 were registered in schools, and only 60 per cent of those registered actually attended classes. See *El Mercurio*, August 12, 1910. See also Luis Alberto Cariola, "La instrucción popular," in *Contribución del Centro Industrial y Agrícola del IV Congreso Científico y 1° Panamericano* (1908).

Cariola was a professor of administrative law at the Catholic University, and for years the principal editor of the conservative daily, *La Unión* of Valparaíso.
[149] Other conservative Chileans expressed similar fears. See Guillermo González Echenique, *Verdades amargas: estudio crítico sobre instrucción pública* (1918), and Alejandro Silva de la Fuente, "Legislación social," *Revista Chilena*, Año III, Tomo VII, no. XXIII (July, 1919).
[150] Donoso, *Desarrollo*, p. 110.
[151] Ramírez, *La misión civilizadora del estado ante las escuelas individualista y socialista* (1901).
[152] *El Heraldo*, July 20, 1910.
[153] *El Mercurio*, January 3, 1923.
[154] See Enrique Molina, "La fisolofía en Chile en la primera mitad del siglo," Universidad de Chile, *Desarrollo de Chile en la primera mitad del siglo xx*, II, 448 ff. See also Molina, *De California y Harvard* (1921), *Por las dos Américas: notas y reflexiones* (1920), and *Por los valores espirituales* (1925).
[155] The cult of Hispanism that began to flourish in Chile during the parliamentary period contributed to the prevalence of this attitude. See Chapter V, the concluding section, entitled "Fear of United States Cultural Penetration," and notes 256-258.
[156] Works which reflect the attitudes of the "respectable reformers" referred to in the text include the following. Víctor J. Arellano, *El catolicismo y el socialismo: réplica a la pastoral del arzobispo de Santiago, don Mariano Casanova* (1893). Esequiel de la Barra Orella, *Necesidad de la reforma social* (1911). Juan Agustín Barriga, *Del Partido y de los intereses Conservadores* (1896). Luis Felipe Contardo, *El catolicismo ante la vida moderna* (1912). Javier Díaz Lira, *Observaciones sobre la cuestión social en Chile* (1904). Isidoro Errázuriz, *Discursos parlamentarios*, 2 vols. (1910). Adeodato García Valenzuela, *Breves reminiscencias sobre la cuestión social* (1907). Alejandro Huneeus G. H., *Estudios sobre cuestiones sociales* (1902). Francisco Huneeus, *Por el orden social* (1917). Tito V. Lisoni, *La revolución social: páginas para Chile. Exposición y crítica de teorías anarquistas* (1903). Padre Luis Guillermo Márquez Eyzaguirre, *Antología de oradores y escritores chilenos*: Vol. I, *Oradores sagrados* (Talca, 1925). Augusto Orrego Luco, *La cuestión social* (1897). Bartolomé Palacios Silva, *El Partido Conservador y el Partido Radical frente a frente* (1918). Palacios strongly favors the Conservatives. Jorge Gustavo Silva, *La cuestión social y la legislación social en Chile* (1915), and *El liberalismo político* (Valparaíso, 1914). *La Revista Católica: órgano de la provincia eclesiástica chilena*. This was a weekly, published 1843-1919. José Luis Riesco Larraín, *La cuestión social* (1922), and *La revolución social: de su génesis y de su desarrollo* (1924). Francisco Rivas Vicuña, *La democracia cristiana* (1915), *Economía nacional* (1914), and *Política nacional* (1913). Martín Rücker Sotomayor (ultimately Bishop of Chillán), *Conferencias populares* (1911), and *Problemas sociales* (1913). Enrique Tagle Rodríguez, *Liberales y Conservadores* (1917). G. Tonido, *La verdadera democracia: noción de la democracia cristiana* (1898). Alberto Vial Guzmán, *Constitución cristiana del estado* (1905). Benjamín Vicuña Subercaseaux, *El socialismo revolucionario y la cuestión social en Europa y en Chile* (1908). Guillermo Viviani Contreras, *Nuestras clases sociales* (1919).
[157] Arturo Olavaría Bravo, *La cuestión social en Chile: los partidos políticos chilenos frente a la cuestión social*, pp. 90 ff. This is the most useful book published on the subject in Chile. Olavaría was a great admirer of the then-president of Chile,

Arturo Alessandri, and dedicated the book to him. He broke with Alessandri during the 1930's. See Olavaría, *Debe y haber* (1936). See also Oscar Alvarez Andrews and Moisés Poblete Troncoso, *Legislación social obrera chilena* (1924), and Eduardo Pantaleón Fontecilla, *La reforma legislativa y política y nuestra cuestión social* (1907. *Memoria de Prueba*).

[158] Examples of sincere and progressive Nationals were Enrique Zañartu Prieto, Enrique Balmaceda Toro, and Roberto Sánchez García de la Huerta.

[159] Amunátegui, *La democracia*, p. 324.

[160] The remarks of Walker are reported in *La Libertad Electoral*, September 25, 1896. See also the favorable biography by archconservative Pedro N. Cruz, *Carlos Walker Martínez* (1904). Venegas, *Sinceridad*, pp. 210-211, condemned the Conservative Party and the Church for trying to solve the social problem by inducing the workers to think only of the next world. This attitude does seem apparent in the speeches of staunch Conservative Abdón Cifuentes. See his *Colección de discursos*, 3 vols. (1916).

[161] See Borja Echeverría, *Terrenos fiscales y colonización* (1886). Late in the parliamentary period, several other moderate and conservative public figures were advocating land redistribution. Francisco Antonio Encina led in attacking these reformers, arguing that if in Chile there was only one landowner for every forty-one inhabitants, it was because only this small percentage had the desire and aptitude to own land. See Encina, Guillermo Subercaseaux, Enrique Zañartu, Alejo Lira, and Raimundo Larraín, "La subdivisión de la propiedad rural," *Revista Chilena*, Año V, Tomo XII, no. 43 (July, 1921).

[162] See Juan Enrique Concha Subercaseaux, *Conferencias sobre economía social* (1918), and *Cuestiones obreras* (1899).

[163] *El Ferrocarril*, November 4, 1904. *El Mercurio*, January 2, 1931. *La Unión*, January 12, 1898.

[164] Other Conservatives interested in social justice included Rafael L. Gumucio, Alejo Lira, Fernando Silva Magueira, Pedro Correa Ovalle, and Gonzalo Bulnes.

[165] See Olavaría, *La cuestión social en Chile*, pp. 59-63. Several important newspapers reflected the Conservative point of view. *El Diario Ilustrado*, founded in 1902, continues to be the voice of archconservatism and clerical interests in Chile. Prominently associated with it in the early days were Ricardo Salas Edwards, Julio Zegers, Paulino Alfonso, Alejandro Silva de la Fuenta, Juan Bardina, Rafael Luis Gumucio, and the immensely talented political cartoonist Jorge Délano (Coke) who joined the staff toward the close of the parliamentary period. *El Porvenir*, the successor to *El Estandarte Católico*, appeared from 1891 to 1906, and profited from the services of Rafael L. Gumucio and Carlos Silva Vildósola, who later became the guiding spirit of *El Mercurio*. *La Unión* of Valparaíso, founded in 1885 and still one of the country's better newspapers, enjoyed the services of Joaquín Walker Martínez, Rafael L. Gumucio, Manuel Foster Recabarren, Alejandro Silva de la Fuente, and Monsignor Rafael Edwards Salas. The famous *El Chileno* appeared between 1883 and 1924. In 1892 it passed into the hands of a group of young Catholics desiring to establish a social and political line somewhat independent of the Conservative Party. For information on the newspapers of this period see Raúl Silva Castro, *Prensa y periodismo en Chile, 1812-1956* (1957), pp. 280-306.

[166] *Nueva República*, January 30, 1896.

[167] See Marcial Martínez, *Nociones sobre la teoría liberal* (1908), and *Postulados de las clases obreras y de los desvalidos y proletarios a presencia de la ciencia social y en especial de la economía política* (1901). See also Francisco Javier Castillo, *La personalidad de d. Marcial Martínez* (1918), and Federico Puga Borne, "Don Marcial Martínez," *Revista Chilena*, Año II, Tomo II, no. 13 (June, 1919).

[168] See Jorge Errázuriz Tagle, *El desarrollo histórico de nuestra cuestión social* (1906), and Errázuriz Tagle and Guillermo Eyzaguirre, *Estudio social: monografía de una familia obrera de Santiago* (1903).

[169] See Tomás A. Ramírez Frías, *El liberalismo y la cuestión religiosa y social en Chile* (1910).

[170] See Olavaría, *La cuestión social en Chile*, pp. 106-110.

[171] In addition to the books cited in notes 167, 168, and 169, see the books mentioned in note 156 written by Liberal Party members Isidoro Errázuriz, Tito V. Lisoni, Jorge Gustavo Silva, and Benjamín Vicuña Subercaseaux. *La Ley* was an important Liberal-Radical newspaper from 1894 to 1910, drawing upon the services of such men as Angel Custodio Espejo, Emilio Rodríguez Mendoza, Alejandro Fuenzalida Grandón, and Abraham König. In 1917 a group of Liberals started *La Nación*, which was probably Chile's best newspaper from 1918 until 1927, in which year President Carlos Ibáñez seized the enterprise. Shortly after the founding of *La Nación*, Eliodoro Yáñez, one of the Liberal Party's finest contributions to the country, became the paper's principal owner and guiding spirit. He was responsible for bringing to *La Nación* one of the geniuses of Chilean journalism, Joaquín Edwards Bello. Finally, on the social consciousness of the Liberal Party, see Arturo Fernández Pradel, *Las tendencias sociales del liberalismo* (1909).

[172] Julio César Jobet, *Ensayo crítico del desarrollo económico-social de Chile* (1955), p. 99.

[173] *El Mercurio*, May 19, 1931.

[174] See *Anales de la Universidad de Chile*, Año CXV, no. 105 (1° trimestre, 1957), which is devoted almost in its entirety to Letelier. See also Gabriela Boza Cadot and Mercedes Uizúa Asúa, *El pensamiento político y jurídico de don Valentín Letelier* (1958. Memoria de Prueba); Alejandro Fuenzalida Grandón, *La evolución social de Chile* (1906); Luis Galdames, *Valentín Letelier y su obra, 1852-1919* (1937); and Carlos Risopatrón, "Observaciones sobre la publicación que esta haciendo el señor Valentín Letelier en los *Anales de la Universidad*, bajo el titulo 'Evolución de la historia,'" *Anales de la Universidad de Chile*, CVI (1° semestre, 1900). This is an outraged conservative attack against Letelier's evolutionary theories on the philosophy of history.

[175] *La Nación*, January 16, 1917.

[176] The initial results of this law were striking. In 1915 there were 322,435 students in public schools; in 1925, the number was 439,937. See Amunátegui, *Democracia*, p. 356. See also Olavaría, *La cuestión social en Chile*, pp. 116 ff.

[177] See the article of Fidel Muñoz Rodríguez in *El Mercurio*, January 1, 1921.

[178] Olavaría, *Cuestión*, pp. 92 ff.

[179] See Malaquías Concha, *La lucha económica: estudio de la economía social presentado al 4° Congreso Científico Americana de 1908* (1910), and *Programa de la democracia* (1894).

[180] Edwards, Frei, *Partidos*, pp. 145 ff.

[181] Oficina Central de Estadística, *Sinopsis estadística y jeográfica de Chile en 1891* (1892), and Dirección General de Estadística, *X censo de la población efectuado el 27 de noviembre de 1930* (1935), III, p. xix.

[182] *Memoria presentada al Supremo Gobierno por la Comisión Central de Censo* (1910), p. 1262. This is the 1907 Census. See also León Alterman P., *El movimiento demográfico en Chile*; Jobet, "Movimiento. . . . ," Universidad de Chile, *Desarrollo de Chile en la primera mitad del siglo xx*, I, 66; Alfredo Rodríguez, *Los movimientos de población* (1900); and Armando Vergara, *La población en Chile* (1900).

[183] Dirección General de Estadística, *X censo*, II, 167. By 1930, fifty-three cities of more than five thousand each were inhabited by 1,684,957 persons, or 41.63 per cent of the population. Moreover, in 1920, only 40 per cent of the active population engaged in agricultural and fishing pursuits, while 30 per cent was employed in industry, 10 per cent in navigation, 4.6 per cent in mining and 4.7 per cent in communications. *Ibid.*, III, p. xix.

[184] For an account of the growing Chilean colony in Paris in the late nineteenth century, see Eduardo Balmaceda Valdés, *De mi tierra y de Francia* (1932).

[185] Oficina Central de Estadística en Santiago, *Sesto censo jeneral de la población de Chile levantado el 26 de noviembre de 1885* (1890), I, p. xiv.

[186] See Domingo Amunátegui Solar, *La formación de la nacionalidad chilena* (1943), p. 8.

[187] Tomás Guevara, *La mentalidad araucana* (1916), pp. 160-161, 167, 168, 169, 203, 205, 211, 217, 233, 237.

[188] *Ibid.*, pp. 237, 239. Additional indications of Indian and mestizo disparagement—which was probably nurtured by the War of the Pacific (see notes 30, 31, 32, 33, Chapter II)—are seen in *El Mercurio*, November 17, 1887, and Emilio Rodríguez Mendoza, "Arauco y la leyenda," *ibid.*, July 8, 1910. In the latter piece, Rodríguez states that the epic poem of Ercilla is so much nonsense. The Indians were never the noble creatures that Ercilla portrays. Similar sentiments are expressed in *El Ferrocarril*, August 3, 1910. See also Rodolfo Lenz, *Estudios araucanos* (1897), p. xiv, who says: "I am acquainted with, but I do not subscribe to, the opinion entertained by so many Chileans, that the Indians are worthless." See also Chapter X, note 91.

[189] For some extremes of laissez-faire thought, see *El Ferrocarril*, December 20, 1891, and April 27, 1898.

[190] See *El Mercurio*, August 12, 1910, and *Memoria presentado . . . por la Comisión Central de Censo* (the 1907 Census), p. 1273.

[191] Julio Heise González, *La Constitución de 1925 y las nuevas tendencias político-sociales*, p. 133.

[192] *Ibid.*, p. 134.

[193] See *El Diario Ilustrado*, October 5, 1914, and Jobet, *Ensayo crítico del desarrollo económico-social de Chile*, p. 139.

[194] Figures of the Oficina Central de Estadística quoted in Jorge González von Marées, *El problema obrera en Chile* (1923. *Memoria de Prueba*), p. 67. Chilean nitrate capital totalled 125,440,080 pesos, foreign capital only 116,797,120. See also Cabero, *Chile y los chilenos*, pp. 310-311.

[195] Jorge González, *op. cit.*, pp. 68-70. See also Dr. F. Landa Z., "Nuestra sistema . . . ," *El Mercurio*, January 1, 1922, who estimated that of the total of 465,849,-

765 pesos of eighteen pence invested in mining and metallurgy in Chile, 243,732,-765—or 52.32 per cent—were in Chilean hands. See also F. Javier Cotapos Aldunate, *El aporte del capital extranjero en la industria minera de Chile* (1947). [196] Jorge González, *op. cit.*, pp. 70-72. See also note 183 for this chapter; *El Mercurio*, January 1, 1922 and June 6, 1926; Oscar Alvarez Andrews, *Historia del desarrollo industrial de Chile*, pp. 184-194; and Angel C. Vicuña Pérez, *Proteccion-ismo aplicado a la industria chilena* (1905. *Memoria de Prueba*).

[197] For acquisition of land by new classes see Humberto Fuenzalida Villegas, "La conquista del teritorio y la utilización durante la primera mitad del siglo xx," Universidad de Chile, *Desarrollo de Chile en la primera mitad del siglo xx*, I, 11-34; and Cámara de Senadores, *Boletín de sesiones extraordinarias*, Sesión 40°, January 8, 1895. Moreover, Carlos Keller, *La eterna crisis chilena*, estimates that between 1880 and 1930, 70 per cent of Chilean territory was claimed and/or occupied for the first time. See also José Gómez Gazzano, *La cuestión agraria en Magallanes* (1938); Marcos Goycolea Cortés, *Colonización de Magallanes y Aysén* (1947); and Agustín Torrealba Z., *La propiedad rural en la zona austral de Chile* (1912).

[198] Carlos Contreras Puebla, an aristocrat who wrote an interesting reply and rebuttal to the *Sinceridad* of Venegas, made this point tellingly. See Contreras (pseud. Juvenal Guerra), *Verdad: réplica a 'Sinceridad' del doctor Julio Valdés Canje* (1911). See also the interesting plea of Juan Agustín Barriga in 1896 that Chile's upper classes continue to woo the rising middle classes: *Del Partido y de los intereses Conservadores: carta que el Diputado de Concepción dirige al sus colegas del Dirección General*.

[199] In brief confirmation of this see Jorge Ahumada, *En vez de la miseria* (1958), p. 53; and Edwards, Frei, *Partidos*, pp. 145-163. More important, consult Chapter X, notes 55-74.

[200] The following works are among those providing some information about Chilean immigration, a topic that has not yet received adequate study. Pedro Pablo Figueroa, *Diccionario biográfico de extranjeros en Chile* (1900). Alberto Hoerll, *Los alemanes en Chile* (1910). Mark S. W. Jefferson, *Recent Colonization in Chile* (New York, 1921). Amadeo Pellegrini C., *El censo comercial industrial de la colonia italiana en Chile* (1926). Pellegrini and J. C. Aprile, *El progreso alemán en América*. Vol. I, *Chile: resumen general de las actividades que ha desarrollado en Chile la colonia alemana* (1934). These two works on Italian and German immigration are quite extensive, between them amounting to over 1800 pages of text. Salvador Soto Rojas, *Los alemanes en Chile, 1541-1917: progreso y servicios que les debe la república* (Valparaíso, 1917), and "Los ingleses en Chile," a series of articles in *El Mercurio*, beginning January 21, 1918. Both of the Soto Rojas pieces are superficial.

[201] Forty-five thousand of the active foreign-born population of 60,000 were registered in the 1930 census as above the *obrero* or laborer class (most of the foreign-born *obreros* were accounted for by Peruvians and Bolivians in the nitrate pampa), and 85 per cent of foreigners above the laborer level resided in cities. Therefore, some 38,250 foreigners were in the Chilean urban middle class. Roughly 1,000,000 of the total national population were in the active population, and of these, 450,000 were middle-class or above. About 50 per cent of those in this category resided in the cities, in short, some 225,000. The foreign-born, middle-class urban population therefore represented 17 per cent of the total urban middle

class in Chile. Computation is based on figures found in Dirección General de Estadística, *X censo de la población* . . . *1930*, II, 167, and III, v-xix.

CHAPTER 5

[1] See Carlos Morla Vicuña, Chilean envoy in Washington, to Chilean Ministry of Foreign Relations, November 7, 1898, *Legación de Chile en EE. UU. de Norte América, 1898*, 2° Tomo, AMRE.
[2] See *El Ferrocarril*, editions of November and December, 1898.
[3] *El Mercurio*, Valparaíso, March 21, 1899.
[4] The Chilean commission was made up of Enrique Mac-Iver, Julio Zegers, Eulogio Altamirano, Luis Pereira, and Eduardo Matte.
[5] *El Heraldo*, Valparaíso, March 27, 1899. For additional information see Oscar Espinosa Moraga, *La postguerra del Pacífico y la Puna de Atacama: 1884-1899* (1958). This excellent monograph is the most complete treatment of the matter to appear in Chile.
[6] *La Unión*, Valparaíso, March 26, 1899.
[7] *El Ferrocarril*, March 28, 1899. See also *El Mercurio*, Valparaíso, March 27, 1899.
[8] Cámara de Diputados, *Boletín de sesiones secretas*, Sesiones of September 5, 6, 10, 12, 15, and 18, 1898.
[9] For accounts of deputy resistance to ratification, see *El Porvenir*, January 16, 1902. This Conservative organ supported the Federico Errázuriz administration, and fully justified the Puna de Atacama decision.
[10] Jaime Eyzaguirre, *Chile durante el gobierno de Errázuriz Echáurren, 1896-1901* (1957), p. 225.
[11] See Gonzalo Bulnes, "Artículos sobre la Puna de Atacama," *El Ferrocarril*, October 22, 23, and 25, 1898. See also the Bulnes article in *ibid.*, February 5, 1902. For additional indications of anti-Buchanan sentiment see Cámara de Diputados, *Boletín de sesiones extraordinarias*, 1902, Anexo de sesión 88 extraordinaria, January 13, 1902, cited in Eyzaguirre, *op. cit.*, and Carlos Morla Vicuña to Federico Errázuriz, February 23, November 8 and 27, 1898, Archivos del Presidente Errázuriz, cited in *ibid*.
[12] See Diego Barros Arana, "La verdad sobre la entrega de la Puna de Atacama," *La Ley* (Santiago daily), January 22, 1902.
[13] For a spirited defense of the Errázuriz administration in the Puna de Atacama matter, see Conservative historian Jaime Eyzaguirre, *op. cit.* See also his "En el cincuentenario del arreglo de la Puna de Atacama," *Boletín de la Academia Chilena de la Historia*, Año XVI, no. 40 (1° semestre, 1949). The Eyzaguirre position is strongly attacked by liberal historian Ricardo Donoso, "Omisiones, erores y tergiversaciones de un libro de historia," *Atenea*, XXXIV, no. 377 (September-October, 1957), and no. 378 (November-December, 1957). Another Conservative defense of the negotiations is Carlos Walker Martínez, *Política internacional de la administración Errázuriz en 1898* (1902).
[14] Fernando Matte Hurtado, writing much later, probably summed up' general Liberal sentiment in Chile: "The Buchanan decision gave most of the territory to Argentina, and produced grave discontent in Chile." See his *El arbitraje en América*,

especialmente en Chile (1922. *Memoria de Prueba*), p. 37. See also Domingo Amunátegui Solar, *La democracia en Chile* (1946), p. 310. On the final settlement, consult *MMRE*, 1903-1905, pp. 6, 81-84, 89-103. For further material on the Puna de Atacama issue consult the following works: Eduardo de la Barra, "Artículos sobre la Puna de Atacama," *La Libertad Electoral*, October 5, 7, 12, 15, and 18, 1898; *Documentos relativos a la Conferencia de Buenos Aires* (1899); Luis Riso-patrón, *La linea de frontera en la Puna de Atacama* (1906); Eliodoro Yáñez, *Apuntes sobre la Puna de Atacama* (1898). Chilean concern over the matter is also referred to in José Zamudio, *Isidoro Errázuriz, Ministro en Brasil, 1897-1898* (1949).

[15] Ramón Subercaseaux to the Chilean Ministry of Foreign Relations, May 4, 1898, *Legación de Chile en Alemania*, 1898, AMRE.

[16] For indications of Chile's hostile attitude toward arbitration at the time see the following works: Enrique Lagos Valenzuela, *El arbitraje internacional en América* (1938), Nemisio Martínez Méndez, *El Congreso Internacional Americano en Washington* (1892), and *El arbitraje obligatorio ante los congresos panamericanos* (1910); Fernando Matte Hurtado, *El arbitraje en América*; Luis Orrego Luco, *Los problemas internacionales de Chile: la cuestión boliviana* (1900), and *Los problemas internacionales de Chile: el arbitraje obligatorio* (1901); Gaspar Toro, *Notas sobre arbitraje internacional en las repúblicas latino-americanas* (1898); José Urrutia, *La evolución del principio de arbitraje* (1908).

[17] *MMRE*, 1901, pp. 30-35.

[18] Morla Vicuña to Chilean Ministry of Foreign Relations, November 8, 1898, *Legación de Chile en EE. UU. de N. América*, 1898, 2° Tomo, AMRE.

[19] Continuing United States pressure for an immediate reply remained a sore point for some time with the Chilean Ministry. Only six days after the Executive Commission had drawn up a tentative and very vague agenda, Henry Lane Wilson was again urging Chile to reply at once by cable. See *MMRE*, 1901, pp. 40-45. Chile was gratified when United States Secretary of State John Hay agreed with Morla Vicuña that a delay in responding to the invitation was fully justified. See Emilio Bello Codesido, *Memoria presentado al Departamento de Relaciones Exteriores por el Enviado Extraordinario i Ministro Plenipotenciario de Chile en México*, 1902, p. 29, and Jaime Eyzaguirre, *El gobierno de Errázuriz*, pp. 290 ff.

[20] See José Alfonso, *El arbitraje internacional en la Conferencia Americana de Washington* (1892), Estanislao Zeballos, *Conferencias americanas* (1898), and Javier Vial Solar, *Páginas diplomáticas* (1900).

[21] *El Ferrocarril*, July 6, 1901. Throughout June, July and August, Orrego Luco published antiarbitration articles in this paper, and then incorporated them into a book that appeared toward the end of 1901: *Los problemas internacionales de Chile: el arbitraje obligatorio*.

[22] *La Nueva República* (Santiago daily), January 14, 1901. Even the London *Times*, September 23, 1901, had observed that Chile, if represented at the Mexico City Conference, would become a center of controversy. See *El Ferrocarril*, November 7, 1901.

[23] See Marcial Martínez, *Segunda Conferencia Internacional Americana tenida en México, 1901-1902* (1902), and Javier Vial Solar, *El problema del norte* (1898). Chile also decided to augment its stock of arguments against compulsory arbitration. In this regard the Foreign Ministry instructed Ramón Subercaseaux in Berlin

to obtain complete reports on the 1899 Hague Convention—the precedent-establishing agreement based upon voluntary arbitration. See the report of Subercaseaux on "Conferencias de la Haya," dated August 7, 1899, and included in MMRE, 1899, II, 241 ff. See also the article of Luis Orrego Luco in El Ferrocarril, August 22, 1901.

[24] Eyzaguirre, El gobierno de Errázuriz, p. 300. See also the instructions of Foreign Minister Rafael Errázuriz to Morla Vicuña, October, 1900, in MMRE, 1901, pp. 69-71.

[25] See Bello Codesido to Chilean Ministry of Foreign Relations, Paris, July 6, 1901; Alberto Blest Gana to Bello, Paris, June 15; Bello to Ministry, Mexico City, August 9, Legación de Chile en México, 1901-1906, y Delegación a la 2° Conferencia Panamericana, 1902, AMRE. See also La Conferencia Internacional de México (México, D.F., 1902), pp. 15-16. This anonymous publication presents strong internal evidence of Chilean authorship. See also MMRE, 1902, II, and most especially, Bello Codesido, Memoria, pp. 33-40.

[26] Bello to Ministry, August 9, 1901, Legación en México, 1901-1906, AMRE.

[27] Ibid.

[28] Bello to Ministry, October 3, 1901, ibid.

[29] For a tribute to Morla's efforts to make the Mexico City agenda safe for Chile see El Ferrocarril, August 21, 1901.

[30] For the report of Blest Gana, Walker Martínez, Bello, and Matte on the Congress see MMRE, 1902, pp. 301-323. See also Belisario García, Vida contemporánea: cuadros de política internacional sud-americana (1903).

[31] Bello, Memoria, pp. 46-55.

[32] Other United States representatives included John Barrett, Henry G. Davis, Volney W. Foster and Charles Pepper.

[33] La Conferencia Internacional de México, pp. 33-35, 108. Bello also referred to the United States as "a powerful source of aid to the Chilean position." See his letter of December 14 to the Chilean Foreign Ministry, Legación en México, 1901-1906, AMRE. See also El Ferrocarril, December 10, 1901, for praise of the United States position.

[34] Argentina, Mexico, Peru, Bolivia, Uruguay, Paraguay, Guatemala, the Dominican Republic, El Salvador, and Venezuela supported compulsory arbitration, although Venezuelan support was later withdrawn. See Marcial Martínez, Segunda Conferencia Internacional Americana, pp. 8-9.

[35] El Ferrocarril, January 17, 18, and 19, 1902.

[36] Ibid., January 8, 1902.

[37] Not a single country ever ratified the compulsory arbitration instrument. See MMRE, 1927, p. 247. For accounts of the bitter debates on the arbitration issue at Mexico City see Bello, Memoria, pp. 60 ff.; El Ferrocarril, December 2 and 3, 1901; and MMRE, 1902, pp. 168-190.

[38] El Ferrocarril, January 22, 1902.

[39] El Salvador, Costa Rica, Ecuador, Guatemala, Nicaragua, Venezuela, and Honduras.

[40] For a general coverage of the Calvo Clause and Doctrine see C. G. Fenwick, International Law (New York, 1948), p. 285; J. B. Moore, A Digest of International Law (Washington, D.C., 1906), VI, 1044; Donald R. Shea, The Calvo Clause: a Problem of Inter-American and International Law and Diplomacy (Min-

neapolis, 1955); and Kurt von Schuschnigg, *International Law* (Milwaukee, 1959), pp. 179-180. For the Chilean account of the Calvo Clause and Doctrine debates at the Mexico City Conference see *La Conferencia Pan-Americana de Buenos Aires: informe presentado por los delegados de Chile* (1911), pp. 161-173; Martínez, *Segunda Conferencia Internacional Americana*, p. 16; and Benjamín Vicuña Suber-caseaux, *Los congresos pan-americanos* (1906), pp. 45, 60. See also Alejandro Alvarez, *L'histoire diplomatique des républiques américaines et la Conférence de México* (Paris, 1902), and "Congreso Panamericano de México," *La Revista de Chile*, VIII (1901).

[41] *El Mercurio*, Santiago, April 1 and 2, 1902. Unless specifically stated otherwise, all *El Mercurio* references after 1900 will refer to the Santiago, not the Valparaíso, edition.

[42] Bello described Argentine delegate Martín García Merou as Chile's chief adversary at the Mexico City Conference. He noted how during the course of the proceedings García Merou went to Washington, hoping to persuade the United States State Department to come out in favor of a broad arbitration agreement. See Bello to Chilean Ministry of Foreign Affairs, December 14, 1901, *Legación en México*, 1901-1906, AMRE. For García Merou's point of view, see his important work *Historia de la diplomacia americana: política internacional de los Estados Unidos*, 2 vols. (Buenos Aires, 1904).

[43] Germán Riesco, *Presidencia de Riesco*, 1901-1906 (1950), p. 269.

[44] *El Ferrocarril*, on January 26, 1902, quoted a Mexico City newspaper which opined that Argentina and Peru had scored a significant diplomatic victory over Chile simply by bringing the matter of compulsory arbitration before the conference, and initially obtaining eight other favorable votes.

[45] *MMRE*, 1902, p. 190.

[46] Martínez was especially suspicious of an agreement signed in Mexico City providing that pecuniary claims could be submitted for settlement to the Hague Permanent Court or to an inter-American Tribunal that would be especially created. Inclusion of the second possibility, to Martínez, represented a Yankee plot to extend hegemony over Latin America. *La Segunda Conferencia Internacional Americana*, pp. 178-180.

[47] Although lacking positive information, Chilean diplomats on the eve of the Mexico City Conference had vaguely suspected that John Barrett was prepared, with the full backing of President Roosevelt, to suggest cooperative hemisphere action to force a settlement of the Chile-Peru dispute, should the American states deem it likely that the issue might lead to renewed warfare. See Miguel Cruchaga, Ambassador of Chile in the United States, to the Chilean Ministry of Foreign Relations, Washington, D.C., August 15, 1932, *Correspondencia: Embajada de Chile en EE. UU.*, 1932, 2° Tomo, AMRE. See also N. Martínez Méndez, *El arbitraje obligatorio*, pp. 23-25, and F. Matte Hurtado, *El arbitraje en América*, pp. 17-18, for indications of Chilean suspicions of United States designs.

[48] To some extent, this change of attitude is indicated in Vicuña Subercaseaux, *Los congresos pan-americanos*.

[49] Also in 1904, a supposedly definitive peace treaty had been signed with Bolivia.

[50] Joaquín Walker Martínez to Chilean Ministry of Foreign Relations, Washington, D.C., December 22, 1904, *Legación de Chile en EE. UU. de N. América*, 1904, AMRE.

[51] Walker Martínez to Ministry, January 22, 1906, *Legación de Chile en EE. UU. de N. América*, 1906, AMRE.

[52] *El Mercurio*, July 25, 1906.

[53] At the Hague Conference, 1907, a dispute arose between Chile and the United States over the Drago Doctrine. The doctrine was originally formulated by Argentine statesman Luis María Drago, who had been concerned over a joint European naval expedition sent to Venezuela in 1902 to pressure that country into resuming the servicing of its foreign debt. The doctrine advanced the principle that matters of debt and pecuniary disputes could not occasion armed intervention in American Hemisphere republics. Chilean diplomats felt that, but for United States highhandedness at the Hague Conference, their country would have received credit for a compromise proposal that was instead attributed to a Yankee delegate at the Hague and that has been known ever since as the Porter Convention. This provided that indebtedness and pecuniary disputes could not occasion intervention if the debtor country agreed to submit the matter to arbitration, and then abided by the arbitration decision. See Alejandro Alvarez, *Le panamericanisme et la VI conférence panaméricaine* (Paris, 1928). See also Luis Aldunate Echeverría, *La Conferencia de la Haya* (Iquique, 1910), Evaristo Molina, *La Doctrina Drago* (1908), and James Brown Scott, *The Hague Peace Conferences of 1899 and 1907* (Baltimore, 1909), I, 96-100, and 415 ff.

[54] Walker Martínez to Chilean Ministry of Foreign Relations, Rio de Janeiro, August 7, 1906, *Legación de Chile en EE. UU. de N. América*, 1906, AMRE; and Manuel J. Vega, secretary of the Chilean Legation in Washington to his Foreign Ministry, May 8, 1906, *ibid.*

[55] Chile was represented by J. Walker Martínez, Adolfo Guerrero, Anselmo Hevia, and Luis A. Vergara.

[56] Walker Martínez to Chilean Ministry of Foreign Relations, Rio, August 7, 1906, *op. cit.*, note 54. See also *El Mercurio*, September 8, 1906.

[57] *El Ferrocarril*, August 2, 1906. *El Mercurio*, August 2, 1906.

[58] Manuel J. Vega to Chilean Ministry of Foreign Relations, July 11, 1906, *op. cit.*, note 54.

[59] Vega to Ministry, September 19, 1906, *ibid.*

[60] Alejandro Alvarez, *Le droit international américain* (Paris, 1910), p. 247.

[61] Julio Pérez Canto prepared an interesting book for presentation to Root upon his arrival in Chile: *Economic and Social Progress of the Republic of Chile* (1906).

[62] *El Mercurio*, September 3, 1906.

[63] *Ibid.*, September 5, 1906.

[64] *La Ley*, September 4, 1906. For additional favorable comments on Root and the United States see: *El Diario Ilustrado*, August 24, 1906; *El Diario Popular*, July 21, 1906; *El Mercurio*, July 6, 1906. See also Alberto Yoacham, Chilean chargé d'affaires in Washington, to his Ministry of Foreign Relations, December 8, 1906, *Legación de Chile en EE. UU. de N. América*, 1906, AMRE, and Emilio Rodríguez Mendoza, "Los congresos pan-americanos," *El Mercurio*, July 6, 1910. In this article, Rodríguez states that Blaine conceived the Pan-American movement in the spirit of imperialism. But Root, by his actions at the Rio Congress and his visit to Chile, heralded the dawn of a new United States attitude and the repudiation of the Blaine methods.

[65] See Alejandro Alvarez, *Las conferencias panamericanas* (1911), and R. Parraguez, *Aspectos jurídicos del antiguo y del nuevo panamericanismo* (1947).

[66] *La Conferencia Pan-Americana de Buenos Aires*, pp. 217-218, 221-222, contains the text of the letters exchanged between Agustín Edwards and Lorenzo Anadón, the Argentine envoy in Santiago.

[67] *Ibid.*, pp. 117-118.

[68] Aníbal Cruz to Chilean Ministry of Foreign Relations, November 11, 1909, *Legación de Chile en EE. UU. de N. América*, 1909, 2° semestre, AMRE. See also *MMRE*, 1910, pp. 301-306.

[69] The other members of the Chilean delegation were Emilio Bello Codesido, Antonio Huneeus, a former Minister of Foreign Relations and professor of natural law at the University of Chile who had to withdraw from the sessions due to sickness, Beltrán Mathieu, a former Minister of State and envoy to Ecuador as well as to Bolivia who would later serve as ambassador in Washington, and Aníbal Cruz. Alejandro Alvarez, by now a member of the permanent arbitration tribunal at the Hague, was named technical advisor. For biographical sketches of these delegates see *El Ferrocarril*, July 7, 1910.

[70] The only countries that had ratified an equal number of agreements were Ecuador, El Salvador, Honduras, and Panama. See *La Conferencia Pan-Americana de Buenos Aires*, pp. 256-257.

[71] See, for example, *El Mercurio*, June 20 and July 6, 1910.

[72] Aníbal Cruz to the Chilean Ministry of Foreign Relations, May 20, 1910, and Alberto Yoacham, Chilean chargé d'affaires in Washington to his Ministry, June 29, and August 11, 1910, *Legación de Chile en EE. UU.*, 1910, 1° semestre, AMRE. One of the most popular diplomats in Washington, Cruz was a close personal friend of Philander C. Knox. When Cruz died in Washington in December 1910, President Taft, his cabinet, the judges of the Supreme Court, many senators and representatives, and the entire diplomatic corps attended his funeral. Cardinal Gibbons participated in the funeral Mass at St. Matthew's Cathedral in Washington and the pallbearers included Knox, Elihu Root, John Barrett, and the heads of the Foreign Relations Committees both of the Senate and of the House. See Yoacham to Ministry, December 24, 1910, *ibid.*, 2° semestre.

[73] *El Mercurio*, August 21, 1910. For a description of the proceedings in Buenos Aires, see also the following sources: Alberto Cruchaga Ossa, *Derecho internacional* (1944), and *La responsibilidad de los estados* (1942); reports prepared by Miguel Cruchaga Tocornal, July 30 and August 2, *Correspondencia del Ministro de Chile en Argentina*, 1910, 2° semestre, AMRE. Also useful is Miguel Cruchaga, *Nociones de derecho internacional* (1915). Appearing in its first edition in 1899, Cruchaga's book is one of the best works on international law published in Chile since the writings of Andrés Bello in the mid-nineteenth century. It contains an excellent summary of the Pan-American conferences. Miguel Cruchaga joined with Aníbal Cruz, Emilio Bello Codesido, Beltrán Mathieu, and Alejandro Alvarez to prepare the *Informe presentado a la IV Conferencia Pan-Americana por la delegación de Chile* (Buenos Aires, 1910). Finally, see Emilio Rodríguez Mendoza, "Las conferencias pan-americanas," *El Mercurio*, July 6, 1910.

[74] *El Heraldo*, Valparaíso, September 14, 1910. Not all later writers have felt that Chile's confidence in the Pan-American movement at this time was justified.

See Galvarino Gallardo Nieto, *Panamericanismo* (1941), pp. 12-13, expressing the belief that throughout the 1906-1910 period the goal of Yankee statesmen was still "cooperation of the American states . . . under the hegemony of the United States."

[75] See *El Diario Ilustrado*, September 6, 1914, and *La Nación*, October 11, 1919.

[76] See Eduardo Suárez Mujica, Chilean ambassador in Washington, to his Foreign Ministry, May 15, 1914, *Embajada de Chile en EE. UU., y Legación en México*, 1914, AMRE, Guillermo Edwards Matte, *El Club de la Unión en sus ochenta años: 1864-1944* (1944), p. 84; *El Diario Ilustrado*, May 18 and October 6, 1914; and *El Mercurio*, May 3, 1913, and March 3, 1916.

[77] See, for example, Ramón Bustos García, *Nociones sobre la intervención* (1944).

[78] *La Libertad Electoral*, probably because of its strong anti-British bias, was the major paper that backed the United States stand. See its editions of December 25 and 27, 1895, and January 1, 1896.

[79] Adolfo Carrasco Albano, "Chile y el conflicto americano: La Doctrina Monroe," *El Ferrocarril*, December 28, 1895.

[80] *Ibid.* Galvarino Gallardo, writing in 1941, also concluded that United States actions in 1895 revealed the desire to dominate all Latin America. See his *Panamericanismo*, p. 30. See also Víctor Eastman, *La Doctrina Monroe* (1897).

[81] Domingo Gana to the Chilean Ministry of Foreign Relations, April 24, 1895, *Legación de Chile en EE. UU. de N. América, 1895*, AMRE.

[82] Gana to Ministry, December 29, 1895, *ibid.*

[83] Gana to Ministry, February 18, 1898, *Legación . . . , 1898*, AMRE.

[84] *El Ferrocarril*, May 14, 1898.

[85] *El Porvenir*, April 10, 15, 19, 21, and November 8, 1898.

[86] *La Unión*, Valparaíso, April 1, 13, 14, and 15, 1898. In sharp contrast to the attitudes revealed by most Chilean writings at the time, *Caracteres de la guerra hispano-americana* (1898), by Belisario García, justified the United States in the war with Spain. In acknowledging a copy of the book sent him by the author, United States Envoy in Santiago Henry Lane Wilson accorded it fulsome praise. See *El Ferrocarril*, June 2, 1898.

[87] See *El Chileno*, November 27, 1903. This represented an editorial change of heart, for on November 12 *El Chileno* had severely criticized the United States. For additional indications that the press did not pity Panama see *El Ferrocarril*, November 18, *El Porvenir*, November 12, and *La Tarde*, November 12, 1903.

[88] *El Ferrocarril*, November 5, 1903. See also *ibid.*, November 9. *El Mercurio*, January 18, 1904, declared that the only way to judge the Panama affair was in terms of how it affected the commerce and prosperity of Chile.

[89] *El Diario Popular*, November 26, 1903.

[90] *El Imparcial*, November 12, 1903.

[91] *El Diario Ilustrado*, November 6, 1903.

[92] *El Imparcial*, November 5 and 9, and *La Ley*, November 11, 1903.

[93] Walker Martínez to the Chilean Ministry of Foreign Relations, January 4, 11, 18, 20, March 7, and August 18, 1904, *Legación de Chile en EE. UU. de N. América*, 1904, AMRE. Additional anti-United States sentiments arising from the Panama affair are found in the anonymous, *La Doctrina Monroe y la política Roosevelt en Panamá* (1913).

[94] In a letter of January 20, 1904 to his Ministry, *op. cit.* note 93, Walker

Martínez described the extent to which Germán Kohl, a Chilean living at the time in the United States, had been alarmed and incensed about the Panama affair. Arming himself with a pistol, Kohl had gone to the White House and demanded to see Theodore Roosevelt. Apprehended and placed in jail, he was judged to be mentally unbalanced.

[95] See, for example, S. A. Vicuña, *La Doctrina Monroe* (1905. *Memoria de Prueba*).

[96] Walker Martínez to Ministry, December 26, 1904, *op. cit.*, note 93.

[97] *Ibid.*

[98] *El Imparcial*, December 10, 1904.

[99] Benjamín Vicuña Subercaseaux, *Los congresos panamericanos*, p. 79.

[100] Augustín Edwards to Seth L. Pierrepont, November 19, 1909, MMRE, 1910, p. 99.

[101] See Carlos Morla Vicuña, Chilean envoy in Washington, to his Ministry of Foreign Relations, September 5, 1898, *Legación de Chile en EE. UU. de N. América*, 1898, 2° semestre, AMRE; Alejandro Alvarez, *Informe presentado al Ministerio de Relaciones Exteriores sobre las gestiones del gobierno de Estados Unidos en favor de Alsop y Cía.* (1910); Agustín Edwards, *Circular extraordinaria sobre el asunto Alsop* (1909); and MMRE, 1910, pp. 76-100.

[102] Aníbal Cruz to Chilean Ministry of Foreign Relations, April 16, 19, and 23, 1909, *Legación de Chile en EE. UU. de N. América*, 1909, 1° semestre, AMRE. See also MMRE, 1910, p. 84.

[103] Cruz to Ministry, September 23, 1909, *op. cit.*, 2° semestre.

[104] Cruz to Ministry, November 5, 1909, *ibid.*

[105] A later Chilean envoy to the United States, Eduardo Suárez Mujica, referred to Huntington Wilson as the guiding spirit behind United States dollar diplomacy, a man who backed every Yankee pretext abroad regardless of how it damaged the rights of foreign countries. Suárez Mujica to Chilean Ministry of Foreign Relations, March 22, 1913, *Legación de Chile en EE.UU. y México*, 1913, AMRE.

[106] Cruz to Ministry, November 18, 1909, *Legación* . . . , 1909, 2° semestre.

[107] See MMRE, 1910, pp. 94-95; Cruz to Ministry, November 18, 1909, *op. cit.*; Knox to Cruz, November 17, 21, 24, *ibid.*

[108] Telegram of Nabuco to the Brazilian Ministry of Foreign Relations, Washington, D. C., November 23, contained in *Legación de Chile en EE. UU.*, 1909, 2° semestre, AMRE.

[109] *The Lusiads*, by L. V. de Camoëns, is considered the greatest poem in Portuguese literature.

[110] Nabuco to Root, November 21, 1909, *Legación de Chile en EE. UU.*, *op. cit.*, note 108.

[111] Root to Nabuco, *ibid.*

[112] Cruz to Ministry, November 27, 1909, *ibid.*

[113] Cruz to Ministry, January 21, 1910, *Legación de Chile en EE. UU. de N. América*, 1910, 1° trimestre, AMRE.

[114] Cruz to Ministry, February 12, 1910, *ibid.*

[115] The ultimate award of King George V called upon Chile to pay 187,000 pounds sterling. Manuel Foster Recabarren, representing Chile in London for the arbitration proceedings, complained of the difficulty of obtaining a fair judgment in a country that was so influenced by the wishes of the United States in regard to

American Hemisphere diplomacy. He also claimed Chile should have settled the matter during the presidency of Riesco (1901-1906). See El Ferrocarril, September 12, 1910. See also The Alsop Claims: Counter-case presented by the Government of Chile to his Britannic Majesty King George V, in the Arbitration to which the Government of Chile and of the United States have Submitted the Matter of the Claims of Alsop & Co. (London, 1910).

[116] El Ferrocarril, September 12, 1910.

[117] MMRE, 1910, p. 71.

[118] Cámara de Diputados, Boletín de sesiones extraordinarias 1909-1910, Sesión of November 19, 1909, pp. 567-568.

[119] Thomas Dawson, shortly before his departure for Santiago as United States envoy had dropped such a hint in an interview with Aníbal Cruz. See Cruz to the Chilean Ministry of Foreign Relations, September 10, 1909, Legacion de Chile en EE. UU. de N. América, 1909, 2° semestre, AMRE.

[120] Cruz to Ministry, November 4, 1909, ibid.

[121] Miguel Cruchaga, Chilean envoy in Buenos Aires, to his Foreign Ministry, June 5, 1909, Legación de Chile en Argentina, 1909-1911, Sección Confidencial, AMRE.

[122] Cruz to Ministry, May 1, 1909, op. cit., 1° semestre. See also Alejandro Alvarez, El libro de la Cancillería Chilena sobre el problema de Tacna y Arica (1912), and Luis Espinoza y Saravia, Después de la guerra: las relaciones boliviano-chilenas (1928).

[123] Cruz to Chilean Ministry of Foreign Relations, April 11, 1910, Legación . . . , 1910, 1° trimestre, AMRE. See also Cruz to Ministry, February 5, June 4, and July 9, 1909, Legación . . . , 1909, 1° semestre. For additional indications of Chilean distrust of United States attitude in the Tacna-Arica matter see MMRE, 1909, pp. 219 ff.; El Mercurio, June 15, 1910; and Emilio Rodríguez Mendoza, "El capital norte-americano en sud américa," ibid., June 19, 1910.

[124] Trancredo Pinochet Le-Brun, "La diplomacia y el nuevo gobierno norte-americano," El Mercurio, June 17, 1913, hoped Wilson would correct some of the lamentable policies of the previous administration.

[125] See Rafael Escobar, La Doctrina Monroe (1921), p. 41.

[126] El Diario Ilustrado, April 14, 1914.

[127] See Félix Nieto del Río, "Cuestiones pan-americanas," ibid., April 7, 1914. This was one of a lengthy series of articles all bearing the same title. In them, Nieto del Río hurled almost every conceivable charge against the United States.

[128] Interview with Marcial Martínez, La Nación, January 22, 1917.

[129] Vicuña Subercaseaux, Los congresos pan-americanos, p. 14, and El Diario Ilustrado, April 7, 1914.

[130] El Mercurio, November 20, 1913. For Chilean preparations for Roosevelt's visit see ibid., November 14.

[131] Theodore Roosevelt, "Discurso en la sesión solemne de 21 de noviembre de 1913, celebrado en su honor," Revista Chilena de Historia y Geografía, IX (1° trimestre, 1914). In the same source see "Discurso de Moisés Vargas en la sesión solemne de 24 de noviembre en honor de Mr. Teodoro Roosevelt." Vargas, incidentally, was another Chilean intellectual noted for his anti-Yankee attitudes.

[132] El Mercurio November 23, 1913.

[133] Enrique D. Tovar y R., *Raza chilena a través de la sociología y de la historia de Chile* (Lima, 1926).

[134] *El Mercurio*, November 24, 1913.

[135] *Ibid.*, February 26, 1914.

[136] *El Diario Ilustrado*, April 7, 1914.

[137] *El Mercurio*, November 25, 1913. See also "Discurso de Gonzalo Bulnes en la sesión solemne de 24 de noviembre de 1913 en honor de Mr. Teodoro Roosevelt," *Revista Chilena de Historia y Geografía*, IX (1° trimestre, 1914).

[138] Eduardo Suárez Mujica to the Chilean Ministry of Foreign Relations, January 15, 1914. *Correspondencia de Embajada de Chile en EE.UU. de N. América, 1914*, AMRE. See also his letter of January 14 in which he states that Wilsonian policies represent an expansion of the Monroe Doctrine's pretenses.

[139] Roosevelt's visit by no means, however, produced unrelieved discord in Chile. He got along well with the social and political notables appointed to entertain him, and decided that Chile was the most beautiful land in the world. The over-all impact of his visit has probably best been described by a March 8, 1914, *El Mercurio* editorial: "Given the peculiarities of his character which created difficulties for traditional Latin hospitality, he nonetheless left among us a favorable impression."

[140] For expressions of Chilean dislike of the new Wilsonian recognition policies see: Carlos Rivas Arangua, *La intervención: doctrinas de Monroe, Drago y Tobar* (1924); Luis Guillén Atienza *El principio internacional de no intervención y las doctrinas americanas* (1949. *Memoria de Prueba*); *El Mercurio*, July 25, 1913; Ricardo Montaner Bello, "Nuevas prácticas internacionales," *ibid.*, October 10, 1930; Aquiles Navarrete Arias, *Los gobiernos 'de facto' ante el derecho internacional* (1939); Ramón Soto Maldonado, *¿Existe en materia internacional el derecho de intervención de los estados?* (1931. *Memoria de Prueba*).

[141] Galvariao Gallardo, *Panamericanismo*, pp. 146-147. Statesman-writer Luis Aldunate produced an analysis of the Mexican crisis that was as highly inaccurate as it was unfriendly to the United States. According to him, an aroused Mexican citizenry, tired of United States economic imperialism, forced Porfirio Díaz to take a strong stand against the northern capitalists. United States business interests then financed the Madero revolution. "Los orígenes del conflicto mejicano," *Pacífico Magazine* (July, 1914).

[142] *El Mercurio*, January 11, 1914.

[143] *Ibid.*, August 26 and 27, 1913. See also *ibid.*, November 9, 1913, and February 27, 1914.

[144] *El Diario Ilustrado*, April 25, 1914.

[145] *Ibid.*, May 27, 1914.

[146] See MMRE, 1911-1914, pp. 239-279.

[147] The United States, assisted by Argentina and Brazil, had attempted to mediate this dispute, and had prevailed upon Chile to persuade Ecuador to be amenable. See Alberto Yoacham, Chilean chargé d'affaires in Washington, to his Ministry of Foreign Relations, June 29, 1910, and Huntington Wilson, First Assistant Secretary of State, to Yoacham, July 13, 1910, *Legación de Chile en EE. UU., 1910*, 2° trimestre, AMRE.

[148] MMRE, 1911-1914, p. 249, and *El Diario Ilustrado*, June 26, 1915.

[149] The ABC powers were represented by their envoys in Washington: Chile by

Eduardo Suárez Mujica, Argentina by Rómulo Naón, and Brazil by (Ambassador) Dominico da Gana.

[150] See Félix Nieto del Río, "El ABC en México y el principio de no intervención a través de la prensa de la época," *Boletín de la Academia Chilena de la Historia,* Año II, no. 4 (2° semestre, 1934); *El Diario Ilustrado,* April 26 and June 26, 1914; and *MMRE, 1911-1914,* pp. 263-275.

[151] Eduardo Suárez Mujica to the Chilean Ministry of Foreign Relations, May 8, 1914, *Correspondencia de la Embajada de Chile en EE. UU. y Legación en México,* 1914, AMRE.

[152] See *MMRE, 1915-1919,* prepared by Luis Barros Borgoño, p. 114.

[153] *El Diario Ilustrado,* May 21 and June 26, 1914; *El Mercurio,* October 27, 1915.

[154] *El Diario Ilustrado,* June 27, 1914.

[155] Nieto del Río, "El ABC en México . . . ," *op. cit.,* pp. 204, 215.

[156] *El Mercurio,* March 15, 1916.

[157] Lauro Müller of Brazil, José Luis Muratore of Argentina, and Alejandro Lira of Chile.

[158] See *Las Ultimas Noticias* (Santiago daily), March 18 and May 24, 1915.

[159] *MMRE, 1915-1919; El Mercurio,* January 5, 1929.

[160] "Hace trece años un chileno vio el ABC," *Zig Zag,* no. 534 (May 15, 1915), tells how Alejandro Alvarez, thirteen years earlier, had foreseen the utility of ABC unity in standing up to the United States. See also Nieto del Río, "El ABC en México . . . ," *op. cit.*

[161] Suárez Mujica to Ministry, March 7, 1913, *Legación de Chile en EE. UU. y México,* 1913, AMRE.

[162] Gallardo, *Panamericanismo,* p. 149.

[163] Carlos Castro Ruiz, "El pacto Wilson y las Memorias de Coronel House," *Revista Chilena,* Año X, no. 79 (September, 1926), pp. 2-4. This article, the most valuable exposition of national attitudes toward the Pan-American Pact written by a Chilean, was continued in no. 80 (October, 1926) of the *Revista Chilena,* edited at the time by Ernesto Barros Jarpa.

[164] *Ibid.,* p. 4.

[165] *Ibid.,* p. 13.

[166] *Ibid.,* pp. 13-14.

[167] *El Mercurio,* May 17, 1916.

[168] Gallardo, *Panamericanismo,* p. 150. *El Mercurio,* May 12, 1916, also argued that Chile did not wish to be tied by international treaties guaranteeing republican institutions. "Each nation, by its own sovereign actions can best protect its republican form of government, as well as its territorial integrity."

[169] See the tribute that Barros Jarpa (Arturo Alessandri's first Minister of Foreign Relations) pays Castro Ruiz for his role in thwarting the Wilson plan, appearing as an introduction to the second installment of the Castro Ruiz article on the Pan-American Pact: *Revista Chilena,* no. 80 (October, 1926).

[170] Castro Ruiz, *op. cit.,* no. 79, p. 22.

[171] *Ibid.,* pp. 24-25. Gallardo, *Panamericanismo,* p. 154.

[172] Fletcher sent his report in April, 1914. See Castro Ruiz, *op. cit.,* no. 79, p. 25.

[173] The First Pan-American Scientific Congress was held in Santiago, 1908-1909.

See *Cuarto Congreso Científico* (1° *Pan-Americano*) *celebrado en Santiago de Chile del 25 de diciembre de 1908 al 5 de enero de 1909* (1909); Tomás A. Ramírez Frías (compiler), *Trabajo del Cuarto Congreso Científico-Americano* (1° *Pan-Americano*), VI *Sección, Ciencias Jurídicas* (1910); "Los trabajos del cuarto Congreso Científico (1° Pan-Americano) celebrado en Santiago de Chile del 25 de diciembre de 1908 al 5 de enero de 1909," in Jorge Errázuriz Tagle (director), *Derecho internacional, constitucional y histórica* (1912).

[174] Gallardo, *Panamericanismo*, pp. 158-162. See also *Las Ultimas Noticias*, February 9, 1916; Suárez Mujica to the Chilean Ministry of Foreign Relations, December 27, 1915, *Embajada de Chile en EE. UU. y Legación en Uruguay, 1915*, AMRE; and *Proceedings of the Second Pan-American Scientific Congress* (Washington, D. C., 1917).

[175] Gallardo, *Panamericanismo*, pp. 155-158.

[176] Alfredo Irarrázaval Zañartu, Chilean envoy to Brazil, carried the brunt of the battle in Rio, while Emilio Figueroa Larraín, envoy to Argentina, fought for his country's interests in Buenos Aires.

[177] See telegram of Alfredo Irarrázaval to Ramón Subercaseaux, February 28, 1916; telegram of Subercaseaux to Irarrázaval, March 3; telegram of Irarrázaval to Subercaseaux, March 9; telegram of Suárez Mujica to Subercaseaux, March 10; telegram of Irarrázaval to Subercaseaux, March 14; and telegram of Suárez Mujica to Subercaseaux, March 26, all in *Oficios dirijidas a las legaciones de Chile en América, 1916*, under Brasil, AMRE.

[178] There are indications that some Argentine opinion began to swing around to the Chilean point of view in regard to the Wilson Pact. On February 5, 1917, the Buenos Aires *La Prensa* voiced the suspicion that the Wilson Pact had been devised as a means of forcing Latin America to enter the war on the side of the United States—in the event the United States should declare war against Germany—under the obligation of protecting that country's territory against possible attack from abroad. Miguel Cruchaga, Chilean envoy in Berlin, noted that Germany had a similar opinion concerning the basic motivation of the Pan-American Pact. See his letter of May 3, 1917, to the Chilean Foreign Ministry, *Legación de Chile en Alemania, 1917*, AMRE. See also Carlos Castro Ruiz, "La Doctrina Monroe y el gobierno de Chile," *Revista Chilena*, Año I, no. 3 (June, 1917).

[179] Wilson's increasing preoccupation with Mexican and European affairs also contributed strongly to this decision. But Chile was convinced that it had been primarily responsible for the pact's defeat. See G. Munizaga Varela, Chilean chargé d'affaires in Washington to his Ministry of Foreign Relations, August 9, 1916, and September 5, 1916, *Embajada de Chile en EE. UU., 1916*, AMRE. In these letters, Munizaga claims the United States press generally conceded that Chile was responsible for the failure of the pact. See also *El Mercurio*, April 7, 1916.

[180] Castro Ruiz, *op. cit.*, note 163, p. 28, quotes the February 29, 1916, dispatch of Suárez Mujica to the Foreign Ministry.

[181] *El Mercurio*, March 8, 1916.

[182] Among the many works that allude to German teaching activity in Chile is Alejandro Fuenzalida Grandón, *La enseñanza en Alemania* (1913).

[183] See Miguel Cruchaga to the Chilean Ministry of Foreign Relations, Berlin, May 30, 1914, *Legación de Chile en Alemania y Austria-Hungría, 1914*, AMRE;

El Diario Ilustrado, April 2, 3, 4, and 5, 1914; Gallardo, *Panamericanismo,* p. 103; and Armando Donoso, *La nación alemana: homenaje a SS.AA.RR.: los principios de Prusia* (1914).

[184] For some of the sources in which these points are made see the following: Arturo Alessandri, interview, *La Nación,* February 26, 1917; editorial, *El Diario Ilustrado,* April 3, 1914; Gallardo, *Panamericanismo,* p. 90; Roberto Huneeus Gana, *Por amor a Chile y por gratitud a la Alemania* (1917), pp. 10-11; editorial, *Las Ultimas Noticias,* September 27, 1917; article by Renato Valdés, *El Diario Ilustrado,* September 18, 1917; Javier Vial Solar, *Conversaciones sobre la guerra* (1917). Like the Huneeus book, this is one sustained outpouring of admiration for Germany. The extremely popular German envoy in Santiago, Friedrich C. von Eckert, played an important part in fanning pro-German sentiments. Eckert remained in Chile after the war and died there in 1923, "sincerely mourned by Chileans." See *MMRE,* 1919-1923, pp. 19-21.

[185] Gallardo, *Panamericanismo,* pp. 73 ff. Another dispassionate and reasonable defense of Chilean neutrality was Alejandro Alvarez, *La grande guerre européenne, et la neutralité du Chile* (Paris, 1915). See also *La Nación,* February 6, 1917. A somewhat less elevated justification for neutrality was advanced by Ismael Tocornal. He appeared almost gleeful over the likelihood of United States entry into the war, gloating over the nitrate profits that a neutral Chile could make by selling its products to both belligerent groups. See *La Nación,* February 8, 1917.

[186] Gallardo, *Panamericanismo,* p. 140.

[187] *La Nación,* April 19, 1917; Huneeus, *Por amor a Chile,* p. 55; and *La Nación,* April 22, 1917.

[188] See interview of Armando Donoso with Arturo Alessandri, *La Nación,* May 6, 1917. Donoso noted that Alessandri became most heated when making his pro-neutrality, anti-United States observations. See also the article by Alessandri in the February 26, 1917, *La Nación.* Defending neutrality in this piece, Alessandri gives vent to strong anti-British feelings. Probably it was politically expedient to be anti-British when one's political career depended upon the votes of the northern nitrate region—where there was bound to be enthusiastic response to charges of labor exploitation by British capitalists.

[189] See the numerous pro-German utterances of Barros Jarpa in the editorials of *La Nación,* 1917 and 1918, written under the pseudonym of William Temple. For the Martínez stand see the article by Omer Emeth, *El Mercurio,* November 17, 1917. Emeth was the pseudonym employed by the French priest Emilio Vaïsse, who was the literary critic for *El Mercurio.*

[190] *La Nación,* of which Yáñez was the principal owner, strongly reflected this outstanding Liberal's belief that neutrality was necessary if Chile hoped to escape from overweening United States influence.

[191] Huneeus, *Por amor a Chile,* p. 55. See also *La Nación,* April 23, 1917.

[192] All of these men would have agreed with Galvarino Gallardo: "Neutrality for Chile is tantamount to preserving its sovereignty." See *Panamericanismo,* p. 136. Arturo Alessandri himself stated: "Solidarity with the United States would imply the tutelage of the United States." See *La Nación,* May 6, 1917. Gonzalo Bulnes was also convinced that a pro-Allied declaration by Chile would have compromised its honor and rights of self-determination. See Armando Donoso, *Recuerdos de cincuenta años* (1947), pp. 280-284.

[193] *La Nación,* February 10, 1917.

[194] *El Diario Ilustrado,* July 5, 1933. See also Joaquín Edwards Bello, "Si Alemania hubiera ganada la guerra," *La Nación,* November 18, 1933.

[195] Javier Vial Solar, *Conversaciones,* pp. 66-70, acknowledged this fact. United States Secretary of State Robert Lansing noted that all of Latin America, except Mexico, Chile, and Argentina, favored the United States in the war. See Gallardo, *Panamericanismo,* p. 83. Also, the German press indicated its conviction that Chile strongly favored the Central Powers. See Miguel Cruchaga, Chilean envoy in Berlin, to his Ministry of Foreign Relations, June 7, 1918, *Legación de Chile en Alemania, 1918,* AMRE.

[196] Edwards Bello, *op. cit.,* note 194.

[197] As early as 1892, Gonzalo Bulnes had praised the religious revival in Germany and the fact that the emperor was turning to the Catholic Church as the means of combating socialism and other extremist, materialistic philosophies. Because of this, said Bulnes, the emperor stood side by side with Pope Leo XIII. See Bulnes, Chilean envoy in Berlin, to his Ministry of Foreign Relations, March 18, 1892, *Legación de Chile en Alemania,* 1892, AMRE. It was also Bulnes who began the policy of bringing Catholic German teachers to Chile, thus preparing the way for the establishment of close ties between German educators and militantly Catholic groups in Chile. See Eduardo de la Barra, *La vida nacional: el embrujamiento alemán* (1899), pp. 43-45. Being a staunch anticlerical, de la Barra strongly resented this aspect of German education in Chile. See also the interview with Gonzalo Bulnes in Donoso, *Recuerdos de cincuenta años.* Alberto Vial Guzmán had also noted the tendency of the German state in the 1890's to align itself once more with the Church. See his *El clero católico en alemania* (1893). This influential book, which went through its third edition in 1895, underlined the Church-State rapprochement that had occurred in Germany, and went a long ways toward convincing many Chileans that the emperor was Catholic at heart. Sentiments of this sort are revealed by the Catholic priest Alejandro Vicuña in his pamphlet, *El origen de la guerra europea* (1917). *El Mercurio,* February 5, 1917, noted: "Almost all the clergy is pro-German and passionately so . . . especially the Spanish clergy."

[198] *El Mercurio,* February 5, 1918.

[199] Cruchaga to Ministry, October 31, 1917, *Legación de Chile en Alemania, 1917,* AMRE; and Cruchaga to Ministry, February 19, September 26 and November 16, 1918, *Legación . . . , 1918.*

[200] Cruchaga to Ministry, June 16 and July 30, 1918, *ibid.* Judging from the material he enclosed in his reports in 1917 and 1918, Cruchaga was firmly committed to the German cause. The legation staff in Berlin prepared during the war a pro-German study, *Alemania antes y durante la guerra.*

[201] See Gallardo, *Panamericanismo,* pp. 35-36, and Agustín Torrealba Z., "Germanes y alemanas: a mis compatriotas de origen alemán," *Las Ultimas Noticias,* January 6, 1919. Torrealba also published articles under the same title in *Las Ultimas Noticias* of January 3, 8, 11, 13, 15, 18, 21, 24, and 25. After this last date, the articles abruptly ceased appearing, perhaps because Chile had by then embarked upon a propaganda campaign to prove that its neutrality had not been pro-German in orientation.

[202] *El Mercurio* was the only major newspaper that was favorable throughout the war to the English-French-United States cause. In 1917 it engaged in a running

debate with the pro-German *El Diario Ilustrado*. See *El Mercurio*, October 19, 21, 24, and 25, and *El Diario Ilustrado*, October 20, 22, 23, and 25, 1917. For additional pro-German writing in *El Diario Ilustrado*, see the letters of Roberto Huneeus, October 14, 15, and 16, 1917; the articles of Luis Orrego Luco, April 14, 15, and 18, 1917; the articles of Renato Valdés, beginning October 11, 1917; and the article of Javier Vial Solar, April 26, 1917. Additional material not already cited pertaining to Chile and the First World War includes the following works: Anonymous, *Le Chili germanophile* (Cahors, France, 1919). The book reveals considerable bitterness over the allegedly pro-German sentiment of Chile. Ricardo Cox Méndez, *A través de la europa en guerra* (1916). The distinguished Conservative Party stalwart in this book reveals his passionate pro-German feelings. No less devoted to the German cause was Galvarino Gallardo Nieto. See his *Neutralidad de Chile ante la guerra europea* (1917). On the other hand, there was Alberto Mackenna Subercaseaux, one of Chile's few articulate Francophiles. See his *Le triomphe du droit* (Paris, 1916). An excellent and objective account of Chilean neutrality, the author of which is not identified, is "La neutralidad de Chile en la guerra mundial," *Economía y Finanzas*, Año II, no. 23 (September, 1938). Carlos Silva Vildósola, an important member of *El Mercurio's* staff, reflected his paper's pro-Allied attitudes in his *La guerra mundial vista por un chileno* (1916). Diametrically opposed was the outspoken Germanophile and Conservative Party publicist, Eduardo Solar Correa. See his *Algo sobre derecho internacional marítimo* (1916), and *La cuestión submarina ante el derecho internacional* (1917). Salvador Soto Rojas, in *Los Alemanes en Chile, 1541-1917: progreso y servicios que les debe la República* (Valparaíso, 1917), strongly implies that Chilean progress was owing almost exclusively to German influence. In a series of *El Mercurio* articles on the English in Chile published early in 1918, the same author attributes Chilean greatness to the British influence. See his "Los ingleses en Chile," beginning in the January 21, *El Mercurio*. Gerardo Vergara Blanco, *Crisis de la neutralidad* (1943. Memoria de Prueba). In this study of the neutrality crisis of the Second World War the author deals briefly with the 1914-1918 antecedents and justifies Chile's policy. Javier Vial Solar, Galvarino Gallardo Nieto, Roberto Huneeus, and Luis Orrego Luco, *Las repúblicas sudamericanas, Chile, Argentina y Uruguay ante la guerra* (1917). This work consists of essays by several of Chile's most outspoken Germanophiles.

[203] See letter of Alberto Mackenna Subercaseaux to Carlos Silva Vildósola, *El Mercurio*, May 5, 1917.

[204] Roberto Huneeus, *Por amor a Chile*, p. 63. See also p. 7.

[205] Those signing the message were Manuel Antonio Prieto, Alberto Mackenna Subercaseaux, Ismael Tocornal, Juan E. Tocornal, Enrique Tagle M. (Chief Editor of the always extremely pro-German *El Diario Ilustrado*), Emilio Rodríguez Mendoza, Guillermo Pérez de Matta, Carlos Edwards, Eduardo Eastman, Fernando Tupper, Javier Díaz Lira, Ernesto Montenegro, Raimundo del Río, Manuel Foster Recabarren, Paulino Alfonso, Jorge Gustavo Silva, Jorge Huneeus, Emilio Bello Codesido, and Salvador Izquierdo. See *La Nación*, September 29, 1918.

[206] Gustavo Munizaga Varela, Chilean chargé d'affaires in Washington, to his Ministry of Foreign Relations, November 27, 1918, *Embajada de Chile en EE. UU.*, 1918, AMRE.

[207] *MMRE*, 1915-1919, p. 315. Argentina also believed war between Chile and Peru might be imminent and offered good offices. This was spurned by the Chilean envoy in Buenos Aires, Emilio Figueroa, who insisted that Chile would work out its own solution with Peru. Figueroa added that the war rumors were wild exaggerations. See his *Memoria, 1918*, p. 35, in *Correspondencia de las Legaciones de Chile en Argentina, Colombia y Costa Rica, 1919*, AMRE.

[208] *MMRE*, 1915-1919, pp. 316-317.

[209] See *El Mercurio*, February 1, 1919. For other indications of alarm over Peruvian propaganda see Beltrán Mathieu to the Chilean Ministry of Foreign Relations, April 14, 1919, *Embajada de Chile en EE.UU, 1919*, AMRE; Jaime de la Lastra B., *Historia diplomática de la cuestión de Tacna y Arica* (1951); Marcial Martínez, *Opúsculos sobre asuntos internacionales* (1919), vol. III of *Obras Completas*; Emilio Rodríguez Mendoza, "Como nos juzgan desde Europa," *El Mercurio*, February 20, 1919; and "Chile, Perú y Bolivia: actividades de la diplomacia peruana: los delegados a las conferencias de la paz," *ibid.*, April 23, 1918.

[210] Arturo Alessandri, "Defendamos nuestra soberanía," *La Nación*, February 26, 1919. Arteaga Alemparte (pseud.), *El problema del Pacífico* (1919). Emilio Bello Codesido, *Anotaciones para la historia de las negociaciones diplomáticas con el Perú y Bolivia, 1900-1904* (1919). Anselmo Blanlot Holley, *Historia de la paz entre Chile y el Perú, 1879-1884* (1919). *La cuestión chileno-peruano: una circular del Ministro de Relaciones Exteriores de Perú, d. Francisco Tudela; respuesta del Ministro de Relaciones Exteriores de Chile, d. Luis Barros Borgoño* (1919). Adolfo Calderón Cousiño, *La cuestión chileno-peruano* (1919). Juan Ignacio Gálvez, *Conflictos internacionales: El Perú contra Colombia, Ecuador y Chile*, 4 vols. (1919). Amanda Labarca Hubertson, "Chile y Perú en los Estados Unidos," *El Mercurio*, February 16, 1919. Alberto Mackenna Subercaseaux, "La situación de Chile ante la conferencia de la paz," *El Mercurio*, February 1, 1919. Ernesto Montenegro, *La cuestión chileno-peruano* (1919). Adolfo Ortúzar, *Cuestiones americanas: Chile-Perú, 1819-1919* (San Sebastián, 1919). Julio Pérez Canto, *El conflicto después de la victoria* (1918). Joaquín Walker Martínez, *Caminos descaminados* (1918), and *La cuestión del Pacífico: clamores de intervención diplomática* (1919).

[211] See Beltrán Mathieu, "La neutralidad de Chile durante la guerra europea," *Revista Chilena*, Año II, Tomo IX, no. 30 (April, 1920), for the major arguments used by the ambassador in Washington. A significant book published both in French and English in 1919 (Paris and New York) was Enrique Roucant, *The Neutrality of Chile*. The book stoutly maintains that Chilean neutrality was devoid of anti-United States, or pro-German aspects.

[212] "Cuestiones americanas," appearing in *El Diario Ilustrado* during April, 1914.

[213] Nieto del Río also published an article asserting: "The new spirit of Chile is due, in large measure, to English and North American influences exerted upon a race which possesses certain acquired qualities of push and ability to assimilate." This appeared in the *Acts of the Pan-American Commercial Congress*, and a copy of the piece was enclosed with the November 12, 1919, correspondence of Mathieu to his Ministry of Foreign Relations, *Embajada de Chile en EE. UU., 1919*, AMRE. Additional references to the activities of Nieto del Río, as well as clippings of various of the articles he published in the United States press, are found in the letters of

Mathieu to the Chilean Ministry of Foreign Relations, April 5 and 14, August 31, and September 3, *ibid.* See also Nieto del Río, "Relaciones entre Chile y los Estados Unidos," *El Diario Ilustrado,* May 19, 1919.

[214] See *La Prensa,* New York City, April 14, 1919. See also Mathieu to Ministry, no date but communiqué received by Foreign Ministry September 5, 1919, *Legación . . . ,* 1919, AMRE.

[215] Labarca had been in the United States previously and knew the country well. See her *En tierras extrañas* (1915), and *Actividades femeninas en los Estados Unidos* (1914).

[216] Accompanying Yáñez on his mission, which lasted from April to December, 1919, were Juan Enrique Tocornal and Augusto Villanueva. See Cámara de Senadores, *Boletín de sesiones extraordinarias,* 1919-1920, Sesión of December 15, pp. 614-615.

[217] See Carlos Vicuña Fuentes, *La libertad de opinar y el problema de Tacna y Arica* (1921).

[218] *La Unión,* Valparaíso, April 21, 1898. Chilean exports to the United States had been worth about $720,000, and imports from the United States some $2,280,-000.

[219] Frank G. Carpenter, "Entre los Yankees de sud-américa," *El Ferrocarril,* October 21, 1898. At later times, two short pieces commented upon expanding United States influence. See *El progreso norteamericano en Chile,* a pamphlet published in 1920; and "Norteamericanos en Chile," *El Mercurio,* September 12, 1927.

[220] Chilean exports to France in 1910 amounted to about $4,807,000.

[221] *Anuario Estadístico la República de Chile,* Año 1910, XXX, 589. See also Adolfo Ortúzar, *Informe comercial del Consulado General en Estados Unidos, 1905* (1908), and William Roderick Sherman, *The Diplomatic and Commercial Relations of the United States and Chile, 1820-1914* (Boston, 1926).

[222] *Memoria, Ministerio de Hacienda,* 1915-1919, pp. 396-397.

[223] See address of Benjamín Cohen, first secretary of the Chilean embassy in Washington, to the Pan-American Commercial Council, Atlanta, Georgia, which met October 1-4, 1924. The text of this address is included with the February 26, 1925, letter of Ambassador Mathieu to the Chilean Ministry of Foreign Relations, *Correspondencia de las Legaciones de Chile en Argentina y Estados Unidos, 1925,* AMRE. See also *Anuario Estadístico de la República de Chile,* 1920, II, 195, and *La Nación,* August 28, 1917. The *Memoria, Ministerio de Hacienda, 1916,* p. xxxii gives valuable information on Chilean commerce during the middle years of the First World War.

[224] Julio César Jobet, *Ensayo crítico del desarrollo económico social de Chile* (1955), p. 153.

[225] See *El Mercurio,* July 28, 1913, and May 18, 1915, on early Guggenheim activity in the Chilean copper industry. See also La Falange Nacional, *Una política del cobre* (1953), which provides information about early United States copper operations in Chile. Largely thanks to United States investments, Chilean copper production rose from 42,726 metric tons in 1909 to 79,580 in 1919. Total world production in the latter year was 925,551 metric tons. See *Anuario Estadístico,* 1920, II, and Carlos G. Avalos, "La introducción de capitales americanos en Chile," *Pacífico Magazine* (December, 1914).

[226] *New York Sun,* March 10, 1919.

[227] Alberto Márquez, et al., Libro internacional sudamericana (1914), and El Mercurio, January 17, 1916.

[228] Investment in industry was only nominal. See Anuario Estadístico, 1920, II, 48-51.

[229] Address of Benjamín Cohen, op. cit., note 223.

[230] Ibid. See also Henry Clay Evans, Jr., Chile and its Relations with the United States (Durham, North Carolina, 1927).

[231] See address of Deputy Vicente Adrián, Cámara de Diputados, Boletín de sesiones extraordinarias, 1919-1920, Sesión 29° of December 11, 1919, p. 948. For additional attacks on the alleged labor exploitation by United States firms see: Alberto Durán B., El estado libre de El Teniente y la vida obrera de las minas (1919); Marcial Figueroa and Eulogio Gutiérrez, Chuquicamata: sus grandezas y sus dolores (1920); Alejandro Fuenzalida Grandón, El trabajo y la vida en el mineral El Teniente (1919); Laura Jorquera, Tierras rojas (1921); and Trancredo Pinochet Le-Brun, 'El Infierno' del Dante y la pampa salitre (1918).

[232] Domingo Amunátegui Solar, La democracia en Chile, p. 287. La Nación, February 1 and 3, 1917.

[233] See El Mercurio, December 10, 1903, and Suárez Mujica to the Chilean Ministry of Foreign Relations, February 20, 1913, Legaciones de Chile en EE. UU. y en México, 1913, AMRE.

[234] El Mercurio, March 16, 1916. See also Trancredo Pinochet, La conquista de Chile en el siglo xx (1909), pp. 56-57, Manuel Hernández Trejos, Las conferencias internacionales americanas y su contenido económica (1947), and Ismael Huidobro P., Las cuestiones aduaneras ante los congresos pan-americanos (1911).

[235] El Mercurio, April 4, 1916. See also Luis Izquierdo Fredes, Augusto Villanueva G., and Gonzalo Bulnes Vergara, Conferencia financiera panamericana reunida en Washington: informe de la delegación de Chile (1916).

[236] See Guillermo M. Bañados, Chile y los problemas de la post-bellum (1919).

[237] La Nación, October 16, 25, and November 7, 1919.

[238] See Emilio Rodríguez Mendoza, "El capital norteamericano en sud-américa a propósito de la declaración de Mr. Knox," El Mercurio, June 19, 1910.

[239] Economic nationalism had been championed sporadically around the turn of the century, but without noticeable impact. See El Ferrocarril, January 24 and May 21, 1895; El Imparcial, December 22, 1903; La Patria, Valparaíso, May 17, 1895; and El Porvenir, December 2, 1903.

[240] Alejandro Venegas, Sinceridad (1910), pp. 233-235, 271, stated that the predominance of foreign capital was in part responsible for Chile's social problem and the heartless exploitation of labor by capital.

[241] El Diario Ilustrado, October 11 and 13, 1915. See also Guillermo Subercaseaux, Nuevas orientaciones de política internacional sud-americand (1917).

[242] La Nación, August 12, 1917.

[243] El Mercurio, June 17, 1913. The newspaper La Opinión, which Pinochet ran between 1915 and 1920, expounded a strong line of economic nationalism. See also J. Raimundo del Río, "La nacionalización de nuestro comercio," La Nación, August 28, 29, and 30, 1917; and El Mercurio, March 28, 1915.

[244] The work was first published in 1912 and a second edition appeared in 1955.

[245] Pinochet La conquista, pp. 63, 110-115, 171-177.

[246] Ibid., p. 212.

[247] Quoted by Fernando Alessandri Rodríguez in the prologue to Luis Valencia Avaria (compiler), *Anales de la república* (1951).

[248] Works of Errázuriz which set the colonial period in a different light than that projected by Diego Barros Arana and fellow liberal historians include: *Don García de Mendoza, 1557-1561* (1916); *Historia de Chile sin governador: 1554-1557* (1912); *Historia de Chile: Pedro de Valdivia, 2 vols.* (1911); *Orígenes de la Iglesia chilena* (1873); *Pedro de Villagra, 1563-1565* (1916); *Seis años de la historia de Chile: diciembre de 1598-abril de 1605, 2 vols.* (1908). Works of conservative historian Ramón Sotomayor Valdés also spoke glowingly of Spanish colonial traditions, and of the statesmen during the early republican period who sought to perpetuate them. See his *Historia de Chile bajo el gobierno del General d. Joaquín Pinto*, 4 vols. (1900-1903); *Historia de Chile durante los cuarenta años trascurridos desde 1831 hasta 1871*, 2 vols. (1875, 1876); *El Ministro Portales* (1954 edition). Ramón Angel Jara, one-time bishop of Ancud, was another precursor of Hispanism. See his *Celebración del 4° centenario del descubrimiento de América por Colón* (1890). See also Jorge Huneeus Gana, *Estudios sobre España*, 2 vols. (1889), and Rafael Sanhueza Lizardi, *Viaje en España* (1886).

[249] See Alejandro Fuenzalida Grandón, *Lastarria y su tiempo (1817-1888); su vida, obras e influencia en el desarrollo político e intelectual de Chile*, 2 vols. (1911). In this highly laudatory biography, Fuenzalida reveals the new trend of thought in Chile by taking exception to his hero's anti-Spanish bias. The time for such attitudes, states Fuenzalida, has passed. Spain has made vast contributions to Chile and there should be close ties of friendship between the two countries. See vol. I, 354-374.

[250] *El Ferrocarril*, April 22, 1898.

[251] For accounts of the various Spanish and pro-Spanish groups in Chile see *ibid.*, March 29 and April 27, 1898. See also *La Voz del Sur*, April 26, 1898.

[252] See Ramón Subercaseaux, Chilean envoy in Berlin, to his Ministry of Foreign Relations, August 10, 1898, *Legación de Chile en Alemania, 1898*, AMRE. See also *El Porvenir*, April 22, 24, and 25, 1898.

[253] *La Libertad Electoral*, July 18, 1898. The quotation is taken from an unidentified number of the Paris *La Nouvelle Revue*. For similar sentiments see *El Ferrocarril*, April 27, 1898. See also Antonio M. Carmona, "Recuerdos gloriosas de España," *ibid.*, April 26, 1898. The battle of Manila Bay was referred to by *La Unión*, May 3, 1898, as "The Battle of the Titans." It maintained that Spaniards deserved this denomination because of their heroism and incredible courage in the face of inevitable disaster; and the Yankees, only because of their material might.

[254] See *El Ferrocarril*, November 2, 1901. See also *La Libertad Electoral*, June 18, 1898; *El Porvenir*, April 10, 1898; and *La Unión*, April 21, 1898. For additional indications of anti-United States feelings in the newspapers see *El Ferrocarril*, March 26, 27, and 28, April 7, 9, 21, and 22, June 18 and July 22, 1898; and *La Unión*, December 20, 1898.

[255] *La Libertad Electoral*, July 7, 1898. See also Adolfo Murillo, "La liga de la paz y de la unión latinoamericana," *ibid.*, December 13, 1898, and *El Porvenir*, April 22, 1898.

[256] Tito V. Lisoni, Liberal Party politician and Catholic intellectual, referred to Rodó's masterpiece, *Ariel y Calibán*, as a gospel for Latin-American youth. He confessed that it reawakened in him the higher aspirations, and added that the book should inspire all Latin Americans to resist succumbing to the influence of extreme

positivism that characterized the North Americans. "Yankee utilitarianism destroys all higher ideals." See Lisoni, El Libro "Ariel": conferencia dada en el Ateneo de Santiago en la sesión de 12 de julio de 1905 (1905), pp. 17-23, 72. See also Armando Donoso, Homenaje al Rodó (1917); E. L. G., "Apuntes sobre Ariel de José Enrique Rodó," La Revista de Chile, VI, no. 2 (2° quincena de enero, 1901); Elvira Santa Cruz Ossa, "José Enrique Rodó," Revista Chilena, Año I, Tomo II, no. 6 (September, 1917); and Julio Vicuña Cifuentes, "José Enrique Rodó," ibid., Año I, Tomo I, no. 4 (May, 1917). See also La Nación, May 4, 1917.

[257] La Unión, December 20, 1898. For similar reactions evoked by the Spanish-American War see the same daily, April 21, May 1, 3, 4, 14, and 29, and June 24, 1898. See also El Porvenir, April 10, 15, 19, 21, 22, 24, and 25, 1898.

[258] Some of the works published in Chile before 1920, glorifying the spiritual superiority of traditional patterns and warning against the penetration of United States culture, include the following: Juan Bardina, Leyenda perjudicial: la supuesta inferioridad de los españoles (1918). An important Spanish immigrant to Chile, Bardina did much to popularize Hispanism in Chile, frequently using the pseudonym of "Lautaro" for his publications. Antonio de Benavides, Por españa y por la raza española (1900). Benavides, a Spaniard who had lived in Chile, rejoiced over the expanding influence there of Hispanism. Francisco Bulnes Correa, El porvenir de las naciones hispanoamericanos (1903. Memoria de Prueba); Aliro Carrasco, Letras hispanoamericanas (1919); Jorge Huneeus Gana, Estudios sobre España, 2 vols. (1898); Fernando Márquez de la Plata, "Recuerdos del Iltmo. Sr. d. Martín Rücker en España," Boletín de la Academia Chilena de la Historia, Año III, no. 5 (1° semestre, 1935). This piece reveals the dedicated Hispanism of Bishop Rücker. Magallanes Moure, a distinguished poet, was among the earliest supporters of Hispanism in Chile. See his Almas y panoramas (1910); Le Chili et la France (Paris, 1919); and Tierra de reliquias (Valencia, Spain, 1912). El Pensamiento Latino: Revista Internacional Latino-Americano Europea. Published 1900-1901 in Santiago, this was an instrument of Hispanism. Trancredo Pinochet Le-Brun, Como construir una gran civilización chilena e hispanoamericana (no date). In this and other works, Pinochet defends traditional Chilean-Hispanic values. See also his El diálogo de las dos américas (Habana, Cuba. Probably 1919). Jorge Gustavo Silva, "La rectificación de la historia de América," Revista Chilena de Historia y Geografía, XXXII (4° trimestre, 1919). This article refers to the fact that Domingo Amunátegui Solar had translated E. G. Bourne, Spain in America, into Spanish. Appearance of this book in a Santiago edition led some Chileans to say that North Americans were pioneers in the move to counteract the Black Legend of Spanish depravity in colonial times. Silva disagrees, claiming that Chileans had dispelled the Black Legend long before Bourne. See also Omer Emeth, "Filosofía norteamericana: el pragmatismo," El Mercurio, August 21, 1910.

[259] Trancredo Pinochet, El diálogo de las dos américas, and the same writer's letter in El Mercurio, October 12, 1912.

[260] El Mercurio, August 21, 1910. For reference to some of Molina's works see Chapter IV, note 154.

[261] Emeth, "Filosofía norteamericana," ibid., November 8, 1920. For an article that is similar in tone see conservative pensador J. M. Echenique Gandarillas, "La influencia del divorcio . . . ," El Imparcial, November 17, 1933.

[262] El Mercurio, December 21, 1925.

[263] Interview with Moisés Vargas, *El Ferrocarril*, November 18, 1904.

[264] *La Unión*, August 2, 1898.

[265] Suárez Mujica to Chilean Ministry of Foreign Relations, January 7, 1913, *Legación de Chile en EE. UU., 1913*, AMRE.

[266] Carlos Walker Martínez, *Historia de la administración Santa María* (1890), esp. p. 63.

[267] For indications of this disparaging attitude toward other Latin-American republics see the following sources. *El Diario Illustrado*, December 12, 1904. *El Ferrocarril*, December 9, 1904. The point of view expressed in the editorial is that Roosevelt's "Big Stick" policy applies only to the turbulent Caribbean republics, which fully deserve such treatment. *MMRE*, 1902, I, 189-190. Here, Eliodoro Yáñez says that other Latin-American republics are not yet sufficiently advanced to render Chilean cooperation with them fruitful. *El Mercurio*, November 26, 1903, November 9, 1904, December 8, 1904, and May 26, 1914. In the last-cited edition we read: "There is need to keep in mind the distinction between the honest, stable governments on one hand, and those of the small and improperly called 'republics' of the tropical zone, utterly incompetent and anarchistic, on the other." See also Vicuña Subercaseaux, *Los congresos pan-americanos*, p. 45.

[268] For the anti-Yankee implications of Chilean recommendations of Latin-American unity see the following sources: *El Ferrocarril*, September 4, 1895, and October 10, 1901; address of Marmaduke Grove, Cámara de Senadores, *Boletín de sesiones extraordinarias, 1942-1943*, Sesión 4°, May 11, 1943. *El Imparcial*, November 5, 9, and 19, 1903; Ricardo Salas Edwards, "El porvenir de Chile en América," *El Mercurio*, February 10, 1919; Javier Vial Solar, *El problema del norte*. This latter book, published in 1898, urged that Chile develop its own economic resources through a union with Latin-American countries that specifically excluded the United States. See also Joaquín Walker Martínez to Chilean Ministry of Foreign Relations, December 1, 1903, *Legación de Chile en EE. UU., 1903*, AMRE, and January 20, February 15, and April 11, 1904, *Legación . . . , 1904*.

[269] Chile's desire to use the ABC power-bloc as a force for offsetting United States influence is revealed in the following sources. Domingo Amunátegui Solar, *La democracia en Chile*, p. 351. Miguel Cruchaga, Chilean envoy in Buenos Aires, to his Ministry of Foreign Relations, February 4 and 5, July 10, September 11 and 25, 1909, *Legación de Chile en la república de Argentina, 1909-1911, Sección Confidencial*, AMRE. See also Cruchaga to Ministry, September 8, 1910, *Correspondencia del Ministro de Chile en Argentina, 1910, 2° semestre*, AMRE. *El Diario Ilustrado*, September 19, 1916. Emilio Figueroa Larraín, *Memoria de la Legación de Chile en La Argentina, 1914-1915*, in *Correspondencia de las Legaciones de Chile en Argentina, Bolivia, y Brasil, 1916*, AMRE. *La Ley*, November 11, 1904. *La Nación*, November 10, 1917. Emilio Rodríguez Mendoza, "La guerra y la América," *Revista Chilena*, Año III, Tomo IX, no. 28 (December, 1919), and *Alfredo Irarrázaval Zañartu* (1925). Irarrázaval was an important diplomat and journalist who served as envoy in Brazil toward the close of the nineteenth century. Eduardo Suárez Mujica, Chilean envoy in Washington, to his Ministry of Foreign Relations, March 15, 1913, *Legaciones de Chile en EE. UU. y en México, 1913*, AMRE. Eliodoro Yáñez, *La sociedad de las naciones latino-americanas* (1919). South American unity, stated Yáñez, would be necessary to offset the

influence of the United· States. Yáñez also criticized the League of Nations Charter for its recognition in Article 21 of the Monroe Doctrine.

[270] The accord between Chile and Argentina came virtually to an end in 1919 when Argentina offered good offices in the dispute between Chile and Peru. Chile regarded this action as impertinent meddling. See Eduardo Ruiz Vergara, secretary of the Chilean Legation in Buenos Aires, to his Ministry of Foreign Relations, March 1, 1919, Correspondencia de las Legaciones de Chile en Argentina, Colombia y Costa Rica, 1919, AMRE.

[271] For indications of the desire to cement ties with Europe so as to escape United States tutelage see El Ferrocarril, December 28, 1895, and May 14, 1898; El Mercurio, January 13, 1913, and April 20, 1916; Gallardo, Panamericanismo, pp. 27, 148-149; Gaspar Toro, "Notas sobre el arbitraje internacional de las repúblicas latino-americanas," published in installments in El Ferrocarril, September and October, 1898. See especially, Joaquín Walker Martínez, Chilean envoy in Washington, to his Ministry of Foreign Relations, Legación de Chile en EE.UU., 1904, AMRE. See also Pierre Leroy Beaulieu, "Las dos Américas y el Congreso Panamericano," El Ferrocarril, October 10, 1901. This French writer enjoyed a large following in Chile. He constantly urged Latin America to form closer ties with Latin Europe, in order to avoid the cultural and economic penetration of the United States.

[272] El Mercurio, November 10 and 11, 1903.

CHAPTER 6

[1] Luis Galdames, A History of Chile, translated and edited by Isaac Joslin Cox (Chapel Hill, North Carolina, 1941), p. 444.

[2] Alessandri's university dissertation, Habitaciones para obreros (1893), was based on the argument that workers should be given adequate homes before they became powerful enough to demand them.

[3] Alessandri, Recuerdos de gobierno (1952), p. 35. See also Alessandri's El Presidente Alessandri y su gobierno (1926), a compilation of various of his articles and speeches of the 1920 electoral campaign and first presidential term.

[4] See Federación de la Clase Media, Manifesto: estatutos generales y documentos que sirven de base para la organización de la Federación de la Clase Media de Chile (1919).

[5] Emilio Castelar, Los valores españoles (1923), p. 103. See also Chapter VIII, note 15, reference to Juan Bardina, Leyenda perjudicial.

[6] Constitutional reform to do away with parliamentary rule had long been favored by Conservatives, anxious for a return to Portales traditions. Monetary stabilization had as many adherents among the Conservatives as any other political group. Income and other taxes aimed at ending reliance on nitrate export taxes appealed to rich northern interests, while governmental decentralization won the support of the well-to-do but politically slighted southern landowners.

[7] Alessandri, Recuerdos, pp. 43-44. Moreover, the Conservative Party had until this time had one of the most distinguished records in supporting social justice legislation. See the excellent study of Arturo Olavaría Bravo, La cuestión social en Chile (1923).

[8] Ricardo Donoso, *Desarrollo político y social de Chile desde la constitución de 1833* (1942), p. 117.

[9] Julio César Jobet, "Movimiento social obrero," Universidad de Chile, *Desarrollo de Chile en la primera mitad del siglo xx* (1953), I, 77.

[10] Alberto Edwards and Eduardo Frei, *Historia de los partidos políticos chilenos* (1949), pp. 183-191. Frei wrote all of that portion of the book that deals with political history after the overthrow of Balmaceda. The work will be referred to hereafter as *Partidos*.

[11] *El Mercurio*, November 3, 1925. See also José Luis Castro, *El sistema electoral chileno* (1941), and Ricardo Cruz-Coke Madrid, *Geografía electoral de Chile* (1952).

[12] Alberto Edwards, *La fronda aristocrática* (1959 edition), p. 183.

[13] Dirección General de Estadística, *X censo de la población efectuado el 27 de noviembre de 1930* (1935), III, pp. vii-xix. Other valuable census sources are: Dirección General de Estadística, *Censo de población de la república de Chile, levantado el 15 de diciembre de 1920* (1925); and Servicio Nacional de Estadística y Censos, *XII censo de población i de vivienda, levantado el 24 de abril de 1952*, 6 vols. (1957).

[14] *X censo*, III, 50.

[15] *Ibid*. Valparaíso had in 1930 a population of 193,205, while neighboring Viña del Mar had soared to approximately 50,000. Concepción's population was 78,000, and that of Iquique 47,000.

[16] *El Mercurio*, January 4, 1931. See also Rodolfo Gamboa, "Población i inmigración en Chile," *Atenea*, Año VI, no. 60 (December, 1929), which shows that Chile's annual increase in population, 1900-1920, was considerably lower than that of Argentina and Brazil, and Arturo Lyon Peña (President of the *Caja de Colonización Agrícola*), "Inmigración y colonización," *Economía y Finanzas*, Año I, no. 14 (December, 1937). Another indication of urban growth was that between 1915 and 1925, Chilean capital invested in nonextractive industry more than tripled, rising from 500 million to 1800 million pesos. For material on industrial growth see the following works: Pedro Aguirre Cerda, *El problema industrial* (1933); Alfredo Aldunate, *Régimen legal de las sociedades en Chile: estudio jurídico sobre sociedades anónimas, bancos, instituciones hipotecarias, cooperativas, con insersión de textos legales y con explicaciones para el cumplimiento de las leyes tributarias y sociales* (1927); Oscar Alvarez Andrews, *Historia del desarrollo industrial de Chile* (1936); Ernesto Barros Jarpa, Alberto Edwards, Luis Pérez, Galvarino Gallardo Nieto, *Chile: geografía económica* (1923); Carlos Keller, "Estructura económica de Chile," *Atenea*, Año II, no. 6 (August, 1925); Walter Müller H., "Industria nacional," *Economía y Finanzas*, Año I, no. 1 (January, 1937).

[17] Edwards, *Fronda*, pp. 206-212. For general background material on Chilean politics and political figures during the early 1920's, see the following works: Alberto Luis Cabero, *Recuerdos de don Pedro Aguirre Cerda* (1948); *Diccionario biográfico de Chile* (various editions); Luis Durand, *Gente de mi tiempo* (1953); Januario Espinosa, *Figuras de la política chilena* (1944); Emilio Rodríguez Mendoza, *Como si fuera ayer* (1919), and *Como si fuera ahora* (1929); Carlos Silva Vildósola, *Retratos y recuerdos* (1936); Salvador Valdés Morande, *Semblanzas de chilenos ilustres* (1954).

[18] Cámara de Diputados, *Boletín de sesiones extraordinarias*, 1920-1921, Sesión 68°, May 12, 1921, pp. 2604 ff.

[19] *Ibid.*, Sesión 40°, December 24, 1919.

[20] Jaime Larraín García Moreno, *Chile, avanzada de occidente en el Pacífico sur* (1955), p. 17.

[21] See the article by Fidel Muñoz Rodríguez in *El Mercurio*, January 1, 1922.

[22] An example of a progressive Democrat interested in reform was Guillermo M. Bañados, president of the Democrat Party at the time of the 1920 elections. Bañados soon grew disillusioned with Alessandri. See his *Avancemos* (1924), *Casas para empleados y obreros* (1923), *Combatiendo la tiranía* (1926), and *La verdadera democracia* (1922).

[23] See *El Mercurio*, May 21, 1919, and *El Diario Ilustrado* of the same date.

[24] *El Mercurio*, January 1, 1922. See also *El Diario Ilustrado*, August 9, 1925.

[25] See Arturo Alessandri, "Actualidades económicos," *Atenea*, Año I, no. 2 (May, 1924).

[26] See *El Mercurio*, January 1, 1922.

[27] *Las Ultimas Noticias*, January 4, 1922. See also José Joaquín Prieto M., *La industria salitre: su historia, legislación y desarrollo* (1945. Memoria de Prueba), and Jorge Gustavo Silva, "Del problema social en la zona salitre," *Revista Chilena*, Año X, no. 75 (May, 1926).

[28] *Las Ultimas Noticias*, January 4, 1922.

[29] Frank Fetter, *Monetary Inflation in Chile* (Princeton, N.J., 1931), pp. 13-14. The peso was worth 12-1/16 pence in 1920, and 5-7/8 pence in 1925.

[30] According to Alvarez Andrews, *Historia del desarrollo industrial*, p. 221, the cost-of-living index increased from 100 to 248 between 1913 and 1923. During this same period the index of nominal wages rose from 100 to 138, but that of real wages declined from 100 to 90.

[31] Julio César Jobet, *Ensayo crítico del desarrollo económico-social de Chile* (1955), pp. 159-163. See also *El Mercurio*, January 1, 1922; Donoso, *Desarrollo político y social*, p. 120; and Edwards and Frei, *Partidos*, p. 190.

[32] Edwards and Frei, *Partidos*, pp. 183-190.

[33] See address of Ismael Edwards Matte, Cámara de Diputados, *Boletín de sesiones extraordinarias*, 1929-1930, Sesión of November 12, 1929, pp. 770 ff. In this address, Edwards refers to the discontent in 1923 of some Radicals, especially Santiago Labarca and Ramón Luis Ugalde.

[34] *La Nación*, July 12, 1923.

[35] Edwards, *Fronda*, pp. 221-223; Edwards and Frei, *Partidos*, pp. 183-191.

[36] Donoso, *Desarrollo político y social*, p. 120, and Edwards and Frei, *Partidos*, pp. 216-217.

[37] Edwards and Frei, *op. cit.*, p. 187.

[38] For material on the September 5 *coup* see the following works: Raul Aldunate Philipps, "La revolución de los tenientes," *Zig Zag*. This fine series of articles began on August 3, 1957, and continued in subsequent editions. *Discursos pronunciados en la Casa del Pueblo con motivo del aniversario del 5 de septiembre* (1930); Francisco Javier Ovalle Castillo, *Personajes chilenos para escribir los anales de Chile contemporánea: los orígenes de la revolución de septiembre de 1924* (Talca, 1926); Emilio Rodríguez Mendoza, *El golpe de estado de 1924: ambiente*

y actores (1927); Carlos Sáez M., *Recuerdos de un soldado: el ejército y la política,* 3 vols. (1933-1934). General Sáez has written one of the best available sources on the events leading up to the 1924 *coup* and the subsequent participation of the military in politics. Rafael Vargas Prado (editor), *Chile ante el nuevo régimen* (1929). This work, analyzing events from September 1924 to December 1925 is in general favorable to the role played by the army. Alejandro Vicuña, *Política chilena, 1924-1925* (1925). Father Vicuña shows great uneasiness over the developments of this period.

[39] Congress, for example, had refused to act on a measure for raising officers' expense accounts. After the September 5 *coup*, quick approval was given. See *Lei de Presupuestos, 1923-1924,* "Ministerio de Guerra," p. 11. Officer discontent arose from the long delays between promotions, resulting from the fact that the higher ranks were filled. Ibáñez was forty-seven in 1924 and only a major.

[40] See Tobías Barros Ortiz, *Vigilia de armas: charlas sobre vida militar* (1920). This book caused a sensation among the younger officers. It asserted that the military could play a part in the regeneration of Chile. Throughout his life, Barros Ortiz was a staunch supporter of Ibáñez.

[41] See Emilio Bello Codesido, *Recuerdos políticos: la junta de gobierno de 1925: su origen y relación con la reforma del régimen constitucional* (1954), pp. 6-7. Bello's work is one of the most valuable studies on events in the troubled 1920-1925 period. The author played a major role in shaping political developments at this time. See also Donoso, *Desarrollo político y social,* p. 121, and *El Mercurio,* September 7, 1924.

[42] Edwards and Frei, *Partidos,* p. 194.

[43] *Ibid.,* pp. 197 ff.

[44] See Yáñez to Edwards Bello, Santiago, January 9, 1925, in "Eliodoro Yáñez, epistolario: la personalidad íntima del estadista a través de su correspondencia," *Anales de la Universidad de Chile,* Centenarios, Edición Extraordinaria (1959, 1960). For a good insight into the social consciousness of Yáñez, see also his *Política de previsión y de trabajo* (1920). For other indications of consternation over the attempt to install Ladislao Errázuriz as president see the interview with Pedro Aguirre Cerda in Buenos Aires, reported in *El Mercurio,* September 20, 1924, and René Montero, *Confesiones políticas* (1959), pp. 26-27. Even arch-Conservative Alberto Edwards realized that the junta, given the times, inclined unrealistically toward the right. See his *Fronda,* pp. 227-234.

[45] See Arturo Ahumada, *El ejército y la revolución del 5 de septiembre de 1924* (1931). Written by an important participant in the events, this is one of the more valuable works on the entry of the military into politics. The same appraisal applies to General Juan Pablo Bennett, *La revolución del 5 de septiembre de 1924* (1926). Some background indications of political stirring in the Chilean army can be found in Oscar Fenner, *Observaciones sobre la labor que corresponderá a la comisión revisora de las leyes de justicia militar* (1922. *Memoria de Prueba*). Fenner, a lifelong supporter of Ibáñez, was an active socialist in the early 1930's. See also Arturo Olavaría Bravo, *La cuestión social en Chile: los partidos políticos chilenos frente a la cuestión social* (1923), pp. 33-51, and Renato Valdés, *Tres cartas* (1932), p. 7.

[46] Ahumada, *El ejército,* pp. 110-111.

[47] *Ibid.,* p. 96. Edwards and Frei, *Partidos,* pp. 195-199.

⁴⁸ Ahumada, *op. cit.*, pp. 121-126. This bulletin was written by Bartolomé Blanche. See also his 1924 pamphlet, *Heridas abiertas*, noting that it was necessary to apply balm to the wounds which unscrupulous capitalists had inflicted upon the laboring classes, and *Circular a todos las unidades del ejército* (1931). In this last pamphlet, Blanche again urges the army to fulfill its destiny in bringing about national regeneration.

⁴⁹ Ahumada, *op. cit.*, pp. 134-136. Bello, *Recuerdos políticos*, p. 4. Edwards and Frei, *op. cit.*, pp. 195-199. Julio César Jobet, "Notas sobre la historiografía chilena," in Ricardo Donoso, *et al.*, *Historiografía chilena* (1949), p. 376. Montero, *Confesiones*, p. 17. Even conservative Jorge de la Cuadra Poissón, *La revolución que viene* (1939), pp. 27 ff., indicates his faith in the integrity and sincerity of the military junta. See also *El Mercurio*, September 11, 1924.

⁵⁰ The military junta made an exception in the case of left-wing Radical leader Santiago Labarca and held an important conference with him. Ahumada, *op. cit.*, p. 149.

⁵¹ Bello, *Recuerdos políticos*, pp. 26-52.

⁵² Edwards and Frei, *op. cit.*, pp. 198-199.

⁵³ Edwards, *Fronda*, pp. 235-241. Jobet, *Ensayo crítico*, p. 168.

⁵⁴ Bello, *Recuerdos políticos*, pp. 69-77. See also Coronel Ortiz Woomald, *¿Que nos pasa?* (1925). Rafael Luis Gumucio, director of *El Diario Ilustrado*, continued to try to spark a new rightist power-grab by publishing provocative and even libelous rumors about the governing junta that succeeded Altamirano, Bennett and Neff. Because of this, *El Diario Ilustrado* was temporarily closed in February of 1915.

⁵⁵ The junta was made up of Emilio Bello Codesido, General Pedro Pablo Dartnell and Admiral Carlos Ward. In addition to works previously cited, see Guillermo M. Bañados, *Combatiendo la tiranía* (1926).

⁵⁶ See Patricio Barros Lynch, *Un cuarto del siglo de legislación tributaria chilena* (1927), and Armando Holzapfel Alvarez, *La traslación y evasión de los impuestos* (1934).

⁵⁷ Donoso, *Desarrollo político y social*, p. 123, and Enrique L. Marshall, "Finanzas y sistema monetario," Universidad de Chile, *Desarrollo de Chile*, I, 263-289.

⁵⁸ Some of the works on the 1925 constitution include the following: Facultad de Derecho de la Universidad de Chile, *La constitución de 1925 y la facultad de ciencias jurídicas y sociales* (1951). J. Guillermo Guerra, *La constitución de 1925* (1929), *Temas constitucionales* (1928), and "Origen y caida de la constitución de 1833," *Revista Chilena de Historia y Geografía*, LXIV (May-August, 1933). A staunch Ibañista, Guerra felt the 1925 constitution and subsequent political events brought about a return to the ideals of Balmaceda. René López Vargas, *Estudio sobre las reformas constitucionales promulgadas el 18 de septiembre de 1925 y sobre los efectos que produjó el parlamentarismo en Chile* (1927. *Memoria de Prueba*). Guillermo Nebel, *Los secretarios de estado en las constituciones de 1833 y 1925* (1936). Hugo Zañartu Irigoyen, *La constitución de 1925 y parlamentarismo en Chile* (1926. *Memoria de Prueba*).

⁵⁹ See Oscar Alvarez Andrews, *La asistencia judicial: estudio sobre la situación de las clases pobres ante el derecho procesal común especial* (1927. *Memoria de Prueba*); Diego Guzmán Pérez (Subsecretary of the Ministry of Labor), "Legislación social obrera," *Economía y Finanzas*, Año II, no. 11 (April, 1938); Oficina

Central de Estadística, *Veinte años de legislación social* (1945); Moisés Poblete Troncoso, *Evolución del derecho social en América* (1942); Jorge Gustavo Silva, "Enuncio y contenido de la legislación social chilena," *Revista Chilena*, Año XIII, nos. 108-109 (April-May, 1929). Francisco Walker Linares, *Apuntes de economía y legislación del trabajo* (1930).

[60] Donoso, *Desarrollo político y social*, pp. 125-127, and Edwards and Frei, *Partidos*, p. 204. See also Julio Heise González, *La constitución de 1925 y las nuevas tendencias político-sociales* (1951). This is probably the best account of the 1925 constitution and the new social forces that it embodied.

[61] Vicuña, *La separación de la Iglesia y el estado* (1922). See also the April, 1923, editions of *El Diario Ilustrado*.

[62] *El Mercurio*, April 17, 1923.

[63] *Ibid.*, April 22, 1923.

[64] *Loc. cit.*

[65] The pastoral was printed in *El Mercurio*, April 25, 1923.

[66] *El Diario Ilustrado*, April 2, 1924. Ricardo Cox Méndez stated separation would result in the atheistic state, *ibid.*, July 22, 1925. Similar opinions were expressed by such distinguished Chileans as Gonzalo Bulnes, Abdón Cifuentes, Joaquín Walker Martínez, Antonio Varas, Manuel Rivas Vicuña, Rafael Luis Gumucio, Joaquín Irarrázaval, Alberto Cariola, Germán Riesco Errázuriz, Enrique Correa, and Augusto Vicuña Subercaseaux.

[67] See Carlos Sáez Morales, *Recuerdos de un soldado: el ejército y la política*, 3 vols. (1933, 1934), and *El Diario Ilustrado*, July 22, and August 2-30, 1925.

[68] Donoso, *Desarrollo político y social*, p. 125.

[69] *El Diario Ilustrado*, July 31, 1925.

[70] Approximately 134,000 of a registered electorate of 302,304 went to the polls. About 127,000 voted for unqualified approval of the constitution. See *El Mercurio*, November 3, 1925.

[71] Joint pastoral of September 20, 1925, published in *La Nación*, September 20, 1925. See also Fidel Araneda Bravo, *El arzobispo Errázuriz y la evolución política y social de Chile* (1956); Fr. Alejandro Cox Méndez, et al., *Historia eclesiástica de Chile*, 1536-1945 (1946); Roberto Peragallo, *Iglesia y estado* (1923); Fr. Alejandro Vicuña, *Pueblos encadenados: el origen de la actual constitución chilena: el fascismo; el sovietismo* (1926). In addition to the pastoral, the cited works by Fidel Araneda Bravo and Alejandro Cox regard the separation with calmness. Peragallo and Vicuña consider it little short of diabolical. Perhaps Eduardo Frei has made the most penetrating observation upon the whole matter: "Separation of Church and state is logical when those who govern are not Catholics." Edwards and Frei, *Partidos*, p. 205.

[72] The following are some of the works that consider the first Alessandri administration. Arturo Alessandri, *Rectificación al tomo IX de la historia de América* (1941). In this, Alessandri tries to correct what he considers the false interpretations and downright calumnies contained in Ricardo Donoso, *Desarrollo político y social de Chile desde la constitución de 1833*. Donoso's work originally was published as volume IX of the *Historia de América bajo la dirección superior de Ricardo Levene* (Buenos Aires, 1940). Donoso, whose anti-Alessandri bias probably arose during the second Alessandri administration (1932-1938) when he was not named director of the National Library, later published a far more vicious and

emotional attack against the "Lion of Tarapacá." See Donoso, *Alessandri, agitador y demoledor: cincuenta años de historia política de Chile*, 2 vols. (Mexico, D.F., 1953, 1954). Another Alessandri-authored work is *Recuerdos de gobierno* (1952). This first volume of a projected two-volume set, carries the Alessandri story only to the September 5, 1924, coup d'etat. Unfortunately, Alessandri died before writing the second volume. Armando Donoso, a distinguished Chilean journalist, has recorded very favorable impressions of Alessandri. See Donoso, *Conversaciones con d. Arturo Alessandri* (1934). Luis Durand, who was Alessandri's secretary during the second administration, has written *Don Arturo* (1952), and *Gente de mi tiempo* (1953). In the 1940's Durand joined the socialist movement in Chile. Inés Echeverría de Larraín (pseud., Iris), *Alessandri evocaciones y resonancias* (1932). In this work one of Chile's most famous woman-journalists has produced a warmly sympathetic character sketch of Alessandri. Eduardo Enríquez Veloso, *Ensayo de historia política y jurídica chilena* (1935. *Memoria de Prueba*). Guillermo Feliú Cruz, "Alessandri, demoledor, constructor y consolidador de un pueblo," *Atenea*, Año XXVII, nos. 302-303 (August, 1950), and *Alessandri, personaje de la historia* (1950). Clarence H. Haring, "Chilean Politics, 1920-1928," *Hispanic American Historical Review*, XI, no. 1 (February, 1931). Julio Heise González, 'El liberalismo y las tendencias políticas de la post-guerra," *Atenea*, Año V, no. 2 (March, 1929). Augusto Iglesias, long a leading Chilean journalist as well as a talented amateur historian, has recently published the first volume of a study that is as unobjectively favorable to Alessandri as the Ricardo Donoso effort is hostile. See Iglesias, *Alessandri: una etapa en la democracia en América* (1959). Fidel Muñoz Rodríguez in "Un año que se va," *El Mercurio*, January 1, 1922, wrote an excellent summary of the first year of Alessandri's rule. René Olivares, *Alessandri: precursor y revolucionario* (1942). Published privately, this is a strongly pro-Alessandri work. Enrique Oyarzún, *El radicalismo ante la revolución actual* (1925). Oyarzún, a reform-minded Radical, was Minister of Treasury under Alessandri. The cited pamphlet reveals what some of the more progressive Radicals desired at the time in the way of change. For somewhat the same approach see Carlos Pinto Durán, *La revolución chilena* (1925), in which the author warns particularly about the dangers of executive tyranny as a reaction to the excesses of parliamentarism. Armando Rodríguez Rodríguez, *Régimen presidencial y sistema parlamentario* (1936. *Memoria de Prueba*). Aquiles Vergara Vicuña, *Tres años en el frente político: recopilación de discursos y artículos políticos* (1925).

[73] *La Nación*, September 30, October 1 and 2, 1925.
[74] Edwards and Frei, *Partidos*, pp. 207-210.
[75] *La Nación*, October 25, 1925.
[76] Edwards and Frei, *op. cit.*, pp. 210 ff.
[77] *El Mercurio*, December 12, 1925.
[78] Edwards and Frei, *op. cit.*, pp. 215-217.
[79] Bello, *Recuerdos políticos*, pp. 218-219.
[80] Conrado Ríos Gallardo, *Chile y Peru: los pactos de 1929* (1959), p. 143. Ríos, who served as Minister of Foreign Relations under Ibáñez, never misses an opportunity in this book to praise the wily ruler.
[81] Some of the literature favorable to Ibáñez includes the following works: Ricardo Boizard, *Cuatro retratos en profundidad: Ibáñez, Lafertte, Leighton, Walker* (1940); Augusto Iglesias, "Revolución ideológica, 1891-1923," *La Nación*, Janu-

ary 3, 6, 11, 14, 19, 24, 28, February 3 and 8, 1928; René Montero, *La revolución ideológica y constitucional de Chile* (1928), and *La verdad sobre Ibáñez* (1952); Juan Antonio Ríos, *Durante el gobierno del General Ibáñez: actuación de la Junta Central Radical* (1931). Ríos reveals that he was far from being the only Radical to cooperate with Ibáñez, and he maintains that much good came from the regime. Jorge Gustavo Silva, *Deberes cívicos de los Chilenos* (1928). All of these works are in stark contrast to the bitter, unbalanced attack against Ibáñez written by Ernesto Würth Rojas: *Ibáñez, caudillo enigmatico* (1958).

[82] Cámara de Diputados, *Boletín de sesiones extraordinarias*, 1925-1926, Sesión 7°, April 16, 1926, pp. 386 ff.

[83] This was the opinion of Emilio Tagle Rodríguez. See *El Mercurio*, May 22, 1927. Alberto Edwards concurred fully. See his *Fronda*, pp. 264-274. Two articles published in 1923 had implied Chile must return to the firm methods of Portales. See Francisco Araya Bennett, "El aniversario de la muerte de don Diego Portales," *Revista Chilena de Historia y Geografía*, XLVI (2° trimestre, 1923), and R. L. Barahona, "Portales: su época y su obra," *ibid.*

[84] *El Diario Ilustrado*, April 11, 1929.

[85] *El Mercurio*, May 6, 1927.

[86] See Montero, *Confesiones políticas*, p. 54.

[87] *El Mercurio*, May 15, 1927.

[88] Jorge Gustavo Silva, *Nuestra evolución político-social: 1900-1930* (1930), pp. 61-62.

[89] Cámara de Diputados, *Boletín de sesiones extraordinarias*, 1929-1930, Sesión 11°, November 12, 1929, pp. 770 ff.

[90] *La Nación*, May 22, 1929.

[91] *El Mercurio*, January 3, 1929.

[92] For the Silva statement see *ibid.*, February 12, 1928. For the Iglesias statement see "Revolución ideológica," cited in note 81. This series of Iglesias articles was one indication of the trend in the 1920's to glorify José Manuel Balmaceda. Both Alessandri and Ibáñez took pride in proclaiming themselves followers of the Balmaceda tradition. For additional indications of the hero worship accorded Balmaceda at this time see *La Nación*, September 4, 1925; Iris, "Lección de historia," *ibid.*, October 4, 1925; and Félix Pinto Ovalle, *Vindicación de Balmaceda: documentos, autografos y grabados inéditos de la revolución del '91* (1925).

[93] *El Mercurio*, April 8, 1923, and *Las Ultimas Noticias*, January 4, 1923.

[94] *El Mercurio*, May 4 and 9, 1926. Armando Donoso, attached to the *El Mercurio* staff, was in Spain early in 1926, and published many articles in the paper singing the praises of Primo de Rivera and Spanish-style fascism. See also the letter of Javier Vial Solar praising fascism in Spain and in Italy, *ibid.*, May 8, 1927.

[95] *El Diario Ilustrado*, June 12, 1924, contains the text of the pastoral.

[96] See Rücker's review of the book by Father Guillermo Viviani Contreras, *Doctrinas sociales*, in *El Mercurio*, February 5, 1928.

[97] See Viviani, *La cuestión social en Chile* (1919), pp. 7-10, and his pamphlets *La democracia* (1919), *Nuestras clases sociales* (1919), and *El sindicalismo* (1919). Similar views were expressed by L. R. Ramírez in the pamphlet, *Socialismo y maximalismo* (1919).

[98] See the articles by Viviani in *El Mercurio*, August 18, and 21, 1926. See also his "La crisis del régimen parlamentaria," *ibid.*, February 5, 1928. In addition see

his books, *La organización social corporativa* (1928. *Memoria de Prueba*), and *Sociología chilena: estudio de sociología general aplicada a nuestra país* (1926).

[99] *El Mercurio*, February 13, 1929.

[100] *La Revista Católica: organo de la provincia eclesiástica chilena*, February 16, 1929.

[101] *Ibid*. See also *El Diario Ilustrado*, March 8, 1929.

[102] Bishop of Concepción Gilberto Fuenzalida Guzmán, in his previously cited pastoral of April, 1923 (see note 63), had made this fact unmistakably clear, noting that Chile had declined because the Church was no longer so influential in the political order, and affirming that only the pro-Church Conservative Party, during its days of power, had brought progress to Chile.

[103] This appraisal was overtly presented in 1936 by Catholic Conservative leader Sergio Fernández Larraín. In *Posiciones católicas ante lo económico social* (1936), Fernández Larraín maintained that the great need in Chile was to fight state intervention, because the government of the country was no longer Christian. Rather, it was in the hands of Radicals and Masons, declared enemies of the Church. At the time Fernández Larraín hoped that Catholics as such would regain control of the state. Meanwhile, he advised that every effort be made to reduce state power.

[104] The social justice work which the Church intensified after 1925 had its origins in the early twenties when the Conservatives had begun to contend with Alessandri for lower-class support. The first "Social Week," held under Church auspices in May, 1922, had advanced a highly paternalistic platform opposed to the concept of the open society. See *El Diario Ilustrado*, May 7, 1922, and subsequent May editions. See also the August 9, 1925 edition. Soon the movement had its own publication, the weekly *Justicia Social* under the direction of Alejandro Walker Valdés. For additional material, see Alfredo Silva Santiago (now archbishop of Concepción and rector of the Catholic University of Chile), *Nociones de acción católica* (1933), and notes 157 and 159.

[105] See the interview with an unidentified major in the Chilean army, *El Mercurio*, February 3, 1927.

[106] Ríos Gallardo, "Tenemos que empeñarnos en hacer vivir nuestro glorioso pasado," *ibid*., June 1, 1927, and MMRE, 1927, p. 365.

[107] *El Mercurio*, November 18, 1928.

[108] See Augusto Iglesias, "Ahora Mussolini," *La Nación*, January 20, 25, and February 3, 1929, and "Nuevas orientaciones de la vida publica," *ibid*., October 20 and subsequent editions, 1929; Jorge Gustavo Silva, "La reacción contra los vicios del parlamentarismo," *ibid*., December 7, 1929. In addition consult Silva, *Examen del nacionalismo económico* (1934), and *El gobierno representativo: su evolución histórica y sus nuevas tendencias en la post-guerra* (1931).

[109] See *La Nación*, January 1, 1928, and January 3, 1929.

[110] See address of Ismael Edwards Matte who was one of Ibáñez' most trusted supporters, Cámara de Diputados, *Boletín de sesiones extraordinarias, 1929-1930*, Sesión 5°, November 5, 1929, p. 575.

[111] See Miguel Cruchaga, Chilean ambassador in Washington, to his Ministry of Foreign Relations, July 22, 1927, *Correspondencia recibida de la Embajada de Chile en EE. UU., 1927*, AMRE.

[112] See Enrique Villegas, Chilean ambassador in Rome, to his Ministry of Foreign Relations, November 20, 1928, *Correspondencia recibida de la Embajada de Chile*

en Italia, 1928, AMRE. See also the pro-fascist memorandum prepared by Villegas, "Memoria de la Embajada de Chile en Italia, 1927," in *ibid.*

[112] See Emilio Rodríguez Mendoza, Chilean ambassador in Madrid, to his Ministry of Foreign Relations, September 17, 1928, *Correspondencia recibida de las Legaciones de Chile en España y en Portugal,* 1928, AMRE. See Rodríguez, *En España* (1932), and *La España que ví y viví* (1948). The sort of concern Rodríguez felt for his country in 1920, which helps account for the fact he later became an Ibañista, is revealed in his *En horas de inquietud* (1920).

[114] "El tecnicismo del estado: estudio político-económico del primer secretario de la Legación de Chile en España, señor Leonidas Irarrázaval Barros, enviado al Ministerio de Relaciones Exteriores de acuerdo con el artículo 4° del decreto ley No. 577," and attached to the January 16, 1928, letter of Rodríguez to his Ministry of Foreign Relations, *Correspondencia recibida de las Legaciones de Chile en España y en Portugal,* 1928, AMRE.

[115] Edwards Bello, "La evolución del pueblo hispano-indio," *La Nación,* February 27, 1928.

[116] Montero, *Confesiones políticas,* pp. 64-65.

[117] Carlos Keller, *La eterna crisis chilena* (1931), p. 32, regarded this as one of the great weaknesses of Ibáñez.

[118] See Domingo Melfi, *Dictadura y mansedumbre* (1931), *Indecisión y desengaña de la juventud* (1935), and *Sin brujela* (1932). See also Jobet, "Movimiento . . . ," Universidad de Chile, *Desarrollo,* I, 83, and Edwards and Frei, *Partidos,* pp. 210-217.

[119] Agustín Edwards, *Recuerdos de mi persecución* (1932). See also his *Algunas reminiscencias y observaciones sobre Chile* (1932), and Francisco Latorre and Manuel Marchant, *Apuntes biográficos de don Agustín Edwards Mac-Clure* (1937).

[120] Eliodoro Yáñez, *La autoridad y la libertad en la constitución política del estado* (Paris, 1928), tells part of the story of the confiscation of *La Nación.* Yáñez was in exile at the time. In 1944 he published a revised, enlarged, and more moderate edition of the same work, which stands as a notable exposition of his political credo. Despite later attempts of Yáñez to reacquire the paper, *La Nación* has remained ever since the Ibáñez seizure the property and journalistic organ of the government.

For some of the works written by Chileans in exile who condemn the dictatorial features of the Ibáñez regime, see the following: Heriberto Bucarel (pseud.), *Vida y hechos de San Carlos Baromeo* (Buenos Aires, 1930); Dr. Alejandro Bustamante C., *Mi medicación: gotas de sangre* (Guayaquil, 1930); Marmaduke Grove, *A mi patria* (Paris, 1928); Father Alejandro Vicuña, *Carta abierta* (Paris, 1928). Other attacks against the dictatorship include: Víctor Contreras Guzmán, *Bitácora de la dictadura: administración Ibáñez, 1927-1931* (1942); Diego Muñoz, *La avalancha* (1931); Arturo Olavaría Bravo, *Durante la tiranía* (1931); Aquiles Vergara Vicuña, *Ibáñez, César criollo,* 2 vols. (1931); Carlos Vicuña Fuentes, *En las prisiones políticas de Chile* (1932), and especially *La tiranía en Chile,* 2 vols. (1938, 1939). The last work, although much of it is written in a highly impressionistic manner, is one of the more penetrating studies of the Ibáñez dictatorship and of the entire stream of Chilean history since independence.

[121] See Angel C. Espejo, *Chile nuevo* (1930), in which a prominent Radical praises the Ibáñez policies.

[122] Donoso, *Desarrollo política y social*, p. 133. Edwards and Frei, *Partidos*, pp. 214-217. Keller, *La eterna crisis chilena*, p. 34.

[123] The Caja de Crédito Agrario was created in 1926 and the Caja de Colonización Agrícola in 1928. See Felipe Herrera Lane, *Manuel de política económica* (1937), II, 177.

[124] See McBride, *Chile, Land and Society* (New York, 1936). See also Guillermo Gandarillas and Guillermo Izquierdo, "El problema de la repartición de la propiedad en Chile," *Economía y Finanzas*, Año II, nos. 18 and 19 (April, May, 1938).

[125] For an excellent summary of the Ibáñez administration's institutional reforms, see *El Mercurio*, January 1, 1929.

[126] "El problema educacional: carta de don Roberto Espinoza al Ministro del Interior Carlos Ibáñez y respuesta de este último," *Atenea*, Año IV, no. 11 (May, 1927), provides an excellent insight into the educational goals of Ibáñez. See also Ministerio de Bienestar Social, República de Chile, *La legislación social y la educación cívica* (1928), and *Revista de Educación*. Published first in 1928, this review contains many fine articles on the previous deficiencies of education and on the new orientation Ibáñez hoped to provide.

[127] Prior to this, little attempt had been made to train public school students in industry, commerce, mining, or agriculture: See Julio Vega, *Bosquejo de una política educacional* (1938), pp. 6 ff. Some of the additional works pointing out the faulty structure of Chilean education during this period include the following: Rubén Enrique Concha Arenas, "Don Darío E. Salas y la ley de instrucción primería obligatoria," *Occidente* (May-June, 1957); Eliodoro Domínguez, *El problema de nuestra educación pública* (1933); Dr. F. Landa Z., "Nuestro sistema educacional y la pasividad económica de la población de Chile," *El Mercurio*, January 1, 5, 8, 15, 16, 24, and 25, 1922; Enrique Molina, *De California a Harvard* (1921). Molina warned that unless the orientation of university education is changed in Chile to give the student more initiative and responsibility and less disdain for modern capitalistic values and hard work, the country's social problem would become worse. Moisés Mussa B., *Nuestro problema educacional* (1932); Mariano Navarrete C., *Los problemas educacionales* (1934); Carlos Oliver Schneider, *Hacia la cultura colectiva* (1932); Oriol Renín Vieille, *La educación primera en Chile, 1810-1953* (1956. Memoria de Prueba); Claudio Salas F., *Nuestro problema educacional* (1933); *Segunda Conferencia Interamericana de Educación*, 2 vols. (1934); D. Valencia, *La experiencia pedagógica en Chile* (1933).

[128] See Galdames, *La reforma de la educación secundaria en 1928* (1932); Mistral to Emilio Rodríguez Mendoza, September 26, 1928, *Correspondencia recibida de las Legaciones de Chile en España y Portugal*, 1928, AMRE; and *El Diario Ilustrado*, August 10, 1931.

[129] Julio Ruiz Bourgeois, "Desarrollo de la minería chilena en la primera mitad del siglo XX," Universidad de Chile, *Desarrollo*, I, 216.

[130] Already by 1928, industrial capital amounted to 2.2 billion pesos of 6 pence, or 12¢, each while capital invested in agriculture was about an even 2 billion. Money invested in transportation amounted to nearly an additional 2 billion, while mining investments had soared to 10.5 billion pesos. See Ministerio de Relaciones Exteriores, *Los capitales en Chile* (1928), pp. 6-7.

[131] Donoso, *Desarrollo política y social*, p. 133.

[132] *La Nación*, February 9, 1928, and Aida Vuscovic Bravo, *Participación del*

capital extranjero en la economía chilena (1957. *Memoria de Prueba*), p. 45. See also *El Diario Ilustrado*, August 18, 1930.

[133] Comisión Económica para América Latina de las Naciones Unidas (CEPAL), *Antecedentes sobre el desarrollo de la economía chilena, 1925-1952* (1954), I, 24.

[134] *Ibid.*, I, 84.

[135] The ratio was 1.2 billion pesos of foreign to 1.0 billion of native capital.

[136] The ratio was 6.0 billion pesos of foreign to 4.5 billion of native capital.

[137] The ratio was 39 million pesos of foreign to 50 million of native capital. For these statistics see Ministerio de Relaciones Exteriores, *Los capitales en Chile*, pp. 6-7.

[138] Keller, *La eterna crisis chilena*, pp. 215-216. Julio Ruiz Bourgeois, "Desarrollo de la minería . . . ," Universidad de Chile, *Desarrollo*, I, 222. *El Diario Ilustrado*, in the months immediately following the overthrow of Ibáñez, gave the most complete account to appear in the Chilean press of the COSACH organization, violently attacking practically every aspect of the company. See, for example, the August 12, 1931, edition. Also in August, *El Diario Ilustrado* published a series of articles by the bishop of Iquique, Carlos Labbé, strongly criticizing the company. See also *El Mercurio*, November 8, 1931, and November 3, 1932. Carlos Dávila, ambassador in Washington for the Ibáñez administration, played a vital role in negotiating for the formation of COSACH. See the Dávila correspondence with his Ministry of Foreign Relations in the months of February and March, 1929, *Correspondencia: Embajada de Chile En EE. UU., 1929*, AMRE.

[139] Montero, *Confesiones políticas*, pp. 73-76. René Montero is not, in my opinion, a reliable source. His works reveal colossal conceit and opportunism. Still, in the present instance, his account has the ring of authenticity.

[140] See Alberto Edwards, *Recuerdos personales sobre los sucesos que ocasionaron el derrumbe de la administración Ibáñez* (1932); Clarence H. Haring, "The Chilean Revolution of 1931," *Hispanic American Historical Review*, XI, no. 2 (May, 1933); Raúl Marín Balmaceda, *La caída de un régimen* (1933); and H. Ochea Mena, *La revolución de julio* (1931).

[141] Alvarez Andrews, *Historia del desarrollo*, p. 232, estimated that as of 1930, 3,900,000 of the 4,289,445 Chileans lived in misery. Javier Vial Solar, *El Diluvio: estudio político* (1934), complained that in March, 1933, 77,865 beggars were licensed in Santiago—one tenth of the city's population. The following works all give valuable information on the continuing social problem from 1920 through the early 1930's: *Acción Social*, published as a monthly during the first Ibáñez administration by the Caja del Seguro Obligatorio, contained much material on social and economic conditions. Arturo Alessandri, "Las cuestiones económicos, el régimen parlamentario, y la cuestión social en Chile desde 1891 hasta 1925," *Atenea*, Año XVII, no. 299 (May, 1950). This is one of the two-time president's most valuable pieces of writing. Oscar Alvarez Andrews, *Bases para una constitución funcional* (1933). Leopoldo Arce G., *La crisis chilena: estudio político, social y económico del país* (1932); Waldemar E. Coutts, *Estudio comparativo de la frequencia y marcha de las enfermedades venéreas durante el año 1929* (1930). Karl Brünner, "Problemas actuales de urbanización," Universidad de Chile, *Conferencias de Extensión Universitaria* (1930); Antonio Cabellos Soriano, *Trabajo asalariado* (1934. *Memoria de Prueba*); Eduardo Cruz-Coke, *Medicina preventiva y medicina dirigida* (1938); Renato Donoso Henríquez, *Consideraciones acerca del problema*

inmigratorio (1928); Carlo Dragoni and E. Burnet, *L'alimentation populaire au Chili: première enquête générale de 1935: texte complet présenté au gouvernement du Chili* (1938). This is a classic report on the undernourishment of the Chilean masses, prepared by foreign technicians commissioned by President Alessandri. Jaime Feferholtz Bernstein, *Nutrición y estado económico social* (1939. *Memoria de Prueba*); Soli O. Friedenthal, *El problema del aborto: estudio médico-jurídico-social* (1937. *Memoria de Prueba*); Guillermo García Burques, *Desocupación y miseria* (1932); Osvaldo Gianini Piga, *Civilización y alcoholismo* (1930. *Memoria de Prueba*); Vicente Huidobro, *La próxima: historia que pasa en poco tiempo mas* (1934). The famous poet turned to political analysis in the troubled 1930's. Jose Husslein, *La evolución del trabajo: estudio práctico de historia social* (1932). *La Información*, a monthly published in Santiago, 1916-1928, concentrated on the social-economic-educational problem in Chile and elsewhere in the world. Raquel Kogan Bercovich, *Estudio social y jurídico del problema de la esclavitud blanco* (1934); Constantino Macchiavello Varas, *Contribución al estudio de nuestro problema de la carestía de la vida frente al problema de las subsistencias* (1933. *Memoria de Prueba*); Santiago Macchiavello Varas, *Política económica nacional: antecedentes y directivas* (1929); Guillermo Mann, *Chile luchando por nuevas formas de vida* (1935); Domingo Melfi, "Proceso de las generaciones jóvenes de Chile," *Atenea*, Año XII, no. 121 (July, 1935). Gabriela Mistral, "Christianismo con sentido social," *Atenea*, Año II, no. 9 (November, 1925); Eduardo Moore, "Causas que producen la degeneración de la raza," *Atenea*, Año I, no. 5 (June, 1924). This article, by the distinguished Liberal Party leader, is probably the best study of the period on venereal disease. Moore estimated that 13,300 died each year in Chile because of venereal diseases. Luis Arturo Moraga, *Riqueza nacional: alcoholismo y prostitución* (1937); Nicolás Novoa Valdés, *Problemas sociales* (1927); H. Orrego Puelma, *Organización y financiamiento de la lucha antituberculosa* (1937). This reveals the tremendous extent of tuberculosis in Chile during the 1930's. Valentín Panzarasa, *La justicia social* (1938); Francisco A. Pinto S.C., *Habitación popular* (1935. *Memoria de Prueba*), and *La tremenda lección* (1933). The second book deals with the decline of the national spirit, blaming it largely upon the inadequacy of the educational system. Jaime Pi-Suñer, "El problema económico de la alimentación," *Atenea*, Año VII, no. 79 (September, 1931); Moisés Poblete Troncoso, *Ensayo de bibliografía social de los paises hispanoamericanos* (1936), and *Problemas sociales y económicas de América Latina* (1936); Luis Prunes, *La prostitución* (1926). Guillermo Puelma, *Estudios médicos, sociales y morales*, 2 vols. (1932). *Revista de la Habitación: organo del Consejo Superior de Bienestar Social*. This monthly, published in Santiago, 1920-1926, contains excellent information on the housing problem. José Luis Riesco, *La revolución social* (1924). Riesco states there are only two classes in Chile: the educated, selfish upper classes, and the lower classes which, though illiterate and indolent, are bound to rise in importance. Javier Rodríguez Barros, "Hacia la despoblación: mortalidad general y mortalidad infantil: alcoholismo, esterilidad voluntaria," *Anales de la Universidad de Chile*, 2° serie, I (3° trimestre, 1923); Irma Salas Silva, *The Social-Economic Composition of the Secondary School Population in Chile* (1930). In this study, the prominent Chilean educator shows the absence of lower-class elements in secondary education enrollment. Ramón Sánchez del Pozo, *El ebrio en la legislación chilena* (1934. *Memoria de Prueba*); Horacio

Serrano, ¿Hay miseria en Chile: una respuesta (1938). Servicio Social: organo de la Escuela de Servicio Social. This useful publication first appeared in 1927. Dr. Lucas Sierra, "Es un mito la higiene pública en Chile," El Mercurio, February 18, 1926, and Nutrición: problema de transcendental importancia: ¿como se alimenta nuestro pueblo? (1930). Long a prominent doctor and government official, Sierra's studies reveal the shocking lower-class health problems. Inés Torres M., Alimentación de las clases populares (1938); Alejandro Walker Valdés, Los parlamentarios de hoy y de mañana (1921). Walker foresaw violent social upheaval if the social problem was not ameliorated. Santiago Wilson Hernández, Nuestra crisis económica y la desocupación obrera (1933. Memoria de Prueba). A few of the novels reflecting the troubled conditions of the times are: Augusto D'Halmar, Juan Lucero (1926); Joaquín Edwards Bello, El roto (1932), and Valparaíso, ciudad de viento (1931); Eugenio González, Hombres (1935)—far from being a good novel, this work by a prominent socialist at least gives an interesting insight into the struggle between anarchists, socialists and nazis; Manuel Rojas, Hombres del sur (1926) and Travesía (1934), works by a man who rose from the lower classes and understood their problems; Alberto Romero, La mala estrella de Perucho González (1935), La novela de un perseguido (1931), and La viuda del conventillo (Buenos Aires, 1930); Carlos Sepúlveda Leyton, Hijuna (1934), and La fábrica (1935).

[142] El Diario Ilustrado, August 3, 1931.

[143] Ibid., August 5, 1931.

[144] Among those making this assertion had been prominent Catholic University professor Luis Alberto Cariola, statesman-diplomat Joaquín Walker Martínez, and distinguished conservative writer Ricardo Cox Méndez. See ibid., August 9, 1925. Javier Vial Solar reached similar conclusions in a book published in 1934, El diluvio.

[145] La Nación, March 26, 1923.

[146] See the article of Rafael Luis Gumucio in El Diario Ilustrado, October 16, 1932.

[147] Edwards and Frei, Partidos, p. 226. See also Héctor Rodríguez de la Sotta, Crisis política, económica y moral: discurso al convención que celebró el Partido Conservador en Santiago (1932) and Víctor Despassier, Muerte del anarquismo (1921), p. 48.

[148] El Diario Ilustrado, August 24, 1930.

[149] Ibid., November 15, 1933.

[150] Ibid., December 20, 1933.

[151] Additional works by authors almost blindly defending the status quo, unwilling even to allow slight modifications, and often advocating a return to the customs of the past include the following. Miguel Luis Amunátegui Reyes, "Oligarquía," El Mercurio, November 2, 1932; Sergio Amunátegui, La propiedad (1932. Memoria de Prueba); José María Cifuentes, Estudio sobre la propiedad (1932); Jorge de la Cuadra Poissón, La revolución que viene (1931), and La verdad sobre las incidencias milicianas (1935); Juan Díaz Salas, Bosquejo histórico del Partido Conservador (1936); José Miguel Echenique Gandarillas, Los demoledores (1928); Diego Espoz, Ante el abismo: ¿está o no Chile al bordo de la revolución social? (1936); Sergio Fernández Larraín, Posiciones católicas ante lo económico-social (1936); Guillermo González Echenique, Refleciones de la hora presente (1934); Víctor Heuertz, "Los

peligros de la gratuidad de enseñanza," *El Imparcial*, October 6, 1933; Antonio
Huneeus Gana, "La constitución de 1833," *Revista Chilena de Historia y Geografía*, LXXIV (May-August, 1933); Jaime Larraín García Moreno, *Orientación
de nuestra política agraria* (1932); Pedro Lira Urquieta, *El futuro del país y el
Partido Conservador* (1934); Arturo Lyon Peña, "En defensa de nuestra democracia," *El Diario Ilustrado*, November 15, 1933, Father Raimundo Morales, "Socialismo y catolicismo," *El Mercurio*, July 8, 1932; Arturo Piga, *Humanismo y espíritu
nacionalista* (1927); Martín Rücker (ultimately bishop of Chillan), *Conferencias
populares, segunda serie* (1921); Alejandro Silva de la Fuente, *De medio siglo*
(1935); Eduardo Solar Correa, *La muerte de humanismo en Chile* (1934); Agustín
Zegers Baeza, *Reflexiones de actualidad* (1934) and *Sobre nuestra crisis política y
moral* (1934).
[152] *El Mercurio*, January 8, 1933.
[153] Although in general opposed to democratic processes, Liberals devoted themselves more to attacking government economic intervention than to condemning
democracy. In 1932, for example, Liberals founded the Biblioteca de Estudios
Sociales, dedicated to spreading the ideas of classical liberalism. The first publication of the group was the pamphlet by LAC (standing for Luis Arrieta Cañas),
El liberalismo y la cuestión social (1933). See also the same author's *El Marxismo
y la cuestión social* (1932). This pamphlet was warmly praised by Augusto Orrego
Luco, "El marxismo y la cuestión social," *El Mercurio*, March 11, 1933.
[154] See Raúl Marín Balmaceda, "Balmaceda y nuestro sistema política," *El Diario
Ilustrado*, July 16, 1933. In glorifying Balmaceda, Marín conceded he was a dictator: "In the 1890 crisis Congress defended the more advanced and democratic
principles. Balmaceda defended the sort of government most suited to the Chilean
character." Marín clearly felt that a dictator was what Chile needed in 1933.
[155] Other writers who implied the need for dictatorship in order to counteract the
tendency toward popular participation in the government were Francisco Antonio
Encina, *Portales*, 2 vols. (1934), commented upon favorably in the nazi publication *Acción Chilena*, II, no. 5 (May 23, 1934), and Alberto Edwards, *El gobierno
de Manuel Montt* (1933. Posthumous), commented upon favorably in *Acción
Chilena*, I, no. 3 (February 7, 1934). See also José María Cifuentes, "Portales,"
Boletín de la Academia Chilena de la Historia, Año V, no. 8 (1° semestre, 1937);
Aurelio Díaz Meza, *El advenimiento de Portales* (1932); and José Miguel Yrarráza-
val, "Portales, 'tirano' y 'dictador,' " *Boletín de la Academia Chilena de la Historia*,
Año V, no. 8 (1° semestre, 1937); Domingo Melfi, *Portales* (1930); General
Carlos Sáez Morales, *Y así vamos . . . ensayo crítico* (1938). In this, one of
Chile's most important military leaders suggested that heavy-handed political rule
and certain fascist patterns might be necessary to put Chile on the road to progress.
Finally, see *El Mercurio*, Nov. 27, 1932.
[156] See Guillermo Subercaseaux, *Historia de las doctrinas económicas en América
y en especial en Chile* (1924).
[157] See *Unión Social*, an annual published by the Unión Social Católica beginning in 1925. See also *Justicia Social*, a weekly published by Catholic elements beginning on May 1, 1922; "La Iglesia chilena y la cuestión social: carta pastoral,"
El Mercurio, September 25, 1932; Francisco Rivas Vicuña, *Nacionalismo social o
ecuaciones del sistema* (1932), and *El porvenir agrícola de Chile: introducción al*

curso de economía rural de la Universidad Católica (1930). A long-time leader in the Conservative Party, Rivas Vicuña served his country in various ministry posts and in Congress.

[158] Santiago Macchiavello Varas in his pamphlet *La tecnocracia* (1934), pp. 5-7, expressed a belief common among many Catholics that individualistic capitalism was an inherently evil system while socialism rested upon a broad humanitarian basis and never lost track of human values. For additional references to early Christian socialism in Chile see Chapter IX, notes 2-14.

[159] Catholics who would fit into this category included: Alfredo Barros Errázuriz, Clotario Blest (president in the 1920's of the *Unión de Centros de la Juventud Católica* and in the 1950's head of the Marxian labor confederation *Central Unica de Trabajadores* or CUT), Francisco Bulnes, Francisco Castillo M., Monsignor Antonio Castro, Juan E. Concha, Jorge Délano, Father Samuel Díaz Ossa, Ismael Edwards Matte, Monsignor Rafael Edwards, Father Jorge Fernández Pradel, S.J., Manuel Foster Recabarren, Eduardo Irarrázaval, Guillermo de la Jara, Jaime Larraín García Moreno, Pedro Lira, Ricardo Latcham, Bishop Rafael Lira Infante, Father Miguel Miller, Bartolomé Palacios, Trancredo Pinochet, Luis Recabarren Vial, Ricardo Salas Edwards, Emilio Tizzoni, and Joaquín Walker Martínez. Some of the more notable literature in this movement includes the following: Pedro Bustos, *La acción católica: a los intrépidos obreros de la U.S.C. Chuquicamata* (1931); Guillermo Echeverría Moorhouse, *El catolicismo ante los problemas sociales* (1933); Rafael Edwards, *Catecismo social* (1925), and *Necesitamos un público católico* (1937); Jorge Fernández Pradel, *La URSS* (1932)—in which the Jesuit argues that greater social justice is necessary in Chile to prevent the adoption of Russian models; Bartolomé Palacios Silva, *El Partido Conservador y la democracia cristiana* (1933), and *Renovación del mundo económico y social: comentario completo de las enciclicales "Rerum Novarum" y "Quadragesimo Anno"* (1934); Julio Philippi, *Economía dirigida* (1933), and *El espíritu de la acción social católica* (1935).

[160] The following are some of the works recommending that moderate concessions be made so as to preserve as much of the status quo as possible: Ladislao Errázuriz Pereira, *La doctrina liberal y la cuestión social* (1935); Gabriel González Videla, *El Partido Radical y la evolución social de Chile* (1938); René León Echaiz, *Evolución histórica de los partidos políticos chilenos* (1939), and *Liberalismo y conservatismo* (1936); Arturo Olavaría Bravo, *Debe y haber* (1936); Partido Liberal, *La crisis* (1932); Carlos Pinto Durán, *Plan de gobierno de la república: única manera de dar fin a cuarenta años de crisis* (1932)—dedicated to Arturo Alessandri; Arturo Prat Carvajal, *Artículos económicos* (1936), and *Causas políticas de la crisis* (1935); Armando Quesada Acharán, *El socialismo: la cuestión social en Chile* (1932). Quesada, a onetime diplomat and president of the Radical Party, served as rector of the University of Chile during the first Ibáñez administration. Germán Spoerer C., *Simbiosis del capital y el trabajo: la función armónica del capital y el trabajo como solución del problema social* (1938); Luis Pizarro Espoz, *La propiedad* (1926. *Memoria de Prueba*); Guillermo Subercaseaux, *La política social nacionalista moderna: a la juventud chilena que estudia y piensa* (1932); R. V. Ugarte, *La lucha de clases y su verdadera solución* (1932); Enrique Zañartu Prieto, *Hambre, miseria e ignorancia* (1938).

[161] Jobet, "Movimiento . . . ," Universidad de Chile, *Desarrollo*, I, 72-80. By 1925 there were in existence some 204 individual unions with a combined mem-

bership of around 200,000. The total active population, about 30 per cent of the national population, was just over 1,000,000. In 1925, there was founded the *Federación Obrera Regional Chilena*, representing an opposition movement to the I.W.W. influence in other labor unions.

[162] For some works dealing with the labor movement in Chile during this period see: Oscar Alvarez Andrews, *Los problemas fundamentales del sindicalismo* (1933); Octavio Cornejo Bravo, *Tendencias modernas del movimiento de asociación profesional* (1948); Aristodemo Escobar Zenteno, *Compendio de legislación social y desarrollo del movimiento obrero en Chile* (1940); Bernardo Gentilini, *Sobre comunismo, huelgas, politiquerías y otros tópicos sociales* (1927); Tuilo Lagos Valenzuela, *Bosquejo histórico del movimiento obrero en Chile* (1941. *Memoria de Prueba*). Carlos Orrego Barros, *La organización gremial y el poder político* (1932). Moisés Poblete Troncoso, *La organización sindical en Chile y otros estudios sociales* (1926).

[163] Jobet, *op. cit.*, pp. 80-85. In 1933, there were 209 industrial syndicates with close to 35,000 members, and 340 professional syndicates claiming 34,000 members. *Ibid.*, p. 93. Labor organization had clearly not yet recovered either from the blows sustained under the Ibáñez regime or from the depression.

[164] Jobet, *op. cit.*, pp. 75 ff. Edwards and Frei, *Partidos*, pp. 229-231. In 1932, the Communist Party elected two deputies to the national Congress. Later in the 1930's, communists scored a notable victory on the labor front by gaining control over the *Confederación de Trabajadores de Chile*. Founded in 1936, the CTCH had soon absorbed the majority of industrial and professional syndicates.

[165] The socialist parties were: the *Partido Socialista Marxista*, the *Partido Socialista Unificado*, the *Orden Socialista*, and the *Nueva Acción Pública*, the latter founded by Alberto Martínez—a friend and companion of the late Luis Emilio Recabarren —and Eugenio Matte Hurtado.

[166] Jobet, *op. cit.*, pp. 89-90. By 1937 the Socialist Party had elected three senators and nineteen deputies. See Edwards and Frei, *op. cit.*, p. 232. The literature pertaining to Chilean socialism and communism from 1920 to the early 1930's includes the following works: Luis M. Acuña, *Doctrinas sociales de Marx: las grandes lineas de la economía social* (1933); Mario Bravo Lavín, *Chile frente al socialismo y al comunismo* (1934); Clodomiro Cabezas Cabezas (an important socialist of the period), *Nuestro socialismo* (1932); Eduardo Cavada Riesco, *El comunismo y su propaganda en Chile* (1933). *Consigna* was a weekly socialist publication appearing in the 1930's. Carlos Contreras Labarca, *América latina invadida por el facismo* (1938). This is one of many pamphlets of the period by the secretary general of the Communist Party. Eliodoro Domínguez, *Un movimiento ideológico en Chile* (1935). Domínguez glorifies the socialist movement. *En defensa de la revolución: informes, tesis y documentos presentados al Congreso Nacional del Partido Comunista a verificarse el 19 de marzo de 1933* (1933). Marcial Figueroa (a militant socialist), *La reconstrucción chilena* (1932); René Frías Ojeda, *Consideraciones sobre nuestra política comercial exterior* (1934. *Memoria de Prueba*). This is an early effort by a man who is now a prominent figure in the Communist Party. César Godoy Urrutia (an active communist during the period), *Manifesto al magisterio de Chile* (1931) and *Los sucesos del 5 de septiembre* (1939); Gregorio Guerra (a socialist writer), *Revolución y crisis de la racionalización* (1932) and *Hacia la formación de un verdadero partido de clase* (1933). Herein are contained the resolutions of the 1933 national conference of the Chilean Communist Party.

Manuel Hidalgo and Emilio Zapata (the two communist deputies in the national Congress), *Dos discursos en el parlamento* (1933. Vol. 57-a, Colección de folletos, Biblioteca del Congreso); Julio César Jobet, *Significado del Partido Socialista en la realidad nacional* (1940). Jobet, one of the leading Marxian-socialist intellectuals in Chile, produced here a valuable work on the early history of the Chilean Socialist Party. Osvaldo Labarca Fuentes (a Marxian propagandist), *Los enanos de la libertad: los crímenes de la Corte Suprema y del gobierno de derecho contra la constitución* (1932); Alberto Mackenna Subercaseaux, *La furia roja* (1937). In this work, a distinguished member of the aristocracy writes on the communist menace. *La Opinión*, founded by Juan Bautista Rosetti, was a socialist daily, 1932-1957. Atilano Oróstegui (apparently a Marxist), *Como se vive en la pampa salitrera . . . a despertar la conciencia pampina* (Antofagasta, 1934). Eugenio Orrego Vicuña, *Tierra de aguiles* (1928). The author, a member of the aristocracy, visited Russia and upon his return wrote one of the first balanced accounts to appear in Chile on the Soviet system. Partido Communista de Chile, *Contra le dictadura fascista de Ibáñez* (1931); *Programa del Partido Social Republicana* (1931); Oscar Schnake Vergara, *Política socialista* (1938); Luis Valencia Courbis, *Sobre las rutas del porvenir* (1931). Typical of much of Chilean thought at the time, this book asserts that the future inevitably holds more socialism, less individualism. *Wikén*, a socialist weekly published 1932-1934, featured the political cartoons of Jorge Délano and occasional articles by Carlos Dávila and Joaquín Edwards Bello.

[167] See Joaquín Edwards Bello, *El nacionalismo continental*, con un prólogo por Gabriela Mistral (1935). Pedro E. Muñiz, *Penetración imperialista* (1935), also follows the Aprista line. In 1933, Alberto Grieve Madge was named secretary general of the Aprista committee in Santiago. See *La Nación*, December 1, 1933.

[168] Edwards and Frei, *Partidos*, p. 241.

[169] See Gabriel Amunátegui Jordán, *El liberalismo y su misión social* (1933).

[170] For the exposition of the nazi program, see the two major works of Jorge González von Marées: *El mal de Chile: sus causas y sus remedios* (1940), and *El problema obrera en Chile* (1923. Memoria de Prueba). The second work anticipates many of the notions that González later developed as head of the nazi movement. González also published a number of pamphlets: *La hora de decisión* (1937); *La mentira democrática* (1936); *El movimiento Nacional Socialista de Chile como única solución de la crisis política y social de Chile* (1932); *Nacismo o comunismo* (1936); *Tres discursos parlamentarios: posibilidades económicas de Chile; la verdad sobre el complot nazi y la "quinta columna;" solución del problema de la defensa nacional* (1941). Even more important are the works of Carlos Keller, who was the guiding intellectual spirit of the nazi movement. See especially his excellent study, *La eterna crisis chilena* (1931). See also his pamphlets *Como salir de la crisis* (1932); *Un país al garete* (1932); *Una revolución en marcha: el Movimiento Nacional Socialista ante la política del país* (1938). In addition, see his book *Spengler y la situación política cultural de la américa ibérica* (1927) in which, among other points, he argues for the necessity of a social hierarchy to preserve the cultural values of Ibero-América. For additional material on the nazi ideology in Chile see the prologue which onetime nazi Fernando Ortúzar wrote for *Mussolini define el fascismo* (1933). See also F. J. Díaz, "Los nazis," *El Mercurio*, June 26, 1932, and "Los nazis y la colectividad alemana," *ibid.*, July 29, 1932, and *Ideario Nacista: colección de artículos publicado en la página Nacional Socialista del diario*

"El Imparcial" (1933). This book is a compilation of nazi propaganda originally published in *El Imparcial*, largely written by Fernando Ortúzar Vial and René Silva Espejo.

[171] Originally appearing to be fervently sincere in his reform aspirations, González probably became obsessed with holding and extending his power, until by 1938 he showed signs of having become a cynical opportunist who was, at least temporarily, emotionally and nervously unbalanced. The finest treatment of the González personality is the Carlos Keller novel, *La locura de Juan Bernales* (1949). The protagonist of the novel, Juan Bernales, is meant to be Jorge González von Marées.

[172] In the early 1930's, *El Imparcial*, which often supported right-wing Liberal Party policy, was strongly pro-nazi. Its editorials averred that democracy had failed, and advocated the corporate state. In 1933, René Silva Espejo (today associated with *El Mercurio*), Fernando Ortúzar Vial, and Huberto Grez Silva—all of them respected intellectuals and journalists—helped found *El Debate* which was avowedly dedicated to the nazi cause. Toward the end of 1933, Ortúzar and his associates on *El Debate* broke with González von Marées, accusing him of betraying the real spirit of nazism. *El Debate* continued briefly as the alleged organ of true nazism. See *La Opinión*, December 21, 1933. *Acción Chilena*, edited by Carlos Keller and published weekly from January 24, 1934, to November, 1937, and sporadically in 1941 and 1942, was one of the official organs of the Nazi Party. Another nazi publication was *El Trabajo*. Starting as a weekly in 1933, it shortly became a daily and continued publication until 1938. Keller was prominently associated with the paper.

[173] *El Diario Ilustrado*, October 10, 1932. Ricardo Boizard, "Nazis," *ibid.*, June 30, 1933. Letter of Osvaldo F. de Castro, *ibid.*, August 26, 1933. *El Mercurio*, November 8, 1932.

[174] One of these was Guillermo Subercaseaux. See the letter of F. J. Díaz in *El Mercurio* July 29, 1932. See Subercaseaux, "El calificativo de socialista dada a nuestra república," *El Mercurio*, July 1, 1932, stating that nazism was in harmony with the culture of the German people. Enrique Zañartu Prieto, Minister of the Treasury, also admired nazi proficiency. See his *Una exposición completa del Ministro de Hacienda sobre la convertibilidad en oro* (1932). See also *El Diario Ilustrado*, October 22, 1932.

[175] Speech of González, Cámara de Diputados, *Boletín de sesiones ordinarias*, 1938, Sesión 9°, p. 502.

[176] The anti-Semitic aspect of nazi propaganda, however, would not necessarily have been repugnant to Chileans. Extreme rightist Ricardo Latcham was strongly anti-Semitic and in his book *Chuquicamata: estado yankee* (1926), esp. p. 51, blamed many of Chile's troubles on the "Wall-Street Jews." The priest Emilio Vaïsse (pseudonym, Omer Emeth) also disliked Jews. See his article in *El Mercurio*, May 29, 1927. Even socialist Deputy Humberto Casali charged the second Alessandri administration with favoring the exploitation of Chile by Jewish imperialists. See Cámara de Diputados, *Boletín de sesiones ordinarias*, 1933, Sesión 4°, May 29, 1933. Besides consulting *Acción Chilena* and *El Trabajo*, especially after 1936, for signs of nazi anti-Semitism in Chile, see the one-page hate sheet put out by the National Socialist Party in 1933: *Nuestra industria salitrera agoniza bajo garras del judaismo internacional; el país no puede tolerar la resurección de la COSACH*. Nor would the nazi attack against Masons (See *El Trabajo*, March 12, 1937, for

example) have disturbed the more conservative Catholic elements. Even in the early 1920's, *El Diario Ilustrado* looked upon most of Chile's ills as resulting from various Masonic plots. See the April 6, 1923, edition. See also the June 3, 1920, attack on the Masonic journal edited by Luis A. Navarrete y López, *La Verdad*, and the June 30, 1920, attack on Enrique Molina, partly on the grounds that he was a Mason.

[177] *El Trabajo*, March 19, 1937.

[178] *Ibid.*

[179] For additional material pertaining to Chilean nazism see Miguel Cruchaga Ossa, *El tercer reich* (1934), and Cruchaga, *et al.*, *Ibero-américa y alemania* (Berlin, 1934). Cruchaga Ossa was fanatically pro-nazi. Luis D. Cruz Ocampo, "El fracaso de la democracia," *Atenea*, Año X, no. 100 (August, 1933), asserted that democracy was dead and argued in favor of fascistic patterns. Guillermo Izquierdo, *El gobierno representativo* (1931), and *La racionalización de la democracia* (1934). An important nazi in the 1930's, Izquierdo was later a supporter of Peronismo and *justicialismo* and of the neo-fascistic movement in Chile. Gabriel González Videla, "Los procedimientos de los nacistas criollos," *La Nación*, September 3, 1933. González Videla was one of the most outspoken anti-nazis in Chile. Juan Noé, "¿Un estudio del fascismo en su X aniversario?" *El Mercurio*, December 5, 1932. Italian-born, but long a resident in Chile, Noé was a strong champion of fascist government in Chile. Nucleo Nacista de Temuco, *Nacismo chileno: un estudio social* (Temuco, 1933). *Reportage conservador al Jefe del Nacismo* (1936). Manuel Antonio Vittini, *¿Panamericanismo o zollverein americano? Crónicas internacionales desde la conferencia panamericana de Santiago hasta la conferencia de Buenos Aires*, con prólogo por Guillermo Izquierdo (1938).

[180] Jobet, "Movimiento . . . ," Universidad de Chile, *Desarrollo*, I, 84.

[181] Quoted in Francisco A. Pinto S.C., *Estructura de nuestra economía* (1948), p. 215.

[182] *El Mercurio*, July 7, 1932, quotes this conclusion of D. S. Iglehart, voiced in New York City.

[183] Pinto, *op. cit.*, p. 216. By 1932 the total value of Chilean exports fell to one fourth of what it had been in 1929. CEPAL, *Antecedentes sobre el desarrollo de la economía chilena, 1925-1952*, I, 33.

[184] Pinto, *op. cit.*, p. 216, gives figures to show that imports in 1932 were only 10 per cent of the 1929 level. CEPAL, *op. cit.*, p. 32 presents figures that represent closer to 20 per cent. Enrique Marshall, "Finanzas y sistema monetario," Universidad de Chile, *Desarrollo*, I, 269 ff., supports the CEPAL figures.

[185] Francisco Walker Linares, "Evolución social," Universidad de Chile, *op. cit.*, I, 38. See also Rodrigo Aburto, "Los empleados cesantes y la colonización," *El Diario Ilustrado*, July 23, 1933.

[186] Oscar Parrao S., *Las cooperativas del consumo ante el problema del encarecimiento de la vida* (1934), p. 6. Parrao was at the time chief of the governmental Department of Cooperatives and his figures are based on official government statistics.

[187] Marshall, "Finanzas y sistema monetario," Universidad de Chile, *op. cit.*, I, 270. Other useful works on the effects of the depression in Chile include the following: Merwin L. Bohan (commercial attaché of the United States Embassy in Chile), "Chile ante el mundo: la situación económico de Chile," *Economía y finanzas*, Año II, no. 15 (January, 1938); *Chile Financiero y Económico* was a fortnightly that

appeared first in 1930; Alberto Cruchaga C., "La crisis y sus realidades," *Economía y Finanzas*, Año I, no. 2 (primera quincena, February, 1937); Manuel Francisco Sánchez, *Política, economía y corporaciones* (1936. *Memoria de Prueba*); Manuel Silva Balbuena, *La especulación en la economía* (1939); Charles Alexander Thomson, "Chile Struggles for National Recovery," *Foreign Policy Reports*, IX, no. 25 (February 14, 1934).

[188] Emilio Bello, *Recuerdos políticos*, pp. 218-220. Edwards and Frei, *Partidos*, pp. 212-214.

[189] Montero had shown little concern for lower-class living conditions in his 1901 *Memoria de Prueba: La responsibilidad del ebrio*.

[190] Edwards and Frei, *op. cit.*, pp. 216-217.

[191] See Manuel Aránguiz Latorre, *El 4 de junio* (1933); Alfredo Guillermo Bravo (Minister of Education under President Montero), *4 de junio: festín de los audaces* (1932); and Jorge Grove V. (a socialist senator in the 1930's), *Descorriendo el velo: episodio de los doce días de la República Socialista* (Valparaíso, 1933).

[192] *El Diario Ilustrado*, September 4, 1932.

[193] See speech of Gabriel González Videla, Cámara de Diputados, *Boletín de sesiones ordinarias*, 1938, Sesión 25°, July, 1938, pp. 1183 ff.

[194] *El Mercurio*, November 1, 1932.

[195] Rodríguez de la Sotta received over 46,000 votes, and Zañartu Prieto nearly 43,000, *ibid.*, November 1, 1932.

[196] Grove won the impressive total of 60,965, while Lafertte received only 4,652. See *ibid.*

[197] See the biweekly publication of the Republican Militia, *Boletín Informativa*, appearing 1933-1936. Terrance Tarr, on the basis of research conducted while in Chile on a Doherty Foundation award, has written a doctoral dissertation, completed in 1960 at the University of Florida, on the Republican Militia. See also Francisco Huneeus, *Actitud de las fuerzas armadas* (1932). The conservative Huneeus abhorred the influence of the military in politics.

CHAPTER 7

[1] Bolivia and Peru did try to enlist the aid of the League of Nations in their dispute with Chile. But by 1922, Chile had defeated these endeavors, with Agustín Edwards taking a leading part in arguing the Chilean case before the League. See *MMRE, 1919-1923*, pp. 124-125, 393-447.

[2] These had occurred in 1893-1894, 1898, 1900-1901, 1902, 1905-1907, 1908-1910, 1912, and 1919. See *MMRE, 1923-1926*, pp. 48-207.

[3] Historian Guillermo Feliú Cruz delivered the reply to the paper entitled "La 'segunda independencia'" read by Barros Jarpa in 1956 upon his reception into the Chilean Academy of History. In this reply, Feliú Cruz referred at length to the new international thought which Barros Jarpa had succeeded in introducing into Chilean foreign affairs beginning in 1920. He noted that since the time of his *Memoria de Prueba* published in 1914, Barros Jarpa had been a strong critic of Chile's traditional antiarbitration policy. Feliú Cruz strongly implied that what Barros Jarpa had in mind was South and even Latin-American unity as a means of opposing the overweening influence of the United States. Barros Jarpa, *La 'segunda*

independencia' (1956), pp. 109-111. See also Barros Jarpa, *Hacia la solución* (1921), a strong justification of the new tendencies in Chilean diplomacy. Important also is the same author's *Esquema de derecho internacional pública* (1938).

⁴ Beginning again in 1919, Chile had begun to fear renewed Argentine support for the Peruvian position. This had undermined the Argentine-Chilean rapport that had proved so useful in dealing with the United States during the Wilson regime. See Eduardo Ruiz Vergara, secretary of the Legation of Chile in Buenos Aires, to his Ministry of Foreign Relations, March 1, 1919, *Correspondencia de Legaciones de Chile en Argentina, Colombia y Costa Rica, 1919*, AMRE. At this time, the Chilean Legation in Buenos Aires had begun publication of *La defensa de Chile*, designed to explain and justify Chile's position to the Argentines. In his March 15, 1919, letter to his Ministry, Ruiz enclosed the fifth number of the publication.

⁵ Fernando Matte Hurtado, *El arbitraje en américa, especialmente en Chile* (1922. *Memoria de Prueba*), pp. 45-49.

⁶ MMRE, 1919-1923, pp. 487-490. In the book by Conrado Ríos Gallardo, *Chile y Perú: los pactos de 1929* (1959), the portion of the narrative covering these events is taken largely from this carefully written 1919-1923 *Memoria*.

⁷ Beltrán Mathieu to Chilean Ministry of Foreign Relations, May 2, 1921, *Embajada de Chile en EE. UU. y Legaciones en Ecuador, Panamá y México, 1921*, AMRE.

⁸ See telegrams of Barros Jarpa to Peruvian Foreign Relations Minister Alberto Salomón, December 12 and 26, 1921, MMRE, 1919-1923, pp. 492-498, 506-507.

⁹ See Joseph Shea to Barros Jarpa, January 18, 1922, and Barros Jarpa to Shea, January 18, *ibid.*, pp. 513-515. See also Mathieu to Chilean Ministry of Foreign Relations, February 10 and 15, 1922, *Embajada de Chile en EE. UU. y Legación en Japón, 1922*, AMRE, as well as the January 19 and 20, 1922, edition of *El Diario Ilustrado, El Mercurio,* and *La Nación,* all of which are favorable to the United States offer.

¹⁰ As delegates plenipotentiary, Chile appointed Carlos Aldunate Solar and Luis Izquierdo. The appointment of Aldunate, who carried the brunt of the load in arguing the Chilean position, was a shrewd move by Alessandri. For many years a distinguished statesman and politician, Aldunate had served both as a national deputy and senator, and as Minister of Foreign Relations—a post that Izquierdo had also filled. Aldunate had also been a professor of civil law at the University of Chile and at the Catholic University. More important, in 1921 he had been elected president of the Conservative Party. By appointing him to represent Chile in the Washington discussions, Alessandri apparently hoped to overcome the anticipated Conservative opposition to the entire proceedings. Two indications of the Conservative opposition that did develop are the books published in 1922: Luis Barros Borgoño, *La cuestión del Pacífico y las nuevas orientaciones de Bolivia,* and Joaquín Walker Martínez, *La Cuestión del Pacífico: una revancha con sangre ajena.*

Alejandro Alvarez (see note 38) accompanied Aldunate and Izquierdo to Washington in the capacity of counselor. The Peruvian delegation was made up of Melitón F. Porras, Hernán Velarde (delegates plenipotentiary) and Solón Polo (counselor). See Arturo Alessandri, *Recuerdos de gobierno* (1952), pp. 134-147; Ministerio de Relaciones Exteriores de Chile, *Las conferencias de Washington:*

antecedentes reunidos por orden del Ministro de Relaciones Exteriores, don Ernesto Barros Jarpa (1922), p. 5; and *MMRE*, 1919-1923, pp. 517 ff.

[11] Ministerio de Relaciones Exteriores de Chile, *loc. cit.*

[12] The climate of discussion was not improved by the propaganda war to which the regularly accredited diplomatic agents of Peru and Chile in Washington resorted. See, for example, Mathieu to the Chilean Ministry of Foreign Relations, May 11, 1922, *Embajada de Chile en EE. UU. y Legación en Japón*, 1922, AMRE. This letter tells of the preparation and distribution of 3000 copies of *Tacna and Arica and the Washington Negotiations* (Washington, D.C., 1922), aimed at counteracting the "lies" of Peruvian propaganda efforts. See also the Mathieu letter of October 10, 1922, describing the use he was going to make of the recently received pamphlet of Monsignor Rafael Edwards, *Rélations entre le Chili et le Pérou* (1922).

[13] Mathieu to Ministry, June 21, 1922, *ibid.*, AMRE. See also Luis Barros Borgoño, "Las negociones chilenos-peruanos en Washington," *Revista de Política Internacional*, I (1° trimestre, 1922), and Ministerio de Relaciones Exteriores de Chile, *op. cit.*, pp. 31-46. For the Chilean case presented in Washington see *MMRE*, 1923-1926, pp. 47-207. For the Peruvian case, see *ibid.*, pp. 210-266. See also *MMRE*, 1919-1923, pp. 565 ff.

[14] See Ministerio de Relaciones Exteriores, *op. cit.*, pp. 46-51, 71-101, and *MMRE*, 1919-1923, pp. 552-554.

[15] See Adolfo Calderón Cousiño, *Breve historia diplomática de las relaciones chileno-peruanas* (1926).

[16] Included in this category would be such men as Eliodoro Yáñez, Gonzalo Bulnes, and Guillermo Rivera, all on the Senate Committee on Foreign Relations at the time, and Ladislao Errázuriz, Joaquín Walker Martínez, Maximiliano Ibáñez, Galvarino Gallardo Nieto, President of the Senate Luis Claro Solar, and Enrique Mac-Iver. Mac-Iver's last important political efforts were directed toward preventing ratification of the 1922 protocol. He spoke against the instrument on August 11 and 12, 1922. See Cámara de Senadores, *Boletín de sesiones ordinarias*, 1922, Sesión 43°, and 44°. On August 21, the elderly Radical Party leader died.

[17] For information on this opposition see Alessandri, *Recuerdos*, pp. 150 ff., and *La Nación*, July 14, 19, 22, and August 20, 1922. See also Luis D. Cruz Ocampo, "No mas doctrina de Monroe," *Atenea*, Año I, no. 5 (August, 1924).

[18] *El Mercurio*, January 1, 1923.

[19] The deputies debated the protocol ratification issue for thirty-eight sessions, finally approving it 78-27. See Cámara de Diputados, *Boletín de sesiones extraordinarias*, 1922-1923, Sesión 48°, November 14, 1922. The Conservative deputies were split on the matter, twelve voting against, twelve in favor of the protocol. The twelve who voted negatively represented the largest numerical bloc of any single political party in opposition to the protocol. The Conservative split was reflected in *El Diario Ilustrado* which during October and November could not decide whether to oppose or favor the protocol.

[20] For the Chilean argument presented before the president of the United States see: *Alegato de la república de Chile presentado al señor presidente de los Estados Unidos en su carácter del arbitrio de acuerdo con las disposiciones del protocolo y acta complementaria subscritos por Chile y el Perú en Washington el 20 de julio de 1922* (1922), *Anexos del alegato de la república de Chile presentado al presi-*

dente de los Estados Unidos como arbitrio (1924), and Arbitraje sobre Tacna y Arica, 3 vols. (1924).

[21] At the time of the Coolidge decision, the provisional junta of Emilio Bello Codesido, General Pedro Pablo Dartnell and Admiral Carlos Ward was awaiting the return of Arturo Alessandri, who resumed his rule on March 20. See Bello, Recuerdos políticos: la junta de gobierno de 1925, su origen y relación con la reforma del régimen constitucional (1954), pp. 151-153, and Ríos Gallardo, Chile y Perú, p. 76.

[22] MMRE, 1923-1926, p. 269.

[23] This was the conclusion reached on October 20, 1925, in secret session by the Chilean delegation at Arica. Presided over by Agustín Edwards, the delegation included Samuel Claro Lastarria, Manuel Foster Recabarren, Manuel A. Maira, Galvarino Gallardo Nieto, Víctor Robles, José Luis Santa María, Héctor Claro Solar, Guillermo Guerra, Antonio Planet, Guillermo Garay, Jorge Aldunate, Luis Arteaga, Luis Barcelo, and Emiliano Bustos. See Ríos Gallardo, Chile y Perú, pp. 105-106.

[24] Agustín Edwards, Recuerdos de mi persecución (1932), pp. 23-33.

[25] See Alessandri, Recuerdos, p. 170, Ríos Gallardo, op. cit., p. 83, and El Mercurio, November 1, 1925.

[26] See Edwards, Memoria presentada al Supremo Gobierno por el miembro Agustín Edwards en la Comisión Plebiscitaria (1926).

[27] MMRE, 1923-1926, pp. 279, 324, 326, 327-329. Ríos Gallardo, op. cit., p. 97. El Mercurio, November 29, 1925.

[28] El Mercurio, November 12, 24, and 29, 1925. See also Cuestiones plebiscitarias (Tacna, 1926), an excellent collection of the editorials of the Arica daily La Aurora (1914-1929) defending the Chilean position in the Tacna-Arica plebiscite proceedings.

[29] El Mercurio, December 26, 1925.

[30] Ibid., December 4, 1925.

[31] See Ríos Gallardo, op. cit., pp. 98-99.

[32] MMRE, 1923-1926, pp. 346, 355-356. See also Miguel Cruchaga, Chilean ambassador in Washington, to Secretary of State Frank Kellogg, August 14, 1926, Correspondencia de la Embajada de Chile en EE. UU. y Legación en Japón, 1926, AMRE, with accompanying memorandum prepared by Samuel Claro.

[33] See J. Luis Fermandois, "La historia se repite: otra vez un hombre norteamericano contra Chile," El Mercurio, June 13, 1926. See also Joaquín Edwards Bello, Tacna y Arica (1926), and José Sáenz, He visto y acuso: motivos plebiscitarios (Iquique, 1926).

[34] El Mercurio, June 11, 1926.

[35] Ibid., May 11, 1926.

[36] Ibid., June 18, 1926, report of a United Press interview with Alessandri who was in Washington at the time. It was also during this period that Alessandri referred to the United States as a nation of giants ruled by pygmies. See Washington Evening Star, December 24, 1932. Moreover, in 1926 such Chilean political leaders as Agustín Edwards, Jorge Alessandri Rodríguez, and Jorge Matte C. engaged with United States Ambassador William Miller Collier in an unfortunate and extremely heated newspaper debate over plebiscite proceedings and good offices. See El

Mercurio, June 1, 2, 3, and 7, 1926; Alessandri, *Recuerdos*, p. 186; and Edwards, *Recuerdos*, pp. 23-25. In particular, former Minister of Foreign Relations Barros Jarpa carried on an acrid and widely publicized exchange with Collier. See *El Mercurio*, June 1, 1926, and Barros Jarpa, "La situación internacional: la extraña irrupción de los 'buenos oficios'; el proceso de la invitación; el desarrollo de las negociaciones; la marcha del plebiscito," *Revista Chilena*, Año X, no. 74 (April, 1926).

[87] *MMRE*, 1919-1923, p. 12.

[88] Alvarez had represented his country at the 1901-1902 Mexico City Pan-American Conference. In 1906, he had been named juridical adviser to the Ministry of Foreign Relations, a post he held for six years. To help prepare his country's delegation for its part in the Second Hague Conference, he published in 1907 *Chile ante la segunda conferencia de la Haya*. In the same year he was named a member of the Hague Permanent Court of Arbitration, a post he continued to hold until 1920. In 1910 he was a member of the Chilean delegation to the Buenos Aires Pan-American Conference. From 1916 to 1918, under the auspices of the Carnegie Endowment for International Peace, he delivered lectures at United States universities and before learned societies on "International Law and Related Subjects from the Point of View of the American Continent." In 1922, he published a book of this title (Washington, D.C.). In the same year he served as counselor of the Chilean delegation sent to Washington to discuss settlement of the Tacna-Arica controversy. From that time on, Alvarez increasingly spent his time abroad, holding a faculty post at the *Institut des Hautes Etudes Internationales*. In 1962 he was living in Paris, still intellectually active, and a judge of the International Court of Justice. A sketchy biographical study of Alvarez is Fernando Gamboa Serazzi, *Alejandro Alvarez: su vida, su obra* (1955. *Memoria de Prueba*). See also the preface by Carlos Castro Ruiz to Alejandro Alvarez, *La reconstrucción del derecho de gentes: el nuevo orden y la renovación social* (1944); Percy Alvin Martin, editor, *Who's Who in Latin America* (2nd edition, 1940); and José María Velasco Ibarra, *Experiencias jurídicas hispanoamericanas: Bolívar, Alejandro Alvarez, Alberdi* (Buenos Aires, 1934). In this, the several-times president of Ecuador presents a penetrating study of Alvarez' contributions to American international law. A few of the many works by Alvarez not cited elsewhere in this chapter's notes include: *L'esprit américain et la vie internationale* (Paris, 1928); "Influencia de la América Latina en la future vida internacional," *Anales de la Universidad de Chile*, 2° serie, Año I (1° y 2° trimestres, 1923); "International Life and International Law in America, their Development during the Last Fifty Years," *Bulletin of the Pan-American Union, Commemorative Issue of the Fiftieth Anniversary of the Pan-American Union* (April, 1940); "Latin America and International Law," *American Journal of International Law*, III (April, 1909); *Le nouveau droit international public et sa codification en Amérique, plan developpé des matières d'un ouvrage en 2 volumes, devant paraître sous ce titre, et être présenté à l'Assemblé des Juristes Américains, à Rio de Janeiro en 1925, pour la Codification du Droit International* (Paris, 1924); "El panamericanismo y la política internacional de América," *Revista Chilena*, Año VI, Tomo XV, nos. 59, 60 (March, April, 1923); *Le panaméricainisme et la VI conférence panaméricaine* (Paris, 1928). The most valuable account in English of the development of the concept of American international law and of the activities

of the Rio Commission of American Jurisconsults is Samuel F. Bemis, *The Latin American Policy of the United States* (New York, 1943), esp. Chapters XIII and XIV.

³⁹ See Chapter I, notes 77, 78 and 83-86. See also Alvarez, *L'histoire diplomatique des repúbliques américaines et la conférence de Mexico* (Paris, 1902). In this book Alvarez maintains that the United States has abused the Monroe Doctrine in the interest of imperialism. The 1889 Washington Conference, according to Alvarez, marked the inception of United States imperialism. See also Alvarez, *The Monroe Doctrine: its Importance in the International Life of the States of the New World* (New York, 1924), and *La nueva tendencia en el estudio de derecho civil* (1900).

⁴⁰ See Chapter I, notes 96-98.

⁴¹ President Ramón Barros Luco had come to the same conclusion in 1915, averring that the Latin-American states must accept the inevitability of dealing and co-operating with the United States in some sort of a common hemisphere policy. See *El Mercurio*, January 1, 1916. Similar sentiments were expressed by the philosopher-educator and traditional friend of the United States Enrique Molina, "El nacionalismo y la solidaridad americana," *Atenea*, Año II, no. 2 (April, 1925).

⁴² In *Le droit internationale américain* (Paris, 1910), Alvarez asserted that United States policy in Latin America was one of imperialism, based upon the desire for hegemony. See especially Chapter V of the Alvarez work. United States actions in connection with the Alsop Company dispute (1908-1909) had intensified this conviction. Alvarez had helped devise in Washington a fair and just settlement of the matter, only to see his efforts nullified by the truculent dollar diplomacy pursued by Secretary of State Philander C. Knox. For information on the Alsop case, the reader is referred to Chapter V of this book, notes 101-103. See also Alvarez, *Las conferencias panamericanas* (1911), in which the author expressed his hostility to the United States. In addition, see Gamboa Serazzi, *Alejandro Alvarez*, p. 40.

⁴³ Sergio Fernández Larraín, *América y el principio de no intervención* (1947), avers with some justification that in Chile the notion of American international law was devised as a means of combating United States encroachments.

⁴⁴ *MMRE*, 1927, p. 210. This *Memoria* contains one of the best accounts published in Chile on the development of the American international law concept in that country. See also Miguel Cruchaga Tocornal, *La responsibilidad internacional de los estados* (1942), *Nociones de derecho internacional* (1899), and Miguel Cruchaga and Alberto Cruchaga Ossa, *Derecho internacional* (1944).

⁴⁵ J. Ruiz Gamboa, Chilean chargé d'affaires in Rio, to his Ministry of Foreign Relations, April 10, 1906, *Legación de Chile en Brasil*, 1906, AMRE.

⁴⁶ Gamboa Serazzi, *op. cit.*, p. 43.

⁴⁷ *Le droit internationale américain.*

⁴⁸ By this time also the Pan-American movement had begun seriously to concern itself with the concept of American international law. The Rio Commission of American Jurisconsults presented a report on the codification of private and public international law applicable in America at the 1910 Buenos Aires meeting of American states. With Alvarez presenting some of the most cogent arguments, the Rio Commission at Buenos Aires asserted the existence of American international law. Two years later the Commission of Jurisconsults met in Rio, where Alvarez again argued strongly for the principle of American international law. See Gamboa Serazzi, *op. cit.*, p. 82. See also Alvarez, *Las conferencias panamericanas*; *La*

Conferencia Pan-Americana de Buenos Aires: informe presentado por los delegados de Chile (1911), p. 50; Miguel Cruchaga, Chilean ambassador in Washington, to his Ministry of Foreign Relations, June 21, 1927, *Correspondencia de la Embajada de Chile en EE. UU.*, 1927, AMRE; Fernández Larraín, *América y el principio de no intervención*, pp. 13-16; Luis Guillén Atienza, *El principio internacional de no intervención y las doctrinas americanas* (1949. *Memoria de Prueba*), pp. 89 ff.; and José M. Saavedra Viollier, *Las conferencias panamericanas y el derecho internacional privado* (1955. *Memoria de Prueba*).

[49] Alvarez gave the most concrete exposition of this thesis at the 1917 Havana meeting of the American Institute of International Law, in a paper entitled, "The Fundamental Rights of the American Continent." Alvarez and his United States friend James Brown Scott had taken the first steps in 1912 to create the Institute of American International Law. Scott served as the first president and Alvarez as the first secretary of the Institute. Active also in the Institute were Luis Barros Borgoño, Eliodoro Yáñez, and Antonio Huneeus. See Fernández Larraín, *op. cit.*, p. 14; Gamboa Serazzi, *op. cit.*, pp. 11 ff.; Guillén, *op. cit.*, p. 79; MMRE, 1927, pp. 600-601.

[50] At the Buenos Aires Pan-American Conference, and at the Rio Meeting of Jurisconsults, respectively.

[51] Guillén, *op. cit.*, p. 82. See also Ramón Bustos García, *Nociones sobre la intervención* (1944), and Manuel Guzmán Vial, *La intervención y la no intervención* (1948. *Memoria de Prueba*). At the 1912 meeting of the Rio Commission of American Juriconsults, John Bassett Moore had presented the United States arguments against the notion of American international law.

[52] As early as 1903, Alvarez had been an advocate of ABC unity, hoping that strength could thereby be achieved for dealing with the United States on terms of equality. See "Hace trece años un chileno vió el ABC," *Zig Zag* (May 15, 1915); Gamboa Serazzi, *op. cit.*, pp. 121-131; and *El Mercurio*, December 15, 1904.

[53] Cruchaga had been the Chilean envoy in Argentina, 1909-1911, and a delegate to the Fourth Pan-American Conference in Buenos Aires, 1910. He was serving as Chilean envoy to Germany and Austria-Hungary when war erupted in 1914. In the same year he was appointed for a six-year term to the Hague Permanent Court of Arbitration. An author and professor of international law at the University of Chile, Cruchaga played an important role in the solution of the Mexican Church-State controversy, 1927-1929. Twice an ambassador to the United States (1926-1927, 1931-1932) Cruchaga served as the first Minister of Foreign Relations for the second Arturo Alessandri administration. For some of his publications, see Note 44. See also Alfonso Bulnes, "Don Miguel Cruchaga Tocornal," *Boletín de la Academia Chilena de la Historia*, Año XVI, no. 40 (1° semestre, 1949), and Conrado Ríos Gallardo, "Don Miguel Cruchaga, el diplomático," *ibid.*

[54] See Ricardo Montaner Bello, *Derecho internacional* (1916), *Negociaciones diplomáticas entre Chile y el Perú* (1934), and "Nuevas prácticas internacionales," *El Mercurio*, October 10, 1930.

[55] As early as 1919, in fact, Alvarez himself had considered the League a potentially valuable means of offsetting United States control of Latin America. See the *La Nación*, December 26, 1919, report on a conference given by Alvarez at the Academy of Political and Moral Sciences in Paris. For an expression of similar sentiment see the speech of Senator Carlos Aldunate Solar, Cámara de Senadores,

Boletín de sesions ordinarias, 1919, Sesión of August 4, 1919, pp. 669-679. See also Agustín Edwards, *La américa latina y la liga de las naciones* (1937), p. 7. Edwards refers to the League as having represented in its initial stages a possible counter-influence to the United States in Latin America. Moreover, Carlos Arangua Rivas, *La intervención: doctrinas de Monroe, Drago y Tobar* (1924) and Francisco Rivas Vicuña, *La politique chilienne de coopération internationale* (Tokyo,. 1919), both regarded the League in the same light. See also Luis Barros Borgoño, *La liga de las naciones* (1920). Arturo Alessandri, upon becoming alarmed by what he considered the prejudiced attitude of Pershing in the Tacna-Arica plebiscite commission, had attempted to enlist the aid of the League of Nations to prevent the United States from exceeding the scope of the Coolidge arbitration decision. See Alessandri, *Recuerdos*, p. 199.

The most notable instance in which Chile turned to the League as a possible counterbalance to the United States occurred in connection with the Geneva Protocol of 1924. This instrument provided for arbitration of disputes that the League Council could not settle and extended the compulsory jurisdiction of the World Court. Article XVI of the protocol provided that a. nonsignatory state should be invited to accept the conditions of the protocol in case of conflict with a signatory. If the state so invited refused and resorted to war against a signatory state, the League could apply sanctions against it. This article obviously created the possibility that a Latin-American signatory state might seek League support in a dispute with the nonsignatory United States. As a result, the United States regarded the Geneva Protocol as a threat to the Monroe Doctrine and succeeded in persuading Great Britain to take the lead in opposing adoption of the instrument. In the meantime, Chile had become one of the most enthusiastic supporters of the protocol, not only because it excepted from arbitration matters previously settled by treaty and therefore backed the Chilean position vis-à-vis Tacna and Arica, but also because the instrument opened the way for enlisting League influence in disputes with the United States. For an excellent description of the protocol and United States attitudes toward it see David D. Burks, "The United States and the Geneva Protocol of 1924, 'A New Holy Alliance?'," *American Historical Review*, LXIV, no. 4 (July, 1959), 891-905. For indications that Chile regarded the protocol as a means of bringing about League intervention in the American Hemisphere to offset United States influence see *V Asamblea de la Sociedad de las Naciones, Memoria de la delegación chilena*, 1924, AMRE, pp. 36, 37, 39. The head of the Chilean delegation to the Fifth League Assembly was Enrique Villegas. Representing Chile at the Sixth Assembly (1925), both Eliodoro Yáñez and Emilio Bello Codesido praised the protocol, and voiced regret that the British attitude had temporarily killed the project. See *MMRE*, 1923-1926, pp. 444, 447, 457-459. In one of his speeches, Yáñez implied resentment that behind-the-scenes United States actions had been responsible for rejection of the protocol. See *ibid.*, pp. 459-460. See also Alejandro Alvarez, *La réforme du part de la Societé des Nations sur des bases continentales et régionales* (Paris, 1926), pp. 170-174; Beltrán Mathieu to Chilean Ministry of Foreign Relations, December 8, 1924, *Correspondencia de las Embajadas de Chile en Brasil y EE. UU.*, 1924, AMRE; interview with Agustín Edwards in London, reported in *Las Ultimas Noticias* and *El Mercurio*, September 3, 1924; interview with Enrique Villegas in *La Nación*, September 28, 1924; *El Diario Ilustrado*, February 11, 1923. See also the *El Mercurio* report, September 22, 1924, on a Geneva newspaper observation that Latin America had become interested in the League, seeing in it the means of escaping United States tutelage, and Martín Drouilly, "Sin la Liga de las Naciones, el caos," *ibid.*, January 1 and 2, 1920.

[56] The Alvarez line of reasoning described in the text emerges when one reads carefully between the lines in two of his works: *La réforme du part de la Societé des Nations*, pp. 160-174, and *La cinquième conférence panaméricaine et la Societé des Nations* (Paris, 1924).

[57] The conference convened on March 25, 1923. Chile was represented by Agustín Edwards, Carlos Aldunate Solar, Luis Barros Borgoño, Emilio Bello Codesido, Antonio Huneeus, Manuel Rivas Vicuña, Alcibiades Roldán, Guillermo Subercaseaux, and Alejandro Alvarez as technical advisor and secretary. See *MMRE*, 1919-1923, p. 257; Miguel Cruchaga Tocornal, "Las conferencias panamericanas," *Revista Chilena*, Año XI, nos. 86-87 (June-July, 1927), and nos. 88-89 (August-September, 1927); "La quinta conferencia panamericana," *ibid.*, Año VI, nos. 59-60 (March-April, 1923); and the giant, eighty-eight page edition of *El Mercurio*, March 25, 1923.

[58] Izquierdo was at the time Chile's Minister of Foreign Relations. Augustín Edwards was elected permanent president of the proceedings.

[59] *MMRE*, 1919-1923, pp. 236-238.

[60] Alvarez, *La codificación del derecho internacional en américa* (1923).

[61] See the excellent study by Thomas McGann, *Argentina, the United States and the Inter-American System, 1880-1914* (Cambridge, Massachusetts, 1957).

[62] See Gamboa Serazzi, *Alejandro Alvarez*, pp. 47-48. For a complete exposition of the Antokeletz position, see his *Tratado de derecho internacional público*, 2 vols. (Buenos Aires, 1928). At least Chile did succeed at the 1923 Conference in helping to reactivate the Rio Commission of American Jurisconsults. It was further agreed at Santiago, in spite of Argentine opposition, that this Commission, inactive since the 1912 Rio meeting, should attempt to proceed gradually and progressively toward the codification of American international law, taking as the basis for its efforts the Alvarez report, "La codificación del derecho internacional en América." See *MMRE*, 1919-1923, pp. 325-326. See also Fernández Larraín, *América y el principio de no intervención*, p. 15, and Guillén, *El principio internacional de no intervención*, pp. 85-94. In addition it was stipulated at the 1923 Santiago meeting that the work of the newly reconstituted Commission of Jurisconsults would be considered at the next Pan-American Conference, scheduled for 1928 in Havana. See Miguel Cruchaga to Chilean Ministry of Foreign Relations, June 21, 1927, *Correspondencia de la Embajada de Chile en EE. UU.*, 1927, AMRE.

[63] An even more bitter source of dispute between Argentina and Chile at the 1923 Pan-American Conference had been the disarmament issue. Argentina felt that Chile was in collusion with Brazil and the United States in a plot to allow Brazilian naval power to outstrip Argentina's. The resulting clashes between Chile and Argentina were extremely heated and in part were responsible for the unimpressive accomplishments of the 1923 Conference. See *MMRE*, 1919-1923, pp. 268-272. See also Beltrán Mathieu to Chilean Ministry of Foreign Relations, February 16, 1922, January 17, and February 1, 1923, *Embajada de Chile en EE. UU. y Legación en Japón*, 1922, and *ibid*, 1923, AMRE, and interview with Mathieu in the *Philadelphia Public Ledger*, May 19, 1923; Cámara de Diputados, *Boletín de sesiones extraordinarias*, 1924-1925, Sesión 125°, May 9, 1925, pp. 2386 ff., in

which Minister of Foreign Relations Luis Izquierdo gives an excellent account of the disarmament controversy; Alberto Cruchaga Ossa, "Chile y el desarme internacional," *Boletín de la Academia Chilena de la Historia*, Año I, no. 1 (1° semestre, 1933); *El Mercurio*, December 12, 1959; and *La Nación*, May 4, 1923. In spite of the strained atmosphere produced by the clashes between Chile and Argentina, the Fifth Pan-American Conference made some positive headway by approving the Gondra Convention for the peaceful solution of disputes. Chile ratified the Gondra Convention on September 23, 1925. See MMRE, 1919-1923, pp. 273-280, and *ibid.*, 1923-1926, p. 474.

[64] See *El Mercurio*, January 18, February 8, and 26, 1931.

[65] See Alfredo Irarrázaval, Chilean ambassador in Rio de Janeiro, to his Ministry of Foreign Relations, April 18, 1927, *Congreso de Jurisconsultos, Rio de Janeiro, 1929*, AMRE. Irarrázaval referred to Pan-Americanism simply as a cloak for United States designs to gain hegemony over Latin America, and described the attempts to codify American international law as dangerous and utopian. Irarrázaval also had a very low opinion of Alejandro Alvarez—one that Alvarez reciprocated in full. See *La segunda asamblea de jurisconsultos de Rio, informe del delegado de Chile, Alejandro Alvarez*, 1927, AMRE, pp. 133-145.

[66] MMRE, 1927, p. 214.

[67] Carlos Dávila, who was received as Chilean ambassador in Washington on October 6, 1927, replacing Miguel Cruchaga, apparently reflected official Chilean thought when he said: "Chile does not recognize it [the Monroe Doctrine], does not accept it, and does not need it. It is not a regional pact. . . and if the United States has proclaimed it and applied it and reserved even under President Wilson the exclusive right of interpreting it, Chile has not proclaimed it, has not accepted it, does not wish to share in it, does not judge it in any manner necessary, and does not desire to interpret it." See Dávila to Ministry of Foreign Relations, September 3, 1928, *Correspondencia de la Embajada de Chile en EE. UU.*, 1928, AMRE. In this respect the administration was in accord with an important opposition figure, Agustín Edwards, who had much the same thing to say about the Monroe Doctrine. See his *La américa latina y la Liga de las Naciones*, p. 21. See also *La Nación*, February 23, 1928.

[68] See letter of Irarrázaval to his Ministry of Foreign Relations, April 18, 1927, *Congreso de Jurisco::sultos, Rio de Janeiro, 1929*, AMRE.

[69] *La segunda asamblea de jurisconsultos de Rio, informe del delegado de Chile, Alejandro Alvarez*, 1927, AMRE, p. 14.

[70] The Rio meeting took as its point of departure a study prepared by Alvarez, *Los proyectos de derecho internacional público y derecho internacional privado*. See MMRE, 1927, p. 216. This *Memoria* also contains the "Extracto del informe del delegado de Chile a la asamblea de jurisconsultos de Rio de Janeiro, señor Alejandro Alvarez," pp. 209-260. Alvarez reveals some degree of megalomania in this report, as well as in the already cited *La segunda asamblea*, AMRE, pp. 12 and 25 where he acknowledged that he was the guiding spirit of the entire proceedings at Rio, as well as the intellectual father of the project of American international law.

[71] For some indications of Chilean thought on diplomatic recognition see Aquiles Navarete Arias, *Los gobiernos de facto ante el derecho internacional* (1939), and

Germán Vergara Donoso, "Reconocimiento de gobiernos 'de facto'," *Revista Chilena*, Año XIV, nos. 125-126 (September-December, 1930).

[72] In other words, the Rio Jurisconsults included in their codification of American international law the principle of the Calvo Clause, named after the Argentine statesman, Carlos Calvo. See *La segunda asamblea*, AMRE, p. 62, and Chapter V, note 40.

[73] *Ibid.*, p. 130. See also pp. 30-34.

[74] *Ibid.*, pp. 129-130. In addition to Alcorta, Argentina was represented in Rio by Carlos Saavedra Lamas. For an interesting indication of the Chilean position that Latin-American unity, especially close accord with Argentina and Brazil, was an important counterweight to United States influence, see Dávila to Ministry of Foreign Relations, March 19, 1929, *Correspondencia recibida de la Embajada de Chile en EE. UU.*, 1929, AMRE, and Alfredo Irarrázaval to Ministry, May 9, 1929, *Congreso de Jurisconsultos, Rio, 1929*, AMRE.

[75] *Correspondencia prestada por el secretario de la delegación de Chile a la VI Conferencia Internacional Americana, La Habana, 1928*, AMRE, p. 83. See also Miguel Cruchaga, "Las conferencias panamericanas," *Revista Chilena*, Año XI, nos. 86-87 (June-July, 1927), and nos. 88-89 (August-September, 1927), providing background material on the earlier conferences and indications of what to expect at Havana, and Germán Vergara Donoso, "La sexta Conferencia International Americana," *ibid.*, Año XII, nos. 95-96 (March-April, 1928).

[76] See the very valuable book of Lira, *Memorias* (1950), describing among other points his efforts toward ABC unity in 1915, and the Chilean role at the 1928 Havana Conference. In Havana, Chile was also represented by Carlos Silva Vildósola, Manuel Bianchi, and Alejandro Alvarez.

[77] The most valuable source revealing this attitude is *Correspondencia prestada por el secretario de la delegación de Chile a la VI Conferencia Internacional Americana, La Habana, 1928*, AMRE, esp. pp. 82-87. See also MMRE, 1928, pp. 253 ff.; Miguel Cruchaga to Chilean Ministry of Foreign Relations, June 28, 1927, *Correspondencia recibida de la Embajada de Chile en EE. UU.*, 1927, AMRE, concerning primarily the economic matters to be discussed at Havana; and Dávila to Ministry, December 3, 1927, *ibid.*, noting the care with which the United States was selecting its delegation because of the realization that its policies would be under sharp attack by the Latin-American champions of the new principles of American international law. Dávila reported that President Coolidge would address the conference, and that the United States delegation would be headed by Charles Evans Hughes, and include Henry P. Fletcher, Dwight Morrow, James Brown Scott, Oscar W. Underwood, Morgan J. O'Brien, Leo S. Rowe, and Ray Lyman Wilbur, president of Stanford University. In addition see Enrique Villegas, ambassador of Chile in Rome, to his Ministry of Foreign Relations, March 5, 1928, *Correspondencia recibida de las Embajadas de Chile en Italia y Santa Sede, 1928*, AMRE, noting that all Europe was interested in the Havana meeting and voicing hope that Latin-American republics would be insistent upon the matter of nonintervention. For important *El Mercurio* stories on the conference, which tend to reveal that Chilean public opinion was more hostile to the United States than was the official Chilean delegation at Havana, see the editions of January 15, 17, 18, 19, 24, 26, February 11, 15, 17, 18, and 24, 1928. Finally see Galvarino Gallardo Nieto, *Panamericanismo* (1941), p. 13.

[78] *MMRE*, 1928, pp. 364-367. Chile was represented by its ambassador in Washington Carlos Dávila and by Antonio Planet. Only thirty-four at the time of the Washington Conferences, Planet was appointed Minister of Foreign Relations by Ibáñez in 1931.

[79] *Ibid.*, pp. 267-268.

[80] *MMRE*, 1929, p. 159. This section of the *Memoria* reproduces the Dávila-Planet report on the conference. See also Dávila to Ministry of Foreign Relations, February 6, 1929, *Correspondencia recibida de la Embajada de Chile en EE. UU.*, 1929, AMRE.

[81] *MMRE*, 1929, pp. 107-108. By 1930, countries that had ratified the Treaty of Conciliation were the United States, Cuba, El Salvador, Chile, Guatemala, and Mexico. By December, 1931, Brazil and the Dominican Republic had also ratified. See *MMRE*, 1932, p. 35. At the time of the 1933 Montevideo Conference, Argentina, Bolivia, Colombia, Costa Rica, Honduras, Paraguay, Peru, Uruguay, and Venezuela had still not ratified. See *MMRE*, 1933, p. 203.

[82] By 1933, Chile was beginning to wonder how generous and sincere the shift really was, for the United States had still not ratified the Arbitration Treaty that, along with the Conciliation Treaty, had been formulated at the 1929 Washington Conference. See Benjamín Cohen, Chilean chargé d'affaires in Washington, to his Ministry of Foreign Relations, April 3, 1933, *Correspondencia: Embajada de Chile en EE. UU.*, 1933 (2° trimestre), AMRE. In effect, the United States had agreed in the Arbitration Treaty to compulsory arbitration of disputes of a "justiciable" nature, even though the arbitration tribunal might be a specially created five-man board, three of whose members would be Latin Americans. Finally, in 1935, the United States did ratify this treaty. See Samuel Flagg Bemis, *The Latin American Policy of the United States* (New York, 1943), pp. 253-254.

[83] At one point of the Washington Conference Chile was fearful that irresistible pressure would be applied, especially by the United States, for a Tacna-Arica settlement. Chile succeeded, however, in mitigating this pressure by leading the Latin-American nations in a move to insist that arbitration and conciliation agreements recognize the Calvo clause. This move split the conference by bringing several Latin-American nations into dispute with the United States and thus spared Chile the embarrassment of being the sole objector to the apparently generous arbitration and conciliation terms favored by the United States. Along with Chile, Colombia, Costa Rica, the Dominican Republic, Ecuador, El Salvador, Mexico, Uruguay, and Venezuela attached reservations to the January 5, 1929, Treaty of Inter-American Arbitration, asserting the principles of the Calvo Clause. See *MMRE*, 1929, pp. 107-109, 111-117, and 163; *Conferencia de Conciliación y Arbitraje, informe sobre, Washington*, 1929, AMRE, esp. pp. 8, 14-18; *El Mercurio*, January 5 and 6, 1929; and *La Nación*, January 6, 1929. See also Enrique Lagos Valenzuela, *El arbitraje internacional en américa* (1938. Memoria de Prueba).

[84] See *La segunda asamblea de jurisconsultos de Rio, informe del delegado de Chile*, AMRE, pp. 92-96. See also Alfredo Irarrázaval to Chilean Ministry of Foreign Relations, April 18, May 6 and 9, "confidencial," *Congreso de Jurisconsultos, Rio*, 1929, AMRE.

[85] Ríos Gallardo, *Chile y Perú*, pp. 178-179.

[86] Dávila was instructed also to try in the meantime to prevent the boundary commission, holding sessions in New York City since the departure of Lassiter

from Arica in 1927—in accordance with the process of United States good offices agreed to by Chile—and presided over by Jay Morrow, from taking any action unfavorable to Chile. See *ibid.*, pp. 288-292. See also *MMRE*, 1928, pp. 9-15, and Félix Nieto del Río, "Tacna-Arica: comisión especial de limites," *Revista Chilena*, Año XI, nos. 88-89 (August-September, 1927).

[87] Ríos Gallardo, *op. cit.*, pp. 180-181.

[88] Chilean accounts do not accord just recognition to the efforts of Kellogg in facilitating a final agreement. For an accurate description of the Kellogg role, see L. Ethan Ellis, *Frank B. Kellogg and American Foreign Relations, 1925-1929* (New Brunswick, N.J., 1961), the chapter devoted to Tacna-Arica, the Havana Conference, and the Clark Memorandum.

[89] Ríos Gallardo, *op. cit.*, p. 199, and *MMRE*, 1928, pp. 14-15, 223. Newspaper response to renewed relations was highly favorable. See *El Diario Ilustrado*, July 15, 1928; *El Mercurio*, July 14; *El Sur* (Concepción), July 17; and *La Unión* (Valparaíso), July 14.

[90] A typical example of this is *El Mercurio*, February 19, 1929.

[91] *MMRE*, 1929, p. 10. Ríos Gallardo, *op. cit.*, pp. 315-316. See also *El Diario Ilustrado*, February 5 and April 12, 1929.

[92] On this matter see Juan Bernal Benítez, *El tratado de Lima de 1929* (1938. Memoria de Prueba); *Chile-Perú: Tratado Chileno-Peruano y Protocolo Complementario, subscrito en Lima el 3 de junio de 1929* (1930); M. Donoso Vargas, *El arbitraje de Tacna y Arica* (1937. Memoria de Prueba); Jaime de la Lastra, *Historia diplomática de la cuestión de Tacna y Arica* (1951); and R. Montaner Bello, *Negociaciones diplomáticas entre Chile y el Perú* (1934).

[93] Ríos Gallardo, *op. cit.*, pp. 306-327. The Chilean Chamber of Deputies ratified the agreement on July 1, by a vote of 71-8, while the Senate approved 27-2. *Ibid.*, pp. 328-330.

[94] *MMRE*, 1929, p. 109.

[95] See Domingo Barros Parada, *Relaciones entre Chile y el Perú: Arica* (1934).

[96] See Conrado Ríos Gallardo, *Después de la paz: las relaciones chileno-bolivianas* (1926).

[97] Armando Donoso, *Recuerdos de cincuenta años* (1947), p. 284.

[98] *La Nación*, May 18, 1929.

[99] *MMRE*, 1929, p. 19.

[100] For a tribute to Carlos Ibáñez as a sincere Americanist who consistently sought New World unity, see Tobías Barros Ortiz, "El día de las Américas," *Atenea*, Año XXXI, no. 346 (April, 1954). Throughout his life, Barros Ortiz was a staunch Ibáñez supporter. For a strong attack on the arrangement with Peru achieved under Ibáñez see Ernesto Barros Jarpa, "El desastre: a propósito del tratado de Lima," *El Diario Ilustrado*, August 19, 1931.

[101] See the Buenos Aires *La Prensa*, December 21, 1928.

[102] See Bulnes to Chilean Ministry of Foreign Relations, May 19, 1928, *Correspondencia recibida de las Embajadas de Chile en Argentina y México, 1928*, AMRE. See also *El Mercurio*, January 10, 1928, commenting upon the contributions of Bulnes to Chilean-Argentine solidarity.

[103] See *La Nación*, December 27 and 30, 1926, January 12, 1928, and January 5, 1929. In this last edition, *La Nación* editorialized that Chile had now embraced a new American Hemisphere policy, one that caused it to assume interest in all the

New World republics, including those of Central America. See also Ernesto Tor-realva, "Nicaragua y la VI Conferencia Panamericana," *ibid.*, January 15, 1928. Condemnation of United States imperialism in Nicaragua is also found in *El Mercurio*, January 12, February 25, 1927, January 6, 15, 18, 1928, and January 8, 1931. See also Gonzalo Bulnes to the Chilean Ministry of Foreign Relations, January 9, 1928, *Correspondencia recibida de las Embajadas de Chile en Argentina y México, 1928,* AMRE.

[104] These comments were prominently featured in the official newspaper, *La Nación*, November 10, 1929. Eliodoro Yáñez, owner of this paper before its con-fiscation by Ibáñez in 1927, had long entertained similar views. See his series of articles appearing in the December 1926 editions.

For additional Chilean literature advocating Latin-American unity as a means of curbing United States influence see: Mario Antonioletti, "Gestación de un movimiento político-social de unidad americana," *Acción Social*, nos. 122-123 (March-April, 1948); Guillermo M. Bañados, *Embajadas en las repúblicas del Brasil y Argentina* (1922); Luis D. Cruz Ocampo, "Hacia la solidaridad americana," *Atenea*, Año I, no. 2 (May, 1924); Joaquín Edwards Bello, "La evolución del pueblo hispano-indio," *La Nación*, February 27, 1928; Onofre Lindsay, *El problema fundamental: la repoblación de Chile y los estados unidos de sudamérica* (1925); Félix Nieto del Río, "Las relaciones de Chile con la república argentina," *Revista Chilena*, Año XIII, nos. 113-114 (September-October, 1929); and Emilio Rodríguez Mendoza, "Notas sobre la Argentina," *La Nación*, December 23, 1930.

[105] See interview with Ibáñez, *El Mercurio*, July 7, 1930.

[106] *MMRE*, 1919-1923, p. 7.

[107] *El Diario Ilustrado* estimated the 1925 total to have been $365,000,000, citing figures provided by the United States Commercial Attaché in Santiago, Ralph Acker-man. See the July 5, 1925 edition. *El Mercurio*, November 8 and 18, 1928, estimated the value at $440,000,000. Of this amount, it was said that some $300,000,000 was invested in mining. Additional sources of information on the increase of United States investments, especially in mining, include the following: Ignacio Aliaga Ibar, *La economía de Chile y la industria del cobre* (1946); Oscar Ilabaca León, *Breve estudio sobre los fundamentos económico-sociales de nuestros empréstitos externos* (1925); Santiago Macchiavello Varas, *El problema de la industria del cobre en Chile y sus proyecciones* (1923); Sady Padilla Z., *Política económica minera de Chile* (1935. *Memoria de Prueba*). Particularly useful is F. Javier Cotapos Aldunate, *El aporte del capital extranjero en la industria minera de Chile* (1947. *Memoria de Prueba*). The 1920-1928 period witnessed the most dramatic rise of United States investments in Chile during the entire twentieth century. After that period, and especially until 1945, the rate of increase in these investments was unspectacular. By 1940, total United States investment in Chile was $592,000,000, compared to $614,000,000 in Cuba, $573,500,000 in Argentina, $492,100,000 in Brazil, and $385,000,000 in Mexico. See the Santiago monthly *Occidente* (September, 1948), p. 10.

[108] Augusto Santelices, *El imperialismo yanqui y su influencia en Chile* (1926), p. 23.

[109] Aida Vuscovic Bravo, *Participación del capital extranjero en la economía chilena* (1957. *Memoria de Prueba*), p. 41. See also M. B. Donald, "History of the Chile Nitrate Industry," *Annals of Science*, I, no. 2 (April, 1936).

[110] Vuscovic Bravo, *op. cit.*, p. 58. See also Julio César Jobet, *Ensayo crítico del desarrollo económico social de Chile* (1955), pp. 174-176, and "Movimiento social obrero," Universidad de Chile, *Desarrollo de Chile en la primera mitad del siglo xx* (1953), I, 75.

[111] In 1929, the United States exported $63,347,161 worth of goods to Chile, and the United Kingdom only $34,811,279. The total value of Chilean imports, 1925, 1929, and 1930 was $148,885,075, $228,644,827, and $377,529,902 respectively. See Pan American Union, *Latest Reports from Chilean Official Sources* (Washington D.C., 1932).

[112] The value of Chilean exports to the United States did not always exceed that of goods sent to the United Kingdom. In 1926, 1927, 1928, and 1929, the value of Chilean exports to the United States was $96,932,557, $63,758,147, $81,161,-468, and $70,886,599 respectively. In the same years, the value of exports to the United Kingdom was $52,153,602, $73,355,718, $82,092,988, and $37,296,682 respectively. For additional material on United States-Chilean economic relations see: Norman Armour (ambassador of the United States to Chile at the time), "Las relaciones económicas chileno-americanas," *Economía y finanzas*, Año II, no. 19 (May, 1938); *Chile*, a circular put out by the Ministry of Foreign Relations for distribution to all Chilean consuls, beginning at the end of 1925; Chile-American Association of New York, *Reciprocal Trade and Resources of Chile and the United States* (New York, 1924); "Deudas latinoamericanas a los Estados Unidos," *Economía y Finanzas*, Año III, no. 27 (January, 1939); and Charles A. McQueen, "Principal Features of Chilean Finances," United States Department of Commerce, *Trade Information Bulletin*, no. 162 (November 26, 1923).

[113] Quoting from a protest prepared by the Chilean Labor Federation (*Federación Obrera de Chile*), Deputy Cárdenas charged that the Chilean army, in connivance with United States capitalists, had driven 3,500 entire families—men, women, and children—out of the Chuquicamata area, forcing them to shift for themselves without shelter or food in the northern pampa. This brutal action had been taken, according to the report, simply because the heads of these families had participated in strikes. See address of Cárdenas, Cámara de Diputados, *Boletín de sesiones extraordinarias*, 1919-1920, Sesión 64°, January 20, 1920, pp. 2050-2052.

[114] See *El Mercurio*, April 17, 1923. The same paper on November 29, 1920, had published a letter from Raúl Ramírez, a Chilean temporarily residing in Berkeley, California. In this letter, Ramírez stated that although the United States had now abandoned its desire for Latin-American territory, it was working toward political and economic control over the area. See also the strong plea for economic nationalism published by Dr. F. Landa Z., "Nuestro sistema educacional y la pasividad económica de la población de Chile," *ibid.*, January 1, 5, 8, 15, 16, 24, and 25, 1922, and Amanda Labarca Hubertson, "Nuestra situación y la de otras mujeres," *ibid.*, a series of articles beginning February 27, 1922, and "Una embajada de mujeres," *ibid.*, February 26, 1923. Additional works advocating economic nationalism in the 1920's, prior to and during the Ibáñez regime, include the following: Marcial Figueroa, *Chuquicamata: la tumba del chileno* (1928), and *Tras del espejismo de la pampa: estudio sociológico en los obreros de la región de salitre* (1931) —both works have a Marxist slant; Eulogio Gutiérrez, *Chuquicamata: tierras rojas* (1926); Daniel Martner, *Estudios de política comercial chilena e historia económica nacional*, 2 vols. (1923), in which the German-trained economist who served as

Minister of Treasury during the first Arturo Alessandri administration reveals his strong economic nationalism; Ernesto Montenegro, article in *La Nación*, January 26, 1928; and Augusto Santelices, *El imperialismo yanqui y su influencia en Chile*, who concludes that the dominance of United States capital is caused by the absence of the "capitalist virtues" in the Chilean people and their resulting economic inferiority. For an earlier manifestation of this viewpoint in Chile see Chapter V, notes 244-246.

[115] Latcham, *Chuquicamata, estado yankee: visión de la montaña roja* (1926). This is one of the strongest attacks against the United States to be written in twentieth-century Chile by a noncommunist.

[116] Bulnes to Ministry of Foreign Relations, May 12, 1928, *Correspondencia recibida de las Embajadas de Chile en Argentina y México, 1928*, AMRE.

[117] The following works all voice strong sentiments of economic nationalism. Alberto Cabero, "El consejo de economía nacional," *El Mercurio*, July 19, 1932. *Camaradas Universitarias.* This one-page publication issued by an organization called the *Comité de Estudiantes Universitarias* several times in 1931 demanded the overthrow of Ibáñez. It was an extreme left-wing publication which delighted in attacking Ibáñez, Pablo Ramírez, Osvaldo Koch, Bartolomé Blanche, Raúl Simón, Pedro Aguirre Cerda, Rodolfo Jaramillo, and others because of their "sell-out" to Wall Street. In 1933 the anonymous book *Washington Carousel* was translated into Spanish and published in Santiago. With much space devoted to an attack against United States imperialism, the book was avidly read in Chile. *Ideología de la Acción Nacionalista de Chile* (1932). Santiago Macchiavello Varas, *Nacionalismo económica* (1932), and *La tecnocracia* (1934). Daniel Martner, *Economía política* (1934). *Memorandum relativo al impuesto sobre el capital declarado de las sociedades extranjeras, que establecía el Art. 43 de la Ley no. 3091 de 5 de abril de 1916* (1934). This government report concerns the dispute raging in Chile at the time over whether the Braden Copper Company had been making adequate tax payments. Julio Pérez Canto, *La industria salitrera y la intervención del estado* (1933). Pérez Canto served as Minister of Treasury in both the provisional government following the overthrow of Ibáñez and the Socialist Republic regime. An economic nationalist, Pérez Canto strongly attacked the Guggenheims and Pablo Ramírez for the COSACH arrangement. *¿Por que cayó Grove?* (1932). This strongly-worded pamphlet blames the maneuverings of United States capital for the fall of socialist Marmaduke Grove. *Programa del Partido Social Republicano* (1931). This party, founded to oppose the allegedly fascistic tendencies of Ibáñez, included among its leaders such men as Horacio Hevia, Enrique Bravo, Carlos Vicuña, and Arturo Olavarría. Jorge Gustavo Silva, *Examen del nacionalismo económico* (1934).

[118] It is significant that in 1933 José Enrique Rodó's *Ariel* was published in a new Santiago edition that was quickly exhausted. In a conference presented late that year, professor Arturo Piga praised Rodó's book inordinately and dismissed the United States as a cultural nonentity, motivated only by materialistic considerations. See *El Mercurio*, November 21, 1933. Also referring to Rodó's classic, *La Nación*, May 1, 1929, predicted that the growing strength of Latin America would permit Ariel (the Latin countries) to prevail over Caliban (the United States). Galvarino Gallardo Nieto, "¿Democracia o plutocracia?" *El Mercurio*, November 4, 1932. Gallardo Nieto, the veteran diplomat and writer who had been one of his

country's delegates to the ill-fated Tacna-Arica plebiscite commission, maintained that the United States was not a democracy, but rather a plutocracy in which, more than in any other country, money determined everything. In his opinion, money had become the only moral value in the United States. At this time also, a group of writers was active in championing the cultural and spiritual values of Hispanism (see Chapter V, notes 247 and 248), and urging closer ties with motherland Spain (see Chapter VIII, note 15). *El Mercurio*, February 5, 1928, referred to the rising cult of Hispanism in Chile, and *La Nación*, February 9, 1928, reported an interesting interview in which Foreign Minister Ríos Gallardo praised Hispanic cultural values and advised closer ties with the motherland.

[119] See the attack in *El Mercurio*, July 23, 1932, for a typical Chilean reaction to the Hawley-Smoot tariff. See also Alejandro Silva de la Fuente, "La cuestión de las tarifas norteamericanas," *ibid.*, July 14, 1929, and Guillermo Subercaseaux, "El patrón de oro: necesidad de una política de armonía y cooperación internacional," *Anales de la Universidad de Chile*, 2° serie, VII (3° trimestre, 1929).

[120] See *El Diario Ilustrado*, July 1, 1931, and *El Mercurio*, June 23, 1931.

[121] Galvarino Gallardo Nieto, although he liked the idea of union, felt it should be limited to Chile, Argentina, and Brazil. Gallardo still clung to the traditional Chilean disdain for the Indian republics of Spanish America. See his "Dificultades del panamericanismo," *El Mercurio*, December 15, 1933, and "Relaciones chileno-argentinas," *ibid.*, March 21, 1932.

[122] Desiderio González Ossandón, *Consideraciones alredor de la producción y del comercio* (1936), p. 7.

[123] See Francisco Javier Fermandois, "Latinoamericanismo," *La Opinión* (Santiago socialist daily), October 7, 1933, and the article by O. Pachotal in the right-wing *El Imparcial*, December 28, 1933.

[124] *El Mercurio*, December 21, 1932.

[125] Schneider Labbé, "Sudamérica ante la crisis mundial," *ibid.*, December 13, 1932.

[126] Article by Schneider Labbé, *ibid.*, December 27, 1932. For additional indications of the desire for Ibero-American unity as a means of ending United States influence, see: Alfredo Gabino Vázquez A., "Al margen de las conferencias panamericanas," *La Opinión*, December 15, 1933; José Ramón Gutiérrez Allende (Minister of Foreign Relations at the time), "Política económica de Chile en la esfera internacional," *Economía y Finanzas*, Año I, no. 7 (May, 1937); Eugenio Orrego Vicuña, "Sociedad de naciones americanas," *Anales de la Facultad de Ciencias Jurídicas y Sociales*, I (January-June, 1935); Emilio Rodríguez Mendoza, "Notas sobre la Argentina," *La Nación*, December 28, 1930; Alberto Sayán Vidaurre, *Por la cooperación interamericana* (Valparaíso, 1935); Emilio Tagle Rodríguez, "Relaciones comerciales con Argentina," *El Mercurio*, April 10, 1932, and "La unión aduanera de sudamérica," *ibid.*, April 18, 1932. See also *ibid.*, December 27, 1932.

[127] See letters of Cruchaga to his Ministry of Foreign Relations, January 4, 7, 9, 15, June 17, and July 20, 1932, *Correspondencia recibida de la Embajada de Chile en EE. UU.*, 1932, AMRE. See also Benjamín Cohen, Chilean chargé d'affaires in Washington, to his Ministry, December 7, 1932, and March 24, 1933, *ibid.*, 1932, and 1933, AMRE. In addition, see address of Democrat Deputy Saturio Bosch, Cámara de Diputados, *Boletín de sesiones ordinarias*, 1933, Sesión 31°, July 19, 1933, pp. 1550 ff.

[128] *El Mercurio*, December 26, 1932.

[129] Cruchaga was accompanied to Mendoza by Subsecretary of the Ministry of Foreign Relations Germán Vergara, by Ministry counselors Félix Nieto del Río and Alberto Cruchaga Ossa, and by Subsecretary of Commerce Desiderio García.

[130] *MMRE*, 1933, p. 375. *El Mercurio*, January 30, 1933.

[131] Argentina, Brazil, Chile, and Peru were attempting to resolve the Chaco dispute, and resented the efforts of a bloc led by the United States and including Mexico, Cuba, Uruguay, and Colombia to achieve the same end. See *El Diario Ilustrado*, September 10, 1932 and July 27, 1933; Osvaldo González Forster, *La neutralidad de Chile en el conflicto del Chaco* (1936. *Memoria de Prueba*); *La Guerra en el Chaco y la Liga de las Naciones: recopilación de artículos del diario chileno "El Imparcial"* (1935); *El Mercurio*, January 2 and 5, 1929, August 5, 1932, and January 2, 1933; *La Nación*, January 5, 7, and 13, 1929; J. Isidro Ramírez, *El panamericanismo, el arbitraje y la agresión boliviana en el Chaco* (1933); and Aquiles Vergara Vicuña, *Bolivia y Chile: lecciones del pasado, advertencias para el porvenir* (1936). See also *MMRE*, 1933, pp. 13-49, 78-90, 97.

[132] On October 10, 1933, the representatives of Chile, Mexico, and Argentina met at Rio de Janeiro and, along with the delegate of Brazil, signed the Saavedra Lamas Pact. President Agustín P. Justo of Argentina flew to Rio to sign the instrument personally. Chile was represented by its ambassador in Rio, Marcial Martínez de Ferrari. The signing of the pact was interpreted by the Chilean press as an important step toward Ibero-American unity in a move ultimately designed to limit the influence of the United States in hemisphere relations. See *El Imparcial*, October 11 and 13, and December 13, 1933; *La Opinión*, October 10, 1933, and *La Nación*, October 8, 10, 13, 17, and December 2, 1933. The last edition praised Miguel Cruchaga for his contributions to Argentine-Chilean rapprochement, declaring that there had never existed greater accord between the two countries. See also *MMRE*, 1933, p. 381.

[133] For a good description of the opening stages of the negotiations that led to the commercial treaty, see *El Mercurio*, November 2 and 13, 1932, and March 24, 1933.

[134] Cámara de Diputados, *Boletín de sesiones ordinarias*, 1933, Sesión 45°, August 17, 1933, pp. 2245 ff.

[135] Illanes Benítez, *Nuestros tratados de comercio* (1933).

[136] Cámara de Senadores, *Boletín de sesiones ordinarias*, 1933, Sesión 39° ª, August 17, 1933, pp. 1212 ff. The Senate ultimately ratified the Treaty 22-19. See *El Diario Ilustrado*, July 18 and 19, 1933. For additional indications that Chile regarded the commercial treaty that went into effect on October 23—having been ratified by Argentina—as at least in part an anti-United States instrument see: Luis Alberto Cariola (ambassador of Chile in Argentina), "El tratado de comercio chileno-argentino," *La Nación*, September 2, 1933; Galvarino Gallardo Nieto, "Relaciones chileno-argentinas," *El Mercurio*, March 29, 1932; and Emilio Tagle Rodríguez, "Relaciones comerciales con Argentina," *ibid.*, April 10, 1932. The same concept was at least implied in the May 21, 1934, message of President Alessandri when he referred to the new commercial treaties celebrated by Chile with both Argentina and Peru. See his *Mensaje leído por S. E. el Presidente de la República . . ., 21 de mayo de 1934*, pp. 11-12.

[137] See Eugenio Orrego Vicuña, *Los problemas de la unificación americana* (1933).

[138] When Miguel Cruchaga departed from Washington in December 1932 to serve as his country's Minister of Foreign Relations, the embassy was left in the care of Benjamín Cohen, acting as chargé d'affaires. Cohen had come to Washington first in 1922 as second secretary of the embassy. A talented linguist who was fluent in French, Spanish, English, Portuguese, and Italian, he served frequently as interpreter at various inter-American conferences. Both he and Ambassador Cruchaga had resigned their posts in 1927 shortly after Ibáñez assumed power. Cohen served as chargé d'affaires from December, 1932, until the following October when Manuel Trucco—a distinguished leader of the Radical Party—presented his credentials in Washington as Chile's new ambassador.

[139] See Cohen to his Ministry, January 12, March 14, and especially May 18, 1933, *Correspondencia recibida de la Embajada de Chile en EE. UU., 1933, 1° and 2° trimestre*, AMRE. Cohen also interpreted as a favorable sign the manner in which Carleton Beals and a host of other writers had begun to attack some of the old-style Yankee practices in Latin America. See his March 24, 1933, letter, *ibid.* *El Mercurio* shared Cohen's optimism over the new United States attitudes. See its editions of November 10, 1932, and April 14, 1933. See also *La Nación*, December 30, 1933, for a favorable commentary on the apparent United States abandonment of imperialism.

[140] See *La Nación*, November 5, 1933.

[141] *MMRE*, 1933, p. 206. See also *La Nación*, December 9, 1933, for an account of the strong speech in favor of the Saavedra Lamas pact delivered by Miguel Cruchaga at the Montevideo Conference.

[142] *MMRE*, 1933, p. 195.

[143] In addition to Chile, nine other countries sent delegations headed by their Ministers of Foreign Affairs: Argentina, Brazil, Guatemala, Mexico, Nicaragua, Panama, Paraguay, the United States, and Uruguay. Besides Cruchaga, the Chilean delegation included the president of the Radical Party, Senator Octavio Señoret; the journalist, professor, and congressman, José Ramón Gutiérrez; the political counselor of the Ministry of Foreign Relations, Félix Nieto del Río; the president of the Chamber of Deputies, Gustavo Rivera; Chile's envoy to Uruguay, Francisco Figueroa Sánchez; and the counselor of the Chilean embassy in Washington, Benjamín Cohen. See *MMRE*, 1933, p. 214, and *La Nación*, September 9, 1933.

[144] Gamboa Serazzi, *Alejandro Alvarez*, p. 19.

[145] *MMRE*, 1933, p. 197.

[146] See the articles of Domingo Melfi who covered the Montevideo Conference for *La Nación*, particularly the December 11, 14, 15, 21, and 24 editions of that paper. See also the articles of Rafael Maluenda who reported on the conference for *El Mercurio*, especially the December 15 edition. In addition, see the *El Mercurio* editorial, December 30. Gonzalo Quintero, covering the conference for *El Diario Ilustrado*, had words of praise for the attitudes of Hull in his paper's December 15 and 16 issues.

[147] *El Diario Ilustrado*, December 21, 1933. *El Imparcial*, December 29, interview with Cruchaga on his return from Montevideo. *La Nación*, December 29, 1933.

[148] *El Imparcial*, December 29. Through O. Pachotal, its special reporter sent to Montevideo, *El Imparcial* provided excellent coverage of the conference. Extreme socialists were, of course, dismayed that the United States had gotten along so well with Latin America in Montevideo and tried to picture the conference as a failure. See "Fracaso de la Conferencia de Montevideo," *Hoy* (January 19, 1934). *Hoy* was a lively socialist weekly published in Santiago, 1931-1942. See also Helmut Brünner, *Aspectos del sistema internacional americana* (1938).

[149] See "Homenaje al Domingo Melfi," *Atenea*, Año XII, no. 249 (March, 1946).

[150] *La Nación*, December 17, 1933.

CHAPTER 8

[1] The neofascistic movements in Chile here referred to are characterized by: (1) suspicion of democracy; (2) dedication to a rigid elitist structure; (3) bitter opposition to government regulation of business and belief in the desirability of government-protected, privately-controlled monopolies in the economic order; (4) advocacy of a "Third Position" distinct from both the despised United States and Russian models; (5) glorification of the medieval guild system and desire to see Chile adopt the corporate-state political structure; (6) a strong insistence upon a government that maintains a professedly Christian—actually, a Catholic—position, and a rabid intolerance of pluralism, either in the religious or social spheres; and (7), a belief that Spain and Portugal are the only untainted countries in the modern world. Works exemplifying these points, in addition to those of Jaime Eyzaguirre and the Hispanists cited in notes 11 and 15 respectively, include the following. Acción Católica Chilena, *La Iglesia y el fascismo* (1946). *Bandera Negra* is a sporadically published circular of the MRNA (*Movimiento Revolucionario Nacionalsindicalista*), an admittedly fascistic group of little influence and few members. *El Debate*, a Santiago daily appearing from 1950 to 1957, was an organ of far-right Catholic advocates of the corporate state. *Estanquero*, a 1949-1954 weekly, was the organ of ex-nazi Jorge Prat who during the second Ibáñez regime (1952-1958) was for a time the most influential cabinet member. José García González, "Entrevista," *Vea*, September 17, 1952. José García, a prominent member of the *Partido Agrario Laborista* (PAL), outlined in this interview the party's platform which, among other features, favored the corporate state. PAL was a rightist, nationalist group founded in 1945. It supported Ibáñez in 1952 and in the 1953 congressional elections won the largest share of votes of any party. It returned to the status of a minority party with the decline in popularity of Ibáñez, and after 1958 ceased to exist independently. Guillermo González Echenique, *El corporativismo* (1942). Diego Guillén Santa Ana, *Política económica: sociología, corporativismo* (1940), and *Filosofía de la democracia cristiana* (1948). Alejandro Hales S., *El corporativismo en el pasado y en el presente* (1945. *Memoria de Prueba*). An important member of the PAL, Hales was a staunch backer of the corporate state. He served as ambassador to Brazil during the second Ibáñez administration. Jorge Iván Hübner Gallo, *Los católicos en la política* (1959), and *El nuevo estado español* (1952). This professor of juridical and social sciences at the University of Chile is a leader in extreme rightist Catholic intellectual circles. Particularly obnoxious to Hübner are the concepts not only of democracy, but of pluralism, tolerance, prag-

matism, and the open society. See also his "Una nueva doctrina económica-social: la tecnocracia," *Anales de la Universidad de Chile*, 4° serie, C (3° & 4° trimestre, 1942), in which he voices a plea for the corporate state. *El Imparcial*, a daily published in Santiago from 1926 to 1953, was a consistent advocate of the corporate state and in general expressed the right-wing Catholic position. Guillermo Izquierdo Araya, *Partido Agrario Laborista: su posición ante las facultades extraordinarias* (1955), and *Política y derecho en los nuevos tiempos* (1945). These works show that ex-nazi Izquierdo, like many other members of the PAL, believed in the hierarchical social order and therefore espoused the corporate state. Jaime Larraín García Moreno, *Chile, avanzada de occidente en el Pacífico sur* (1955), *El mejoramiento de la vida campesina* (1936), and *Orientación de nuestra política agraria* (1932). On the basis of these books, espcially the first cited, Larraín—who in 1960 became the president of the Catholic Church-oriented *Instituto de Educación Rural*—emerges clearly as a neofascist. Partido Agrario Laborista, *Congreso General Extraordinario* (1952). This document clearly shows that the corporate state ideal and the devotion to traditional values continued to characterize the PAL, even after the 1952 departure of Larraín. Alejandro Silva Bascuñán, "Notas para una crítica de la constitución," *Anales Jurídico-Sociales de la Facultad de Derecho de la Universidad Católica de Chile*, no. 10 segundo, Año XXX (1957). The article suggests that events since 1925 have proved the evils of labor-union participation in political activity. Unions should be incorporated into the management of industries, as a step toward the corporate state. *Veinte años: 5 de septiembre 1938 —5 de septiembre, 1958*. A tribute to the nazi "martyrs" of 1938 (see text of this chapter pertaining to the election and rule of the Popular Front, 1938-1941), this publication called for revival of the old movement, condemned the United States, and praised Spain and Portugal. See also *La Tercera de la Hora* (the Santiago daily reflecting Radical Party opinion), January 4, 1960, describing the attempts of Jorge Zamorano and others to revive Chilean nazism.

[2] Address of Ricardo Boizard, Cámara de Diputados, *Boletín de sesiones ordinarias, 1938*, Sesión 57°, August 30.

[3] Luis Galdames, *Historia de Chile* (1944 edition), p. 577.

[4] Alvin Cohen, *Economic Change in Chile, 1929-1959* (Gainesville, Florida, 1960), pp. 12-13. Corporación de Fomento de la Producción, *Cinco años de labor, 1939-1943* (1944), pp. 20-21. Herman Finer, *The Chilean Development Corporation* (Montreal, 1947), pp. 14-15. Kalman Silvert, "The Chilean Development Corporation" (doctoral dissertation, University of Pennsylvania, 1948), p. 32.

[5] Stevenson, *The Chilean Popular Front* (Philadelphia, 1942).

[6] Cámara de Diputados, *Boletín de sesiones ordinarias, 1948*, Sesión 26°, July 27.

[7] Cohen, *op. cit.*, p. 38. An outstanding study of the second Ibáñez administration is Donald W. Bray, "Chilean Politics During the Second Ibáñez Government, 1952-58" (doctoral dissertation, Stanford University, 1961).

[8] See *El Mercurio*, March 7, 1960. In the March 1961 congressional elections Liberals won 220,894, and the Conservatives 196,965 votes. The Radical Party obtained the highest vote of any single party: 295,970. Total votes cast in the election were 1,330,465. See *El Mercurio*, March 8, 1961. Conservative-Liberal strength has, however, declined. In 1957, the Conservatives elected six senators and twenty-two deputies; in 1961, they elected four and seventeen respectively (there are forty-five senators and 147 deputies in the Chilean Congress). Liberals in

1957 elected nine senators and thirty-two deputies; in 1961 they elected nine and twenty-six respectively. The Communist, Socialist, Radical, and Christian Democrat parties in 1961 scored impressive gains over 1957 electoral results.

Some basic works covering the political history alluded to in this and the ensuing chapter include the following titles. Gabriel Amunátegui Jordán, *Partidos políticos* (1952). Hernán Amaya Videla, *Morande 80* (1952). Much of the political gossip of the González Videla administration (1946-1952) is included by the author, a public information officer at the time. Oscar Bermúdez Miral, *El drama político de Chile* (1947). Ricardo Boizard, *Historia de una derrota* (1938). The work analyzes the defeat of Gustavo Ross in his presidential bid. Alberto Cabero, *Recuerdos de don Pedro Aguirre Cerda* (1948). This is a favorable biography, written by a man who was long an important literary figure and Radical Party leader. Ricardo Cruz-Coke, *Geografía electoral de Chile* (1952). This is an invaluable study of voting patterns according to geographical regions. The author has continued his research in two later articles, "La elección senatorial de Santiago," *Política y Espíritu*, Año IX, no. 102 (October 15, 1953), and "Geografía electoral de Chile," *ibid.*, no. 101 (October 1, 1953). Jorge de la Cuadra Poisson, *Magia financiera*, con un prólogo por Enrique Zañartu Prieto (1938). This is a favorable analysis of the financial policies of Gustavo Ross. Florencio Durán Bernález, *El Partido Radical* (1958). Written by an important member of the Radical Party, this not always reliable work deals with the period since 1938. *Ercilla*, 1935—. This valuable, often lively, weekly gives a good coverage of political events. Januario Espinoza, *Figuras de la política chilena* (1945). *Frente Popular*, a Santiago daily, was published 1936-1940. Juan Antonio Gómez Andrade, *El derecho de sufragio* (1958. *Memoria de Prueba*). Sergio Guilisasti Tagle, *Caminos de la política* (1960). This useful work is made up of essays by two members of each of the major political parties. René Montero Moreno, *Confesiones políticas* (1959). Long the private secretary of Ibáñez, Montero explains his defection from the president during his second administration on the grounds that Ibañismo was swinging too far to the left. Arturo Olavaría Bravo, *Casos y cosas de la política* (1950). The author flirted with socialism in the early 1930's, then supported Alessandri but broke with him in 1935. He served briefly as Minister of Foreign Relations in the second Ibáñez administration. Roger Sotto Marín (pseud., Próspero), *Visión espectral de Chile* (1955). This highly readable book emphasizes some of the racier aspects of contemporary politics. Luis Palma Zúñiga and Julio Iglesias Mélendez, *Presidencia de Juan Antonio Ríos* (1957). Darío Sainte Marie S., *El presidente Ibáñez* (1957). Sainte Marie, who uses the pseudonym Volpone, was director of the government paper *La Nación* during the second Ibáñez regime, and more recently has directed one of the "yellowest" papers in Chile, *Clarín*. He regarded Ibáñez as perhaps the greatest master of practical politics that Chile has ever produced. Alfonso Stephens Freire, *El irracionalismo político en Chile: un ensayo de psicología colectiva* (1957). *Topaze*, 1931—. This weekly humor magazine contains some of the finest political cartoons to be found in Latin America. *Vea*, 1939—, is another weekly that contains valuable coverage of the political scene, although its level of reporting may have declined in recent years. Ernesto Würth Rojas, *Ibáñez, caudillo enigmático* (1958). Würth did not like Ibáñez and makes little attempt to be objective.

* Writing in 1852 from Georgetown University, young Isidoro Errázuriz told his father, Ramón: ". . . the faults of the United States spring from the characteristics of Anglo-Saxon blood, leading those possessing it always to seek liberty for themselves, and slavery for others. . . . Between Chile and the United States there is a difference as great as that between Greece and ancient Persia, between light and shadow, between liberty and despotism." See the April 15, 1852, letter of Isidoro to Ramón Errázuriz, reproduced in *Revista Chilena de Historia y Geografía*, LVIII (3° trimestre, 1928).

[10] See *Colección de ensayos i documentos relativos a la unión y confederación de los pueblos hispano-americanos* (2 vols., 1862, 1867), I, 257-274. See also Juan Enrique Lagarrigue, *La religión de la humanidad* (1884). Lagarrigue was one of the principal propagators of positivism, "the religion of humanity," in Chile and his suspicious attitudes toward the United States were similar to those of Bilbao. In the 1920's, Radical Deputy Alberto Cabero also criticized the United States for its lack of culture. See his *Chile y lo chilenos* (1926), esp. pp. 10-11. The great poetess Gabriela Mistral also frequently indicated her preference for the light, the graceful, the cultural, and the artistic over what was merely powerful, strong, and brutish. She referred also to industry as a corrupting influence, and often extolled the superiority of Latin over Anglo-Saxon blood. See her *Recados contando a Chile*, vol. IV in *Obras selectas* (1957), pp. 14-16, 84, 131. In a revealing letter of late 1928 to Emilio Rodríguez Mendoza, who was serving as Chile's ambassador to Spain, Mistral admonished the diplomat that his fundamental failing, and also that of the president he served—Carlos Ibáñez—was the desire to make Chile a materially powerful country. Mistral felt that Chile should not aspire to economic grandeur, but should concern itself with developing even more fully its spiritual superiority over other American nations. See her September 26, 1928, letter to Rodríguez, enclosed with his letter of November 7, 1928, to the Chilean Ministry of Foreign Relations, *Correspondencia de las Legaciones de Chile en España y Portugal, 1928,* AMRE.

[11] Eyzaguirre, "Presencia histórica de hispanoamerica," *Estudios,* no. 141 (October, 1944). Eyzaguirre was the guiding spirit of the extremist right-wing journal *Estudios,* published in Santiago, generally as a monthly, from 1932 to 1955. See also Eyzaguirre, *La fisonomía histórica de Chile* (1948). This is one of the most challenging and best written interpretations of Chilean historical evolution, but tends to glorify a semi-medieval, feudalistic social structure.

[12] See Carlos Keller, "Spengler y el último occidente," *Occidente* (February-March, 1948).

[13] See Chapter V, section entitled "Fear of United States Cultural Penetration," and notes 247 and 248.

[14] See Emilio Rodríguez Mendoza to his Foreign Ministry, April 20 and June 18, 1928, *op. cit.,* note 10.

[15] A very inexhaustive list of the more avowedly Hispanist writings since 1920 would include the following works. *América,* a monthly published in Madrid beginning in 1930 and dedicated to spreading Hispanism in the New World, enjoyed wide popularity in Chile. The September 1930 number was dedicated to Chile and expressed satisfaction with the large number of devoted Hispanists in that country. General Francisco Araya Bennett, *Hispanismo* (1929). Manuel Atria R., Roberto Barahona, and Antonio Cifuentes, *Hacia una cultura ibero-americana* (1944). The volume is comprised of three strongly Hispanist essays, calling for cultural integra-

tion between Hispanic America and mother Spain. Eduardo Balmaceda Valdés, *Anhelo y visión de España* (1958), and *De mi tierra y de Francia* (1932). Juan Bardina, *Leyenda perjudicial: la supuesta inferioridad de los españoles* (1918). An important Spanish immigrant to Chile, Bardina did much to popularize Hispanism in his newly-adopted country, frequently using the pseudonym Lautaro. Among those Chileans whom Bardina listed as fervent Hispanists were: Carlos Silva Vildósola, Guillermo Pérez de Arce, Julio Pérez Canto, Carlos Varas (pseud., Mont Calm), Rafael Luis Gumucio, Nataniel Yáñez Silva, Ricardo Valdés, Rafael Maluenda, Víctor Domingo Silva, Víctor Silva J., Trancredo Pinochet, Ernesto Barros Jarpa, Joaquín Edwards Bello, Víctor de Valdivia, Claudio Arteaga Infante (pseud., Clarín), Enrique Tagle Moreno (pseud., Víctor Noir), Emilio Rodríguez Mendoza, Galvarino Gallardo Nieto, and Fidel Muñoz Rodríguez. Alfredo Benavides Rodríguez, "En torno a la imaginería española e hispano-americana," *Boletín de la Academia Chilena de la Historia*, Año XVI, no. 40 (1° semestre, 1949). Francisco Contreras, *L'esprit de l'amérique espagnole* (Paris, 1931). Perhaps the leading Hispanist in Chile at the time, Contreras advocated Hispanic-American unity to resist United States culture. Pedro N. Cruz, *Estudios sobre literatura chilena* (1949 edition), 3 volumes. José Miguel Echenique Gandarillas, *La inquietud religiosa en España* (1931). Jaime Eyzaguirre, *Hispanoamerica de dolor* (Madrid, 1947), and "Hacia la unidad de los pueblos hispánicos," *Estudios*, no. 167 (December, 1946). *Indice*, a monthly published 1930-1932, was the organ of a young and enthusiastic group devoted to Hispanic values and Hispanic-American unity to protect a superior culture against United States influence. One of the principal founders and guiding spirits was the Venezuelan Mariano Picón Salas, who for many years made his home in Chile. Carlos Keller R., "Darwin y Chile," *Anales de la Universidad de Chile*, *Centenario, Edición Extraordinario* (1959-1960). Keller concluded this important article by rejoicing that the youth of Chile have rejected the materialism of Darwinism which still enjoys vogue in other countries. Ricardo Latcham, *Doce ensayos* (1944). Latcham has long been a glorifier of traditional, Hispanist values. Osvaldo Lira, *Hispanidad y mestizaje y otros ensayos* (Madrid, 1952), and *La vida en torno* (1949). Anything that deviates from the traditional sociopolitical patterns of pre-Bourbon Spain is apparently suspect to the priest who is an influential voice in far-right Chilean intellectual circles. Pedro Lira Urquieta, *Temas hispano-americanos* (1942). A leading Hispanist and extreme rightist, Lira expresses his disdain for the materialism associated with non-Latin cultures. Walter Meyer Rusca, *Con los ojos abiertos sobre las tres américas* (1946). The book contains a Chilean traveler's impressions of the United States, Mexico, and Peru. Acrid criticism is accorded the first. "Monumento a Rodó: palabras pronunciadas por el Réctor de la Universidad y del Canciller Uruguayo, don Alberto Guani," *Anales de la Universidad de Chile*, 4° serie, III & IV, nos. 47 & 48 (1942). *Mundo Español* was a monthly that began publication in Santiago in 1925 and emphasized the contributions of Spanish culture to Chile. Eugenio Orrego Vicuña, "Destino de Chile," *Estudios*, no. 140 (September, 1944). Hispanic-American unity is advocated as the only means for defending superior values. See also his "Sociedad de naciones americanas," *Anales de la Facultad de Ciencias Jurídicas y Sociales*, I (January-June, 1935). Roberto Peragallo, *Grandeza futura de la lengua española* (1937), and *Por españa* (1941). The author was for forty years an influential professor of the law faculty of the

Catholic University of Chile and always a staunch Hispanist. See also "Homenaje a don Roberto Peragallo," *Anales Jurídico Sociales de la Facultad de Derecho de la Universidad Católica de Chile*, Año XXXIX, no. 10 (primero, 1954-1957). Jaime Peralta Peralta, *España, potencia americana* (1958). A member of the faculty of the school of law of the University of Chile, Peralta hoped a Latin-American union, based on the ideals of Spanish culture, would render the area safe from the influence of the United States. Mariano Picón Salas, *Hispanoamérica: posición crítica* (1931). See above reference to Picón Salas in this note in connection with citation of the journal *Indice*. In *Ensayos escogidos* (1958) Picón Salas continued his Hispanist tirades, averring that Wall Street and London were the symbols of all that had ruined civilization, while Spain continued to be the symbol of eternal values. Arturo Piga, *Crisis y reconstrucción de la segunda enseñanza: un problema hispanoamericana* (1940), and *Humanismo y espíritu nacionalista* (1927). Through education, Piga advised, Latin America should more fully develop and nourish its spiritual superiority over non-Latin areas. Trancredo Pinochet Le-Brun, *Como construir una gran civilización chilena e hispanoamericana* (no date). *La Raza*, a Santiago monthly, appeared first in 1922. Decidedly Hispanist in tone, it urged closer ties between Spain and Latin America. *Rodó* was another monthly published in Santiago, beginning in 1924. An organ of Hispanism, it frequently attacked the United States and was concerned over the alleged cultural imperialism of the Colossus.

[16] Cruz-Coke L., *Discursos: política-economía-salubridad-habitación-relaciones exteriores-agricultura* (1946), p. 7. Enrique Mac-Iver, long-time leader of the Radical Party, felt during the second decade of the twentieth century that ruin was coming to Chile because the masses were being aroused to challenge the only classes that knew how to govern. See Jaime Larraín García Moreno, *Chile, avanzada de occidente en el Pacífico sur* (1955), p. 17. Throughout his life Alberto Edwards Vives was in agreement with this appraisal. For the eloquently expressed political ideas of Edwards Vives, described by some as the last defender of monarchical principles in Chile, see especially his *La fronda aristocrática* (1959 edition). See also *Bosquejo histórico de los partidos políticos chilenos* (1903), *La organización política de Chile* (1943 edition), *Páginas históricas* (1945 edition), and *Recuerdos personales sobre los sucesos que ocasionaron el derrumbe de la administración Ibáñez* (1932).

[17] *El Diario Ilustrado*, November 15, 1933.

[18] Amunátegui Reyes, "Oligarquía," *El Mercurio*, November 2, 1932.

[19] Víctor Heuertz, "Los peligros de la gratuidad de enseñanza," *El Imparcial*, October 6, 1933.

[20] Cámara de Diputados, *Boletín de sesiones extraordinarias*, 1957-1958, Sesión 18ª, April 25, 1958. The professor that Gumucio had in mind was probably Alejandro Silva Bascuñán. Other deputies denied that such remarks had been made at the Catholic University.

[21] *The Revolt of the Masses* by José Ortega y Gasset is popular in Chile—it went through its second Santiago edition in 1934, and its third in 1936—in part because it is looked upon as proving that democracy is inimical to culture and contrary to common sense. See the article of Héctor Rodríguez de la Sotta, *El Diario Ilustrado*, September 26, 1932. Houston Stewart Chamberlain, moreover, exercised a powerful influence on many Chileans including Alberto Edwards, con-

firming this ultraconservative *pensador* in his belief that the masses must be kept politically silent. See *El Mercurio*, April 17, 1932. For additional expressions of dislike of democracy in the 1930's, see Chapter VI, notes 142-155.

[22] Letter of Subercaseaux, March 25, 1928, *Correspondencia recibida de las Embajadas de Chile en Italia y Santa Sede*, 1928, AMRE.

[23] A. The reader is referred to the following notes in this chapter: 1, on neofascism; 10, dealing with Alberto Cabero and Gabriela Mistral; 12, pertaining to Carlos Keller; 16, on Cruz-Coke, Larraín García Moreno, Mac-Iver, and Edwards Vives; 22, on Ramón Subercaseaux; and 24, on Rodríguez de la Sotta and Marín Balmaceda.

B. In addition, the reader is referred to notes in preceding chapters. Chapter IV: notes 156-165, 168-171, citing early twentieth-century works rejecting social and political alteration, but frequently urging some measure of paternalistically-administered reform. Chapter VI: notes 2-7 on the conservatism of Alessandri; 94-109 on fascism; 152-155 advocating dictatorship; 157 on Catholic action and the social problem; 158 and 159 pertaining to social modifications through implementation of the Christian social gospel; 160, listing works that favor slight modification in order to keep the social structure essentially intact; and 170-173 on the Chilean nazi movement. See also Chapter IX: note 19, dealing in part with Conservative opponents of the Christian Democrats.

C. In addition, the following more recent works manifest, either explicitly or implicitly, strong distaste for United States social and political patterns. José María Cifuentes, *Cuestiones contemporáneas* (1956), *El Partido Conservador Tradicionalista: su programa y su acción* (1953), and *Ensayo sobre el capitalismo* (1948). In these works, the extremely conservative Catholic University professor defends the old order. Crescente Donoso Letelier, *Portales y García Moreno: paralelo político y psicológico* (1955). Marcial Sanfuentes Carrión, *El Partido Conservador* (1957). Alejandro Silva de la Fuente, *Punto final* (1956). Alfredo Silva Santiago (now archbishop of Concepción and rector of the Catholic University, Santiago), *Estudio sobre la manera práctica de combatir el comunismo* (1937). Ramón Subercaseaux, *Memoria de ochenta años: recuerdos personales, críticas, reminiscencias históricas, viajes, anecdotas*, 2 vols. (1936).

D. There are also authors exhibiting a more liberal thought than that of those cited above in part C, but still thoroughly unwilling to tolerate direct democracy, genuine class competition, or the open society, and therefore basically opposed to United States patterns. The following titles are indicative of this approach. Daniel Armanet, "Economía social; el organismo económico; política; monetaria; la única solución; ¿cuanto durará la prosperidad?" *Economía y Finanzas*, Año XI, no. 128 (June, 1947). The distinguished economist and director of *Economía y Finanzas* ridicules the reform aspirations of certain young Conservatives. José María Caro (late cardinal-archbishop of Santiago), *La Iglesia está con el pueblo* (Valparaíso, 1939), and *El misterio de la masonería* (1926). In the latter, the archbishop held the Masons responsible for many of the ills of Chile. Jorge Fernández Pradel, S.J., *Acción católica* (1941), *Hacia un nuevo orden por un catolocismo social auténtico* (1952), and *Un nuevo orden social* (1940). Father Fernández was a leader in Catholic social justice movements beginning even before the 1920's. Lorenzo Fernández Rodríguez, *La justicia social eterna* (1949). The author seems to feel that justice cannot exist in a pluralistic, open society. Alberto Hurtado Cruchaga,

S.J., *¿Es Chile un país católico?* (1941), *El orden social cristiano en los documentos de la jerarquía católica,* 2 vols. (1947), and *El sindicalismo* (1950). The beloved Father Hurtado, known as the "labor priest," did outstanding work in encouraging social justice. Like Fernández Pradel, above, and like today's Christian Democrats in Chile, Hurtado felt that social justice based on merely pragmatic considerations and lacking theological roots was bound to be inadequate. See the sympathetic biography by Alejandro Magnet, *El Padre Hurtado* (1954). Marcelo Miranda Gancia, *El pensamiento social cristiano en la economía* (1947. *Memoria de Prueba*). Julio Philippi and Sergio Contardo, "Relaciones entre la personalidad y la sociedad," *Anales Jurídico-Sociales de la Facultad de Derecho de la Universidad Católica de Chile,* Año XLI, no. 13 (1957). The article suggests that if a social system is not expressly based on the teachings of St. Thomas, it is suspect. José Pizzardo, *La acción católica y la asistencia religiosa a los obreros* (1937). Guillermo Rebolledo López, *La Iglesia y la cuestión social* (1945). Carlos Vial, *Caudernos de comprensión social* (1952), and *Cuaderno de la realidad nacional* (1952). A liberal Catholic, a successful businessman, and in 1950 a frustrated Minister of Treasury, Vial argues for social reform as administered from above, rather than as demanded by the masses from below.

The authors cited above cannot in every instance be accurately described as rightists. Men like Caro, Fernández Pradel, Hurtado Cruchaga, and Vial certainly desired genuine change and reform. Their suspicions of the United States social system would be occasioned by their spiritually motivated distrust of pragmatism. Chilean intellectuals in general demand an over-all, total philosophical position as the foundation for their attitudes toward life. United States lack of concern with broad, philosophical speculation and its dedication to pragmatism stand as imposing obstacles in the way of any attempt to justify its position among a people demanding philosophical-theological ultimates.

[24] Examples of this sort of nonsense are provided by Conservative Party stalwart Héctor Rodríguez de la Sotta, *O capitalismo o comunismo: o vivir como en Estados Unidos o vivir como en Rusia* (1952), and by the late, influential, right-wing Liberal Raúl Marín Balmaceda, *Derechas o izquierdas* (1948) and *No demagogia* (1955).

CHAPTER 9

[1] Silva, *Nuestra evolución político social, 1900-1930* (1930), p. 107. For earlier works suggesting that socialism was the system most in accord with Christian and moral principles see Chapter VI, note 158, and Chapter VIII, note 23, part D.

[2] *El Mercurio,* August 26, 1932.

[3] For material on Latcham, see Chapter VII, note 115.

[4] Morales, "Socialismo y catolocismo," *El Mercurio,* July 8, 1932.

[5] *Wikén,* January 9, 1932.

[6] *Ibid.,* January 23, 1932.

[7] An interesting, semiautobiographical work by Délano is *Yo soy tu* (1952).

[8] See, for example, the pamphlet by Pinochet, *Por que soy amigo de la Unión Soviética* (1941).

[9] See Vicuña's *Pueblos encadenados* (1926), and *La separación de la iglesia y el estado* (1922).

[10] See *El Mercurio*, January 9, 1932.

[11] See José Inalaf Navarro, *Rol económico, social y político del indígena en Chile* (1945. *Memoria de Prueba*), pp. 75-76. Inalaf was a student in the classes of Walker Linares at this time, and includes extracts from classroom lectures in his book.

[12] Gallardo Nieto, "¿Democracia o plutocracia?" *El Mercurio*, November 4, 1943.

[13] See Heise González, *La constitución de 1925 y las nuevas tendencias político-sociales* (1951).

[14] *El Mercurio*, March 8, 1960.

[15] Gómez Millas, *Habla Juan Gómez M.* (1942).

[16] On the formative years of the National Falange, see Alejandro Silva Bascuñán, *Una experiencia social cristiana* (1949). Silva Bascuñán is now a prominent professor of constitutional law at the Catholic University, Santiago, known for his conservative viewpoints. See also Alberto Edwards and Eduardo Frei, *Historia de los partidos políticos chilenos* (1949), in which Frei writes the section of the book dealing with twentieth-century Chilean politics.

[17] See *Me defiendo* (1939), in which Gumucio defends himself against the numerous attacks that were occasioned by his joining the Falange. Gumucio is the father of Rafael A. Gumucio, an important figure in the Christian Democratic movement in the 1950's and early 1960's.

[18] *El Mercurio*, March 8, 1961. The total vote cast in the elections was 1,330,464.

[19] Angry books and pamphlets produced by the conflict between the Conservative and Christian Democrat parties include the following. Carlos Aldunate Errázuriz, *División de los católicos: refuta una carta de don Rafael Luis Gumucio* (no date, probably early 1940's), *Intervención de la iglesia en cuestiones sociales* (1940), and *Polémica sobre Maritain* (1940). The author strongly attacks the *Falange Nacional*, which he regards as heretical because of its belief in democracy and the open society. Jacques Maritain is regarded as tainted because of his "secularist" leanings and his acceptance of pluralism and democracy. An opposite point of view is presented by Christian Democrat Jaime Castillo, *En defensa de Maritain* (1949). Falange Nacional, *El Partido Conservador* (1938). This is a spirited attack upon the social and political backwardness of the Conservative Party. Sergio Fernández Larraín, *Falange Nacional, democracia cristiana, y comunismo* (1958). Staunch Conservative Fernández feels the Christian Democrats have sold out to the communists, in part because of their acceptance of pluralism and their attacks upon the traditional Chilean elite. See the same author's *Aspectos de la división del Partido Conservador* (1950). Jorge Iván Hübner Gallo, *Los católicos en la política* (1959). This is one of the strongest attacks published against the "heretical" inclinations of the Christian Democrats. Monsignor Luis Arturo Pérez, *Maritain* (1938), and *Estudio de filosofía político social* (1948). These works vigorously attack Maritain and the Chilean Falange as the agents of pluralism, laicism, secularism, and the like.

[20] Castillo, *Comunismo y democracia* (1951).

[21] Chonchol and Silva Solar, *Hacia un mundo comunitario: condiciones de una política social cristiana* (1951).

[22] Important works of Frei include: *Aun es tiempo* (1942); *Chile desconocido* (1937); *Pensamiento y acción* (1958); *La política y el espíritu*, con prólogo por

Gabriela Mistral (1946); *El régimen asalariado y su posible abolición* (1933); and *La verdad tiene su hora* (1955).

[28] Máximo Pacheco Gómez, *Política, economía y cristianismo*, con prólogo por Eduardo Frei (1947), p. 184.

A few of the many important works pertaining to Chile's Christian Democrat movement are listed below. Ricardo Boizard, *Cuatro retratos en profundidad: Ibáñez, Lafertte, Leighton, Walker* (1950). This work, by an important journalist once associated with the ultraconservative *El Diario Ilustrado*, but as of 1960 with the Radical organ, *La Tercera de la Hora*, contains an interesting sketch of early Falange leader Bernardo Leighton. Ismael Bustos, *Introducción a la política* (1961). Christian Democrat Bustos argues that communitarianism which provides in all spheres a unifying, humanistic, fraternal sense is superior to pluralism which merely supplies society with a multiform state adequate to accommodate the actual diversity of different religious, social, and functional-interest groups. The acquisition of property as the legitimate fruit of labor is justified, but there is said to be a need for the fundamental revision of property concepts, both as they apply to industrial and landed wealth, in order that all men may be assured material well-being adequate to protect their dignity. Falange Nacionale, *El Cobre* (1953). Nationalization of the copper mines is the ultimate goal, but the Christian Democrats are willing to proceed gradually. Manuel Garreton Walker and Radomiro Tomic Romero, *Definición de una actitud: tres discursos*, con un prólogo por Eduardo Frei (1942). The book consists of essays by two Christian Democrats. A leading member of his party, Tomic is regarded by some Chileans as an extremist and a demagogue. His anti-United Statesism is certainly more virulent than Frei's. Other works of Tomic include *Fundamentos cristianos para una nueva política en Chile* (1945); *Comunismo, capitalismo y democracia cristiana* (1948); and *Chile y la guerra* (1942). Rafael A. Gumucio and Eduardo Frei, *21° aniversario de la Falange Nacional* (1956). Monsignor Manuel Larraín Errázuriz (bishop of Talca) is one of the few advocates of the Christian Democrat Party among members of the Chilean hierarchy. His writing includes *La hora de la acción católica* (1956) and *La iglesia ante el problema social* (1941). Bernardo Leighton has published the following pamphlets: *Los conflictos del trabajo y su significado social* (1945); *Cuenta política del Presidente Nacional, 4° Congreso Falangista, 13-14 abril* (1946); *Labor Falangista en el Ministerio de Educación Pública* (1952); and *Problema internacional* (1947). See also Leighton's *Memoria de Prueba, Propiedad rústica y gremios agrarios* (1933). Marcelo Martínez Candía, *El pensamiento social-cristiano en la economía* (1957. *Memoria de Prueba*). Jaime Ross Bravo, *Bases para una filosofía de la ley* (1945. *Memoria de Prueba*). Christian Democrat sentiments are also found in the widely publicized March 1, 1960, letter addressed by the Chilean University Student Federation (FECH) to President Eisenhower while the latter was in Chile. The FECH was at this time controlled by students affiliated with the Christian Democrat Party. Patricio Fernández, a Christian Democrat and then president of the FECH, is generally acknowledged as the author of the letter although there were some claims that Radomiro Tomic actually wrote it. For the text of the letter, see *El Mercurio* or *El Diario Ilustrado*, March 2, 1960.

Christian Democrat periodicals are: *La Libertad*, an interesting and often provocative daily founded in 1958; *La Voz*, a weekly directed by Alejandro Magnet; and *Política y Espíritu*, a semimonthly which appeared first in 1945. See also the 1960 book of Sergio Guilisasti Tagle, *Caminos de la política*, containing interviews with two of the leading spokesmen of each of the major political parties in Chile.

[24] Cámara de Diputados, *Boletín de sesiones ordinarias*, 1933, Sesión 25°, July 11, 1933, pp. 1310 ff., and Sesión 34°, July 26, pp. 1724 ff. Also, the Santiago daily *Extra*, published in 1946 and 1947 by left-wing elements in the Radical Party, contained frequent allegations that the conservative Radicals had consistently betrayed the interests of the masses.

[25] Cámara de Diputados, *Boletín de sesiones extraordinarias*, 1955-1956, II, Sesión 15°, November 22, 1955, p. 1177.

[26] See Guillermo F. Bañados, *La verdadera democracia* (1922), in which the onetime president of the Democrat Party advocates socialism. See also the speech of Socialist Deputy Humberto Casali, Cámara de Diputados, *Boletín de sesiones ordinarias*, 1933, Sesión 31°, July 19, 1933, p. 1555.

[27] Muñoz, "Un ano que se va," *El Mercurio*, January 1, 1922.

[28] In the 1950 municipal elections, the Popular Socialist Party won more than 16,000 votes, and the Socialist Party only slightly over 10,000.

[29] The most active historian of Chilean socialism is Julio César Jobet. His works include: "Alejandro Venegas Valdés, precursor del socialismo," *La Opinión* (a Santiago socialist· daily), September 20, 1947; "Las concepciones historiográficas de F. A. Encina," *Occidente* (September-October, 1958), in which Jobet accuses Encina of advocating racism and in general all that is out of date and decaying in the sociopolitical order; *Ensayo crítico del desarrollo económico social de Chile* (1955), perhaps Jobet's major work; "Hacia el reestructuramiento económico social de Chile," *Occidente* (February-March, 1940); *Luis Emilio Recabarren: los orígenes del movimiento obrero y del socialismo chileno* (1955); "Movimiento social obrero," Universidad de Chile, *Desarrollo de Chile en la primera mitad del siglo xx*, I (1953); "Notas sobre la historiografía chilena," in Ricardo Donoso, et al., *Historiografía chilena* (1949); *Los precursores del pensamiento social de Chile*, 2 vols. (1955, 1956); *Significado del Partido Socialista en la realidad nacional* (1940); "Síntesis interpretativa del desarrollo histórico nacional durante la segunda mitad del siglo XIX," *Atenea*, Año XXIII, no. 250 (April, 1946), and no. 251 (May, 1946); "Síntesis interpretativa histórico de Chile durante el siglo XX," *ibid.*, Año XXIV, no. 264 (June, 1947), and no. 265 (July, 1947); *El socialismo en Chile* (1956); and *Socialismo, libertad y comunismo* (1958). See also Pablo García, "Realidad y perspective de la obra de Julio César Jobet," *Atenea*, Año XXIX, nos. 329-330 (November-December, 1952).

[30] *El Mercurio*, March 8, 1961.

[31] See Jobet, "Socialismo y comunismo," *Occidente* (April-May, 1951), in which the Marxian socialist author expresses his hatred of communism.

[32] The results of the September 4, 1958, presidential election were: Jorge Alessandri, 387,297; Salvador Allende, 352,915; Eduardo Frei, 255,168; Luis Bossay, the Radical Party candidate, 190,832; and Raúl Antonio Zamorano, 41,268.

[33] Below are listed a few of the titles in the vast literature of communism and Marxian socialism in Chile. Humberto Abarca, *Informe del Secretario de Organización del Comité Central a la XII sesión plenaria del Partido Comunista de Chile* (1943). Luis M. Acuña, *Doctrinas sociales de Marx: las grandes lineas de la economía social* (1933). Fernando Alegría, *Recabarren* (1938). This is a well-written, favorable biography of one of the earliest socialists who ultimately became

a communist. Salvador Allende, the prominent socialist senator and medical doctor who has twice been an unsuccessful presidential candidate has written various pamphlets, a typical one being *La contradicción de Chile: régimen de izuquierda, política económica de derecha* (1943). Allende's major work is *Realidad médico-social chilena* (1939). Oscar Alvarez Andrews, *Apuntes históricos del movimiento sindical* (1936). This provides, much information on socialist-anarchist-communist penetration in labor organization. Raúl Ampuero, *La juventud socialista en el frente del pueblo* (1940). This is one of the early political pamphlets of the energetic Marxian socialist, now a Socialist Party senator. Ampuero was a leading figure in the *Partido Socialista Popular* during the 1940's and 1950's. *Así Es*. A left-wing daily, this was published in Santiago, 1938-1947. José Cademartori, "Análisis del proyecto de reconstrucción y fomento que el gobierno envió al Congreso," *La Ultima Hora*, July 8, 1960. Cademartori, a young communist deputy, a professor of economic theory at the School of Economics, University of Chile, and formerly Chief of Planning of the government Development Corporation (CORFO) advances the party-line approach to the Chilean earthquake disaster (March, 1960): high taxes on the rich and on United States firms, loans primarily from socialist countries, and economic planning for all of Chile, not just the afflicted area. Juan Casiello, *Lo que ha hecho el comunismo* (1942). Alejandro Chelén Rojas, *En defensa de la minería chilena* (1957). This work is of pronounced Marxian orientation. Carlos Contreras Labarca has been one of the leading communists since the late 1920's. The onetime senator is the author of a large number of pamphlets, including the following: *Alessandri, portavoz de las fuerzas reaccionarias y profascistas* (1935); *América-latina invadida por el fascismo* (1938); and *La Lucha del pueblo por la reorganización de Chile* (1946). Luis Corvalán in 1960 was secretary general of the Communist Party in Chile. See his *Informe del Comité Central al 11° Congreso del Partido Comunista de Chile* (1958). Sergio Fernández Larraín, *Informe sobre el Comunismo reunido a la Convención General del Partido Conservador Unido el 12 de octubre, 1954* (1954). The work lists all of the groups that Fernández suspects of being tainted by communist orientation, as well as all of the men he suspects of being communists. A list of communist-line periodicals is also included. Fernández, appointed Chilean ambassador to Spain in 1958, is the self-professed number-one communist hunter of Chile, often referred to as the McCarthy of Melipilla. For him, anyone who appreciates the poetry of Pablo Neruda is suspect. Ricardo Fonseca, *Chile es capaz de resolver sus problemas* (1947). In this work, a former leading communist extols the Communist Party. René Frías Ojeda is a fast-rising communist in the Chilean political arena. An early work of his is *Consideraciones sobre nuestra política comercial exterior* (1934. *Memoria de Prueba*). César Godoy Urrutia, a communist, has published interesting works, among them *Adonde va el socialismo* (1940) and *Los sucesos del 5 de septiembre* (1939). Armando González Rodríguez, *Comunismo y democracia* (1951). Middle-ground, freethinker González has produced a strongly anticommunist study, with some valuable insights into the Chilean situation. Eugenio González Rojas, onetime senator and secretary general of the *Partido Socialista Popular*, is the author of several political tracts, among them *Socialismo y liberalismo; posición del Partido Socialista Popular frente a la situación nacional* (1957) and *El PSP lucha contra las facultades extra-ordinarias* (1949). *Hoy*. Published as a weekly in Santiago, 1931-1942, this was a socialist organ famed in its early days for the editorial writing of Carlos Dávila.

Raúl Irarrázaval Lecaros, *El comunismo en Chile* (1948). This is a strongly anti-communist pamphlet. Elías Lafertte, who died in 1961, was long one of Chile's leading communists and served a term as president of the Communist Party. See his *Como triunfaremos en las elecciones de 1941* (1941), *Hacia la transformación económica y política de Chile por la via de la Unión Nacional* (1945), and *Vida de una comunista: páginas autobiográficas* (1957). The last work contains reminiscences of the nitrate pampa, Recabarren, the political struggle before and during the 1930's as well as in the 1940's, prisons and exile, and the Popular Front and the FRAP. Humberto Mendoza, a Marxian socialist, has written, *¿Y ahora? El socialismo movil de post guerra*, con prólogo por Julio César Jobet (1942) and *Socialismo, camino de la libertad* (1945). Manuel Francisco Mesa Seco, *El comunismo ante la ley chilena* (1947). Salvador Ocampo P. and Elías Lafertte, *El cobre de Chile: nacionalización de Chuquicamata, Potrerillos y Sewell* (1951). *La Opinión.* Published in Santiago, 1932-1957, this was an important socialist daily. Partido Comunista de Chile, *Ricardo Fonseca, combatiente ejemplar* (1952). Between 1941 and 1947, the Central Committee of the Communist Party of Chile published *Principios: Revista mensual teórica y política.* In September 1958 appeared the first edition of the monthly *Problemas de la Paz y del Socialismo: Revista Teórica y de Información de los Partidos Comunistas y Obreros. ¿Qué Hay?* A leftist weekly, this was published in Santiago, 1951-1958. *La Raspa.* This was a leftist humor review published in Santiago in 1949. Sergio Recabarren, a socialist, frequently advocates in print the cause of Latin-American unity as a means of counteracting United States imperialism. See his *Latinoamerica y imperialismo* (1949), *progreso y destino cultural latinoamericano* (1950), and *La solidaridad continental* (1951. *Memoria de Prueba*). Aniceto Rodríguez, a Marxian socialist senator and a skilled orator, has written *América latina entre la miseria y el miedo* (1957), *Forjando la unidad popular* (1956), and, with Raúl Ampuero, *Democracia y revolución* (1955). *Rumbo.* This socialist monthly was published in Santiago, 1939-1940. *Saca Pica.* Published in Santiago, 1942-1945, this was a leftist weekly. Oscar Schnake Vergara, an important socialist political figure, has published such works as *América y la guerra; sensacional discurso* (1941), *Chile y la guerra: hacia una democracia dirigida—discurso del Ministro de Fomento* (1941), and *Política socialista* (1938). Marcelo Segall, a professor and leading figure in the Instituto Marx-Engels-Lenin in Santiago during the 1940's, has written *Desarrollo del capitalismo en Chile: cinco ensayos dialécticos* (1953). This is an extensive examination of Chilean economic development, especially in the nineteenth century, from a Marxian point of view. *El Siglo.* This is the communist daily, published in Santiago, 1940-1948, and 1952—. Sergio Sotomayor A., *Carta abierta de un ex-militante al Partido Comunista de Chile* (1953). Valodia Teitelboim, one of Chile's leading communist figures, has written *Hijo del salitre* (1952), a social commentary novel of life in the nitrate pampa, *El amanecer de capitalismo y la conquista de América* (1943), and *El pueblo y el terremoto* (1960). *La Ultima Hora.* Published in Santiago since 1945, this socialist organ is one of the liveliest Chilean newspapers. Antonio de Undurraga, *Recabarren o el lider de sudor y oro* (1947). *Vistazo.* A weekly propagating the FRAP line, this has been published in Santiago since 1954. Oscar Waiss, an eminent Chilean socialist who was once the leader of the Trotskyist movement in his country, wrote *El drama socialista* (1947). In it, he expressed disillusionment over the internal dissension that ravaged the Communist

Party in Chile and the manner in which party bureaucrats betrayed the cause. There is also a valuable epilogue which singled out for praise the men who had rendered loyal service to Chilean Marxism. See also the same author's *Un fantasma recorre el mundo* (1938), a novel which proclaimed the teachings of Trotsky, *Nacionalismo y socialismo en américa-latina* (1954), and *Antecedentes económicos y sociales de la constitución de 1833* (1934. *Memoria de Prueba*).

For the beginnings of Marxian and communist infiltration, see Chapter IV, notes 136-138. For Marxian and communist literature of the 1920's and early 1930's, see Chapter VI, notes 162-167. See also Robert J. Alexander, *Communism in Latin America* (New Brunswick, New Jersey, 1958), especially Chapter X, and S. Cole Blasier, "Chile: a Communist Battleground," *Political Science Quarterly*, LXV, no. 3 (September, 1950).

[34] Prologue by Feliú Cruz to Julio César Jobet, *Ensayo crítico del desarrollo económico-social de Chile*.

[35] The Jobet work referred to is the *Ensayo crítico* (1955), that of Ramírez is *La guerra civil de 1891* (1951), while that of Heise González is *La constitución de 1925* (1951). It is particularly significant that Jobet and Ramírez are among the few historians who concern themselves with the attempt to use scientific methods of investigation. Unfortunately, most non-Marxian historians content themselves largely with the methods of the essayist and the polemicist.

[36] Armando González Rodríguez, "El drama del catolicismo social," *Occidente* (September-October, 1955), argues that Christian socialists are being dangerously naive in cooperating even temporarily with communists. However, he concedes that, given the enormity of the problems reformers face in bringing change to Chile, their willingness to cooperate in the short run with communists is at least understandable.

[37] Silva de la Fuente, *Punto Final* (1956), p. 157.

[38] See González R., "Un falso dilema: catolicismo o comunismo," *Occidente* (December, 1942).

[39] For this sort of description of United States capitalism see Jaime Eyzaguirre, *Elementos de la economía* (1954 edition), Chapter I.

[40] The book was published in 1951. See also Jaime Castillo, "Un dilema falso: o comunismo o liberalismo," *Política y Espíritu* (February, 1947). Another important article is José Léniz Prieto, "Capitalismo, no; comunismo, no; entonces, ¿qué?" *Occidente* (October, 1948). Léniz avers that capitalism does not have the answer because it accepts ownership of land and does not recognize the capital value of man. This leads to the enslavement of the masses and accumulation of wealth in the hands of a few. Léniz was a booster of the Christian Democrats until 1947 when, upon being admonished by Archbishop Caro of Santiago, they withdrew from an alliance with the communists. This convinced Léniz that the movement was too much controlled by traditionalist churchmen to offer a real solution for Chile. On the other hand, in *O capitalismo o comunismo: o vivir como en Estados Unidos o vivir como en Rusia* (1952), rightist Héctor Rodríguez de la Sotta argues that there can be no middle position between the United States and Russia. In maintaining that Chileans should follow United States models he unfortunately presents a very outdated description of that country's socioeconomic structure.

⁴¹ See in particular, Jorge González von Marées, *El mal de Chile* (1940), and Carlos Keller, *La eterna crisis chilena* (1931).

⁴² Conviction that foreign capital's dominance is a symptom of Chilean decadence is an important aspect of Christian Democrat ideology. The works cited below reveal a similar belief. Enrique Bunster, "Problema fundamental de Chile," *Occidente* (December, 1949). The article, by one of Chile's most popular writers, is a good review of the social problem. The real evil, as the author sees it, is that Chile is not independent. Dependence on foreign capital has interfered with the finding of fundamental solutions to the major national problems. Horacio Serrano Palma, *¿Por qué somos pobres?* (1959). This book adheres closely to Encina's thesis in *Nuestra inferioridad económica* (See Chapter IV, notes 61 and 62). Foreigners are taking over because of Chilean economic inferiority and lack of imagination. Enrique Oyarzún, *El radicalismo ante la revolución social* (1925). This staunch supporter of the first Ibáñez administration regarded foreign capital's dominance as a galling reminder of national stagnation. A similar thesis is developed in Augusto Santelices, *El imperialismo yanqui y su influencia en Chile* (1926).

For some of the literature that blames Chile's educational system for having fostered economic inferiority and facilitated the takeover by foreign capital, see Chapter IV, note 62, and Chapter X, notes 76-79.

⁴³ The following works all express sentiments of economic nationalism. Arturo Aldunate Phillips, *Estados Unidos, gran aventura del hombre* (1943) and *Un pueblo en busca de su destino: Chile, país industrial* (1947). In the first of these books, Aldunate, although extremely lavish in his praise of the United States, warned Chileans that they would probably be ignored by that country after the Second World War, and advised them to take steps to reduce their dependence on foreign capital. Ignacio Aliaga Ibar, *La economía de Chile y la industria del cobre* (1946). Oscar Alvarez Andrews, *Historia del desarrollo industrial de Chile* (1936). Oscar Alvarez Gallardo, *Condiciones de vida y trabajo del obrero de las minas en Chile* (1952). Luis Amadeo Aracena, *Ensayos económicos, políticos y sociales* (1941). René Arriagada and Sergio Jarpa, *Por una política nacional* (1952). Gonzalo Bulnes Aldunate, *El catastro de las minas y algunos aspectos del régimen de concesión minera* (1942). Santiago del Campo, "Política económica interamericana," *Occidente* (August, 1949). Círculo de Economía, *Dos problemas nacionales: (a) Realidad del cobre; (b) Convenio con Argentina* (No date, probably 1953). This is a valuable exposition of the copper industry and the position of the United States in it. The pamphlet voices economic nationalism, suggesting the United States had not paid sufficiently for its concessions. Aníbal Pinto is the man primarily responsible for this report. Renato Echiburu Bassi and Hernán Tike Carrasco, *La gran minería del cobre: proyecciones nacionales* (1957). Julio Heise González, *La constitución de 1925 y nuevas tendencias politico-sociales*. Fernando Illanez Benítez, *La economía chilena y el comercio exterior* (1944). Aníbal Pinto Santa Cruz, *Chile: un caso de desarrollo frustrado* (1959); *Cuestiones principales de la economía* (1955); and *Hacia nuestra independencia económica* (1953). One of Chile's leading economists and a guiding spirit of the excellent review *Panorama Económica*, which started in 1948 as a monthly and now appears semi-monthly, Pinto is a strong economic nationalist and something of a socialist. He is bitterly opposed to the tendency of the United States and the International Monetary Fund to make aid dependent upon internal monetary stabilization programs. See his *Ni estabilidad*

ni desarrollo: la política del Fondo Monetario (1960). In these sentiments, Pinto is joined by Felipe Herrera Lane, first president of the Inter-American Development Bank. See Herrera's *Desarrollo económico o estabilidad monetaria* (1958). Another work in the same vein is Agustín Bruce Depolo, *El Fondo Monetario Internacional y su intervención en la economía chilena* (1958. *Memoria de Prueba*). Francisco Antonio Pinto S.C., *Estructura de nuestra economía* (1948) and *Política económica* (1959). Aida Vuscovic Bravo, *Participación del capital extranjero en la economía chilena* (1957. *Memoria de Prueba*). Enrique Zañartu Prieto, *Hambre, miseria e ignorancia* (1938) and *Manuel Aristides Zañartu, o historia y causas del pauperismo en Chile*, con prólogo por Emilio Rodríguez Mendoza (1940). Long prominent in political circles, Enrique Zañartu argued that lack of tariff protection and other measures of economic nationalism were responsible for national poverty.

For earlier indications of economic nationalism see Chapter V, notes 240-246, Chapter VI, note 138, and Chapter VII, notes 113-118, and 127. Greater economic nationalism is advocated by Hispanists (see Chapter VIII, notes 13-15), by Christian Socialists, by Christian Democrats, by many Radicals, and, naturally, by Marxian socialists and communists.

[44] See in particular the eloquent article by the principal economist of the Radical Party's left wing, Alberto Baltra, "Los factores sociales y el desarrollo económico," *Panorama Económico*, no. 182 (December 20, 1957). See also Carlos Arangua R., "Analizando los problemas: la situación del cobre," *ibid.*, beginning in no. 163 (March 29, 1957), and running through no. 182 (December 20, 1957). This is one of the more thorough studies of the copper industry in Chile from the days of early independence to the present time.

[45] See *Vea*, May 30, 1956, p. 8, for criticism of the mission by the Radical Party's Luis Bossay. Donald Bray appears to be correct when he observes: "The United States mission did, indeed, become a hated symbol among the lower-income groups. . . . The Radical Party, playing upon the public dislike of the mission, assumed a position of defending the people against the harsh Klein-Saks program." Bray, "Chilean Politics during the Second Ibáñez Government, 1952-1958" (Stanford University doctoral dissertation, 1961), p. 118. Thus, a hypocritically assumed posture led to much Radical criticism of the mission.

[46] A principal critic of the Klein-Saks mission was Flavian Levine Bawden, a prominent Chilean businessman and the guiding spirit of the Huachipato steel plant. See his "Analizando los problemas: erores que se repiten," *Panorama Económico*, no. 178 (October 25, 1957).

[47] For earlier manifestations of Chilean desire to achieve Latin-American unity as a means of offsetting United States influence see Chapter I, notes 79-94, Chapter V, notes 268 and 269, Chapter VII, notes 52, 74, 95, 101-104, and 128-137. Moreover, senate debates in 1942 clearly suggest that Chile's neutrality during the early stages of the Second World War resulted in part from the hope of a few highly-placed policy directors that they could establish freedom for their nation from United States influence by maintaining an alliance with neutralist Argentina. If the Chilean-Argentine neutralist front could be sustained despite United States displeasure, it was anticipated that it would provide the nucleus for an expanding bloc of Latin-American nations that could disregard United States pressures. Passages in senate debates that reveal this spirit include: remarks of Senator Enrique Bravo, *Cámara de Senadores, Boletín de sesiones extraordinarias*, 1942-1943, Sesión 3°,

November 24, 1942, pp. 116 ff.; remarks of Senator Oscar Valenzuela, *ibid.*, Sesión 4°, November 25, pp. 139-140; remarks of Senator Humberto de Pino, *ibid.*, Sesión 6°, December 2, pp. 193 ff.; remarks of Senator Gustavo Rivera, *ibid.*, Sesión 7°, December 9, p. 217; remarks of Senator Fidel Estay, *ibid.*, Sesión 9°, December 21, p. 237; and remarks of Senator Carlos Contreras Labarca, *ibid.*, Sesión 10°, December 22, p. 329. See also Eugenio Orrego Vicuña, "Destino de Chile," *Estudios*, no. 140 (September, 1944). This article expressed pride in the strength of Presidents Barros Luco and Sanfuentes in maintaining Chilean neutrality during the First World War, as well as regret that neutrality had not been preserved in the Second World War. Had it been, Orrego felt South American countries might finally have achieved independence from the United States. No. 104 of *Estudios* (September, 1941) was almost entirely dedicated to urging Chilean neutrality and close cooperation with Argentina as a means of helping Latin America ultimately to become independent from the United States.

[48] Although the specter of direct United States intervention in Latin America is diminishing as a cause of anti-United Statesism among Chileans, several authors have in recent times expressed concern over the matter. A few of their works are cited below. Ramón Bustos García, *Nociones sobre la intervención* (1944). Sergio Fernández Larraín, *América y el principio de no intervención* (1947). Eduardo Frei, *Las relaciones con los Estados Unidos y el caso Guatemala* (1945). Luis Guillén Atienza, *El principio internacional de no intervención y las doctrinas americanas* (1949. *Memoria de Prueba*). Manuel Guzmán Vial, *La intervención y la no intervención* (1948. *Memoria de Prueba*). Sofía Ibarra Pensa, *Paralelo entre el sistema interamericana y las Naciones Unidos* (No date. *Memoria de Prueba*). Juan Bosco Parra Alderete, *Los sucesos de Guatemala—de junio de 1945—y el derecho internacional público* (1957. *Memoria de Prueba*). R. Parraguez Acevedo, *Aspectos jurídicos del antiguo y del nuevo panamericanismo* (1947).

Two works which reveal that fear of direct United States intervention in Latin America is no longer the cause for concern it once was in Chile are: Samuel Walter Washington, "A Study of the Causes of Hostility toward the United States in Latin America: Chile" (Washington, D.C., 1956. Processed), an external research paper; and Alain Girard and Raúl Samuel, *Situación y perspectivas de Chile en septiembre de 1957: una investigación de opinión pública en Santiago* (1958).

[49] *Habla Juan Gómez M.*

[50] The widely-read book of Carlos Dávila, *We of the Americas* (New York, 1949; Spanish edition in Santiago, 1950), is frequently interpreted in Chile as a call for Latin-American unity to escape economic dependence upon the United States. See "Ardiente guerra en marcha," *Ercilla*, June 14, 1949, and the report of the 1959 lecture presented by Carlos Sander in *El Mercurio*, December 12, 1959. Other works which seem to desire a Third Position include the following. Carlos Arriagada Hurtado, "Un plan Marshall para America Latina," *Occidente* (May, 1949). The author complained of United States neglect, and suggested that Latin-American union was in order. Ernesto Barros Jarpa, "Nuevos aspectos del orden internacional especialmente en América," *Las actuales orientaciones del derecho* (1942). The author, a long-time champion of Latin-American unity, seemed to anticipate the Third Position approach. Alejandro Magnet, *Orígenes y antecedentes del panamericanismo* (1945). The Third Position approach is implicitly advocated in this work by an important member of the Christian Democrat Party. Carlos Keller, "Spengler

y el último Occidente," *Occidente* (February-March, 1948). Ricardo Krebs, "La época del imperialismo," *Estudios*, no. 163 (August, 1946). Ricardo Latcham, *Chile en frente a su destino* (1944). Cristina Sanz, *El plan Marshall y américa-latina* (1954). Luis Urrutia Ibáñez, *Federación iberoamericana* (1942). Eduardo Yrarrázaval Concha, *América latina en la guerra fría* (1959). The author urged closer economic ties to match the cultural bonds already existing between Europe and Latin America. Economic integration among Latin-American nations was also stressed. See the same author's *El hemisfero postergado* (1954), in which he argued that United States policies were largely responsible for Latin America's slow progress.

CHAPTER 10

[1] Reported in *El Mercurio*, September 20, 1931.

[2] *Ibid.*, January 8, 1932. Approximately 20,000 Chileans at this time enjoyed an annual income of between 10,000 and 30,000 pesos, while some 3,000 annually gained in excess of 50,000.

[3] See for example, Ernest Feder, "Feudalism and Agricultural Development: the Role of Controlled Credit in Chile's Agriculture," *Land Economics*, XXXVI, no. 1 (February, 1960).

[4] McBride, *Chile, Land and Society* (New York, 1936).

[5] Bowers, *Chile through Embassy Windows, 1939-1953* (New York, 1958).

[6] *The Atlantic Monthly*, November, 1959.

[7] Bellesort's book was published in Paris in 1923. See also Julio César Jobet, "Notas sobre la historiografía," in Ricardo Donoso, Luis Durand, Alberto Edwards Vives, Francisco Antonio Encina, Jaime Eyzaguirre, Guillermo Feliú Cruz, Luis Galdames, Juan Gómez Millas, Jobet, Mariano Latorre, Domingo Melfi, and Eugenio Pereira Salas, *Historiografía chilena* (1949), pp. 354-366.

[8] Cámara de Senadores, *Boletín de sesiones extraordinarias, 1937-1938*, Sesiones of November and December, 1937.

[9] Corporación de Fomento de la Producción, *Cuentas nacionales, 1940-1954* (1957), and *Renta nacional, 1940-1954*, 2 vols. (1956). See also Aníbal Pinto, *Chile, un caso de desarrollo frustrado* (1959), p. 185, and Félix Ruiz C., "Por que no estoy de acuerdo con el profesor Levine," *Panorama Económica*, no. 179 (November 8, 1957). In this article, Ruiz affirms that during the preceding eighteen years manual laborers have been the hardest hit of any functional-interest group through loss of real purchasing power.

[10] Jadue, *Redistribución probable del ingreso de las personas en Chile: período 1940-1954* (1960). See especially the chapter entitled, "La distribución del ingreso de las personas por tramos de renta." Of the active population, says Jadue, 78.3 per cent receives 33.1 per cent of the national income.

[11] Varela, "Distribución del ingreso nacional," *Panorama Económica*, no. 208 (December, 1959), p. 405. Francisco Cuevas Mackenna, vice-president of the *Sociedad Nacional de Minería*, using elaborate charts to corroborate his position, has asserted that between 1956 and the end of 1959 the purchasing power of salaried groups declined 19 per cent. See the summary of the Cuevas findings in *La Ultima Hora*, April 20, 1960.

On this theme, there are many other interesting works which the reader could consult. Helio Varela, *Estratificación social de la población trabajadora en Chile y su participación en el ingreso nacional, 1940-1954* (1958). Manuel Silva Balbuena in *La especulación en la economía* (1939) noted that those benefiting from gains in the Chilean economy were not the workers, but a parasitical speculating class. The essay by Max Nolff in the book *La inflación: naturaleza y problemas* (1954)— with chapters contributed by Nolff (the most substantial work in the volume), Jaime Barrios, Eduardo Frei, Felipe Herrera Lane, Pedro Irantel, Sergio Molina, and Aníbal Pinto—points out that as of 1951 the Chilean lower classes had failed to benefit from Chile's economic development.

[12] Juan Crocco Ferrari, *Ensayo sobre la población chilena* (1947. *Memoria de Prueba*), p. 332. This is one of the best surveys of the Chilean social problem, and probably the best Chilean *Memoria de Prueba*, or university dissertation, encountered by the author.

[13] Nicholas Kaldor, *Economic Problems of Chile* (1956. Mimeo.). Kaldor wrote his fine study on the basis of *Corporación de Fomento* and Economic Commission for Latin America (ECLA, or CEPAL in Spanish) figures. The work was not published in Chile, but a mimeograph copy is in the ECLA Library in Santiago. The treatise was substantially reproduced in *Trimestre Económico*, XXVI, no. 2 (México, D.F., April-June, 1958).

[14] International Bank for Reconstruction and Development, *Situación y perspectivas económicas de Chile* (1957. Mimeo.). See also the summary of this work in *Panorama Económico*, no. 166 (May 10, 1957), p. 204.

[15] These figures, based upon information in a 1953 *Informe* of the International Monetary Fund, are supplied by the Austrian economist-diplomat Carl Hudeczek, *Economía chilena: rumbos y metas* (1956), p. 157. Hudeczek once served as Austrian ambassador in Chile.

Careful studies of the Chilean tax structure have also been made by Enrique Piedrabuena Richard. See his *Compendio de legislación tributaria chilena* (1945), and *Manuel de derecho financiero* (1950). An obvious bias in favor of the upper-income groups sometimes leads Piedrabuena to questionable conclusions; and his assertions that Chileans are overtaxed, with business initiative thereby being stifled, are in clear conflict with information provided by the United Nations (see note 16).

Moreover, the regressive features of the Chilean tax structure result in a situation in which the lower classes actually bear the heaviest proportional burden in financing the widely-heralded social security system. The general inadequacies and occasional injustices of the Chilean social security system are treated in: Joseph Grunwald, *Limitaciones económicas del sistema de seguridad social chileno* (1958); Instituto de Economía de la Universidad de Chile, *Perspectivas económicas del problema de las pensiones* (1958) and *Antecedentes legales de ocho cajas de previsión chilenas existentes en 1957* (1958); Waldo Pereira A., *La seguridad social en Chile* (1950); and Francisco A. Pinto S.C., *Seguridad social chilena* (1950).

[16] United Nations, Economic Commission for Latin America, *Estudio económico de América Latina, 1950: hechos y tendencias recientes de la economía chilena* (1951), p. 16.

[17] Alberto Baltra, "Los factores sociales y el desarrollo económico," *Panorama Económico*, no. 181 (December 6, 1957), and no. 182 (December 20, 1957). See

especially the latter number, p. 818. See also Kaldor, *op. cit.*, p. 21, and Aníbal Pinto, *Hacia nuestra independencia económica* (1953), pp. 68-69. Pinto states that Chile in recent years has invested only some 11 per cent of her gross national product, as compared to Norway with 30 per cent, Holland with 23 per cent, Brazil with 13.9 per cent, and Mexico with 15.3 per cent.

[18] See *El Mercurio*, July 3, 1960.

[19] Ahumada, *En vez de la miseria* (1958), pp. 74-75.

[20] Baltra, *op. cit.* (see note 17), no. 182.

[21] Armanet, "Peligros de la estabilización," *Economía y Finanzas*, Año XXIV, no. 282 (April, 1960).

There are many other useful works dealing with the general economic factors of the social problem. Some of these are cited below. Enrique Alcalde Irarrázaval, *Aspectos actuales de la inflación chilena* (1957). Miguel García Corcés, *Cálculo de gastos en alimentación, bebidas, tabacos y alojamiento de la población chilena, 1940-1950* (1953. *Memoria de Prueba*). Hilda González, *El problema económico como factor determinante del caso social* (1945. *Memoria de Prueba*). Instituto de Economía de la Universidad de Chile, *La situación económica de los empleados particulares* (1953). Julio César Jobet, "Hacia el reestructuramiento económico social de Chile," *Occidente* (February-March, 1940). Zarko Luksic, "La inflación monetaria en Chile," *Economía: Revista de la Facultad de Ciencias Económicas de la Universidad de Chile*, Año XIII, no. 42 (April, 1953). Moisés Poblete Troncoso, *Standard de vida y desarrollo económico social* (1956) and *El subconsumo en la América del sur: alimentos, vestuario y vivienda* (1946). Enrique Solari Mongrio and Roberto Alvarado Córdoba, *Introducción al panorama económico de nuestra salud* (1957). José Vera L., "Aspectos sociales del desarrollo económico," *Economía: Revista de la Facultad de la Universidad de Chile*, Año XIX, no. 63 (2° trimestre, 1959). Ernesto Wagemann, *La población en el destino de los pueblos* (1949).

Some of the primary sources dealing with Chilean economic development are listed next. Banco Central de Chile, *Boletín Mensual*. Corporación de Fomento de la Producción, *Geografía económica de Chile*, 2 vols. (1956). Additional works published by the *Corporación de Fomento* have been cited in the notes above. Corporación de Reconstrucción y Auxilio, *Memoria, estadística y balance correspondiente a los años 1939, 1940, 1941* (1942). This work is mainly concerned with the reconstruction that followed the 1939 earthquake. The *Dirección General de Estadística* has, since 1928, published yearly reports under each of the following headings: *Agricultura e industria agropecuarias; Comercio exterior; Comercio interior y comunicaciones; Demografía y asistencia social; Estadística chilena; Finanzas, bancas y cajas sociales; Industrias; Minería; Política, administración, justicia y educación.* A valuable Santiago monthly which began publication in 1941 is *Economía: Revista de la Facultad de Ciencias Económicas de la Universidad de Chile*. The journal is generally inclined to favor reform and bold experimentation. It publishes valuable book reviews and summaries of the *Memorias de Prueba* that pertain to economics. Another Santiago monthly, which began publication in 1937, is *Economía y Finanzas: Observador Internacional*. This is a valuable source not only for articles, but for statistics, and for information on mining, agriculture, livestock, and commerce. Useful economic indices are frequently included. The general orientation leans somewhat toward the classical liberal point of view, but there are often exceptions. The *Instituto de Economía de la Universidad de Chile* has put out many excellent studies, some of which have already been cited. Additional works published by the *Instituto* include: *Boletín Informativo, hechos y perspectivas de la economía chilena vistos al 1 de abril de 1958* (1958); *Chile y la inflación* (1955); *Desarrollo económico de Chile, 1940-1956* (1956); *La migración interna de Chile en el período 1940-1952* (1960); *Ocupación y desocupación, Gran Santiago, Valparaíso, Viña del Mar, zona de Concepción, Valdivia, Los Lagos, junio de 1959* (1959); *Perspectivas del comercio exterior chileno y sus efectos sobre el desarrollo económico, 1959-1965* (1959); and *Research, Publications and other activities* (1959). Beginning in 1948 as a Santiago monthly, *Panorama Económico* is now a semimonthly. It is a valuable, lively review of discussion, as well as of straight economic information. In 1960 the director was Mario A. Sáez, the Radical Party deputy representing Concepción. *Precios: Revista oficial de la Bolsa de Comercio de Santiago y Bolsa de Corredores de Valparaíso*. Starting as a weekly in 1933, this publication ended as a quarterly in 1954. Sociedad de Fomento Fabril, *Hoja de Información Económica*. This appears sporadically. As of April 1960 thirty-nine numbers had been published. United Nations, Economic Commission for Latin America, *Antecedentes sobre el desarrollo de la economía chilena, 1925-1952*, 2 vols. (1954) and *Estudio económico de América Latina* (1956). The Economic Commission for Latin America has its headquarters, as well as a valuable library, in Santiago. This library, together with those maintained by the *Corporación de Fomento de la Producción* and the *Instituto de Economía* of the University of Chile, provide the economist with much better facilities for study than he is apt to encounter elsewhere in Latin America. Universidad de Chile, *Seminario de problemas regionales de Atacama* (1957); *Seminario de problemas regionales de Antofagasta* (1957); and *Seminario de investigaciones de la provincia de Aisén* (1959). These publications are careful surveys of social as well as economic problems in three of Chile's trouble areas.

[22] For 1930 figures, see Dirección de Estadística, *X Censo de la población efectuado el 27 de noviembre de 1930* (1935), II, 309. For 1952 figures, see República de Chile, Servicio Nacional de Estadística y Censos, *XII Censo general de población y de vivienda, levantado el 24 de abril de 1952* (1955), I, 159. The 1952 figure does not include those who may in the future learn to read and write. Neither, however, does it include those who having once learned these skills have now forgotten them. Thus, 25 per cent probably represents a fairly accurate illiteracy statistic for 1952. Eduardo Hamuy, "Educación elemental, analfabetismo y desarrollo económico," *Boletín de la Universidad de Chile* (May, 1960), p. 14, held 19.8 per cent to have been the accurate illiteracy figure. The census taken in that year revealed also that of the approximately 1,100,000 children between ages seven and fourteen, only 718,394 attended school, leaving 321,789 who were receiving no education. See *El Mercurio*, December 20, 1959. Economist Jorge Ahumada estimated in 1958 that only 13 per cent of the population then above six years of age had received or would receive instruction. See his *En vez de la miseria* (1958), pp. 28-29.

[23] República de Chile, Servicio Nacional de Estadística y Censos, *op. cit.*

[24] Caja de Habitación, *Memoria de 1950* (1952). The pages of this work are not numbered.

[25] Caja de la Habitación, *El problema de la habitación en Chile* (1945), p. 93.

[26] Cámara de Senadores, *Boletín de sesiones extraordinarias*, 1942-1943, Sesión 7°, May 18, 1943, p. 1015.

[27] República de Chile, Servicio Nacional de Estadística y Censos, *Primer censo nacional de vivienda* (1955).

[28] See Raúl Sáez S., *Casas para Chile: Plan Frei* (1959), containing the Eduardo Frei plan on Chilean housing and copious explanatory notes. This work is one of the richest sources on the current housing crisis in Chile and contains a fine bibliography.

[29] Antigoni Stogianis, *Ingreso familiares y gasto en vivienda para el área urbana de Chile* (1957). Some additional works on Chile's housing problem are here listed. Hugo Galdames Avendaño, *El problema de la vivienda popular en Chile y Argentina* (1949. *Memoria de Prueba*). Instituto de Economía de la Universidad de Chile, *Un aspecto de la situación habitacional de Chile en 1952* (1958). David L. Krooth and Arthur H. Courshow, *Report of Housing Finance Team* (1958). Teófilo Mansilla, *La crisis de la vivienda* (1957). Olgo López Muñoz, *El problema de la vivienda en Chile* (1946). Luis F. Luengo Escalona, *El problema de la vivienda* (1946).

[30] See Enrique Rosenblatt B., *El problema del alcoholismo* (1958), p. 7.

[31] *Ibid.*, pp. 354, 379.

[32] Elías Mehgme Rodríguez, *La economía nacional y el problema de las subsistencias en Chile* (1943), II, 922, estimates that 90 per cent of accidental deaths in Chile are caused by intoxication.

[33] Other works dealing with the problem of drunkenness include: Daniel Camus Gundián, *Alcoholismo, problema médico-social* (1951), which is probably the best study published in Chile on the topic; Armando Maldonado San Martín, *La ley de alcoholes y los problemas del alcoholismo* (1949); and the arrestingly entitled pamphlet of Luis Arturo Moraga, *Riqueza nacional—alcoholismo y prostitución* (1937).

[34] Lautaro Ojeda Herrera, *Esquema del hambre en Chile* (1959). This valuable book reviews most of the important material written on the subject in the past thirty years.

[35] Cámara de Senadores, *Boletín de sesiones extraordinarias*, 1942-1943, Sesión 5°, May 12, 1943, pp. 919 ff.

[36] See *La Libertad*, March 26, 1960, and Carlos Jorquera, "Chilenos pierden su dimensión," *Ercilla*, April 6, 1960. Additional works dealing with the problem of undernourishment are cited here. Ricardo Cox and Jorge Mardones, *La alimentación en Chile* (1942). Jaime Feferholtz Bernstein, *Nutrición y estado económico social* (1939). Raúl Molina Schulz, *La economía y el problema de la alimentación en Chile* (1954). Alfredo Riquelme, *Panorama de la alimentación en Chile* (1958). Julio Santa María, *¿Podemos alimentarnos mejor?* (1954). Inés Torres M., *Alimentación de las clases populares* (1954).

[37] In 1942, tuberculosis caused 276 of every 1000 deaths in Chile, according to Arturo Aldunate Phillips, *Estados Unidos, gran aventura del hombre* (1943), p. 121. In 1941, some sources estimated life expectancy at 33.6, compared to Panama with 50.2, Uruguay with 50, and Brazil with 37.4. See Daniel Camus Gundián, *op. cit.* (note 33), p. 111. A more recent and more optimistic appraisal put Chilean life expectancy at approximately 52. See United Nations, *Informe sobre*

la situación social en el mundo (1953), p. 19. For general health conditions in Chile, consult the work by medical doctor and socialist Senator Salvador Allende, *Realidad médico-social chilena* (1939), and the excellent study of Juan Crocco Ferrari, *Ensayo sobre la población chilena* (1947). See also Crocco Ferrari and Flavián Levine B., *La población chilena* (1945), and Eduardo Cruz-Coke L., *Medicina preventiva y medicina dirigida* (1938). Reformist Conservative Cruz-Coke was, as a senator, largely responsible for the enactment of Chilean public health legislation.

[38] Books cited in note 37 contain information on infant mortality. Gabriel Gutiérrez Ojeda, "Nuestra crisis permanente," *Occidente* (November, 1945), gave the findings of an inspection of the Quinta Normal, a slum area in Santiago, conducted by the University of Chile: infant mortality among the 66,942 residents was 200 for every 1,000 born alive. República de Chile, Servicio Nacional de Estadística y Censos, *Demografía y asistencia social, año 1951* (1952), p. 86, gave figures showing that during 1951 deaths at under five averaged slightly less than one for every five births. Given these figures, the estimate of one death out of every four among urban lower classes seems conservative enough as of 1951. More recent statistics might show an improvement. Still, in 1959 in Santiago province alone it was said that 10,000 children of less than one year's age died because of lack of food and care, and that 7,000 were born dead. See Daniel Armanet, "Peligros de la estabilización," *Economía y Finanzas*, Año XXIV, no. 282 (April, 1960).

Additional works, dealing not only with health and infant mortality, but with the entire scope of urban social problems, are listed next. León Alterman P., *El movimiento demográfico en Chile* (1946). Oscar A. Alvarez Gallardo, *Condiciones de vida y trabajo del obrero de las minas en Chile* (1952). Luis Amadeo Aracena, *Ensayos económicos, políticos y sociales* (1941). Luis Arrieta Cañas, *Majaderías socialistas* (1942). Arrieta grants the existence of the social problem and argues that socialism is not the solution. He is a prolific defender of economic liberalism. See also his *El liberalismo y la cuestión social* (1942). Another defender of modified liberalism as the proper means for solving the social problem is Paul Aldunate Phillips, *Sentido moderno de liberalismo* (1943). Alfredo Bowen, "Perspectivas cristianas del sindicalismo," *Estudios*, no. 102 (June-July, 1941). Bowen, at the time professor of labor law, School of Social Service, Catholic University of Chile, called attention to the failure of organized labor in the country. A similar theme is found in Octavio Cornejo Bravo, *Tendencias modernas del movimiento de asociación profesional* (1948) dealing with certain phases of labor organization since 1920. "Desarrollo de la educación chilena desde 1940," *Boletín Estadístico de la Universidad de Chile*, III, no. 1 (1959). The article deals with the continuing lack of educational facilities and with the consequent deterioration of social and economic conditions. Joaquín Edwards Bello, "¿Como combatir la terrible depresión de nuestro caracter?" *La Nación*, March 19, 1936. Edwards was concerned over the lack of optimism and gaiety in Chile, and over the absence of concerted effort to improve the social and economic plight of the masses. Alfredo Gaete Berrios, *Derecho del trabajo* (1943). This is a carefully annotated study of an important aspect of the Chilean legal structure. Rebeca Gañer, *El abandono de hogar del menor de sexo femenina* (1941. *Memoria de Prueba*). Jorge González von Marées, *El mal de Chile: sus causas y sus remedios* (1940). Héctor Humeres Magnán, *La huelga* (1957) and *Patrones y obreros* (1953). Abelardo Iturriaga J., *Características psico-sociales del niño chileno abandonado y delincuente*, con la colaboración de María Quesada N. (1944). Julio César Jobet, "Movimiento social obrero," in Universidad de Chile, *Desarrollo de Chile en la primera mitad del siglo xx* (1953); "Síntesis interpretativo histórico de Chile durante el siglo xx," *Atenea*, Año XXIV, no. 264 (June, 1947), and no. 265 (July, 1947). Amanda Labarca Hubertson, "Evolución femenina," in Universidad de Chile, *Desarrollo*. Tulio Lagos Valenzuela, *Bosquejo histórico del movimiento obrero en Chile* (1941. *Memoria de Prueba*). Mariano Latorre, *Chile, país de rincones* (1957 edition). The Spanish author who spent most of his life in Chile and became one of the country's best writers, explored various features and characteristics of Chile and Chileans, focusing attention on aspects of the social problem. Lucy Luco, "El obrero chileno y sus problemas," *Estudios*, no. 97 (January, 1941). This is an outstanding analysis of many phases of the social problem, including education, health, alcoholism, undernourishment, infant mortality, housing, and workers' wages. Many reliable and useful statistical tables are included. *Mensaje*. This monthly which began publication in 1953 is a Jesuit organ that stresses the need for social justice and reform. Silvestre Molina Urrua, *Condición económico-social de los mineros en la zona carbonífera* (1948. *Memoria de Prueba*). The study suggests that working conditions in mines owned by Chilean nationals are generally worse than those in the foreign-owned operations. Oficina Central de Estadística, *Veinte años de legislación social* (1945). Trancredo Pinochet Le-Brun, *Este Chile que es tu patria* (1945). The well-known author made a passionate plea for social reform and national revitalization. Olga Poblete de Espinosa, *Cuaderno de estudios sociales* (1953). Moisés Poblete Troncoso, *El movimiento obrero latinoamericano* (México, D.F., 1946). *Previsión Social*. This monthly was published in Santiago, 1935-1952, by the *Ministerio de Salubridad, Previsión y Asistencia Social de Chile*. Floreal Recabarren, *Historia del proletariado en las provincias de Tarapacá y Antofagasta* (1954. *Memoria de Prueba*). Blanca Rengifo Pérez, *El niño por nacer y el derecho a la vida* (1947. *Memoria de Prueba*). *Revista de Asistencia Social*. This was a Santiago monthly published 1932-1944. *Revista del Trabajo: publicación mensual: Organo oficial de la Inspección General del Trabajo*. This invaluable source of information on working conditions has been appearing since 1931. Kalman Silvert, "An Essay on Social Structure," American Universities Field Staff Letter, Santiago de Chile, November 25, 1956. This, and other Field Staff letters by Silvert in 1956 and 1957 are valuable sources of information. Hernán Troncoso, "Situación sindical de Chile," *Política y Espíritu*, no. 208 (September 15, 1958). This is an excellent article on the inadequacies of the organized labor movement. Universidad de Chile, *Boletín Informativo del Departamento de Extensión Cultural, dedicado a la 2° y 3° etapa del seminario del Gran Santiago* (1958). The work deals with many aspects of the social-economic problem in greater Santiago. Lina Vera de Vieira, *Panorama de servicio social* (1960). The work summarizes the achievements of social workers in Latin America, and especially in Chile. Graciela Vivanco Guerra, *Bosquejo del problema social en Chile* (1951. *Memoria de Prueba*). Francisco Walker Linares, "Evolución social," in Universidad de Chile, *Desarrollo*, I, 35-49. See also the same author's, *Panorama del derecho social chileno* (1947).

[39] Two examples of books of this sort are: A. Acevedo Hernández, *La raza fuerte* (1922), a novel on the Chilean *rotos*, and Roberto Hernández C., *El roto chileno:*

bosquejo histórico de actualidad (Valparaíso, 1929). One should also consult the text of the play *Perejíl*, produced in Santiago in 1960. The author of the text and the creator of the comic strip entitled "Perejíl" that appears in *El Mercurio* and depicts the adventures of the *roto* Perejíl, is Mario Rivas-Lugose. The moral of the play seems to be that *rotos* are fine, wonderful, and magnificent people, and that Chile could not get along without them. However, they must know their place and stay in it, work hard, and avoid being "climbers." A more realistic work dealing with the *rotos* is Lautaro Yankas, *Rotos* (1954). Written by one of Chile's best novelists and short-story authors, this work is a skilful collection of character sketches of various types of Chilean *rotos*.

[40] See *Panorama Económica*, no. 209 (December, 1959), 405. Francisco Walker Linares, "Evolución social," *op. cit.* (note 38), p. 41, states that unlike the situation in other countries, it is in Chile very rare for a member of the proletariat to advance to bourgeois status.

[41] See Chapter IV, notes 200 and 201.

[42] Julio Vega, "La clase media en Chile," in *Materiales para el estudio de la clase media en la américa latina* (Washington, D.C., 1950), pp. 81-82.

[43] Mistral and Guillermo González, *Deber cristiano* (1922). See also Mistral, "Cristianismo con sentido social," *Atenea*, Año II, no. 9 (November, 1925).

[44] Ernest Feder, "Feudalism and Agricultural Development: the Role of controlled credit in Chile's agriculture," *Land Economics*, XXXVI, no. 1 (February, 1960), 92. Based in part on a research study entitled "Controlled Credit and Agricultural Development in Chile," to be published in Spanish by the *Instituto de Economía de la Universidad de Chile*, the Feder article is one of the very best that can be found on Chilean agriculture. The failure in Chilean agricultural development was noted also in two other basic sources: the 1952 *Informe* prepared by a mission of the International Bank for Reconstruction and Development in cooperation with the FAO of the United Nations; and the 1955 *Censo Agrícola*. See also David Felix, *Desequelibrios estructurales y crecimiento industrial: el caso de Chile* (1958), pp. 20-21.

[45] Instituto de Economía de la Universidad de Chile, *Desarrollo económico de Chile, 1940-1956* (1956), pp. 111, 115, 116. Alberto Baltra, "Los factores sociales y el desarrollo económico," *Panorama Económico*, no. 182 (December, 1957), estimated that in the fifteen years previous to 1957 agricultural production increased 1.69 per cent annually, while consumption of agricultural products went up 2.3 per cent. See also Ministerio de Agricultura, *La agricultura chilena en el quinquenio 1951-1955* (1957), p. 29. Another indication of the failure of Chilean agriculture is the fact that in 1910 there were some 2,676,000 head of cattle in the country. Forty years later the number was 2,344,000. In the same time-span, the human population increased some 80 per cent. See Francisco Rojas Huneeus, "Chile en su aspecto agrícola," in Universidad de Chile, *Desarrollo*.

[46] Feder, *op. cit.*, p. 92.

[47] See the 1955 *Censo Agrícola*, as well as Instituto de Economía de la Universidad de Chile, *Desarrollo económico*, and Aníbal Pinto, *Chile: un caso de desarrollo frustrado*, p. 164.

[48] Universidad de Chile, *Desarrollo económico*, p. 107. Recent and thoroughly documented studies show that between 1925 and 1960 some 60 per cent of the arable land in Chile's central valley changed hands. See Thomas Frank Carroll,

"Agricultural Development in Chile" (1951. Unpublished doctoral dissertation, Cornell University), and especially Gene Ellis Martin, *La división de la tierra en Chile central* (1960), p. 11. Martin's study was originally written as a doctoral dissertation at Syracuse University under the direction of Preston James, with research in Chile made possible in part by a Doherty Foundation grant. In his work, Martin shows that the new landowners have been mainly urban middle-class elements, with primary interest in making a quick economic gain from their properties, and/or acquiring greater social prestige. The new middle-class owners have emulated the inefficient, absentee ownership patterns of the old landowning aristocracy, and often the productivity of the lands they acquire has declined. Also, land has been taken by its recent purchasers from the production of basic nutrition crops, and shifted to the raising of more remunerative fruit products. Moreover, the 1925-1960 redistribution has not benefited the rural workers who actually live in the area, as 95 per cent of those permanently residing in the central valley's farm areas are not landowners. Frequently, land acquisition by new urban middle sectors has resulted in deteriorating conditions for the agrarian laborers (Martin, *op. cit.*, pp. 133-136). Thus, it is not fair to blame the traditional landowning aristocracy alone for the plight of agriculture.

⁴⁹ Feder, *op. cit.*, pp. 94-106, and P. Ríos C., *et al.*, *El crédito agrícola en Chile, 1940-1955* (1957).

⁵⁰ See Alfredo Bowen, "El problema de la sindicalización campesina," *Estudios*, no. 165 (October, 1946) and the address of Deputy José Cruz Delgado, Cámara de Diputados, *Boletín de sesiones ordinarias*, 1943, Sesión 3°, June 1, 1943, p. 149. The following is a list of additional works dealing with the lamentable agrarian situation in Chile. O. Alvarez A., "El problema agrario en Chile," *Revista Mexicana de Sociología* (January-April, 1958). V. Bacigalupo, *El control restrictivo del crédito como se ha aplicado por el Banco del Estado* (1958. Mimeo.). Jorge Baraona Urzúa, *El inquilinaje en Chile antes la historia y antes el derecho* (1953. Memoria de Prueba). Ana María Barrenechea and Tulio Lagos Valenzuela, "Panorama de la vida rural chilena," *Occidente* (July-December, 1957). The last two works are good accounts of the miserable conditions in which the rural laborer toils and, after a fashion, lives. Other works dealing with the same topic are: Guillermo Corona Carreño, *El problema de la habitación campesina* (1951); Isabel Gundelach Faúndez, *El obrero agrícola ante la legislación del trabajo* (1955. Memoria de Prueba); Amanda Labarca, *Mejoramiento de la vida campesino* (1936); Jaime Larraín García Moreno, *El mejoramiento de la vida campesina* (1936); Bernardo Leighton, *Propiedad rústica y gremios agrarios* (1933. Memoria de Prueba); René León Echaiz, *Interpretación histórica del huaso chileno* (1954); Olga López Muñoz, *Las colonias escolares y su misión higiénico social* (1948); Moisés Poblete Troncoso, *La economía agraria de América Latina y el trabajador campesino* (1953); and Betty Woscobosnik Bassis, *Inquilinaje en el medio rural de Puente Alto: estudio económico-social* (1941).

The United Nations Economic Commission for Latin America as of 1962 was engaged in preparing a study to be entitled *Desarrollo de la agricultura chilena*. Finally, the reader is directed to the fine essay by Humberto Funezalida Villegas, "La conquista del teritorio y la utilización durante la primera mitad del siglo XX," in Universidad de Chile, *Desarrollo*.

⁵¹ Gabriela Mistral, *Recados contando a Chile* (1957), p. 18.

[52] The 1960 preliminary report of the *Comisión de Reestructuración Social y Económica de la Agricultura* stresses the need to assimilate agrarian laborers, representing 35 per cent of the population, into a modern society.

[53] Previously cited Census reports indicate that in 1930, 49 per cent of the population was urban; in 1940, 52.5 per cent, and in 1952, 60.2 per cent. In 1930, there was an urban population of 2,119,221 in a total population of 4,287,445. In 1952, it was 3,573,112 in a total population of 5,932,995.

[54] For a description of the futile, fragmentalized urban labor movement see Hernán Troncoso, "Situación sindical de Chile," *Política y Espíritu*, no. 208 (September 15, 1958).

[55] When aristocrat Luis Orrego Luco published his powerful novel *Casa grande* (1908), in which he attacked the vices of the oligarchy, it was primarily middle-class writers who rallied to the defense of their allegedly affronted brethren. See Domingo Melfi, "La novela *Casa grande* y la transformación de la sociedad chilena," *Anales de la Universidad de Chile*, CXI, nos. 69-72 (1948).

[56] See Ricardo Valdés, "Sobre el siútico criollo," *Pacífico Magazine* (January, 1919).

[57] For material on the origins of the middle class-upper class alliance in Chile, see the concluding section of Chapter IV, "The Rural-to-Urban Transition."

[58] *El Mercurio*, January 14, 1919.

[59] *Ibid.*, January 19 and February 28, 1919.

[60] *El Diario Ilustrado*, May 19, 1919.

[61] Macchiavello, *Política económica nacional* (1929).

[62] *El Mercurio*, April 1, 1932. See also *ibid.*, January 24, 1933, noting the election of Rafael Maluenda as president of the *Unión de la Clase Media*. The *Unión* was dedicated to maintaining the established order, and its membership agreed that class conflict could not be tolerated in Chile.

[63] Silva, *Nuestra evolución político-social, 1900-1930* (1930), p. 100.

[64] Mistral, *Recados*, pp. 92-93 (see note 51).

[65] *Ibid.*, p. 99.

[66] Melfi, *op. cit.* (see note 55).

[67] *La Nación*, November 28, 1930.

[68] Alarcón Pino, *La clase media en Chile* (1947. Memoria de Prueba), p. 95.

[69] *Ibid.*, pp. 98-99.

[70] Pinto Salvatierra, *El clase media y socialismo* (1941), p. 9.

[71] Vega, *op. cit.* (see note 42), p. 80.

[72] *Ibid.*, p. 87.

[73] Heise González, *La constitución de 1925 y las nuevas tendencias político-sociales* (1951), pp. 159, 161. Pagination is based on the work as first published in the *Anales de la Universidad de Chile*, no. 80 (4° trimestre, 1950).

[74] The following is an inexhaustive bibliography of works not mentioned in the text which indicate a belief by the respective authors that the middle class has in general sided with the aristocracy and ignored the interests of the lower classes. Oscar Alvarez Andrews, "Las clases sociales en Chile," *Revista Mexicana de Sociología*, XIII, no. 2 (May-August, 1951). T. R. Crevenna, *La clase media en Bolivia, Brasil, Chile y Paraguay* (Washington, D.C., 1940). Jorge de la Cuadra Poisson, *Prolegómenos a la sociología y bosquejo de la evolución de Chile desde 1920* (1957). The noted conservative author pays homage to social standpattism and to

middle-class contributions to this cause. Luis Durand (d. 1954) has been one of Chile's principal authors in this century and served as presidential secretary during the second Arturo Alessandri administration (1932-1938). Disillusioned with the middle-class betrayal of the lower classes, he joined the *Partido Socialista Popular* in the 1940's, but soon became convinced that this party also was betraying its social mission. Two of Durand's works are *Alma y cuerpo de Chile* (1947), a fine collection of short stories depicting national customs and traditions (one of the best sketches is entitled "El país del patrón y del sirviente"), and *Frontera* (1949 edition), considered his masterpiece. Alberto Edwards Vives and Eduardo Frei, *Historia de los partidos políticos chilenos* (1949). In describing political development from 1891 to 1949, Frei comments at length on the rapport between Chilean middle and upper classes and notes the insecurity and lack of permanence characterizing the middle class. Januario Espinosa, "La clase media en la literatura chilena," *Atenea*, Año X, no. 100 (August, 1933). Among other points, the work comments upon the importance of the founding (1905) of the weekly *Zig Zag*, claiming the journal was an outlet for Chilean middle-class expression. *Zig Zag* has almost always been characterized by its careful, if not stuffy, devotion to the values of the aristocracy. Amanda Labarca H., "Apuntes para estudiar la clase media en Chile," *Atenea*, nos. 305 and 306 (November, December, 1950). Labarca argues that one of the main characteristics of Chilean middle-class members is their expectation of belonging to the upper class in the next generation. In the 1920-1950 period, says Labarca, when the middle class was wielding political power, it did nothing substantial to purify political processes or to aid the lower classes. Jaime Larraín García Moreno, *Chile, avanzada de occidente en el Pacífico sur* (1955) and *Evolución social de Chile* (1950). Aristocrat Larraín favors strengthening the traditional ties between upper and middle classes. Pedro I. Ljubetic V. and Marcia Ortiz, *Estudio sobre el origen y desarrollo del proletariado en Chile* (1954. *Memoria de Prueba*). Jorge Millas, "Ortega y la responsibilidad de la inteligencia," *Anales de la Universidad de Chile*, CXIV (1° trimestre, 1956). Millas shows great distrust of the masses and feels that middle-class intellectuals should have very little to do with them. Enrique Molina, "Ciencia e intuición en el devenir social," *Atenea*, Año XXII, no. 240 (June, 1945). Molina suggests that Chile's failure to develop the discipline of sociology may lie in upper- and middle-class lack of interest in the lower classes. In *Confesión filosófico y llama a la superación de la américa-hispana* (1942), Molina also comments upon lack of middle-class attentiveness to lower-class problems. Benjamín Subercaseaux, *Contribución a la realidad* (1939). In a series of essays dealing with such topics as sex, the *siútico*, the *rotos*, Chilean psychology, and the dehumanization of the upper and middle classes, Subercaseux provides the reader with one of the best portrayals of Chile and its people. Julio Vega, "Algunos característicos fundamentales del pueblo chileno," *Occidente* (October, 1950). Carlos Vial, *Cuaderno de comprensión social* (1952) and *Cuaderno de la realidad nacional* (1952). Successful businessman and frustrated Minister of Treasury in 1950, Vial blames the social problem upon ingrained attitudes of the upper and middle classes and in particular censures the Radical Party. Carlos Vicuña Fuentes, *La tiranía en Chile*, 2 vols. (1938, 1939). In volume I of this valuable but often impressionistic work, Vicuña Fuentes upbraids the middle class for its disassociation from the lower classes.

For another example of middle-class betrayal of the lower classes and national interests, see note 48 in this chapter. Finally, for an excellent bibliography of Chilean works pertaining to the classes and to social mobility see Antonio Ruiz Urbina, Alejandro Zorbas S., and Luis Donoso Varela, *Estratificación y movilidad sociale en Chile* (Rio de Janeiro, Brazil, 1961). This study of over 150 pages was sponsored by the *Centro Latinoamericano de Investigaciones en Ciencias Sociales*.

[75] *El Mercurio*, February 10, 1916.

[76] See Cámara de Diputados, *Boletín de sesiones extraordinarias*, 1922, Sesión 34°, November 3, 1922, pp. 361 ff. Among the deputies most vocal in raising these charges were Emilio Tizzoni, Wenceslao Sierra, Santiago Labarca, Joaquín Irarrázaval, and J. Ramón Herrera Lira. One of the many writers who agreed with these congressional charges in the 1920's was Trancredo Pinochet Le-Brun. See his *Como construir una gran civilización chilena e hispanoamericana* (no date) and *La conquista de Chile en el siglo XX* (1909).

[77] See Amanda Labarca H., *Bases para una política educacional* (Buenos Aires, 1944); *Historia de la enseñanza en Chile* (1939); and *Realidades y problemas de nuestra enseñanza* (1953).

[78] See Vega, *op. cit.* (note 42). There is a lengthy list of works suggesting that the educational structure in Chile foments class prejudice, leading the middle class to shun labor and the laboring classes, while striving to emulate the aristocracy. For the works published prior to the mid-1930's on this topic, see Chapter IV, note 62, and Chapter VI, notes 126-128. Many of the works criticizing the educational structure also contain strong expressions of economic nationalism (see Chapter IX, note 43) calling for a revision of education so as to train Chileans to manage their own economy. Critical works of the educational structure published in 1933 or later are listed below.

Carlos Atienza (National Director of Secondary Teaching at the time), "Entrevista," *La Nación*, September 29, 1933. Atienza stated that Chilean secondary education produced only nonproductive entities, with disdain for labor and technical proficiency. The middle classes were interested only in the humanities, as learning in this field enabled them to be taken for members of the aristocracy. Octavio Azócar Gauthier, *La enseñanza industrial en relación con la economía nacional* (1951). Eliodoro Domínguez, *El problema de nuestra educación pública* (1933). Domínguez, a prominent educator at the time, delivered a forceful indictment of Chilean instruction, basing his complaints on the considerations outlined above. Florencio Durán Bernales, *El Partido Radical* (1958). This book has a good section on the education reforms attempted by the Popular Front, 1939-1941. It is extremely unfortunate that the Radical Party, whose members in general control the bureaucratic structure of public education and furnish probably the majority of teachers, has done so little to revitalize the educational system. Juan F. Fernández C., *Pedro Aguirre Cerda y el Frente Popular chileno* (1938). Eduardo Hamuy, "Problemas de educación elemental y desarrollo económico," *Economía: Revista de la Facultad de Ciencias Económicas de la Universidad de Chile*, Año XVIII, nos. 60 and 61 (3°, 4° trimestre, 1958). Hamuy is one of the best informed writers on Chilean education. Amanda Labarca H., "Educación," in Humberto Fuenzalida Villegas, *et al.*, *Chile: geografía, educación, literatura, legislación, economía, minería* (Buenos Aires, 1946). Written by some of the leading Chilean authorities in their respective fields, this book reaches generally pessimistic conclusions. E. Maguire Ibar, *Formación racial chilena y futuras proyecciones* (1949. *Memoria de Prueba*). Particularly on p. 53 Maguire laments the impractical nature of Chilean education, holding this to be responsible in part for the lack of a stable middle class with its own traditions and values. Luciano Martínez Echemendia, "Necesidad de transformar todas las escuelas tradicionales o intelectuales en las escuelas progresivas," in *Segunda conferencia inter-americana de educación*, vol. II (1934). Roberto Munizaga Aguirre, *Algunos grandes temas de la filosofía educacional de don Valentín Letelier* (1952) and *El estado y la educación* (1953). Moisés Mussa, "Chile necesita de una política educacional," *Occidente* (April, 1949) and "Nuestra educación y la realidad económica de Chile," *ibid.* (March, 1945). In these articles, another prominent educator argued that the antiquated educational structure accounts for much of Chile's economic backwardness, and for the preservation of an archaic social structure. See the same author's earlier *Nuestra problema educacional* (1932). Mariano Navarrete C., *Los problemas educacionales* (1934). Luis Oyarzún, "El pensamiento educacional de don Simón Rodríguez," *Atenea*, Año XXIV, no. 266 (August, 1947). The article deals with the reforms which this early director of the *Oficina del Trabajo* wanted introduced into Chilean education, so as to make the country more productive and to overcome the gulf between the classes. Octavio Palma, José Herrera, and María Etcheverry, *El problema de la enseñanza científica en el liceo* (1958). Francisco A. Pinto S., *La tremenda lección* (1933). The prominent sociologist argued that educational inadequacies have forced Chileans to rely excessively on foreigners and foreign capital and have caused social stagnation. Antenor Rojo, "La educación pública y la realidad económica de Chile," *Occidente* (January, 1951). The article criticizes the almost exclusively humanistic curriculum of secondary education. Darío E. Salas, *Nuestra educación y sus deficiencias* (1933). Irma Salas Silva, *The Socio-Economic Composition of the Secondary School Population of Chile* (1930). Miss Salas, who is now prominently associated with the *Instituto Pedagógico* of the University of Chile, pointed out the prevailing absence of lower-class elements in the secondary education institutions. It would be worthwhile to make an up-to-date survey of this sort. D. Valenzuela, *La experiencia pedagógica en Chile* (1933). Julio Vega, *Bosquejo de una política educacional* (1938) and *La racionalización de nuestra enseñanza* (1954). Vega feels that the 1928 Ibáñez reforms represented almost the only attempt to rectify the sort of educational shortcomings that have been described, and regrets the failure of the endeavor to produce lasting results.

[79] See Ernest Feder, "Do-Gooders in Latin America: Variations on a Theme," *Prairie Schooner*, XXXIV, no. 3 (Fall, 1960), 230.

[80] Aníbal Pinto, *Hacia nuestra independencia económica*, p. 77 .

[81] Molina, *Confesión filosófica y llama a la superación de la américa-hispana* (1942), p. 102.

[82] The Palacios work was published first in 1911.

[83] The racist slant is particularly strong in vol. III, Chapters III, IV, and V of F. A. Encina, *Historia de Chile desde la prehistoria hasta 1891* (1943). The twentieth and last volume of this work was published in 1952.

[84] Jobet, "Notas sobre la historiografía," Ricardo Donoso, *et al.*, *Historiografía chilena*, pp. 354-355.

[85] Edwards and Keller were both strongly influenced by Oswald Spengler's *El*

hombre y el técnico, which preached the supremacy of the white over colored races. This book, the most widely read of Spengler's in Chile, appeared in its first Santiago edition in 1932. Three years later, the third edition was already exhausted.

[86] Cabero, *Chile y los chilenos* (1926).

[87] Gallardo Nieto, "Dificultades del panamericanismo," *El Mercurio*, December 15, 1933.

[88] *Ibid.*, July 8, 1933.

[89] Emilio Rodríguez, *Alfredo Irarrázaval Zañartu* (1932), pp. 145-146.

[90] September 26, 1928, letter of Mistral to Rodríguez, accompanying the November correspondence of Ambassador in Madrid Rodríguez to the Chilean Ministry of Foreign Relations, in *Correspondencia recibida de las Legaciones de Chile en España y Portugal, 1928*, AMRE.

[91] The following is a bibliography of books not cited elsewhere in the notes which display, or comment upon, the prevailing anti-Indian bias. Jerónimo de Amberga, "Estado intelectual, moral y económico de Araucano," *Revista Chilena de Historia y Geografía*, XLV (3° trimestre, 1913). This presented a pessimistic appraisal of the Araucanians. Renato Donoso Henríquez, *Consideraciones acerca del problema inmigratorio* (1928). Donoso urged that Chile encourage foreign immigration, as the native Indians and mixed bloods were inferior. Joaquín Edwards Bello, *El nacionalismo continental* (1935). Brilliant journalist Edwards Bello urged Chileans to follow Víctor Raúl Haya de la Torre and the "Aprista" movement, but conceded that the anti-Indian bias in Chile might render this course of action impossible. Tomás Guevara, for many years an influential professor at the University of Chile, openly professed the inferiority of the Indian. Among Guevara's many works on the Indians of Chile, several of which were first published in the *Anales de la Universidad de Chile*, are: *La etnología araucana en el poema de Ercilla* (1924); *Folklore araucano* (1911); *Historia de la justicia araucana* (1922); *La mentalidad araucana* (1916); *Psicología del pueblo araucano* (1908); and *Raza chilena* (1905). Carlos Larraín de Castro, "Carta a Omer Emeth," *El Mercurio*, May 29, 1927. Larraín argued that the Chilean race was superior to that of other Latin-American republics because the conquerors and seventeenth-century Basque merchants largely refrained from marrying the inferior Indians. Emeth agreed, but cautioned that the Basques were not quite the super-race sometimes pictured, as they were "tainted" by Jewish blood. Jaime Larraín García Moreno, *Chile, avanzada de occidente en el Pacífico sur*. Larraín discussed the inferiority of Indian blood (pp. 26-27), and stated that the genius of Diego Portales was most apparent in his desire in 1837 to crush the Bolivia-Peru confederation led by General Andrés Santa Cruz. This confederation might have imposed Indian rule over Spanish Chile. Ricardo E. Latcham, *Prehistoria chilena* (1936 edition) and *Los primitivos habitantes de Chile* (1939 edition). In these and other works Latcham, a British engineer turned ecologist whose writings in their original editions appeared around the turn of the century, defended the Indians and asserted that Chilean prejudices against them were unjustified. Ricardo E. is not to be confused with Ricardo A. Latcham, the author-diplomat frequently mentioned in the text and notes. Rodolfo Lenz, a German professor of languages at the University of Chile, often expressed indignation over the anti-Indian biases which he encountered in Chile. See his *Estudios araucanos* (1897) and *Estudios sobre los Indios de Chile* (1924). One of the most active combatants against Indian prejudice in mid-twentieth-century Chile has

been Alejandro Lipschutz, an intellectual of German-Jewish extraction noted for his far-left political ideas. See his *La comunidad indígena en américa y en Chile* (1956) and *El indoamericanismo y el problema racial en las américas* (1944). Wilhelm de Moesbach, *Vida y costumbres de los indígenas araucanas en la segunda mitad del siglo XIX* (1936 edition). In the prologue which he wrote to this edition of the classic study, Rodolfo Lenz stressed that the vices and faults often noted by Moesbach were the result of the unjust treatment which the Indians had received, and not, as commonly assumed, the consequences of racial inferiority. Carlos Munizaga A., *Vida de un Araucano: el estudiante mapuche* (1960). The work revealed some of the tribulations faced by an Araucanian as of the 1950's in his quest for education. J. M. Muñoz, *Estudio de antropología jurídica o medicina legal* (1912). The work commented at length on the common Chilean assumption of Indian inferiority. Carlos Oliver Schneider, *Los Indios de Chile: lo que actualmente se sabe sobre ellos* (1932). The work argued that the Indians might not be, as it was overwhelmingly assumed in Chile that they were, hopelessly degenerate and racially inferior. Through education, the author felt, Indians could be assimilated into society. Emilio Rodríguez Mendoza, "Arauco y la leyenda," *El Mercurio*, July 8, 1910. Rodríguez asserted the unreliability of that portion of the Alonso de Ercilla epic poem, "La Araucana," which glorified the Araucanians. Rather, the Araucanians were in reality always inferior and incapable of improvement. The same thesis was advanced by Eduardo Solar Correa, *Semblanzas literarias de la colonia* (1933). Benjamín Subercaseaux, "¿Hay prejuicio racial en Chile?" *Zig Zag*, October 12, 1957. Subercaseaux is strongly affirmative in replying to this question, Víctor de Valdivia (pseud.), *La europeanización de sudamérica* (1923) and *El imperio iberoamericano* (Paris, 1929). A long-time University of Chile professor, utilizing the pseudonym of Valdivia, maintained that increasing Europeanization was the only hope for Latin America. He believed that the Indians are a degenerate race whose blood corrupted those who shared it.

For earlier indications of anti-Indian bias, see Chapter II, notes 30-33, and Chapter IV, notes 186-188. Moreover, the anti-Indian prejudice gained impetus in the mid-nineteenth century with the rise of the cult of positivism. Juan Enrique Lagarrigue, the great popularizer in Chile of the "Religion of Humanity," implied in his *La religión de la humanidad* (1884) that only the Teutonic, Anglo-Saxon, and French "races" are capable of progress.

[92] León Alterman P., *El movimiento demográfico en Chile* (1946. *Memoria de Prueba*), p. 60.

[93] Enrique L. Marshall, *Los araucanos ante el derecho penal* (1917. *Memoria de Prueba*), p. 41.

[94] E. Maguire Ibar, *Formación racial chilena y futuras proyecciones* (1949. *Memoria de Prueba*), pp. 13, 64.

[95] Arturo Ahumada, quoted in *El Mercurio*, March 4, 1928.

[96] Onofre Lindsay, *El problema fundamental: la repoblación de Chile y los Estados Unidos de subamérica* (1925), p. 38.

[97] Francisco Javier Díaz Salazar, *La influencia racial en la actividad económica de los indígenas chilenos* (1940. *Memoria de Prueba*), p. 13.

[98] Humberto Gacitúa Vergara, *Estudio social y consideraciones legales del problema indígena en Chile* (1916. *Memoria de Prueba*), p. 4.

[99] José Inalaf Navarro, *Ros económico, social, y político del indígeno en Chile* (1945. *Memoria de Prueba*), p. 9.

[100] Cámara de Diputados, *Boletín de sesiones extraordinarias, 1929*, Sesión 15°, November 20. As of 1960, there were approximately 200,000 pure-blooded Araucanians in Chile. See L. C. Faron, *Mapuche Social Structure: Institutional Reintegration in a Patrilineal Society of Central Chile* (Urbana, Illinois, 1961), p. 5.

[101] Subercaseaux, "La super gente bien," *Zig Zag*, March 27, 1954, p. 51.

CHAPTER 11

[1] As early as 1926, Father Guillermo Viviani Contreras, *Sociología chilena: estudio de sociología general aplicada a nuestra país*, pp. 162-163, observed this fact.

[2] The archconservative *El Diario Ilustrado* was quick to react against the United States when that country began timidly to advocate reform in Latin America. See the editorials and articles appearing throughout the August and September 1961 editions. To a large degree the future success of the United States in escaping from its guilt-by-association position in Chile could be measured by the intensity of attacks from such sources as *El Diario Ilustrado*.

[3] That traditional practices have produced this effect was indicated by the letter sent to President Eisenhower during his visit to Chile by the University Student Federation (FECH). One of the letter's cardinal points was that the United States appeared to be primarily interested in protecting the wealth of privileged elements within the existing order. See Chapter IX, conclusion of note 23.

[4] Alvin Cohen, *Economic Change in Chile, 1929-1950* (Gainesville, Florida, 1960), pp. 5-6.

[5] Mimeographed letter of Tom Scanlon, a Peace Corps volunteer serving in Chile, December 31, 1961.

[6] See "Soviet Political Warfare in Latin America," *Intelligence Digest*, no. 278 (London: January, 1962), p. 11.

[7] The quotation is from William P. Glade, "The Economic Costs of Social Backwardness and the Economic Value of Social Reform," a paper presented to the second annual Conference of the Midwest Council of the Association for Latin-American Studies, October 12-14, 1961, at the University of Illinois. The paper was subsequently published in *Inter-American Economic Affairs*, XV, no. 3 (Winter, 1962). A 1960 United States Senate study on Latin America also noted that certain elements of progress may be felt more directly and may create a greater feeling of social and economic advance than do some of the basic elements customarily associated with a rise in per-capita gross national product. The Senate study stated that Latin America can and must proceed more rapidly toward achieving these elements of progress, among which would be included better health, higher quality of commodities and services, improved working conditions, and above all, a feeling that one is not being discriminated against by the government or any social class. See *United States Senate, 86th Congress, Second Session, Subcommittee on American Republics' Affairs of the Committee on Foreign Relations*, Document 125, August 31, 1960, pp. 599-600. The study, entitled "Problems of Latin-American Economic Development," was prepared by the Institute of International Studies and Overseas Administration of the University of Oregon.

INDEX OF NAMES

www.ingramcontent.com/pod-product-compliance
Lightning Source LLC
Chambersburg PA
CBHW050226270326
41914CB00003BA/582